Communication Skills
for *Business*
and Professions

Paul R. Timm
BRIGHAM YOUNG UNIVERSITY

James A. Stead
UNIVERSITY OF PHOENIX

PRENTICE HALL
UPPER SADDLE RIVER, NEW JERSEY 07458

Library of Congress Cataloging-in-Publication Data

Timm, Paul R.
   Communication skills for business and professions / Paul R. Timm,
James A. Stead.
      p.   cm.
   Includes bibliographical references and index,
   ISBN 0-13-348608-7
   1. Business communication.   2. Communication in management.
3. Interpersonal communication.   I. Stead, James A.   II. Title.
HF5718.T535   1996
650.1′3—dc20   95-41679
                                                               CIP

PRODUCTION EDITOR: **Adele Kupchik**
MANAGING EDITOR: **Mary Carnis**
ACQUISITIONS EDITOR: **Elizabeth Sugg**
DIRECTOR OF MANUFACTURING & PRODUCTION: **Bruce Johnson**
MANUFACTURING BUYER: **Ed O'Dougherty/Ilene Sanford**
MARKETING MANAGER: **Frank Mortimer, Jr.**
EDITORIAL ASSISTANT: **Kahdijah Bell**
FORMATTING/PAGE MAKE-UP: **The Clarinda Company**
PRINTER/BINDER: **R.R. Donnelley & Sons, Willard, Ohio**
INTERIOR & COVER DESIGN: **Sheree Goodman Design**
ILLUSTRATIONS: **Mark Ammerman**
COVER PHOTO: **Tommy Flynn/Photonica**

© 1996 by Prentice-Hall, Inc.
A Simon & Schuster Company
Upper Saddle River, New Jersey 07458

Chapter Opener Photo Credits:

Chapter 1, photo by Alese/Mort Pechter, courtesy of The Stock Market; Chapter 2, courtesy of Honeywell; Chapter 3, photo by John Coletti, courtesy of Stock Boston; Chapter 4, photo by Jon Riley, courtesy of Tony Stone Images; Chapter 5, photo by Bruce Ayers, courtesy of Tony Stone Images; Chapter 6, courtesy of Sun Microsystems; Chapter 7, courtesy of United Nations; Chapter 8, photo by Stephen Frisch, courtesy of Stock Boston; Chapter 9, courtesy of Comstock; Chapter 10, photo by Frank Siteman, courtesy of Monkmeyer Press; Chapter 11, photo by David R. Frazier, courtesy of Tony Stone Images; Chapter 12, courtesy of Superstock; Chapter 13, photo by John Lund, courtesy of Tony Stone Images; Chapter 14, courtesy of The Travelers; Chapter 15, courtesy of Superstock; Chapter 16, photo by Ted Horowitz, courtesy of The Stock Market; Chapter 17, photo by FourByFive, Inc./Superstock; Chapter 18, photo by Tim Brown, courtesy of Tony Stone Images; Chapter 19, courtesy of IBM; Chapter 20, photo by Henley & Savage, courtesy of The Stock Market.

Printed in the United States of America

10 9 8 7 6 5 4 3 2

ISBN 0-13-348608-7

Prentice-Hall International (UK) Limited, *London*
Prentice-Hall of Australia Pty. Limited, *Sydney*
Prentice-Hall Canada Inc., *Toronto*
Prentice-Hall Hispanoamericana, S.A., *Mexico*
Prentice-Hall of India Private Limited, *New Delhi*
Prentice-Hall of Japan, Inc., *Tokyo*
Simon & Schuster Asia Pte. Ltd., *Singapore*
Editora Prentice-Hall do Brasil, Ltda., *Rio de Janeiro*

DEDICATION

To our fathers:
Roy C. Timm (1907-90)
Albert Stead

CONTENTS

PART TWO

Communication: Consistency amid Change 53

CHAPTER THREE

Human and Organizational Needs: Communication, Motivation, and Success 54

Appropriate Language Use: The Way We Word   80

Proven Communication Principles: Four Pillars of Effectiveness   110

**CHAPTER
SIX**

Media and Technology: Quantum Leaps Daily   136

CHAPTER NINE

Projecting Professionalism: Writing with Class   214

CHAPTER TEN

Writing Routine, Informative, and Goodwill Messages: Simple, Quick, and Powerful   238

CHAPTER ELEVEN

Writing Disappointing or Unfavorable Messages: Clarity with Sensitivity   276

CHAPTER EIGHTEEN

Delivery of Oral Presentations: Conveying Your Message with Impact   498

PART SIX

Reference Tools for Communication Effectiveness amid Change   565

PREFACE TO THE STUDENT

We think books should be fun. Perhaps that's a radical idea, especially for a textbook, but we state that up front for a reason. A textbook succeeds only if it teaches the reader. Teaching and learning, as current literature on "learning organizations" notes, occur when the process allows for creativity, empowerment of all participants, and even entertainment. Hence, we have attempted to make this book as stimulating and enjoyable as possible for you.

Having exerted our efforts to make this book useful and fun, we ask only that you read and use it to your best advantage. To do this, it will be helpful to understand the features of the book and a tip for getting the most from your study of business and professional communication skills.

Some Book Features

1. *Macroview.* Business and professional communication is more than letter and report writing, as important as these may be. Many books emphasize these functions without fully considering the context in which they and other forms of communication occur. Professional people communicate in response to and anticipation of organizational needs. The broader matters of organizational and marketplace success provide the real catalyst for communication activity. Early chapters delve into this context to provide students with real-world understanding of the complexity of the topic.

2. *Interesting sidebars.* We have included many "sidebar" devices that will both entertain and enlighten. Stories, quips, quotes, and cartoons enliven the information giving and stimulate reflection. Take time to read and ponder them.

3. *Highlighted terms.* We believe that much of the benefit of reading—any kind of reading—is the expansion of one's vocabulary. Unfortunately, many readers, on encountering an unfamiliar term, do not look it up. They guess at its meaning instead, and, in so doing, miss the opportunity to add it to their personal lexicon. So we have decided to highlight potentially unfamiliar terms.

4. *Emphasis on today's skills.* We have tried to keep our focus on the kinds of communication skills needed in today's and tomorrow's business and professional world. Your career or profession will also entail the learning of many specialized concepts. The information in this book will provide you with a powerful foundation of usable skills that have been shown to boost peoples' careers in dramatic ways.

5. *Friendly tone.* We have tried to write in ways that sound like a friendly mentor and teacher. Our language level may surprise you at times. It is likely to be more informal and conversational than many textbooks you have read. We do not apologize for that. We have found that the best wisdom and insight can be explained in simple terms.

6. *Ideas, not rules.* We present you with tools and ideas, not hard-and-fast rules. Although correct grammar and usage has its place in the tool kit of any profes-

sional, this book does not dwell on these aspects of communication. We do provide you with excellent reference materials in the appendices that will serve you well as needed. The book is primarily about communication, a broader and infinitely more interesting and creative process than a mechanical, rule-driven production of documents and presentations.

7. *Interaction.* We want you to interact with this book. The layout is designed so you can scribble notes in the wide margins and personalize the ideas presented so that you can use them now. "Communicator's Journal" activities will help you personalize and employ key text ideas. All learning involves translating what is read or heard into information applicable to us as individuals. Look for your applications, and note them in this text. Don't just read the book, *use* the book.

This book is the product of countless hours of work and study as well as the combined business and professional experiences of your authors. We quickly admit that we don't have all the answers to all possible problems. (That's one point experience teaches clearly!) We do sincerely believe that the ideas presented in this book will help you develop the crucial tools needed for optimal success in careers for 2000 and beyond.

In short, helping you develop real-world communication skills is the goal of this book.

Communication Skills for Business and Professions captures the dynamics of today's business realities. The business world at the upcoming turn of the century will call for communication skills different from those used in the past decades. After you take this course, you will have the necessary skills.

PAUL R. TIMM, *Ph.D.*
JAMES A. STEAD

PREFACE TO THE INSTRUCTOR

Communication Skills for Business and Professions shows students the process of communicating as real-world professionals do it *today*. It contains only essential hard-and-fast rules and few absolutes. The book offers guidelines and examples of applications used in modern organizations and, it encourages a process of creative communication as we compete for attention in an information-saturated world. The outcome of this process is skill building without rigidity and learning with versatility. Countless variations are available to the creative, adaptable professional.

Here are some specific elements that illustrate differences between this and other texts on the market.

1. **Consistency amid change.** Readers are given a strong overview of what is different and what remains the same—*consistency amid change*—in business communication. Among the things that remain consistent are human and organizational needs, appropriate language use, and proven communication principles. Change is most evident in media and technology use, and audience diversity and expectations. Awareness of this material provides an exceptional foundation for today's business and professional communicator.

2. **Focus on the communicator.** Readers are taught about the *mental processes that cut across communication efforts*. They are shown the myriad factors that can and will determine communication success or failure. They are forewarned that communication is an art, not a science; and that the choices they make in initiating, developing, and transmitting messages will have enormous impact on their likelihood for success.

3. **Outcome tests.** Readers are constantly reminded that business and professional communication is *functional*—centered on the results—and that literary qualities or even the "correctness" of their message is secondary in importance to whether or not it worked. The ultimate test of a message is the following: Did it get the receiver to do what you wanted?

4. **Media selection.** Readers are taught to *consider the media* they use. Too many texts assume that a business letter or report is called for in a given situation when, in the real world, it would never be used. Written correspondence is tremendously expensive—a cost of doing business that cannot always be economically justified. Student writing assignments calling for a letter to a customer whose washing machine is broken are laughable. Appliance dealers don't do that. They pick up the telephone, visit the customer, or meet with dissatisfied buyers and quality-control people—but they rarely write letters.

   If anything, businesses today are reticent to put much of anything in writing. In our increasingly litigious society, putting information in writing can be dangerous. A classic example is when people ask for a written recommendation for a job applicant—perhaps one your company terminated. Today's business people have learned to be careful.

5. **Quality communication.** Readers are taught how *communication is an important aspect of any business's major responsibility: satisfying customers.* The entire book builds on the premise that customer satisfaction is absolutely essential to business and professional success. This focus is a distinct departure from the traditional text and is grounded in the realities of today's business world.

6. **Process writing.** Writing is still the best way for one to organize thoughts and digest ideas. Readers are taught the *composition process from ideation to finished document.* Patterns of arrangement for various types of messages are illustrated with a wide range of real examples. Advantages and disadvantages are assessed. So, yes, the book teaches writing—in a pragmatic, functional manner.

7. **Quick reference tools.** The reference materials provided suggest approaches to almost any kind of business communication situation. Tried and tested patterns for "bad-news" messages (ones that disappoint readers and those that convey unfavorable information about people or organizations,) persuasive messages (including sales materials,) and goodwill messages that boost relationships are illustrated extensively.

   Sticky grammatical problem solutions, format questions, documentation tips, and the ever-present editing symbols are available in the Reference Tools, which are easily accessed in the back of the text.

8. **Presentation.** Readers are encouraged to develop skill in the use of *visual communication media.* These, in connection with both oral and written communication, are concisely shown with numerous examples.

9. **Employment.** Readers are taught about *job-getting communication* (a subject of immediate concern to many students), which is covered with the same kind of creativity shown throughout the book. Experienced recruiters tell us that there is no "one right way" to design a resume or cover letter. In fact, people who do use standard formulas have a cookie-cutter similarity that often disqualifies them from serious consideration. This book shows a range of possible tactics for the job-search process from identifying prospects to preparing one's "sales literature" to handling interviews and follow-up.

10. Finally, readers are reminded throughout the book of the *broader communication tasks faced by professionals: building cooperation, leading and participating in meetings, using today's technology, and dealing with a diverse range of individuals.*

Teaching Aids and Supplemental Materials

Communication Skills for Business and Professions is offered with the most extensive array of teaching materials of any current text. All materials were developed at the same time as the book to ensure a perfect match between text content and supplements.

Teaching Aids

Teaching Aid materials include the following:

- **Real-world cases** illustrating communication challenges of businesses of all sizes and shapes—not just major corporations.

- **Performance Challenge**
  Guidance for polishing skills.

- **Communicator's Profile**
  Communication advice from successful business people.
- **Communicator's Journal**
  Cases detailing critical issues in preparing a message.
- **Tables and Checklists**
  Easy reference throughout the book and in the Appendices.
- **Cartoons**
  Lively humorous illustrations of key concepts.
- **Understanding the Basics**
  End of chapter summary and review questions.
- **Another Look**
  Actual business examples with guided practice.
- **Performing on the Job**
  Real-world cases requiring decision-making and problem-solving
- **Video-clip library** with materials created exclusively for the book as well as a range of related stories from the archives of journalism.

New Approach

Most books on the market today assume that the student will be employed in a large, traditionally structured organization. In reality, the greatest number of career opportunities lie in the less structured, more fluid world of entrepreneurship, rapid innovation, independent distributorships, and even telecommuters. Further, today's world organizations increasingly deal in the dynamic world of information and services, and less often in tangible products and traditional manufacturing.

Some quickly evident characteristic of these "information age" organizations are that they seldom, if ever, create long, formal reports. Their correspondence is more likely to be brief and electronically transmitted. Their decision-making documentation is more likely to rely heavily on graphics with less text. The text that is delivered is more likely to be oral rather than written. Rapid changes demand rapid communication.

Traditional business communication texts seem reticent to acknowledge these changing realities, clinging instead to the ways the course has been taught for decades.

The book does not concentrate on formal reports as do so many other texts. Long-written reports are the anathema to quick-moving, dynamic organizations. By the time a traditional report is completed, it is likely to be obsolete. Today's companies move faster. Even highly paid consulting firms seldom provide detailed written reports. They are much more likely to present their findings and recommendations orally with graphic support, leaving the client with only the presentation visuals and supporting data.

Supplements

Supplemental materials include:

- **Study Guide** available both in print and electronic media assists student review of the topics presented in each chapter. The Study Guide includes a reference of sample documents.
- **Instructor's Resource Kit** that offers a complete package for teaching in a lecture hall or through Distance Learning programs.
  - Course outlines, suggested syllabi, and scores of proven in-class activities guaranteed to bring a lively atmosphere to any classroom.

- Suggested grading guidelines for assignments. What to look for and how to evaluate student papers has never been simpler. Guides also make for more consistent, less subjective grading—thus overcoming a major student complaint.
- Notes for an easy transition from other nationally recognized textbooks to *Communication Skills for Business and Professions.*
- Video guide for using video in the classroom.
- Colorful, interesting **classroom visuals** available on both acetates and Power-Point disks.
- Extensive **test bank** (both on hard copy and disk) that allows instructors to tailor their examinations to their students and their courses.
- **Video program** keyed to the text and the **JWA Video offer**—a complete set of lecture-based videos based on Paul Timm's creative teaching style and correlated to parts of the textbook.
- An **on-line help line** through America-on-Line or Prentice Hall's College On-line World-Wide Webb site that puts teachers in touch with the authors for answers to their specific questions about classroom approaches.
- **Pheedback Newsletter** subscription with regular updates about new material available to instructors who adopt the book. These range from teaching tips and idea sharing among instructors to new video clips, updated visuals, and cases and illustrations from today's news media.

Final Note

A lively, conversational style is a hallmark of the book. The text strives for a 10th- to 11th-grade reading level—about the same as the *Wall Street Journal.* It speaks clearly without talking down to the reader. To your authors, there is no higher compliment than to hear students say, "They write the way they talk." We hear that often.

We sincerely hope that you enjoy the book and would be delighted to receive your feedback. Please drop us a note or send a fax.

PAUL R. TIMM
JAMES A. STEAD

Paul R. Timm, Chair
Department of Management Communication
590 Tanner Building
Brigham Young University
Provo, UT 84602
Fax: (801) 378-8309

ACKNOWLEDGMENTS

The authors express special thanks to all who have helped develop this book and its supplemental materials.

We express special appreciation to Julia Bottita who managed to pull together all the details while still handling her duties as executive secretary. All of this she did with efficiency, thoroughness, and good humor. Thanks, Julia.

We also appreciate the work of Roger Terry who wrote some of the cases and instructional materials which students will find of enormous value as they develop their communication skills.

Likewise, the team at Prentice Hall deserves special recognition for their excellent work, often done on short deadlines. Elizabeth Sugg, Roberta Moore, Adele Kupchik, Teri Stratford, and Frank Mortimer, Jr. deserve special mention for their outstanding professionalism.

Reviewers of early drafts of the manuscript provided valuable help in developing the finished product. We especially appreciate the thoughtful efforts of

Ellis Buchanan, University of Texas at San Antonio, Texas

Roosevelt D. Butler, Trenton State College, New Jersey

Janet Ciccarelli, Herkimer County Community College

Patricia Combies, Salve Regina University

Randy E. Cone, University of New Orleans, Louisiana

Wells F. Cook, Central Michigan University, Michigan

Billie Millie Cooper, Consumnes River College, California

Linda W. Crumb, University of Science and Arts of Oklahoma, Oklahoma

R. Neil Dortch, University of Wisconsin-Whitewater, Wisconsin

Karen Gurchick, Lansing Community College, Michigan

Sandra Hanner, Meredith College

Sherron Kenton, Emory University, Georgia

Martha Kuchar, Roanoke College, Virginia

Thomas Lloyd, Westmoreland Community College, Pennsylvania

Thaddeus McEwen, Eastern Illinois University, Illinois

Thomas A. Maik, University of Wisconsin-La Crosse, Wisconsin

Francis R. Mazzaglia, Boston University, Massachusetts

Paula J. Pomerenke, Illinois State University, Illinois

Sally Tarley, Fairmount State College, West Virginia

Hilda Turner, Arkansas Tech University, Arkansas

Jack Welch, Abilene Christian University, Texas

Finally, we thank our families for their support and patience as we put in the extra hours necessary to write this book.

ABOUT THE AUTHORS

Paul R. Timm, Ph.D. is Chair of the Department of Management Communication in the Marriott School of Management, Brigham Young University. Paul's career has included leadership positions at Bell South, Xerox Corporation, and several entrepreneurial companies as well as 20 years as a university professor. He is an active consultant in communication, human relations, and customer satisfaction. Dr. Timm had written 29 books and scores of articles. He also wrote and appears in six videotape training programs sold worldwide.

James A. Stead teaches management and communication courses at the University of Phoenix. He is the Vice President for Human Resources at Universal Campus Credit Union. His experience includes 27 years in the financial industry. Jim has written a number of training programs and instructional manuals. He has been a trainer for several major training companies, directing seminars throughout the United States and Canada.

PART ONE

Communication and Professionalism

Excellent communication skills can do more to advance a promising career than almost any other factor. Ask managers, lawyers, systems analysts, secretaries, health care providers, retailers, and business people what can make or break a career—handling the technical part of their job or dealing with people—and they'll agree on the latter.

Every day you face challenges like getting and giving correct information, developing strong working (or personal) relationships, attracting new customers and satisfying those you have, working in teams, solving disputes, building consensus for decisions, reducing hurt feelings, giving constructive criticism, "picking other people's brains" for useful ideas, "working around" difficult people, conveying new ideas to others, instructing people, and building a network of friends and coworkers.

All this requires communication skills. Unfortunately, many people never really take a good, objective look at the way they communicate. Many may assume that because they were the life of the party last night, they'll be great communicators at work the next day. Others may conclude that because they tend to be quiet or reserved, they'll never be effective leaders or motivators.

These assumptions are erroneous. Each person develops a unique communication style. That's part of what makes people so interesting and diverse. This part of the book views communication as a broad process that impacts daily life in dramatic ways. You learn ways to make the most of a knowledge of communication in business and the professions as you jump-start, or turbocharge, your career—and your life.

CHAPTER 1

Consistency amid Change: The Future Is Today

CHAPTER 2

The Need for Communication Skills: Career Builder or Career Breaker

Consistency
amid Change:
The Future is Today

L E A R N I N G   G O A L S

After you have studied this chapter, you should be able to:

- Appreciate the impact of technology on communication in business and professions.

- Recognize your attitudes toward communication better.

- Articulate several personal goals for communication skill improvement.

- Understand the value of one-to-one messages in building rapport and life-long relationships.

- Recognize the difference between "share of the market" and "share of the customer."

- Describe some social, economic, and organizational shifts influencing today's business communication.

- Become aware of the new realities of professional communication.

- Define the object of communication.

- Understand the three important expectations in effective communication.

- Cite some myths related to communication in the workplace.

- Commit to excellence in mastering business and professional communication skills.

The Way It Is . . . Back from the Future

For more than 150 years, the telegram communicated immediacy, urgency, and importance. But in 1991, Western Union closed down its telegraph service around the world. It could no longer compete with a newer technology: the fax.

The shift from telegram to facsimile transmission illustrates what some business consultants term a **paradigm shift**—a sudden change in the assumptions about the otherwise steady march of business progress.

The demise of the telegraph industry is only one of countless examples of so-called paradigm shifts—new ways of thinking about and doing business. The list of obsolete products and services replaced by new, previously unimagined ones is long. The pace of these changes seems ever increasing. As recently as 1980, many of today's commonplace devices were not yet used. For example, automatic teller machines, laser printers, or cellular telephones were largely unheard of. Even more incredible, "the number of televisions with remote control devices was statistically insignificant. There were no compact disks, almost no videocassette recorders, and no video rental stores. Only restaurants had microwave ovens. Facsimile machines cost several thousand dollars each, took five minutes or more to transmit a single page, and were found only in very large companies. No one had a personal computer."[1]

Electronic communications ushered in the information age as surely as the automobile propelled the industrial age. The automobile radically transformed both the economy and society. When the automobile first appeared, it seemed to be merely a horseless version of the well-known carriage. Few people then would have imagined that a noisy, smelly, unreliable machine would eventually be responsible for the creation of the suburbs; the undreamed of mobility of families; and the growth of supermarkets, malls, and the interstate highway system—and drive-through fast-food restaurants.

Today's information technology is of no less epic proportions, and most of us are not even remotely prepared. The old business paradigm relying on mass production, media, and marketing is being replaced by a totally new paradigm: a one-to-one economic system propelled by **one-to-one communication** capabilities.

This one-to-one future will be characterized by customized production, individually addressable media, and one-to-one marketing, totally changing the rules of business competition and growth. Instead of market share, the goal of most business competition will be share of the customer—one customer at a time. For example, products will be increasingly tailored to individual tastes, electronic information will be inexpensively addressed to individual consumers, and many products ordered over the telephone will be delivered to the home in eight or fewer hours.

In the one-to-one future, businesses will focus on the kinds of profits that can be realized from long-term customer retention and lifetime values.

Social and Economic Shifts for the New Future

Technology has changed our lives dramatically in the past few decades.

It is easy to find **characteristics of new** technology that seem to reflect huge changes in your way of life. Perhaps just as significant are the **social, economic, and political shifts** that impact business, the professions, and the exchange of ideas.

These kinds of changes will be every bit as disruptive to your lives, and as beneficial, as the Industrial Revolution was to the lives of your great-grandparents. The way you compete will change dramatically enough during the next few years to alter the very structure of society, empowering some and disenfranchising others.

The one-to-one future holds immense implications for individual privacy, social cohesiveness, and the alienation and fractionalization that could come from the breakdown of mass media. It will change forever how many seek information, education, and entertainment, and how people pursue happiness. In addition to the "haves" and "have nots," new class distinctions will be created between the "theres" and "there nots." Some will have jobs that require them to *be there*—somewhere— whereas others will be able to work mostly from their homes or cars, without having to be *anywhere*.

It would be difficult to underestimate the cataclysmic changes that will jolt society as a result of this paradigm shift, which will disrupt everything. Ultimately, one-to-one technology will create an entrepreneurial froth of opportunities. When the dust has settled, millions of new businesses, not even conceived today, will have sprung up across the economic landscape as naturally and randomly as wild flowers after a severe winter.

In a world in which communication and information are practically free, the economic system will be driven more than ever before by genuine innovation and human creativity. In such a world, ideas will be the medium of exchange.[2]

On the social and economic scene, substantial demographic shifts have occurred. Work forces are increasingly diverse—made up of people from a wide range of economic circumstances, cultures, religions, and both genders. Today's work force consists of more two-income families and single parents with the associated family responsibilities this poses. An increasingly educated work force exists and its people are less tolerant of mindless, repetitive work. People expect today to be more involved in organizational decisions and have their input considered.

Politically, organizations face changing government regulations (from further restrictions to deregulation) that reflect levels of social awareness previously not considered in the business world. Equal employment opportunities for people of all backgrounds, persons with disabilities, and gender equity are among the more notable changes of recent years. Similarly, concern for the environment, employee health and safety, and even emotional well-being have become hallmarks of today's successful businesses. Caring companies attract better employees and ultimately succeed in the marketplace.

Your Personal Shifts for the Future

Are you ready to grab onto the whirlwind of change and be a player in this exciting time of business and professional changes? Many people resist or even fear change of the kinds described. It pushes them outside their comfort zone and demands that they learn new skills. Consequently, many people are left behind. Will you be one of them?

Take a few moments to assess your attitudes toward business and professional communication today using the following self-analysis.

Later in this chapter, you learn how this self-test can be useful in setting personal learning goals.

Gaining a better understanding of your communication skills and attitudes is an important first step toward preparing for today's business and professional communication challenges and opportunities.

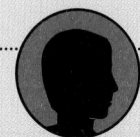

A Look Inside . . . Communication Skills

Communication skills and attitudes improve by shining the light of self-awareness on them. This self-inventory will help identify where you are now. After you've finished reading and applying the material in this book, retake this self-quiz and see how much you've grown.

This measurement, like others in this book, will be useful if you are totally honest in your answers. You need not show this to others; use it as an honest look within yourself.

The following checklist shows how you now see yourself as a communicator. Read each statement, and circle yes or no. After answering yes or no, review each answer, and circle the (+) or (−) to indicate how you feel about your answer. A plus means you are satisfied; a minus means you wish you could have answered otherwise.

Answer honestly based on how you actually feel or act, not how you wish you would.

1. I often have great ideas that I like to explain to other people.

    yes   no   (+)   (−)

2. I am often the person who initiates communication in groups and even with people I don't know.

    yes   no   (+)   (−)

3. When I stand up to speak before a group or in a meeting, I feel a lot of "stage fright."

    yes   no   (+)   (−)

4. Before trying to influence others, I make it a point to be certain that I know as much as possible about their needs and wants.

    yes   no   (+)   (−)

5. When I disagree with others, the argument often becomes too heated, and afterward I regret what I've said.

    yes   no   (+)   (−)

6. I am good at persuading others to my views.

    yes   no   (+)   (−)

7. I would have more influence in my job and social settings if I could communicate my feelings and ideas better.

    yes   no   (+)   (−)

8. I enjoy learning and using new communication technology.

    yes   no   (+)   (−)

9. I regularly clip and save ideas from things I read, or note good ideas I hear.

    yes   no   (+)   (−)

10. I always encourage feedback from others to see if my message is clear to them.

    yes   no   (+)   (−)

11. While listening to others, I try to identify and organize the main ideas being expressed.

    yes   no   (+)   (−)

12. When communicating, I consider feelings and attitudes to be at least as important as facts and ideas.

    yes   no   (+)   (−)

13. In comparison with others, I think I listen more carefully than they do.

    yes   no   (+)   (−)

14. In comparison with my peers, I think that I generally write more effectively than they do.

    yes   no   (+)   (−)

continued on page 7

COMMUNICATOR'S INVENTORY *continued from page 6*

15. I have a good vocabulary.

    yes   no   (+)   (−)

16. I am eager to hear helpful criticism from others after I speak up.

    yes   no   (+)   (−)

17. Improving my professional communication skills is one of my highest priorities.

    yes   no   (+)   (−)

18. I like dealing with people from a wide range of ethnic or cultural backgrounds.

    yes   no   (+)   (−)

19. I eagerly learn and use the latest writing techniques, graphic design ideas, and visuals.

    yes   no   (+)   (−)

20. I know how to use Internet or on-line information services comfortably.

    yes   no   (+)   (−)

This chapter introduces you to the demands of today's and tomorrow's changing workplace. Later chapters in the book detail ways to make the most of such changes. Let's first look at the communication impact of technology changes.

New Media for the Future

One-to-one, tailored messages can now be sent to huge audiences.

In addition to the speed and efficiency advantages of today's media, other considerations have an impact on human understanding. One of the most significant trends is in the increasing ability to generate efficiently personalized, one-to-one messages tailored to the needs and wants of individuals, especially customers, coworkers, and associates.

The power of customized messages should not be underestimated. In an organization's marketing function, for example, there has been a shift from mass marketing—sending the same messages to a massive number of people in hopes that some of them will respond favorably—to individualized marketing—sending a unique message to each individual. This personalization began with word processing, which gave us the ability to produce "merge" letters that include personalized sections interspersed with the generic message.

Today, mass mailers take advantage of this ability to personalize sales letters, sweepstakes entry forms, and even the envelopes they are sent in. Further, some are now including past buying information to convey a personal effect.

There is a progressive movement toward what some experts call one-to-one marketing. The intent of one-to-one marketing is to create long-term relationships with customers and provide for a wide range of their needs. This is a departure from traditional mass marketing.

Mass marketing has used broadcasting, widely distributed print media advertising, and junk mail to gain a larger *share of the market*. If, for example, your store accounts for 10 percent of all the men's wear sold in your town, mass marketing will try to get that share up to 12 or 15 percent. The assumption is that a larger share of market means more profits, but this is becoming less of a sure thing. Adver-

Technology is redefining communication for future employees. (Photo by Bruce Ayres, courtesy of Tony Stone Images.)

tising costs have increased, and results have dropped. It costs more and more money to get a new customer into your store using traditional communication approaches.

One-to-one marketing builds relationships that allow businesses to earn a larger share of the customer's business.

The one-to-one marketing differs from mass marketing. It focuses on establishing and strengthening an ongoing relationship with your existing customers. You do this by gathering as much information about them as possible and responding to their needs. A men's wear store today may do little mass advertising and still be profitable by keeping close to its customers and meeting all their clothing needs. A bank or credit union may expand its services eventually to handle all their customers' financial needs. This is called getting a larger *share of the customer* and has been profitable.

It is today's communication media that make this one-to-one process possible. In the past, keeping track of customer names and addresses, sales data, and personal preferences was a complex and time-consuming process. As the number of customers grew, the task became impossible. Today's computers and point-of-sale electronic recording devices make it easy. You can now track individual preferences, poll customers about their needs, and customize services and products to meet those needs. In short, you can better understand your customers.

(Reprinted by permission: Tribune Media Services.)

Put yourself in Yvonne's position, and respond to the following questions:

1. Why should you be concerned about the problems described?
2. How could team leaders best come up with some helpful possibilities for solving the problems?
3. Do you think you should meet with employees face to face to discuss their concerns? Why? Why not?
4. As a customer, what concerns you when you get slow response or poor service from telephone representatives?
5. How does this case illustrate the importance of communication professionalism in organizational success?

CHAPTER TWO

The Need *for* Communication Skills:

Career Builder or Career Breaker

LEARNING GOALS

After you have studied this chapter, you should be able to:

- Identify the critical role of communication in defining successful individuals and organizations.

- Compare your skills with those required in today's workplaces.

- Understand the personal costs of poor communication skills.

- Describe the four directions organizations must communicate and understand the organizational costs of poor communication.

- Recognize the crucial role of feedback in the learning process.

- Describe the four stages of individual and organizational learning.

- Identify the universal characteristics of managerial work and organizational success.

- Accept the notion that the receiver determines the success of communication.

- Better understand your own comfort zone and your tendencies in reacting to feedback.

The Way It Is . . .
The Best of Companies

In the ten-year period between the first and second editions of their best selling book, *The 100 Best Companies to Work for in America* (1994), authors Robert Levering and Milton Moskowitz have noted positive changes in the best organizations in five key areas. Notice how communication plays a role in defining successful companies that attract workers.

- *More employee participation.* A rarity in the early 1980s, genuine employee involvement in decision making about their jobs is a reality among the best companies. Ironically, this change has often occurred because of layoffs. With fewer supervisors, many companies have been forced to reorganize how work is accomplished. In some cases, the quality movement—the management philosophy of the 1990s—provided specific techniques for increasing employee participation. Effective participation calls for open and honest communication. As Chapter 1 discusses, bosses cannot rely on one-way, top-down communication in today's organizations.

- *More sensitivity to work/family issues.* Many of the best companies have made tremendous strides toward dealing with the problems of working mothers and fathers, offering a variety of child care options and flexible work schedules. Flexibility presupposes that the needs of the individual and the company are clearly understood.

- *More two-way communications.* Accessibility of the top executives is much more common today than in the early 1980s. Even many large firms offer employees opportunities to ask questions—and get answers—directly from their CEOs. In the past, accessibility was too often more symbolic than real. Every manager proclaimed an "open door policy," but many put up intangible barriers that made true openness unlikely.

- *More sharing of the wealth.* Profit-sharing and gain-sharing programs have increased dramatically, as have employee stock ownership plans. Some companies are even extending stock options, typically reserved for a handful of top executives, to everyone in the ranks. Openness about organizational results—good and bad—are now more appropriately communicated to employees at all levels.

- *More fun.* In many more companies, having fun seems to be part of the corporate mission. Fun is not inconsistent with operating a serious, profit-making business. Watch out for companies where there is no sense of humor. Hoopla, celebration, and good-natured fun are a hallmark of top companies.

- *More trust.* Finally, there is a more fundamental characteristic of the new workplace style. In the best workplaces, employees trust their managers, and the managers trust their employees. The trust is reflected in numerous ways: no time clocks, meetings where employees have a chance to register their concerns, job posting (so that employees have first crack at openings), constant training (so that employees can learn new skills), and employee committees empowered to make changes in policies, recommend new pay rates, or allocate the corporate charity dollars. Trust, in the workplace, simply means that employees are treated as partners and recognized as having something to contribute beyond brawn or manual dexterity or strong legs and arms.[1]

How do your skills measure up against the requirements of the new workplace? What skills will best serve you in participating in and leading the companies and professions of the 21st century? Do you know how to generate trust, fun, empowerment, and openness?

Career Success and Your Ability to Communicate

Career success ultimately depends on the ability to help achieve the kinds of conditions described by Levering and Moskowitz. Effective communication is the tool of choice. More than ever before, one's ability to communicate well affects one's capability to thrive in today's organizations and professions. If a person could strive for expertise in but one competence, communication would be the wise choice.

Pretty strong statements, you may say. Consider the following evidence:

- Ninety percent of those who work in careers and professions, do so in organizations. Organizations cannot exist or function without communication.

- Most employees serve customers in their work. Customers cannot be served without communication.

- Professions are constantly creating new knowledge and information breakthroughs. This result could not occur without communication.

- Agencies of government, religion, social action, and education could not accomplish their agenda without communication.

Indeed, the biblical story of God's confounding the language of a wicked people, whether interpreted literally or metaphorically, illustrates the ultimate impediment to human advancement: lack of communication!

In short, communication skills are fundamental to the human experience. The better the skills, the richer the experience.

COMMUNICATOR'S JOURNAL

Rate Your Employer

In your journal, rate the degree to which your employer (or, if you are not employed now, a former employer or your school) measures up to the communication roles of successful companies. List what they seem to be doing (or failing to do) in the areas of participation, sensitivity to family, two-way communication, sharing the wealth, fun, and trust. Use two columns as shown subsequently.

What would you do differently if you were in a position to make changes?

	What They Do	What I'd Do
Participation		
Sensitivity to family		
Two-way communication		
Sharing wealth		
Fun		
Trust		

Good communication skills lead to richer life experiences. (Photo by Walter Hodges, courtesy of Tony Stone Images.)

This chapter attempts to convince you of these facts and motivates you to pursue your personal plan of action enthusiastically to improve your business and professional communication skills.

Today's business and professional success calls for better communication skills than ever before. Several reasons support this claim.

1. Businesses demand more participation and mental involvement from employees and associates at all levels. Companies no longer employ "hired hands" for routine mechanical tasks. They hire the whole person including the brain. (Mechanical tasks are done by machines.)

2. The "hired brains" convey ideas for better organizational success via communication. Progressive companies *listen* to the ideas of their people as well as their customers and other stakeholders. This listening is a crucial communication skill.

3. Because good organizations are more open to ideas, your ability to *articulate* such ideas is increasingly important. Being an active participant in a company, organization, or profession requires active communication.

4. People with poorly developed communication skills can add little to group success. Employers with poor language facility resulting from lack of vocabulary, years of speaking nonstandard English, or not enough reading to appreciate language as the expression of ideas are of little value to a business or organization.

People who develop facility in thinking, articulating, listening, and sharing information find their careers taking off. No set of skills will do more for one's success in life.

Personal Costs of Poor Communication

Writing is a particularly challenging skill for many people.

Written communication is especially troublesome for many people. It's the last of the four major communication functions (listening, speaking, reading, and writing) that most of us learn, and it is probably the most difficult. Written communication problems are widespread. Otherwise intelligent people seem to have enormous difficulty expressing even fairly simple ideas in writing. For some, the problem stems from a lack of vocabulary and working knowledge of sentence structure. More often, however, the problems are emotional in nature: People suffer "writer's block," or they fear that their written words will show them in an unfavorable light.

Let's consider the following scenario as illustrative of typical daily occurrences in companies:

> **"You know, Tom, eight months ago I didn't even think I'd want a career in retailing, and starting Monday I'll be managing my own department," said Carol Watson-Thomas, Mayko's department store's newest manager. "This is almost too good to be true!"**

> **"Don't be so humble, Carol. You've worked hard and you've been a darn good employee for Mayko's," responded Tom. "You'll be a terrific manager."**

> **"I really hope so, Tom. I want the home electronics department to be the best and most profitable department in the store. And you know what else? I want to be a corporate officer some day.**

> **"You've got my support, Carol. Go for it! But first, you'd better be thinking about managing your department. We still need that additional part-time clerk."**

> **"Right, Tom. I'll get on it immediately."**

Carol remembered the new applicant folders that the personnel department had sent to her. She began to leaf through them and was drawn to the striking differences in the letters of application written by the job seekers.

The first letter was from Sandra O'Neil, who said the following:

> **I am deeply interested in a career in retailing with a major department store such as Mayko's. My work experiences in selling shoes and running my own successful A'boné cosmetics business (see enclosed resume for details) taught me the importance of customer satisfaction.**

The other letter, from Clyde Price, included the following sentence:

> **One reason I've held several jobs in the past two years is because none of these jobs afforded me sufficient opportunity to make the kind of money I am capable of earning.**

The rest of the information in the applicant's folders confirmed to Carol the initial impressions created by these short excerpts. Whom do you think Carol will hire?

A second decision Carol faced was the selection of an assistant department manager. Several people seemed to be qualified for the promotion. Again, her decision was heavily influenced by the candidates' communication skills.

Application letters can have a lasting impression on the person making a hiring decision. (Courtesy of Jose L. Pelaez/The Stock Market.)

Earl Wooley looked like the logical choice for the job—he is bright and ambitious with a good head for figures. He can estimate the department's profits with uncanny accuracy, and he has made great buying decisions that produce a lot of income for the store. Earl is not an effective communicator, though, and sometimes lacks subtlety.

Last week, for example, a good customer of Mayko's called to question why the home computer she bought a year ago could not be returned for a full credit. She wanted the new, higher-speed system, but she wanted the full purchase price of her earlier system applied to the cost of the new one.

Earl tried to explain how computers become rapidly obsolete as newer models become available and that her old 386 model was worth little now. In addition, Mayko's doesn't take trade-ins. Ms. Van Dyke argued that Mayko's policy on merchandise returns had always been liberal—no questions asked. She then cut off the conversation saying, "I'll be on vacation at our cabin in the mountains. Would you please send me a letter explaining your inflexibility?"

Earl did not see his response as "inflexible," and he resented having to write the letter. Here is a copy of what he sent to the customer.

Earl mailed the letter and sent a copy to Carol, who just about had a heart attack. She immediately sent a follow-up letter apologizing for Earl's ill-prepared message. It took Carol a full hour on a follow-up telephone call to attempt to save Ms. Van Dyke from becoming a former customer.

Now what do you think of Earl's chances for promotion?

These episodes point to one conclusion: Poor communication skills can quickly sabotage one's career. Even people with good skills in other areas of the business will be severely handicapped by the inability to speak and write effectively.

Mayko's Department Store
North City Mall
East Parkway Drive
Morristown, NJ 07960

July 28, 199x

Ms. Juliette Van Dyke
104 Remote Cabin Road
Boonies, NC 38911

Dear Ms. Van Dyke:

I tried to explain to you on the phone that there
is no way we can trade in your old 386 computer
system. It isn't worth much, and our generous
return policy doesn't apply to antiquated
electronic equipment. This isn't like returning a
dress or sweater. If we took your old computer
back, we'd lose a lot of money.

I personally resent your demand that I explain my
"inflexibility." I'm flexible. But I can't give away
the store's money. You should have known the old
386 computer you bought would be out of date soon.
That's the way it goes with computers—they keep
getting faster and better.

I will be happy to show you our newer systems, but
I can't take the old one back. You got a good deal
on the old one, so I'd be satisfied with that and
understand the realities of this business.

Thank you for shopping at Mayko's, and have a nice
day.

Very truly yours,

Earl Wooley

Earl Wooley
Personal Electronics Specialist

(Reprinted by permission of Johnny Hart and Creators Syndicate, Inc.)

Other business skills will not override the need for good communication skills.

Later examples in the book show you how to respond to a request like Ms. Van Dyke's.

Walter J. Neppl, former president of the J. C. Penney Company, has said:

Possession of even the highest level of business acumen doesn't mean much unless it's accompanied by the ability to communicate clearly and concisely. The man or woman who attempts a business career without firm command of both spoken and written language is like an aspiring pilot who taxis for takeoff without the benefit of flying lessons. In either case, survival would be a miracle.[2]

To carry the flying metaphor a step further, a person entering a business or professional career with no training in communication is about as likely to succeed as a 1920s barnstormer in the age of the space shuttle. No one can realistically "fly by the seat of his pants" in our complex society.

Many people think they are good communicators, but most can improve.

The problem with communication is that most people think they are pretty good at it. Many assume that because their messages make sense to them, their communications also make sense—and are accepted by—others. Some aren't aware of what they don't know. Blundering along without understanding the quality of communication is the worst form of myopia. Like the ostrich, this kind of communicator always leaves one end exposed!

The challenge for each person is one of constant refinement and improvement.

COMMUNICATOR'S JOURNAL

How Does Earl's Letter Strike You?

Let's pause and take a closer look at Earl's letter. How would you feel if you received this from Mayko's? List your specific responses.

What phrases or words particularly upset you? List them.

Now, what would you say to Ms. VanDyke if one of your employees had written this message? Jot down a few ideas—you need not write a whole letter.

What did you learn from this exercise?

Organizations Must Communicate to Survive

Communication creates sustained patterns of action among people in organizations. Without effective communication, coordinated action would be impossible.

Organizations by their very nature must create and sustain patterns of coordinated action among people; they must get people to understand and work together to reach group goals. These action patterns are created and maintained by ongoing communication.

Organizations Communicate in Four Directions

To operate effectively, organizations must communicate effectively in four directions (Figure 2–1).

1. *Downward communication.* This type of communication consists of messages sent from the company's leaders to subordinates. Executives convey directions to managers who pass on information to supervisors who, in turn, communicate with nonmanagement employees. Effective bosses communicate with different subordinates in different ways depending on their perception of the receiver's needs. The trend is toward more frequent and honest downward communication. People at all levels in organizations have a right to know what is going on and successful companies keep them informed. One communication axiom is that there really is no such thing as a secret in an organization–at least not for more than forty-eight hours or so.

2. *Upward communication.* This type of communication consists of messages sent up the line from subordinates to bosses. As we saw in the ideas from *The 100 Best Companies to Work for in America* cited earlier, openness to ideas and input from people in lower organizational levels is often the hallmark of healthy and enjoyable companies. People at all levels can and will have ideas for organizational improvement. Companies that tap into those ideas can benefit tremendously. Companies that do not allow for easy upward com-

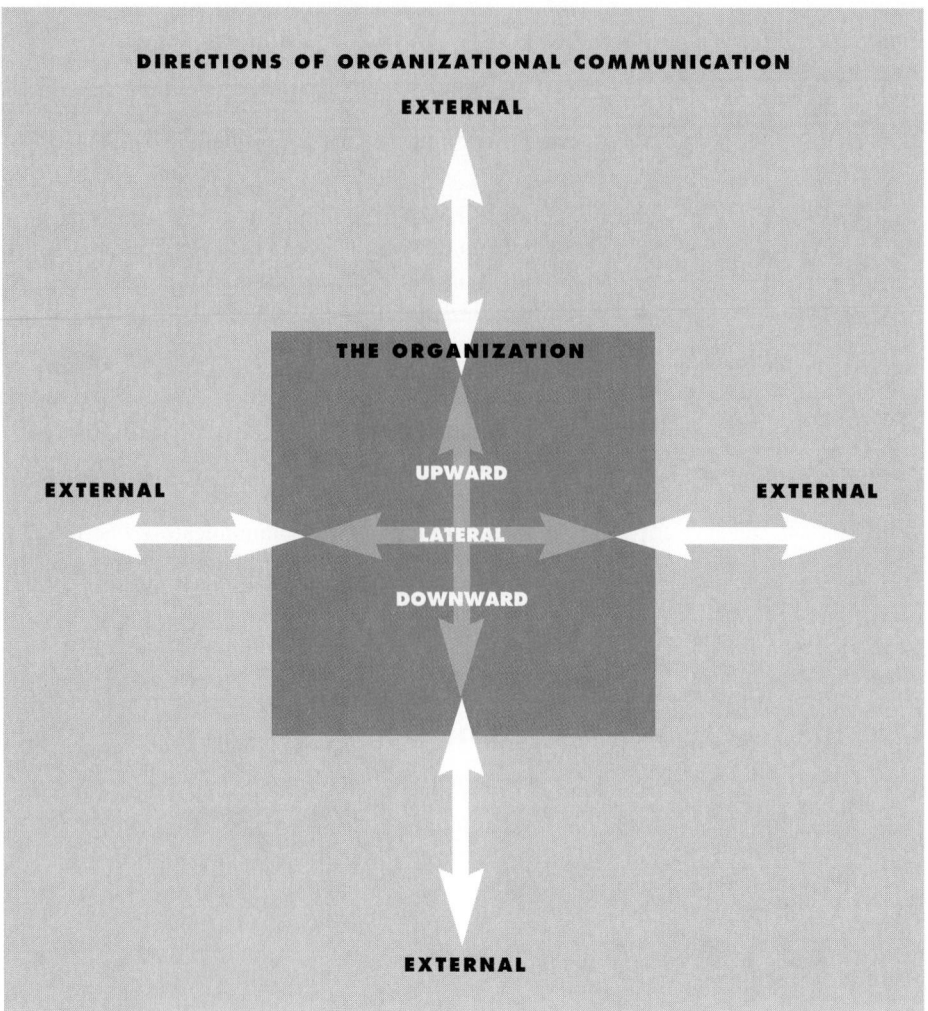

DIRECTIONS OF ORGANIZATIONAL COMMUNICATION

EXTERNAL

THE ORGANIZATION

EXTERNAL   UPWARD   EXTERNAL

LATERAL

DOWNWARD

EXTERNAL

FIGURE 2–1
Four directions of
communication.

All four types of
communication are
necessary for
organizational success.

munication miss the opportunity to tap into a critical resource: their people's ideas.

3. *Lateral communication.* This type of communication occurs when people on the same organizational level share information. One characteristic attributed to successful Japanese companies in the 1980s was their lateral openness. Even private offices were discouraged so that people would talk with their peers freely and openly when they worked in a large "bullpen" setting. Self-directed teams create situations in which lateral communication can flourish.

4. *External communication* is the sharing of messages with people outside the organization, especially customers, suppliers, and other **stakeholders**—people who hold a stake in the success of the company. Sociologists call this "boundary-spanning" communication because it crosses the bounds between the organization and its many publics. In recent years, companies have made extraordinary efforts to get input from outsiders, especially customers.

One Advantage of Bad Writing[3]

The only benefit we have seen from bad writing is that it can be funny. An insurance company claims adjuster collected the following gems received from people who had had accidents and were asked to explain what happened in writing:

- Coming home, I drove into the wrong house and collided with a tree I don't have.
- The other car collided with mine without giving warning of its intentions.
- A pedestrian hit me and went under my car.
- The guy was all over the road: I had to swerve a number of times before I hit him.
- I was on my way to the doctor's with rear-end trouble when my universal joint gave way, causing me to have an accident.
- I told the police that I was not injured, but on removing my hat I found that I had a skull fracture.
- The pedestrian had no idea what direction to go, so I ran over him.
- I saw the slow-moving, sad-faced old gentleman as he bounced off my car.
- The indirect cause of this accident was a little guy in a small car with a big mouth.
- The telephone pole was approaching fast. I was attempting to swerve out of its path when it struck my front end.

Organizational Costs of Poor Communication

When any of these four kinds of communication are poor, organizations wallow in "wheel spinning," persistent misunderstandings, and ineffective information sharing. The results can be chaotic instead of productive.

Here is an example of a typical problem arising from a "simple" memo. Notice how poor downward communication has a dramatic effect on external communication—and company goodwill.

A company memorandum discussing a new policy on customer credit limits was issued with the following apparently innocent sentence in it:

Let's apply this new credit policy with discretion right across the board.

The writer meant that the new policy should be applied in all appropriate cases, but that there would be some cases in which it was not applicable, and care should be taken to handle such cases discreetly.

That was not the impression created in the minds of the people who received the memo. They understood the order to mean that the new credit policy was to be applied to all the company's customers, "right across the board," and the words "with discretion" merely meant they were to be polite about it.

It took just two days for the earthquake to develop. Outraged customers demanded to know what the company meant by refusing to extend the usual credit terms. Tempers were lost. Orders were canceled. Before the tangle was straightened out, it was told, the company had lost $50,000 worth of business.

Management, Professionalism, and Communication Skills

Many readers of this book are preparing for or currently in management positions in organizations. How do management responsibilities affect the need for communication skills? The manager's job calls for a higher level of communication sophistication. That's why managers are typically paid more and why skilled managers are always in demand.

The Functions of Management

The notion that the manager's job consists of certain key functions was articulated early in the twentieth century by Henri Fayol, an early management theorist. He classified these functions as planning, organizing, commanding, coordinating, and controlling. Remarkably, his list has endured through the years with only minor changes. Let's look at each function as it relates to communication.

1. **Planning** is a thinking process—a sort of internal communication within one's mind. The manager looks ahead to what must be done to maintain and improve performance, solve problems, and develop personal competence. To plan, a manager sets objectives in each area that is to be pursued this week, month, and year. Having set these objectives, the manager then thinks through such questions as the following:

   - What has to be done to reach these objectives?
   - How will these activities be carried out?
   - Who will do them?
   - When will these activities occur?
   - Where will this work be done?
   - How much of what kind of resources will be needed?

   Such planning is a communication process of asking questions and creating understanding, sometimes done within one's own head but more often after gathering input from other people.

2. **Organizing** involves arranging the work sequence and assigning areas of responsibility and authority. Having decided the objectives and activities of the work unit, the manager must do the following:

   - Assign these responsibilities to unit staff.
   - Ensure that all responsibilities and supporting authorities are assigned, that none is "uncovered," and that there is no overlapping of responsibilities.

   Downward communication is prevalent in this function.

3. Fayol's principles of **commanding and coordinating** are often summed up in the term *leading,* an area where the manager has the following functions to enable the unit to achieve its objectives:

   - Indicate the direction in which subordinates must go.
   - Generate the energy (motivation) that subordinates must feel.
   - Provide the needed resources.

   Downward, lateral, upward, and external communication determines success in leading.

4. **Controlling** is the function ensuring that the manager and the work group are working toward the selected objectives. It involves comparing actual results to expected or planned-for results so as to identify any deviation from plan. Typically, any deviation from plan leads to a replanning of activities so as to close the gap, although sometimes the objectives themselves are changed in order to be more realistic.

Upward communication of results is critical to this function.

The essence of the manager's job is to accomplish work with and through other people.

The Common Thread in Management Functions

Each of Fayol's functions involves *people*. Herein lies the universal characteristic of the manager's job: It always includes working with other people. Only when managers *accomplish work with and through other people* are they doing the job correctly.

How do you convey to other people what needs to be done or how a task should be done? You accomplish this goal through *communication*.

The Nature of Organizations

Business and professional communications always occur within or in association with organizations. To recognize the nature of such communication better, you should understand some things about the nature of organizations.

In the modern world, you spend most of your lives in some sort of organized activity. At birth you are introduced to an organization called the hospital staff.

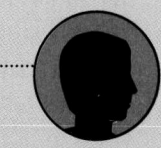

COMMUNICATOR'S PROFILE

Steven R. Mecham, School District Superintendent

Steve Mecham is widely known for being a friendly, pleasant, and highly effective executive. Administering a large school district with many stakeholders (students, teachers, parents, administrators, and the community) calls for constant demands on his communication skills.

Among the characteristics Steve describes for the highly effective business communicator are the following:

1. Keep people informed through constant formal and informal contact.
2. Seek to understand before being understood.
3. Establish relationships of trust as you work to resolve concerns.
4. Keep the mission of the organization in focus, and always remember that the customer comes first.

The greatest challenge Steve faces is in making decisions that "have universal buy-in. Diversity of issues and interests make decisions tough to come by. It can be like herding cats. But when the community starts to see the big picture, not just their own pet view, decisions can be made with everyone's needs in mind."

Within a few days, you actively join an organization called a family. For the rest of your days, your needs and wants are fulfilled directly or indirectly by organizations. Manufacturing, farming, mining, and distribution organizations bring you products to satisfy your material needs. Schools, churches, clubs, and informal social groups serve your needs for information, understanding, personal growth, and affiliation. Governments are organized to provide essential services for the public good.

In contemporary society, there are few legitimate hermits. You can run, but you can't hide. Being a recluse from organizational life is becoming increasingly more difficult.

All people are affected by organizations throughout life.

A Universal Characteristic of All Organizations

When you think about organizations, you may picture the physical aspects like buildings, office space, machines and tools, or capital assets as described in an annual report. Organizations, though, can exist without any of these. Many people work in small organizations with only a few others. But anytime you work with even one other person, you create an organization. The crucial characteristic is that you have *people assembled (physically or figuratively) to achieve some agreed-on purpose.*

This process of assembling and agreeing-on purpose comes about through communication. In more complex organizations, people are called on to be managers. The role of managers—getting things done through the efforts of others—is essentially one of organizing and communicating. The communicating breathes life into the organizing.

Three Organizational Failures

Organizational failures arise when too little communication occurs, too much communication is attempted, or ineffective communication is widespread.

Too Little Communication. Crumbling relationships and dysfunctional families often result from too little communication. Countless numbers of marriages fail primarily because couples withhold expressions of appreciation, concern, or ideas. People who cannot express their feelings to each other in marriage seldom succeed as a family organization.

Keeping people informed and getting a constant flow of information from stakeholders are characteristics of strong organizations.

Likewise, businesses where people have insufficient knowledge of company goals, how its various departments function, or what consumers want run a huge risk of internal confusion and poor market acceptance of their products or services. Good organizations keep their people informed of all appropriate information. Great organizations constantly solicit feedback from stakeholders (all people who share an interest in the company's success) and act on it.

Too Much Communication. The problem of overcommunication may be less commonplace in small companies but can be enormous in larger ones. A common frustration expressed by people in organizations is the feeling that they are saturated by information—much of which requires a decision. People today receive literally thousands of messages each day. They wake up to radio commercials, see signs and billboards on the way to work or school, receive dozens of pieces of mail, flyers, or announcements. One midlevel manager working in the high-technology industry said that after returning from a one-week vacation he had more than 200 electronic-mail (e-mail) messages to review!

Each message calls for one or more decisions. First, you must decide if you are going to pay attention to it at all. Next you decide if it has any relevance and, then whether you should do something it requests. Each decision point complicates your life and demands mental activity. People who find themselves bombarded with enormous amounts of information, much of it irrelevant, may collapse under the load.

This is the organizational equivalent of the old quip: "I asked him what time it was, and he told me how to build a watch." Smart companies keep people informed of things they need to know or may want to know, but don't bombard them with trivia. Unfortunately, one side effect of more efficient media is overload. With the advent of photocopiers in the late 1950s, everyone now had the power to be a publisher. With e-mail, everyone can now be a "broadcaster."

The executive who takes home a bulging briefcase full of "must-do" work each night feels a great deal of stress. Organizations may fail if that stress reaches a breaking point. In Chapter 7, you learn about the increasingly difficult problem of information overload in today's businesses. It can be crippling.

Communication overload can cripple an organization and damage employee productivity.

Widespread Ineffective Communication. Widespread ineffective communication also results in organizational failure for several reasons. Among the most common are unclear direction or coordination, inadequate processing of important data, and missed organizational opportunities. Much of this book is aimed at reducing the chance that your communication will add to this organizational problem.

Successful Organizations Are Continually Learning

Successful organizations are learning organizations.

Today's successful organizations are ones where constant learning is occurring. Enlightened employees at all levels know the importance of constant improvement by discovering and applying new ideas. This process requires good communication.

Stages of Learning

Knowledge for individuals and organizations typically evolves through four **stages of learning.** Notice how the stages relate to communication skills (Figure 2–2).

Without feedback, many people remain in learning stage 1.

STAGE 1: **You Aren't Aware that You Don't Know.** To understand this point, consider the example of an energetic two-year-old boy who wants to ride a bike that he sees his older brother riding. He doesn't know, however, that he doesn't know how to ride it. All he says is, "Mommy, I want to ride the bike." Most people in busi-

FIGURE 2-2

Learning evolves through four stages.

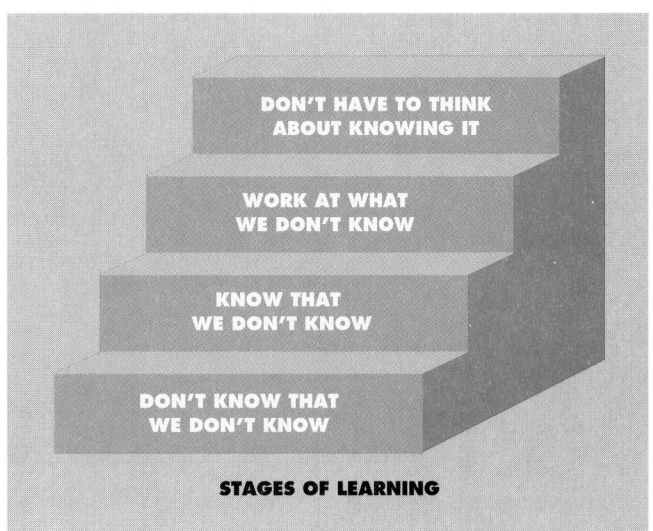

DON'T HAVE TO THINK ABOUT KNOWING IT

WORK AT WHAT WE DON'T KNOW

KNOW THAT WE DON'T KNOW

DON'T KNOW THAT WE DON'T KNOW

STAGES OF LEARNING

ness who do not receive detailed feedback about their communication skills are at this state of unconscious incompetence. They simply are not aware of their interpersonal communication habits.

STAGE 2: **You Are Aware that You Don't Know.** Here you learn that you are not competent at something. This often comes as a rude awakening. For example, a two-year-old boy gets on a bike and falls off. He has immediately gone from stages 1 to 2 and knows that he does not know how to ride a bike. A writer whose tone is offensive (like Earl's letter to the Mayko customer) or a speaker whose mannerisms are annoying makes this shift to stage 2 when the problem is pointed out and accepted as true. A company climate of openness where honest criticism is given freely and with sincere intent, and where people are willing to accept criticism without undue offense helps us move into stage 2.

STAGE 3: **You Work at What You Don't Know.** At stage 3, you consciously make an effort to learn a new skill. Practice, drill, and repetition are at the forefront. This is where most learning occurs. It takes effort and work. The little boy carefully steers, balances, and pedals, and thinks of what he is doing, step by step. The writer or speaker consciously works at changing a distracting habit. An employee takes the time to develop proficiency with new communication media, such as e-Mail, the Internet, and various software programs.

STAGE 4: **You Don't Have to Think about Knowing It.** Here the skill set happens automatically at an unconscious level. For example, a little boy rides his bike without even thinking about it. He can whistle, talk, sing, or do other things with his mind at the same time. A speaker with a distracting habit who has learned to overcome it through practice doesn't have to concentrate on not doing the distracting habit. The business writer feels comfortable in composing a memo or letter.[4]

People and learning organizations evolve through these stages constantly as they adapt to the realities of our fast-changing world.

An example of such a learning effort was undertaken by a company that found a significant communication problem arising from one of its officers who wrote too many poor-quality memos. Much organizational effort was being wasted in (1) trying to figure out what the memo meant, and (2) gathering information and preparing a response to the memo. This officer was a corporate vice-president who had 15 division directors reporting to him. He was unaware of the problem he was creating (stage 1). Consultants Jerry B. Harvey and C. Russell Boettger were called in to assess the situation.

The consultants found the large quantity and poor quality of memos generated by this one vice-president to his 15 division directors was a source of considerable frustration and organizational waste. Harvey and Boettger collected sample copies of the "most confusing, irrelevant, or nonessential" memos. They made transparencies of these, which were projected on a screen in a meeting of the vice-president and his division directors. Participants were then asked to summarize the following in writing on a 3- × 5-inch card:

1. What the reader thought the memo said to do
2. What action the reader would take in response to the memo
3. What priority the reader would give the memo—high, medium, or low

A Look Inside . . . Feedback Receptiveness

Take a moment to answer this short self-quiz. Circle a 5 if the statement is almost always true, a 1 if it's almost never true, and some number in between if it's sometimes true.

A. I feel embarrassed when people point out my mistakes.

    5   4   3   2   1

B. I resent people telling me what they think of my shortcomings.

    5   4   3   2   1

C. I regularly ask friends and associates I trust to comment on how I am doing.

    5   4   3   2   1

D. I know how to offer constructive criticism to others in a sensitive way.

    5   4   3   2   1

E. I like having people tell me their reactions to my activities because it helps me adapt my future behavior.

    5   4   3   2   1

If you scored 4 or 5 on items A and B, you may be putting up some resistance that could deter you from getting useful feedback. People are normally uncomfortable when they receive harsh or insensitive feedback, but even that can be useful if they wring out the emotion and look at the giver's perspective. Even their worst critic can provide a gift of good advice if they do not allow emotion to blind them. Successful communicators learn to look for good advice even when it's buried under a lot of worthless noise.

If you answered 4 or 5 to items C and D, you are creating a climate where helpful feedback is expected and accepted. People and organizations who foster such openness can benefit from others' advice.

If you answered 4 or 5 to item E, you are probably a little unusual. But you are on the right track.

Remember, being open to feedback does not mean that you necessarily agree with it. But if you get little or no feedback, you have nothing to sort out, apply, or learn from.

The consultants collected the cards and led a discussion of the different perceptions compared with what the executive said he intended. In stage 2 what emerged was the fact that the memos were frequently misunderstood—a situation that was costly to the organization.

The consultants then calculated the costs of such misunderstanding—a step researchers too often neglect. Before the memo problem was brought to the awareness of the organization, the average people costs (the vice-president's dictation time, the secretary's transcription time, and the professional staff members' time to collect data and respond) of a sample of memos came to $31 each. The vice-president was generating an average of 61 such memos each month (367 in the six-month period studied). This executive was taught to write more clearly and he practiced his new skills. This took him through the first three stages of learning, and the results for him and the organization were dramatic. Eventually, the executive felt comfortable (stage 4) in sending clearer messages.

A sample of memos analyzed after the consultants' efforts showed the average cost had dropped to $9 each. The company saved about $20,000 per year by reducing the total number of memos and by cutting the costs per note of just this one executive.[5]

Here is an important point: Harvey and Boettger reported this study more than 20 years ago. Adjusting for inflation, the costs would easily be three to four times that today, starting at almost $100 per memo being reduced to $36 each. The $20,000 could easily be $75,000 or more in today's dollars.

It pays to invest some time and effort to move through the four stages of learning. Your success depends on it.

The Critical Need for Feedback

Learning cannot occur without feedback. Unfortunately, many people and organizations do little to encourage or cultivate useful feedback. They "protect" themselves from getting their feelings hurt. Many tune out anything that might undermine their self-confidence. In doing so, they also forfeit an enormous opportunity for growth.

No one needs to agree with all feedback. In fact, you'd be foolish to do so. An attitude of feedback receptiveness, though, is vital to the development of your communication skills.

People and Organizations That Communicate Well

Think for a moment about the places where you regularly do business. Perhaps a supermarket, restaurant, convenience store, or service station comes to mind. Now think further about why you continue to patronize that place of business.

Thousands of people at training sessions thought this way and gave specific reasons why they kept going back to a particular organization. In every group, the responses were the following:

- The waitresses (or proprietors or clerks) are really friendly. They call me by name and seem genuinely interested in me.
- Old Phil at the gas station waves when I drive by.
- Mike the butcher listens to me when I ask for a special cut of meat.
- Sarah's so friendly—she's always willing to help.
- Doc Peterson's nurses are really nice. They seem to take a real interest in the kids.

The words are different, but the theme is almost always the same: The organization, through its people, communicates a sense of caring. Conversely, studies conducted by the Forum Corporation interviewed customers lost in business-to-business relationships. The research concluded that 69 percent of those customers who stopped buying were lost not because of product quality or cost, but because they felt poorly treated.[6]

When people consider what organizations they "hate to do business with," respondents often cite government agencies or departments within a company with a worker who conveys a sense that "I really don't care about you"; "I hate my job and it's partly your fault"; or "I can't be bothered with you now." These employees don't verbalize such statements, but they do convey these impressions.

An obvious and significant challenge for managers is to be sensitive to the ways their organizations (companies, division, work groups, and individual represen-

Tips for Encouraging Feedback[7]

1. *Do not be defensive: listen—do not explain or justify.* Learn to withhold your response. When someone is criticizing you, it is not the time to explain or justify your actions, even if you think the criticism is unwarranted or stems from a misunderstanding. Listen now, and explain later. Being defensive stifles feedback. It tells others you are more interested in justifying yourself than in understanding what is being said.

2. *Ask for more information, especially specifics.* This is a good opportunity to obtain more information. Honest questions will support and encourage the continued flow of feedback. For example, say, "That is helpful; tell me more. Is there anything else I should know about that?"

3. *Express an honest reaction.* You certainly have a right to express your feelings about the feedback received. You may well say, "I am a little surprised you said that, but you may have a point," or "I am not sure what to say. I never even thought of that, but I will from now on."

4. *Thank those providing feedback, and plan for the future.* Let people know that you realize how risky giving feedback can be and express your appreciation for their efforts. This might also be a good time to plan for future feedback sessions. These will be less disturbing and more productive than the first one because you have demonstrated your receptiveness.

You should realize that few people can handle the four points presented. Not because they would not benefit from them, but because it takes a lot of courage to seek out and really hear feedback—especially criticism. The successful communicator is willing to do what the unsuccessful communicator is not. Getting feedback is a classic example of such an action.

Although you cannot ultimately control communication, you can learn effective ways to influence it.

tatives) communicate. Be alert to problems, and be willing to correct and improve communication as an ongoing management activity. This book shows you some ways to do so.

Determining Communication Success

Communication skill building arises from constant learning or attempts to create clear understanding coupled with the awareness that you really can't *control* communication. Yet you can, and must, seek to influence it. This is a frustrating state of affairs for people who want to be dictators, persuaders, or motivators. Many people want to get subordinates to produce more, peers to accept their viewpoint, customers to buy, and bosses to be impressed with them. But ultimately this will happen only when *your message receiver determines the meaning of your messages.*

Getting Out of Your Comfort Zone

Real communication improvement often means letting go of old assumptions and getting out of your **comfort zone** of communicating as usual. Improvement has little to do with talking louder, more emphatically, or more earnestly. It has little to do with increasing the amount of information you project to others. It has little to do with making the message sound better but has everything to do with *developing more understanding.* This means looking at the world through the eyes of others and walking the proverbial mile in another's moccasins. Most people are hesitant to do this, but it is exactly through this kind of empathizing that meaningful improvement of communication occurs.

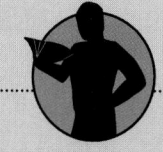

COMMUNICATOR'S
JOURNAL . . . IDEAS
YOU CAN USE NOW

Managing with Questions

Make a copy or write the questions above in your journal for use when you are in a leadership position.

The ongoing process of creating a climate for understanding is no small task. Creation of a garden where understanding grows begins with self-analysis. It matures as we develop empathy for others. It requires extensive effort, and the individual willingness to step outside one's comfort zone. It involves giving of one's self to an extent that many are unwilling and perhaps unable to do.

As with any skill development, great communicators are willing to do that which poor communicators are unwilling to do. They understand the process and work the problem without excessive "pride in authorship" in the ways they've always done things.

> Great communicators are willing to do what poor communicators are unwilling to do: understand their audience.

Why Communication Is an Art

Communicating with another person is not a science. No magic checklist of precise and exacting procedures exists. Specific, sound principles and themes can be learned, but there are thousands of variations on these themes. Thus, it is an art to use your skills and capabilities to best advantage within the framework of the principles outlined in this book.

And like any art, the subtle differences make huge differences in the quality of the finished product.

What makes great art? Often it is the blending of simplicity, clarity, texture, color, sounds, and composition. As communicators, people have access to a vast pallet of color, a wide open canvas, and a world of imagination.

Complex things are easy to do. Simplicity's the real challenge.[9]

Before artists become masters, they became experts in basic brush strokes. They learned the principles of painting. Only then were they *free* to create masterpieces. This book can provide the brush strokes; what you do with them is your choice.

How Can You Become a Better Communicator?

Improving communication skills is a somewhat difficult task for one major reason: You communicate the way you do because you are comfortable doing so. Communication style is a natural part of your personality. When someone says, "You should change the way you communicate," that person is asking you to change your normal behaviors—a most difficult task. But you can improve the effectiveness of your communication if you do the following:

- Acquaint yourself with a wide range of options that can be applied in a given communication situation.
- Try some new approaches to communication.
- Observe the results and make further adjustments as needed.

This book acquaints you with many ideas, all of which are based on accepted communication theory. From these you may select several options worth exploring, but remember that communication is more art than science. There is seldom one foolproof, absolutely right way to communicate. Flexibility and sensitivity are needed to learn to communicate effectively.

Understanding the Basics

SUMMARY OF KEY IDEAS

- The best companies to work for, and the companies that attract the best employees are those that exhibit the following:
    - More employee participation
    - More sensitivity to work/family issues
    - More two-way communications
    - More sharing of the wealth
    - More fun
    - More trust
- All of the preceding characteristics require good communication in four directions: downward, upward, lateral, and external.
- Much of workers' career success hinges on communication skills. Poor skills will damage people and organizations.
- The common thread in the key functions of management (planning, organizing, leading, and controlling) is communication. Communication is the essence of what managers do.
- Organizational failure can stem from
    - Too little communication
    - Too much communication
    - Widespread ineffective communication
- Successful people and organizations are constantly learning.
- Learning cannot occur without feedback.
- The message receiver ultimately determines the success of communication.
- Real communication improvement requires getting out of one's **comfort zone** and trying new behaviors.
- Communication is an art, not a science. There are no magic tricks or foolproof procedures.

feedback receptiveness

downward, lateral, upward, and external

customer service

stages of learning

receiver determines communication success

stakeholder

planning

organizing

commanding and coordinating

controlling communication overload

comfort zone

QUESTIONS FOR FURTHER THOUGHT

1. Why does the message receiver always determine communication success?

2. Who are your customers, right now?

3. How could you possibly exceed the expectations of one of your customers today?

4. What happens when an organization overcommunicates?

5. How successful are most companies at keeping secrets? How does such undercommunicating cost organizational effectiveness?

6. Why is trust so important in making an organization a good place to work? What role does communication play in creating a trusting environment?

7. What's wrong with Earl's letter to Ms. VanDyke (page 31)?

8. Give three examples of each form of communication that might occur in a business you are familiar with: downward communication, upward communication, lateral communication, and external communication.

9. Why is communication regarded as the common thread woven through each of the principles of management?

10. What are the ways that organizations can fail to make the most of communication? How can each be remedied?

11. Describe an example in which you've experienced the four stages of learning.

12. How can you personally encourage additional feedback from others?

Morale as a Competitive Weapon

At Chevron, says Judy Shah, a quality improvement analyst in the company's information technology arm, the morale of the troops is getting more attention than it has in some time. Chevron has cut its staff by about 6,500 workers in the past two years, and employee loyalty and morale took a nose-dive. Now, Shah says, *with a better understanding that productivity and quality gains are often the function of happier workers, the company has started regular checkups on worker morale—called "employee commitment surveys"—and is posting results in lobbies and internal newsletters for all to see.* "The commitment index went down after the downsizing and reorganization," Shah says, "but the company has a new strategic direction of creating more committed workers and teams. To have happier customers, you need happier employees."

Good service performance requires understanding and supportive management—and management that is not threatened by being challenged, say Len Schlesinger, a professor at the Harvard School of Business, and Bill Fromm, president of a Kansas City marketing firm. Management "needs to help its service stars do their best work. These folks are not always the easiest employees to have, but that's only because they never settle into complacency."

The authors say too many service companies (department stores and fast-food restaurants in particular) still operate under the assumption that labor is an "expendable, renewable resource—and then they create unmotivated, underpaid employees who couldn't care less about how well they treat customers."

Experts say some of the most effective morale-boosting tactics are often low-cost, everyday things management can do to let workers know their work is appreciated, their concerns and fears are being heard, and what they should expect in the future. Honest communication usually tops the list. *People simply want an honest appraisal of any changes that will affect them—with no management doublespeak—and to be shown lines of communication can run both ways.* One manager told [the author that] every bad decision he's ever made was because "I didn't really talk to the people directly involved in a project or a change process."

And taking as a given that workers are fairly compensated, most employees just want to hear periodically from someone who matters to them that their work makes a positive difference, or their career development goals are taken seriously.

Of course, there are other things companies can do to ease the stress of those in customer contact positions. Many companies no longer require more than three or four hours of customer contact during a service representative's eight-hour work day; those in the fast-food and airline industries often give their front-liners this kind of break. Businesses with intensive customer contact need to take care to devise schedules so employees who have been "on stage" too long are rotated away from customers for a while.

At the Home Shopping Network (HSN), executives are increasingly aware that the morale of front-line workers determines what kind of service customers receive. Call centers are notorious for burnout, with annual rates of 80% common. HSN's turnover is a well-kept secret, but is generally regarded as among the lowest in the business. One reason is the company "tries to treat the whole employee," claims Melanie McCarthy, formerly a training manager and now director of interactive operations. In ongoing stress management training for phone reps, for instance, trainers now conduct visualization exercises to help workers cope with stress, and use role-plays featuring worst-case scenarios with irrational customers, "so individuals realize this happens to everyone and isn't a personal thing," says McCarthy.

She says the company's top executives are "acutely aware" of how morale issues can affect corporate performance—especially customer satisfaction. HSN works hard to break down management-employee barriers and build trust levels. Executives regularly visit the call centers, sometimes serving phone representatives popcorn from a cart. "It gives them a chance to talk with workers in a very unthreatening way, and hear their concerns," McCarthy says.

Another program, called "In Touch"—a brainchild of the CEO—asks executives at the director level and above to spend a full day in the call center listening in on customer calls, and then taking a few calls themselves. The program not only sends a message to front-liners that management cares about what they do, McCarthy says, it also gives executives an in-the-saddle perspective of the quality of worklife on the front lines and service issues customers are concerned about.

At the Coleman Co., a maker of camping and recreational equipment in Wichita, KS, one way front-line morale issues are addressed is by giving workers more variety in their day-to-day work and increased decision-making power. Kathy Welch, director of worldwide customer service, says she has taken the initiative to form self-directed work teams in her unit.

"We had always informally worked in teams and been cross-trained extensively to back each other up—it was just a matter of making the team structure more formal," she says.

The role of team facilitator rotates among team members. Many in her department also serve on cross-functional teams including employees from shipping, traffic, warehouse, and credit, with the purpose of finding ways to streamline processes and improve internal service. Customer service workers also attend sales meetings, and report that they enjoy the change of pace and chance to interact with workers from other departments in both duties, Welch says.

Service representatives are encouraged to periodically get away from the phones by visiting with their regular customers face-to-face or traveling to trade shows. There are also frequent celebrations and service awards given in Welch's unit.

Welch says it's something of a morale lift when Coleman's executives make a point of visiting her area to chat with workers, "asking them what kind of customer concerns they're hearing, what they might change in processes, what's keeping them from doing a good job."

Making work more interesting and varied is also key to improved morale at Taco Bell, a fast-food subsidiary of PepsiCo. The company historically relied completely on the command-and-control style of supervision—one manager for each restaurant, one area manager for every six restaurants, and one mind-numbing job for each employee. But

following companywide reengineering, many Taco Bell outlets now operate without traditional managers; self-directed teams manage inventory, schedule work, order supplies, and train new employees. *These team-managed restaurants have lower employee turnover and higher customer satisfaction scores than do the remaining traditionally-run restaurants, Taco Bell reports.*

Excerpted from Dave Zielinski, "Companies Make the Link: Happy Employees Create Satisfied Customers," *The Service Edge,* Vol. 7, No. 8 (August 1994): pp 2–3. Reprinted with permission of Lakewood Publications.

Applying Your Knowledge

1. How are "Employee Commitment Survey" results communicated to employees?

2. What are some low-cost, everyday things management can do to let workers know their work is appreciated?

3. Do you agree with the article that honest communication tops the list of what employees need to boost morale? Why?

4. How do HSN executives attempt to break down management-employee barriers and build trust levels?

5. List similarities from this article to the five positive changes in successful organizations discussed in the chapter.

Applying Your Skills

ACTIVITY 2-1: Feedback Receptiveness Is an Attitude

Think back to the last time you received criticism from someone else. To what degree did you

1. Hold back on defending or explaining yourself until the full criticism was fully expressed?

2. Work to understand the critiquer's viewpoint as best you could?

3. Ask for elaboration or clarification without being overly defensive?

4. Express an honest reaction?

5. Thank the person for the feedback?

For most people, *giving* criticism (even in a constructive way) is risky. When people first offer

such feedback, they watch closely to gauge the receiver's responses. The reaction they receive will usually determine whether they will offer feedback again. This means that *you* have the opportunity to avoid turning off future feedback that could be valuable to you.

ACTIVITY 2-2: Breaking Out of Your Comfort Zone

1. Describe something you recently did to push yourself outside your comfort zone (for example, introduced yourself to a stranger, asked for a date, participated in a city council meeting, called in to a radio talk show, tried a new skill, gave a talk, or sang before an audience).

2. How did you feel about this step outside your comfort zone before you did it? (Be specific about your apprehensions.)

3. How did you feel after you accomplished it? (Be specific.)

Even if you didn't totally succeed at what you tried, you should feel good about making the effort.

Once you push out of your comfort zone, you are ready to try new behaviors. This book provides many ideas about new communication behaviors that work for people. Try them, and then look at your results. Think about what went well, what didn't go so well, and how to try it a little differently next time.

Life is a constant process of experimentation and learning. Life is a do-it-to-yourself project; the more you learn to do, the more successful you will be. Because so much of life involves communication, doesn't it make sense to build your communication skills?

ACTIVITY 2-3: Fixing Earl's Letter

Go back to the letter on page 31 written by Earl Wooley to the customer of Mayko's. Rewrite the content of that letter to convey the message more tactfully.

PERFORMING
on the Job

CASE 2-1 The Give-Me-Feedback CEO

You are a member of the management team for WHAM Financial Services. You and the other six members of the team have been employed at WHAM for a minimum of ten years each. The CEO was recruited from outside the organization more than three years ago. The CEO is a "get-things-done" type with a dominant personality. He meets problems head on and has accomplished what the board of directors requested in terms of company profits and expense reduction. The management team meets weekly and sometimes more often depending on the issues.

For the past few months you have noticed the CEO requesting feedback, during meetings, on issues, and the following characteristics occur:

1. Interrupts speaker with an idea or thought unrelated to requested feedback.
2. Repeats ideas just given by the speaker as if he had not heard a word.
3. Physically preoccupied with note taking and side conversation while speaker is attempting feedback.
4. Defensively questions the feedback, often interrupting before the speaker is finished.

In your observations, you have noticed that the other members of the team are hesitant to give information or ask questions. It appears that improved communication is needed for the organization to continue functioning successfully. You become aware, in a discussion with two other team members, that they are experiencing frustration and are losing their desire to even try to communicate or to give feedback. There seems to be an attitude of "Whatever the CEO wants is fine with me," and a feeling that feedback is not really wanted.

Case Questions

1. What problems do you see in the communication behavior of the CEO?
2. What do you think might be the reasons for such behavior?
3. How would you feel about discussing your observations with the CEO?
4. Would you be willing to give feedback in this situation?
5. If the behavior is affecting the management team, do you think it would be affecting the rest of the staff? Why or why not?

CASE 2-2 A Distracted Employee

John Jenkins supervised the human resources function at Smooth Ride Helicopter (SRH). SRH is a medium-sized aircraft leasing company employing 150 people. The human resources department consists of John, Cynthia, and Tracy. In addition to supervising, John is responsible for personnel policy and procedure, legal aspects of employment, and overseeing the hiring and firing of employees. Cynthia's responsibilities include employee documentation, benefits, time keeping, payroll, and employee files. Tracy is responsible for training and development. All three people have expanded their positions as SRH has grown and the need has become apparent for definite human resource functions.

Within the last year John has noted a change in the working habits of Cynthia. She was remarried a year and a half ago, and her priorities have shifted away from her duties. She moved approximately 50 miles away from SRH, which created a one-hour minimum commute each way to work. John and Cynthia have visited informally about the situation. He has expressed concern about her on-time record and her ability to assist employees in her areas of responsibility. Several employees have complained to John that Cynthia is often not available, and when she is, she is "short" in patience with them and fails to meet their needs.

John realized he had to try a different approach to communicate his concerns to Cynthia. Rather than a face-to-face discussion, he put a list of concerns in a memo to Cynthia. The concerns included the following:

- Availability for employees (schedule)
- Difficulty of the daily commute
- Treatment of employees

He requested that she review the memo before a meeting to discuss the issues. Cynthia seemed to appreciate getting the information in writing, and did take the time to ponder her situation and make recommendations to improve.

Case Questions

1. What were John's discussions with Cynthia lacking?
2. Did John have adequate information regarding Cynthia's behavior before writing the memo?
3. Would it be appropriate for John to ask Cynthia, "Do you want to be here?"
4. How can Cynthia improve her communication with employees?
5. Why is communication from the human resource department to employees important to the operation of the organization?

PART TWO

Communication:
Consistency
amid Change

New technology and expectations, and different ways of doing business
have largely improved our ability to deliver
products, services, and information in ways
undreamed of even a decade ago. The human
side of communicating, the purposes of information sharing, and the desire to achieve
professionalism and efficiency continue to motivate successful people to build and enhance
their skills and understanding.

The chapters in this part look at communication
and the impact of technology changes facing
today's businesses and professions. Although
technology advancements play a major role,
they are not the only changes. Nor should we
assume that all things have changed. Clearly,
much of what makes up good communication
is rooted in consistencies—factors that have
and will remain the same.

This part of the book is about those elements
that change and those that remain the same,
and how these affect business and professional communication.

Human *and* Organizational Needs:
Communication, Motivation, and Success

LEARNING GOALS

After you have studied this chapter, you should be able to:

- Recognize the basic human needs that can be satisfied via effective communication.

- Comprehend the role of communication in people's needs for achievement, affiliation, and power.

- See that the fundamental need of business and professional organizations is to identify and meet customer needs.

- Profit from the application of a total quality service model in any kind of organization.

The Way It Is . . . Give the Teller a Smile[1]

The next time you go to your bank, give the teller a smile and an encouraging word. He or she could probably use it. Meager pay, minimal raises, expanded duties, and the specter of layoffs are hanging like a dark cloud over many employees on banking's front lines. "Morale stinks," says one assistant branch manager bluntly.

It used to be a job at a bank was pretty much a guarantee of lifetime employment, with weekends and evenings free to spend with the family, and with good prospects for moving into senior management. Cashing checks, taking deposits, and asking about the kids were a teller's main duties.

These days, banks are closing branches and squeezing costs. Those that remain have extended hours during weekdays—and now demand even weekend duty. With automated teller machines (ATMs), telephones, and computers handling a growing number of everyday transactions, banks are loading tellers up with new tasks.

It's not unusual, for example, for tellers to get weekly sales quotas on the number of accounts or certificates of deposit they're expected to open, or the number of referrals or contacts they're expected to make. Some banks even demand tellers call customers at home to push new products like mutual funds. At some banks, tellers aren't even tellers anymore but "associates." They don't work in branches but in "sales offices."

"When I first started, it was a bank. You cashed people's checks and helped them with a problem. You didn't have to push a product of the month," says a fifteen-year veteran who was among scores of midlevel managers laid off recently as part of a cost-saving consolidation of branch duties at her bank.

Banks contend that they deal with employee rancor by involving branch employees in ways to schedule workers, award incentive pay, and handle other hot-button issues. "It's critically important to me that our employees . . . feel they have a stake in our success," says an executive vice-president of retail financial services. Banking's need to change employees' roles and expectations is no different from other industries' need to confront the cold realities of the leaner-and-meaner American workplace. Many companies have gone through prolonged downsizings and restructurings that, at the cost of massive layoffs, have helped automakers, computer chip manufacturers, and other U.S. industries boost productivity and recapture lost market share.

Now it's banking's turn. After decades of acting like marble monoliths that dictated to their customers, only to see their share of U.S. financial assets fall from nearly 90 percent at the beginning of the century to less than 40 percent by the 1990s, banks are changing their tune. They're asking customers what they want, and targeting small businesses and affluent individuals—two segments of the population with which banks have maintained relationships.

All this has banks striving to retain and win back customers lost over the years to mutual funds, insurers, brokerages, and finance companies with a zeal reminiscent of the late Sam Walton, the enthusiastic founder of retail giant Wal-Mart. "We must be a low-cost provider"; "we must focus on the customer"; and "we must sell, sell, sell" are the mantras of many banking executives these days.

Unfortunately for tellers and other branch workers, this new paradigm doesn't bode well. A study last year found that one-half of all bank customers prefer conducting transactions outside of branches—and that more than one-half of all retail banking transactions, such as deposits and withdrawals, already are done at ATMs, by telephone, or by computer.

The same study estimated the average cost of a transaction is $1.07 if done by a teller, $.35 if done by phone, and $.27 if done at an ATM.

Not surprisingly, banks are pushing nonbranch alternatives in a big way while they close branches. That's not to say that branches will become a thing of the past. "Branches are not going to go away in our lifetime," says a principal in

continued on page 57

PERFORMANCE CHALLENGE *continued from page 56*

the San Francisco office of McKinsey & Co., a consulting firm. "People can eat at home or eat takeout but they still choose to go to a restaurant. You can buy almost anything you want—a software program, or suit, or dress—at a mall or by phone. But people still choose to shop in person. When people have problems, they still like to talk to someone face to face."

To offset the higher cost of operating a branch, however, banks will have to push more product, he said. This will require branch workers to be more flexible and to learn multiple tasks—such as handling loan requests, generating sales of mutual funds and other nontraditional products, and working odd hours to match the ebbs and flows of customer traffic.

How banks involve branch employees in making these changes will be a key to how well their strategy works, consultants agree. "If you end up demoralizing the employees, you can end up losing business."

What banks can't do, says Robert Kelley, a business professor at Carnegie Mellon University, is tell employees this is the way it is and leave it at that. "Those organizations that have a weak relationship between the employee and management almost always have a weak link between employees and the customer," he says.

The changes described in banking are not unlike those found in a wide range of businesses. These changes are almost always rated in changing needs. In this case, the banks need

1. To compete more effectively with other financial institutions
2. To adjust to changing customer demands for longer hours and different services
3. To keep costs down to remain competitive

These changing organization needs impact individuals working in the banks. They are now required to adjust their needs for

1. Job security and predictability
2. Advancement opportunity
3. Opportunity for personal interaction with customers
4. Convenient work hours
5. Salesmanship as a job requirement

This opening scenario is a way of introducing the fact that people and organizations all have needs that, if not satisfied, will lead to stress, frustration, anger, hurt, inability to compete, and general disruption of the status quo.

Communication and Human Needs[2]

Let's look first at some universal human needs and talk about their relationship to business, professions, and communication. First, some basics about needs.

Basic Needs Everyone Has

Maslow's hierarchy of needs was a major contribution to our understanding of motivation.

Psychologist Abraham Maslow believed that behavior can best be explained in terms of individuals seeking need satisfaction.

He also saw that different needs work on people at different times and that some needs are more generic to all people than others. Until basic or "lower-order needs" are satisfied, "higher-order needs" cannot and will not motivate a person.

Maslow boiled down his list of needs to five: survival, security, belonging, esteem, and self-fulfillment (Figure 3-1).

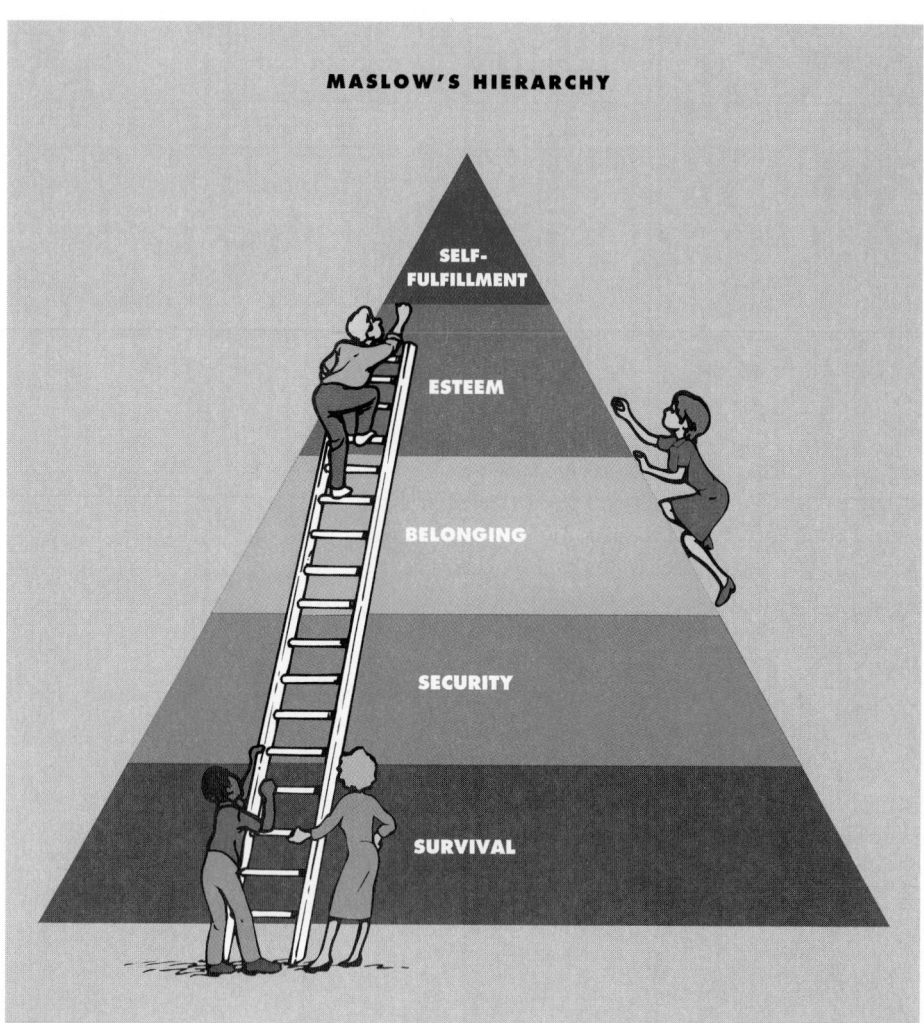

FIGURE 3–1
Maslow's hierarchy of needs.

You cannot be motivated by higher-level needs if these most basic needs are not met.

Survival Needs. The human need to be physically comfortable is the most basic type of need, according to Maslow. Whenever you put on mittens in cold weather, replenish your body with food and water after exercise, or step outside for a breath of fresh air, you are seeking to satisfy these physical needs.

Most can understand how difficult it would be to pay attention to other types of needs if such basic needs are not met. Consider trying to listen to a class lecture, for example, while you are hungry or uncomfortable in a hot, stuffy room. These unsatisfied physical needs are likely to dominate your thoughts and behavior, even though you'd prefer to concentrate on your higher goal of studying effectively. If you get a pizza or get out of the room, then you can think about the higher need to learn from the lecture.

You may quit a job that you see as too dangerous.

Security Needs. The next level of needs in Maslow's hierarchy deals with safety and security: freedom from fear of physical danger, the need for self-preservation, and the concern for the future. In the early years of the industrial revolution, many workers were fearful of injury or even death on the job. These concerns, in part, led to the organization of labor unions and other pressure groups. Fear of being a crime victim caused workers to push for better security in convenience stores.

People respond to unmet needs for security in several ways. They may quit a job if it is too physically dangerous. They may be especially motivated to observe certain safety precautions to reduce the chance of accident or injury. Others may save some money from paychecks just in case their income is cut off. Once people feel reasonably secure, still higher needs become primary motivators.

Most people need good relationships with others.

Belonging Needs. Some of us do prefer to be left alone, but most people have a basic yearning for relationships with others. For example, people who are imprisoned, such as the prisoners of war in Vietnam, demonstrate the **need for affiliation.** These prisoners relate that after being kept in isolated captivity for many months, they worked out a crude code system that allowed them to send messages by tapping on the wall of their dungeons. Their reaction was nearly ecstatic when they could "talk" to others and reaffirm that they were not alone. As a less dramatic example, studies have shown that employees who work away from others, such as toll takers or bank tellers who work in isolated, drive-in facilities, tend to be less satisfied on the job. They typically cite the lack of interaction with other employees as a source of their dissatisfaction.

Recognition and rewards can satisfy our need for esteem.

Esteem Needs. People feel varying levels of a need to be recognized. Many like to receive "strokes" that tell them, "Your efforts are appreciated, and you are valued." Subtle rewards, such as private offices, carpeting, or a more desirable location in a workroom, can communicate this recognition and sense of worth to individual employees.

Status symbols, such as new automobiles, jewelry, and expensive clothing, are attempts to communicate our esteem.

Self-Fulfillment Needs. Maslow coined the term **self-actualization** to identify the need to maximize one's potential. The artist who produces her best painting and the author who creates what he regards as a literary masterpiece are examples of self-actualized people.

The employee who seeks to satisfy self-fulfillment needs strives to produce the best possible job. This employee is best motivated by supervisors who are supportive by providing an environment where self-directed work may occur. Communication to the self-actualized employee is much different from communication to people at lower need levels.

Other Needs That Affect Human Behavior

Some people have an exceptionally high need to achieve.

People are also motivated by a variety of social needs including the drive to achieve certain goals or objectives, the need to affiliate with others in meaningful activity, and the need for power or status.

Need for Achievement. David C. McClelland has spent a lifetime studying the human urge to achieve. His research has led him to believe that the **need for achievement** is a distinct human motive that can be a dominant drive in certain people. The need for achievement has been studied in a wide range of experiments. One typical experiment went something like the following:[3]

Participants in the experiment were asked to play a ring-toss game. Their objective was to throw the rings so that they would hook on a peg. That was the only instruction given to participants. The variable that the experimenters looked for was how close to the peg the individual subject stood when tossing the rings. The subjects could stand anywhere they wanted to.

Most people tended to throw randomly, first standing very close and later perhaps stepping back. But people with a high need for achievement seemed to measure

carefully where they were most likely to get a sense of mastery—not too close to make the task ridiculously easy or too far back to make it impossible. They set moderately difficult but potentially achievable goals.

People with a high need for achievement tend not to be gamblers. They prefer to work on a problem rather than leave the outcome to chance. They don't mind taking moderate risks, but they want to have as much control as possible over the outcome. They plan, gather information, and communicate to gain skills needed.

Achievement-motivated people gain satisfaction from the accomplishment itself. They do not reject rewards, but the rewards are not as essential as the achievement itself. Such people get a bigger kick out of winning or solving a difficult problem than from the money, praise, or other rewards they may receive.

These people enjoy and appreciate receiving concrete feedback. They respond favorably to getting information on how well they are doing on the job. However, they tend to resent comments or information not directly relevant to the work. They want task-relevant feedback so they can know the score.

From this description, one can see that achievement-motivated people would be desirable in organizations. As managers, however, high achievers may be overly demanding or have unrealistically high expectations of others. How they communicate these expectations can help or hinder cooperation with others.

Need for Affiliation. Another driving need identified in some individuals is the **need for affiliation.** Some people have an unusually high desire to be accepted by others. They conform to what they believe other people want from them. If the work group has high goals, effective work habits, and other organizationally desirable characteristics, the group will tend to pull the individual member up to a high level of per-

People with a high need for achievement appreciate task-relevant feedback.

Some people have an exceptionally high need to be accepted.

Some people have a driving desire to achieve goals. (Photo by Michael Ponzini, courtesy of Focus on Sports.)

formance. Likewise, low performance can result from group pressures in the opposite direction.

A cartoon showing a work foreman talking to another is captioned: "Posting individual productivity reports has really created a competitive spirit among employees . . . they boast about who does the least." That outcome may be the result of high needs to be accepted by the group, even at the cost of poor achievement.

Research on affiliation needs suggests that a common goal among people who have a high need for affiliation is social interaction and communication with others. Such people dislike being alone or being left in the dark.

In some cases, affiliative behavior is linked with the need to reduce anxiety. People may interact with others because they have fears or stresses that can be relieved, in part, by others. It's the "misery loves company" idea. In other cases, individuals simply enjoy being with people.

People with a high need for affiliation seek the company of others and take steps to be liked by them. They try to project a favorable image, and they will work to smooth out disagreeable tensions in meetings or teams. They help and support others and want to be liked in return.

Some people have an exceptionally high need to exert power.

Need for Power. A third type of driving need considered here is the **need for power.** Some individuals have a strong need to dominate people, win arguments, persuade others, and prevail in every situation. These people are likely to be driven by a high need for power.

Many people have a high need for affiliation. (Courtesy of General Electric Company.)

A strong power drive is not necessarily undesirable.

The concept of a need for power is not new. Machiavelli, a sixteenth-century philosopher and politician, was a master at using power to get his way. In fact, his name has become synonymous with a personality type that likes to manipulate others. A strong power drive, however, is not necessarily undesirable or reflective of a character defect. In its positive sense, power is the process by which a leader's persuasive and inspirational behavior evokes a "can-do" feeling in subordinates. Power can build confidence in people. The active leader who helps a group set and achieve goals uses power constructively.

Managers should strive to recognize the effects of needs on people.

There is nothing wrong with having a high need for power, affiliation, or achievement. Each can be useful and productive to an organization. The key is to recognize the influence of these needs on the behavior of employees—especially communication behavior.

Growing Trend toward Self-Actualization

Today, work is seen as more than just a source of income.

One distinct trend of the past decades is the movement toward increasing emphasis on self-actualization. This trend is marked by several shifts in what had been traditional thinking.

The first shift is that people are viewing work as a source of more than just financial income. In their book *Re-inventing the Corporation*, John Naisbitt and Patricia Aburdene explain the trend this way.

> There is a new ideal about work emerging in America today. For the first time, there is a widespread expectation that work should be fulfilling—that work should be fun.
>
> Thirty years ago, that would have been an outrageous notion. . . . Nevertheless, people know intuitively that work ought to be fun and satisfying, even when it is not.
>
> Today . . . the same forces which are re-inventing the corporation are transforming this deep human need into a realistic expectation in the workplace. The economic demands of the information society together

with the new values of the baby boom generation are fostering the "work should be fun" idea.[4]

The second shift in traditional thinking lies in the ways people view job security. Today, relatively few people can expect to join a corporation after graduation from school and remain securely there until retirement. With so many companies being re-structured or taken over, or simply going out of business, old-fashioned job security with a big corporation is largely a myth.

As a result, more people are recognizing that job security is achieved by developing excellent and marketable skills that are in demand. In addition, many more people are starting their own businesses. Entrepreneurs often gain feelings of control over their own destiny and freedom that are not available in traditional organizations.

The final shift is that people are rethinking the broader issue of balancing career and other life activities. People need to feel fulfilled in all areas: career, family or relationships, self-development, and so forth. People are increasingly recognizing the need for self-management and life balance.

As one author put it, "We have the same amount of mental energy and the same number of hours in a day as people of other generations and other locations, but we have so many more demands, so many more things. We live in the first time and place in the world's history and geography where challenges stem not from scarcity but from surplus, not from oppression but from options, and not from absences but from abundance."[5]

The senior editor of *Training* magazine, Ron Zemke, sums up a shift toward different motivators in the 1990s: "Personal growth and life satisfaction are back [as important motivators]."[6]

Our point in this chapter is that human needs remain fairly consistent and that these must be considered in any communication attempts.

The bank tellers in our opening story are facing changes in the workplace yet their underlying needs remain constant. As individuals, they will have been known to psychologists for some time. Among these needs are survival, security, belonging, esteem, self-fulfillment, achievement, affiliation, power, and a broader sense of self-actualization and balance in their work and personal life.

Messages aimed at impacting people's behaviors must appeal to the appropriate need(s).

The next section considers the needs of organizations.

Communication and the Ultimate Organizational Need

Regardless of the type of organization or profession you are engaged in, one fundamental need lies at the core of its success: the need to create and maintain *customer satisfaction* through quality products, service, and information. Business and professional communication is critical to this process.

Linking Communication, Customer Satisfaction, and Quality

Customer service and organizational quality depend on effective communication. When you get right down to the basics of professional success, satisfying customers is pivotal. You can gain tremendous benefits from recognizing the link between communication skills and success with customers. The remainder of this chapter describes that critical link and shows you some examples. The important theme of customer satisfaction continues through the remainder of this book.

The Widespread Concern about Customer Satisfaction

Customer service horror stories are everywhere. People are fed up with a lack of communication, concern, courtesy, and competence displayed by employees who are supposed to serve. A lot of people agree with management guru Tom Peters who sums up the frustration of consumers when he says "customer service stinks."

In the manufacturing age, managers focused their efforts on reducing product defects. In the information age, they are refocusing on efforts to avoid customer defections. It's not unusual for a typical company to lose 10 to 30 of its customers each year. Most of these defecting customers do so because of dissatisfaction with the company's service. In today's business environment, people can buy the same kinds of products from many different places. The determining factor that will cause them to buy from one place over another is how well they are treated.

The Price of Failing in Customer Satisfaction

The failure to build strong customer relationships will destroy your chances for success. No matter what else the company is doing well, poor service will drag it down. Consider the following:

- It costs five times as much to attract a new customer as it does to keep an old one. Ironically, few companies have a systematic strategy for **customer retention.**

- If an unhappy customer tells eleven others about a bad experience and these eleven each tell five others, 67 people will get the bad word about a company. These are typical ripple effects of bad service.

- Sixty-eight percent of customers who stop doing business with an organization do so because of company indifference.

- It takes twelve positive incidents to make up for one negative incident in the eyes of the customer. Nevertheless, 95 percent of complaining customers will give you another chance *if you resolve their problems promptly.* Unfortunately, most organizations have no reliable mechanism for receiving complaints in time to fix them.

- Only 4 percent of unhappy customers even bother to complain. For every complaint heard, 24 others go uncommunicated to the company—but not to other potential customers.

Recognizing customer service as the core organizational need can focus you on an exceptional opportunity for distinguishing yourself and your organization and for gaining a significant profit advantage (Figure 3-2).

By increasing the rate of customer retention by as little as a few percentage points, organizations have seen their profits jump by 25 to 100 percent, according to one consulting executive.[7] Likewise, companies that excel at customer service do a much better job of retaining employees. A direct correlation has been shown between the customer-retention rate and work force stability.

Why can't the boss simply order people to give good customer service as some naive leaders have been heard to do? Because customer service, like other kinds of communication, is a complex process. If it were easy, every company would excel at it. It isn't easy, however, and they don't—therein lies the golden opportunity.

The organizations that succeed at reducing customer defections will unquestionably thrive and prosper; others can look forward to only diminished success.

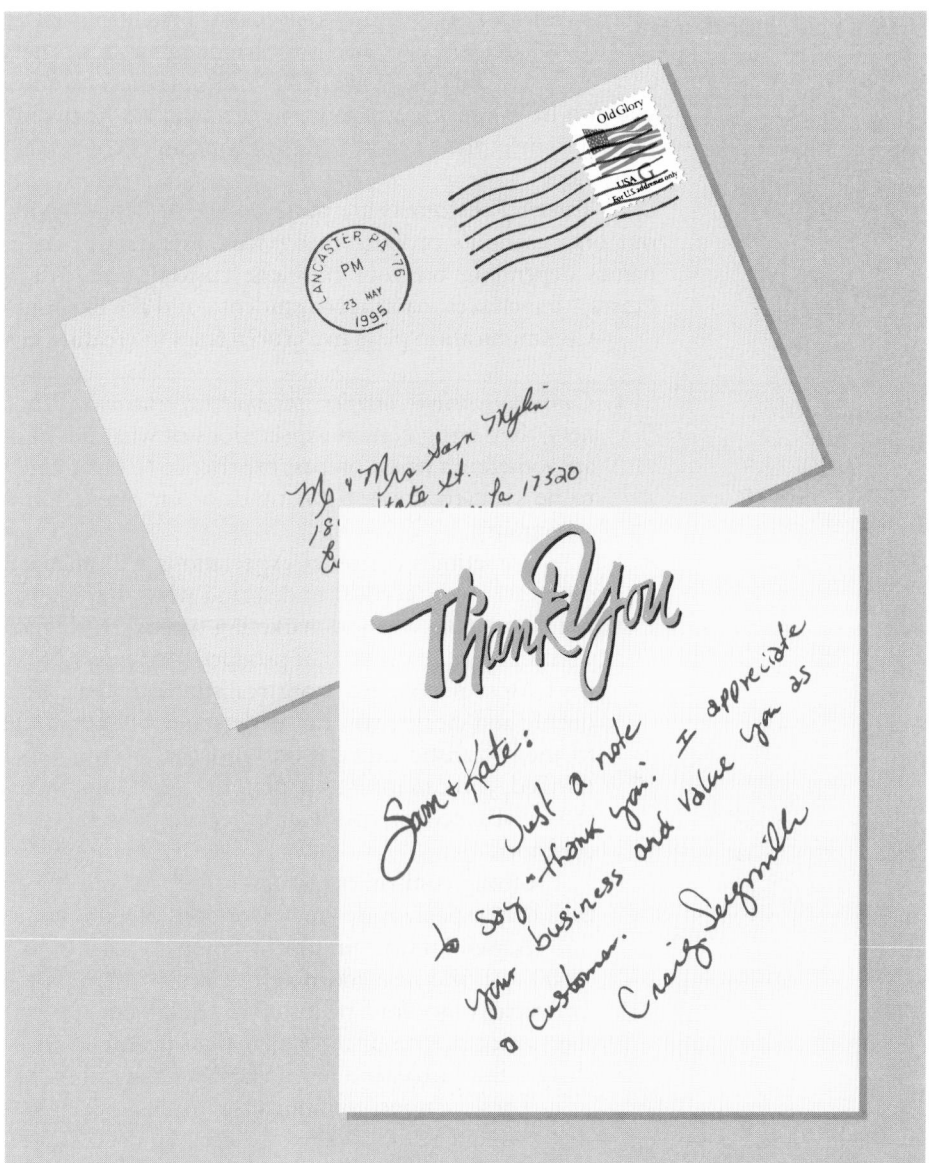

Communication and the Need for Customer Satisfaction

The following are five ways that communication plays a major role in customer satisfaction. Incidentally, in organizations, customers take two forms: **internal and external.**

Internal customers are those people, departments, or organizations served by what we do. The only person who might have no internal customers is the individual who works completely alone.

For example, a word-processing clerk or copy-center worker within a company serves other workers' needs to produce documents for the organization. A personnel office worker serves employees' needs for benefits information, management's needs for staffing, and company needs for handling various paperwork requirements.

As individuals, you have at least one internal customer: your boss; as a manager, you also have internal customers in the form of the people you supervise. They rely on you to meet their needs. Effective companies communicate this notion of internal customers.

External customers are those people or departments who are the end users of our organization's product or services. Frequently you call these people different names depending on your business: customers, clients, guests, patients, patrons, "cases," franchisees, passengers, students, and the like, but they are all customers.

Communication plays five crucial roles in creating customer satisfaction.

1. *Communication clarifies customer expectations.* Whenever customers do business, they bring certain expectations of what it will be like. These expectations are sometimes based on past experience (I was treated well last time and expect to be similarly treated this time) or on reputation (Sarah says this is a great restaurant).

   Sometimes customer expectations are unrealistic and cannot be met. In such cases, you need to understand what they want and explain why that may not be possible. Cynical marketing types often bemoan the fact that customers want immediate delivery of products that never break, and they want them for free! Most people are more realistic than that, however. By communicating openly and clearly, you can understand what your customers want and convey to them realistic expectations about what you can or cannot provide. Once clarified, you can meet—or, better yet, exceed—these expectations through our service. Exceeding customer expectations is the surest way to create a repeat customer.

   Strong companies constantly look for ways to give customers a little more than they expect. Here are descriptions of a few companies that have done so.

   A well-known air freight company claims to deliver your packages by 10:00 A.M. the next morning but usually delivers them by 9:00 or 9:30 A.M.. The repair office for a major office equipment company makes it a point to have the service person arrive earlier than promised. A successful repairman often charges the customer a few dollars *less* than estimated.

   These actions communicate to customers that the company is serious about winning their loyalty by exceeding expectations.

   What can you do to overdeliver? Here are some ideas.

   - *Provide it faster.* If you say "by noon," have it by 11:45 A.M.; if it's due next Friday, get it done on Thursday.
   - *Offer to deliver it.* You might say, "I'll drop it off at your house on my way home this evening."
   - *Offer to handle the transaction efficiently.* You might say, "You just fill in this part [of a form], and I'll handle the rest."
   - *Take a trade-in.* Offer to dispose of the old one.
   - *Offer to handle additional paperwork.* You might say, "I'll get the license forms taken care of for you."

   Use your imagination. Remember, the strongest way to build customer loyalty is to exceed expectations. Without effective communication, you could not even know your customers' expectations, let alone exceed them.

Understanding and exceeding expectations is the key to successful customer relations. Some companies are able to achieve this at a very high level. (Photos courtesy of Al Grillo/ SABA Press Photos, Inc., Martha Bales/Stock Boston, and Lionel Delevingne/ Stock Boston.)

Communication can open up feedback channels for customers to be heard.

2. *Communication can reduce customer annoyance.* A second way communication plays a role in customer satisfaction is by identifying customer peeves. Through listening, focus groups, or surveys you learn what people dislike. Surveys give customers opportunity to express irritation at sales telephone calls during dinner, prerecorded solicitation messages, and waiting in line when other windows or registers are closed.[8]

Other research reveals consumer irritation over employees who are poorly trained; who talk on the telephone while waiting on customers; who say, "It's not my department"; and who talk down to people by using phrases, such as "What do you mean you don't understand?"

Once known, companies can overcome customer annoyance by simply explaining service taboos to all employees. Managers should make clear from the first day of employment that there are specific things that are simply not to be done in their organization.

For example, in a supermarket, checkout clerks are told repeatedly of this taboo: They must absolutely avoid chatting with each other about personal matters when a customer is present. This supermarket placed special emphasis on this taboo because it employs a cashier-bagger team at each checkout counter. The danger in this is that the checker and bagger, often young people, enjoy each other's company and may find themselves talking to each other and ignoring the customer. Therefore, management simply told each employee that if there are no customers around it's acceptable to chat while you're working; however, when the customer appears, all personal discussions must stop. Taboos should be clearly communicated. Some examples might be the following:

- Never make fun of a customer.
- Never accept a tip or gratuity from a customer.
- Never respond sarcastically to a customer comment.
- Never sit down on the job.
- Never allow the telephone to interrupt a face-to-face conversation with a customer.
- Never degrade a competitor's product, customer's trade-in, or customer's expressed preference.

3. *Communication creates better customer understanding.* A health care executive talks specifically about the need for good communication to build understanding:

> Patient accounting departments deal with collecting and disseminating information. Their communication occurs with consumers, such as patients, physicians, and payers, as well as other healthcare staff members.
>
> The effectiveness of their communication determines whether consumers understand services being requested, recommended, or rendered. It also affects payment for services and creates positive or negative attitudes about how future experiences might by handled.
>
> Healthcare employees perform their tasks in a complicated environment. They deal in Greek and Latin medical terminology.
>
> They must understand a variety of technical codes, abbreviations and acronyms. They use releases, certifications, authorizations, and attestations. And they produce invoices. They also must read and understand how to interpret information in health insurance manuals, intermediary notices, and state and federal registers.[9]

The executive goes on to show that inadequate staff training makes many of these problems worse. The patient (customer) becomes frustrated and angry. Calming the upset customer consumes even more time and resources.

4. *Communication is crucial to calming upset customers.* Communication is the most important of the "recovery skills" needed to bring back an unhappy customer. To do so, first recognize that upset customers want you to

- Listen and take their concerns seriously.
- Understand their problem and the reason they are upset.
- Compensate them or provide restitution.
- Feel their sense of urgency; get their problem handled quickly.
- Avoid inconveniencing them further.

- Treat them with respect.
- Have someone punished for the problem.
- Assure them that the problem will not happen again.

5. *Communication lets us tell customers our story.* Finally, part of customer relations is public relations, and the first rule of public relations is to *let good deeds be noticed*. If a customer has a problem and you fix it, tell that customer, and, in some cases, tell other customers too.

> **Example: An auto service department replaced my car's radio immediately rather than removing it and sending it off for repair. The service manager said he didn't want me to be "driving around with a hole in my dashboard" A reminder that he'd given me good service.[10]**

Communication implements a continuous improvement cycle.

Communication skills clearly play an important role in successful customer service, which, in turn, meets the ultimate organizational need. Managers cannot just demand good service from their employees. They must treat customers as they expect employees to treat them. The entire organization must be focused on the customer. This focusing can be seen as a continuous improvement cycle. The remainder of this chapter discusses a model of this cycle with an eye toward the roles of communication in implementing the process.

Continuous Service Improvement and Communication Skills

The following model describes a strategy for best meeting the organizational goal of customer satisfaction. Only through clear communication can the answers to the model's key questions be obtained (Figure 3-3).

1. *What do our customers want?* The starting point of the **continuous improvement cycle** requires that we know what our customers want. In times past, businesses assumed they knew what customers wanted. Henry Ford offered his Model T in any color a customer could want so long as it was black. Later, mass marketing polled customer needs and then gave everybody the product that most people seemed to want. But that was then, this in now. We live in an age where the customer's *individual* wants and needs are considered and acted on. The one-to-one relationships discussed in Chapter 1 are rapidly becoming reality.

   Here are three ways to get at customer wants and needs.

   - *Communicate with customer focus groups.* **Focus groups** are discussion sessions used for marketing research, but they can also play an important role in understanding customer expectations.

     Here is the procedure: Companies select a random sample of customers and invite them to join in a feedback sharing session. Usually the company selects from its better customers by qualifying them according to how much they spend.

     They formally invite the customers to participate telling them when and where as well as how long the session will take. They let them know the reason: they are attempting to better understand customer needs and how to be of better service to them.

CHAPTER THREE **Human and Organizational Needs** **69**

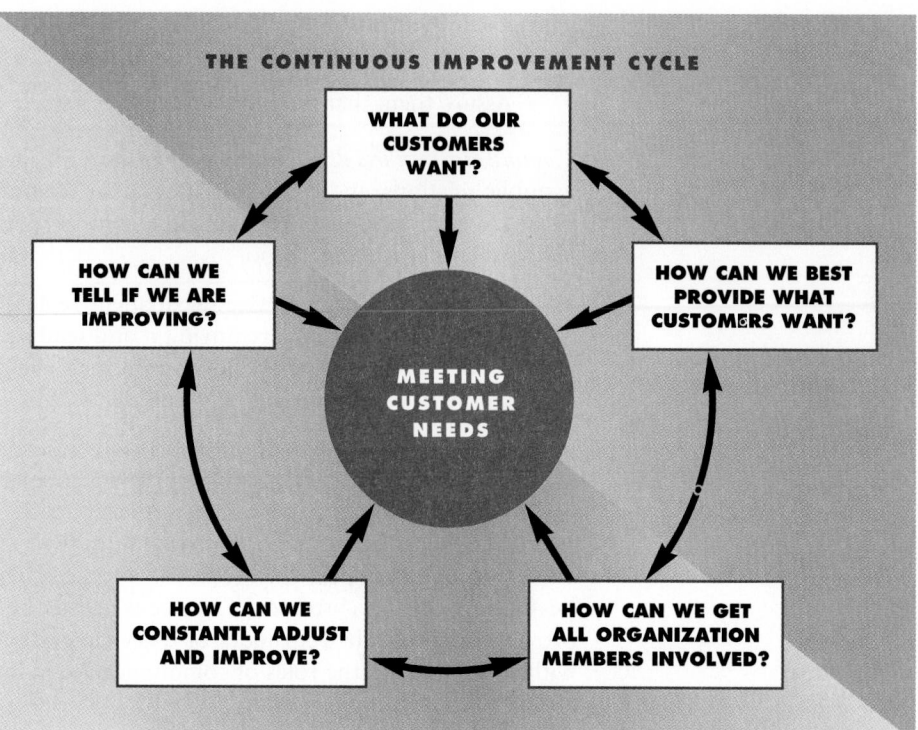

FIGURE 3–3

The Continuous
Improvement Cycle

Participants are generally given a gift certificate, a free dinner, or even cash. This creates some obligation in them to contribute thoughtful ideas and time. The focus group discussion then focuses on listening and not trying to defend or argue a viewpoint.

- *Communicate by fishing for feedback.* A less formal way to get feedback is to let the customer know that you are receptive to it, and to provide ways for him or her to give it to you easily. In dealing with individual customers, the use of open-ended questions is particularly important. An **open-ended question** is one that cannot be answered with a simple yes, no, or one-word response. The following are some common questions you hear every day in businesses that can be easily changed to open-ended ones:

> "Can I get you something else?" can become "What desserts would you like to order?"
>
> "Will that be all?" can become "How else might we serve you today?"

Opening the communication channels gives customers opportunities to *complain,* which is good.

Why do we want to give customers easy opportunities to complain? Because studies have shown that customers who do complain and have their problems resolved have a 95 percent chance of coming back.

When you fish for feedback, take it seriously, don't be overly defensive, and thank people for their comments and criticisms.

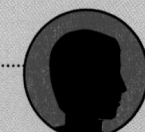
John Wade, Media Consultant, Educator, Coach

It is no exaggeration to say that John Wade is one of the country's leading authorities on dealing with mass media. He has interviewed thousands of people on local, national, and international television programs. He has questioned and conversed with every imaginable type of media guest—from presidents and famous actors to animal trainers and eccentric inventors—covering topics from the tragic to the most frivolous and funny.

John has also appeared on the *Tonight Show* and guest-hosted major morning television shows. He now serves as moderator/host for business management videoconferences that are seen live via satellite across North America. As a personal communication skills coach, John teaches business clients how to best communicate with today's media.

John's years of communication experience have helped him develop a natural ability to get the most out of a conversation. He explains it this way: "People open up to me. I'm complimented that they instinctively trust me."

His rule of thumb: "There is no 'one size fits all' set of rules for being an effective communicator. Each person possesses a combination of traits and capabilities, some helpful, some harmful."

- *Communicate via comment cards and surveys.* Written feedback cards or telephone surveys can gather considerable data on how you are doing. Use open-ended response opportunities whenever possible. Make it easy to complete and not too long.

Each of these techniques will help answer the question: What do our customers want?

Successful companies use several techniques to determine what the customer wants.

2. *How can we best provide what customers want?* The second step of the continuous improvement cycle points up the need for using input from organization members to develop and refine strategies for meeting—or better yet,

Large retailers put a human face on the company with greeters. (Copyright ©1994, Washington Post Writers Group. Reprinted with permission.)

Pickles by Brian Crane

Getting the Most from Focus Groups

Focus groups are a powerful communication tool. In marketing, customer satisfaction and any situation that calls for creativity to solve problems and improve processes, focus groups can provide excellent ideas. Here are some ways to make the focus group successful.

- Set the stage by having someone from top management moderate the group.
- Create an open atmosphere where participants will feel comfortable giving you all kinds of feedback. Be polite, open, encouraging, and *receptive*.
- Don't ever cut people off when they're making a critical comment, and *do not, above all, be defensive of the way you're doing things now,* when in the eyes of the customer it's not working.
- Listen, and keep any follow-up questions open-ended.
- As focus group members express compliments, these should be acknowledged and thanked. However, the emphasis needs to be on negative feedback, that is, areas where changes could be made to meet the needs of the customers better.
- Limit the group to a set amount of time. Typically, a one-hour or (maximum) 90-minute session works best. People will start losing interest if you go any longer than that.
- Tape record the entire focus-group session and transcribe key notes for review. As you analyze the results of this group session, look for key words that might tip you off as to what the customers are looking for. If, for example, concerns about the amount of time needed to complete their transaction come up repeatedly, you might make the mental note of how we can best meet customer needs more quickly.
- At the end of the focus-group session, be sure to thank the participants for their input.

exceeding—customer expectations. One approach is often to agree on a theme. Get all employees pulling in the same direction. Here are some ways to articulate a unifying theme.

- Commit to identifying a succinct, clear, description of your uniqueness. What do you have to offer the customer?
- Gather ideas from customers. Ask them, "What five things do you want as customers in doing business with us?"

Why People Don't Complain

There are two main reasons people do not complain when they are dissatisfied.

- They think the complaint will do no good.
- They aren't sure how to voice their complaint.

Show that complaints do make a difference (by responding when problem areas have been corrected) and to make it easy for them to complain.

- Gather people together in the organization and ask, "If you were a customer, what five things would you like to get from our company?" Ask people to respond quickly. Jot down the language, and then collect all of the words.

As you gather perceptions from customers and employees, you'll notice that some terms come up repeatedly. These typically are the kinds of words that will reassure your customer. These are good words to put into your customer service theme.

As you draft a theme for your organization, remember the following:

- Write several rough drafts of the theme; don't be too quick to come up with the finished version. Phrase the final version in seven words or fewer.
- If possible, try to make the theme into an acronym, where the first letters of each word form a word in themselves.

"What good does it do just to be able to repeat some theme?" The answer is that it's a start. Repeating some words may seem meaningless at first, but most organizations fall far short even of that level of agreement. Focusing people on a common theme can be well worth the effort.

Associates at some Wal-Mart stores wear a "Chant" button to remind themselves that "Customers Have Names, Too."[11]

3. *How can we get all organization members involved?* The next step in the cycle shows a need to train and retrain to build employee competence. People quickly forget ideas conveyed to them in training sessions. Repeated exposures to the same ideas are almost always necessary for people to apply those ideas. Training cannot be a one-shot affair. Training cannot be a once-a-year retreat. Training must be ongoing.

Training need not always be formal, classroom-style sessions. Often the best training happens in small groups or one-to-one communication among associates in an organization.

Some supervisors spend about ten minutes each morning before opening to the public to remind service representatives of the skills and behaviors they need to apply. Like a coach warming up a star athlete, the good supervisor will train and retrain on a regular basis.

Remember, too, that training is much more than just telling. It involves "hands-on" practice, critiques, and regular follow-up.

Sometimes, some good old-fashioned cheerleading works. The legendary Sam Walton would lead cheering sessions at Wal-Mart company meetings. He'd raise his right hand and lead his associates (employees) in the "Sam's Pledge":

> **From this day forward, every customer that comes within ten feet of me, regardless of what I'm doing, I'm going to look him in the eye, I'm going to smile, I'm going to greet him with a "Good morning," or "Good afternoon," or a "What can I do for you?"—so help me, Sam![12]**

4. *How can we consistently adjust and improve?* Team building and open communication are crucial as people at all levels seek to improve processes and services. Companies that open the upward communication channels from employees as well as from external customers will get the most and best improvement ideas.

Often communication is the reward as well as the tool for continuous improvement.

Strong organizations reward good ideas. Often this reward is itself a communication. Complimentary letters and memos, recognition announcements, newsletter write-ups, and spoken expressions of appreciation are among the most powerful motivators.

5. *How can we tell if we are improving?* Without ongoing measures and tracking, customer satisfaction becomes no more than a short-term "program." Organizations that do track service create the ongoing emphasis needed to achieve competitive advantage.

Among the scores that could be tracked are the following:

- Average scores received on shoppers' surveys. (People posing as customers evaluate the service received.)
- Number of customer complaints received and handled.
- Number of company-initiated calls to customers to assess satisfaction.
- Office accessibility (how many times customers experience a busy signal or long lines).
- Random observations of employee behaviors. Count such things as eye contact time, smiling, efficiency of handling transactions, courtesy, thanking customers, and so forth.

Excellence in customer satisfaction is an ongoing process, just as is good communication. Success with customers is a fundamental need of all organizations. Communication provides the key vehicle to satisfying this need.

Understanding the Basics

SUMMARY OF KEY IDEAS

- Communication is fundamental to expressing and meeting human and organizational needs.
- Basic and secondary needs affect human behavior in profound ways.
- Today's organizations are recognizing the growing trend toward self-actualization, and most are opening the communication process to permit more satisfaction of this high-level need.
- The ultimate organizational need is to create and maintain customer satisfaction. Many companies fail to achieve this as fully as possible.
- Communication can create customer satisfaction in the following five ways:
  - Clarifying customer expectations
  - Reducing customer annoyance

- Creating customer understanding
- Calming upset customers
- Telling the organization's story

- Continuous service improvement strategies work best when the answers to key questions are communicated. These questions follow:
  - What do our customers want?
  - How can we best provide what our customers want?
  - How can we get all organization members involved?
  - How can we consistently adjust and improve?
  - How can we tell if we are improving?

KEY TERMS AND CONCEPTS

Maslow's hierarchy of needs	internal and external customers	service taboos
need for affiliation	continuous improvement cycle	focus groups

open-ended questions   exceeding customer expectations   customer retention

need for achievement   self-actualization

need for power   customer service theme

QUESTIONS FOR FURTHER THOUGHT

1. Think about places you prefer to do business (stores, restaurants, gas stations, banks, etc.). List three such places, and then list, specifically, what little things make you want to come back. Then put a star next to the factors that are clearly communication related.

2. Why does customer satisfaction demand good communication skills from both the organization and its external customers?

3. Think about a company or organization that you think produces strong customer satisfaction. Compare what they do against the continuous improvement cycle. How do they measure up? What further communication actions might they take to improve further?

Changing the Role of Top Management: Beyond Systems to People

Top-level managers in other companies are coming to the same conclusion: Personal relationships are much more effective in communicating complex information, sensing subtle signals, and transferring embedded knowledge. Anita Roddick, the founder and managing director of the Body Shop International, abhors formal systems. She believes that communication is much more effective than reports at capturing employees' attention and triggering action. Her organization is designed "to maintain a constant sense of change, even anarchy," she says. As a way to convey her excitement about the products and her interest in customers to the employees and franchises in 700 Body Shops in more than 40 countries, Roddick has installed a bulletin board, a fax machine, and a videocassette recorder in every shop. She continually bombards her employees with images and messages designed to get them talking. She visits stores to tell stories and listen to employees' concerns, and she holds regular meetings with cross sections of employees, often at her home. In all her personal communications, Roddick taps into the organization's informal networks, even by planting ideas with the office gossips. She encourages upward communication through a suggestion scheme run by the irreverently named Department of Damned Good Ideas. Another process allows any employee to bypass the formal systems and communicate directly with a director-level executive on any issue.

Ingvar Kamprad, founder of Ikea, also prefers to communicate through personal networks rather than formal systems. Throughout his 30-year lead-ership of the company, Kamprad has transferred priorities on what he describes as a "mouth-to-ear basis." He seeds the organization with "culture bearers," individuals who exhibit management potential and share the company's values. Throughout the 1980s, Kamprad led weeklong training sessions on Ikea's history, culture, and values. Then, the company assigned the ambassadors who attended the sessions to key positions worldwide. By the early 1990s, more than 300 cultural agents were serving as nodes in a personal communication network that could collect and transmit information without the distortion that more formal information systems often introduce.

Most managers also realize, however, that the challenge goes beyond creating their own communication links. They must build a network through which all members of the organization can exchange information, develop ideas, and support one another. To do so, they must nurture the horizontal information flows that vertically driven, financially biased formal systems long ago short-circuited.

At Becton Dickinson and Company (BD), a health-care products company, domestic and international managers had long been insulated from each other, despite the existence of an information system that was designed to prevent that problem. Although formal reports could identify common problems and opportunities and assess their importance, they could not easily communicate their causes and potential solutions. Such subjective information required personal interaction.

For example, when BD's blood-collection product, Vacutainer, performed below expectations in Europe in the mid-1980s, the U.S.-based product development managers refused to modify it. Their formal reporting system confirmed the lower-than-forecast European conversion rate, but it did not help them understand the cause of the problem. The European managers knew that their customers were worried about the safety of the new product, but U.S. managers had dismissed that explanation as an excuse for poor marketing implementation. And although the system was able to calibrate precisely the shortfall in market penetration, it was never able to bridge that gap in communication. Not until AIDS made blood-handling safety a larger concern in the United States did BD's domestic managers understand what the European managers had tried to tell them.

Such incidents convinced the company's top management that its heavy reliance on formal, systems-driven communication was restricting its ability to learn from its overseas managers. Ray Gilmartin, who was BD's CEO at the time, helped create global teams in each of its businesses in the hope that improved communications would lead to more effective cooperation between domestic and international managers. The supposition has proved to be accurate. The worldwide blood-collection team and others like it have helped develop cross-border strategies and launch global products. Team membership has become a mark of status, and a global network has become an important career asset. Indeed, Gilmartin cites such cross-border relationships as one of the keys to BD's success in expanding its international sales from less than 30% to almost 50% of the company's total sales in just six years.

At BD, ABB, and most of the companies that we studied, executives have been rethinking their role in managing organizational information. Instead of building systems to collect data solely to help them make top-level decisions, they now realize that they must ensure that all employees have access to information as a vital organizational resource. In the information age, a company's survival depends on its ability to capture intelligence, transform it into usable knowledge, embed it as organizational learning, and diffuse it rapidly throughout the company. In short, information can no longer be abstracted and stored at the corporate level; it must be distributed and exploited as a source of competitive advantage.

(Excerpt from Christopher A. Bertlett and Sumatra Ghoshal, "Changing the Role of Top Management: Beyond Systems to People," *Harvard Business Review* [May–June 1995]: pp 140–41.)

Applying Your Knowledge

1. What conclusions are top-level managers coming to regarding personal relationships and communications?

2. List some behaviors of Anita Roddick that illustrate her style of communication.

3. Why are employees of the 700 Body Shop franchises allowed to bypass formal systems and communicate directly with a director-level executive on any issues? Do you think this is a wise practice?

4. Discuss possible advantages and disadvantages of Ingvar Kamprad's "culture bearers" at Ikea.

5. At Becton Dickinson and Co., what happened to convince top management their information system was restricting its ability to learn from its overseas manager?

6. According to this article, what does a company's survival depend on in today's information age?

Applying Your Skills

ACTIVITY 3-1: Analyzing a Customer Dispute

If you have business experience, think back on a situation in which you tried to use recovery skills to handle an upset customer. If you have no such experience, recall a situation in which you were the upset customer. Answer as many of the following questions as you can. Then summarize how you might have communicated differently to reconcile the dispute.

1. What was the nature of the customer complaint?

2. How did the customer see the problem? Who was to blame, what was most irritating, why was he (she) angry or frustrated?

3. How did the other party seem to see the problem? Was there any way in which you were partially to blame?

4. What did you say that seemed to help to remedy the situation?

5. What (if anything) did you say that seemed to aggravate the situation?

6. Do you think this customer was "recovered?" Why or why not?

What would you do differently in light of what you've learned in this chapter?

ACTIVITY 3-2: Writing to Customers

1. Suppose that you own a small retail business. Why would it—or would it not—be a good idea to send handwritten thank you notes to as many customers as possible? Describe the advantages and disadvantages of this suggestion.

2. Write a simple note that could be used as a model by your employees. Allow for personalization to each customer if possible. Make your note concise but sincere in tone.

3. Exchange your note with another student. Ask for a good critique. Fish for specific feedback that could help you improve the wording, style, and so forth.

CASE 3-1 What's a Manager to Do?

One man told us this story that illustrates how little things communicated (remember the meaning is in the receiver) can destroy a business relationship:

> A few weeks ago my teenage daughter, Erika, made a small deposit to her savings account at a local savings and loan. The teller continued chatting with another employee and virtually ignored Erika. She didn't say hello or thank you. She rolled her eyes at the small transaction and made the customer feel unimportant.
>
> Erika came home incensed. "I hate that place," she told me. I want to close out my account and go to a bank that wants my business." After finding out what happened, I agreed that she should do business where she wants to. I signed for her to withdraw her savings, and we opened a new account at another bank.
>
> Later that week Erika and I happened to talk with the manager of the original bank. He was an old friend, and I frankly felt a bit uncomfortable as Erika, a fairly outspoken teenager, explained her actions. She told him that she felt she had been treated poorly and then said, "I'm sure this is no big deal to you. I had only $370 in my account."
>
> But it was a big deal to the manager. He said to Erika, "I'm very disappointed in our company. You're 17 years old. We could have had you as a customer for 60 or 70 years! And besides, you'll tell other people about our services, and we may not get their business—or the business of your friends, your children, and your grandchildren! You better believe I'm upset. Is there anything I can do to get your business back?"

Let's consider what happened here. The message received by Erika was that she was not valued as a customer. Some things the teller did—or failed to do—conveyed that. (Remember, the meaning of a message is always assigned by the receiver.)

The manager's reaction points to another communication challenge. Although he felt strongly about the importance of good service, he could not control that teller's behavior. He regretted the lost customer but has limited power to do anything about it.

What would you do if you were that manager? Be specific and complete.

CASE 3-2 TEAM: New Employee Orientation

Prime Option is a credit card issuer. Like any business extending credit, there is a department of people responsible for collecting on delinquencies. The task of collecting on slow and late payments is difficult and challenging for employees. Most of their interactions deal with sensitive money matters of customers who may be either embarrassed or frustrated by their situation. Prime Option believes that in order for the employees to be productive, they must be treated fairly and with respect. Employees were given an opportunity to vote on their job title. The collectors call themselves account managers, who work on a "cradle-to-grave" arrangement—meaning that once they start working an account, it is theirs to work until it is collected or charged off to losses.

Prime Option has an extensive new employee orientation program called Training Empowerment and Motivation (TEAM). The focus of this training is geared toward the development of skills in communication, conflict resolution, and rapport with people. It is designed to set the stage for employees to know how to carry out difficult duties. It helps establish a positive work environment, mutual respect, trust, integrity, and open communication.

Case Questions

1. What is Prime Option communicating with the TEAM program?

2. Are the outcomes of the TEAM program possible in the "collections" environment when so much of the contact with customers can be perceived as negative?

3. Who do you think is best to deliver the TEAM program to new employees? Why?

Appropriate
Language Use:
The Way We Word

LEARNING GOALS

After you have studied this chapter, you
should be able to:

- Recognize how perceptions and
  language use affect communication.

- Understand the functions of language
  and some common misconceptions
  about how words "work."

- See how language labels can lead to
  self-fulfilling expectations.

- Identify the dilemma in attempting to
  enforce "speech codes" or
  "politically correct" language rules.

- Understand how personality
  problems can arise from the
  misuse of language.

- See the role of nonverbal
  communication in written documents.

- Describe the kinds of nonverbal
  communication that arise in business
  communication.

The Way It Is . . . The Way We Word

Individual styles of communicating vary as do personalities. No one is exactly like another person physically or psychologically. Yet you attempt to convey your unique "worlds" of experiences to others through a common language.

Although you may take the whole process pretty much for granted, the way language works is not well understood by most people. Language use affects the way you think and the way others relate to you.

It may strike you as ironic that language—the very essence of what many view to be communication—poses one of the most common sources of misunderstandings. The problem (and opportunity) lies in recognizing how language works.

Chapter 1 indicated that absolute, 100 percent understanding between two or more people is practically impossible. This chapter elaborates on that thought.

In addition, another reality of communication remains constant, as does the function of human and organizational needs (discussed in Chapter Three). This reality is referred to as "the way we word."

Why Communication Styles Are Unique

You develop your own ways of using words (or symbols). How you process and arrange words is your personal language structure. Your perceptions of the world (ideas, thoughts, or feelings) to which you attach words and symbols is like the data input for a computer. But your language structure, the way you use words, is like the software—the program that tells the system what to do with the data.

A shared semantic code is the agreement people hold about what things mean.

Two things can be done to improve language use skills: (1) broaden a person's vocabulary so that more precise, raw data can be described; or (2) improve the match between the semantic code (the agreement between people on what words "mean") and reality. Increasing someone's vocabulary is usually a far less fruitful approach than clarifying the semantic code. Only when vocabulary is seriously inadequate is emphasis on improved vocabulary significantly valuable.

The semantic codes shared by participants—their agreement on what words "mean"—determine the clarity of communication. Yet these codes often go unrecognized. You may assume that your meaning is self-evident and could not possibly be interpreted otherwise—therein lies the potential for miscommunication.

We Function in Two Worlds

You function in a world of your experiences and a world of your words. The words are the labels that you assign to things you experience. *You can literally call things anything you want to.* You can use words in any way to convey an idea. Ideally, your words will at least be similar to those your receivers would use. Nevertheless, it is your decision how you choose to label your experience.

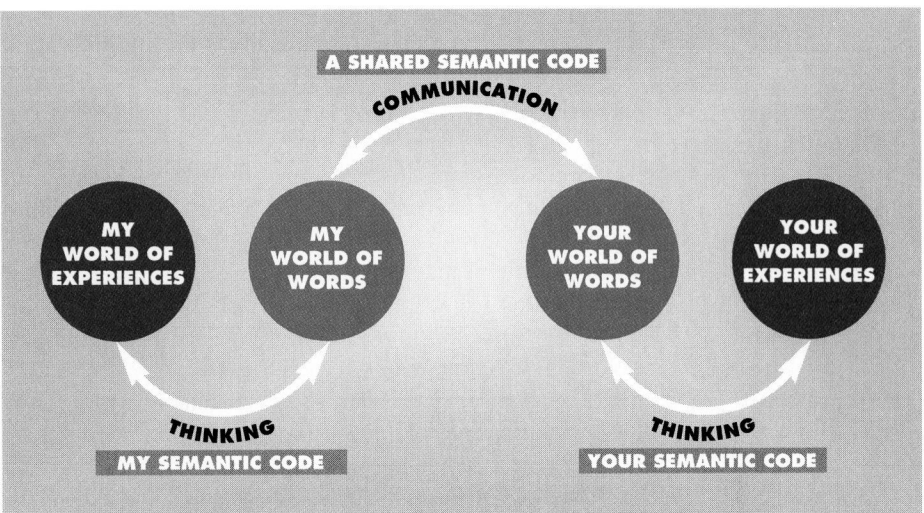

Figure 4-1 shows how our world of experiences and our world of words interact in the communication situation. Note that the only link between any two people is through their worlds of words.

To the extent that you use words in such a way that another person gains some similar meaning from them, you can be successful in communication.

Language experts have identified several assumptions and *misassumptions* about word use that may cause serious problems in the way people communicate. Recognizing these limitations of language use can help the business communicator become more effective.

Words Do Not Have a "Right" Meaning

Communication is not a transfer of meaning.

Words do not have an inherent, "right" meaning. They only have the meaning that people assign to them. People can and do assign different meanings to the same words as already discussed. Understanding this important point will help you avoid an oversimplification that can be dangerous. Communication is not a transfer of meanings from one person to others. The term "transfer" conjures up images of simply carrying a package (message) from one point to another.

A sender cannot really transfer meanings; rather, the mind of the receiver *creates* meanings. The sender's task is to use symbols that trigger responses that accurately create meanings similar to the sender's.

W. Charles Redding, a pioneer in organizational communication, taught that understanding of this viewpoint is essential to anyone who communicates in organizations—business people and professionals.

> The failure to observe the notion that the meanings are *created* in people is probably the cause of one of the most pervasive errors in everyday communication. This error has been labeled the *content fallacy*. It is the common assumption that there must be some way of so wording our messages that . . . our ideas will be "transferred" to the minds of the receivers. . . . What happens all too often is that we keep tinkering with the contents of the message-sender's message rather than trying to find

more ways of making sure that the message-receiver's responses are appropriate. This content fallacy leads us to believe that we are "getting through" to our audience merely because we are getting through to ourselves.[1]

Suppose that I, as a manager, enthusiastically announce that we are going to *re-engineer* the company to achieve greater *cost-effectiveness*. ("Re-engineer" was a popular business buzzword in the early 1990s that meant reorganize. "Cost-effectiveness" meant profitability.) As one of my employees, you have a rough idea what those terms mean, but in the last company where you worked, what they called "re-engineering" amounted to nothing more than mass layoffs and cost-effectiveness was the excuse your old boss used for cutting your pay.

Under these circumstances, it is probably not very likely that you'll share my enthusiasm for the new project. My word choice—which I thought was pretty sophisticated, even trendy—may well be viewed by you as something ominous and threatening. This situation involves a good setup for a communication failure.

Meanings do not reside in the words themselves but in the minds of the word's users. Associations conjured up cannot always be predicted.

Several Common Word Use Problems

The following is a brief discussion of some of the most commonplace language use problems.[2] As you read these, think of examples you've experienced.

Confusion of Facts with Opinions or Inferences

To assume that people, in general, know an absolute fact when they see one can be dangerous.

In truth, most information you receive is opinion or inference, not fact. An inference is defined as a conclusion based on incomplete information. Something you personally observe or experience can be regarded as fact, at least for us. Just about anything else, however, should be considered inference or opinion.

The problem is that language does not automatically make clear the distinction between inference and facts. So we must make an effort to do so.

For example, under normal circumstances, you can state direct observations—"I saw Tom leave school at five o'clock"—as facts. But if you say "I saw Tom leave school to go home at five o'clock," it becomes an inference. You have now added a new dimension to the message that may or may not be true. Did Tom leave school? Yes, I saw him do so (fact). Did Tom go home? Maybe, but I cannot really be sure. I just assume that is where he went (inference).

You communicate inferences all the time. Problems arise when your message receivers are unclear as to whether you are inferring or speaking fact. There is nothing wrong with drawing inferences. Inferences are necessary for people to make day-to-day sense of the world. The important point is that you recognize inferences as such and that you word them in ways that will help us and our listeners avoid confusing them with facts. Failure to do so can often lead to confusion and argument.

An inference can be clarified as such by adding some reference to yourself. For example, if you say, "That new policy is outdated," it sounds like a fact. It is our inference or opinion, but it sounds like a fact. If you add a phrase, such as "to me," or "I think," your listener understands that this is your inference or opinion, not an absolute fact.

Think of how you would respond to the previous statements if you disagreed, if you thought the policy was a good one. In the first form, "The policy is outdated," you would be likely to argue the point because you see it otherwise. In the second form, you would perhaps disagree, but you would recognize that as just one person's impression of the policy.

Nobody can argue with what you like. If you say, "I do not like that decision," that is your right, and other people—it is hoped—will respect it. But if you say, "That was a rotten decision," then others may be put on the defensive if they liked (or made) the decision.

Whenever you make a statement you reveal something about your personal values and attitudes. Here is an example.

If you state the opinion that "Vernon is incompetent," it may appear on the surface that incompetence is some key characteristic of Vernon. But what you are really saying is that

- Your personal experience has supplied you with a meaning for the word incompetent.
- You have seen Vernon's behavior as fitting your view of the concept of incompetence.
- Therefore, you conclude that Vernon is incompetent.

Notice that the words "you" and "your" enter into this analysis throughout. When you conclude that Vernon is incompetent, you are really talking about something *you've* done. You've related Vernon and incompetence. You have related them in your world of words; whether or not they are related in the "real world" remains unclear.

So, in essence, every opinion you offer is a statement about yourself. This is so because

- You can never say all there is to say about any topic. It would take too long.
- Those things you do choose to discuss and those you choose to ignore involve a selection process on your part, based on your experiences.
- Each of us had had unique experiences, and no two people have experienced the same things.
- You have created your own unique way of attaching words or labels to your world of experiences.
- When you combine several of these labels into a message, you are saying little about objective reality and instead are describing something that is of great importance to you *personally.*

Thus, when you conclude that Vernon is incompetent, you are reporting on some word associations that you have made. This statement doesn't really say much about Vernon, but it does say some interesting things about you.

A simple remedy for this problem of expression is to make clear the fact that you recognize this process. You can do so by converting these opinions into facts. "I think that Vernon is incompetent" is stating a fact. "I've observed Vernon doing things I consider incompetent" is stating a fact.

This changing of terms often results in greater accuracy and clarity of expression. Failure to so clarify your messages can lead to considerable embarrassment, incorrect conclusions, and serious potential harm to your credibility.

Words always distort reality somewhat. But distortion is not as much of a problem as the failure to recognize the inevitability of distortion

Oversimplified Categories

The tendency to oversimplify the categories into which many mentally sort things is another common problem in the way language is used. Often, these categories are too simple—black or white—when people really should describe shades of gray.

Many people rely too heavily on polar terms, words that force us to choose between extremes—good or bad, always or never, weak or strong, big or little—and that tend to oversimplify. In reality, most things in life are better described in fine variations among events or experiences than by either/or categories. To illustrate, take simple **either/or questions,** such as the following:

1. Are you a good student or a bad student?
2. Are you big or little?
3. Are you liberal or conservative?
4. Are you attractive or ugly?
5. Are you a success or a failure?

Either/Or Interview Question

A nationally prominent governor was interviewed on television. The interviewer repeatedly asked a variation of the same questions, "Did you go to Washington to dramatize a problem and serve the people of your state or to advance your own presidential ambitions?" The politician's answers proved frustrating to the reporter and perhaps seemed to be evasive, but the questions could not accurately be answered when cast in an either/or form: "serve the people" *or* "advance presidential ambitions." Finally, the politician simply stated that he did not look at the world in such simplistic black or white terms, and that there were many reasons behind his actions. Probably the best answer in this case was, "both," although the politician had not yet announced his candidacy for president and stopped short of saying that.

People often ask questions just as absurd as these. The appropriate response would be *compared to what (or whom)?*

Do not let yourself get painted into a corner with someone else's oversimplified questions. If you are really interested in creating understanding—in really communicating—avoid these simplistic polar terms.

In a work organization, this process may mean avoiding the tendency to classify workers as industrious or lazy, productive or unproductive. In one company, a sales manager actually had a chart on his wall with the names of all his salespeople boldly displayed under the headings "heroes" and "bums."

The problem is that when your language reflects such either/or logic, other possibilities are overlooked. If you classify a manager only as a "good leader" or a "bad leader," you leave out a lot of other possibilities. Maybe he or she is effective in some dimensions of the job but ineffective in others.

Sales representatives and other persuaders often use this either/or forced choice to their advantage. "Would you like to accept delivery next Monday or Wednesday?" attempts to preclude the option of not taking delivery at all.

Your credibility can be seriously damaged when listeners recognize these kinds of oversimplified language structures. Whenever you hear yourself or others sending either/or messages, you might be wise to consider the following:

- Are all the options covered?
- As compared with what (or whom)?

Words Can Lead to Self-Fulfilling Expectations

Managers who see their subordinates as heroes or bums are not relating to reality. It is far more realistic and hopeful to think in terms of people who can and will change their work performance. Today's hero may have been yesterday's bum if managers

Self-fulfilling expectations are results that come true because you think they will.

have been able to avoid the related problem of self-fulfilling expectations—results that come true because you think they will.

Your mind tends to pay attention to events that "fit" what you expect. For example, a person who is biased against workers from one ethnic group will be more likely to notice poor behavior from people in that group. This reinforces an attitude the biased person holds. Likewise, if you expect your child to be the star of the school play, she probably will be just that (especially in your eyes).

These filters grow out of individual experiences, background, and values. Over time, you develop a "filter" through which you view the world. The filters of your mind place labels on the world you encounter, and determine what you select to perceive. When you can make no sense out of some thing or event—that is, if it doesn't fit your world view—you tend to reject it.

It can be disconcerting, for example, to find that the worker you've labeled as "rebellious" is suddenly vigorously defending the company. It is also unsettling to find that "nice, pleasant" reception person suddenly shouting angrily at a visitor. You'd prefer to reject or explain such discrepant observations because they just don't jibe with "the way things are" in your mental world.

Good communicators keep labels somewhat loose. They maintain some language flexibility so that unanticipated changes in things, events, and people can still fit into their mental world. Words do not automatically allow for such flexibility and change, so we need to.

Words Have Emotional Connotations

Many terms carry **emotional connotations** that can excite, anger, offend, or create pleasant or unpleasant associations in people. An obvious example is the profane expletive, which, for example, could be extremely embarrassing or offensive to a group of worshippers while being a source of considerable amusement to a group of heavy-metal music fans. The word itself doesn't change, only the receiver's associations, and, in this case, the context in which the term is used.

Semanticist Stuart Chase used the terms "purr" words and "slur" words. This was a catchy way of describing euphemisms and dysphemisms. A **euphemism** is a term that creates a more pleasant or less objectionable association in minds of its users. A **dysphemism** is the opposite; it conveys a more negative or unpleasant association. The degree of pleasantness or unpleasantness will depend on people's attitudes.

Here are a few examples.

Euphemism	Neutral	Dysphemism
Emotionally challenged	Hard-to-manage child	Brat
Luxury automobile	Standard-sized car	Gas guzzler
Go powder my nose	Go to the rest room	Go to the toilet (or worse)
Passed away	Died	Croaked
Sizzling steak	Cooked meat	Flesh of a steer

Some humorous exchanges can arise when you use euphemisms or dysphemisms in unexpected ways. A cartoon showed a woman talking to a man who was carefully inspecting his food. She said, "That yellow scum on top happens to be Hollandaise sauce." Another illustration of slur words came from one of MacNelly's "Shoe" cartoons.

[NEWSPAPER EDITOR TO WRITER:] Senator Belfry's office is complaining again about our unfair treatment of the distinguished senator in our editorials. . . .

[WRITER:] Baloney! I'm never unfair in any of my editorials! Which one are they talking about, anyway?

[EDITOR:] The one called, "Bozo the Clown goes to Congress."

Politically Correct Language

The creation of speech codes and the encouragement of **politically correct language** is largely an attempt to override undesirable effects of dysphemisms. Words seen as potentially offensive are discouraged. Users of terms deemed inappropriate are subject to punishment, counseling, sensitivity training, and the like. Although some speech goes too far and examples of politically correct language are sometimes extreme, the intent is generally to reduce offense to others.

Although this intent to eliminate terminology that may offend other people is noble, it is simply impossible. Remember, the words do not have meaning; people assign meanings. The impact of a term varies widely depending on who says it, how it is said, and countless other variables. For example, an insult hurled at a person in the heat of an argument has a totally different impact from the same term used in a joking, lighthearted, or teasing manner.

Successful professionals develop a high level of sensitivity to emotional loadings or the potentially offensive terms.

Clever . . . or Offensive?[3]

William Carlin thought he had a great idea for an enjoyable business—and a catchy name to boot. As a sideline business, he and his wife would arrange golf events for corporations at various private clubs. The New York company's name, Fore Play Golf Inc., surely would get attention.

It did. "We spent days and months chasing leads and couldn't even get appointments, " Mr. Carlin recalls. "We had no business at all for months on end."

In mid-1992, however, the Carlins found that a little punctuation can be crucial to business success. They changed the company name a bit to "Fore! . . . Play Golf Inc." Since then, they have been organizing golf events for a dozen companies, including International Business Machines Corp., Mr. Carlin says. The Mistake: The Carlins initially chose a name that could only make their staid target customer base nervous. "My wife and I struggled with the name," Mr. Carlin says. "We had hoped it would be a catchy name, but it was just too risqué. We sure found out the name makes a difference."

Language Misuse Can Be a Symptom of Personality Problems

As suggested in this chapter, many communication problems arise from a lack of awareness of how language works. In the extreme, when people are oblivious to relationships between words and reality, they may experience serious social problems. Indeed, psychologist William Pemberton[4] suggests that maladjusted people typically exhibit tendencies such as these:

1. They tend to assume that everyone is having the same experiences at the perceptual level as themselves—that there is only one "right" way to look at or feel about anything.

2. They tend to assume that if they talk long enough, loud enough, or "reasonably" enough, they will be able to influence others to their way of thinking.

3. They tend to assume that the characteristic by which something is named, labeled, or judged is *in* the object, that what they say about it is in the "right" characteristic, "real" name, or "real" meaning.

4. They tend to make generalized conclusions from few experiences in such a way that new experiences have to fit old conclusions or remain ignored.

5. They tend to shut out further consideration of a problem with, "That's all there is to it."

(Note: Pemberton's list is not meant to suggest that anyone exhibiting such behavior is "maladjusted." Many are guilty of occasional misassumptions. Maladjusted people, however, persistently think and act as described.)

Words Sometimes Conceal Rather than Reveal

Sometimes people don't say what they really mean. It's shocking but true! Actually, there are good reasons for being less than totally truthful on occasion. The situation may make people feel awkward, or they might simply keep their real thoughts to themselves for other reasons. In such cases, some may rely on clichés or platitudes, which are acceptable to those they interact with even though these words convey little or no real information. Consider the following dialogue between a manager who wants to promote a worker and the employee's immediate supervisor, who would love to get rid of him.

[MANAGER:]	Kim, I'm looking at your man Harrison for that programming job over on the Placebo Project. What do you think of him?
[SUPERVISOR:]	Harrison? Sure, he's a good dude.
[MANAGER:]	Do you think he can handle it?
[SUPERVISOR:]	No problem. He's really with the program. He's been one of my big guns ever since he came here. He's a stand-up guy.

| [MANAGER:] | Thanks, Kim. I appreciate your being up front with me on this one. I'll push things along, and we'll get some action on it real soon. |
| [SUPERVISOR:] | Cool. |

Whatever factual information might have been exchanged here was completely muddled by the clichés or trendy language. What did these people really say to each other? Not much. Their true meaning will be determined by each individual, but clearly, there is little attempt to create common understanding. The supervisor's agenda is to avoid saying anything that may have him stuck with Harrison, not to create accurately a common semantic code.

Carefully listen to your own language use.

Anticipating how people will associate your words with meanings you want to convey is tricky. One key is to reduce the emotionalism in language when clear, objective decisions and actions are required. A good starting point is to listen carefully to your own language first.

Nonverbal Communication Can Be Louder than Words

As important as it is to develop sensitivity and skill in using language, it's equally important to remember that both verbal and nonverbal communication creates meaning. Nonverbal cues, many of them subtle, are a form of language—they create meaning in others.

What you do almost always overrides what you say.

The sobering reality is that what you *say* is almost always overridden by what you *do*. Although the language you use conveys certain objective information, your body conveys how you *feel* about what you say. Whenever you perceive a discrepancy between the words and nonverbal cues you receive, you usually assume that the nonverbal message is the "real" meaning. Your actions speak so loudly in others' ears that they can't hear what you are saying.

Nonverbal communication is that which does not use words or common symbols.

Just what is nonverbal communication? It is probably easier to describe what it does *not* include than to specify all that it does. Most scholars who study nonverbal communication agree that the term excludes communication using words, numbers, or normal written or oral language. Instead, it focuses on all the other things that cause meanings to be created in people.

The ways that people attach meanings to messages can readily be influenced by any of these unspoken, and often unnoticed, nonverbal characteristics. The following is a closer look at some nonverbal elements that frequently influence business and professional communication.

Distance	Situation
Touching to about	
18 inches	Lovers, close friends, or conspirators
2 to 4 feet	Normal social conversation
4 to 12 feet	More formal business conversation, meetings
12 or more feet	Public or presentational speaking

"What's the fish like today?"

Environment and Space

People have a need to define their own territorial boundaries—their personal bubble—and establish conversational distances among themselves. Communication researchers know that proximity is a potent variable in developing contact with another person. In North American cultures, relationships and situations determine the distance from each other as they communicate.

In normal conversation, a person who moves in closer than arm's length is seen as pushy or aggressive. A person who stands back a bit farther than "normal" conveys aloofness.

When your space expectations are violated, you get uncomfortable. For example, observe the behavior of people crowded into an elevator. Their normal social distance is suddenly reduced to intimate distance. Most people respond by looking up at the floor indicator or otherwise distracting themselves.

Crowded elevators violate our "personal space." (Courtesy of Barbara Alper/Stock Boston.)

Spatial and environmental behaviors can reflect our style of leadership. For example, the arrangement of one's office furniture can create impressions of status differences or openness. The manager who talks to an employee from behind his or her desk comes across differently from the manager who crosses the room to sit next to the employee (Figures 4-2 and 4-3).

In customer relations, environmental barriers can cause problems. An auto dealership removed the sales representatives' desks from their cubicles and replaced them with small round tables. The impact on sales was dramatic. Customers seemed to see the round-table environment as far less threatening.[5]

Another example of space as a nonverbal communication dimension is found in the ways you position yourself when speaking to others.

Organizational rank often affects space expectations. Many assume that higher-level executives will have more spacious offices. Their space is also more likely to be "protected" via closed doors, reception rooms adjoining their office, and sometimes even their position in the building—they are often on or near the top floor.

Although it's perfectly appropriate for the executive to "invade" the work area of a lower ranking employee, don't try barging in on the boss.

Remember that these nonverbal conditions are culturally defined. The preceding examples apply to United States, Canadian, and most European cultures. Arabic, Latin, and Asian countries have their own nonverbal cues and traditions.

The "culture" of the organization also affects nonverbal communication. In organizations in which an "informal chaos" nurtures creativity, it may be just fine to barge into the boss's office with a hot idea.

Physical Appearance and Dress

If you arrive at a meeting dressed in a business suit and find the other participants in jeans and sneakers, you may feel awkward. The key variable is *appropriateness* to the occasion. You'd look out of place at a funeral in casual clothing but equally out of place working in a surf shop in a suit. Dress standards vary widely even in the business world. California high-technology firms are often noted for casual dress, whereas corporate employees in New York dress in standard business attire.

1. People (whether in a doctor's office, in the boss's office, or at home) are more comfortable conducting *conversation* when they are at right angles (90° or 45°) and approximately 4 feet apart.

2. When working closely together, *cooperating* on a task, people prefer corner seating or side-by-side seating.

3. When people are working on different tasks, *co-acting*, but need to be in close proximity to each other, they prefer distant seating.

4. *Competing* people also prefer to sit opposite each other.

5. People sitting side-by-side (on a sofa for example) often prefer to converse with those across or at right angles to them.

6. Individuals in a group are more likely to participate if the group is seated in a circular pattern rather than in a rectangular pattern or in straight rows.

7. When a group sits in a circle, individuals are more likely to ask questions of or make comments to the persons with whom they can make eye contact. Again, they are less likely to communicate with those sitting the closest to them.

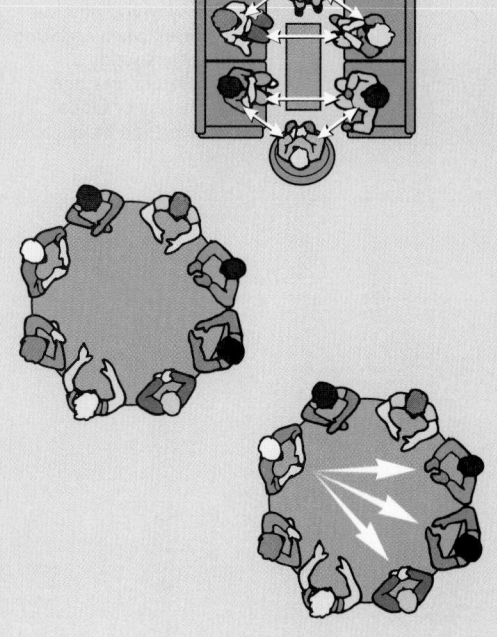

FIGURE 4–2
Seating arrangements.

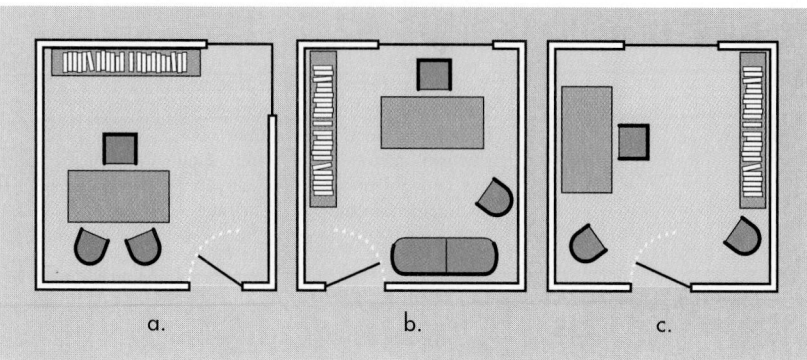

FIGURE 4–3
Office arrangements.

Many companies designate casual days—usually Fridays—when employees are invited to dress comfortably in informal clothing. Closely related to appearance and dress are the artifacts that people display. Jewelry, office decorations, and attractive personal belongings tell others something about you. The absence of such personal artifacts may convey a different message. Either way, the impression formed from such nonverbal cues will be in the mind of the observer.

Physical Behaviors

Nonverbal physical behaviors include the positioning and movement of the arms, legs, and posture. "Body language" can parallel or override the spoken language. Body movements often communicate unspoken messages such as the following:

1. Like or dislike for another
2. Reminders of status differences

The way you position yourself when speaking to others sends a nonverbal message. (Courtesy of Gabe Palmer/The Stock Market.)

3. Personal moods

4. Approval seeking or a need for inclusion

5. Quasi-courtship behavior (flirting)

6. Deception

7. Interpersonal warmth or affection

Included among these physical behaviors would be nervous mannerisms, shuffling from position to position, frequent looking at one's watch, and posture or position when seated.

One type of physical behavior that also ties in with the spatial variables is touching behaviors. Although a literal pat on the back or a reassuring handshake is often appreciated, some people get a reputation for being "touchy-feelie." Many people feel uncomfortable with excessive touching.

Touching can be construed as sexual in nature and seen as harassment, so it makes sense to limit touching to a handshake, pat on the back, or the like. Lingering touch conveys a more intimate relationship and should be avoided. Table 4-1 summarizes some common nonverbal cues.

TABLE 4-1
COMMON NONVERBAL CUES

Nonverbal Communication	Signal Received	Reaction from Receiver
Manager looks away when employee is talking	I do not have this person's undivided attention.	Supervisor is too busy to listen to my problem or simply does not care.
Failure to acknowledge greeting from fellow employee	This person is unfriendly.	This person is unapproachable.
Ominous glaring (i.e., the evil eye)	I am angry.	Reciprocal anger, fear, or avoidance depending on who is sending the signal in the organization.
Rolling of the eyes	I am not being taken seriously.	This person thinks they are smarter or better than I am.
Deep sighing	Disgust or displeasure	My opinions do not count. I must be stupid or boring to this person.
Heavy breathing (sometimes accompanied by hand waving)	Anger or heavy stress	Avoid this person at all costs.
Eye contact not maintained when communicating	Suspicion or uncertainty	What does this person have to hide?
Manager crosses arms and leans away	Apathy and closed-mindedness	This person already has made up his/her mind; my opinions are not important.
Manager peers over glasses	Skepticism or distrust	He or she does not believe what I am saying.
Continues to read a report when employee is speaking	Lack of interest	My opinions are not important enough to get the manager's undivided attention.

Expressions of Face and Eyes	Facial expressions and movements of the eyes are especially important ways people convey a variety of emotions ranging from fear or anxiety to happiness, relief, or requests for additional information. Scientists have found that dilation of the pupil may indicate emotional arousal, interest, or attentiveness.
Vocal Cues Accompanying Spoken Words	People stereotype others on the basis of their voices: The man with a lisp is a sissy. The lady with slurred speech is assumed to be drunk. The woman with a husky or breathy voice is aggressive or sexy. Although these stereotypes are unfounded, studies have shown that a person can judge with fair accuracy the age, sex, and status of others from the sound of their voices alone. Also, people make judgments about one's trustworthiness, likability, competency, and dynamism on the basis of voice.

The messages we receive are colored by these and undoubtedly other nonverbal factors.

Functions of Nonverbal Communication

Nonverbal communication serves six major functions.

Repeat Function. As you give directions at the nearest gas station to a lost motorist, you may *repeat* the information by using hand gestures, such as pointing south. Likewise, the restaurant maître d' repeats his message that this is a formal restaurant and "gentlemen are requested to wear ties" by himself being attired in a dinner jacket and a tie.

Substituting Function. "Staring daggers" at another person via a facial expression that conveys anger is an example of substituting. No spoken words may be needed. Likewise, a friendly wave, a thumbs-up gesture, or a warm handshake can send a clear, positive message. (Thumbs up, however, is considered an obscene gesture in Australia!)

Complementing Function. If you saw a worker talking to a supervisor, and his head was bowed slightly, his voice was slow and hesitating, and he shuffled slowly from foot to foot, you might conclude that he felt embarrassed about something he did. The nonverbal behaviors you observed complemented the spoken apology. They may also make a statement about the worker-supervisor relationship.

Accenting Function. Just as italic or bold print highlights parts of written messages, so can nonverbal cues accentuate parts of spoken messages. Pointing an accusing finger adds emphasis to criticism (as well as probably creating defensiveness in the receiver). Shrugging one's shoulders accents confusion, and hugs can highlight excitement or affection.

Regulating Function. Nonverbal cues can regulate a conversation. By allowing one's voice to trail off at the end of a sentence, the speaker indicates that another person may now talk. Also, nonverbal cues that say "I still appreciate you" (like a pat on the back after a chewing out) can regulate or soften the spoken message that said "I'm upset with what you did."

Contradicting Function. Perhaps the most significant function—and the function that can get the insensitive communicator in the most trouble—is the contradicting function. Nonverbal cues often contradict or veto the verbal message they accompany.

The nonverbal veto occurs when a person barks "I'm not upset" at another person, or when the company's slogan, "The customer always comes first," is proudly displayed above the parts counter where the clerks are chatting among themselves and ignoring a customer. The conflicting messages conveyed can be confusing and upsetting.

To increase effective understanding you need to develop sensitivity to both nonverbal cues and hidden meanings in language. Your personal **communication style** can be refined to look beyond the obvious messages and attach accurate meanings to the enormous numbers of communication cues present in any organizational setting.

Nonverbal Communication in Written Media

Don't mistakenly assume that **nonverbal elements in written communication** apply only in spoken or face-to-face situations. Among the nonverbal cues that can come across in written media are the following:

- The appearance of the document. Paper quality and color, typefaces, spacing, and accompanying art all convey meaning.
- The tone of the message. Is it conversational and friendly? Stuffy and formal? Difficult to understand or clear?
- The signature (or lack of one); attachments or enclosures.

Clearly, communication is affected by myriad small and often subtle points. Pay attention to detail.

Word Choice Affects Writing Style[7]

In organizations everywhere, people play games with letters. They bounce them back and forth between the people who write them and the people who sign them. It's a game nobody likes, but it continues, and companies pay for it. Why? Are there problems with typos? Factual misstatements? Poor format? Not usually. The real reason is that the signer doesn't like the writer's *style*. Organization members may make the following comments:

- "It takes new assistants about a year to learn my style. Until they do, I have no choice but to bounce letters back for revision. I won't sign a letter if it doesn't sound like me."
- "I find it difficult, almost impossible, to write letters for my boss's signature. The boss's style is different from mine."

John S. Fielden, writing in the *Harvard Business Review*[8] offers this working definition of style in the context of business writing.

> **Style is that choice of words, sentences, and paragraph format which by virtue of being appropriate to the situation and to the power positions of both writer and reader produces the desired reaction and result.**

Style 1

August 5, 199X

Mr. Ted Bennion, Owner
Bennion Motors
1334 Tandamount Highway
Bison Breath, NE 33445

Dear Mr. Bennion:

Please inform me of how I can get an appointment with you. I wish to discuss with you how Primo Auto Detailing can save you time and money.

Perhaps you do not see a need for auto detailing, but please allow me to show you how we can work together to improve your performance. Even if you are pleased with your current approach to auto detailing, I would appreciate your letting me show you why we at Primo Detailing can offer you a better value.

We have served people like you for more than seven years. We provide the finest-quality auto cleanup, paint restoration, interior shampoo, and deep polishing available at any cost. Can we please talk about how we can make the appearance of Bennion's used cars second to none at a very economical price?

I would appreciate the opportunity to speak with you. When I call within the next week to arrange an appointment, please take my call. I promise to be brief; if I take more than 20 minutes of your time, I will contribute $100 to the High Hopes Foundation in your name. My goal is your total satisfaction.

Sincerely,

Mark Benson

Mark Benson
Primo Auto Detailers

Style 2

August 5, 199X

Mr. Ted Bennion, Owner
Bennion Motors
1334 Tandamount Highway
Bison Breath, NE 33445

Dear Ted:

What'll it take to get an appointment with you?
Whatever it is, hey, I'll do it. Why? Because I
know Primo Auto Detailers can save you time and
money.

If you're thinking, "But I don't need auto
detailing," let me show you how we can work
together to improve your sales. Or even if you're
happy with your current approach to cleaning up
used cars, let me show you why using Primo is a
better value.

We've served people like you for more than seven
years. We provide the best in auto cleanup, paint
restoration, interior shampoo, and deep polishing.
Can we talk about how we can make Bennion's used
cars the sharpest on the market at a fraction of
the cost you'd expect to pay? In fact, a Primo
Detailing job pays *you* in sharply increased resale
value.

I'd like to talk to you. When I call within the
next week to arrange an appointment, please take my
call. If I take more than 20 minutes of your time,
I'll contribute $100 to the High Hopes Foundation.
My goal is your satisfaction.

Sincerely,

Miles Benson

Miles Benson, Head Guy
Primo Auto Detailers

Word choice is one important part of style. Later chapters will discuss other elements of style.

To illustrate how the style of a message can change with word choice, look at the two versions of the same letter on pages 98–99. Both letters attempt to serve the same purpose, but the tone is different. Which style do you like better?

Which letter did you like the best? Which sounds most like you? What specific language differences cause these letters to sound different?

To most people style 1 sounds a bit more formal and, perhaps, a bit more respectful of the reader. Style 2 is more casual and conversational, using contractions (you're, we've, I'd), which sound like the way we talk. The "Dear Ted" salutation is more familiar. This could be seen as friendly or possibly overly familiar and somewhat disrespectful by the reader.

Subtle word choices convey a different tone in letters.

The Need for Sensitivity

Successful communicators are sensitive to the differences that verbal and nonverbal cues can make in even the simplest messages. This is an aspect of communication that remains unchanged, despite technological or societal changes. The professional communicator knows how to adjust his or her style to the demands of the situation.

Often you can and should be conversational. On certain occasions, you need to adjust; the failure to do so can be embarrassing. For example, at a college banquet, a

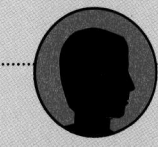

COMMUNICATOR'S PROFILE

J. Richard Staley, Loan Officer
Medallion Mortgage Co.

Rich, a former attorney, left his law practice to enter the highly competitive mortgage business. As a loan officer, his job is to help people arrange financing for their homes—a process that can involve quite a bit of stress for the person who is signing a long-term obligation. Consequently, Rich must work hard to explain the process and answer borrower concerns.

When explaining a mortgage agreement, Rich will often ask his customers to repeat back to him in their own words the information he gave them. He does this in a pleasant manner, but with serious intent: to be sure the customer is fully informed.

Rich thinks that the highly successful business communicator is one who "comes to the point quickly, then waits for feedback to be sure he or she is understood." Such people also "write in a fashion that is easily understood and take the time to make sure grammar and spelling are correct."

Rich spends about half his work day in face-to-face communication and another 35 percent handling written and telephone communications.

graduate student was introducing the state's governor. She had spoken to our rather youthful, 40-something-year-old governor and worked with him in developing a youth program. In introducing him at the governor's honors academy for outstanding high school students, she said, "We want to thank Mike for being here today." "Governor Michael Leavitt" would have been the appropriate introduction. The governor seemed unaffected by this casual introduction, but you could sense a gasp in the audience.

Language sensitivity and the flexibility to apply appropriate styles for various situations are hallmarks of the good business and professional communicator. Awareness of and flexibility in language use—both verbal and nonverbal—continue to be consistent needs in today's business and professional communication.

Understanding the Basics

SUMMARY OF KEY IDEAS

• The way you use language reveals much about the way you see the world. Each person relates his or her world of experiences to others through his or her "world of words."

• You can be a better communicator by recognizing the following limitations and characteristics of language:

  • Words do not have inherent meaning; they mean different things to different people.

  • Words do not *automatically* separate facts from inferences.

  • Words tend to push things into either/or categories.

  • Words can lead to self-fulfilling expectations.

  • Words have emotional "loads."

  • Words can sometimes conceal more than they reveal.

  • Words often carry hidden meanings.

• Nonverbal communication conveys as much or more meaning than does verbal communication. When verbal and nonverbal contradict each other, people are more likely to believe the nonverbal.

• Nonverbal cues can be projected in written documents as well as spoken communication via appearance and tone.

• Word choice is an important element of writing style.

• Language sensitivity and flexibility are keys to creating effective tone in written as well as spoken communication situations.

• Despite other changes in the ways we communicated, language use skills remain constant in today's business world.

KEY TERMS AND CONCEPTS

nonverbal veto

content fallacy

oversimplified categories

self-fulfilling expectations

euphemism

politically correct language

communication style

metatalk

semantic code

inference

either/or questions

emotional connotations

dysphemism

categories of nonverbal cues

nonverbal elements in written
  communication

1. Consider your nonverbal communication and how you come across to others. Make a list of adjectives that describe your image. Ask several associates to make a similar list about you. How do these lists compare?

2. It has been said that language does as much to conceal as to reveal. How would you respond to that idea? Does nonverbal behavior work the same way?

3. Much has been said about so-called "politically correct" language in recent years. Describe the positives and negatives of politically correct language as you see them.

"Metatalk"

Gerald I. Nierenberg and Henry H. Calero's popular book called *Meta-Talk: Guide to Hidden Meanings in Conversations*, describes some functions of conversational expressions. They categorize verbal responses as softeners, foreboders, continuers, interesters, downers, convincers, strokers, and pleaders. These categories and some additional examples follow as a guide to word functions.

(This reading is excerpted from ideas discussed in Gerald I. Nierenberg and Harry H. Calero, Meta-Talk: *Guide to Hidden Meanings in Conversations* [New York: Trident Press, 1973], pp 15–16.)

Softeners

Intended to influence the receiver in a positive way—to soften him or her for the "real" message.

Expression	Purpose or Real Meaning
"You're going to like what I'm about to tell you."	Prepares the receiver for what we believe will be good news for him or her.
"It goes without saying."	Attempts to get agreement by assuming it to be so.
"I venture to say"; "off the top of my head"; "I'm sticking my neck out"; or "at first blush."	The message sender is about to draw a conclusion based on incomplete data.
Use of acceptance or agreement statements followed by *but, yet, however, still,* etc.	The message sender does not feel the receiver is right but wants to soften the flow of disagreement.

Foreboders

Put listeners in a negative or anxious frame of mind; can lead to unpleasant encounters or psychological games.

Expression	Purpose or Real Meaning
"Nothing is wrong" (accompanied by a look of anxiety).	There is something wrong, but I don't want to talk about it; or there is something wrong and I want you to show concern and probe further.
"It really doesn't matter."	It matters.
"Don't worry about me."	Please do.
"I have nothing more to say."	I'm about to blow up and argue.
"I'd rather not discuss it."	I want to talk to someone about it but probably not you.

Continuers

Attempt to get the listener to disclose more information. Often viewed as supportive but can be counterproductive when people go on too long.

Expression	Purpose or Real Meaning
"What else is new?"	Introduce another topic for conversation.
"Go on"; "That's very good"; "Now you're talking"; or "I like that.	Please elaborate on your point. I agree with what you say.
"Why don't you go with that line of thought," or "Tell us more about that idea."	You don't make much sense to me yet, but this could become productive if you go on.

Interesters

Statements and questions that attempt to arouse interest. Often add nothing to the conversation and can become something of a verbal "tick" for speakers; can also annoy listeners.

Expression	Purpose or Real Meaning
"And do you know what?"	Are you still listening?
"Guess what happened!"	The speaker must demand the listener's attention by getting him or her to say, "What?"
"What do you think of [some emotion-loaded term or expression] . . . ?	I hope you'll agree with my stand on this issue.
"I could say something about that!"	I don't want to cause trouble, but I will anyway.

Downers

Used to intentionally put the listener in a defensive state of mind. Often used when a speaker is in a win-lose situation and is moving in for the kill. Vocal tone and facial expression can add considerable power to the downer; often the tone is sarcastic.

Expression	Purpose or Real Meaning
"Are you happy now?"	You have just humiliated me and caused great anguish, and you should feel miserable too.
"Don't make me laugh."	A mean-hearted reaction to another's request, demand or opinion.
"Don't be ridiculous."	You have said something I disagree with, and I will now attack you as a person.
"Put it to music. . . ."	I have heard your excuse, and I'm not sympathetic.
"That's the way it is, pal."	I am totally unsympathetic to your plight.

Convincers

Often used as substitutes for logical argument. When a speaker is having trouble making a sensible case, convincers can cause listeners to forget the logical inconsistency.

Expression	Purpose or Real Meaning
"That's the *only* way we can do business in this city."	Justification of an unethical or illegal act.
"Why, anyone can do it!"	The task is so simple that even a moron could accomplish it. (This can also be a downer when the listener has just failed the task in question.)
"Anyone can follow my line of reasoning."	Persuades by intimidation; I find it simple and so should you.
"I think we all agree that. . . ."	Appeals for consensus or tries to smooth over conflict.
"Let me make one thing perfectly clear. . . ."	Introduces a conscious deception or tries to hammer home a belief.
"Everybody I know agrees. . . ."	Therefore, you should agree, too; or therefore, it must be true.
"Believe me, . . ."	Please agree with me, I'm desperate for your acceptance.

Strokers

Used to elicit approval statements—positive strokes—or to give strokes: to tell people that they are special.

Expression	Purpose or Real Meaning
"How do you like my new outfit?"	I need reassurance that I look nice.
"What do you think of my plan? I didn't go too far, did I?"	Although I don't want criticism, here is a double-barreled question that invites you to praise and be critical.
"I shouldn't tell you this, but. . . ."	You'll enjoy hearing this gossip, and I want to make you happy and strengthen our relationship.
"I heard some really good things about you. . . ."	Here are some positive strokes; be prepared to be modest.

Pleaders

Reflect the emotions of the speaker—may be envy, uncertainty, discomfort, concealed aggression, or expressions of superiority.

Expression	Purpose or Real Meaning
"I certainly wouldn't parade around in a revealing dress like that." (Envy)	I wish I had a figure like hers
"He's pretty obnoxious with all his jokes." (Envy)	I wish I could be the life of the party.
"I'll do my best." (Uncertainty)	My best probably won't be good enough.
"Do you mind if I ask you. . . ." (Followed by a penetrating or accusing question, which is concealed aggression)	Now I've got you; my disdain is now made visible.
"That's nothing, you should see. . . ." "Don't you know that?" or "It may interest you to know. . . ." (Superiority)	I'm smarter; I'm more in-the-know; or I'm better.

Applying Your Knowledge

1. Review the list of metatalk expressions. List the ones you use for each category.

2. Pair off with another person, and ask him or her to respond to each phrase. Does your partner see any problems in your use of these phrases? Which, if any, should you probably avoid? Which, if any, seem to be useful in conversation?

Applying Your Skills

ACTIVITY 4-1: Can Language Sensitivity Go Too Far?

Among the many stories about politically correct language and the attempt to avoid hurting anyone's feelings are these examples cited in a recent *Wall Street Journal* article.[9]

• Coca-Cola is criticized for "reverse sexism" because a diet Coke commercial shows a group of women ogling a beefy construction worker as he strips off his T-shirt.

• A Nynex spot was criticized by animal-rights activists because it showed a rabbit colored with blue dye.

• A Burger King commercial stirred controversy because it showed a mother teaching her grown son to memorize and recite the company's advertisement slogan to get a discount meal. After people with learning disabilities objected, the advertisement was pulled.

• A commercial for Black Flag insecticide was altered after a veteran's group protested the playing of taps over dead bugs.

• The Alliance for the Mentally Ill of New York State picketed a Daffy's discount clothing store because of a billboard showing an empty straitjacket with the headline, "If you're paying more than $100 for a dress shirt, may we suggest a jacket to go with it?"

Recognizing that advertising is a unique and often "off-the-wall" form of business communication, what might you do if confronted by people offended by your advertising?

What does this say about meanings of words? Is there a right or wrong meaning?

How do such criticisms pose problems for advertisers and creative writers? What would you do if faced by such a complaint about your company's advertising?

ACTIVITY 4-2: Which Letter Sounds Right for You?

Review the two letters on pages 98 and 99. Which style do you prefer? Which sounds more like the way you'd write such a letter?

Imagine that you are writing a similar sales letter but for a different kind of business. What style would you use if you were

1. A funeral home

2. An investment advisory service

3. A country music act

4. An upscale restaurant and banquet service

5. A city tourist's bureau

Choose one of the preceding and draft a letter to be used to solicit new business.

PERFORMING
on the Job

CASE 4-1 Sanitization of Speech

A teachers' organization in Canada consisting of nearly two thousand educators are encouraging the avoidance of violent images in everyday language. They are recommending the use of language in "better taste" when working with students in the classroom. Some traditional expressions to avoid include the following:

1. "More than one way to skin a cat"
2. "Don't shoot yourself in the foot"
3. "Killing two birds with one stone"

Another suggestion is rather than "hitting" the computer keys on the keyboard, "tapping" may be more appropriate.

The teachers' group is being criticized for its stance to sanitize speech. Opponents are saying the group is trying to murder the language and leave it "poetically challenged." In addition, these critics believe that the group is stifling creativity.

Case Questions

1. Is the teachers' group justified in its efforts to change language in the classroom? Why? Why not?
2. List why you agree or disagree with the opponents of this issue.
3. List why you agree or disagree with the teachers' group.
4. How could this issue be relevant in other business organizations or settings?
5. List some phrases, clichés, or colloquialisms you think relate to this issue and some alternative suggested wording.

CASE 4-2 School Teacher Customer Service Representative

Betty Wilson is a customer service representative (CSR) for Highpoint Office Supply Company. She has worked in a variety of positions at Highpoint for more than five years, with the past two years as a CSR. Her work involves answering questions, resolving problems, explaining products, and cross-selling various services—all over the telephone. There is no face-to-face contact with customers. CSRs must be knowledgeable of products and services; proficient at problem solving; and able to communicate in a friendly, intelligent manner.

Lisa Olsen supervises the twelve CSRs at Highpoint. Of the twelve CSRs, Betty has been in the work force the longest, with several years' work experience as an elementary school teacher earlier in her career. Lisa has been getting periodic complaints from customers saying that Betty "talks down" to them. She sounds preachy and even a bit sarcastic at times. At times she has been heard telling customers that they should "please be quiet while I explain this to you." Several customers refuse to speak with Betty because of past experiences. Lisa has discussed Betty's behavior with her several times. Each time Betty improves, but then, after a few months, customer complaints begin again.

Betty believes that she is performing her duties according to company policy and proper procedures. She handles more than the required number of calls, and earns monthly incentives from selling customers additional products and services. She realizes that occasionally customers need to be "guided" in their decisions and instructed how to use certain products more prudently. She believes that her efforts are helpful to the customers she assists.

Case Questions

1. Describe how Lisa might explain complaints of Betty "talking down" to customers.

2. How can nonverbal messages be communicated over the telephone?

3. How would you explain the concept that communication is not always what you say but how you say it?

4. Should Betty continue as a CSR? Why? Why not?

CHAPTER FIVE

Proven Communication Principles:
Four Pillars of Effectiveness

LEARNING GOALS

After you have studied this chapter, you should be able to:

- Recognize the importance of the four pillars of communication effectiveness.

- Argue for the importance of strong ethical standards in communication.

- Describe the crucial role of perception in creating understanding or failing to do so.

- Understand the importance of verifying perceptions before jumping to conclusions.

- See how different attitudes, beliefs, and values can be potential barriers to clear communication.

- Recognize communication barriers caused by noise, channels, and lack of feedback.

- Discover key reader or listener characteristics through audience analysis.

The Way It Is . . . Four Pillars of Communication Effectiveness

This chapter considers four key principles of communication effectiveness. These four, taken together, can be seen as pillars supporting the overall objective of quality business and professional communication. The four pillars are the following:

1. Ethics
2. Analysis
3. Awareness
4. Axioms

Ethics can be defined from many perspectives. Classical ethics is a division of philosophy that deals with character and conduct. People who enter certain professions or work for certain employers automatically agree to assume certain moral duties as a part of their work. Doctors, attorneys, police officers, clergy, military officers, and public officials take oaths to save lives, uphold the public welfare, abide by rules of confidentiality, and otherwise fulfill the responsibilities of their profession in an honorable manner.

Business communicators sign no oath of ethical conduct but, ultimately, make numerous decisions about ethical standards as a part of their work. In a great measure, ethics represents who people are not only the defined standards of some profession or the generalized norms of society. Ultimately, a person's ethics define that person's values.

Strong ethics is also good business. Communicators who adhere to a high sense of moral values will ultimately be more successful than the person whose ethics are "flexible" or "situational." In short, ethical communicators are more successful.

Analysis, the second pillar, refers to understanding the audience, or the audience being addressed. Although the term **audience analysis** sounds like something public speakers do, it is a broader concept than that. Receivers of all types of messages in any medium—spoken, written, visual, or electronic—will respond more appropriately if the communicator has analyzed the audience and made some careful guesses about its likely reactions to the message.

The third pillar, **perceptual awareness,** refers to a communicator's understanding of perceptual differences among people. As Chapter 2 discussed, we all have a unique way of looking at the world and expressing our understanding of it. Communicators who ignore or take lightly the reality of perceptual differences run a huge risk of miscommunication.

Finally, the fourth pillar, called **axioms of communication,** are accepted, proven rules or laws that hold up time after time (Figure 5-1). In the field of communication, several such axioms exist and are discussed later.

Ethical Communicators Are More Effective

Some of the most vigorous debates about communication ethics arise in the field of advertising. Some would argue that advertising is a world unto itself and that it does not reflect typical business communication. Advertising can also be seen as high-stakes communication that must be cost-effective. Thus, the temptations to relax ethical standards may appear attractive. Consider the outcome, however, by reviewing

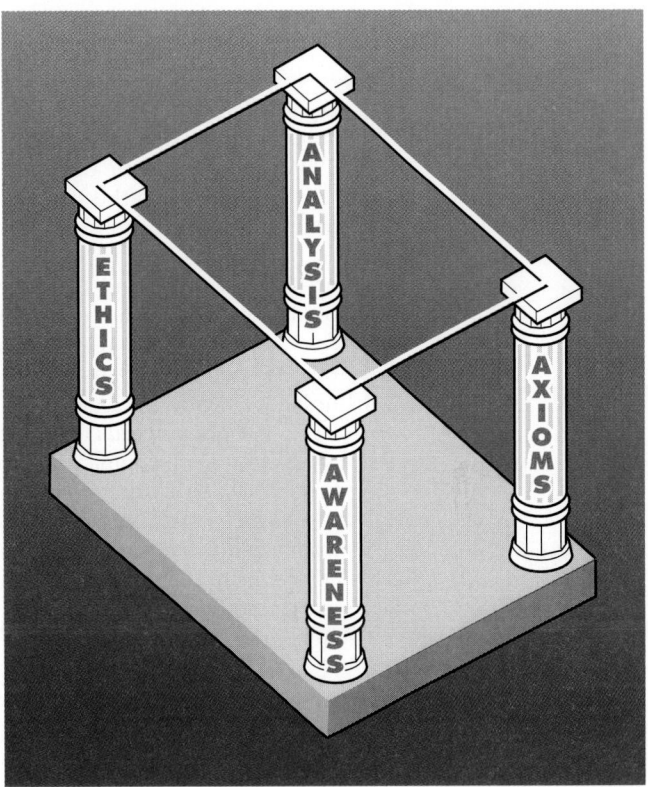

FIGURE 5-1

the news article on page 114 about advertising. How would you feel as an executive in the companies described?

The companies cited in the article are, of course, good companies. None would intentionally set out to lie or cheat their customers. They know better than that. But, at least in the eyes of one watchdog organization, they overstepped the bounds between truth and distortion in some of their advertising messages.

What do misleading advertisements have in common? Some people would say that they use the power of communication to deceive rather than to enlighten. The ethical element—the need to communicate what is honestly regarded to be true—is subordinated to the desire to get people to do something (i.e., buy their product).

How do you avoid the pitfall of unethical communication? Ultimately, the communicator's purpose plays a major role. If you seek to persuade another person at any cost, you increase the likelihood of stooping to unethical methods. If you honestly think that your message receiver will benefit from your communication, but that he or she remains free to make that decision (and you can handle it if they don't agree with you), you are more likely to keep your communication within ethical bounds.

Ethical communicators persuade but do not manipulate.

So, what is your intent? Manipulation or sincere persuasion? What is your motivation? Your advantage, or the mutual benefit to you and your receiver? How willing are you to allow the receiver freedom to choose?

These are some of the questions that will largely shape your attitudes toward communicating ethically.

Applying clear ethical standards helps you avoid the distortion, confusion, and ambiguous communication that damages your credibility. And without strong credibility, your likelihood of communication effectiveness is greatly diminished. Ethical

Dubious Award for Ten Advertisers[1]

WASHINGTON (Reuter)—Simba from "The Lion King" and "Mary Poppins" actress Julie Andrews were involved in two of the most deceptive or misleading ads of 1994, according to the Center for Science in the Public Interest [CSPI].

Andrews was the spokesperson for a television ad hawking an arthritis pain reliever that the center charged was overpriced.

The Walt Disney Co., maker of the wildly successful "Lion King," was criticized for its 60-second TV commercials that appear to be objective movie reviews of Disney films, but are really quotes made up by the advertisers.

Center officials told a news conference they wanted to help consumers "level the playing field" against "reputable companies and their marketers that seek to, or inadvertently, deceive consumers."

In a mock awards ceremony, the center said the "winners" of its lemon award were well-known companies. They included Walt Disney Co., General Motors Corp., Prudential Securities, and R.J. Reynolds Tobacco Co.

The center slammed pitches for products and services in nine areas, ranging from alcohol and food to tobacco and toys.

One of the more notable targets was Van Den Bergh Food, maker of Promise margarine, whose ads warn about the dangers of heart disease and advise consumers to "get heart smart."

In reality, the CSPI said in a statement, "Promise margarine is high in total fat and high-fat foods promote obesity, a risk factor in the development of heart disease."

The center said that while the margarine's claims have already been banned on labels by the Food and Drug Administration, they still appear in advertising, which is regulated by the Federal Trade Commission.

A center spokesman said the awards, called the Harlan Page Hubbard Lemond Wards, are named after a turn-of-the-century ad executive who pioneered modern national advertising and was also a snake oil salesman.

communicators are invariably more successful communicators. The manipulator may win a short-term gain, but the business and professional communicator knows the value of the long pull. Inevitably, unethical communication catches up with its user, damaging credibility beyond repair. Arni Sigurdsson, chairman, Iceland Media and Marketing says, "Trust is the foundation of good business communication, [it is] not a highly impressionable image or front. The substance of true impressiveness is courage, character, and a charitable mind.

Personal Ethical Standards

Notions of what is right and fair, or wrong and unjust color people's attitudes. People who have a clear set of ethical standards have the advantage in building a strong self-concept and positive attitudes.

Management writer Kenneth Blanchard and personal motivation expert Norman Vincent Peale say that

> **ethical behavior is related to self-esteem. We both believe that people who feel good about themselves have what it takes to withstand outside pressure and to do what is right rather than do what is merely expedient, popular, or lucrative. We believe that a strong code of morality in any business is the first step toward success. We believe that ethical managers are winning managers.**[2]

The ability to maintain an objective focus and not have perceptions distorted by outside pressure is a powerful tool. It helps you create confidence in your ability and reduces self-doubt.

"People with self-doubt usually don't like themselves very much and they don't trust their own judgment. As a result, they are driven by a desire to be liked and accepted by others."[3] The results are distorted perception and unproductive attitudes, which inevitably emerge in their communication behaviors.

Eight Rules of Ethical Thinking[6]

Almost every decision has ethical implications. The "right" thing to do often isn't clear.

To "do the right thing" begins with thinking rightly, say authors Robert Solomon and Kristine Hanson.

To think ethically means to steer your thoughts toward *compliance* with the rules, *contributions* you can make, and harmful *consequences* to avoid. Robert C. Solomon and Kristine Hanson boil down their study of ethical thinking into the following eight rules:[4]

1. Consider the well-being of others, including nonparticipants.

    Follow the golden rule, without sacrificing your own interests. As far as is reasonable, contribute to the general good and avoid consequences that hurt others.

2. Think as a member of the business community, not as an isolated individual.

    Business has rules of propriety and fairness that allow it to prosper. Respecting contracts, paying debts, and selling decent products at a just price underpin the business community's existence.

3. Obey, but do not solely depend on, the law.

    Ethical thinking goes beyond mere legal compliance. Many things that are not illegal, such as taking advantage of trust, are unethical.

4. Think of yourself and your company as part of society.

    Business people are citizens, and business thrives because it serves society. Business is subject to the same ethical rules as the rest of society. Ignore social problems and you invite government regulation.

5. Obey moral rules.

    This is the foundation of ethics. German philosopher Immanuel Kant called moral rules "categorical imperatives." They are unqualified commands—no exceptions, even for busy executives on the cusp of a profitable deal.

6. Think objectively.

    To be disinterested, or think from a neutral perspective, is essential to determine whether an action is truly right and not just rationalized self-interest.

7. Ask, "What sort of person would do such a thing?"

    Ethics derives from the Greek *ethos,* which means "character." Ethics is not so much obedience to rules as it is the upkeep of your personal and company character—your "good name." Peter Drucker summarizes business ethics as "being able to look at your face in the mirror in the morning."

8. Respect others' customs, but not at the expense of your own ethics.

    The hardest ethical dilemmas involve not a conflict between ethics and profits but one between two ethical systems. "When in Rome . . ." is a good rule of thumb. But if following a community's customs violates your moral values, stick to your own principles.

Ethical thinking, then, merely means considering oneself and one's firm as citizens of the business community and the whole society. Concern for others' well-being also mirrors your self-respect. This need not preclude financial success. Indeed, ethical thinking is essential to viable strategic plans. Media consultant John Wade explains it this way: "The best communicators are those people whom you naturally like, respect, and trust for themselves and their characters rather than for their accomplishments. Speaking in terms of the true meaning of 'goodness,' the better a person is, the better communicator that person will be on subjects believed to be of importance."

Audience Analysis Is Crucial to Communication Success

Dr. Herb Gilruth is a psychology professor at State University. His niece, Sarah, teaches eighth grade at Washington Junior High. As a young, progressive teacher, Sarah thought it would be interesting if uncle Herb would talk to her class about psychology.

Dr. Gilruth responded to her invitation and prepared a half-hour presentation on psychology basics.

"Kids," he began, "I'm going to talk with you about psychology, the study of mental processes that impact your everyday life in myriad ways, ranging from your self-concept to your socialization skills. I'll illustrate my main points by citing empirical research that I'm sure you'll find interesting."

How's he doing so far?

After several more minutes of "explanations of the parameters of clinical, abnormal, and social psychology phenomena," the kids started to squirm. He droned on, however, oblivious to the fact that no communication was occurring. Sure, he was talking, but no information was being shared. Why not?

The problem here was that Dr. Gilruth was simply out of touch with his listeners. He normally spoke to college students and was completely unaware of (or insensitive to) his young audience. He failed to discover his listeners.

The great statesman William Penn once said: "Better say nothing than not speak to the purpose. And to speak pertinently, consider both what is fit, and when it is fit to speak." How do you determine "what is fit," so that you might speak "pertinently"? The answer to this lives within your listeners.

The word "pertinent" might be replaced with terms like understandable, useful, or necessary. The process of discovering "pertinence," called audience analysis, is perhaps the most important communication skill you can learn.

Audience analysis means making guesses based on as much information as you can reasonably gather. From these guesses, you can determine how best to construct your message for maximum impact.

The process is not mysterious; you make guesses about others' behaviors every day. When you walk down a busy street, you guess that others will go to one side of the sidewalk or the other. You anticipate the possibility that the person walking in front of you may suddenly stop to look in a shop window.

More to the point, when you bring a message to someone, you picture mentally—or anticipate—how that person is likely to react.

Audience analysis is a process of making guesses about our audience and adjusting our message to best meet their needs.

You constantly do audience analysis, perhaps unconsciously, as you anticipate responses from others. What kind of reaction would you anticipate if you made the following statements to the people indicated?

1. *To your parent or roommate.* "My brother is out of work and needs to stay with us for about a month."

2. *To your bookstore customer.* "That textbook is out of stock, but I can order it for you. You'll have it in about three weeks, and it'll cost $55."

3. *To a customer who returned an unsatisfactory product.* "Your refund check is in the mail."

4. *A letter to your classmates at the university.* "I want to invite everyone to the St. Mary's Church young singles group Bible study next Wednesday evening."

5. *A sign posted in the window of your business.* "Billy-Bob's Bar 'Happy Hours' have been extended. They now start at noon on Friday and go until eight in the evening. Half-price drinks!"

Sales professionals learn to anticipate buyer objections ("It'll only get 16 miles to the gallon") and have carefully prepared responses ("But with its larger gas tank, the Speedfire V-8 can go more than 500 miles between fillups!").

Audience analysis and the prediction of responses is a natural activity for people. How do you learn to predict listener or reader responses accurately? The best approach is to empathize—to constantly put yourself into your listeners' shoes. In so doing, you try to:

1. Recall how you have responded when you received similar messages

2. Understand the actions, thought, values, and emotions of your listeners, or other people who are similar to your listeners.

Four Approaches to Discovering Your Audience Members

Audience analysis is a questioning process.

Because each communication situation and each person is unique, you cannot predict responses with 100 percent accuracy. You can profitably look for common reactions likely to be found in most cases, however. Several approaches to audience analysis are suggested subsequently. A combination of these may yield the best results. Remember, audience analysis is a questioning *process*. The answers aren't always clear, yet the process continues to be essential to successful communication—perhaps more so than ever in this age of one-to-one communication.

Approach 1: What Do They Need or Want to Know?

You've been asked to communicate (either in an oral briefing or written report) on a rather broad topic such as "technology developments in office equipment." You can't say everything there is to say about such a topic. You need to choose from the mass of available information some facts you think will be useful and interesting. You will not select these solely on the basis of your interests; you will attempt to anticipate your listeners' needs as well.

- First, make careful guesses about listener *interests and information needs*. These guesses are based on what you know about the listeners or others like them. For example, say that in talking with employees, you have noticed that people really seemed to perk up when you talked about computer networking. In your conversations with managers, they have expressed a need for faster computers. You have recently attended an "office of the future" trade show where you saw software that could enhance the storage capacity of your computers, a problem people in your organization have. Ideas about what material to cover will come from these kinds of data.

- Second, you need to have a good idea of *how much they already know* about the subject you will discuss. You will lose your audience fast if you tell them too much of what they already know. They will feel you are talking down to them or, worse, insulting their intelligence.

  Conversely, it is just as bad to talk about complex information to people who don't yet know the basics. Listeners or readers who are, for example, new to computer technology need to be brought up to date about exactly what small computing systems can do before they are likely to get very excited about purchasing one.

  Dr. Gilruth, in our earlier example, apparently thought eighth graders understood the psychological terms he used. This guess was incorrect, however.

- Third, you must find out *how much detail they want or need* to know about the topic. Giving detailed information to people who just want an overview of the material may annoy or bore them. When a person just needs to know what time it is, don't explain how to build a watch! Here, it is important to use the **what-they-need-to know approach.**

  When communicating with people within your own organization, you have a distinct advantage over the outsider in such analysis. To get clear answers to these questions, you can often simply go to the people you will be speaking or writing to, and ask them! You can also draw from day-to-day interaction with them at work to get important clues about their needs.

Approach 2: What Do They Expect?

Audience expectations have a way of being self-fulfilling, as Chapter 4 discussed. People hear what they expect to hear, even if they have to distort a communicator's real message to make it fit what they anticipated. In this case, it is best to use the **what-do-they-expect approach.**

When your message coincides with what the listener expected, your success is enhanced, unless your message receiver makes an "I've heard all this before" assumption. In such cases, details of your message may be lost because your listener or reader thinks he or she already knows what you are saying.

If your message presents a viewpoint different from what your audience expects from you, it pays to clarify early the fact that this message may not be the one they anticipated. In fact, creating "content set" to clarify what will be covered in your message is a powerful idea that Chapter Eight discusses further.

How do expectations arise? One source may be a person's organizational role. For example, a sales representative is expected to try to sell you something, whereas a labor leader will probably talk about employee needs that are not being met by management. The accountant is likely to have an eye on financial considerations, and the guy from the computer center is expected to talk in technical computer-speak.

All these are, however, stereotypes that may be false. The point is, people's organizational roles provide a preview of what they are expected to talk about. When these expectations are not met—the hard-nosed assembly line foreman gives a humorous pitch about the company picnic or the computer wiz talks to us in down-to-earth, simple language—the results can take you by surprise.

Personality, past behavior, appearance, age, sex, ethnic origin, race, and countless other factors provide clues that translate into expectations. The leader interested in getting across ideas that vary from these expectations may need to shock the audience into a recognition that the unexpected is being presented. The sales representative may open a customer letter with: "I'm not writing to sell you anything today. In fact, I won't even accept an order from you." This is likely to cause the purchasing agent to expect and prepare for an unusual type of presentation. Similarly, the systems analyst who announces that "I'm not here to talk about computers" may spark curiosity as well as adjust expectations.

It pays to ask yourself: "What do my audience members expect from me?" If your topic is consistent with what they anticipate, use this to strengthen your message. If your topic is different, be sure to help them readjust their expectations lest they mentally distort your message and miss the point entirely.

Approach 3: Nature of the Audience

Other people's reaction to a message may affect your reaction.

When listeners come together for the purpose of information sharing, you have an audience. When another person reads your written message, you have an audience. Certain roles generally emerge in such situations. In oral communication, audience members normally accept the role of a listener; they are quiet and defer to the speaker. The speaker recognizes his or her role as the one speaking. For written documents, the receiver usually tunes out other distractions and pays attention to your message—at least momentarily.

In either situation, a lot more interaction—two-way communication—may be going on than may meet the eye. The alert receiver carries on a mental dialogue with the sender and with his or her own thoughts. The alert message sender gets nonverbal feedback from listeners in the form of facial expressions, body movements, laughs, and grunts or yawns. The reader creates mental impressions from the nonverbal aspects of a document (it's appearance, tone, visuals, etc.). Finally, there is interaction between the audience members when more than one person gets the same message. The listener who sees others dozing off, or becoming agitated or enthusiastic may be affected by these reactions. Whispered remarks or snickers among audience members can quickly degrade the effectiveness of a serious presentation. The reader may well ask others their reactions to a document before forming a conclusion.

The type of audience you face affects these roles. William Brooks[5] identifies several different types of audiences for oral presentations. Parallel cases for receivers of written messages can be imagined.

First among these is the *casual* audience, which he also refers to as the *pedestrian* audience. An example of this may be shoppers who momentarily watch or listen to a demonstration of a particular product in a department store. For written messages, a pedestrian audience might be the recipient of a piece of "junk mail." Before any further communication can occur, the sender must get the receiver's attention.

A second type of audience is the *passive or partially orientated* audience. This audience is often made up of "captive" receivers—people who have been invited or perhaps required to attend a presentation, or who feel a duty to read your message.

A third type of audience is the *selected* audience. This audience is composed of people who have gathered for some purpose that they clearly understand. Usually the audience here has been especially invited to a meeting or selected to receive a document because they have some special interest or expertise.

A fourth audience is the *concerted* audience. These audience members have a clear understanding of why they've come together and are actively engaged in accomplishing clearly defined goals. It is their duty to read the document or participate in a presentation.

A fifth type of audience is the *organized* audience. This might be typified by a class in school, an athletic team, a military unit, or a department within a business.

Members of this type of audience are completely orientated toward the message sender whom they see as the leader or specialist with particular expertise. A memo from the boss reaches an organized audience.

The type of audience you face will determine your first priority task. For pedestrian audience members, you must grab their attention. Fail in this, and the receivers will simply leave or toss your letter! Passive audience members are less likely to walk out on you or throw away your document, but you need to gain their interest in the topic early, or they'll mentally tune you out. For selected audiences, there is generally some degree of interest already established. Here, you need to make a favorable impression and establish credibility early in the process. For the *concerted or organized audience*, your primary task is to elicit understanding, commitment, and specific action.

Approach 4: Demographics

The **demographic approach** to audience analysis gathers as much information as possible about key characteristics of the people with whom you are communicating. These characteristics may include age, sex, socioeconomic status, political philosophy, occupation, hobbies and activities, educational level, and so forth. From these data, the comunicator can draw certain inferences about his or her audience. Consider what these demographic characteristics might say about people.

1. *Age.* A person communicating with teenage employees should probably structure his message differently from the one for older employees. Several studies have indicated that younger people tend to be more frequently idealistic, more impatient, and often more optimistic than older people. Older employees think more in terms of past experiences. They often consider new ideas in light of past failures and may prematurely write off a suggestion with, "We've tried that before, and it didn't work." Researchers conclude that, "As a general rule, . . . a young audience will respond well to challenges and exciting new ideas while an older audience will respond more favorably to appeals to tradition and to moderate reforms with extensive practical justification."[6]

   In addition to adjusting the content of your message in the light of your audiences' age, the delivery of oral messages might also be adjusted. In general, older people tend to prefer a slower, more deliberate style of speaking. The younger audience will tend to prefer a faster, more lively pace. In addition, younger employees tend to have a higher dependence on visuals to accompany both written and oral messages.

2. *Gender.* Communication studies have shown that male and female audiences often respond differently to the same message. (There's more on this fascinating subject in Chapter 7.) Although **gender differences** are changing, past studies have indicated a tendency for women to be more easily persuaded than men. Some evidence suggested that men tend to reason more objectively, whereas women are more responsive to emotional appeals. Women have also been shown to retain more specific information about a particular message than do men.

   Deborah Tannen's best-selling books,[7] *You Just Don't Understand: Women and Men in Conversation* and *Talking from 9 to 5* reinforce the fact that men and women communicate differently. Among gender differences are that women communicate to express themselves and ultimately to connect with other people—to create genuine understanding. Men, conversely, are more likely to use communication to solve problems and exert control.

   Understanding male-female communication differences is a fruitful area for further study. Says Tannen, "if we recognize and understand the differences

Males and females tend to communicate differently, according to some studies.

Advertisers have a keen awareness of audience demographics. (Photo courtesy of David Austen/Stock Boston.)

between us, we can take them into account, adjust and learn from each other's styles."[8]

3. *Socioeconomic status.* Good communicators must consider the capability of an audience to understand their message. People from lower socioeconomic classes tend to be less educated and have more difficulty understanding complex ideas. Our capabilities for understanding are based on our experiences. An individual who was raised in a socially deprived situation has had considerably different experiences from the educated person from a more advantageous social background.

For example, college graduates may view the world as a fairly pleasant place with lots of opportunities for growth, whereas high school dropouts with poor literacy skills will see their lives from a less optimistic perspective. They see the future as an endless continuation of the humdrum present.

In communicating with such people, appeals to high levels of personal growth may fall on deaf ears. They'll understand your words but will reject the notion that something positive could happen to them. (See the discussion of different need levels in Chapter Three.)

Demographic differences affect people's values and attitudes.

Such demographic characteristics as age, gender, socioeconomic class, and so forth are not, of themselves, significant to the communicator. Their significance lies in the fact that these factors affect receivers' values and attitudes, which, in turn, affect the way they interpret messages. New, incoming information is filtered through existing beliefs to determine if it makes sense. If it is deemed sensible, is it pleasant, neutral, or unpleasant to the audience? The result will be an audience that is either positive, neutral (disinterested), or negative toward the information you present.

When your audience is neutral or indifferent to what you have to say, your primary concern is to get them interested. Indifferent listeners are likely to ask themselves, "What's in this for me?" or "Why do I need to know this?" In such situations, the communicator takes on the role of an instructor; he or she must teach receivers how this information is of value to them.

When dealing with hostile or excessively negative people, another problem arises. The person presenting information to such an audience should be aware that attitude changes come about slowly and that the message sender should be realistic about the goals for the communication effort. In dealing with a potentially hostile audience, it is useful to establish some sort of common ground on which the audience and the sender can agree.

Awareness of Different Perceptions

The third pillar of communication effectiveness is perceptual awareness. By this we mean that good communicators are sensitive to, and account for, the fact that people see the world differently. *No two people perceive the same event in the same way.* The images in people's heads are formed through the process of perception by which people take in, organize, and make sense of information from the world around them. Understanding this can help the communicator adjust his or her messages for maximum effectiveness.

Cartoonist Charles Schulz, the creator of the "Peanuts" comic strip, once depicted this scene: Three "Peanuts" characters—Lucy, Linus, and Charlie Brown—were lying on their backs on a grassy hill. They were looking up to the sky as this conversation occurred.

[LUCY:]	**If you use your imagination, you can see lots of things in the cloud formations. What do you think you see, Linus?**
[LINUS:]	**Well, those clouds up there look to me like the map of the British Honduras on the Caribbean. . . . That cloud up there looks a little like the profile of Thomas Eakins, the famous painter and sculptor. . . . And that group of clouds over there gives the impression of the stoning of Stephen. . . . I can see the apostle Paul standing there to one side.**
[LUCY:]	**Uh-huh. . . . That's very good. What do *you* see in the clouds, Charlie Brown?**
[CHARLIE BROWN:]	**Well, I was going to say I saw a duckie and a horsie, but I changed my mind!**

As usual, Charlie Brown is feeling a bit of peer pressure in this conversation; nevertheless, the key point is that, as he and the others look at these clouds, they, in fact, see different images. No two people see the clouds, or for that matter, any other object or idea, in exactly the same way. People perceive—that is, they make sense out of things—according to their own field of experience. The differences in people's perceptions are natural and inevitable. The communicator most likely to run into trouble is the one who has absolutely firm faith in the "truth" of his or her own perceptions.

The following are descriptions of common communication barriers. Awareness involves planning for these possibilities and adjusting one's message to minimize the damage.

Barriers Arise from Perceptual Errors

Picture this case. You are the new manager of a small manufacturing company that has had some profit difficulties recently. Your feeling is that the organization needs to be "tightened up" to become more productive. You walk into the machine shop of your company one day, and only three people are there. One man is sitting on a bench next to his machine, leaning against the wall. He appears to be almost asleep. Another employee is fixing a child's bicycle. The third person is talking on the telephone to someone he addresses as "honey." It's 9:30 A.M. on a Tuesday. What do your immediate impressions tell you about this scene? (Take a moment or two, and jot down what conclusions you might draw from this brief description.)

"A bunch of goof-offs," you might say. "I'll bet their supervisor's away. If I really were the manager there, I'd probably fire them."

Perhaps your perceptions are accurate, but if you act on this picture of reality without further investigation, you could be making a big mistake. Here's what was really happening at that machine shop. The first employee had worked all night to get out a special rush order. He hadn't slept in more than 26 hours, and he was taking a 15-minute break. The man on the telephone had also been at work through the night. This was the first chance he'd had to call his wife to see how their sick four-year-old daughter was responding to new medication. The third worker was taking time on his normal day off to work on the company-sponsored "Toys for Poor Kids" Christmas project.

Does that change your perceptions of this scene a bit? What might have happened if you had, indeed, just been appointed as a new efficiency manager, and you'd ordered everyone back to work?

The point is this: Don't take initial perceptions at face value. Get as much information as possible before you firm up perceptions into opinions that influence your actions and the ways you communicate.

People who fail to recognize the complexity of human perception often fail as communicators. An oversimplified or self-centered view that "what I see is reality," coupled with the failure to recognize that others have different pictures of reality, leads to closed-mindedness and communication failures.

Failure to recognize the complexity of human perception often results in failed communication.

Barriers Arise from Different Fields of Experience

Attitudes, beliefs, and values shape an individual's field of experience.

Our individual field of experience is a composite of our unique **attitudes, beliefs, and values.**

A belief is a conviction that something is true or false, or that it is probable or improbable. The conviction may be based on evidence, experience, or faith and confidence. Although some beliefs may be based on false evidence or incomplete data, or may be distorted by emotion, they all play an important role in perception and communication. If I absolutely believe that tax cuts will invigorate the economy but you believe that they will not, we will probably experience a barrier to understanding as we communicate about this topic.

Attitudes are our tendencies to respond positively or negatively to persons, objects, or situations. Attitudes are always directed toward something. To ask a person, "How's your attitude?" is a meaningless question unless "attitude toward _____" is understood.

Attitudes are triggered by *beliefs*. People who believe that product shortages were caused by companies' cutting back on production to create scarcity and price increases generally hold negative attitudes toward such companies. People who believe that mass media advertising is manipulative or untruthful will hold negative attitudes toward such messages.

Values are general notions of what is good or bad, of what is to be preferred or rejected. They serve as the foundation for beliefs and attitudes, and are highly resistant to change. Although you may have an almost infinite number of attitudes and beliefs, you tend to hold fewer values. Dominant values can often be described in concise phrases. You may, for example, profess to value such qualities as self-reliance, kindness, a reverence for nature, love of family, faith in democracy, loyalty, desire to help others, attitude of "looking out for number one," or survival of the fittest. Even a short list of possible values, such as this one, should suggest how conflicts and miscommunications arise. A "survival-of-the-fittest" person may see one who "helps others" as soft-hearted and foolish.

Barriers Arise from Noise

Anything that detracts from a message can be seen as "noise."

Noise is a term we use to refer to any kind of distortion or disruption of the communication process. Physical factors, such as the rumble of machinery, excessive smoke, or heat and the like, as well as other subtler types of noise can affect communication. A typographical error, misspelling, bad enunciation, or an ambiguous sentence are examples of writer- or speaker-caused noise. Message receivers can also create noise by their bad reading habits, deficient hearing, weak vocabulary, or failure to pay attention to the ideas conveyed.

The sloppy appearance of a letter can create noise by distracting the reader from what is said in it, just as the sloppy appearance of a speaker can cause a listener's thoughts to wander.

Barriers Arise from Lack of Feedback

When accurately interpreted by the message senders, feedback can tell them how successful they've been. If the message does not seem to be "getting across," the careful communicator will make readjustments (restate ideas, stress key points, adapt the message to the listener or reader, and so on) to improve the chance of accurate communication.

Media choices affect the kind and quality of feedback you are apt to receive. Written messages allow little or no immediate reaction. Face-to-face conversations allow for a great deal of feedback including direct questions, comments, and nonverbal reactions, such as a frown, smile, or nod of the head.

Whenever possible, it makes sense for a speaker or writer to solicit feedback by asking people to respond to the message so that accurate understanding can be established. Loan officer Richard Staley says, "My pet peeve is when people don't observe or request feedback." Electronic media, such as e-mail, make responding to written messages easy.

"Know your audience" should be the motto of anyone sincerely interested in being a better communicator. Efforts spent in a careful, probing analysis of your message receivers will pay handsome dividends in helping you communicate pertinently and to the purpose.

The need for audience analysis remains the same despite any technological or environmental changes in business and professional communication.

Axioms of Communication Effectiveness

Several **axioms of communication** have been shown to be consistently true. These have been tested and shown effective through years of communication research. The remainder of this chapter summarizes some of these principles.

Axiom 1: Message Senders with High Credibility Are More Effective at Getting Ideas Across

Credibility is a function of trustworthiness, expertise, and, to a lesser extent, dynamism and similarity. When people show themselves to be honest with you and to have no hidden motives that would benefit them at your expense, you are more likely to believe them. When people are seen as having expertise in the particular topic that they are communicating about, they are likely to be more persuasive. When people are seen as dynamic, sincere, and enthusiastic, they are often seen as more credible. Finally, when people are seen as "like us," having similar standards, values, or interests, you are more likely to believe them.

How can communicators build such credibility? The following are a few ideas:

To Build Credibility in	Communicators Might Try to
Trustworthiness	Acknowledge any possible conflicts of interest; avoid downgrading competing products or ideas; offer a balanced evaluation.
Expertise	Show that they understand competing ideas or products; explain how they gained their knowledge; cite authoritative sources
Dynamism	Use lively language to express enthusiasm and sincerity; use vocal variation and nonverbal cues to convey excitement
Similarity	Cite common ground with message receiver; acknowledge similar experiences, disappointments, and successes; be "down to earth"

Axiom 2: A Well-Organized Message Communicates Effectively.

Organizing ideas into comprehendible sentences, paragraphs, and documents or presentations make the likelihood of success much greater. People hold certain expectations about how a message is likely to be—or should be—structured. Chapter 8 shows you some patterns for organizing messages that boost communication effectiveness considerably.

Axiom 3: Repetition Helps People Remember a Message

If you've heard people paged at an airport or store, you'll notice that the page is almost always repeated.

> **Will arriving passenger Thomas Jones please go to Delta baggage service? Arriving Delta passenger Thomas Jones, please go to the Delta baggage service.**

Why do we repeat the same message (although perhaps in slightly different words)? Simply because some **redundancy** is needed. Remember the advice in Chapter Two: Expect to be misunderstood—then work to reduce the likelihood through repetition. If the person didn't hear a part of the first page, he will likely be able to hear the message when repeated.

Who Has Credibility?

Your choices will likely come from the degree of trustworthiness, expertise, dynamism, and similarity to yourself that you perceive in these people.

- Rush Limbaugh
- Hillary Clinton
- Bill Gates
- Kathy Lee Gifford
- Dan Rather
- Clarence Thomas
- Oprah Winfrey
- Newt Gingrich

Why do you think these people are high or low in credibility? Consider the four elements of credibility just discussed.

Even in written messages, some repetition is often needed to reduce the likelihood of mistakes. Often, visual displays of information repeat and reinforce text. In some cases, speakers or writers use a lot of repetition to create a theme or aid in remembering. Recall the famous "I Have a Dream" speech of Dr. Martin Luther King. He consistently repeats the phrase "I have a dream' as he builds the momentum of his message.

Advertising jingles rely on repetition to create a memorable message—sometimes to the point of being obnoxious. Nevertheless, no one can deny the power

Martin Luther King delivering his "I Have a Dream" speech. (Photo by UPI, courtesy of Bettman.)

of repetition in helping people remember a message. It may not make them believe the message any more strongly, nor will it necessarily create understanding, but it will aid recall.

Axiom 4: Two-Way Communication Creates Understanding.

Without two-way communication, you might as well be talking to yourself. Your messages may sound better and better to you, but you have no way of knowing how they will affect your listeners or readers. Great companies and successful individuals constantly test their message effectiveness. As shown in the continuous improvement cycle in Chapter Three, successful companies must constantly test for understanding and process feedback.

A recent article describes how one small business sought to determine if its customers were getting the message and vice versa.

> Training inexperienced salespeople can be difficult. So Richard Cucco, chief operating officer of Camadon Inc., a $25 million seller of fax machines and copiers in Pewaukee, Wis., invites customers or prospective customers into training classes to talk about how purchasing decisions are made. Some keys to a successful session: trainees prepare their questions in advance, and everyone remembers the meeting will not be used for selling.

> What customers have to say has great credibility with students [sales people]. And customers tend to be flattered by the company's interest. "They're talking about themselves for an hour and a half, which everybody likes to do," says Cucco.[9]

This strikes us as an excellent example of creating mutual understanding though useful feedback. Two-way communication expedites the creation of such understanding.

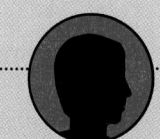
Debby and Steve Kallinikos, Owners, Burgers Supreme

Teamwork and customer care are the keys to Steve and Debby's remarkably successful restaurant. Every day, people line up to sample the wide menu of good food served fast. The customers have come to feel like family, all because of the staff's attention to individual needs.

It's not uncommon for a customer to find that a meal is "on the house," the owner's way of expressing appreciation for the patronage. Every day customers are seen smiling when Steve and Debby greet them by name and anticipate their wants—and earn their loyalty. These unexpected surprises never happen at the competition—the large chain restaurants.

The core values guiding this successful enterprise are honesty and the simple belief in treating everyone the way they want to be treated. The successful communicator at Burgers Supreme anticipates customers' needs before they ask. They keep "very aware of everything going on around the restaurant."

The nonverbal cues projected by busy workers, in their distinctive caps and tee shirts, efficiently bussing tables and hustling to serve, result in a clean, friendly atmosphere.

The greatest communication challenge Debby cites is that "we just don't have enough time. We are so busy helping customers and doing other things that it makes it hard to talk to guests and employees as much as we would like."

But Steve and Debby make the most of each face-to-face encounter and have been richly rewarded with a hugely successful business—a business built on open communication and caring for customers and team members.

Axiom 5: Alterations and Distortions Can Occur as Messages "Flow" from Person to Person

Messages get distorted as they "flow" from person to person.

You may have played the game where one person whispers a message in the ear of the person next to her who, in turn, passes it on to another player, and so on. After 10 or 12 players, the message that is announced aloud is different from the original. Something happens to information as it moves from person to person.

That game illustrates what communication experts call the **serial transmission effect.** The more people a message goes through, the more pronounced the distortions. The reason for this is that each person puts his own "spin" on the message; each interprets it in an individual way and rephrases it in a similarly unique way.

The links in a communication network—the number of receivers and transmitters—determines the degree of distortion.

The business communicator can reduce serial transmission distortion by

• Reducing the number of links in the network

• Selecting communication media that are less susceptible to individual interpretation

Axiom 6: Visual Support Helps People Grasp a Message

Most people working today have been raised in a time when video images have been everywhere. From earliest television to today's dazzling computer images, people have come to expect more information to be communicated via visuals, not just words.

The generic term for such images is *graphics*. Charts, pictures, graphs, full motion video clips—all these have become commonplace in business communication. Although it is still rather rare to use graphics exclusively for delivering a message, they almost always add clarity and interest to both written and spoken messages. Graphics *supplement* the message by

- Helping message receivers visualize complex data
- Emphasizing important points
- Breaking up the text to make a document easier to read
- Condensing and simplifying difficult concepts

This book repeats the topic of visuals. Successful business communicators look for opportunities to use graphics with all types of messages.

Axiom 7: Openness and Assertiveness Make People Better Communicators

Constructive disclosure builds stronger understanding.

Self-disclosure is the degree to which individuals reveal their attitudes and feelings to others. **Assertiveness** means being pleasantly direct in expressing those attitudes and feelings. (Note: To be assertive does not mean being rude, abusive, or even pushy. Instead, assertiveness is a healthy form of self-disclosure, a way to contribute to information sharing.)

Some people are open and expressive about how they feel, whereas others are hesitant to reveal feelings and opinions. Undoubtedly, people can go too far in either direction. The person who has a tough time expressing feelings leaves others in the dark. If that person is in a business organization, he or she creates ambiguity for employees, coworkers and customers. The person who speaks his or her mind openly may run the risk of being offensive to other individuals. If these attitudes or ideas are phrased appropriately, however, the likelihood of offending is greatly reduced. Chapter 20 reveals techniques for accomplishing this goal.

Evidence indicates that healthy, effective interpersonal relationships develop when there is *constructive* disclosure. The more open you are with someone else, the more open the other person will tend to be with you. Two people who share with each other their reactions to an experience are often drawn together. Giving and receiving feedback can lead people to more productive and useful relationships with each other. If you do not know how others feel and how much they are reacting to events, you will not be of much help to those people. Likewise, if you are too hesitant to disclose your own feelings, others may not be able to help you, and you may fail to gain the advantages of that closer relationship.

There are, of course, reasonable limits to disclosure. Few people are interested in the most intimate feelings or fantasies of others, and people have limits on how much they can or will tell. In addition, it is usually a good idea for managers *not* to express their negative feelings toward management policies or about other people. The key word is *constructive*.

Remember our definition of assertiveness: being pleasantly direct. It's important.

Understanding the Basics

• Four pillars of communication effectiveness are ethics, analysis, awareness, and axioms.

• Ethical communicators are more effective because they are perceived as having higher credibility.

• Ethical thinking and actions involve considering the well-being of others, respecting business conventions, obeying the law, seeing yourself and your company as a part of the larger society, obeying moral rules, thinking objectively, maintaining standards of good character, and respecting others' customs.

• Analysis of one's audience can enhance communication effectiveness. Doing this means making careful guesses about what your audience needs, wants, or expects. The nature of the audience and its demographic characteristics can also provide important cues for effectiveness.

• Awareness of different perceptions—that no two people perceive the same event in the same way—highlights possible communication barriers.

• Axioms of communication effectiveness validate the need for strong credibility, good message organization, some repetition, two-way information flow, serial transmission problems, visual support, and open assertiveness.

KEY TERMS AND CONCEPTS

ethics	assertiveness	demographic approach
perceptual awareness	self-disclosure	gender differences
attitudes, beliefs, and values	audience analysis	serial transmisssion effect
noise	what-they-need-to-know approach	redundancy
feedback receptiveness	what-do-they-expect approach	axioms of communication
audience expectations	nature of the audience approach	
credibility		

QUESTIONS FOR FURTHER THOUGHT

1. Why is it important to discover your audiences? Why should this be an ongoing process?

2. What are self-fulfilling expectations? Give an example.

3. Which type of audience (as described by William Brooks in this chapter) would you most and least like to make an oral presentation to? Why?

4. Do you agree with the authors' comments about male/female differences in responding to the same message? Support your position with an example.

5. What is the role of ethics in business communication? How would you describe your own ethical standards regarding communication?

ANOTHER Look

Audience Analysis and the Woman Car Buyer

The following news article illustrates how a segment of one industry is applying audience analysis to improve its communication. Look especially at the crucial role of customer feedback in this process.

Cars have long fascinated Judy Jones, a child of Detroit's golden years in the 1950s and '60s. But until recently, she said, the automobile industry didn't seem too interested in her. Automakers rarely acknowledge in their advertising or sales pitches that women can appreciate cars or that they buy more than a third of all new cars and trucks.

"Women have never been targeted," said Ms. Jones, editor and publisher of Dallas-based *Women's Enterprise* magazine. "It's all men."

That may be changing. A women's advisory committee formed by Dallas-area Lincoln-Mercury officials and dealers has been so successful in heightening the automaker's appeal with female buyers that the company is forming similar committees in other regions of the country.

Besides reviewing advertising and occasionally suggesting changes in wording, the 9-month-old committee "mystery shopped" area Lincoln-Mercury dealers to see how salespeople treated women customers. Their reviwis were videotaped and later played for the dealers, an experience that Dallas Lincoln-Mercury dealer Jimmy Bankston said was "pretty embarrassing for some."

Car buying is unpopular with most people, according to surveys. But women particularly dislike it. Some salespeople treat women with disrespect or skip over technical details when they're dealing with a woman. If a woman customer arrives at the dealership with a man, the salesperson often assumes that the man will make the final decision on a car even when a woman is buying it.

When the 11 committee members began work, they did not expect local dealers and Lincoln-Mercury officials to pay much attention to their suggestions. "I have really been surprised and amazed that they have," said Ms. Jones, a member of the committee.

She probably shouldn't be, some industry observers said. Given the current state of the industry, Lincoln-Mercury and other automakers have plenty of reason to be responsive.

If car makers are to maintain their market share, they can't afford to overlook any segments of buyers. And women are a substantial group. They accounted for 35 percent of all car and truck sales last year, and 33 percent of Lincoln-Mercury sales, said Joel Pitcoff, research and analysis manager at Ford Motor Co.

Bobbie Koehler-Gaunt, general sales manager at Lincoln-Mercury, said women are especially important to Lincoln-Mercury because they figured prominently in the company's slight growth last year. The company won't disclose exact figures on market segments or growth within those segments.

"We knew at Lincoln-Mercury that if we were going to realize our potential, we had to reach women," she said.

Last summer, when Lincoln-Mercury was discussing the introduction of its new midsize sedan, the Mystique, the company said it expected 55 percent of the car's sales to be to women, a percentage that Mr. Boeger described as "pretty high." Lincoln-Mercury said women also account for a "substantial" portion of Sable, Cougar and Tracer sales.

"As I continued to read about the growing influence of women in new-car choices, it just screamed for some sort of action," he said.

Mr. Boeger got volunteers for the committee from a variety of sources, gathering names from local Lincoln-Mercury dealers, as well as other businesses and area women's organizations. Some of the women drive Lincoln-Mercury cars.

They range in age from 25 to 65 and are fairly diverse in ethnicity. Some are professionals, some are homemakers. About half are married.

The committee meets for a couple of hours once every month or six weeks. Most of its efforts have been focused on advertising by local Lincoln-Mercury dealers, with the women making suggestions on phrasing or words.

Recently, for example, the committee was given a list of words such as "performance," "luxury," and "comfort." Committee members were asked what the words meant to them.

"Performance to me as a woman may mean something completely different than to a man," said committee member Sara Reidy, a human resources consultant.

The committee proposed "mystery-shopping" the Lincoln-Mercury dealerships mainly because so many members have had bad experiences with new-car dealerships. "We went around the table and everyone had a horror story," Ms. Jones said.

One major difference between male and female buyers is women "go into the ownership experience with such low expectations that they almost can't be disappointed," Ms. Koehler-Gaunt said.

Committee members each visited a dealership. Shortly after they left the dealership, they sat down before a camera to recount their sales experience.

Many had relatively minor complaints. But most said they felt that they were treated differently than a man would have been.

In Ms. Reidy's case, the salesman pointed out a hook in a car's interior where she could hang her purse, but never bothered to show her the vehicle's engine and did not offer her a test drive of the car. "What he thought was most important to me was the design of the interior," she said.

In the future, Ms. Reidy said, she hopes the committee can make similar "mystery-shoppings" of dealers' service and body shops.

"I have to say I'm really kind of proud to have served on this committee," said Ms. Reidy. "There is going to be a difference. I don't think we're seeing it now, but we're being heard."

"That's the purpose of all this, to educate the dealers on the diversity of who is coming into their dealerships," Ms. Koehler-Gaunt said.

(Excerpted from Terry Box, *The Dallas Morning News,* Knight-Ridder/Tribune Business News, May 28, 1995. Used with permission.)

Applying Your Knowledge

1. What are some assumptions salespeople hold regarding female customers?
2. How would you teach salespeople to serve the female customer better?

Applying Your Skills

ACTIVITY 5-1: What Was Wrong with Herb?

Review the story of Dr. Gilruth and his junior high listeners. Where did he go wrong? List specific terms he used that went over the heads of his audience.

How can we avoid a similar problem?

ACTIVITY 5-2: Types of Audiences and Primary Tasks

Describe a specific example of each type of audience listed subsequently. Then describe the first task you'll need to accomplish to succeed in communicating with these audiences.

	Example	First Priority Task
Pedestrian		
Passive		
Selected		
Concerted		
Organized		

ACTIVITY 5-3: Audience Analysis Approaches

Summarize in your own words, the four audience analysis approaches described in this chapter. Write specific questions you'd like answers to before communicating.

	Approach	Specific Questions
What they need or want to know		
What do they expect		
Nature of the audience		
Demographics		

ACTIVITY 5-4: Audience Reaction[10]

How do you react to some everyday situations? How intense are your feelings about some typical events? Read each of the short incidents described below and select the word that best describes what you would imagine your first reaction would be. . . . You may use the same word more than once. Do not make an in-depth analysis of the situation; just read it quickly and give your first impression.

1. alarm
2. anger
3. concern
4. curiosity
5. disapproval
6. disinterest
7. envy
8. excitement
9. fear
10. gladness
11. gratitude
12. happiness
13. humiliation
14. interest
15. irritation
16. joy

17. kindness   20. sadness

18. love   21. worry

19. resentment

I. While riding the subway, you see a man with three small boys ranging in ages from about two to six. The boys run up and down the aisles, yelling and screaming. The father sits totally oblivious of the behavior of his kids.

II. You are heading home after a hard day's work. You are passed on the freeway by a couple driving a car similar to yours. They are obviously close to each other, in fact, you wonder if he can safely drive the car while she tousles his hair and nibbles his earlobe.

III. While attending the company's family picnic, you overhear a child saying to his parent: "I hate you! You are so mean to me! I hate the way you treat me!"

IV. At lunch time you decide to walk a few blocks for a quick sandwich. As you are crossing the street at a busy intersection, a car races through the intersection, apparently trying to beat the red light. The car comes so close that you literally jump out of the way to avoid being hit.

V. You are on a committee for your service club to interview and select a citizen of the year. During the interviews of candidates, you are informed that a real hero has been nominated and will arrive for an interview shortly. He saved a drowning child last summer and donated the reward money to create a CPR training program for youth leaders. He is kind and courteous.

Before considering your first responses, we'd like you to react to the incidents again, but from a slightly different point of view. Do the same as you did before: read the vignette and select the word that best describes what you think your first response would be. Use the list of words from the preceding page, writing the appropriate word in the space provided. Feel free to use the same words more than once.

I. While riding the subway, you see a man with three small boys ranging in ages from about two to six. The boys run up and down the aisles, yelling and screaming. The father sits totally oblivious of the behavior of his kids. They are on the way home from the hospital where his wife died after weeks of suffering from cancer.

II. You are heading home after a hard day's work. You are passed on the freeway by a couple driving a car similar to yours. They are obviously close to each other; in fact, you wonder if he can safely drive the car while she tousles his hair and nibbles his earlobes. The passenger is your spouse, and it is your car.

III. While attending the company's family picnic, you overhear a child saying to his parent: "I hate you! You are so mean to me! I hate the way you treat me!" The child is your son, speaking to your spouse.

IV. At lunch time you decide to walk a few blocks for a quick sandwich. As you are crossing the street at a busy intersection, a car races through the intersection, apparently trying to beat the red light. The car comes so close that you literally jump out of the way to avoid being hit. The driver is your eighty-year-old mother, who recently had an eye operation.

V. You are on a committee for your service club to interview and select a citizen of the year. During the interviews of candidates, you are informed that a real hero has been nominated and will arrive for an interview shortly. He saved a drowning child last summer and donated the reward money to create a CPR training program for youth leaders. He is kind and courteous, but he was accused of sexually molesting your child, although evidence at the trial was insufficient to convict him.

ACTIVITY 5-5: Your Perceptions

What are your perceptions and attitudes toward the following things? Jot down words that describe your first reaction to the term, then try to explain how beliefs, attitudes, and past experience may influence your perceptions toward the following:

- French poodles
- Rhubarb
- Advanced mathematics
- Middle-aged women
- Snow
- Jogging
- Liberals
- Bull fighting
- Religious people
- Government employees
- Mexican food
- Auto mechanics
- Hairdressers
- Fashion designers
- Textbook authors
- Hockey
- MTV

PERFORMING
on the Job

CASE 5-1 A President's Message

Robert Farley is the president of a small midwestern manufacturing business. The company has 208 employees; many are rather young and just starting out in their careers. Many of the employees are putting a spouse through school at the nearby state university or are working while going to school on a part-time basis. About 15 percent of the employees have been with the company for many years and will probably work there until retirement.

Each month an employee newsletter is published to keep employees informed on matters and issues relevant to the organization. Each month, Mr. Farley writes a "Message from the President" column directed to all employees. This past month, several employees expressed frustration with the president's message. They thought that they were being patronized and spoken down to. Mr. Farley's intentions are to boost morale, not deflate it. He was surprised when he heard of the reactions to his article.

Part of Mr. Farley's latest article told of his friend (John) who needed a $5,000 loan for income taxes. John was approaching the April 15 tax deadline and had been too busy with other matters to investigate the possibilities for a loan. Mr. Farley wrote of how he referred John to his bank where he receives excellent service. Mr. Farley emphasized the importance of customer service in his article and thanked all the staff for their efforts. John was able to get the loan and commented on how nicely he was treated by the bank staff.

Another point made by Mr. Farley in his article announced upcoming on-site seminars to discuss retirement and financial planning. All employees were "strongly encouraged" to attend even if they didn't have a lot of assets.

Mr. Farley ended his article with the sentence he regularly uses to conclude, "Thank you for all you do."

Case Questions

1. Why would some of the staff feel patronized or spoken down to?
2. What do you think Mr. Farley was trying to communicate in his article?
3. What do you think Mr. Farley communicated to the shorter-term employees?
4. What do you think Mr. Farley communicated to the longer-term employees?
5. What can Mr. Farley do in the next monthly newsletter?

CASE 5-2 Vindictive Customer[11]

Jeremy Dorosin is a consumer on a crusade that should strike a chord with everyone ever slighted by a rude clerk or arrogant corporate executive. Dorosin wants a public apology from a business that he believes mistreated him.

Dorosin, a Pinole resident who runs a Walnut Creek scuba shop, is going to extraordinary lengths to achieve his goal. He is running national newspaper advertisements listing a toll-free telephone number to attract other disgruntled customers of the object of his scorn, the popular coffee chain Starbucks Corp.

In the three weeks after Dorosin ran his first ad in *The Wall Street Journal*, Dorosin has apparently touched a nerve. So far, he says he has received more than 3,000 calls and scores of faxed letters from consumers scolding Starbucks for the way that Dorosin says he was treated at the chain's Berkeley store.

What's more, Dorosin says he has lined up enough support to finance his plans to spend up to $5 million on advertisements continuing to skewer Seattle-based Starbucks over the next six months. Dorosin already has spent about $10,000 to pay for four ads in *The Wall Street Journal* and his toll-free number.

Dorosin, age 37, swears he won't go away until Starbucks pays more than $100,000 for a full-page advertisement in *The Wall Street Journal* carrying an apology to him.

"I'm not asking for any money, so they can't say I'm trying to blackmail them," Dorosin says. "This isn't about money. It's about treating people right."

To Starbucks, Dorosin's campaign seems like a tempest in a teapot. The company can't fathom Dorosin's hostility because its customer service department went to great lengths to find a reasonable resolution to his grievances, said Starbucks spokeswoman Cheri Libby.

"We pride ourselves on providing customer satisfaction," Libby said. Starbucks suspects that Dorosin is targeting the company so he can collect material for a book that he is compiling on morality. The company also suggests its competitors in the coffee industry may be bankrolling Dorosin.

Dorosin brands the theory linking the advertisements to his book as "absolute nonsense." He won't identify the companies that have agreed to finance his campaign.

The dispute between Dorosin and Starbucks dates back to his purchase of a $169 espresso machine in Starbucks' Berkeley store. Dorosin picked the machine as a special wedding gift for a female friend who had just survived a bout with cancer.

When the bride opened the gift and found a rusty machine with missing parts, Dorosin became livid. He believed that Starbucks had sold him a used machine.

Libby says the machine may have been tested before reaching the store but stresses that Starbucks would never knowingly sell a used machine.

As compensation for the problem, Dorosin says he asked Starbucks to send the bride a letter of apology accepting blame for the faulty gift in addition to a top-of-the-line espresso machine. Starbucks says Dorosin wanted a $2,500 espresso machine for less than $200. Dorosin says he wanted a $400 machine for the bride. Starbucks finally offered a $269 machine.

When Dorosin couldn't get what he wanted from Starbucks' corporate headquarters, he decided to air his grievances publicly. After his second advertisement appeared, Starbucks tried to mail Dorosin a full refund and give the bride a new machine, but it was too late.

Dorosin will now settle for nothing less than a full-blown apology in *The Wall Street Journal*.

Starbucks, which earned $10.2 million last year on 1994 sales of $285 million, isn't prepared to go to those lengths. "How can we apologize for something that we didn't do?" Libby said.

In the meantime, Dorosin is preparing to buy a full-page ad in *The Wall Street Journal* to publish some of the letters he has received from consumers responding to his previous advertisements.

Starbucks probably won't want to excerpt the letters in its annual report. In one typical diatribe, Santa Clara County management consultant Thomas A. Bottenberg writes, "Starbucks has unleashed the fury of every customer who has ever been approached incorrectly or been taken for granted."

Dorosin is confident he will teach Starbucks an expensive lesson. "Everybody in retailing knows the customer is always right because unhappy customers can do a lot of damage," Dorosin says. "If a customer is dissatisfied, 250 people will probably hear about it. I think I have definitely increased that ratio."

Case Questions

1. Why is Mr. Dorosin doing this? What factors seem to have touched off this vendetta?

2. What attitudes, beliefs, or values underlie Mr. Dorosin's actions?

3. If you were an executive with Starbucks, what would you do about this situation? Be specific about the actions you would take.

4. Explain your view of the ethics of both parties in this dispute.

Media and Technology:
Quantum Leaps Daily

LEARNING GOALS

After you have studied this chapter, you should be able to:

- Better understand the changing realm of communication technology.

- Recognize that the various communication media and approaches have inherent advantages and disadvantages, and that these media should not be used out of habit but rather selected carefully.

- Understand the distinction between communication efficiency and communication effectiveness.

- Become aware of some of the unspoken "ground rules" associated with different communication media.

- Carefully select appropriate media based on speed, feedback capacity, hard-copy availability, message intensity and complexity, formality, and relative costs.

- Identify some ways to mix media to improve effectiveness.

- Become aware of a variety of communication tools used successfully in other organizations.

- Recognize the problem of communication overload and some ways to deal with it.

The Way It Is . . . Communication Media

In business and professions, you have, more than ever, a wide variety of communication **media** at your disposal. Which ones you choose to use for a particular situation can, in itself, communicate. In other words, each form of communication—each **medium** or tool—conveys unspoken messages. For example, a cheap medium, such as a handwritten, photocopied note, might say the following to its recipient:

- This message isn't important. If it were, it would be presented more formally.

- You are not important enough to receive this information from the source personally.

- The message source is too busy to convey this information to you in a more personal way.

- This matter is so urgent, the sender had to sacrifice personalism to get out the information quickly.

- This is routine information that you will readily understand.

An expensive medium, such as a formal presentation to small groups with accompanying color visuals and quality handouts, tells its receivers the following:

- This message is important. The audience is important.

- It is crucial that you receive and understand this information.

- This matter is complex enough to require a careful explanation to groups small enough so that individual questions can be answered.

- The message sender wants to portray a high level of professionalism.

Any or all of these thoughts might enter the minds of the receivers. In doing so, the medium itself makes comment about the contents of the message.

Communication effectiveness improves and communication costs drop when appropriate media are selected. This section first clarifies what is meant by medium (or media) and then discusses the effects of the unspoken assumptions inherent in each.

High-quality visuals send a message: "This presentation is important." (Photo by Dollarhide, courtesy of Monkmeyer Press.)

What Does Media Mean?

Although we often associate the term media with radio/television or with communications hardware such as telephones, videotape recordings, and the like, this discussion of the media of business communication goes beyond the mechanical aspects. The term *media* is being used here in a broad sense, to include the *method, channel,* or *circumstances* under which communication occurs. Although this description includes various types of written, oral, and electronic communication devices, it is not limited to them.

Typically people think of the term medium (the singular form of media) as a channel or mechanism for transmitting or conveying messages from point to point. Although this description may be useful to a point, it implies a mechanical element that doesn't apply to the human side of the communication process. A more useful way to consider media arises from the following definition:

> A medium is defined by a generally accepted set of ground rules for structuring and exchanging messages.

These ground rules today apply to electronic technology as well as writing, speaking, and various forms of interaction to exchange messages. The technology side is the most rapidly changing with the increased availability of e-mail, fax, Internet, teleconferencing, and the like. Nonetheless, the process of selecting appropriate media for given messages remains much the same.

Technology gives us more choices but does not alter the need to make an educated decision about media appropriateness.

Any message, regardless of the care put into its composition, can fall flat if the communicator uses an inappropriate medium. Worse yet, it can backfire. The memo on page 140 is fairly clear, but it fails miserably to accomplish its goal. As you read it, consider some possible outcomes from such a message.

What problems do you see with this message? You could cite its tone, sentence structure, or format. We'll talk about those characteristics at length later in the book.

Despite huge changes in electronic technology, the process of selecting an effective medium is based on many similar concerns.

Sometimes the easy
way creates more
problems than it solves.

But let's look at an even more basic problem that makes the message's success unlikely: the writer's decision to use a broadly disseminated memo in the first place. It's
probably the wrong medium. Wilbur chose the easy way to deal with a problem—
broadcasting his message. But in doing so, he probably created more problems than he
solved.

MEMORANDUM

TO: All employees

FROM: Wilbur Jackson, Supervisor

DATE: August 14, 199X

RE: COFFEE BREAK ABUSE

It has recently been brought to my attention that
department employees are taking excessively long
coffee breaks. This is in violation of company
policy. Employees caught taking more than fifteen
minutes morning and afternoon will be terminated.
If things don't improve, the manager of the Roach
Coach, Inc., will be told to not send their snack
and coffee services to our offices anymore and the
break room will be closed. I trust you will obey
policy in the future regarding this matter.

By choosing a medium that goes to everyone—guilty and innocent alike—
Wilbur chose the easy way. But suppose that you work for Wilbur and that you have
been careful to limit your coffee breaks to fewer than fifteen minutes. Further, suppose that you often forego breaks at all to meet the demands of your job. How would

you react to this message? You'd probably be pretty upset. You'd most likely think that Wilbur isn't the brightest manager.

Some Media Ground Rules

The **"ground rules"** for use of a particular medium are usually assumed by participants rather than prescribed in advance. Communication professor Richard Hatch says, for example, that a casual medium called "polite conversation" (yes, that meets our definition of a medium) usually works under the following ground rules:

- Whoever is talking may continue to talk until he or she appears to be finished.
- No speaker should talk for "very long" at a time, which may vary from a few seconds to two or three minutes, depending on the circumstances.
- Nobody may interrupt the speaker unless he or she agrees to be interrupted.
- When a silence occurs, each participant has an equal opportunity to begin talking, that is, nobody is intentionally excluded.
- Anybody who is talking may change the subject without getting permission from other participants.[1]

When such ground rules are violated, participants in the communication situation are thrown off. Visualize a polite conversation in which any of the rules listed are violated—let's say that interruptions abound—and you're likely to picture an ineffectual and decidedly *im*polite conversation.

Table 6-1 on page 142 suggests additional examples of the kinds of ground rules—generally unspoken—present under several spoken and written/graphic media.

You don't consciously consider each rule every time you communicate, but they are there. They've just become so familiar that you no longer notice them. These rules do, however, provide a rational basis for making decisions about what medium to use for specific messages. If, for example, you need to convey some highly technical, intricate, and complex information, you would be likely to avoid the casual conversation medium. Such messages may involve talking for long periods, and listeners would be expected to refrain from changing the topic. Instead, you'd probably use a formal presentation or written document.

Some communicators overuse a medium without much thought.

Much of the success or failure of functional business communication can be attributed to media selection. Some managers use memos, for example, to convey the darndest things. Like Wilbur in the earlier story, they fail to see the downside of their media selection. They opt for convenience and beget confusion or resentment.

What medium should Wilbur use? Assuming that the problem he sees exists (and is not just a misperception on his part), he should use a medium that

- Avoids implying that all employees are guilty, or
- Permits receivers to respond, explain, justify, or deny the accusation

In all likelihood, a personal one-to-one conversation with suspected offenders would make sense. If he doesn't have any idea who is taking the long breaks—or if the accusation is even true—he might bring up the concern, carefully worded, at a meeting of his subordinates, allowing them to comment or respond.

TABLE 6-1

EXAMPLES OF GROUND RULES FOR MEDIA

Some Possible Ground Rules	Spoken Media				Written/Graphic Media		
	Conversation (Telephone or Face-to-Face)	Interview	Committee or Tele-conference	Presen-tation	Letter/ Memo/ E-mail	Report	Poster/ Display
Receivers may interrupt and/or seek clarification	Yes	Yes	Yes	No	No	No	No
Participants may change the subject	Yes	Some-times	Yes	No	No	No	No
One person may talk for extended periods	No	No	No	Yes	No	Yes	No
Participants have equal opportunity to initiate ideas	Yes	Some-times	Yes	No	No	No	No
Messages are pre-sented in a stan-dard arrangement or format	No	Some-times	No	Yes	Usually	Yes	No
Supporting data of considerable detail are presented with conclusion	Some-times	No	Some-times	Yes	Some-times	Yes	No
Artistic or aesthetic qualities are con-veyed	No	No	No	Some-what	No	Some-times	Yes

These approaches are more time-consuming and costly than a quick memo, but are likely to be much more effective.

The memo isn't the only communication medium that tends to be overused or abused. Consider the use of the infamous "pink slip"—a notice of firing used by some companies—or the informal chat in the rest room where the employee's work quality is critiqued in the presence of others. These communications reflect ignorance of the effects of media. They are apt to have adverse effects on the organization and the person who unwisely selects them.

One common adverse effect is a waste of time or money from poor media use. Here's a personal example from one of your authors.

> I once attended a meeting called by the general manager of the large cor-poration where I worked. About 200 employees, midlevel managers, su-pervisors, and office staff were required to attend. The company rented a meeting room at a hotel near the main office, because we had no confer-ence room large enough. The purpose of the meeting was for the general manager to explain, in a broad sense, the need to economize on our everyday operations. After stating that need and explaining how it re-lated to the company's profit picture, the boss asked if anyone had any comments or suggestions.

One secretary spent several valuable minutes explaining how she had developed a system to save paper clips and cut up paper for scratch pads. Several others took the opportunity to impress the boss with their success stories at conserving office supplies or cutting down on photocopying.

No one seemed to notice, however, the cost of that medium being used: the mass meeting! By the time the people drifted back to their offices, the company had spent more than 300 hours in direct labor costs alone. In addition was the cost of the meeting room, the cost of reduced efficiency back at the offices while all the supervisors were gone, and the incalculable cost of possible lost business or customer resentment created when people wanting to speak to a meeting attendee simply had to wait until our "cost-cutting" meeting ended.

What was the return on this communication investment? Employees learned that the company would like to make a profit (a real eye-opening notion!), and they picked up some tips on saving paper clips. The corporation used a thousand-dollar medium to convey nickel-and-dime ideas. The point is that selection of appropriate communication media can have a huge effect on costs and effectiveness.

The first step to using media effectively is to recognize that the method you choose sends important signals to your receivers. It provides cues about your estimation of the audience's importance as well as the significance and urgency of the message being conveyed. A routinely distributed photocopied memo conveys a different immediate impression from that of a neatly typed and personally signed letter—even though the actual words used in the message may be identical.

The media you choose communicate meaning themselves.

Rating the Medium, Not the Message[2]

How would you rank the following eleven forms of business communication in terms of effectiveness (starting with the least effective)?

Handout (Flyer—randomly distributed)

Advertisement

News item

Brochure

Mass-produced letter

Typewritten letter

Handwritten letter

Phone conversation

Large group discussion

Small group discussion

One-to-one conversation

If you left the above list unchanged, you'd have what market researchers call the "Ladder of Communication Effectiveness," arranged from least to most effective. Here, in a slightly revised and ascending order, is how executive Mark H. McCormack grades each method—and why:

11. *Handout, Grade F:* Flyers are virtually worthless. They're distributed on one street corner and deposited in a trash can at the next.

10. *Mass-produced letter, Grade D minus:* You'll never convince me that mailing 1,000 letters to have 990 ignored is effective communicating. Yet in some direct-mail circles, this 1 percent response is considered great.

9. *Advertisement, Grade C:* Quick! What's the last great advertisement that you can recall?

8. *News Item, Grade C:* High readership, high credibility, but hard to control.

7. *Brochure, Grade C:* Great for image building and selling the pre-sold.

6. *Typewritten letter, Grade C plus:* The standard form of communication. Essential as a means of self-protection. Effectiveness is inversely proportional to its length.

5. *Handwritten letter, Grade B minus:* This personal touch is memorable when you're writing to someone you know. Debatable when you don't.

    I've met many executives socially, but I don't know them well. Yet I suspect they'd take notice if I wrote them a letter in longhand. I know it would make an impression if they communicated that way with me.

4. *Large group discussion, Grade B:* A favorite of self-perpetuating bureaucrats: the less certain they are of what exactly they want to discuss, the more people they invite to discuss it.

    Large discussions are fine for *handing down* decisions, less so for *making* them. They also require ruthless follow-up.

(continued)

(continued)

> **3.** *Small group discussion, Grade B plus:* The preferred method of making internal decisions. To me, an acceptable small group is three people. The ideal is two.
>
> **2.** *Phone conversation, Grade A minus:* As they say, the next best thing to being there. Keep this in mind the next time you debate whether to write or call.
>
> **1.** *One-to-one conversation, Grade A plus:* Not only the best form of communication, but in my experience better than all the other forms combined. Keep this in mind the next time you debate whether to bring an associate or go

Five Ways to Pick the Best Media

With the different impact of various media in mind, how can we choose intelligently among the many options available? Here are some key suggestions.

Understand Efficiency versus Effectiveness

Communication **efficiency versus effectiveness** are two different things. Efficiency is a simple ratio between the resources expended to generate intentional messages (including time, materials, and effort) and the number of people to whom the message is sent. To improve efficiency, you simply increase the number of people reached or reduce the message preparation costs. The widely distributed memo, mass mailing, or large meeting can be *efficient*.

Communication efficiency = costs divided by number of people reached.

$$\text{Communication efficiency} = \frac{\text{Resources (including time) expended}}{\text{Number of recipients reached}}$$

Communication *effectiveness* is another matter. Chapter 1 stressed that communication is the creation of understanding and that only the message receiver will determine success. By that criterion, business and professional communication may be said to be *effective* when a message is

Communication effectiveness happens when a message is received, understood, remembered, and used by the intended audience.

- *Received* by its intended audience (and not by a bunch of others who have no interest or involvement)
- *Interpreted* essentially the same way by the recipients as intended by the sender.
- *Remembered* over reasonable period
- *Used* when appropriate occasions arise[3]

Many communication failures arise from emphasizing efficiency over effectiveness.

The dilemma for the business person is that, in most cases, the communication methods that are most efficient are least effective and vice versa. In almost every case, for example, face-to-face conversation with individuals is the least efficient, least convenient, and most costly method of conveying ideas and creating understanding.

It is also the most effective. And for some types of messages, including Wilbur's problem with the coffee breaks, it is essential. Wilbur's "efficient" memo blast results in a shotgun approach that is likely to hit the wrong people (violating effectiveness condition number one by striking the innocent as well as the guilty). This could cause huge resentment.

For most businesses, face-to-face communication is preferred, but it is not always practical. (Courtesy of Rob Crandall/Stock Boston.)

An unwillingness to pay the price for effectiveness in communication may well be false economy. Management theorist Saul Gellerman concludes:

> "A very large part of the blame for ineffective communication . . . falls on management's persistent efforts to communicate with the most people at the least cost. Alas, communication is one function where it does not pay to be efficient."[4]

In some cases a message is simple or not important enough to transmit via individual, face-to-face interaction. In many cases, organizational size, distance between locations, or complexity forbids it. We must then strike a balance between efficiency and effectiveness. Unfortunately, many people choose a communication method out of habit, without considering the merits or drawbacks of possible alternatives.

Understand the Characteristics and Costs of Various Management Communication Media

A broad description of media is a generally accepted set of ground rules, with specific advantages or disadvantages to each. A wise selection considers the

1. Media characteristics inherent in each
2. Relative costs of written (including e-mail) versus spoken communication

Some of the characteristics of business communication media that make one preferable to others in a given situation follow.

Speed. How fast or slow a medium is depends on several factors including preparation time, delivery time, and assimilation time (the time it takes for the receiver to comprehend the message being delivered).

A mailed letter is generally slow getting from sender to receiver (e-mail users call it "snail-mail"), although overnight services and fax reduce the time problem. An oral presentation of the same information—although instantaneously received—

may take considerably more preparation time, however. Ironically, the time-consuming job of producing a videotape or slide presentation can be offset when repeated showings efficiently reach many employees or customers with the same information.

Normally, the spoken word is faster than a print medium, except, for example, when comparing a formal oral presentation with a hand-written note.

Immediate Feedback Capacity. The amount and promptness of feedback are other media characteristics. Written media elicit no **immediate feedback capacity** from your audience while you are writing the message. By the time you get a response it may be too late to adjust and clarify the original message.

Written media give the least feedback; face-to-face communications give the most.

Telephone conversations provide immediate feedback in the form of questions, comments, tone of voice, pauses, hesitation, and so on. A face-to-face conversation provides all this plus other, nonverbal feedback in facial expression, body movement, and posture.

Hard-copy Availability. Whether or not a permanent record of the message is *normally* retained is another media characteristic. Ordinarily, interviews, informal conversation, and telephone messages leave no record. (These can be recorded, but that is not routine practice in most organizations.)

E-mail messages can be easily printed or filed but otherwise do not leave a hard copy. (They do, however, remain electronically filed, so be aware that what you say can usually be traced back to you. "Flaming," or sending insulting, derogatory messages anonymously, has become a serious problem for some e-mail users, creating a need for additional system security as well as additional capability to trace messages.)

Written communications, such as letters, reports, and most memos, are maintained on computer files and often as paper copies too. An informal note, however, may be discarded and is, therefore, usually a nonrecord medium. This medium can have advantages where candid expression "off the record" is called for. Putting it in writing seems to make the message more formal or "official," a situation that may also call for less openness in expression.

Message Intensity and Complexity. Some media can better convey **message intensity and complexity.** A high-intensity message may be one that conveys unpleasant information or in some way plays on the receiver's emotions. Persuasive messages that require careful explanation of underlying reasoning are often best communicated

FIGURE 6–1

E-Mail screen showing an inter-office memo.

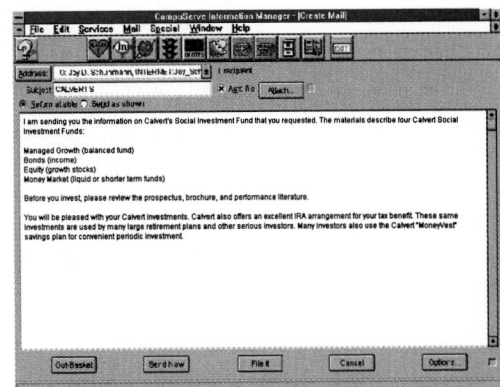

Beware! Your E-Mail Could Haunt You Later

By Sharon M. Haddock

Beware! That light-hearted but pointedly wicked E-mail transmission you just sent to your friend across the country may never die.

And it could show up in court as state's evidence, be published in a free-for-all gossip column or even destroy your company's reputation in the business market. There's no controlling it once it leaves your computer.

Companies and employees must be cautious before they play with E-mail or they'll regret it, says Diane Hartman, president of Quality Training International.

"We know every time a wonderful new invention comes along, it affects people," said Hartman, who researched E-mail policies with Karen Nantz. "We just don't always know in what ways."

Nantz is an associate professor at Eastern Illinois University. Hartman has extensive business experience and focuses her attention on training people to communicate effectively.

Hartman and Nantz surveyed 375 certified executive secretaries across the country in 10 different industries for their three-day study—the results of which showed up in The Wall Street Journal—and found that few companies have definitive, if any, policies on how their employees should use E-mail.

Consequently, hundreds of thousands of electronic messages leave business computers every day. Some are hawking goods, some are friendly letters, others are jokes. Some divulge sensitive information. Still others are trade secrets on their way to the wrong hands.

Many employees, once granted access to the information highway, become E-mail junkies and spend a lot of company time sorting and sending over the wires.

Some even conduct sideline businesses by E-mail.

Whatever the situation, the bottom line is that the company identified on the E-mail salutation is liable for whatever the employee sends out.

Courts are upholding cases where an E-mail missive has hurt business or libeled an individual, said Hartman. In one case, a broker doing illegal trading over the Internet was sued and his company fined $2 million for failing to safe-guard "the company asset"—his E-mail access. . . .

Once created, E-mail lives an average of five years in someone's backup file or memory bank, said Hartman.

Even legitimate E-mail is causing problems when employees don't understand the weight of their words or practice sound communication skills on the line. Comminques full of spelling, grammatical and format errors regularly leave on the E-mail express.

"Paper mentality does not transfer to the soft screen," said Hartman. "And people don't realize how much we communicate non-verbally that doesn't get sent with E-mail. It's sometimes better to talk face-to-face, especially when it's a volatile issue."

A message sent in all capital letters looks angry, for instance. Often, a word can be read more than one way. Sometimes a message is accidentally sent out globally when it wasn't intended to be.

Sometimes not checking the E-mail box can be trouble. One employee piled up 4,000 E-mail messages and crashed his company's system, she said. Employees can use another worker's computer—left temporarily unattended—and send a message under that worker's signature.

Hartman said a good executive or employee will choose E-mail verbiage judiciously and often elect to send his or her message another way.

(continued)

(continued)

For instance, employee evaluations don't belong on the message boards. Nor do memos about impending layoffs or cutbacks.

Most companies today are still busy trying to catch up with their system hardware and software, said Hartman, and haven't taken the time to worry about E-mail policies.

"They will [think about it] once they have a problem," she said.

(Reprinted with permission of Deseret News.)

Some Precautions

- Don't send E-mail when you're angry.
- Don't write anything you wouldn't want published in the company newsletter.
- Realize an E-mail message is no more private than a phone message.
- Plan what you say. No message should be a flaming arrow.

by a medium that can carry complex data in a relatively structured format. Typically, a formal letter, a carefully planned oral presentation, a videotape, a computer disk presentation, or a written report would be best. A casual, unstructured conversation or a brief memo would not be appropriate nor adequate.

Formality. Some media are more appropriate for formal occasions, and others fit well in informal settings. A letter of congratulations to an employee conveys more **formality** and has a rather different effect from, say, a casual, unplanned remark conveying the same information. The letter makes it official. A hand-written note, conversely, sent to the board of directors by a worker may be considered out of line. When the message is intended for internal consumption only (within the "family"), its format may be less formal than if it were to be publicly disseminated outside the organization.

Electronic media (like e-mail) tend to be more informal and conversational. Perhaps this is because people type their own messages and opt for conciseness. Common abbreviations and icons are used as shortcuts. The overall effect seems to be moving business toward greater informality, as Chapter 7 discusses.

Beware of the overuse of technology. This statement from Frank Fountain, Regional Sr. Vice President for Bank of America, points out the downside. "One of my pet peeves is the impersonal nature of some electronic communication, such as voice mail systems that don't allow callers to transfer to an operator, or that are obviously being used to screen calls."

Be Aware of Relative Costs of Media

One further media characteristic is especially important in business: costs. The cost of communicating is not easily calculated, but it clearly affects an organization's budget.

Many different costs should be considered in media comparisons. The greatest expense is usually the **people costs:** the wages and benefits paid to employees. Additionally, we need to count **technical costs,** such as word processing equipment, e-mail networks, modems, telephones, videotape players, and even paper, postage, and photocopies. A simple face-to-face conversation between two executives involves no technical cost but considerable people cost.

The cost of creating and sending a simple, business letter or memo today can exceed $80 according to a recent *Personnel Journal* estimate. Responding to such letters more than doubles the costs, so that internal letters and memos—ones we both generate and respond to in the company—can really sap organizational resources.

The most expensive cost of all—the cost of *ineffective* messages that backfire, because of either a wrong medium choice or poor quality—is not calculated into any of these estimates. These *real* costs can only be guessed.

Table 6-2 summarizes the characteristics and relative costs of eleven commonly used media.

TABLE 6-2
SOME CHARACTERISTICS AND COSTS OF MANAGERIAL COMMUNICATION MEDIA

Media	Fast/ Slow	Feedback (High/Low)	Record (High/Low)	Formal/ Informal	Inside/ Outside	Complex/ Simple	Cost (High/Low)
Informal conversation	Fast	High	Nonrecord	*Informal*	Either	Simple	Low
Telephone conversation	Fast	Medium	Nonrecord	*Informal*	Either	Simple	Low-medium
Formal oral presentation	Medium	High	Nonrecord	*Formal*	Either	Medium	Medium
Informal note	Medium	Low	Nonrecord	*Informal*	Either	Simple	Low
Memo	Medium	Low	*Record*	Informal	*Inside*	Medium	Medium-high
Electronic mail	Fast	Low-medium	Record	Informal	Inside	Medium	Medium-high
Directive	Slow	Low	Record	*Formal*	*Inside*	Medium	Medium
Fax	*Fast*	Low	Record	Either	Either	Medium	Medium
Letter	Slow	Low	Record	Formal	*Outside*	Complex	Medium
Formal report	Very slow	Low	Record	Very formal	Inside	*Complex*	High

Note: *Italicized items are the specific biases that would ordinarily cause a communicator to choose that medium for his or her message.*

(Courtesy of Crisp Publications, Inc., 1200 Hamilton Court, Menlo Park, California 94025.)

TABLE 6-3

COMBINING MEDIA FOR EFFECTIVENESS

Medium	Major Limitations	Supplemental Media
Informal conversation	No record; deals with simple messages	Informal note to acknowledge; additional written information to clarify complex topics
Telephone conversation	Little nonverbal feedback; no record	Informal conversation; memo or note to confirm; tape conversation
Formal oral presentation	Preparation time; no record	Written report of briefing (outline format) to follow up
Informal note	Low feedback; deals with simple messages	Telephone or conversation follow-up
Memo	Low feedback	Telephone or conversation follow-up
Directive	Preparation time; low feedback	Meeting or presentation to amplify and get feedback
Letter	Preparation time and cost; low feedback	Telephone follow-up to test for understanding

Consider Media Mixing: A Sound Alternative

Here is a fourth way to make the most of media. Remember that you are certainly not limited to the use of a single medium. Often a combination of several media does the job nicely. Disadvantages of one medium can be made up by another. For example, the slow-feedback characteristic of written media can be offset by accompanying the message with an oral medium: talk the receiver through the paper or report. Table 6-3 suggests some ways to combine commonly used media to offset such disadvantages.

Understand Media Expectations

One final consideration in media selection is that people come to expect certain types of messages to be communicated via certain media. Habits of communicating develop and become the norm.

To give extra impact to a message, a business communicator may want to use a different medium or different combination of media. Novelty in a message's presentation can also enhance the chances that it will be received. Companies that sell products via direct mail are constantly looking for ways to cut through the clutter of similar mail pieces. They use personalization, color, typefaces, illustrations, and unusual packaging among other tricks.

The latest technology is not necessarily the best media. E-mail use has exploded in recent years. Yet one New York investment banker told us he "never looks at [his huge "stack" of] E-mail. If a guy wants my attention, the best bet is to come by my office and yell in the door."[6]

Creativity, a consideration of media characteristics, and some educated guesses about likely effects of messages provide the manager with some real opportunities to develop an interesting and effective media mix.

Technology and Information Overload

Today's business can drown in an overabundance of information.

Perhaps the greatest impact of the new technologies on business communication lies in the amount of information it makes available. Many organizations face an embarrassment of riches: They are drowning in a sea of information.

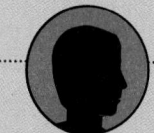
Randy Myers, Director, Investor Service Centers, Charles Schwab & Co.

In Randy's business two distinct processes are used to communicate within the organization. "The first process developed out of the need to exchange large quantities of data involving highly regulated customer account and trading information. The second process is less formal and relatively unstructured, used to communicate general management information between headquarters and remote offices."

Since the company demands precision in handling financial accounts, Schwab uses the latest electronic technology. "Our phone system has a complex array of special features that allow field offices to speed dial to an 'expert.'"

Because of the volume of information handled, Schwab has found it necessary to eliminate as much needless paperwork as possible. This becomes difficult in an industry that is so closely regulated. "The compliance department's requirements sometimes demand hard copies, but we are moving toward more and more electronic data storage."

When asked about future technology, Randy expressed certainty that the industries to watch are those that will provide interactive television. Soon, people will be shopping, dialing up all kinds of specialized information, and receiving the bulk of their education through their TV sets.

Despite the emphasis on technology, Randy feels that the human process of communication will always be critical to business success.

The reasons for this tidal wave of information include the fact that everyone can now become a "broadcaster," sending messages worldwide at low cost. The impact of technology today mirrors the technical advances of the late 1950s and 1960s when photocopying made anyone a publisher. Before that, writers wrestled with carbon paper to make copies of documents. The photocopier, especially those that used plain paper as pioneered by Xerox Corporation, made carbon copies obsolete. (The cc: remains on the letters of many people. Xerox Corporation employees use an xc: instead, and many others are converting to a simple c: for copy).

As photocopiers became widespread, companies worried about copy proliferation. In fact, when IBM entered the photocopier business in the early 1970s, they advertised that their machines printed *slower* than Xerox's, thus reducing copy proliferation!

Eventually, companies got a handle on paper and copying costs—or became resigned to the level of these expenses.

Media and the Changing World of Business Communication

A review of the definition of "media" as "generally accepted ground rules for structuring and exchanging messages" indicates that much changes and much remains consistent in business communication. The greatest changes involve speed and distance. With electronic media, business people dramatically reduce the time required to transmit messages while, at the same time, make distance irrelevant. An Internet message can go halfway around the world about as quickly as across the hall. A teleconference can draw people together from across the country for group discussion without physical proximity.

Once again, however, remember that although technology provides more choices, it does not alter the need to make careful, informed decisions about media appropriateness.

Information overload is a major headache. Another problem is the misuse of business media (see "The Biggest Loser at Solitaire").

The Biggest Loser at Solitaire—The Company[7]

With people and computers working in tandem, the office is a more productive place, right? Well, sometimes. The world of computers has hosts of good fairies, but there are gremlins as well. It's worthwhile to examine some of our preconceptions about computers so that we can keep them from taking a megabyte out of efficiency:

- *People can really focus on computer work.* Not really. A better way of putting it is that people can really focus on computers, but not necessarily on computer work. A peek at the screen can be revealing.

  The hands you see hammering the keyboard may not be nailing down a project. They may be pounding out a code so that their spaceship can dodge asteroids.

  The hand deftly guiding a mouse may not be working on a pie chart. Computer users have even come up with a euphemism for on-the-clock game-playing: "mouse practice." Many computer games come equipped with a "boss screen," an innocuous graph or summary sheet that pops up with the touch of a key to placate probing eyes. . . .

  Based on a recent survey of 6,000 computer users, SBT Accounting Systems reached the sad conclusion that American business loses about $100 billion a year because of PC gaming.

- *Electronic mail makes it easier for people in the office to stay in touch.* Unfortunately, sometimes the people who get in touch are the ones from whom you don't want to hear. Self-important memo writers or idle scribblers can clutter your E-mail with debris. E-mail improves communication only if the people who receive it are the people who need to receive it. Otherwise, E-mail provokes a babble of opinions.

  A client of mine recently returned to his office from an out-of-town conference. Several *hundred* E-mail messages were waiting for him. He spent 10 hours learning, among other things, which team was favored on Monday Night Football and how to make a superb apple cobbler.

- *Computers can store a ton of information.* Yes, and your attic can store a ton of junk. How much do you want to "pile up" in your storage? You can squirrel away item after item in your computer memory. The problem is, will you ever be able to find it again? . . .

(continued)

(continued)

A computer has only so much brain power. The more brain power it uses for remembering, the less it has for thinking (running your software).

- *Computers make people creative.* Not so. Computers are servants. They don't teach you creativity, although they do make it easier for people to turn their creative ideas into results. A graphics program, for example, can draw objects with perfect symmetry, and let you revise work easily.

But computers also make doodling more fun than ever. There are drawings beyond the dreams of madness—intellectual graffiti—scrawled into the image files of many a computer. . . .

A few parting words of advice:

- Purge game applications. There's no nice way of saying it: Work time is for work. Having a card table and video arcade beckoning from a few feet away makes work seem like a world of dreariness.

- Tell people that you don't want *bulletin board* E-mail sent to all and sundry.

- Clean out the attic from time to time. You can do so by throwing obvious junk out—delete it.

- Aspiring artists who weren't hired to do graphic art stay out of harm's way more easily if they don't have an alluring graphic art program.

Follow these rules and you'll cut down on workplace distractions.

Understanding the Basics

SUMMARY OF KEY IDEAS

- The medium chosen to communicate a message will have an impact on the meaning the receiver attaches to the message.

- A communication medium can be viewed as a generally accepted set of ground rules for structuring and receiving messages. These ground rules play a large part in determining the medium's effectiveness in a given situation.

- Among characteristics of a medium that should be considered are *speed, feedback capability, hard-copy availability, message complexity, need for formality,* and *relative cost.*

- The media, methods, or approaches you choose when communicating can enhance or detract from your communication success.

- Communication efficiency is a simple ratio between the total costs of a message and the number of people reached by that message.

- Communication effectiveness is determined by the degree to which a message is *received by the intended audience, interpreted correctly, remembered for a reasonable period, and used when appropriate occasions arise.*

- The amount of information available both to individual contributors and to all levels of management continues to increase at an exorbitant rate.

- Continuous information flow and instantaneous communication within businesses of all types pulls together organizational layers, causing a flattening of organizational charts.

- Mixing several media can offset the disadvantages of one of them, resulting in more effective communication. An oral message followed by written confirmation works best in many situations.

• Today's technology has allowed anyone to become a "broadcaster," just as photocopying permits anyone to be a publisher.

• Information overload and misuse of technology pose major problems for many organizations.

KEY TERMS AND CONCEPTS

media

medium

ground rules

immediate feedback capacity

people and technical costs

information overload

expectations

efficiency versus effectiveness

e-mail, icons, abbreviations

hard-copy availability

media mixing

intensity and complexity

formality

QUESTIONS FOR FURTHER THOUGHT

1. Describe in your own words the dilemma of communication efficiency versus communication effectiveness. Why don't people always use individual, personal media?

2. What kinds of messages can or should be transmitted by the most efficient means? Give specific examples.

3. What kinds of messages require a high degree of effectiveness regardless of efficiency? Give specific examples.

4. Recall an experience you have had in which an inappropriate medium or tool was used to convey an important message to you. Describe what happened in the form of a short case or critical incident description.

Changing Face of Business Communication

By Nicholas D. Wells

In the 1830s, when the first sewing machines were being introduced, it became a matter of pride for business leaders to renounce the new devices as an evil that would leave thousands of families without means of support, because most clothing was made by women working at home with a needle and thread. Yet with populations booming, the need for the new devices became more and more evident. Forward-looking businesses accepted the "evil device," changing the textile industry completely and providing thousands more jobs in industries that were never imagined when the sewing machine was first introduced.

The last few years have seen the emergence of great changes in the ways businesses communicate. First, fax machines began appearing in every office; about the same time Federal Express removed the excuse of mailing delays from the business world. More and more companies began exchanging data electronically to improve productivity. Many firms also began video-conferencing between sites to save travel costs and communicate more frequently. Of late, electronic mail (e-mail) addresses are appearing all over letterheads, business cards, and advertisements. You can't pick up a publication without reading about the growth explosion on the Internet and why you should join the fracas.

Although no one would downplay the importance of communication to the vitality of a business enterprise, fear of the unknown may lead some to rail against the "sewing machines" of our day, which continue to change the very heart of how business is transacted. This article examines four facets of the changing models of business communication that will help you understand how

your organization can benefit from the dramatic changes that are already occurring worldwide.

When we speak of new technologies or new methods of communication, we are speaking generally of electronically linking the world, and the acceptability of using electronic links in conducting all types of business.

The heart of all of these new technologies is the same: removing barriers of distance and time, lowering costs, and improving the overall ability of people to communicate their thoughts and needs. These ideas form the basis for several of the sections below.

The Importance of Information

. . .In the opinion of many futurists, information is the factor that is making the entire economy look like a service industry, ... Major product releases occur infrequently, and most competitors in similar industries soon have technologically similar products (if one were vastly superior in technology, the others would not survive). Consequently, between major breakthroughs, all companies are judged on the same basis: How do they use information to benefit their customers. In effect, they become service industries focused on servicing their products. Thus, the ability to locate information in a timely manner and to distribute it through the correct channels to the correct people is paramount. . . .

Like businesses, individuals are beginning to realize the valuable role information plays in their careers and personal goals. This truth is similar to the importance education has always played in making a successful career, but it stretches further, because we

must continually treat information as an ally in making decisions. . . .

The Breadth of Information

In ages past, great discoveries came from those who saw insights across disciplines, like Isaac Newton "inventing" calculus to solve physics problems. Yet we often have to specialize to such a degree that we lose the benefit of a cross-disciplinary knowledge base. Broad access to information makes us more able to use a generalist's understandings to solve the problems that our specialists face. For example, we can search all medical journals for references to lasers or cigarettes, review or search all White House papers for medical references, or check the complete federal budget.

The amount of information available continues to take our breath away. . . . Any type of technical or product information, private or government statistics, or entertainment of any kind either is now available or will soon be available from a desktop computer, free or for a fee. Putting this information in the hands of everyone, instead of only those who have the time, skill, and systems to find it in obscure places has a profound effect both on management style and on the productivity of individual contributors. . . .

Like a child in a candy store, information workers find they can spend their days snatching up "mind candy" without ever getting down to the task at hand. Highly efficient searching and browsing tools are not widely available for on-line systems; in the meantime, browsing through the electronic stacks to find what is relevant to your work can be as engrossing as picking up the latest business or science magazine and can consume hours.

Security is always a concern as well. With more on-line information available, the risk increases that information will be used without compensation or by the wrong people. Organizations often rush to place information on-line long before they understand either how valuable that information is or who will be able to access it. Even something as simple as reading an employee's e-mail has raised red flags at major corporations. . . .

The Speed of Communication

. . .The speed of communication comes from two sides. First, information producers have the ability to place records instantaneously in the computer as transactions are processed (your grocery store probably updates its inventory the instant the checker scans your box of cereal). Second, very large amounts of that information can be transmitted to any point on the planet at incredible speeds. . . .

Your customers expect you to have complete records of their transactions at your fingertips when they call. This expectation comes not because they know all the technologies involved, but because they see your competitors and others in related industries doing it. They call their credit card company and have all charges and payments available; they call a mail-order catalog and know just what is in stock and when it will arrive at their house; they call their shipper and hear exactly where their package is. Why should this same person call you and tolerate, "I'm not sure how we're doing on your order—can I get back to you tomorrow?". . .

The New Organization

The more technology you have in place, and the more it removes barriers, the less tolerant employees will be of ivory-tower, nonempowered, no-information-flow management. These are the technologies that enable the "empowerment" buzzword, because they furnish lower layers of organizations with enough information to make intelligent (read "empowered") decisions, and then act on them.

Continuous information flow and instantaneous communication within and among businesses pulls together organizational layers, effectively if not literally flattening organizational charts. Managers can provide data that employees need, and employees can quickly resolve concerns with management. The phenomenon of e-mail alone has changed many organizations: anyone can send e-mail to the CEO, and an assistant usually can't intercept it. . . .

People at the bottom of the traditional organizational chart were often the ones in contact with the customer or involved in the hands-on work of the factory. But these were the individuals least likely to have any information to assist them in making decisions. Technology changes that. For example, imagine a Federal Express employee able to access information on a customer's package and act on it, instead of getting the information from a central office, which sends a decision for action along with the data. The old method increases the load on the central office and takes initiative away from the person who is in contact with the customer. . . .

Conclusion

. . .The changes described here are not trivial. When jet airplanes became a travel alternative, they were not just a new method of getting from here to there. Competing industries underwent radical change, and railroads, in particular, struggled in vain to compete. The ability to have breakfast on one coast and dinner on the other soon altered the entire business world. In the same way, new information technologies will radically alter the use of traditional systems such as telephones and U.S. mail, and eventually the entire business world. Where airplanes began the push to remove barriers of time and space, reduce costs, and improve communication, current technologies are set to finish the job.

Neither organizations nor individuals can afford to ignore these new possibilities, while all around them both competitors and colleagues build new relationships and new businesses with capabilities that will soon be as commonplace as the telephone. . . .

(Nicholas D. Wells, "The Changing Face of Business Communication," *Exchange Magazine* (spring 1995): 3–4, 23.)

Applying Your Knowledge

1. How does this article relate to at least two of the technological issues discussed in the chapter?

2. Discuss your understanding of the term *intangibles* and give a specific example.

3. What enables us to make better use of our time even if it is the resource we can't have more of?

4. How is instantaneous communication relevant to the flattening of organizational charts?

5. What does technology do for the people at the bottom of the traditional organizational chart?

Applying Your Skills

ACTIVITY 6-1: How Do You Communicate?

Consider your average day or week, *estimate* the frequency and time spent communicating by way of the following media:

Face to face (conversational)

One on one	Frequency:
	Time:
Small group	Frequency:
	Time:

Written

Memo	Frequency:
	Time:
Letter	Frequency:
	Time:
Reports	Frequency:
	Time:
Other	Frequency:
	Time:
Other	Frequency:
	Time:

Electronic

E-mail	Frequency:
	Time:
Fax	Frequency:
	Time:
Teleconferencing	Frequency:
	Time:
Videoconferencing	Frequency:
	Time:
Classes/Teams	Frequency:
	Time:
Other	Frequency:
	Time:

Now after making an estimate, log your media use for one week to determine how close your estimates match your actual behavior. The frequencies and times will vary depending on your circumstances. This is a good activity for determining and even analyzing what media you are spending time using.

ACTIVITY 6-2: What Media To Use

Describe the type or types of media you would use if you were the presenter in the following three situations.

Situation 1
- Small-group setting (five–seven people).
- You are to present a proposal for a new on-site storage facility for all company office supplies.

Situation 2
- Medium-group setting (twenty–twenty-five people).
- You are to present a change in your company's personnel policies regarding proper dress and grooming.

Situation 3
- Large-group setting (fifty–sixty people).
- You are presenting an estate planning seminar to people in their middle forties.

Why did you pick the media you did for each situation?

Have you considered ground rules for effectiveness and efficiency?

This type of activity will assist you in your next presentation in terms of the media you chose.

ACTIVITY 6-3: Invitation

You are asked by your manager to invite several top-performing employees to a catered lunch with senior management. The lunch is to take place in two weeks on a Friday in the company board room.

How would you go about inviting these employees to the lunch? List some ideas.

Rough out a sample invitation that you think would be well received by the employees receiving it.

ACTIVITY 6-4: Pros and Cons of E-mail and Fax

List some characteristics about using e-mail.

Frustration:

Appreciation:

Do the same regarding your use of fax machines.

Frustration:

Appreciation:

When you use the appropriate medium, it is hoped that frustration is decreased and appreciation increased by both sender and receiver.

ACTIVITY 6-5: Review a Communication Event

Describe an actual event from the past week in which you were involved. How effective was it? Complete the following:

Sender

Receiver (you)

Message

How was it sent? (Medium)

Was it received by the right person(s)?

Was it interpreted clearly?

Was it remembered for a reasonable amount of time?

Was it used?

You should do this off the "top of your head." If it was a "remembered" and "used" message, this activity requires no outside resources.

ACTIVITY 6-6: Cost of Ineffective Messages

Complete the following to estimate the cost of ineffective communication. Identify an ineffective message you have received or sent and complete the following:

The message was (paraphrase the main idea):

It was intended for (audience[s]):

The medium (media) used:

It was ineffective because:

A better way would be:

Estimated cost of ineffectiveness:

Hours @ $ /per hour = Total $

Total $ × Number of people = cost of ineffectiveness

Consider people costs and technical costs (primarily equipment).

PERFORMING
on the Job

CASE 6-1 School Causes Real Stink with Body Odor Letter[8]

Lest you think our earlier Wilbur Jackson e-mail memo was far fetched, here is another example of the problem of broadcasting memos. This story was distributed by the Associated Press news service.

—High school administrators have caused a stink by sending letters about body odor to 16 exchange students.

The letter was sent Sept. 21 after a teacher complained about the hygiene of one of the students, said Airline High School Principal D.C. Machen.

The letter said "Americans find body odors highly offensive" and that the students should adopt "a daily ritual of cleanliness so as not to offend your American hosts."

"I read it and put it in the trash because it was so stupid," said Leo Antunes, a 16-year-old Brazilian.

After three students complained, Machen and counselor Gene Self, who wrote the letter, apologized to all 16 who got the letter.

Self should have spoken with the one student privately, Machen said.

In the letter, Self wrote of her observations while traveling in Europe.

"American girls shaved their legs where European girls, on the whole, did not," the letter read. "Americans seemed to pay more attention to appearance. They were well-groomed, neat, squeaky clean."

Case Questions

1. Was a letter the best medium for this situation? Why? Why not?
2. Can this type of issue exist within the workplace environment?
3. If a situation like the one described exists in a company, how would you recommend a supervisor resolve the issue?

CASE 6-2 Trucking Down the Information Highway

This case involves two departments of a large trucking company (TC) operating throughout the United States. The two departments at TC are safety and management information systems (MIS). The project these departments are to undertake is to develop a new, improved way of sending and receiving information about accidents via the company-wide computer system. This project would allow for report timeliness and accuracy through existing technology. It would also assist in accident prevention by providing a data base of scenarios to learn from.

An employee of MIS spent one day discussing the project with the vice-president of safety and the safety director. This meeting was an overview of what was to be accomplished along with some information sharing about the background of the project. It was agreed that the safety director would work directly with the MIS employee in getting the project under way. In the beginning, they communicated on a daily basis.

After three weeks, the original MIS employee was reassigned to a different project at another company location. A new MIS employee was assigned who was not only new to the company but new to the trucking industry. Thus, the process to speed communication through the use of technology had to begin again to bring the new employee "up to speed." In the midst of this change, a restructure of MIS created a vice-president of MIS/telecommunications. The new vice-president put the project on the back burner, creating more delays. Procedures were implemented that required a form be completed for the safety representative to discuss the project with MIS.

The second MIS employee assigned to the project left the company after six months, which resulted in no contact person in MIS for safety to communicate with in person or in writing. Even with all these setbacks, some progress has resulted from the president and CEO of the company being made aware of accident statistics. They are both anxious to get this project implemented. With this renewed interest, MIS has been instructed to put the project on a front burner and communicate openly with the safety department to ensure completion.

Case Questions

1. Do you think reporting accidents via computer is an effective medium? Why? Why not?

2. Technology is generally implemented to speed processes. What factors slowed the implementation of this project?

3. Would you have approached this project differently if you were the representative from the safety department? Explain.

4. Why would the company executives have such concern regarding this project? How would you recommend the executives communicate their concern to the safety department and MIS?

CHAPTER SEVEN

Communication
with a Diverse Audience:
Cross-Cultural Realities

LEARNING GOALS

After you have studied this chapter, you should be able to:

- Understand the reality of widespread diversity in audiences for business messages.

- Tap into the value of audience diversity.

- Recognize differences in male-female communication tendencies.

- Identify five ways people reduce their power when writing and five ways they can enhance assertiveness. See how these might be especially useful to female communicators.

- Avoid stereotyping potholes, turnoffs, or irritants that can damage relationships.

- Recognize some characteristics of American-style conversation.

- Acknowledge that fun at work can be boosted by healthy communication activities.

- Recognize that more visual variety is generally expected by today's audiences.

The Way It Is . . . I See You[1]

Among the tribes of northern Natal in South Africa, the most common greeting, equivalent to "hello" in English, is the expression: *Sawu bona*. It literally means, "I see you." If you are a member of the tribe, you might reply by saying *Sikhona*, "I am here." The order of the exchange is important: until you see me, I do not exist. It's as if, when you see me, you bring me into existence.

This meaning, implicit in the language, is part of the spirit of *ubuntu*, a frame of mind prevalent among native people in Africa below the Sahara. The word *ubuntu* stems from the folk saying *Umuntu ngumuntu nagabantu*, which, from Zulu, literally translates as: "A person is a person because of other people." If you grow up with this perspective, your identity is based upon the fact that you are seen— that the people around you respect and acknowledge you as a person.

During the last few years in South Africa, many corporations have begun to employ managers who were raised in tribal regions. The *ubuntu* ethic often clashes subtly with the culture of those corporations. In an office, for instance, it's perfectly normal to pass someone in the hall, while preoccupied, and not greet him. This would be worse than a sign of disrespect under the *ubuntu* ethic; it would imply that you felt that person did not exist. Not long ago, an internal consultant who had been raised in a rural village became visibly upset after a meeting where nothing much had seemed to happen. When a project where he had played a key part came up for discussion, his role was not mentioned or acknowledged. Asked later why it bothered him so much, he said, "You don't understand. When they spoke about the project, they did not say my name. They did not make me a person."

Successful business communicators acknowledge and appreciate the people who help make them successful. Today's organizations are far reaching and highly diversified in terms of the people involved. Our operations are much more likely to extend across national boundaries. Our employees, coworkers, customers, and associates are more likely than ever to be from a wide range of backgrounds and cultures. To fail to acknowledge them and address their uniqueness in communication efforts runs the serious risk of discounting them.

Communication to a More Diverse People

Communicating to diverse people is nothing new, although the term *diversity* has become more popular in recent years. In business and professions, people have long experienced differences among message receivers that can cause misunderstanding, underuse of skill and talent, or offense to others. Today's organizations, however, face a shrinking world where cultures and genders mix more freely than ever before. To thrive as communicators, people need to be more cognizant of the differences so that they can better tailor our messages for maximum effectiveness. For many, diversity in the workplace used to mean simply employing women and minorities. Now the term refers to people of various ethnic roots, physical abilities, ages, creeds, sexual orientations, socioeconomic levels, education, and even personality types. The concept has gone beyond hiring and evolved into managing diversity. It involves allowing all kinds of employees to develop their potential and work with others without sacrificing individuality.

Companies are coming to recognize that valuing diversity is good business. Diversity of backgrounds, predispositions, and world views helps people better understand their customers, coworkers, and stakeholders.

Likewise, professionals can tap into the value of diversity by

- Involving many different people in business decisions.
- Sending a message that you value diversity by reaching out to customers of a wide range of backgrounds and characteristics.
- Looking at one's own cultural biases. Assess whether these make sense in light of your audiences.
- Accepting and accommodating variations in approach, style, and pace.
- Training others working with you. Help them recognize their own culturally biased thinking.
- Developing sensitive communication skills.
- Maintaining a sense of humor. The person who looks for examples of offense may find them where none is intended. Relax, and enjoy human differences.

This chapter now looks at several prominent changes in the nature of audiences and expectations that amplify the need for diversity-sensitive communication skills.

Male-Female Communication Differences

The fact that men and women have different communication styles has been the subject of considerable study in recent years. Popular books such as Deborah Tannen's *You Just Don't Understand*,[2] and, even more applicable to our discussion, her *Talking from 9 to 5*,[3] have shed light on many social differences in male and female communication tendencies.

Tannen's writings focus on "patterns of conversational style influenced by gender. Based on the assumptions that people learn styles of interacting as children growing up, and that children tend to play in sex-separate groups in which different styles are learned, practiced, and reinforced, the book proceeded from the metaphor of male-female conversation as cross-cultural communication."[4]

> **Men often put their ideas in the strongest terms possible, then wait to see if anyone shoots them down.**
>
> —Deborah Tannen, *Talking from 9 to 5*

Business Success and Gender Chat[5]

To be truly effective in today's business world, people need to be fluent in both **femalespeak** and **malespeak.** Both communication styles can be valid for various situations. But neither works well in every situation.

Conversation in business is rife with rituals. The rituals typically used by men and women often clash, leading to misunderstanding and, fairly often, hindering women's progress up the male-dominated corporate ladder. Here's an example.

Early in her career, Linda Vandegrift tended to be quiet. She spoke when spoken to and didn't have an opinion or idea that was controversial. This is characteristic of femalespeak.

As time went by, Vandegrift—who is the director of sales and marketing at the Omni/Rosen Hotel in Orlando—learned the importance of communicating assertively. She realized she had to speak her mind, to be upfront and direct. This is common in malespeak.

"Look like a lady; act like a man; work like a dog."

—*Fortune* **magazine's advice to women who want to succeed in the workplace, circa 1990**

"As soon as you start to waiver as a woman in business, you're seen as wishy-washy," she says. Conversational rituals among men are seldom indecisive. Often such rituals involve using opposition such as banter, joking, teasing, and playful putdowns, and expending effort to one-up the other guy in interaction.

Women's rituals, conversely, are often ways of maintaining an appearance of equality, considering the effect of the exchange on the other person, and expending effort to downplay the speaker's authority so they can get the job done without flexing their muscles in an obvious way.

As long as both people in a conversation follow the same conventions, everything is fine. When ways of communicating are not recognized as conventions, however, they are taken literally with negative results on both sides. For example, men who tease or use putdowns may be viewed by women as hostile or arrogant. Women whose conversation conventions seek to avoid appearing boastful or try to be sensitive to others' feelings may be seen by men as insecure or even incompetent.

When male managers use femalespeak conventions, they may be seen as meek or weak by other men, whereas women may praise them for their style. Conversely, or perversely, women managers who use a malespeak style are often criticized by female subordinates for being cold and haughty. This can be a lose-lose situation for women and men.

By being accommodating, women risk being seen as indecisive.

Men who tease or use putdowns risk being seen as hostile or arrogant.

The flexibility to use both male and female communication conventions is called genderflexing.

Experts have reported that men and women have different conversational styles (conventions). (Courtesy of Bruce Ayres/Tony Stone Images.)

Maintaining flexibility to adapt—what Dr. Judith Tingley calls **genderflexing**—seems to be the most useful way out of this dilemma. In the reading at the end of this chapter, Tingley offers tips for genderflexing.

Gender Differences in Written Communication

Writing can convey genderspeak differences as well as conversational speaking. In *Power Writing for Executive Women*[6] Patricia Westheimer aims not at getting women to write like men, but to teach women to strengthen their own style, by eliminating the things that weaken it and building on those that make it strong. She quotes Steve Green, managing editor of Copley News Services in Washington, D.C., who says:

> **Women are more intuitive about the emotional game that is going on in the business world. They tend to tune in to the emotions of a situation more than a man does. By doing that, they are better able to aim their correspondence at the person who will be receiving it. In other words, they know their audience, which is one of the first rules of power writing.**[7]

In her book, *Power Writing for Executive Women,* Patricia Westheimer cautions against phrasing that tends to place the writer in a less assertive light. Among these she cites the following:

- Overusing words and phrases like "I'm sorry," "I apologize," "at your convenience," "if you can," "I hope we can." (It's fine to be polite, just don't overdue it.)
- Using self-deprecating words and phrases such as "I hope you won't think I'm" or "If it wouldn't be too much trouble" (any words that tend to take away from your sense of personal power).
- Using faulty construction such as delaying your main point until the end of the letter, not clearly defining the purpose of your correspondence, covering too many topics or combining unlike topics, and not using transitions between paragraphs.
- Using a false-sounding or unprofessional close: anything other than "Sincerely."
- Presenting more problems than solutions—if you ask more questions than you have provided answers for.

Westheimer says that you boost your power when you do the following:

- Write with brevity and conciseness—if your letter is one page or less.
- Use action-oriented ideas and phrases such as "let's meet and discuss," "thank you for," "attached is," "lets's develop."
- Use action-oriented words like meet, decide, consider, motivate, authorize, act, respond, define, lead, obtain, reduce, consult, build, recommend, study, or use.
- Start each paragraph with a different word.
- Stop when you've finished. Don't add routine formalities like "call if you have any questions," "have a nice day," and so on.

Although people need to be careful of broad-brush generalizations about gender characteristics, much support exists for the kinds of differences just discussed. Business communicators become more effective when they appreciate individual styles and uniqueness, and are willing to recognize their own style while being simultaneously tolerant and accepting of other people's styles. Herein lies an important key to dealing with the changing environment of today's business communication audiences.

Cross-Cultural Communication Challenges

The Workforce 2000 study, commissioned by the U.S. Department of Labor in 1987, identifies seven demographic trends that will revolutionize American business in the twenty-first century:

- A decreasing number of workers
- An increase in the average age of workers
- More women visible on the job
- So-called minorities making up one-third of new workers
- More immigrants in the work force
- An increase in service and information jobs
- A need for higher skill levels

Together, these trends scream out a common urgent need for professional communicators to embrace—and value—diversity.

An important first step is to commit oneself to ongoing learning. To best communicate with more diverse audiences, people need to be aware that there are not only different people, different behavior, and different styles; there are also different ways of looking at them. People look at things from their own viewpoint.

Thus, in supporting diversity in business and the professions, you should strive to see new viewpoints, challenge personal biases, and build new skill sets in terms of interacting with others.

Companies recognize the need to work with employees to promote a culture that appreciates diversity. (Courtesy of John Feingersh/ Uniphoto Picture Agency.)

Arni Sigurdsson, Chairman and Tomas Gudmundsson, President, Iceland Media and Marketing

Iceland Media and Marketing is an integrated communications company that provides seminars, conferences, consultations, public relations, and publications expertise to companies throughout the country. "Our goal is to expand into the broader European market. To be successful in that endeavor we need to be sensitive to cross-cultural challenges and languages. To best meet client needs we are able to speak their native tongue and communicate within their language and cultural framework."

Arni and Tomas have built a successful business, meeting the communication needs of a wide variety of clients. They are "computerized to the hilt."

"Our entire business revolves around communication," says Arni. "We are small, nimble, and fast [at adapting to client needs] and we know that the only constant is change."

"The highly successful business communicator," says Arni, "is a trustworthy, credible, likeable, sympathetic facilitator of human needs [who] constantly strives to provide solutions where others may only see problems."

Their pet peeve is "people who convey the message that they know it all and close themselves off to new solutions." As entrepreneurs, Arni and Tomas disdain people with what they call "a banker's mentality with cold feet" who are "too cautious for their own good and fail to take calculated risk."

Again, the key is learning.

Part of not offending people is getting to know people and asking the question "What is it that you want to be called?" (For example, does a coworker prefer "black" or "African American," or "Hispanic or Latino"?) If you don't know, you have to ask. It's appropriate to do so.

Sometimes you'll make a glaring error. Then, the only thing you can do is correct yourself and move on. When you don't know something, you have to rub elbows a little bit to find out about it.

Today's workforce is more than ever before likely to be composed of a wide range of cultures, races, age groups, and abilities. Minimally, effective communicators will need to know how to avoid relationship-damaging **potholes** in what is said. The following are some such potholes, turnoffs, or irritants expressed by people of various groups.

Conversation, American Style[8]

When people from different cultures interact, they frequently feel ill at ease and they often misjudge or misunderstand each other. To try to reduce the communication problems that arise in multicultural situations, it is helpful if we know something about the communicative styles of the majority of the people we deal with.

Here are some generalizations about the **communicative culture** found in most American businesses.

Racial Stereotyping:
Potholes, Turnoffs, or Irritants

African Americans	Being identified by race (e.g., "Brian Jones, the black teacher," or "Shawna Smith, the African-American dentist")
	Receive less valuable feedback (e.g., nonminority bosses are too hesitant to give straight feedback for fear of offending)
	Experience difficulty of being accepted for personal achievement because of negative attitudes toward affirmative action hiring and promotion practices
	Used to meet Equal Employment goals—tokenism
Asians	Lumped into one group (e.g., assumed to be Japanese or Chinese when actually Korean, Vietnamese, Malaysian, etc.)
	Taken advantage of because of nonassertive cultural training
	Stereotyped as affluent (rich Japanese), mathematical, golf-loving, etc.
Latinos	Lumped together (e.g., assumed to be Mexicans when actually from Argentina, Ecuador, Chile, etc.)
	Assumed to be less industrious
White men	Accused of racism or sexism (assumed to be insensitive to such issues)
	Give less direct feedback to women or minorities for fear of misinterpretation
	Avoid mentoring women for fear of implied sexual relationship
White and minority women	Feel they are not listened to
	Are offended by sexist language, sexual innuendo, or harassment.
	Receive watered-down feedback
	Feel excluded from male dominated subgroups

Age Group Stereotyping:
Potholes, Turnoffs, or Irritants

Older people	Dislike being compared with one's mother or father
	Are assumed to be less technologically literate/skilled; out of touch with the "new"
	Are assumed to be less physically fit or less mentally alert
Young people	Are uncomfortable supervising older workers
	Are assumed to be careless, impatient, have short attention span
	Are assumed to be immature, inexperienced

Disabled Stereotyping:
Potholes, Turnoffs, or Irritants

	Are unduly called courageous or brave
	Are assumed generally incapable or helpless
	Are referred to with improper terminology (e.g., crippled, epileptic, spastic)
	Are subject to lack of basic courtesy (e.g., walking away from a blind person without telling him; standing while talking to a person in a wheelchair)

Alternate Lifestyle:
Stereotyping Potholes, Turnoffs, or Irritants

	Are subject to offensive terminology (e.g., "sexual preference" implies a choice; "sexual orientation" implies an innate condition)
	Are not recognizing them for their diversity
	Feel judged, disdained by others

1. *Preferred topics.* In casual conversation (what we call small talk), Americans prefer to talk about the weather, sports, jobs, mutual acquaintances, and past experiences, especially ones they have in common with their conversation partners. As they grow up, most Americans are warned *not* to discuss politics or religion, at least not with people they do not know well, because politics and religion are considered controversial topics. Sex, bodily functions, and emotional problems are considered very personal topics and are likely to be discussed only with close friends or professionals trained to help.

   By contrast, people in some other cultures are taught to believe that politics and religion are good conversation topics, and they may have different ideas about what topics are too personal to discuss with others.

2. *Preferred forms of verbal interaction.* In a typical conversation between Americans, no one talks for long at a time. Participants in conversation take turns frequently, usually after the speaker has spoken only a few sentences.

American conversationalists tend to take turns talking in short segments.

   Americans prefer to avoid arguments. If argument is unavoidable, they prefer it to be restrained, carried on in a normal conversational tone and volume.

   Americans are generally impatient with ritual conversational exchanges that do not really convey much meaning. Nevertheless, a few of them are common. For example, "How are You?" "Fine, thank you. How are you?" "Fine." Or, "It was nice to meet you." "Same here." Or cliché, "Have a nice day."

   People from other countries may be more accustomed to speaking and listening for longer periods when they are in conversation. They may be accustomed to more ritual interchanges (about the health of family members, for example) than Americans are. They may enjoy argument, even vigorous argument, of a kind that Americans are likely to find unsettling.

3. *Preferred depth of involvement.* Americans do not generally expect very much personal involvement from conversational partners. Small talk—without long silences that provoke uneasiness—is enough to keep matters going smoothly. It is only with very close friends (or professional counselors) that Americans generally expect to discuss highly personal topics. Topics considered highly personal, incidentally, include financial matters. Many Americans are very uncomfortable if you ask how much money they make or how much something they own costs.

   People from other countries may prefer even less personal involvement than Americans do and rely more on ritual interchanges. Others come from countries where much more personal involvement is sought.

4. *Preferred channels.* Most American businesspeople are verbally adept—have a good vocabulary—speak in moderate tones, and use some gestures of the arms and hands. Touching behaviors in normal business communication are usually limited to a handshake or occasional pat on the back.

   By contrast, other cultures may be accustomed to channels that use louder voices, many people talking at once, vigorous use of hands and arms to convey meanings or as emphasis, and more touching between conversation partners.

5. *Level of meaning emphasized.* Americans are generally taught to believe in the scientific method of understanding the world around them, so they tend to look for specific facts and physical evidence to support viewpoints. Compared to Americans, people from other countries may pay more attention to the emo-

tional content or the human feelings aspects of a message and be less concerned with what Americans would call facts.

Many misjudgments and misunderstandings can arise between people who have different communicative styles. Here are some examples.

- Foreign visitors in the United States might hear little but small talk among Americans and erroneously conclude that Americans are not mentally capable of anything more than simple talk about such subjects as the weather, sports, teachers, or their own social activities. The conclusion that Americans are intellectually shallow is also reached by many people who regard argument as a favorite form of mental exercise. They see Americans as too sensitive and not very good at arguing.
- Americans may label people who customarily speak little and who rely heavily on ritual conversation as "shy," "too formal," or "too polite."
- Vigorous arguing (with raised voices, much use of hands and arms, and perhaps more than one person talking at a time) of the kind that is natural to some people may alarm Americans, who expect violence, or at least long-lasting anger, to follow loud disagreements.

Communicating Internationally[9]

A common criticism of some U.S. business people is that although they have the technology and know the business, they are not prepared as a country to deal with cultural differences.

Among the cultural elements that impact cross-cultural communication are language and symbols, time orientation, personal achievement, personal space, social behavior, and intercultural socialization.

Languages don't always translate directly.

Language and Symbols. Of all the cultural elements of cross-cultural business, the language of the host country is among the most difficult to manage. Although it is beneficial for individuals to know the language, one also needs the competency to recognize idiomatic interpretations, which are different from those found in the English dictionary. Words spoken by an American may not have the same meaning when translated into another language.

Furthermore, gestures, facial expressions, and motions send different signals. For example, Americans are often direct in their conversations, expecting the truth with no hint of deception. At the same time, Americans also tend to be uncomfortable with silent moments. People in some other countries, though, may prefer not to be direct and may shift their eyes away from the American. To them this is a sign of respect. To the American, however, it may be seen as a gesture suggesting withholding of information. And in some cultures silence is appreciated, giving discussants or negotiators time to think and evaluate the situation.

One of the most damaging demands that can be made of an Asian is "Give me a yes or no answer." Although an American would view this as a mild form of confrontation and would expect to get a "yes" or "no" response, Asians rarely say no. This is because of their reluctance to displease another with a negative answer and also to save them the embarrassment of having to admit an inability.

In some countries, if a question is asked, the visitor may be told whatever the native thinks the visitor wants to hear. If you ask for directions in Mexico, Lebanon, or Japan, and the natives don't really know the answer, they may still give you one simply to make you happy!

In some Asian countries an attempt to maintain eye contact (as Americans typically do) may be perceived as a sign of aggression. Conversely, in Saudi Arabia, eye contact and gestures of openness are important and could facilitate communications.

Most people who transact business abroad may not be proficient in the spoken language of the host country. However, these kinds of nonverbal issues may be of much greater importance to closing the deal than actually knowing how to speak the native language.

Symbols or trademarks can have an adverse meaning in a different country. For example, the Wise Corporation would have to change or modify its trademark if it decided to test-market potato chips in India. The owl, which is the Wise trademark, is a symbol of bad luck in India even though in America it is associated with intelligence. General Motor's Chevy Nova brand translates into "won't go" in Spanish.

Time Orientation. Americans are clock watchers. They live by schedules and deadlines, and thrive on being prompt for meetings and "efficient" in conducting business. In many parts of the world people arrive late for appointments, and business is preceded by hours of social rapport. In such places, people in a rush are occasionally thought to be arrogant and untrustworthy.

In the United States, a high value is placed on time. If someone waited outside an office for half an hour or so beyond the appointed time, it would be seen as a signal of his or her lack of importance. In the Middle East, a business person may keep a visitor waiting for a long time as a show of respect.

Americans are also deadline oriented. If a deadline is mentioned to an Arab, however, it is like waving a red flag in front of a bull. Forcing the Arab to make a quick decision may very well cost you the deal. Experienced negotiators recommend slowing down and looking for signals that suggest that negotiations are not going well.

Western cultures emphasize the efficient use of time. After all, we often say, "Time is money," and "Time is the enemy." In contrast, Eastern cultures view time as unlimited and unending. In America, meetings sometimes begin with phrases such as "Let's get started" and "Let's dispense with the preliminaries." In Japan, casual conversation precedes business matters, because the Japanese are generally more interested than Americans in getting to know the people involved in the transaction.

Personal Achievement. For the most part, Americans strive to achieve, be competitive, land the best job, earn the most money, and be promoted. They consider their position in the organization for which they work as an indication of status. They are an individualistic society and have built a nation based on our tenacity to get things done in as little time as possible and with minimal disruption.

By contrast, Hindu teachings suggest that acquisition and achievement are not to be sought, because they are the major courses of suffering in one's daily life. In Japanese organizations, positions are not arranged in a status hierarchy, and promotions have often been determined based on seniority rather than merit. Japanese workers are encouraged to work as teams. Cooperation is an art in Asian countries. It is said in Japan that "the nail that sticks out will be pounded down." This illustrates that individual competitiveness is less desirable than teamwork and team spirit.

Even the former Soviet Union encouraged teamwork. If a work group failed to meet production goals, no one was rewarded. But if a group exceeded its quota, everyone would benefit. Although cash rewards are often given to high achievers in America, a Japanese, Chinese, or Yugoslav would be humiliated to receive one.

Not everyone seeks time efficiency.

Personal Space. Different cultures have varying rules on personal space and touching. Americans sometimes touch others on the hand or arm or shoulder when talking. Such behavior would not be appropriate, especially with the left hand, when in the Middle East.

The distance between individuals when talking is another issue that must be known and respected. Most individuals have a specific amount of space that they maintain between themselves and others when conversing (see Chapter 18 for more on personal distances). Americans are typically made uncomfortable by the close conversation distance of Arabs and Africans. Arabs and Africans, however, may feel rejected by the greater personal distance Americans maintain.

Indonesians operate with less empty space than Americans require, and some touching is permissible. However, an Indonesian should not be patted on the head, and a person of the opposite sex should never be touched. In some cases, personal touching can be viewed as an extreme act; in addition to violating the norms of a culture, it may even be viewed as a criminal offense.

Other social behaviors, if not known, will place the American international traveler at a disadvantage. For example, in Saudi Arabia, it is an insult to question a host about the health of his spouse, show the soles of one's shoes, or touch or deliver objects with the left hand. In Korea, both hands should be used when passing objects to another, and it would be considered impolite to discuss politics, communism, or Japan.

When greeting someone, it is appropriate in most countries, as in the United States, to shake hands. In some countries the greeting includes a handshake and more. In Japan, a handshake may be followed by a bow, going as low and lasting as long as that of the senior person. In Brazil, Korea, Indonesia, China, and Taiwan, a slight bow is also appropriate.

In some countries, the greeting involves more contact. For instance, in Venezuela, close friends greet each other with a full embrace and a hearty pat on the back. In Malaysia, close friends grasp with both hands; and in South Africa, blacks shake hands, followed by a clench of each other's thumbs, and another handshake.

In many countries, men do not shake hands with a woman unless she extends her hand first. In India, women, or a man and a woman, greet each other by placing the palms of their hands together and bowing slightly; and in Mexico simply by a slight bow. In some countries, such as India, it is not advisable for men to touch or talk alone with a woman.

Intercultural Socialization. In addition to knowing specific courtesies, personal space, language and communication, and social behavioral differences, there are numerous intercultural socialization behaviors that an international business person should learn.

It is not always necessary for an international business traveler to understand the "whys" of a culture, but it is important to accept them and to abide by them while on foreign soil. However, if the time is available, becoming thoroughly aware of the culture in which you will be visiting or working will pay excellent dividends.

Changes In Communication Expectations

The workplace is changing in ways in addition to the mix of its workers. Generally, workers have come to expect these kinds of communication characteristics.

- Less formality
- More visual attractiveness, variety, and innovation

We'll look at these changing expectations in the following examples.

People Expect Less Formality

A recent clipping appeared on America Online from the Reuters news services.

"What Do You Call Your Boss?"

Should Dagwood Bumstead start calling his cranky boss by his first name Julius instead of Mr. Dithers to improve their working relationship?

"That could be a big step in the right direction," says David "Call me Dave" Morand, a professor of management at Pennsylvania State University.

Morand released a study this week concluding bosses and workers are better off when they call each other by their first names.

"This is a very important device and a symbolic leveling of status," said Dave. "Your relationship is supposed to be collegial; this sets the tone for that."

Dave said his two-year study found first names are much more common in the workplace today than they were 20 years ago as society has grown more democratized.

A boss establishing a first-name basis on the first day of work "would set an immediate positive tone" for an employee, he said.

"That could mean just as much, if not more, to you than the fact that I've eliminated the executive dining and wash rooms, the preferred parking and office spaces, and the time clocks and dress codes," he said.

In fact, in many major companies, reciprocal first-naming is universal from the lowliest maintenance worker or receptionist right up to the chief executive.

Morand's study drew from interviews with employees and officials at Hewlett Packard, Mars Inc., Xerox Corp., and Walt Disney Co.

In those companies, if employees call top officials and the chief executive by a title and last name, they are openly corrected in a friendly way, he said.

At United Parcel Service, he said, there was even an explicit policy calling for all employees to use their first names within the organization.

The vast majority of the hundreds of employees he interviewed preferred being on a first-name basis with their bosses, he said.

(DILBERT reprinted by permission of United Feature Syndicate, Inc.)

Fun at Work[10]

There's no reason that work has to be suffused with seriousness. . . Professionalism can be worn lightly. Fun is a stimulant to people. They enjoy their work more and work more productively.

—Herb Kelleher, CEO, Southwest Airlines

Making work fun is one key to building trust, energy, and interdependence within your company and business network. Intense pressure brings a shift in the body's neuropeptides, which can lead to feelings of exhaustion, depression, and just plain dullness. A deep belly laugh stimulates the brain to produce endorphins. Endorphins renew you physically, mentally, and emotionally; they contribute to feelings of relaxation and refreshment, as well as a positive outlook. Here are ways a Texas-based company has introduced fun into the workplace.

Southwest Airlines: Change the Rules of the Game
Recruit Candidates Who Are Able to Laugh

Southwest Airlines chooses whom to hire based on their ability to make work fun. When recruiting, they give prospective candidates difficult situations to solve. Then they observe who is able to laugh and have fun in the process of searching for solutions. People who get serious and tense while trying hard to get the right answer are much less likely to be hired than those who are honest and open about their abilities, even to the point of making a joke about them. Interviewers also watch for who is rooting for other candidates versus who is competing to be the best. It's the first type whom they believe most likely to be effective team players.

Have Fun

At the beginning of a flight the flight attendants asked for two volunteers from the passengers to make the safety announcements. One volunteer would present the spiel and the other would demonstrate the procedures. Everyone had a great time. There was lots of laughter, hamming it up, and shared fun. Everyone even listened attentively to announcements they would have tuned out ordinarily.

A friend was flying home to New Orleans late on a Friday evening after a long and grueling week in Houston. He was grumpy and exhausted as he dragged himself to the gate area. The flight was slightly delayed due to bad weather so the gate agent invited the passengers to play games. She gave a prize to the person with the largest hole in his sock, to the one with the ugliest photo on his driver's license (impartial judges were chosen from the crowd), to the person with the oldest coin, to the one with the most people in one photo, and to whomever had the strangest item in their purse or pocket. The fun continued on board. By the time they landed in New Orleans my friend was astounded to discover that he was relaxed, refreshed, and in a great frame of mind.

The notion that work can be fun is relatively new. Business and professional communicators can, more than ever before, use humor to communicate. Southwest Airlines is a good example of this line of thinking.

People Expect More Visual Attractiveness, Variety, and Innovation

Along with increasing informality, people have come to expect other things from the communication in their organizations: attractiveness, variety, and innovation.

Today's technology helps us meet these expectations. Below are some examples.

- *Memos and Letters with Illustrations.* Desktop publishing, clip art—even simply pasting a cartoon or illustration to a document—greatly enhances the likelihood that people will read it.
- *Color Copying and Printing* also gets reader attention and can be produced on today's photocopiers and computer printers.
- *Presentation Visuals* are almost mandatory in today's organizations. Virtually any oral presentation is enhanced by multimedia. It's become expected. [See Chapter 19 for more on visuals]

Understanding the Basics

SUMMARY OF KEY IDEAS

- To thrive as communicators, we need to be more cognizant of the differences so that we can tailor our messages for better maximum effectiveness.

- We now have gone beyond just hiring minorities and evolved to the concept of "managing diversity." This management of diversity allows all kinds of employees to develop their potential and work with others without sacrificing individuality.

- Companies realize that valuing diversity is good business because it helps employees understand customers, coworkers, and stakeholders.

- Whether the differences are race, gender, religion, national origin, or age, business communicators become more effective when they appreciate individual styles and uniqueness. They must be willing to recognize their own style while being tolerant and accepting of other people's styles.

KEY TERMS AND CONCEPTS

gender chat	potholes	femalespeak
enjoying human differences	conversational strategies	stereotyping
diversity	malespeak	communicative culture
genderflexing		

QUESTIONS FOR FURTHER THOUGHT

1. What are some of the advantages to diversity in today's business world? To the individual employee? To the organization as a whole?

2. This chapter discusses fun in the workplace. What are some of the issues related to diversity and humor, and what do different people consider funny?

3. Do you agree or disagree with the communicative differences noted between men and women? Why?

4. What is being done in organizations to "manage diversity?"

5. Do you think people are becoming more tolerant of differences or less tolerant? Explain.

For Success at Work, Bone Up on Styles of Gender Chat[11]

The following excerpt from a newspaper column takes a strong position about the masculine communication style. After you read this, respond to the subsequent questions.

While Deborah Tannen contends that both genders can be good communicators, an Orlando management consultant disagrees.

John Curtis, vice president of The Orlando Consulting Group, is un-abashed in saying "men's style is wrong."

"Men are ill-equipped almost from birth to be good communicators," he says. Because of their early socialization, "they're emotionally retarded and psychologically underdeveloped."

Bam! Pow! Thunk!

"Men are hung up with games of power, dominance, ego, manipulation, and wanting to keep score."

All of which is why women "do a better job of bringing to the workplace the masculine and feminine sides of their personalities," Curtis says.

"They can be forceful, stern, direct, and powerful," he says. "But they also do a better job of accessing the kind, caring, sensitive, and empathetic side."

Men, alas, tend to be one-dimensional communicators.

Applying Your Knowledge

1. To what extent do you agree or disagree with Curtis?

2. If his assertions are, in fact, largely true, what could organizations do about it? What would you do if you were the boss?

3. Present a counter argument to Curtis.

Applying Your Skills

ACTIVITY 7-1: Observing Communication

Observe and analyze a communication situation between two or more people of different cultural backgrounds.

- Identify the participants
- Identify the cultural backgrounds
- Describe the purpose of the interaction (any remembered dialogue)
- Describe the outcome
- Identify reasons for its success or failure
- Offer recommendation for improvement

ACTIVITY 7-2: Personal Communication Experiences

List the personal communication experiences you have with any or all of the following:

- People of different national origin
- People of different race
- People of different religion
- Members of the opposite sex
- People older than you
- People younger than you

What kinds of things do you do to help you communicate better in these situations? Do they work? Why?

ACTIVITY 7-3: What Do You Prefer?

Interview three to six people of different races. Ask them which term they prefer when referencing their race or national origin. Let them explain their reasoning and their preferences. List the reasons or preferences and determine if common characteristics exist. Conclude from these commonalities how people can become more proficient at communicating across cultural lines.

ACTIVITY 7-4: Other Potholes?

Review the stereotypes referred to in this chapter. List additional potholes, turnoffs, or irritants you feel should be added to those listed.

Stereotype	Potholes, Turnoffs, or Irritants
Age	
Race	
Alternative lifestyle	

ACTIVITY 7-5: First Names Okay?

From the following list, indicate whether or not you refer to these people by their first name, and why you do or don't.

- Classmates
- Coworker
- Supervisor
- Supervisor's supervisor
- Store clerk
- Cab driver
- Reservation agent by phone

Consider how you could improve your communication skills by using people's name.

ACTIVITY 7-6: American Style

Review the five generalizations listed in the "Conversation, American Style" section of this chapter. Give one to three personal examples of each of the generalizations.

1. Preferred topics
2. Preferred forms of verbal interaction
3. Preferred depth of involvement
4. Preferred channels
5. Level or meaning emphasized

This exercise will help you further identify your communicative style, which assists you in understanding the styles of others.

PERFORMING
on the Job

CASE 7-1 The Joy of Personnel Work

You are the personnel director responsible for the initial screening of job applicants. Once you have screened them, department supervisors further screen with a first interview. Your company sees the importance of involving the supervisors in the hiring process. The president of the company has expressed his desire for employees who are established in the area, have work experience, and are willing to stay with the organization for a reasonable length of time. Your organization has offices in just one state and does business with customers throughout the United States.

Most of the positions being offered are entry level because of company policy of "moving from within" so as higher level positions come available, existing employees have the first opportunity to move into them. This practice has been relatively successful, but it does leave the entry-level positions to be filled from the outside. These positions require constant contact with the public in person and by telephone.

Latta applied for employment six months ago. She is a single parent with two young children. She is seeking full time employment and is settled in the community and plans to make it her permanent home. She has had several years' work experience, and it appears her qualifications are suitable for an entry level position. You have referred Latta to several supervisors who have all interviewed her but have not been interested in making her an offer.

In talking to the supervisors regarding their interviews with Latta, you have discovered the following information:

- She is from India and wears traditional Indian clothing to interviews.
- She has jewelry and marks on her face which are characteristic of her culture.
- Her strong accent makes it difficult to understand what she is saying.
- Her desperate need for a job comes through in the interview to the point that they are uneasy with her responses because they feel she will say anything to get the job.
- She has sent flowers to the female supervisors to thank them for interviewing her.

The supervisors have not been willing to have follow-up interviews with Latta. She calls regularly to let you know that she is still interested in any position and would like to be considered.

Case Questions

1. Are the supervisors justified in not having follow-up interviews with Latta based on the concerns they sight? Explain your reasons.

2. How do you think Latta's desperation is communicated? Verbally? Nonverbally?

3. How do you explain to Latta the concerns of the supervisors? Do you even try?

4. Because Latta meets all the basics qualifications for an entry-level position, should you hire her and assign her to the department with the next opening? What would such an action communicate to the supervisors?

5. Express your thoughts on this case from your perceived viewpoint of the following:

   - Latta
   - President
   - Supervisors
   - Customers

CASE 7-2 Foreign Aid

Many colleges and universities throughout the United States have exchange students from around the world attending their institutions. Most of these students are serious about their studies and work hard to accomplish their degree objectives. Many of these institutions require some sort of public speaking or oral communication class for business majors. The thinking is that once students get established in their careers, they will be required to make presentations of various types in the work environment. Such courses provide students with basic experience in planning, organizing, and delivering a worthwhile presentation to small, medium, and large groups.

Because exchange students majoring in business are required to take such courses as a part of their program, several issues come to light for those instructors responsible for grading these students. Three issues for the exchange students include the following:

- Relating to the audience
- Difficulty with the English language
- Lack of experience in the American business environment

Case Questions

1. Should exchange students be required to complete "cultural" prerequisite classes before the business presentation classes? Why? Why not?

2. Should instructors be a bit more lenient with the exchange students in such required courses? Why? Why not?

3. Should special presentation classes be offered consisting of only exchange students? Explain.

4. Provide a recommended program for dealing with each of the three issues listed in this case.

PART THREE

Document Writing Skills:
Effectiveness *amid* Change

An 18-yr old college freshman once wrote:

Writing is not a natural or spontaneous way to communicate—it's slower than talking, it needs to be more precise, it must be grammatically correct, and it leaves a copy that people can pick apart.

Remember when mom wanted you to write a letter to Aunt Bess thanking her for the birthday gift? Remember applying to a school that asked you to write a personal biography as part of the application? Remember the elementary school "themes" or essays such as "What I did on my summer vacation"? A lot of students groaned at such work. Many professional people still do.

We have met many professional people who have outstanding, interesting ideas that are never applied or tested because the thinker cannot or will not put them in writing so they can be scrutinized, critiqued, refined, and enlarged upon by others. Writing allows for the processing and application of thought.

Although the trend in business is toward less writing quantity (for example formal reports are infrequent), written communication will never be replaced. In today's business environment writing has become more concise, more efficient, more conversational, and often less formal.

CHAPTER EIGHT

Planning
and Managing Writing:
How to Write it Right

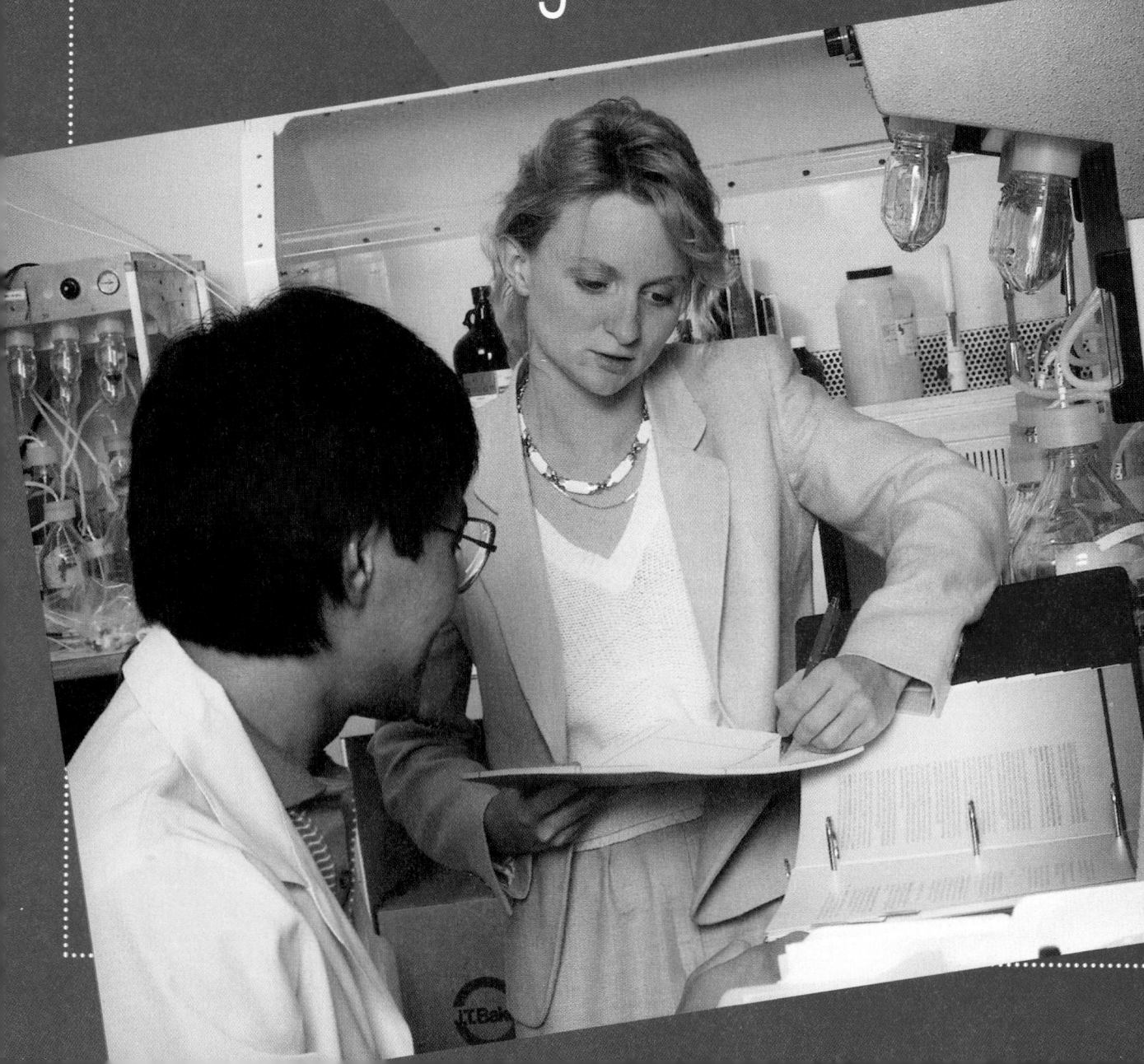

LEARNING GOALS

After you have studied this chapter, you should be able to:

- Recognize the functional nature of business communication.

- Organize a message appropriately using the big-idea-first (BIF) or big-idea-a-little-later (BILL) approach.

- Help your reader get the message by applying content set and access techniques for emphasis.

- Create a conversational and efficient tone in your writing by using simple, familiar wording: concrete nouns, active verbs, and avoiding unnecessary repetition.

- Recognize common failures in wording messages.

The Way It Is . . . The Hated Instruction Manual[1]

Visions of playing with your new toys dance in your head. But first: the instruction manual.

"It's an experience designed to humble and humiliate anyone," says Terry Stewart of Charlotte, N.C., about the manual for the assembly of a home gym. "It looked more like a praying mantis after I got through with it." Mr. Stewart eventually paid someone $150 to put together the $560 machine.

Michael Mooney, a Boston information designer—that's what they call manual writers these days—bought a $65 electronic organizer three months ago. But the calculator-sized gadget is nearly dwarfed by the instruction booklet, which is 117 pages long and contains sentences like, "If there is any secret entry between memos 4 and 5, which is hidden from view by the SECRET function, 'memo 2' will be stored before 'memo 5' but not immediately after 'memo 4.'" Pending a tutorial from an office mate, Mr. Mooney has yet to start using the organizer.

Everyone has felt the aggravation of trying to wade through poorly written documents that serve more to frustrate than to communicate. If these manuals were novels, publishers wouldn't print them, and no one would read them. In short, they'd be a waste of paper. The subject here is not literature, but business communication. Are there differences?

The difference between literature and business writing is like the difference between culture and agriculture. In business, people are concerned with the yield.

This is not to say that your writing should be so utilitarian as to be ugly, coarse, or overly blunt. As a matter of emphasis, though, function is more important than form. Even if beautifully written, a message is of little worth if it doesn't accomplish a task.

Functional writing gets results and accomplishes tasks. It causes readers to *do* something or to *think* in some way they would not if the message were not received.

Two important function questions should be asked about any business writing:

1. Is this document (letter, memo, e-mail message, report, proposal, etc.) necessary?

> Business writing is aimed at getting the reader to *do* or *think* something—usually *do*.

2. Does this document use an appropriate strategy?

Is This Document Really Necessary?

If a situation requires an extensive two-way exchange of information to create understanding, don't rely on writing alone. Call or visit. Sometimes flying across the country for a face-to-face conversation can be "cheaper" than a letter. Such trips would be worthwhile to save a major customer or to influence legislation affecting your business.

If, however, you need to:

1. Convey fairly complex but not highly emotional information (for example, a list of costs and serial numbers of parts)

2. Have a permanent record of what was said (like a proposal for services with prices quoted)

Poorly written documents lead to tremendous frustration. (Reprinted by permission: Tribune Media Services.)

3. Project a somewhat formal message to convey, for example, a contractual agreement,

then go with a carefully written document.

When the case is not so clear-cut, other media may work as well. We could hand write a note, send a preprinted form or information sheet, or—when responding to someone else's written message—simply write a brief reply on the original letter and return it, keeping a photocopy for our own records. An example is shown in Figure 8–1.

The major advantages of written media are their permanent record, relative formality, and capacity of conveying complex data. Disadvantages include high cost, low speed, and lack of immediate feedback. When you need these advantages and can live with the disadvantages, writing makes sense.

Does This Document Use an Appropriate Message Strategy?

Once you have decided that a memo, letter, or report is the best medium, you need to decide the most efficient strategy for conveying your message. This strategy should consider the best *pattern of organization, content setup, accessing techniques,* and *writing style.* The following sections examine each of these four strategy elements.

Patterns of Organization: What's the Big Idea?

The first strategic question writers should ask is, "What's the big idea of my message?" In functional writing, the **big idea** can be defined as the following:

- What you want the reader to *do* as a result of reading this message.
- What you want the reader to think or feel as a result of reading this message.

The big idea of any message is the outcome wanted. What do you want the reader to do, think, or feel?

If you cannot answer one or both of these questions, the big idea is unclear, and you cannot produce a functional message. If you don't know what you are trying to accomplish, there is no way your reader will. So save your time and effort; the message will fail.

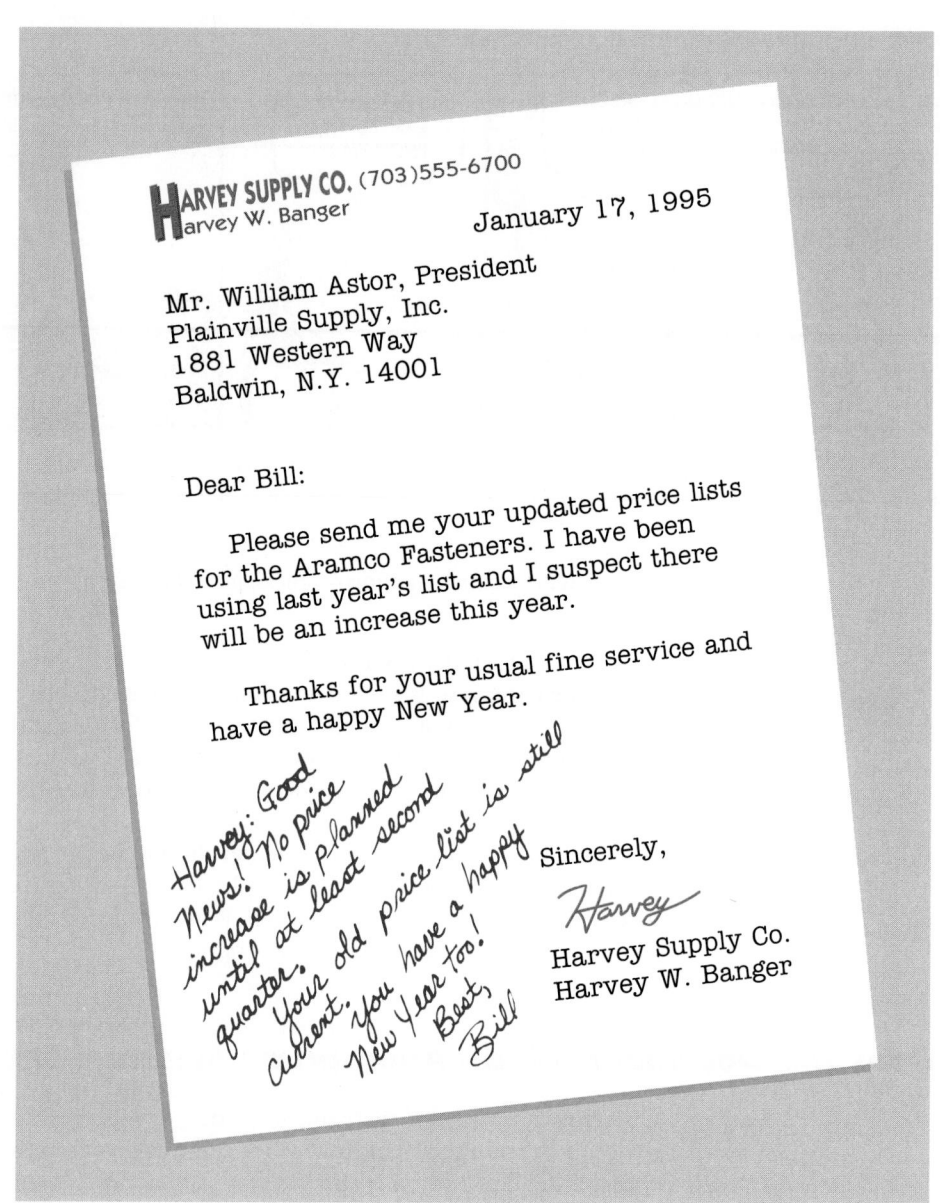

Harvey: Good News! No price increase is planned until at least second quarter. Your old price list is still current. You have a happy New Year too!
Best,
Bill

FIGURE 8–1

A quick reply can be handwritten on a piece of correspondence to save time.

When you are clear about your big idea—you can concisely state it—decide if you want to use a direct or indirect approach: BIF or BILL.

Big-Idea-First Approach

BIF is deductive reasoning, a direct approach.

Messages conveying routine information or information that will be seen as good news by its receiver should almost always use a **BIF approach.** This pattern of arrangement is what logicians call *deductive reasoning*, a direct approach. Start with the major premise—the big idea—and then add detail that explains the major point as needed. These explanatory details should answer any questions you might anticipate from your reader. Figure 8–2 shows an example.

Such good news messages are almost no-brainers. The reader is glad to hear your compliments; even if your form isn't good, the thought is appreciated.

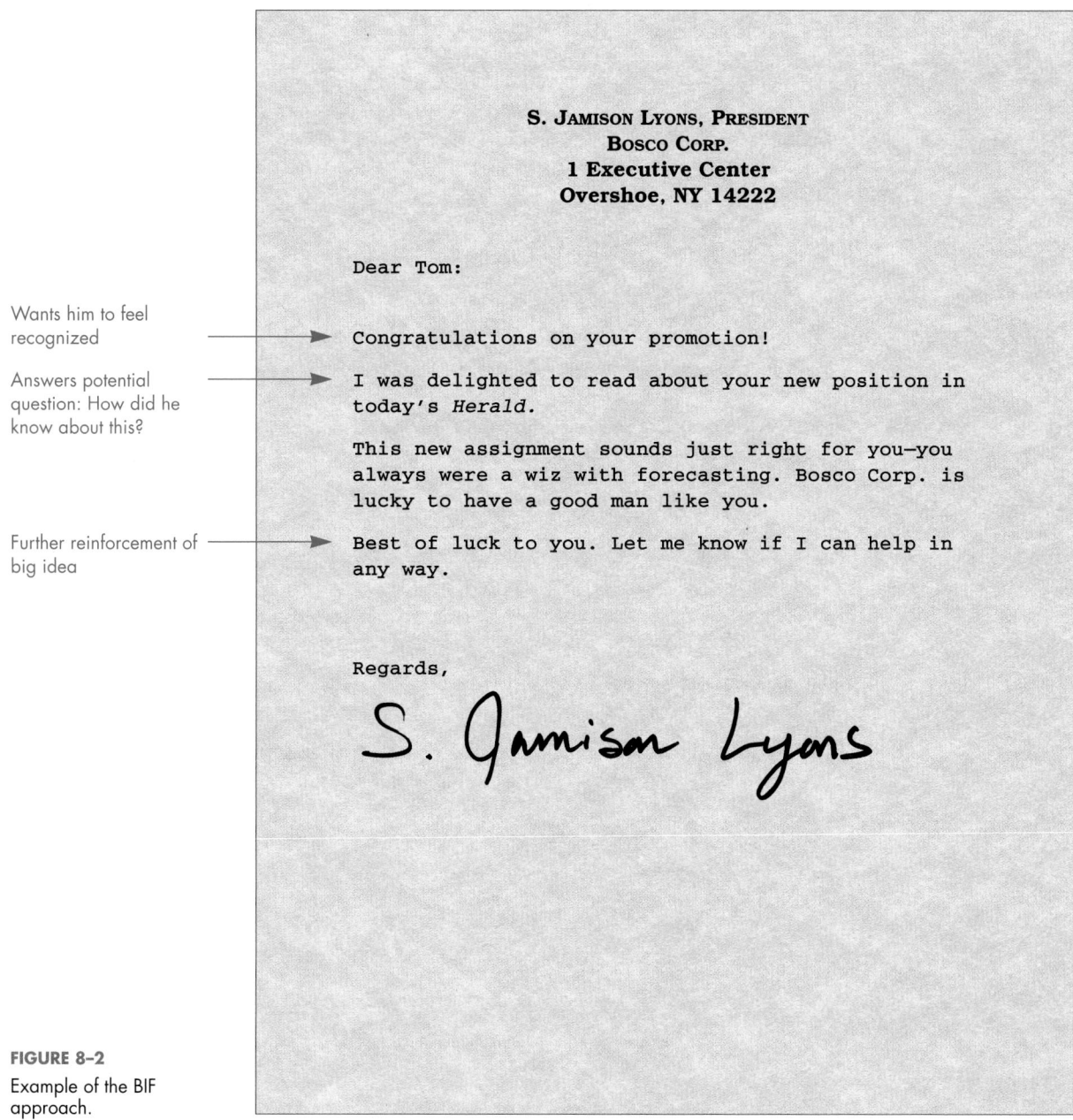

S. JAMISON LYONS, PRESIDENT
BOSCO CORP.
1 Executive Center
Overshoe, NY 14222

Dear Tom:

Congratulations on your promotion!

I was delighted to read about your new position in today's *Herald*.

This new assignment sounds just right for you—you always were a wiz with forecasting. Bosco Corp. is lucky to have a good man like you.

Best of luck to you. Let me know if I can help in any way.

Regards,

S. Jamison Lyons

Wants him to feel recognized

Answers potential question: How did he know about this?

Further reinforcement of big idea

FIGURE 8–2
Example of the BIF approach.

Likewise, BIF letters that request something the reader is happy to provide should look something like the following (Figure 8–3):

In such writing situations, there is no need to be subtle, no reason to hold back your main point. Tell your reader the big idea. Your reader will either be glad to get your message (good news) or at least be interested in what you have to say (routine). Then, anticipate reader questions and meet other information needs he or she might have.

Remember, the big idea is what you want the reader to *do with* or *feel about* the information in your message—your purpose for writing. It is, if you'll pardon the clichés, the bottom line of the message—where the rubber meets the road. If your

GLINNIS MANUFACTURING
1128 Centerville Road.
Cheyenne, WY 88776

November 15, 1997
JWA Video
411 S. Sangamon St.
Chicago, IL 60607

REQUEST FOR COPIES OF VIDEO TRAINING PROGRAMS

Please send me one copy of each of the following
videotape training programs:

THE POWER OF CUSTOMER SERVICE
SUCCESSFUL SELF-MANAGEMENT

I saw these videos previewed at a recent sales conference in Las Vegas and was told I could order
them directly from you. I understand the cost is
$99 each and have enclosed a check for $198.

Please bill me if there is an additional fee for
shipping and handling.

The videos should be shipped to the above address.
For any questions about this order, call me or my
secretary, Terry Rogers at (909) 555-1880.

Sincerely,

Janice T. Booker

Janice T. Booker
Director of Training

Big idea: What you want the reader to do

Supporting detail anticipates possible reader questions

FIGURE 8–3

A request letter using the BIF approach.

reader accepts or acts on the big idea as you wish, your communication attempt has been successful. All the rest of the words used in the writing are just packaging used to wrap the big idea or provide additional, clarifying details. Figure 8–4 shows one more example.

Notice that the closing thought on BIF messages is often a goodwill comment or offer to be of service. This can reduce any abrupt tone that may be conveyed by such brief messages. It provides a smooth closing. Do not, however, use the over-worked

If you have any questions, please do not hesitate to call upon me.

Magnum 44 Recreational Goods, Inc.

M E M O R A N D U M

TO: Sales Managers

FROM: Marion Seestone, Division Manager

DATE: November 15, 1997

RE: SALES RESULTS FOR OCTOBER

Big idea: What she wants reader to do. →

Attached are last month's sales results for your review. Please bring this with you to our staff meeting on Friday, November 20.

Overall, I am pleased with the trends. The Jacksonville team has shown particularly good improvement in unit volume.

Anticipates likely reader questions. →

If you see any glitches in the report, call me, and we'll check them out.

FIGURE 8–4
A memo using BIF.

A goodwill close can smooth over any abruptness in a BIF message.

This line sounds stuffy and insincere. Besides, if taken literally, you may end up with an unwanted pen pal!

Advantages of the BIF Approach. The BIF pattern offers several advantages.

- Because the reader is tipped off right away to what our purpose in writing is, BIF saves valuable time for the reader.
- The direct beginning often attracts the reader's attention. For example, it is easy to keep on reading when the opening of the letter is "Congratulations," "Thank you," or "Please send me. . . ."

- Writers using BIF don't waste time getting started on the letter or memo. Once you know what the big idea is, you can write it with little hesitation. As you think about probable reader reactions and anticipate likely questions, the supporting details will follow naturally.

For all its advantages, however, BIF can create some problems. If you anticipate that a message might be emotionally disturbing (that is, disappointing) to the reader, don't put the bad news (the big idea) in the first line. Likewise, if your message is persuasive and you need to present convincing evidence before you state your conclusion (the big idea), generally avoid BIF. A sales letter that begins, "I want to sell you some insurance" has little chance of succeeding. Try the next approach instead.

Big-Idea-a-Little-Later Approach

A BILL strategy puts the big idea later, using inductive reasoning.

The **BILL approach** prepares the reader for the action or conclusion you are requesting. This uses *inductive* logic, an indirect approach. It provides reasoning or evidence that leads up to the major premise—the big idea. In emotionally sensitive or persuasive situations, you run the risk of turning the reader off if the big idea is presented too soon. Presenting a conclusion without first showing reasoning may not be a good strategy when conveying bad news or a persuasive appeal.

Traditionally, business communication books have advised using an inductive strategy for *all* such letters—especially the bad news message. Others, however, hesitate to make such a blanket statement. Some readers prefer BIF even for bad news, which Chapter Twelve discusses further.

For now, recognize the options. A careful analysis of your reader will give you some clues about what approach makes sense. In some cases, you'll want to use BILL; in others, a more straightforward BIF approach may actually be less distasteful. Here is a situation you may recognize.

MooseLips Corporation has been recruiting on campus. Students have been interviewed, and most will not be offered a position with this prestigious company. They will, presumably, be disappointed by the message saying that.

Using the traditional BILL model, the body of the letter to the rejected students might read something like the following:

> **It was a pleasure to meet you during our recruiting interviews last week on campus. We were most impressed with the student body at Cheney University and generally found each of you well prepared for leadership positions at major corporations.**
>
> **As you know, we were particularly interested in students with experience or special training in complex information systems. Although your academic preparation is impressive, your informations systems experience has been somewhat limited, making your application slightly less appropriate to our current needs. Although a position in this area cannot be offered to you now, we would like to keep your application and resume in our active file for possible matching to a future position.**
>
> **Again, we offer our congratulations to you for your fine college preparation and wish you every success.**

How would you feel as a recipient of that letter? Some would appreciate the writer's sensitivity and attempts to let us down gently. Others might prefer that he get to the point and just indicate if they got the job or not.

In persuasive messages, especially sales letters, the BILL approach is almost always used for the simple reason that it works. Chapter Twelve shows how BILL is often applied to persuasive messages.

Advantages of the BILL Approach. When used well, the BILL approach offers several advantages.

- It can reduce the disappointment felt by a reader in receiving bad news by providing reasons that justify the decision. Ideally, the reader will say: "I'm not happy about the decision, but I guess if I were in the other person's shoes, I'd do the same."
- It demonstrates a writer's empathy and desire to maintain goodwill.
- It reduces the likelihood that the reader will turn off the message before the writer has had a chance to give the big idea.

Content Setup: Preparing Your Reader to Get the Message

Here is the second element of a writing strategy: **content setup.** This is a powerful way to improve the likelihood that your reader will understand your message.

Content Setup or Preview

Documents generate reader expectations even before they are read.

When a reader picks up a report, letter, or other document, he or she immediately begins to anticipate—to form expectations—as to what this writing is about. These expectations are guesses you make about the message even before you receive it. You also make guesses about the person writing, and that person's motives and intentions.

Psychologists believe that expectations can have a strong influence on what people hear or read. In other words, what people expect is often what they get—even when they have to change their reception of the real message to fit preconceived ideas. It makes sense, then, for the writer to create the most appropriate and positive expectations early in the communication.

One of the most effective ways to set the right expectations is simply to tell the reader what the message is about. It's like the old adage of public speaking that gives the three steps to success.

1. Tell them what you are going to tell them.
2. Tell them.
3. Tell them what you just told them.

The first part of that three-step advice is *content preview*. This part tells the reader what's coming up in the document or message.

Content preview can be general or specific. In either case, it sets the stage for what will follow. An example of general content preview follows:

This memo is to provide you with some data you may need for forecasting budgets.

Specific content preview gives more details. Another example follows:

This memo describes your team's product-by-product sales results for last month and the year to date.

In both cases, content preview helps the reader focus on what the message will be about and mentally prepare to deal with it.

In longer documents, the last paragraph of a section should create a content preview for what is to follow. It is often a description of the specific items that will be coming up.

> **This review of sales results will give you an idea of the major challenges we face. The next section of this report will address each of the three most significant problems and provide recommendations for dealing with them.**

As these examples show, the easiest way to create content preview is by simply telling the reader what you plan to say next. This is especially easy to do when the message is direct and to the point (using a BIF approach). Here are some more examples of content preview statements.

- The following report recommends relocating the warehouse to the Westside Industrial Park.
- Enclosed is my contribution to the University Alumni Fund.
- This performance review cites three incidents of substandard performance.
- In response to your request for a transfer, here are the procedures you'll need to follow.
- This business plan shows how an investment of only $10,000 can create a viable vending route that will return monthly income of at least $600.
- Four small business computers are evaluated in this report.

Informative subject lines create clear content setup.

In many cases, the subject line of a memo or letter serves as the content preview. To make this most effective, writers should use *informative* subject lines rather than simple *topical* subject lines. Here is how these differ.

An informative subject line conveys a *complete thought;* a topical subject line does not. In some cases, a topical subject line is no more than a category for filing the memo. Notice the difference between topical and informative subject lines.

Topical	Informative
Guest speaker	Senator Bob Bennett will be guest speaker at our November luncheon.
Air travel on expense account	Reimbursement for business travel will be tourist class fare only.
Advanced management program	You have been selected to participate in the Advanced Management Program on May 28.
New policy on rental car insurance	Don't buy the dollar-per-day supplemental insurance when renting a car.
Staff meeting	All staff members will meet April 26 at 2:00 P.M. in room 374.

In each of the preceding cases, the informative subject line conveys a complete thought. In doing so, it creates immediate content setup for the reader.

In cases for which you have chosen a BILL approach, placing the big idea of your message later (bad news or persuasive messages, typically), you can still use informative subject lines. Some examples follow:

Policy Change Will Affect Sales Compensation

Update on New Pricing Schedule Effective January 199X

Further Details on Last Week's Staff Meeting Topic

These still convey a complete thought without divulging the big idea prematurely.

Strengthening content preview is one of the simplest ways for a writer to improve the chances that the reader will get and use the message. Content preview helps create realistic expectations in the reader's mind. By doing this, you reduce misconceptions and improve the accuracy of communication.

Accessing Techniques Tell Readers What's Most Important

A third strategy element involves "accessing" key information. In any message, certain ideas or bits of information are more important than others. One common mistake made in functional writing is the failure to point out which bits of information are, in fact, more important. Important information should receive a position of prominence—that is, the more the reader will need to understand that information—the more *accessible* you should make it. Your writing should somehow point to key ideas in your message.

Critical information should jump out at the reader.

One of the major differences between literary writing and functional business writing is this notion of accessing. In literature, a reader is expected to read through the whole story to find the important material. The author doesn't normally help the reader to do that efficiently. In business communication, **emphasis techniques (accessing)** are used to highlight key ideas. Ideally, a business report, letter, or memo should be written so that it need *not* be read word for word, but can actually be skimmed. The key bits of information should jump out at the reader.

Three Kinds of Accessing

Three types of emphasis in writing are: verbal, visual, and psychological. Each of these can be used to point to the most important ideas in a message. Some are more subtle than others, and you can use a variety of accessing techniques within the same document.

Verbal Emphasis. One form of verbal emphasis is the use of *word cues* to indicate that a key idea is coming up or has been stated. For example, the writer might say,

"The most important aspect is . . ."

"This last part is particularly important . . ."

"Please read these instructions carefully . . ."

"Of all the options suggested, one stands out . . ."

These overt cues can be used in either written or spoken communication. They provide important road signs for the reader or listener.

A second type of verbal emphasis is the use of *repetition*. When a key idea is repeated several times (preferably phrased a little differently each time), the reader gets the idea that this is, in fact, an important bit of information.

Repetition of key ideas —like these margin notes—helps access important information.

Repetitious phrases can also be used to help organize a message. Perhaps the first few words of a series of headings might be repetitious to show how these headings fit together. In a business report, for example, we may say

- First Important Reason for . . .
- Second Important Reason for . . .
- Third Important Reason for . . .

Visual Emphasis. Several types of visual emphasis can be used to help the reader skim through the message and get the important ideas in it. These visual techniques include

- Enumeration—1, 2, 3
- Listing—such lists are put in columns and can have the following notations:
  1. Numerals
  A. Letters
  * Asterisks or stars
  - Hyphens
  • Bullets

Today's word-processing and presentations software give anyone a wide variety of accessing capabilities once available only to artists and designers (Figure 8–5). Take the time to learn about such capabilities, and you'll give added professionalism to your documents while providing better access for your reader.

Psychological Emphasis. "Pointing" by means of psychological principles entails deciding how to arrange information in the message. Three ways to achieve psychological emphasis are order, space, and freshness.

The *order of information*—when clearly pointed out to the reader—can help the reader anticipate what is coming next and remember what has been said. This form of psychological emphasis helps separate the key ideas from the extraneous. An example follows:

> **This report will give you a chronological look at the history of the problem from 1988 to present [CONTENT SETUP].**
>
> **Possible Headings**
>
> 1988 to 1990 Gradual Reducation in Market Share
>
> 1991 Premature Introduction of the Abacus Product Line
>
> 1992 Resources Spent to Solve Abacus
>
> 1993 Loss of Key Management Personnel

FIGURE 8–5

Most word-processing software programs have a variety of symbols. You can add variety to your documents by making use of them.

Bullets: Symbols that Draw Attention

Symbol	Description	Symbol	Description
•, ○	Solid and hollow bullet	⟩	Right angle bracket
■, ❑	Solid and hollow box	→	Right arrow
■	Small square bullet	▶	Solid triangle right
•	Small bullet	◀	Solid triangle left
◘	Inverse bullet	→	Solid head right arrow
■	Inverse hollow bullet	√	Check mark
◆	Square lozenge	#, ♯	Number or Pound, Sharp

- Capitalizing—the word in CAPS gets the emphasis
- Underlining—with <u>one</u> or <u>two</u> or more
- Borders—such as this
- Type variation—different FACES, *styles,* and SIZES
- Color paper and design borders (which can be purchased at office supply stores ready for your computer printer of photocopier
- Graphics—a picture is worth how many words?
- Shading or highlighting—with color marker
- Varying margin widths to "frame" the message
- The attention-getting power of w h i t e space (including short paragraphs)
- Cartoons or figures, icons, and clipart (all of which are available in software packages)

Other orders of arrangement that are readily recognized by your reader will be places compared ("Districts in the Midwest Region are compared . . ."), or cause and effect.

The discussion of *space* in terms of psychological emphasis refers to the relative amount of space devoted to a particular topic. If, for example, a sales letter for a piece of machinery spends several paragraphs describing reliability and only one short line indicating something about its ease of operation, the reader psychologically determines that reliability is more important than ease of operation.

Finally, psychological emphasis can be achieved through *freshness* by suggesting that the message is a new approach, catchy idea, or particularly innovative notion. Imaginative wording such as identifying a problem by a clever phrase can give psychological emphasis to it. Some examples follow:

It's baaack. . . . The computer-glitch-from-hell has surfaced once again, but network support says it will be fixed by 2:00 P.M. today.

It's new! It's improved! Okay, you've all heard that before. But this time Corporate has really done it: A turbo-charged compensation plan that you will all like.

How many ways can we thank you folks? Last month's results were off the chart!

Efficient Sentences

An average sentence length of about 16 words is appropriate for adult readers.

Long sentences can be useful to de-emphasize information.

Finally, access is damaged by long, complex, or compound sentences that hurt message efficiency. They slow down both reader and writer.

Sentences should convey bite-sized pieces of information that can be digested by your reader one piece at a time. The rule of thumb is that, for most adult readers, sentences should *average* about 16 words in length. Some sentences may have only two or three words, whereas others can run to 30 or so.

One other consideration in dealing with sentence length: different lengths have different effects on readers. Short sentences have punch. They emphasize. They hit hard. The potential disadvantage of using only exceptionally short sentences is that they may sound like you are talking down to the reader. They can create a dog-trot rhythm sounding like a children's book. Longer sentences, conversely, can be useful when you want to de-emphasize information that may be objectionable or unpleasant for your reader.

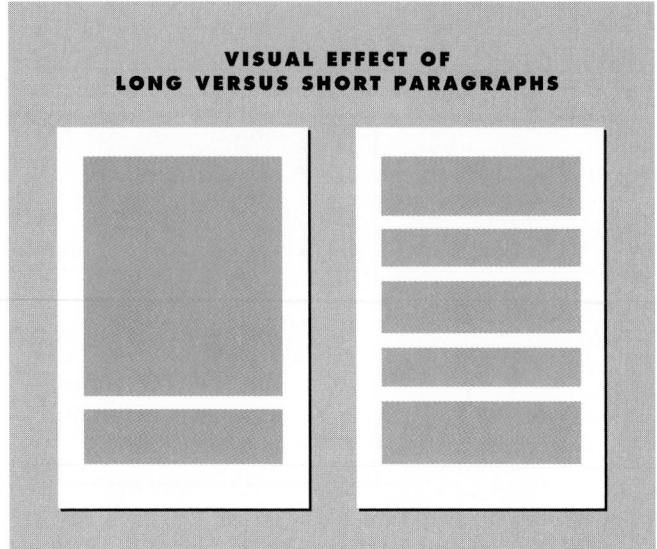

FIGURE 8–6

These outlines show the visual impact on the reader of long versus short paragraphs.

Efficient Paragraphs

No one wants to plow through long, heavy-looking paragraphs.

In business and professional writing, paragraphs should usually be shorter than you'd expect to find in literature, unless de-emphasis is desired. People prefer to read information presented in manageable bits. When people receive a document with long paragraphs—even before reading the first words—they are likely to conclude that this message is going to be difficult to read. Poor accessing, created by long, heavy-looking paragraphs, makes the reader's job more difficult. No one wants to face a page covered with a huge blob of words.

Grammatically, a paragraph should develop one theme. Writers have considerable latitude, however, in choosing when to break to a new paragraph. For business writing, paragraphs should seldom exceed six lines. Figure 8–6 shows the visual effect of different paragraph lengths. Which letter would you prefer to read?

Selection of Appropriate Writing Style

What constitutes a writing "style"? John S. Fielden, in an excellent article in the *Harvard Business Review*[2] article advocates adjusting your writing style to various situations you face. The factors to consider in selecting a style are the following:

- *Nature of the message* you are to convey, especially if it will be seen as good news or bad news by the reader.
- *Likes and dislikes* of the receiver, such as the preference for directness versus the preference for "straight talk."
- *Relative power positions* of the writer and reader. You would probably use a different style in writing to a company president than to a friend or subordinate.

Fielden describes six writing styles.

- Forceful
- Passive
- Personal

- Impersonal
- Colorful
- Less colorful

A letter can, of course, be a combination of these styles. The following chart summarizes much of Fielden's thinking as it applies to business communication. Take a few moments to study the chart so that you will understand some of the "strings to pull" if you wish to adjust your writing style.

BUSINESS WRITING STYLES						
Style	**Forceful**	**Passive**	**Personal**	**Impersonal**	**Colorful**	**Less Colorful**
When to use	Writer is in a position of power Action requests Writing to subordinates	Negative message Writer in lesser power position Avoid the imperative	Good news message Persuasive Action request	Negative message Informative message	Good news message Advertisements, sales	Routine business writing Informative message Technical and scientific writing
How to project	Use active voice Stay with subject-verb order in sentences Step up front and be counted ("I have decided") Don't beat around bush; be direct Avoid "weasel word" (qualifiers) Use a tone of confidence and surety	Use passive voice Attribute negative action to nameless "others" Use "weasel word" (qualifiers) Use long sentences and heavy paragraphs	Use active voice Use persons' names and personal pronouns Use short sentences Use contractions Direct questions to the reader Personalize with specifics applicable only to this reader Conversational tone	Use passive voice Avoid names Use titles Avoid personal pronouns Use complex sentences	Use many adjectives and adverbs Use metaphors and similes Use wit	Avoid adjectives and adverbs Blend impersonal and passive styles Use a tone devoid of wit, liveliness, and vigor

You may not want to use all of these techniques in a document, however.

Unless you have a boss or an organizational culture that dictates something else, most business writing will likely use vitality and economy, simplicity, and conversational tone. The following sections look more closely at these key elements of style.

> A business-writing definition of style:
>
> Style is that choice of words, sentences, and paragraph format which by virtue of being *appropriate to the situation* and to the *power positions* of both writer and reader *produces the desired reaction and result.*

Vitality and Economy of Language

Most business writing is simple, economical, and conversational.

Many phrases that appear in poorly thought-out business writing are there because writers have "always done it that way." Typically inexperienced letter writers check the correspondence files to see how others have been written in the past. So they end up using phrases like the ones in the following rhyme. Although an exaggeration, this poem illustrates how vitality can be sapped out of a message when buried under these overworked expressions:

> We beg to advise you and wish to state
> That yours has arrived of recent date.
> We have it before us; its contents noted.
> Herewith enclosed are the prices we quoted.
> Attached you will find, as per your request,
> The forms you wanted, and we would suggest,
> Regarding the matter and due to the fact
> That up to this moment your order we've lacked,
> We hope that you will not delay it unduly.
> We beg to remain, yours very truly.[3]

In fairness, many of these phrases have evolved over time from what was considered business etiquette. Commerce was rich with formal and excessively flowery phrases in years past. In some cultures, it continues to be so. A recently received letter from a consulting client in Brazil ended with this sentence: "Staying at your disposal, we look forward to hearing from you." In the American business culture, letter writers seldom use such expressions, preferring more economical, conversational language.

To achieve economy of language, work to reduce unneeded repetition and cluttered phrasing. Make sure every word carries its own weight; no free riders are allowed. Here are some economy and vitality boosters.

Avoidance of Unnecessary Repetition. Although repeating an idea can be an effective teaching device (especially in oral communication), and a useful form of verbal accessing, unnecessary repetition distracts the reader.

Needless Repetition	Repetition Eliminated
The *provisions* of the contract *provide* for a union shop.	The contract provides for a union shop.
The new rule will affect *each* and *every* employee.	The new rule will affect every employee.
In my opinion I think the plan is reasonable.	I think the plan is reasonable.
This letter has attempted to answer any possible questions you may have, but if you have further questions, please *do not hesitate to contact us.*	If you have additional questions, please call.

Avoidance of Surplus Words and Cluttered Phrases. Words that add nothing to the meaning of the sentence should be dropped. Phrases that can be replaced by a single word or shorter expression should be changed. Here are some examples.

Cluttered	More Concise
In the event that payment is not received . . .	If payment is not . . .
The report is *in regard to the matter* of our long-term obligations . . .	The report is about . . .
I have just received your letter and wanted to respond quickly.	I wanted to respond quickly to your letter.
The quality of his art work is so good that *it permitted us to* offer him a long-term contract.	His work was so good that the company offered him a long-term contract.

The most economical and vital language results when you write the way you would talk in a planned, purposeful conversation. You wouldn't say, when handing an envelope to a coworker in our office, "Enclosed herewith please find the report I've written." In conversation you'd be more likely to say, "Here's the report I prepared on. . . ." So why not write that way? It gets to the point and conveys your message efficiently. The trend in written communication is to the less formal, more conversational tone.[4]

Improve language efficiency by using clear, specific wording. Concrete words improve efficiency and hold your readers' interest by creating vivid mental images. Often these are short, familiar terms.

Abstract	Specific
A leading student	Ranked second in a class of 80
Most of our people	87 percent of our employees
In the near future	By noon Wednesday
Lower cost than . . .	$43 less than . . .
A sizable increase in sales	Doubled in sales
Low energy consumption	Uses no more power than a 60-watt lightbulb
The cost would be enormous	. . . would cost every taxpayer $286 per year

Use of Active Verbs. Just as concreteness improves nouns and modifiers, use of the active voice adds impact to verbs. The grammatical term *voice* refers to whether the subject of a sentence acts or is acted on. If it is *acted on,* the passive voice is used; if it *does the acting,* the active voice is used. Active verbs make your sentences more

Active voice: The subject does the action. Passive voice: The subject receives the action or is acted on.

- *Specific.* "The board of directors decided" is more explicit than "A decision has been made."
- *Personal.* "You will see an improvement" is both personal and specific; "An improvement will be seen" is impersonal.
- *Concise.* The passive requires more words and thus slows down both the writing and reading. Compare "Toni bought a Chevy" with "A Chevy was bought by Toni."
- *Emphatic.* Passive verbs dull the action. Compare "The strategy gets good results" with "Good results are achieved with the strategy."

The clearer relationship between subject and verb in active voice adds force and momentum to your writing. By closely associating the *actor* (noun) and the *action* (verb), the writer helps the reader visualize more clearly what is happening. In some cases, however, the writer may intentionally want to de-emphasize this association (or remove the actor entirely) by using passive voice. For example, which would you rather report?

I just ran over your cat. (active)

Your cat has been run over. (passive)

Assuming the demise of the cat is bad news to the receiver, you'd probably choose passive voice to de-emphasize the message slightly. For most business writing, however, the active voice is preferred because it adds vitality.

Passive	Active
Each tire *was inspected* by a mechanic.	A mechanic *inspected* each tire.
A gain of 41 percent *was recorded* for paper product sales.	Paper products sales *gained* 41 percent.
A full report *will be sent* to you by the supervisor.	The supervisor *will send* . . .; or you *will receive* a full report from the supervisor.
All figures in the report *are checked* by the accounting department.	The accounting department *checks* all figures in the report.

Here are some other, related ideas on developing a **conversational tone.**

Unspoken Meanings of Some Overworked Expressions

The following are examples of common terms and phrases often used to cloud meaning rather than clarify. The "correct " translation for each is supplied. Don't take these interpretations too seriously—unless you're an incurable cynic. Remember, however, the "between-the-lines" message these expressions might convey to the reader.

Expression	Translation
It has long been known that . . .	We haven't bothered to look up the reference, but. . . .
Your suggestion is being reviewed.	It's so wrapped up in red tape that the situation is almost hopeless.
It is generally believed that . . .	A couple of other guys think so too.
The idea is under consideration.	Never heard of it.
The idea is under active consideration.	We're looking in the files for it.
We will advise you in due time.	If we figure it out, we'll give you a call.
Program	Any assignment that can't be handled by a telephone call.
Consultant (or expert)	An ordinary guy with a briefcase more than fifty miles from home.
We'd like to keep your application on file.	We just threw it away.
After careful review . . .	My secretary skimmed your proposal.
Activate	I made photocopies and tagged them to other people.

Use of Simple Wording. Often a common word can do the job of a multi-syllable jawbreaker.[5] There is a clear correlation between how many syllables are in a word and how difficult it is to read. Lots of big words slow down both the writer and the reader, and they usually don't communicate any more effectively, despite the increased effort. In the following examples, listen to the differences:

Long and Heavy Wording	Short and Simple Wording
Polysyllabic verbiage obfuscates comprehension.	Big words block clarity.[6]
Our *analysis* of the *situation* suggests needed *experiential* training to *optimize* the job performance of our employees.	We think our people need more job training.
John *acceded* to the demands for *additional compensation*.	John agreed to pay them more.
My investment recommendations were *predicated* on *anticipations* of additional *monetary funds* being made available.	I based investment recommendations on an expected increase in money available.
Ramifications of our *performance shortfall* included *program discontinuation*.	Because we didn't reach our goal, the program was discontinued.

Use of Familiar, Conversational Words. A second way to be more conversational is to use everyday language. This helps your reader understand what you are saying. Many business writers think they must use technical or formal language—or the latest buzzwords—to convey the appropriate *image*. You serve only your *illusions* of status with language so technical and stilted that it loses meaning for your receiver. Talk in terms that your reader is sure to understand.

Unfamiliar, Stilted Words	Everyday, Conversational Words
Ascertain	Find out
Terminate	End
Re-engineer	Reorganize
Database	List
With all due dispatch	Quickly
Monetary transaction	Sale or purchase
Occupational position	Job
Financial obligations	Debts
Disproportionate	Unfair
Equity participation	A share of ownership

Use of Some Contractions. In speaking, people constantly use contractions, such as I'll, haven't, can't, shouldn't, and so forth. Using the uncontracted form "I shall, have not, cannot, and should not" can sound more formal—and less conversational.

Clichéd Corporate Conversations from Hell[7]

You don't have to be a rocket scientist to recognize that corporate America is a leading-edge recycler of tired phrases. It's a no-brainer. Pitch artists swearing they walk the talk, bearing offers of win-win situations, are legion. But the bottom line is that you don't want to be left out of the linguistic loop while colleagues who are a bit slower on the learning curve throw out slews of mouth-bitten chichés every time they touch base with you. That's why we ratcheted up our very own Devil's Dictionary—to take you through the worst of the worst just one more time.

Our nation's bulging inventory of business clichés is spun out by pundits, picked up by senior executives, and regurgitated by pilot fish imitating their bosses. The explosion of management tomes and seminars in the past 15 years has fostered a top-down commitment among business folk to pepper their vocabularies with the latest business jargon. As the pace of work becomes lighting-quick, people condense complex historical events into flashy insights. "Just as reading diet books is a substitute for losing weight, reading management books is a substitute for good management," comments Vanderbilt University professor Terrence Deal (whose own *Leading With Soul* is due in bookstores soon).

In this age of clichés, meaninglessness reigns. Does anyone truly know what the "value chain" is? Or exactly what is "empowerment"? Avers Ralph Kilmann, professor at the University of Pittsburgh's business school: "People feel comfortable with these concepts. They think they understand them because they use them in conversations, memos, and publicity statements, but there is virtually no substance to these words." Now that's vision!

The Devil's Dictionary

Team Player An employee who substitutes the thinking of the herd for his own good judgment.

Reengineering The principal slogan of the Nineties, used to describe any and all corporate strategies.

Vision Top management's heroic guess about the future, easily printed on mugs, T-shirts, posters, and calendar cards.

Paradigm shift A euphemism companies use when they realize the rest of their industry has expanded into Guangdong while they were investing in Orange County.

Restructuring A simple plan instituted from above in which workers are right-sized, downsized, surplused, lateralized, or, in the business jargon of days of yore, fired.

Empowerment A magic wand management waves to help traumatized survivors of restructuring suddenly feel engaged, self-managed, and in control of their futures and their jobs.

This is not to say that people always use contractions. Sometimes, for clarity, writers will want to spell out the longer form.

Contractions give the writer an opportunity to create a more conversational tone.

Two Tasks of Correspondence

Every letter or memo attempts to convey a message and projects an image of its writer. Sometimes one task is relatively more important than the other. Figure 8–7 illustrates how these functions could be plotted on a grid. Let's assume that each axis of this grid is calculated between 1 and 9 (low to high), with the vertical axis reflecting the degree of reader understanding—the *accuracy* with which the message has been received—and the horizontal axis reflecting favorableness of the impression created by the writer—his or her *image*. The optimum business letter would be a 9-9 (high-accuracy, high-image) one. A total waste of paper and money would be a 1-1 (low-accuracy, low-image) letter.

You may, however, get by with a 9-1 letter if the overriding task of the letter is to convey accurate information with minimal concern for image projected. A military directive or routine transmittal of some data may be efficient and fairly harmless as a 9-1. At the other end of the grid, a 1-9 letter, one whose message content is less than precise may be well received when it's the "thought that counts." Inadequate but thoughtful expressions of sympathy, or cheerful but rather vague notes of congratulations may be 1-9s.

Business and professional communicators should normally be concerned with both tasks. Going back to our earlier discussion of word choices, the lawyer or stock broker who insists on using professional jargon in an attempt to feed her sense of importance may convey a learned image but will soon turn off the reader who can't figure out what she is saying. Such "impressive"-sounding letters may stroke the writer's ego but only frustrate the reader.

Conversely, the writer who spits out cold, heartless, but fact-filled sentences with great precision may seem like a well-programmed android. Good business letters are more than pure information transfer. They also involve impressions and expressions of humanity. Even when mass printed by a computer, today's professional letters can sound like a neighborly chat over the fence—especially when they employ

FIGURE 8-7

The Image-Accuracy letter grid.

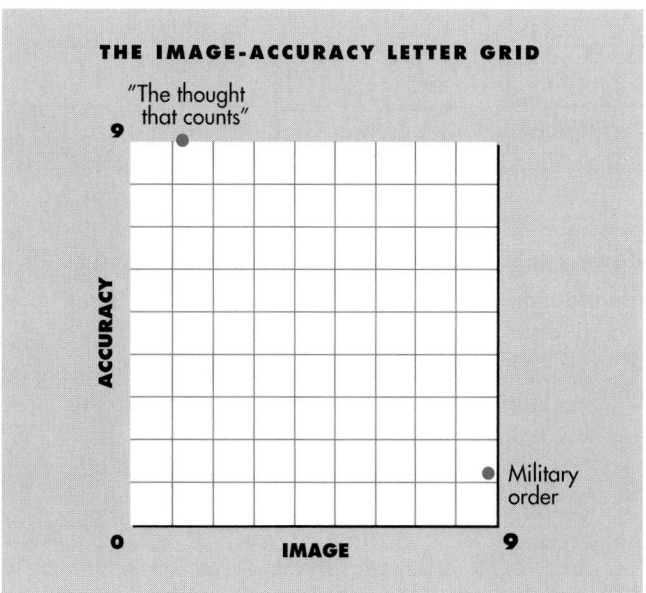

a conversational tone and one-to-one personalization. Letter effectiveness arises from both the informational and the "human" content of the message.

Understanding the Basics

- Business writing is *functional* writing. It should always focus on a particular result. This desired result is the *big idea* of the message.

- These questions should be answered before writing.

    Is this letter necessary (or useful)?

    Is this letter efficient?

- The BIF pattern of arrangement is best for routine or good-news messages, whereas the BILL pattern is usually better for messages that are likely to affect the reader's emotions. The latter situations include some bad-news persuasive messages.

- Good writers learn to adjust their writing style as dictated by the document's purpose, likes and dislikes of the reader, and relative power of the reader and writer.

- Most of today's business writing calls for an efficient, conversational style.

- Message efficiency is achieved through economy of language, simple conversational wording, active voice, and the like.

- Message effectiveness is the degree to which the message is clear, projects a favorable image of the writer, and accomplishes the big idea.

- Content setup creates appropriate expectations in the mind of the reader by previewing the message.

- Accessing adds verbal, visual, and psychological emphasis to important ideas in a message, thus helping your reader to get to the big idea.

KEY TERMS AND CONCEPTS

functional writing	content setup	emphasis techniques (accessing)
BIF approach	contractions	support and texture
BILL approach	big idea	conversational tone
active verbs		

QUESTIONS FOR FURTHER THOUGHT

1. Business communication is or should be more functional than other types of writing. Do you agree or disagree with that viewpoint? Justify your position.

2. Why does a conversational tone generally communicate more efficiently in business letters? Can you think of cases in which tone should be more formal—even "stuffy"?

3. Take a look at some business letters or memos you have received at work or home. What is the big idea of each? Where does the writer position the big idea? Is this the way you would write the letter? If not, what would you do differently? Why?

4. Why do active verbs and concrete nouns communicate more clearly?

5. Why is accessing important? Can you think of times when you may want to avoid accessing key ideas?

ANOTHER Look

Mutually Understood

Buffett Decodes Fund Prospectus

The Securities and Exchange Commission wants mutual funds to write their prospectuses in plain English. . . . To show mutual fund lawyers how to do it, SEC Chairman Arthur Levitt asked Warren Buffett, the legendary investor and CEO of Berkshire Hathaway, to rewrite a typical mutual fund prospectus paragraph. Here is the paragraph—and Buffett's version.

The Original
Maturity and Duration Management

Maturity and duration management decisions are made in the context of an intermediate maturity orientation. The maturity structure of the portfolio is adjusted in the anticipation of cyclical interest rate changes. Such adjustments are not made in an effort to capture short-term, day-to-day movements in the market, but instead are implemented in anticipation of longer term, secular shifts in the levels of interest rates (i.e., shifts transcending and/or not inherent to the business cycle). Adjustments made to shorten portfolio maturity and duration are made to limit capital losses during periods when interest rates are expected to rise. Conversely, adjustments made to lengthen maturation for the portfolio's maturity and duration strategy lie in analysis of the U.S. and global economies, focusing on levels of real interest rates, monetary and fiscal policy actions, and cyclical indicators.

Buffett's Version
Maturity and Duration Management

We will try to profit by correctly predicting future interest rates. When we have no strong opinion, we will generally hold intermediate-term bonds. But when we expect a major and sustained increase in rates, we will concentrate on short-term issues. And, conversely, if we expect a major shift to lower rates, we will buy long bonds. We will focus on the big picture and won't make moves based on short-term considerations.

(Copyright 1994, USA TODAY. Reprinted with permission.)

Applying Your Knowledge

1. How did Mr. Buffett's version improve on the original?
2. What techniques for effective writing did he use?

Applying Your Skills

ACTIVITY 8-1: Letter Tone and Factual Content

Collect examples of five business letters. (Avoid professional sales letters or mass mailings prepared by advertising or public relations (PR) agencies. Instead, get personal business letters addressed to individuals.)

Show where, in your opinion, each letter rates on the grid. Then comment on the relative clarity and image projected by the letter. Why did you rate the letter as you did? How would you rewrite the letter to improve it?

Look at the following letter. Rewrite it to incorporate the ideas in this chapter.

MBA ADMISSIONS BOARD

February 19, 19XX
Mr. Daniel A. Martin
Cedar Grove, Iowa

Dear Mr. Martin:

The admissions board has reviewed your application and has voted negatively on your request for admission. Although I know our decision will come as a disappointment to you, I hope the following comments will help you understand the context in which this decision was made. The admissions board relies on the written application and the supporting documents in their evaluation of candidates for the MBA Program. Using these materials, we collectively consider academic strengths, demonstrated accomplishments, managerial experience, and personal characteristics. This year we will have reviewed some 7,000 applications. We try to offer admission to those individuals we think have the best potential to become general managers. With an entering class limited in size to 780 persons, a great many difficult decisions must be made.

Sincerely,

Romelia M. Porter

Romelia M. Porter
Chairperson

ACTIVITY 8-3: Let's Get Conversational

Replace the big, "impressive" word with a more familiar word or phrase.

Substantiate

Configuration

Modification

Calculate

Orientation

Recalcitrant

Recidivism

Extrapolate

Implement

Optimize

Enhance

Facilitate

Re-engineer

Empower

ACTIVITY 8-4: Mutually Understood

Review the changes made in the fund prospectus shown on page 207. What language efficiencies were achieved in the Buffett version? Make a "before" and "after" list and categorize the items according to the examples shown on pages 199–202 of this chapter.

PERFORMING
on the Job

CASE 8-1 Do You Really Want to Be Here?

Put yourself in the place of the human resources director, Jane, dealing with a long time department employee, Claudia. For the past two years, Jane has noticed Claudia's job performance deteriorating. The two have discussed the issue on several occasions, and Claudia seemed to realize that improvement must occur because employees of the company depend on her. However, after a few months, the deterioration continues. This time, instead of a face-to-face conversation, Jane gives Claudia the following memo written after a telephone call from Claudia indicating she would "not be to work today."

Case Questions

1. Is this an effective memo? Why? Why not?
2. Why might written concerns have a different impact on Claudia than previous discussions?
3. How would you have dealt with Claudia if you were Jane? How would you follow up on this memo?
4. Was Jane too lenient? Should Claudia have been let go based on substandard performance?

CASE 8-2 You Are Invited

Senior management at XYZ have been working to implement a "soft-sell" culture for the past two years. They have implemented sales incentives and stressed the importance of employees making sure customers are informed of all products available from XYZ. The efforts of management and the employees seem to be reflected in a profitable bottom line.

Management's concern is that only a small percentage of employees are receiving sales incentives. They want to get other employees excited about the possibility of earning additional income and maintaining loyal customers because of employee efforts. Their thinking is that some employees may not know how to go about "selling" or "informing" customers. They believe that some assistance from the "top sellers" would be helpful. The invitation below was sent to fifteen of the top incentive earners for one month.

MEMO

DATE: July 7, 19XX

TO: Claudia

FROM: Jane

RE: Various performance issues

After your telephone call today, I wanted to get some things down in writing that are concerning me. I don't mean to appear "cold," it's just that I can think more clearly when putting my thoughts in writing.

1. When you first came to me a couple of months ago, you indicated your scheduling problems would be due to the illness of your mother-in-law. This was after the first of the year when other reasons kept you away from the office quite a bit in January and February. Recently, it seems that more and more different reasons are coming up that are keeping you away.
2. The other day you informed me that you and your husband have purchased a building lot in Baytown (sixty miles away). This indicates to me that settling in Baytown will mean a continuation of your daily commute, and I realize that it is difficult for you.
3. You talked to me a few weeks ago about the concern that you did not have enough to do. I guess this is leading me to ask the question a former boss posed to me a few years ago. Do you want to be here?
4. I have been getting several calls and comments from employees needing assistance and feeling that they can't get their questions answered by you. They have a hard time getting hold of you (even with a cellular telephone). Your position really does require a consistent presence, which has been sporadic for some months.

I have tried to be patient and as understanding as possible. I don't think that the human resources department is providing good service to our staff. Please ponder this memo, and let's discuss future directions.

INVITATION

TO: (Several employees reaching certain sales
       goals)
FOR: "One-Plus" Awards Luncheon
WHEN: Friday, June 23, 1995
TIME: Noon
PLACE: Boardroom

Because of your efforts in providing our customers
with "one-plus" service, senior management would
like to provide lunch for you.

Come and enjoy a catered meal with senior management and others like yourself who are doing an exceptional job in helping our company reach its
goals. Share your success techniques and ideas
about providing "one-plus" service.

RSVP to Janet at ext. 773 by Tuesday, June 20,
1997.

The purpose of the lunch was for employee recognition and idea sharing. Management thought successful ideas could be shared with all employees to assist them in knowing how to "soft sell."

Case Questions

1. How would you feel if you were a top seller and received an invitation to the luncheon?
2. Does the written invitation accomplish management's purpose of encouraging a sales culture? Why? Why not?
3. How would you design such an invitation? How would you word it?

CHAPTER NINE

Projecting
Professionalism:
Writing with Class

LEARNING GOALS

After you have studied this chapter, you should be able to:

- Describe the importance of accuracy and tone in effective correspondence.

- Identify ten common business-writing problems that can impact both accuracy and tone of a document.

- Explain how reader self-interest can be better met by using reader-viewpoint wording.

- Contrast and provide examples of blanket tone versus personal tone and positive versus negative wording.

- Explain how to avoid tone problems, such as abrasiveness, preaching, false sincerity, and sexist language.

The Way It Is . . . Blending Accuracy and Tone

Two elements of any writing will have an overwhelming effect on the writer's professionalism and the document's success: accuracy and tone. **Accuracy** determines the writing's informativeness—how well it explains the ideas it intends to convey. **Tone** is the sum of those characteristics that reveal the writer's attitudes toward his or her subject and readers. Tone largely determines the success with which the writer influences the reader. Attention to these two elements allows the writer to project true professionalism.

Failure to be accurate can lead to all kinds of unwanted consequences ranging from the need to communicate "clarifying information" or corrections to downright embarrassment. Consider how the writer of the following messages must have felt:

Buy one hot dog for the price of two and receive a second hot dog *absolutely free!*

—Restaurant coupon

Our February 9 issue reported our earnings per share as $1.88 billion. The addition of "billion" was a typesetter's error, and we apologize for any ecstasy the error may have caused.

—AT&T employee magazine

There was a typo in lawyer Ed Morrison's ad. His logo is: "Your case is no stronger than your attorney," not "stranger."

—Tulsa, Oklahoma, *Gusher*

Potentially even more embarrassing moments can arise from a message that projects an inappropriate *tone*. For example, Suppose you are chairperson of a neighborhood volunteer committee, and you want to invite members to attend the next meeting. Which of these sentences conveys the best tone?

1. The next planning meeting will be held on May 13.

2. We look forward to working with you again at our next planning meeting on May 13.

3. You are expected to attend our next planning meeting on May 13.

How does each sentence convey a different tone? The tone is partly conveyed by what the sentence implies about the reader's relationship to the writer.

The first example is strictly informational—it conveys no feelings at all. The second seems more positive—it conveys a pleasant tone and an implication that working together in the past has been a pleasant experience. The third strikes us as too dictatorial, too demanding. It seems to indicate a boss-subordinate relationship that is probably inappropriate, especially in a volunteer organization. See how simple changes in even brief messages can change the whole tone?

Some people think they can avoid embarrassing moments by using spell- or grammar-checking software. Even the best of such software, however, fails to catch all polish errors or tone problems.

All Errors Are Not Equal

Writing consultant Gary Blake explains that "[S]ome writing problems may result in embarrassment; others do not necessarily embarrass you but can lead to significant losses of time, money and company stature."[1]

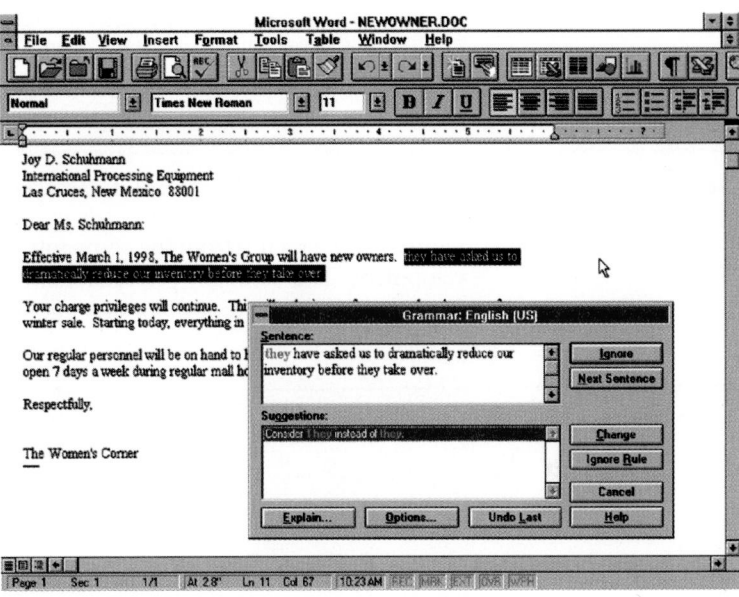

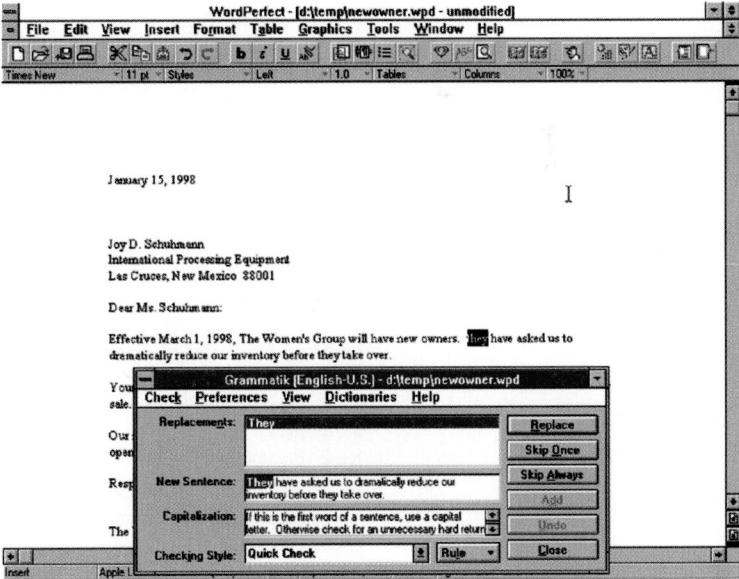

FIGURE 9-1

Grammar/style checker for word processing document.

Blake goes on to rank business writing problems as he sees on a 1- to 10-point scale, with 1 being a minor error that may embarrass but seldom does further damage and a 10 showing a problem likely to do substantial damage. Here is his ranking:

1. Spelling and capitalization
2. Grammar and punctuation
3. Misused words
4. Redundancy
5. Hedging

6. Lengthy paragraphs
7. Lengthy sentences
8. Passive language
9. Inappropriate tone
10. Poor organization

(A copy of Blake's article appears on page 231 at the end of this chapter.)

Later chapters discuss many of these problems. This chapter, however, focuses on projecting professionalism through accuracy and appropriate tone.

Business Communication Is Human Communication

Figure 9-2 is a memo from the company president to the manager of Training and Development. The company president isn't too happy about a recent training program. How do you like the tone of his message? How would you feel if you were Ms. Gardner?

FIGURE 9–2

Sample critique memo.

MEMORANDUM

TO: Training and Development
       c/o Michelle Gardner, Manager

FROM: Butch R. Rocco, President

DATE: February 16, 1998

       MY REACTIONS TO YOUR DEPARTMENT PRESENTATION
       ON TEAM BUILDING

Michelle, as department leader, I want you to convey my message to the other members of the group. Whenever I say "you" in this memo, I am talking to all department members unless otherwise noted. Tell them that.

Overall, I was disappointed in the presentation. It was lousy.

You gave a lot of information but few specifics on how to build and use team efforts. A training session like this needs to focus more on specific behaviors. It is not important that the listeners understand concepts so much. You got into your touchy-feely mode of teaching abstract ideas rather than actions because this is what you people are taught in college. Organizational training follows a different model.

You should have done a better job of identifying what you want us to do before charging forth with the presentation. What is it your employees can *do* now that they couldn't do before your presentation? I'd be hard pressed to answer that question.

Now for some more specific feedback:

1. The baseball metaphor cited from that guy's book was okay, but it reflects mostly just a way to remember that there are four main points—like bases. Just because something appears in a book does not mean it is the best way to present it. Don't blindly accept ideas or organizational patterns just because you see them in print.

2. Preparation would have smoothed out the flow between trainers as well as the individual segments. You didn't practice this, did you? The opening remarks especially should be tight, clear, and attention getting. Virtually all of you started with a simple statement of what you were going to talk about. This tells us a little but in itself doesn't motivate us to participate. Good intros create interest via something more clever than just a simple statement. I thought you learned that in school.

3. Several presenters used the masculine pronouns exclusively. I noticed this especially in Dave and Helton. For Dave, the problem is aggravated when he constantly referred to leaders and managers as "he." We'll catch all kinds of flak from the women's libbers in the company. Get into the habit of mixing gender references now, and you'll save a lot of potential aggravation later.

4. Your attempt to be interactive by asking the audience questions caused loss of control over the flow of the training session. People hate to be asked questions whose answer is totally obvious, e.g., "Why is it better to have a motivated employee?"

FIGURE 9–2 cont'd

5. Work on sticking within time limits. We don't have all day for this kind of training. Even after I told you we were running out of time, you went back to asking questions that went on too long. Let's be flexible, people. Know which points are most important and be able and willing to cut to the short version if necessary when time becomes a factor.

6. All your trainers used too many pauses and filler words. These "ahs" and "ums" drive me nuts. These are always the result of lack of practice or preparation. Avoid my least favorite word: "basically." Ugh! You people are supposed to be professional communicators. After all that's what training is: communication.

7. Handouts did not follow the training. These distracted rather than reinforced the message.

8. Visuals. You did exactly what I hate: You made transparencies out of photocopied pages from a book. These were far too busy.

9. Overall, focus needed. Learn this: *You must focus on a realistic "big idea"—something you can cover thoroughly in the time allowed.* What do you want your listener to *do*?

I am attaching to this memo the comments of the participants.

Let's get this right, people. If you can't handle this simple training, I'll bring in somebody from the outside and abolish our in-house training department. Your next training (in April) better show some substantial improvement. As you know, I am totally committed to a productive, pleasant, and friendly culture in our company.

FIGURE 9–2 cont'd

Apply the same human relations skills to your writing that you do in conversations.

To be effective human communicators, writers need to apply the same human relations skills they would use in a face-to-face encounter. Specifically, writers need to be especially sensitive to people's feelings, interests, wants, and needs. Failure to do so creates unnecessary strains on relationships including those established by the written word. The ability to get along with others, even on paper, is essential in successful business communication.

Although business communication is functional communication—that is, it tries to get something done—business communication is also *human* communication. A business document is a message from a person, a writer, to another person, a reader.

Human relations skills can be conveyed with appropriate tone.

The subsequent sections consider a few principles of human relations and how these might apply in written communication. The first and perhaps most basic principle follows.

People Are Strongly Interested in Themselves

Our primary motivation is self-interest.

It is the nature of the human being—and all other known creatures, for that matter—to be concerned with and motivated by their own personal needs, wants, and interests. This self-centeredness, or **egocentricity,** is normal and not particularly harmful unless carried to the extreme, when there is *no* caring about others.

When people speak or write, they reflect this egocentricity in their language. A study once conducted at a Midwestern university showed that every fifth word written or spoken by a human being is *I* or one of its derivations—*me, mine, my, we, ours, us.*[2]

Even though people are all self-centered to some degree, most learn to temper the tendency to focus on and talk about themselves exclusively. Indeed, the extremely egocentric person is avoided like someone with a contagious disease.

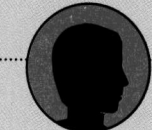

COMMUNICATOR'S PROFILE

Steve Summers, Master Muffler Shops

Steve Summers is president of a chain of muffler shops. Although we might not think of auto repair shops as places where sophisticated business communication takes place, they are. A major factor in the success of Steve's business lies in communicating with his customers, as well as among the different shop locations, efficiently and effectively.

When we asked Steve what communication process has been especially successful for him, he talked of his recent decision to install fax machines at each company location. "We use the machines to send and receive payroll information, vendor invoices with discrepancies, and most importantly, accounts receivable information (data on who owes us money) that must be keyed in at each location individually. Before we installed the machines, much of this communication was done by phone with several errors occurring regularly."

A major challenge occurs when service people fail to take notes on customer needs and work is left undone or done incorrectly. Steve constantly encourages his people to listen carefully and take notes.

Steve's pet peeve is when his people "beat around the bush" or fail to give him the full story when facing uncomfortable situations. Steve spends about 60 percent of his work day directly involved in communication with customers and employees.

Frank Fountain, Regional Senior Vice President, Bank of America.

When we asked executive, Frank Fountain, what makes a successful business communicator, he was quick to cite these characteristics:

- Enthusiasm, energy and commitment
- The ability to keep presentations and discussions relevant, to the point, and brief
- An openness to the involvement of other people and the ability to create opportunities for feedback and participation
- A clear sense of who the audience is and the willingness to personalize messages whenever possible to meet the needs and interests of the audience.

Frank expresses some frustration at the inevitable conflict between the efficiency of electronic media and the relative inefficiency, but greater effectiveness, of more personal forms of communication. Nonetheless, Bank of America is at the forefront of electronic media and "electronic mail has become the standard vehicle for sharing information, largely replacing memos and other interoffice correspondence."

"Despite these technological advances, however, personal conversations still remain a highly effective way to communicate," says Mr. Fountain.

The point here is that business writers can turn this egocentricity into an advantage if they recognize the reader's needs. Effective communicators learn to express concern and appreciation for the views of others in letters, memos, reports, proposals, and other documents.

People Prefer Reader-Centered Messages

The reader-oriented writer thinks of the reader first.

One important way to reflect consideration for your reader is by phrasing your message in terms of reader viewpoint. Expressing appropriate reader viewpoint involves much more than just selecting certain key words. Genuine **reader viewpoint** causes a document's tone to reflect a sincere interest in the reader. Self-centered writers think of themselves first. Reader-oriented writers think of and convey their messages in terms of what the reader wants or needs to know.

One "red flag" that the writer should look for is the words, *I, me, my,* and so forth found in abundance in written messages. Second or third person often conveys more reader interest and objectivity.

Please don't conclude that you should try to eliminate the use of I and its variations. To do so may be impossible in some cases. In other cases, your efforts may result in rather tortured syntax and excessive wordiness. Besides, the use of *I, we,* or *me* does not always indicate a lack of reader viewpoint. For example, the person who says,

"I hope you will be happy with this decision" is not really violating a reader viewpoint even though the sentence begins with the word I. The overall tone and sense of caring for the reader is far more important than simply avoiding the use of first-person pronouns.

Look at the following sample sentences and see the difference in the tone of the reader-oriented version compared with the **I-centered** one:

I Centered	Reader Viewpoint
I'm applying for this job because it would give me some great business experience.	Because you are looking for a person who can step right into the job, I think you'll be interested in my qualifications, which I feel could benefit your company.
I have received your business plan of October 23.	Thank you for your business plan of October 23.
We require that you sign the sales slip before we charge this purchase to your account.	For your protection, we charge your account only after you have signed the sales slip.
I have been a social studies teacher for twenty-two years.	My twenty-two years of experience in teaching social studies provides a strong background for a position in your training department.
I am sending this report back to you for an update.	So that you may update this report with the most current findings, it is being returned to you.
I think you'll be interested in our life insurance plan.	As a young father, you'll be interested in our life insurance plan tailored to the couple with small children and a limited budget.
We are happy to announce that we now offer a twenty-four-hour teller machine.	Now you can bank with us conveniently with a twenty-four-hour teller machine.

Use the reader viewpoint when your communication goals are to be sincere and friendly. The reader viewpoint conveys an interest in your reader and recognizes a principle of good human relations. Another principle to consider follows.

People Want to Be Treated as Individuals

The sweetest sound to most people is the sound of their own names.

You can improve the tone of written documents by phrasing your information as though talking to individuals rather than groups. A personally addressed business letter singles out a reader for individual attention. A letter with a **personal tone** conveys a more sincere regard for the specific person than one addressed to "Dear Customer" or "Dear Fellow Employee."

Names or other information can be easily inserted while most of the letter remains the same for all readers. Explore these possibilities when you consider a mailing.

Avoidance of the "Blanket Tone"

When a document makes the reader feel lost in the crowd, the **blanket tone** is responsible. For example, consider the blanket tone in the following excerpts from letters:

Blanket Tone	Personal Tone
When a thousand requests are received from prospective customers, we feel pleased. These requests show that our product is well received.	A copy of the booklet you requested is being sent to you today. Thank you for requesting it.
The cooperation of our charge customers in paying their accounts is appreciated. By paying on time, they allow us to give better service.	I certainly appreciate your paying the account. Your prompt payment allows us to give you better service.

The blanket tone makes the reader feel lost in the crowd.

Importance of Addressing Your Reader Directly

Strive to express ideas in terms of the individual reader's benefit. One way to do this is through direct address. Here, the writer makes "this means you!" statements. Each day television and radio commercials demonstrate examples of this approach. The announcer "personally" addresses each of the several million people who may be listening and attempts to make them feel that they are spoken to as individuals.

Direct address shows your readers how your message applies to them and how it can meet their individual needs in some way. One way to show this application is to clarify *features* and *benefits*, which Chapter twelve discusses.

People Prefer Positive Information

Positive language has a lot of pluses.

Positive language often conveys more information than does negative language. It also tends to be more upbeat with a more pleasant tone. Rather than telling a person what is *not* or what you *cannot* do, focus on the positive—what *is* or what you *can* do.

If you say "I do *not* live on 14th Street," it conveys very little information. It does not say where you do live; it only rules out one of the possibilities. Conversely, the positive statement, "I live on 20th Street" coveys a great deal more specific information. There is usually more information conveyed in a positive statement.

Positive language also has a more pleasant ring to the ear. Yet many common negative phrases still creep up in business writing. Some examples follow:

We *regret* to inform you that we cannot . . .

We have received your claim . . . (claim has a negative ring for most people)

Your *failure* to comply . . .

We *regret* that we cannot permit . . .

To illustrate the difference in tone between positive and negative word choices, here is an example: A corporate executive had to write to a local civic group denying a request to use the company's meeting facilities. To soften the refusal, however, the executive decided to let the group use a conference room, which might be somewhat small for its purpose, but was probably better than no room at all. Unfortunately, the executive was not sensitive to the effects of negative wording. She wrote the following:

> We <u>regret</u> to inform you that we <u>cannot</u> permit you to use our clubhouse for your meeting, as the Ladies' Book Club asked for it first. We can, however, let you use our conference room, but it seats <u>only</u> 25.

Review of the word connotations clearly brings out the negative (underlined) words; first, the positively intended message, "We regret to inform you," is an unmistakable sign of coming bad news. "Cannot permit" contains an unnecessarily harsh meaning. Notice how the one good-news part of the message is handicapped by the limiting word "only."

Had the writer searched for more positive ways of describing the same situation, she might have written this tactful response.

> As the Ladies' Book Club has reserved the clubhouse for Saturday, we can offer you the use of our conference room, which seats 25.

No negative words appear in this version. Both approaches yield the letter's primary objective of denying the request and offering an alternative, but the positive wording does the better job of building and holding goodwill for the company.

Let's look at some examples of negative and positive sentences. Listen to the tone of each. (The negative words are in italics.)

Negative Wording	Positive Wording
You *failed* to give us the part number of the muffler you ordered.	So that we may get you the muffler you want, will you please check your part number on the enclosed card?
Smoking is *not* permitted anywhere except in the lobby.	Smoking is permitted only in the lobby.
You were *wrong* in your conclusion, for paragraph three of our agreement clearly states . . .	You will agree after reading paragraph three of our agreement that . . .
We *regret* to inform you that we must *deny* your request for credit.	For the time being, we can serve you only on a cash basis.
We *cannot* deliver your order until next Wednesday.	We can deliver your order on Wednesday.

People Don't Like Abrasiveness

If you tend to have a somewhat abrasive personality, this will come across in your writing and can hurt the tone of your message. **Abrasiveness** refers to an irritating manner or tone, the kind of writing or speaking that sounds pushy or critical.

To determine if you tend to have an abrasive personality, you might ask yourself questions such as these.

- Are you often critical of others? When you supervise others, do you speak of "straightening them out" or "whipping them into shape"?
- Do you have a strong need to be in control? Must you have almost everything cleared with you?

Am I Abrasive?

Although it may be useful to ask yourself the preceding questions, a more important exercise is to ask your spouse, people you work with, your friends, or even your subordinates how they might respond to these same questions regarding you. It is often only by the feedback of others that you can get an accurate picture of your own personality. (Don't jump down their throats if they say you are abrasive!)

- Are you quick to rise to the attack and challenge?
- Do you have a strong need to debate with others? Do your discussions often become arguments?
- Do you regard yourself as more competent than your peers? Does your behavior let others know that?

The abrasive personality will tend to communicate in a manner that can be irritating to others. Try to recognize in yourself the degree to which you have a strong need to control or dominate other people. If you suspect that you do have this need, it would be important for you to make an extra effort to soften the abrasiveness of your written communications.

Remember that there is a major difference between being abrasive and being assertive. **Assertiveness** simply means that you express your feelings and observations, normally phrased, in a manner that is nonthreatening to other people. For example, instead of saying to someone, "You don't make any sense," the assertive person would say, "I'm having a difficult time understanding what you're saying." Rather than saying, "Deadbeats like you burn me up," the assertive person might say, "People who consistently make late payments cause us a lot of extra work and lost revenue." Few people get offended by the assertive individual. Indeed, one definition of assertiveness is: "being pleasantly direct."

There is a difference between abrasive and assertive.

I always try to keep my words soft, honeyed, and warm, because I never know when I will be called upon to eat them.

—Senator Everett Dirkson

People Don't Like to Be Lectured to or Preached at

Human beings tend to be independent creatures, and they like to be treated as equals, not talked down to. Thus, writing that suggests that writer-reader relations are not equal is apt to make the reader unhappy.

Usually, preaching in documents is not intended; it occurs when the writer is trying to convince the reader of something, as in this example.

> You must take advantage of savings like this if you are to be successful. The pennies you save pile up. In time you will have dollars.

In this case, the point may be appropriate, but saying something so elementary, as if the reader did not know it, is insulting. Likewise, messages that "remind" the reader of obligations may irritate.

> When you agreed to serve on this committee, you knew that you had a responsibility to meet each week.

> The extension of credit is a privilege we give to those who have shown trustworthiness. Along with this privilege goes the obligation to make prompt, regular payments on your account.

People Can Spot False Sincerity

An overall impression of sincerity—an expression of caring—is a composite of key points in this chapter. Don't overdo the goodwill techniques (like referring too often to your reader by name in the message), but do have a sincere desire to convey the best possible image of your company.

Likewise, avoid terms that suggest **false sincerity.** One example of such exaggeration showed up in a form letter from a company president that was sent out to each person who signed up for a new charge account. This had a touch of unbelievability.

> I was delighted today to see your name listed among Belko's new charge account customers.

Your overall tone can be more important than the words you use. (Cartoon Features Syndicate.)

"I took out the 'sincerely yours' because I don't think you meant what you said."

Consider the following one, taken from an adjustment letter of a large department store:

We are extremely pleased to be able to be of service to you and want you to know that your satisfaction means more than anything in the world to us.

Such obviously false sincerity comes across as pure baloney. Such gushiness sounds condescending and downright silly. That can't help but damage relationships between the writer and reader. Avoid letting goodwill attempts degenerate into false sincerity.

People May Be Offended by Sexist Language

A discussion of appropriate tone for business writing would be incomplete without a discussion of **sexist language.** Historically, language has attributed masculine-gender words to certain jobs (businessman, salesman, stock boy, and so on) and, by doing so, implied that such positions are inappropriate for females. Likewise, the rules of grammar indicated that when you were unclear as to whether a pronoun referred to a man or woman, you should use the male form—for example, "A speaker should avoid overuse of *his* notes.

In recent years, society has become more sensitive to the between-the-lines meanings conveyed by certain language stereotypes. A "speaker" could as easily be a woman, so why refer to "*his* notes"?

Perhaps more important, language gender helps to create stereotypes. Terms like *mailman* imply that all people who deliver mail are (or should be!) men. Some readers are offended by language that seems to exclude one of the sexes. You run the risk of demeaning at least half your readers by using sexist language. Whether or not *you* are offended by such language is irrelevant. Someone you write or speak to could be. Here are some guidelines to help you avoid potentially damaging sexist language.[3]

Some readers are offended by language that seems to exclude one of the sexes.

1. Use *he* or *she* only to refer to a specific man or woman.

    Biased: If a manager knows what *he* is doing, *he'll* be sensitive to *his* workers. (Implies that all managers are men.)

    Specific: *If Mr. Jones,* a manager, knows what *he* is doing, he'll be sensitive to his workers.

2. If gender is unknown or statement may apply to both genders, you may use "he or she."

    Biased: Please ask the receptionists in all offices to count the number of times *she* is asked that question.

    Unbiased: Please ask the receptionists in all offices to count the number of times *he or she* is asked that question.

3. Use genderless terms like *one, person, audience, listener,* or their plurals.

Biased:	The office manager is responsible for harmony. *She* must know *her* job and those of the workers.
Better:	The office manager is responsible for harmony. That *person* must know the workers' jobs.

4. Substitute *the* for *his, her,* or *hers.*

Biased:	The sales manager has to solve many problems with *his* team.
Better:	The sales manager has to solve many problems with *the* team.

5. Use nonsexist plural instead of the universal *man* or *he.*

Biased:	*Man* has certain needs and wants. *His* needs are many.
Better:	*Men* and *women* have certain needs and wants. *Their* needs are many.

6. Eliminate pronouns by rephrasing (a great many variations are possible).

Biased:	Interviews are given when *he* schedules them.
Better:	Interviews are given when scheduled.
Biased:	*Her* performance review showed that *her* productivity was below established standards.
Better:	*The employee's* performance review indicated productivity below established standards.

7. Use job titles and functions instead of sex-specific titles.

Biased:	The *firemen* took turns preparing meals.
Better:	The *firefighters* took turns preparing meals.
Biased:	The department *chairwoman* called the meeting.
Better:	The department *head* called the meeting.

8. Avoid mistakes in the inside address and salutation when you are unsure of the preferred title (Mrs., Miss, Ms.) or gender (names like Lynn, Dana, or Chris; or when initials only are used).

Avoid if unsure:	Mrs. Terry Franklyn
Instead:	Dear Terry Franklyn
Avoid if unsure:	Dear Mr. Jackson
Instead:	Dear T. J. Jackson
	(or omit salutation entirely)

Applying good principles of human relations and avoiding the common pitfalls described in this chapter can do much to create appropriate tone in your messages. Business communication is functional in nature, but it need not lack human qualities. A sensitivity to tone helps a writer to sound human. The positive overall impression created in the minds of your readers will be worth the slight extra effort expended to say it with feeling.

Understanding the Basics

• To create appropriate tone in a message, recognize that business communication is human communication. People's feelings must be considered.

• The ability to get along with people—even on paper—is essential to successful business communication.

• People have strong self-interests and are motivated by their personal needs and wants. Good writers focus on the needs of their readers.

• Writers show consideration for their readers and project a more sincere tone if they phrase ideas in terms of reader viewpoint.

• People don't like to be confused when reading. The skillful writer tries to be clear.

• People prefer to be treated like individuals. Good writers personalize their messages whenever possible.

• Positive language tends to convey more information than does negative language. Positive wording also tends to sound more pleasant.

• Abrasiveness violates human relations principles and can cause serious communication problems.

• Lecturing to or preaching at people damages the tone of a message.

• An exaggerated "sincerity" gives a false tone.

• Sexist language can demean some people and seriously affect the tone of a message.

KEY TERMS AND CONCEPTS

accuracy	assertiveness	blanket tone
message tone	sexist language	abrasiveness
reader viewpoint	egocentricity	false sincerity
personal tone	I-centered	positive versus negative wording

QUESTIONS FOR FURTHER THOUGHT

1.   If tone is so important in written communication, why do you see so much correspondence with inappropriate tone?

2.   Of all the tonal areas discussed in the chapter, which area do you feel will help you the most in your career?

3.   Should you ever write a letter when you are angry? If so, why? If not, why not?

4.   What kinds of terms convey abrasiveness?

5.   How can we be assertive without being abrasive? Write five samples of each.

It is Recommended that you Write Clearly

Some writing problems may result in embarrassment: others do not necessarily embarrass you, but can lead to significant losses of time, money and company stature. To help you recognize the differences. I've ranked major business writing problems on the standard 1–10 scale, with "1" being a problem that will cause minor embarrassment and "10" being a problem that can seriously harm the health of your organization:

1) *Spelling and capitalization.* Misspell an occasional difficult word (e.g., supersede, judgment, questionnaire) or capitalize a few words that shouldn't be, and you may lose face in front of an English major, but you won't lose business—as long as you don't misspell a client's name, that is.

2) *Grammar and punctuation.* The run-of-the-mill error (leaving out an occasional comma or hyphen, splitting an infinitive, using a dangling modifier) isn't going to send customers out the door. I'm not suggesting that all such mistakes are harmless, however. Here's a notorious case in which poor punctuation did result in a business loss: By leaving out a strategic hyphen in the sentence. "I need the six foot long rods by Friday," a supervisor caused a $25,000 mistake. (He needed six-foot-long rods not the six foot-long rods he received.)

3) *Misused words.* Although Mark Twain cautioned us to "use the right word, not its second cousin," business people are forever writing "continual" when they mean "continuous," "i.e." when they mean "e.g." and "anxious" when they mean "eager." As a writing consultant, I place great value on accuracy: as a businessman. I know that the misuse of words rates only a 3 on our scale.

4) *Redundancy.* There are two types of redundancy: a) repeating your thoughts, which stems from a lack of organization, a mistrust that you've explained something well the first time, or an attempt at padding a message, and b) redundant phrases such as "consensus of opinion" or "foreign imports." . . .

5) *Hedging.* When you use "weasel" words and phrases (e.g., "it is my understanding," "possibly," "perhaps," "could"), you drain your writing of authority and cause your reader to regard you as wishy-washy. . . . Customers and prospects become distrustful when they are exposed to a lack of forthrightness.

6) *Lengthy paragraphs.* When business writers create paragraphs that fill up an entire PC screen, their readers frequently find an excuse to avoid reading any further.

7) *Lengthy sentences.* Long sentences, especially ones filled with detailed introductory clauses, can derail your readers' train of thought. In tandem with lengthy paragraphs, they increase the odds that your reader will wind up confused and put off. While you shouldn't feel compelled to create only "the cat sat on the mat" sentences, you must be ready to break up most sentences of 30 words or more.

Now we've come to the problems that affect the—forgive me!—"bottom line":

8) *Passive language.* In technical writing, when what is being done is more important than who is doing it, passive language is not only acceptable—it's preferable. But for the rest of the business world, passive language comes across as weak and tentative.

Thirty-five years ago, the noted lexicographer Eric Partridge referred to passive language as "passing the buck." When you write "It is recommended . . ." instead of "I (or we) recommend," you are walking away from taking responsibility for your actions. . . .

9) *Inappropriate tone, vagueness.* The wrong tone—too abrupt, too negative, condescending, stuffy—can destroy a message and cost you customers. Be on the lookout for writing that adds a negative spin ("John has neglected to show up for the meeting"), makes the writing stuffy or pompous ("We are in receipt of your letter of the 25th"), or overly humble ("Thank you for taking five minutes from your busy schedule to meet with me").

Vague phrases ("ASAP," "at your earliest convenience") lead to lost productivity by inviting follow-up phone calls to clarify the message.

10) *Poor organization.* A business person who writes without organizing his or her thoughts is like a commercial pilot who takes off without a flight plan. In business, failure to come to the point or lead the reader through a document is a recipe for being misunderstood and ignored by prospects, customers and upper management.

Of all the writing problems that plague business people, none is more far-reaching or likely to cripple profits and profitability than lack of organization. Documents that meander usually fail in their attempt to either inform or persuade.

With writing skills, as with so many things, what you don't know will hurt you. Just as the small storm can turn torrential; any of the problems on my scale can become serious, depending on circumstances or on frequency.

Mr. Blake, a writing consultant based in Port Washington, N.Y., is co-author of "The Elements of Business Writing" and "The Elements of Technical Writing" (Macmillan).

Applying Your Knowledge

1. The author of this article cites several examples of misused words. Explain what each term means.
2. Rewrite the examples identified under "inappropriate tone, vagueness," to reflect better phrasing.
3. How can a writer best overcome the problem of poor organization? (Hint review Chapter 8)?

Applying Your Skills

ACTIVITY 9-1: Sentence Rewrites

Rewrite the following sentences to improve the tone. Then explain briefly what tone problems you saw in the original version.

1. I am returning the unused portion of the enclosed Chococrunchy candy bar because I was not fully satisfied with it. I want my money back.

2. I am doing a report on the global strategies the multinational corporations use to monopolize and exploit other countries. Please send me information on everything your company does to others.

3. If you do not pay your overdue account immediately, your credit will be severely damaged.

4. Why don't you answer my application letter for a trainee job with your company? I know I'm the best-qualified applicant you've seen.

5. Remember, it is better to give than receive. For this reason, we want you to give to the annual Clarksville Freedom Festival with all your might, mind, and strength.

6. Like most people, you are probably aware of the great money salesmen in the insurance industry make. For this reason, we want you to come on in for an interview in what may be the greatest career on earth.

7. I'm Ted Simmons, and I want to sell you a car.

8. Because you claim that the package was never received, I'll have my girl deliver a replacement right away.

9. Every salesman in this store is thoroughly trained in providing exceptional customer service. Therefore, it is obvious to me that you must have said something to set off the fistfight.

10. Your damage claim, like all such claims received, will be processed through our normal channels.

11. Obviously your qualifications are significantly less than what we are looking for in this position.

12. You failed to fill out the necessary paperwork for the loan.

13. Women typically have poorer repayment records than men. Therefore, I am rejecting your application for the loan.

14. Because virtually everyone wants to purchase season tickets for the upcoming season, I am sure you can see that we must be very selective of which fans are permitted this privilege.

15. We have had all kinds of people apply for the job: a fireman, a mailman, a busboy, even a stewardess! We cannot consider any more people.

ACTIVITY 9-2: What's Wrong with Butch's Memo?

Let's take another look at Butch Rocco's blistering memo to his training manager (pages 218–220). Consider the tone of his message. What possible problems are likely to arise from this document? Identify examples of

1. I-centered phrases
2. Blanket tone
3. Negative wording
4. Abrasiveness
5. Preachiness
6. False sincerity
7. Sexist language

ACTIVITY 9-3: You're the Critic

Collect a sample of at least three business memos or letters, preferably ones that have been individually written, not produced by an advertising or sales organization. Review each in the same way you did the Butch Rocco memo in Activity 9-2.

ACTIVITY 9-4: Teaching Your Assistant about Tone

The following is the body of a letter written by one of your assistants. He prepared this in response to a customer's request for a credit extension. The customer wanted to make no payment on her account this month but pay extra next month. The customer's credit history has not been outstanding in the past. She has been out of work several times and was, therefore, late in paying twice in the past seven months. Her work situation seems more stable now.

Critique the tone of the letter. Then edit or rewrite the letter. Be prepared to show your assistant (or explain to the class) how you improved the tone.

```
Dear Ms. Hocking:


It is impossible for us to extend you another month
before your next payment on your auto loan. Already
you have been late twice this year. Such behavior
shall have serious detrimental effects on your
credit rating.

I sympathize with your problem. We all have prob-
lems. I find myself short of cash every now and then
too. But I always—always—pay my debts first, before
spending money on luxuries. Your auto loan is a
special obligation; one that should not be taken
lightly.

If we let you off the hook this month, we'd have to
do the same for all of our other thousands of cus-
tomers. I'm sure you see that would be out of the
question because we are in this business to make a
profit.

My suggestion to you (the same suggestion I've made
to other ladies who seem to have such problems) is
to forego some other spending urge and instead make
your car payment on time, as agreed upon.

Thank you for doing business with Steve's Bank and
do have a nice day.



    Sincerely,
```

PERFORMING
on the Job

CASE 9-1 I Must Put It in Writing

The following is a memo to the manager of the department from a member of the team. It was written after a meeting with the whole team in which a proposal was presented by the manager which was somewhat of a surprise to the rest of the group.

MEMO

Date: June 20, 1995

To: Bob [Manager]

From: Jack [One of the team members]

RE: Using Alex's Printing for all copy work

I want to put in writing the concern I expressed in our team meeting this afternoon. The proposed arrangement with Alex's brings back negative feelings of previous experience and is of great concern to me.

I believe we need more flexibility in the use of company resources. Limiting us to one source for all copying and printing is a bad idea. If this issue were put to a vote, mine would be no. I know that your recommendation will be made to top management and that they will, ultimately, make the decision. My request is that they realize that I do not support this recommendation.

Three problems with the proposed contract with Alex's are as follows:

1. The involvement of the company president's son looks unethical.

2. Unclear reasons exist for limiting us to this one vendor.

3. The inconvenience of going "outside" for even small copy jobs is a problem.

I didn't speak up in the meeting because it seemed that you really want this arrangement. If you feel I am being insubordinate, that is not my intention. I'll be glad to discuss this with you at your convenience.

---

1. Describe your perception of the accuracy and tone of this memo.
2. Is the memo professional? Why? Why not?
3. If you were Jack, would you have written such a memo? If so, would it be different? If not, why?
4. If you were a consultant to this organization, and Bob described this situation and let you read the memo, what would you recommend he do?

CASE 9-2 Heated Memo

Marian was steamed. For the third time in as many weeks, she had to reprimand Harry and Sally about their flirtatious behavior on the job. She decided to write a "memo to file"—a memo she would put in their personnel files to document this unprofessional behavior in case further disciplinary action is needed. She also determined that she would give both of them a copy and route another copy to her boss. Here is the body of her memo:

MEMO

I've told you two lovebirds that this crap has got to cease. It's fine to like each other but your constant grinning, fondling (backrubs, brushing against each other, hand holding) and loving looks make you look like a couple of goofballs. Get a clue, people. Our customers don't give a damn about your romantic interests. They want your full attention, not cutesy behavior. Grow up.

If I catch either of you flirting again, I'll fire you.

Case Questions

1. What do you think of Marian's memo? How does it measure up in terms of accuracy? Tone?

2. Assuming that Harry and Sally do, in fact, display flirting behaviors that detract from their job performance, how would you handle the problem?

3. How do you feel about the "memo to file" idea? Would you send a copy to the boss? Why or why not?

CHAPTER TEN

Writing Routine, Informative, and Goodwill Messages:
Simple, Quick, and Powerful

LEARNING GOALS

After you have studied this chapter, you should be able to:

- Recognize how goodwill messages can strengthen relationships.

- Write direct, complete, and friendly routine and goodwill messages.

- Create effective relationship-building messages for personal and organizational purposes.

- Write a news release.

- Understand the role of goodwill messages in professional and organizational success.

- Welcome the opportunities for goodwill message sending.

The Way It Is . . . The Gift of Appreciation

Dennis Boykin will never forget his first two weeks at Mary Kay Cosmetics, where he works on the cosmetics production line. He received a free calculator (given to all plant employees for no lost-time accidents in the previous month), a birthday card (signed by Mary Kay herself), and a Thanksgiving turkey. Boykin told us he was "flabbergasted," having never worked at a company that bestowed gifts for anything.

This barrage of presents is not unusual for Mary Kay. The company runs on a high-octane mixture of recognition and rewards. Founder and chief inspiration/cheerleader Mary Kay Ash wouldn't have it any other way. As she told us when we met her in her Dallas office: "Every single person you meet has a sign around his or her neck that says, 'Make me feel important.' If you can do that, you'll be a success not only in business but in life too. God didn't have time to make a nobody. Everybody is a somebody in my book."

Mary Kay herself spends a lot of time trying to make her employees feel important. The night before we interviewed her, she had been up late signing 400 birthday cards. The cards offered a free lunch for two at the company restaurant (a full lunch here can usually be had for less than $3) or free movie tickets. Ash sends employees gifts on other occasions, too. For a newborn child, she sends a little silver bank shaped like a duck. For newlyweds, she sends a silver bowl. Every employee gets a turkey on the Monday before Thanksgiving because Mary Kay knows it takes a full three days for a frozen turkey to thaw properly. On every anniversary of hire, employees receive a card personally signed by Mary Kay. Employees also receive a $100 U.S. savings bond after every five years of service. Ten-year veterans are profiled in Heartline, the company newsletter, and honored in a special ceremony in Mary Kay's office. She tries to make employees feel impor-

tant even when there's no special occasion by providing fresh flowers and white tablecloths in the cafeteria, and perfume and makeup in the rest rooms. The reason for all this? According to Ash, "Appreciation is the oil that makes things run."[1]

If appreciation is truly the oil that makes things run inside a company, think what it can do for customer relationships. Figure 10–1 shows an example of a thank-you note sent to customers.

Letters like the following one are commonplace in businesses that sell high price items like cars, trucks, appliances, furniture, and the like. Companies are increasingly recognizing the value of the thank you note to buyers of even lower priced items. An example is the thank you note shown in Chapter Three (page 65) written by the owner of an athletic shoe store.

Why do this? The answer is because such correspondence can form the beginning of an ongoing business relationship. It tells the customer that he or she is important to you and that you are available to serve further. Goodwill messages are an often overlooked way to create that all-important one-to-one relationship, thus meeting a basic organizational need.

The letter in Figure 10–1 moves in the right direction but isn't as effective as it could be. The end of this chapter returns to this letter and provides some ideas to strengthen it.

Please remember that there is no absolute, *right* formula for creating such a message. It's effectiveness ultimately depends on the receiver's interpretation.

This chapter considers the power of routine, informative, and goodwill messages. When you have finished this chapter, you should be able to prepare effective one-to-one relationship-building messages with ease.

JAN 6, 1995

Helen L. Timm
Paul R. Timm
81 E. 2000 St.
Orem UT 84058

Dear Paul and Helen:

We appreciate your business and the opportunity to work with you. Below is some information you will find helpful.

We normally receive your license plates about four weeks after all the paperwork from the sale is completed. We will send you a postcard when the plates are ready to be picked up here at our Cashier's window.

The title is issued by the state government and will be sent directly to the firm that loaned the money for the vehicle. If you paid cash, the title should reach you about two months following the completion of the paperwork from the sale.

Our Service and Parts Departments are open Monday through Friday for regular service. A courtesy bus is available at no charge in the Provo-Orem area Monday-Friday. Please call when your car needs servicing to make an appointment in order to minimize delays.

FIGURE 10–1

Companies recognize the value of the customer thank you letter. (Reprinted with permission from Christensen Chevrolet/ Buick/Geo.)

Chevrolet, Buick and Geo all send out important survey forms to a percentage of our customers during the first month after the sale and again at 5 months. We strive to make our customers *very satisfied*. If you are not, please let us know first. When you receive a survey form, please take the time to fill it out and return it in the envelope provided.

We care about you as our customer and look forward to a continued business relationship. Our goal is to be deserving of your future business.

Sincerely yours,

Mike Echevarria

Mike Echevarria

Marc Ensign

Marc Ensign
General Manager

FIGURE 10-1 cont'd

Routine Informative Message

Routine informative messages answer simple questions or grant easy requests.

Routine messages answer reader questions. Typical examples are letters that ask for or offer explanations, or that order a product being advertised. The receiver of such a message is likely to be happy to get it—it conveys good news from his or her perspective. Minimally, it answers a question and often presents an opportunity for relationship building.

Routine letters and memos are an essential part of business. For many companies, they represent the bulk of business writing. Some common topics for routine writing include the following:

- Routine announcements (Figure 10–3)
- Inquiries about products or services (Figure 10–4)
- Transmittal memos accompanying reports (Figure 10–5)
- Letters granting a request (Figure 10–6)
- Letters of introduction (Figure 10–7)
- Requests for credit information (Figure 10–8)
- Acknowledgement letter (Figure 10–9)
- Confirmation letter (Figure 10–10)

Following are examples of each of these types of routine messages. Other routine letters may fall into this category, but these samples give you a sense of the types of messages. Take a few moments to critique these sample letters. How might you change their tone or content to better fit your personal communication style? Remember, just because these appear in print in a book does not mean they are perfect for all occasions and audiences. Your personal touch can dramatically improve these. Remember, communication is an art, and you are the artist.

FIGURE 10–3
Routine announcement.

INTEROFFICE MEMO

TO: All Employees

FROM: P. R. Kershner, Personnel Director

DATE: September 25, 199X

SUBJECT: COLLEGE TUITION PROGRAM NOW AVAILABLE TO ALL EMPLOYEES

Any full-time company employee may now apply for tuition payment for evening classes at Local State University. Courses taken need not be job related.

An orientation meeting will be held to explain this new benefit to interested employees at 5 P.M. on Friday, October 1. The program will be explained at that time. Attending the meeting will in no way obligate you to participate in the program. The meeting will last approximately one hour. Written details, applications, and so on will be furnished.

We hope to see you next Friday.

JULIA BECKER CONSULTING SERVICES
MARKETING RESEARCH SERVICES
332 Severon Street
Chicago, IL 60608

May 2, 1998

Software Specialists
1104 Silicon Lane
Houston, TX 7000

Please send me further information on your new Num-
berKruncher statistical software package. I use an
IBM personal computer with Pentium chip and 12 megs
of RAM. I am looking for easy-to-use software that
will permit me to do statistical analysis of marketing data.

Also, please identify the nearest dealer where I
can see a demonstration of your product.

I expect to make a purchasing decision within 30
days. My office telephone number is (802) 555-0001.

Sincerely,

Julia Becker

Julia Becker
Consultant

FIGURE 10–4

Inquiry about a
product.

MEMORANDUM

TO: Sales Managers, Jacksonville Branch
FROM: Alan Hamarabi, Branch Manager
DATE: March 16, 199X

SALES RESULTS BY TEAMS FOR FEBRUARY, 199X

Attached are the February sales results for each
team in the branch. Overall, I am pleased with the
trends. Four of the five teams have shown increases
in major product sales, whereas the fifth, although
leveling off at essentially the same volume as January, has maintained good results with several new
sales representatives.

Special congratulations go to Brenda Wetherly's
team for a nice improvement in overall volume.

If you have questions or concerns about this report, give me a call.

FIGURE 10–5

Transmittal memo
accompanying a report.

MODERN BUILDER SUPPLY, INC.
Business to Business Materials
Highway 101
Murfreesboro, TN 33778

March 26, 199X
Ms. Jaralyn Reemes
207 W. Seventh
Buffalo, NY 14026

Dear Ms. Reemes:

Thank you for your credit application, and welcome!
We've established an initial credit line of $8,000
for you and Reemes Outdoor Products, Inc. This
should make your day-to-day business with us more
convenient. We'll review your available credit periodically to make sure it sufficiently covers your
purchasing needs.

We have enclosed with this letter a pamphlet explaining the policies and billing procedures for
your new credit account.

We consider it a privilege to grant you credit.
We'll work hard to earn your business and show you
how important you are to Modern Builder Supply.
Just bring the enclosed card to me the next time
you're in, and our staff will do the rest to make
sure you get the special attention you deserve.

Working with us has just gotten a little easier.
Working with you has always been our pleasure!

Sincerely,

Rodney Peterson

Rodney Peterson
President

Enclosures

FIGURE 10-6

Letter granting a
request.

BRONSON SECURITY SYSTEMS

"Keeping an Eye on Your Assets"
1001 Upper Ridge Rd., Suite 665
Wayne, MI 45776

Mr. Blaine Wilson, President
NuWay Technology
12777 Highway 50
Orlando, FL 27002

Dear Mr. Wilson:

At Bronson Security Systems, we're always looking
for better ways to serve your needs for plant security. I think we've found another in Arnold (Bucky)
Corridini.

Bucky has joined us as Coordinator of Surveillance
Services. He will help us maintain, and improve,
the high standard of quality service you've come to
expect from Bronson.

Of all the candidates we considered for this position, we found Bucky offered the best combination
of ability, enthusiasm, and professionalism. Most
important, he is the kind of person we want working
on your account at NuWay Technology—the best.

I'm confident you'll see this valuable addition to
our staff as further evidence that we are committed
to our clients. I've asked Bucky to introduce himself personally to you within the next week. If
there's anything he or I can do for you, please
call.

Thank you for doing business with us.

Sincerely,

Guido Lambini

Guido Lambini
President

FIGURE 10–7
Letter of introduction.

BAUER'S AUTOMOTIVE SUPPLY
1256 Bailey Parkway
Oklahoma City, OK 34567

June 12, 199X
John Stedaman, Manager
Far Western Welding Supply
122 Main Street
Clovis, NM 12345

Dear Mr. Stedaman:

Thomas J. Branner, one of your customers, currently an applicant for wholesale credit at Bauer's Automotive, has provided us with your name as a reference for previous business experience. We distribute custom truck parts and automotive supplies to repair shops and dealers.

Mr. Branner's total expenditures are estimated to average $75,000 each year. We would appreciate any information that could help us make the right decision for our company and our customer. Would you please specify on the enclosed form the length of your business association with Mr. Branner, the approximate volume of business done with you annually, and his manner of handling such business?

Any information you provide will remain in strict confidence, and we'll be happy to assist you with similar references if such an opportunity presents itself.

Thank you in advance for your prompt attention.

Sincerely,

Victor Bauer

Victor Bauer
General Manager

FIGURE 10–8
Request for credit information.

THE LEGISLATURE OF THE STATE OF ARIZONA
Honorable William T. Jackson
District 41 Representative
Phoenix, AZ 77890

Ms. Susan Barker-James
441 Freemont Lane
Oshkosh, AZ 77248

Dear Susan:

I'd be delighted to be part of your club's political action panel to discuss our state's current
budget crisis.

I understand that you'll meet on Thursday, July 14,
at 8:00 P.M. at the Country Club Civic Room.

It is hoped that my comments will be useful to your
club members. I'd be happy to entertain questions
from the audience.

Sincerely,

William T. Jackson

William T. Jackson
State Representative, District 41

FIGURE 10–9
Acknowledgment letter.

PEAT, COOPER, AND SELLS
Security Brokers
11990 Biscayne Blvd.
Miami, FL 32800

February 18, 199X
Mr. William A. Southwood
218 South LaGrange
Tallahassee, FL 32304

Dear Bill:

This will confirm the arrangements made by telephone today for you to visit our office on Monday, March 7, 199X at 9:30 A.M. Our office is located in the Biscayne Tower Building, Suite 2100.

During the time you are with us, Bill, you will meet a number of people operating at different levels of responsibility in the firm. Your day will include having lunch with two of our staff members, giving you the opportunity to talk with some of our recently employed college graduates. You will probably finish the day around 4:00 P.M.

If you have any questions, please call me collect at (305) 374-3951. We all look forward to seeing you on March 7 and discussing with you the opportunities that are yours at Peat, Cooper, and Sells.

Sincerely,

Ralph D. Potter
Managing Broker

FIGURE 10–10
Confirmation letter.

Three General Guidelines for Routine Messages

Writers should apply the following principles when writing routine letters: Be *direct*, be *complete*, and be *friendly*.

Be Direct

A writer can do little to destroy the effectiveness of a good-news letter. The intent is to tell readers something they are glad to hear. Efficiency of communication should be an important consideration here. These letters are generally brief—although not curt—and to the point. A direct order of presentation (BIF) should normally be used; the central point of the letter should come first. If you are writing to order 200 Disco-trimmers, start your letter with, "Please send me 200 Disco-trimmers." The big idea of the letter may then be followed by other relevant subordinate information that clarifies details, such as "I am enclosing a check for $10,496," and "Please ship them to our warehouse at. . . ."

This may seem like a ridiculously simple issue, but many routine letters fail to get directly to the point. They might begin, "We are impressed with your advertisements for the amazing Disco-trimmer," or "We are interested in exploring the possibility of doing business with you." You simply don't need this stuff. Your reader isn't likely to miss the lack of pleasantries because the main thrust of your letter is good news. Enclosing a big check can help a reader overlook any unnecessary verbiage. Get directly to the point.

If you want to order fifty exotic air plants, *don't* start your letter like the following:

Dear Exotic Imports:

We are interested in the possibility of doing business with Exotic Imports. We recently read your advertisement in *Exquisite Homes and Gardens* and were very impressed.

Would it be possible for us to order fifty exotic air plants?

A better way to start would be:

Dear Exotic Imports:

Please send fifty exotic air plants to. . . .

Again, be direct. Put the big idea (what you want the reader to do) first. Then follow up with the details. Surprise endings may have a place in literature and storytelling, but they have no place in business and professional communications.

The preceding samples of routine writing show appropriate directness.

Be Complete

The letter that is incomplete may fail to do the job. Here is a true horror story that illustrates our point: A company's direct mail sales letter, personalized with typed inside address and personal salutation, was to be sent to 100,000 potential customers. The letter ended with the instructions that the reader "could take advantage of the offer" by simply initialing the letter and returning it in the prepaid envelope.

Be sure that even the simplest letter is complete.

However, to save the expense of having typists insert the 100,000 inside addresses and personal salutations, a budget-minded official requested that the entire message be printed and that all inside addresses be omitted. The salutation was changed to the general, printed, "Dear Customer." The result was that the company received more than 11,000 of the letters back, but no one had the slightest idea whose initials they were![2]

Other than firing the "budget minded official" who decided to omit the inside addresses, nothing could be done to recoup the wasted costs of such a mailing. Not only did the company waste the expense of a 100,000-piece mailing (which could cost about $50,000 in today's costs), but it also incurred the displeasure of the 11,000 who expected to get something back but didn't.

Another error committed by some people is to mail a batch of letters without sufficient postage—and have them all come back. The cost of a postal scale is a good investment.

So be complete, and pay attention to details.

Sometimes in an effort to be brief and efficient, a writer forgets to include needed details. Some examples follow:

- The return address is missing (although the reader may need to respond).
- The reader is not told to whom to make a check payable.
- The letter is not signed, implying that it may have been mailed without the writer's final approval. (This problem happens often.)
- Crucial details are left out, such as the address of a meeting place.
- Inaccurate information is included. (A writer confirmed an appointment but for the wrong date, for example.)
- No telephone number is provided, although a telephone call would be the obvious way to handle the response.

> Another, although less common example of a good-news letter that flops is illustrated by one received from the president of a company where a friend of mine had applied for a job. The opening statement read: "You are hereby appointed accounting manager. . . ." The letter sounded more like a coronation than an offer of employment. Although my friend was pleased to be offered the position, the tone clearly assumed that he would jump at the opportunity. Instead, the presumptuous sound of the letter turned him off. He declined the job. Even in good-news letters, some sensitivity to tone is necessary.

Be Friendly

A good friend and colleague opened a letter the following way:

> Dear Paul:
>
> Have you noticed that I ask you for something, then you do it for me, then you don't even hear from me for months? Please *don't* notice that! And I teach my students that a thank you note is the most important letter they will learn to write!

Her personality and sense of humor jumps right off the page. Her conversational tone is delightful and, of course, her "apology" quickly accepted.

A routine letter can fail if you leave out important details.

For routine, informative letters, be *direct* (using BIF), be *complete*—anticipate what the reader will need in order to do what you want—and be *friendly*. Today's business world appreciates a human tone.

Goodwill Letters

A **goodwill letter** is one you write even though you don't have to. Customers who receive sincere, personal messages from people they do business with (like the Chevy dealership letter on pages 241–242) will likely harbor more favorable feelings toward that person and organization.

Likewise, few things make an employee feel better than to receive a brief message of appreciation, congratulations, sympathy, or concern. The notes and small gifts sent by Mary Kay have helped make her company a great place to work. It takes only a minute, yet it can help to develop good employee relations. People love to get goodwill messages, especially when they are not expected. Goodwill messages express feelings of caring and may convey appreciation, congratulations or recognition, and sympathy or condolences.

Appreciation Messages

A note or letter expressing appreciation is always a treat, and opportunities for these are almost unlimited. The format is less important than the tone of such a message. In fact, you can often be casual and creative in such messages so long as you project a pleasant tone. Handwritten notes can be as good as formally typed messages. Personal note paper can be used rather than letterhead. Some business people have special executive-sized letterhead just for handwritten notes.

To strengthen a note of appreciation, do the following:

1. *Mention or describe the specific actions, attitudes, or characteristics that you appreciate.* Just saying "I appreciate you" is nice. But saying, "I appreciate the way you helped us stay on track at our last meeting," or "I appreciate your quick response in providing me with . . ." is likely to have more impact.

2. *Use the person's name in the body of the message.* Don't overdo it, though—it may sound patronizing—but do personalize the message. Address the reader as you would when talking to him or her. Use first name, nickname, or more formal address as appropriate. Don't call the reader "Bill" if you would normally call him "Mr. Kosinski."

3. *Do not send mixed strokes.* A goodwill message should be all positive. If you have negative information to convey, save it for a separate message. Do not say, "Tom, you did a really good job on the Wesson negotiations. I'm always proud to have you representing our company. But will you please quit wearing those loud ties? They made your appearance less than businesslike."

4. *Be conversational.* A goodwill letter should sound the way you would talk. Stuffiness or formality can damage the tone. Contractions are usually fine. Even terms that are ordinarily considered slang can create a pleasant tone ("Way-ta-go!" or "Attaboy!")

The following note may be a bit stuffy for a goodwill note:

Dear Ms. Graham:

I wish to advise you that you have accomplished excellent results with your new marketing projections program. The technical accuracy of your software will be most beneficial to our organization. Sincere appreciation is extended to you and your staff.

The following note is a bit friendlier but still reflects a degree of formality:

Dear Cristine:

On behalf of the development department, I want to thank you for the excellent work you and your people have done in developing the new marketing projections program. I feel certain that your efforts will result in an exceptional product for our clients.

Please accept my sincere thanks.

The following note has a warmer, more personal, informal tone:

> Chris—
>
> You did it again! Your marketing projections program is a home run! Way to go, Chris and the gang.
>
> Thanks to you and your team for giving us a real boost!

The degree of formality you choose will depend on what is comfortable for you. Some people prefer the more formal tone, but many enjoy a more conversational, breezy message.

Congratulations or Recognition Messages

Congratulation messages can follow the same guidelines as the appreciation note, although they may be slightly more formal. Be sure to

1. *Mention the specific actions you are congratulating the reader for* (graduation from the company's advance training program, promotion to vice-president, bowling a 300 game, a son's advancement to Eagle Scout, etc.).

2. *Suggest that you understand some of the effort that went into the achievement* ("I know this reflects many hours of hard work," etc.).

3. *Express pride and support as appropriate* ("I'm proud to have worked with you and want you to know you'll have my continued support in your new position, etc.")

Sympathy or Condolences

Sooner or later, everyone faces the experience of sharing grief. Many need to communicate with those who are dealing with the inevitable process of mourning. It is useful to understand something of the psychology of mourning.

Professor James Calvert Scott explains this process.

> Mourning involves the psychological task of breaking the bonds with that which has been lost and eventually reinvesting that attachment in living people and things. Society's death-related rituals, including the letter of condolence, play a significant role in repairing and restoring the emotional and social damage caused by death.

> Well-meaning family and friends often interfere with the grieving process by avoiding mention of the loss at the very time the bereaved need most to confront it. By doing so, they prevent the bereaved from experiencing the reality of death and the full range of emotions that are necessary in order to accomplish a healthy resolution. Working through grief is the process of consciously admitting and accepting the loss intellectually and emotionally. The ultimate goal of grief work is to be able to remember the loss without emotional pain and to direct emotions to the future.[3]

The psychologically sound letter of condolence should help the bereaved to work through their grief. You can accomplish this by following these guidelines:

1. Avoid euphemisms relating to death and the deceased person.

2. Refer to him or her by name, not "the dearly departed"; say "died" or "passed away," not "expired."

3. Say something brief about your relationship with the deceased person if you knew him or her.

4. Avoid quoting poetry, rhetorical writing, or scripture unless you are certain that it will bring comfort.

5. If you have a personal relationship with the reader, make a specific offer of assistance, if possible. Offer to help with child care or to house visiting relatives, as appropriate. Anticipate your reader's needs and try to be of service.

With business colleagues' families, you may not know the deceased personally. In such cases, a brief note or card is sufficient.

General Pattern of Goodwill Messages

A big idea first usually works best in goodwill messages. Often the first words will be "congratulations," "I appreciate," or "I am sorry to hear. . . ."

The pattern, format, or even the grammar of a goodwill message is less important than is the fact that it was sent and reflects a sense of caring. Typically, a goodwill message will take only a few minutes to produce but will offer a great return in improved relationships.

Follow-Up Notes Are Good Business: A Personal Story from One of Your Authors[4]

When I was a manager trainee in my first job out of college, I sent a letter to the college recruiter who had hired me. The letter was brief—it simply said how much I enjoyed working for the company and how he had helped me. I received a call from him a few days later. He thanked me for the letter and commented that of all the trainees he had worked with, I was the only one who had written to him in this way.

Interestingly, a short while later he was instrumental in my getting promoted to a better position.

Best-selling author, Harvey Mackay talks about "short notes [that] yield long results" in his book *Swim with the Sharks without Being Eaten Alive*. He comments on how few people send follow-up notes to customers, even those who have made a major purchase, like a car. Another glaring omission of many people interviewing for a job is the follow-up thank you note to the interviewer.

Mackay cites many successful people who constantly send out short but effective notes with messages like "I want you to know how much I enjoyed our meeting/interview/your gift/your hospitality" or "Congratulations on your new house/car/tennis trophy."

The moral of the story: Don't hesitate to let people know that you appreciate them, and do it *in writing*. Don't worry too much about formality or business letter protocol. Often a handwritten note, written conversationally, works fine. Just do it.

The following are additional examples of goodwill letters. The first is a note to an employee.

Dear Terry,

I just wanted to drop you a quick line and say
. . . thanks. Thanks for coming to work here at
Left Wave boutique. Your input into this store has
been the prime factor in making our success this
year. You're grrrrrreat!

Appreciatively,

Bonnie

Bonnie

The second example is a note to a consumer from a local merchant.

Dear Mrs. Riebel:

Thank you for stopping in the other day.

We're really glad you found the lamp and end table
you wanted.

If you are ever looking for something we don't have
on display, just ask for it. If we don't have it in
stock, chances are good that we can get it for you
. . . and we'd be more than happy to do it.

It was nice to serve you. Come back again soon, if
only to browse and visit. We do appreciate your
business and want to be of every possible service
to you, Mrs. Riebel.

Sincerely,

Adele Kupcluk

Adele Kupcluk
Store Manager

One young and successful manager makes it a point to send short letters to the homes of employees whose work was exemplary. The payoff for such a simple action is that

1. Employees know he recognizes and appreciates their good work.

2. By sending it home, he allows the employees' family to share in the praise.

3. The letter becomes a part of the employees' personnel file and can be used when preparing a performance review.

4. By noting that copies have been sent to higher levels of management (cc: The Boss), employees know they are getting additional attention.

Ways Organizations Can Create Goodwill

Opportunities for goodwill notes come up almost daily. Write them often. You'll be glad you did. Besides on-the-job performance, personal and family accomplishments can be acknowledged. A daughter's wedding, an impressive bowling score, and recognition for community service can all be opportunities to show you care. Such free expression can build a supportive organizational climate.

Press releases can be a public goodwill message.

The "public" form of a goodwill message may take the form of a **press release**. Here, the intent is to convey good news or to shed light on some positive aspect of an organization via a message broadcast through print or electronic media. Although not personalized, such messages can help create a positive image for the company and attract customers.

Publicity⁵

Follow up any news releases you send to the media.

A properly produced news release can be the backbone of any publicity campaign or image-building effort.

Creating real news about your product or service is actually the first step. The next step is identifying and contacting the appropriate publications or broadcasters to receive your news release. To get the best results, send your news releases to only those media whose audiences are likely to be interested in what you have to say.

Follow up with telephone calls to the media contacts to make sure they received your release, but don't try to pressure them into running it. If they run it, be sure to thank them (another opportunity for a goodwill note). If they don't run it, don't call and complain.

News Release

News releases provide much of the information found in the media.

The basic tool for generating publicity (i.e., public goodwill) is the **news release.** With it companies can get free publicity from newspapers, magazines, radio, and television. Much of the material in newspapers and magazines comes from such releases sent out by companies, government agencies, associations, and various individuals and groups.

A common, easy-to-follow format is used for most successful news releases. It has several key elements: the originator (you), the release date, the contact, a headline, and the double-spaced copy itself.

If you send out the news release on your company stationery, that will take care of the originator. All you have to do is type NEWS or NEWS RELEASE in capital letters at the top of the letterhead.

The release date is the date you want the story released. In many cases, it can say FOR IMMEDIATE RELEASE. This is probably best, unless there is some overriding reason why the story can't be released before a certain date. Also necessary is the name of a person to contact for further information. Along with the name, include the telephone number and area code where that person can be reached.

The headline should appear in capital letters, six spaces below the contact line. It should be as clever and catchy as possible so it captures the attention and arouses the interest of the editor or producer. Newspaper headlines can be used as models of how to write news release headlines. Try for a headline that compels the reader to read the entire release. An example of a press release appears in Figure 10–11.

Customer SatisfACTION Strategies, Inc.   **Contact Kym Fong**
                                                    800-555-5505


```
                     NEWS RELEASE

                 (FOR IMMEDIATE RELEASE)


WHY CUSTOMERS BUY: BEYOND MYSTERY SHOPPING

Customer SatisfACTION Strategies (CSS) announces a
breakthrough technique for determining customer
buying behaviors.

A pioneer in "mystery shopper surveys" in the Los
Angeles area, CSS can now get you, the business
person, far more information than ever before pos-
sible. We will not only tell you how well your em-
ployees treat customers but how effectively your
company's overall strategy motivates your customer
to buy.

Using CSS's exclusive psychology of "Sense-mak-
ing™," trained observers watch and record the most
subtle customer behaviors to tell you exactly what
motivates customers to buy and what does not. When
CSS audits a store or business, it guarantees at
least five specific ideas for boosting sales. And if
the recommendations don't work, they refund the
consulting fee.

CSS President Norman White says that they can offer
such an unheard-of guarantee because of the power
of the new psychology of Sense-making™. Developed
by a Washington psychologist, Sense-making™ studies
subtle, often overlooked nonverbal cues shoppers
use to express approval or disapproval of products,
store layout, displays, and the like. White clearly
states that "If our services don't boost sales, you
owe us nothing."

Companies interested in this breakthrough technique
to boost sales are invited to contact Kym Fong, at
800-555-5505 for further information.
```

FIGURE 10–11

News release.

Eight spaces below the headline, you should begin the body of the release. It should be double-spaced and written like a newspaper article, with the most important information in the first paragraph (a BIF approach), the supporting information next, and the least important information last. A one-page release is usually best. If you do use more than one page, place the word "MORE" at the bottom center of the first page.

News releases are used to announce the start of your company or professional practice, new products and services, speaking engagements, and appearances on radio or television shows, or any other event connected with your company that has potential news value.

Because your release may be reprinted verbatim in some newspapers or organizational newsletters, spend ample time to compose clever, readable releases. In some cases, your release may even be used as the basis for a feature story.

End your news releases with a "For more information" paragraph. Use this to give your company's name, address, and telephone number, and to offer a free brochure or some other kind of promotional material. Doing this encourages people to contact your business, giving you new prospects and an opportunity to gauge the relative impact of that particular coverage.

If you are particularly interested in developing a high media profile, you may also want to add a line at the bottom of your release saying "Media interviews welcome." Professionals and others in personal service businesses can benefit most by being recognized as experts in their field by the media.

Promotion of Yourself with For-Your-Information Notes

Public relations is the art of doing things and letting people know about them. Consider doing your own PR.

You don't need to brag. Instead, use simple techniques to let your boss know what you've been able to accomplish. If, for example, you just untangled a sticky billing problem for a customer, send your supervisor a **for-your-information (FYI) note.**

Mr. Bennion:

As you know, we've been having a major problem with Mrs. Pim's account. Here's what I did: [describe the actions taken.] I hope this solves the problem.

If you have any other ideas or directions on how to deal better with similar situations in the future, please let me know.

This note does several things. First, it keeps the boss informed. Second, it displays some action you've taken. Third, it expresses your openness to feedback from him or her.

Don't report everything you do, just the exceptional work. Often, a supervisor will keep such notes in your personnel file and, when performance review time comes around, will be reminded of just how valuable you are.

Understanding the Basics

SUMMARY OF KEY IDEAS

• The goodwill letter or note is one you send even though you don't have to. This type of message works well in improving employee and public relations.

• Routine and goodwill messages are commonplace in business. To be effective, they should be direct, complete, and friendly.

• Common examples of such messages are announcements, product inquiries, transmittal memos, letters granting a request, introductions, and credit information requests.

• Goodwill messages are exceptional opportunities for relationship building and enhanced professional success.

• The BIF approach works well with good-news and routine business writing.

• BIF can fail if you forget to include *all* the important details.

KEY TERMS AND CONCEPTS

goodwill letter

conciseness

product inquiries

credo

transmittal memo

news release

for-your-information (FYI) note

QUESTIONS FOR FURTHER THOUGHT

1. Describe the key characteristics of an effective routine request letter.

2. Why are goodwill messages useful to business and professional people?

3. How often do you receive goodwill messages? What form do they take? How do they make you feel?

4. How often do you send goodwill messages? Why?

We Thought It Over and Decided Creative Thinking Wasn't for Us

By Steve Stecklow

Some of the world's leading experts on thinking are gathered this week at the Massachusetts Institute of Technology in Cambridge.

Perhaps they should do a little thinking about news releases.

This newspaper received a "personel" invitation to the event—the Sixth International Conference on Thinking—in a letter and news release replete with rather, uh, thoughtless errors.

For instance, former U.S. Surgeon General C. Everett Koop, who was scheduled to receive an award at the conference, was identified as C. Everett Coop.

The event, the press release said, features "world renown" researchers and practitioners in the "field of education, business, medicine and technology." Major awards given at a banquet will recognize "international experts in field of thinking."

The release further explained that a new association, known by the acronym "ACCTION," would be launched at the session. The name, it said, stood for "Assure Creative Thinking in Our Nation."

"I know, I know," said Gela Sulikashvili, a conference spokesman, when asked about the news release. "You know, sometimes people think about things too much. There's quite a ways to go between thinking and actions."

He described the release as a "last-minute production" and said it was not proofread until it was already in the mail. He also said the acronym was correct but the name was wrong. The acronym stands for "Assure Critical and Creative Thinking in Our Nation."

His boss, Robert Swartz, one of the conference's organizers, was not amused. "I didn't see it, and I don't know how that happened," he said.

Mr. Swartz went on to say that the conference, which has attracted about 2,000 researchers, educators, psychologists and business people, is a very serious event. Its purpose, he said is to discuss the latest research into how students and workers can learn to think "more carefully and thoroughly so that their judgments are well-founded."

In the meantime, the press office at MIT has some thoughts on the matter. First, it had nothing to do with the conference's press material. And, a spokesman adds, MIT is only renting out space for the conference.

(Steve Stecklow, "We Thought it Over and Decided Creative Thinking Wasn't for Us," *Wall Street Journal*, July 22, 1994, p. B-1. Reprinted with permission of the Wall Street Journal © 1994 Dow Jones & Company, Inc. All rights reserved.)

Applying Your Knowledge

1. Make a list of the problems with the news release as they are identified in the article.
2. For each problem, suggest a solution that could have prevented it.

Applying Your Skills

ACTIVITY 10-1: Announcement, Alumni Relations

Trustees of Bradenton Community College (BCC), Bradenton, Georgia, recently completed their search for a new college president. They selected Thomas Pierce, retired U.S. Congressman. Since he left the House in 1986, Pierce has been vice-chairman of Zeit Industries, a local plastics manufacturer. He earned a master's degree in public administration from the University of Georgia and, as a congressman, was an active proponent of higher education. Since joining Zeit, he has also been a generous though anonymous contributor to the college endowment, a fact he doesn't want "paraded before the public." Pierce will take a large pay cut in accepting this position but thought it was the right thing to do at this point in his life. He will resign as vice-chairman of Zeit but will remain on the board of directors. He would like to see enrollment and funding increase to the point that BCC can soon become a four-year rather than a two-year college. The trustees support him in this goal.

As director of alumni relations for the college, write a letter to all alumni, announcing the appointment of Pierce as college president. Fill in a few interesting details from the life of President Pierce, remembering that his administrative assistant will want to approve the letter before it is mailed.

ACTIVITY 10-2: Inquiry, Management

You are a sales representative for the Sweatshop, a supplier of athletic wear to college stores. The company has reserved a 10- × 10-foot booth at the upcoming Campus Market Expo (CAMEX) trade show sponsored by National Association of College Stores (NACS). Because of the addition of three new product lines, it now appears that the booth will be too small. CAMEX is scheduled for mid-April; it is now late January, and NACS has informed you that all the 10- × 20-foot booths are already taken. The exhibits manager, however, suggested that one of the other exhibitors, Packmania, might be interested in trading booths. Its owners have complained in the past about lack of sales at the CAMEX show and yet have reserved a 10- × 20-foot booth. She thinks that with perhaps the right monetary incentive, Packmania might be induced to trade booths with the Sweatshop. A 10- × 10-foot booth costs $1,400, whereas a booth twice as large costs $2,500.

You have been asked by Sweatshop owner Jack Cardon to write a letter to Packmania president, Sam Doyle, and inquire about the possibility of switching booths at the upcoming show. "Offer him $1,300, which would put his cost for the smaller booth at $1,200. Mention that the booth is in a high-traffic area. Don't make this sound like a 'take-it-or-leave-it' offer," he warns you, "but at the same time, don't give him the impression that this is an invitation to dicker. We think this is a fair price and a good opportunity for him to move to a better location." Time is also of the essence. To have your new booth location printed in the CAMEX literature, the trade must be finalized by February 15. Packmania is headquartered at 1950 Arlington Road, Bloomington, IN 47402.

ACTIVITY 10-3: Inquiry, Finance

Mercy Hospital in Dayton, Ohio, has been fighting a losing battle in health care cost control. One particularly painful area is the hospital pharmacy which spends $3.5 million on drugs each year. David Rhein, director of finance at Mercy, read about a revolutionary program being tried by the Medical Center at St. Paul State University. This program involves a 920 Compaq computer loaded with software that can evaluate a drug's effectiveness and estimate how the use of various alternatives will impact the hospital's bottom line.

Rhein has asked you to write the pharmacy director at St. Paul State Medical Center (450 Cedar Street, St. Paul, MN 55101) and ask for more information about this program, particularly the cost savings St. Paul has experienced.

ACTIVITY 10-4: Inquiry, Editorial

Karla Cornish, editor of *Alumni Exchange,* a publication of Birmingham College's School of Management, has decided to write two book reviews for each issue of the magazine, which is published twice a year. She called Berrett-Koehler Publishers and asked them to send her a review copy of *We Are All Self-Employed* by Cliff Hakim, a book she thought alumni might find interesting. The Berrett-Koehler publicity manager, Valerie Barth, asked her to submit this request in writing so they could have it for their records.

Compose a letter over Cornish's signature to Berrett-Koehler publicity manager Valerie Barth, 155 Montgomery Street, San Francisco, CA 94104. Include a request to have Cornish's name added to the Berrett-Koehler mailing list so that she will receive their fall, winter, and spring catalogs.

ACTIVITY 10-5: Transmittal, Human Resources

Employease is an employee leasing company that handles payroll and provides benefits to approximately 3,000 employees of small businesses in the Miami area. The company has approved a third health insurance option for its employees. Mary Garcia, vice-president of human resources, has put together a report comparing the costs and comparative benefits of the three options for all employees. She has asked you to write a memo that will be attached to the report which is being sent to all 3,000 Employease employees.

ACTIVITY 10-6: Granting a Request, Customer Service

Brian Numkena, a building contractor in Omaha, Nebraska, wrote to First National Bank of Kentucky and requested an increase in the credit limit on his Visa Gold card from $10,000 to $15,000. His credit record is excellent, though his annual income is borderline. Your supervisor, after looking through his records, has authorized you to grant Brian's request. Write him a letter informing him that his credit limit has been increased. Numkena's address is 432 Grant Avenue, Omaha, NE 68102.

ACTIVITY 10-7: Granting a Request, Management

Carolyn Sambogni is president of the Great Salt Lake Literacy Foundation and author of the popular *High on Books*. She has been invited by the Orem, Utah, Rotary Club to be its luncheon speaker on June 8, 19XX. The topic they wish Ms. Sambogni to address is "Turning Children Off Drugs and On to Books." Carolyn has checked her schedule and can make time for this speaking engagement. She has asked you to send a brief response to the Rotary president, Cal Martin, 559 N. Palisades Drive, Orem, UT 84057.

ACTIVITY 10-8: Introduction, Sales

Sally Chung, an effective sales representative for Sterling Office Supply (SOS) in Boise, Idaho, has just been promoted to sales manager. The sales manager has decided to relocate Karl Stimpson from Montana to Boise, where he will take over Sally's clients, businesses that buy everything from desks to pens from SOS. Knowing how sales success is built on relationships more than anything else, Sally wants to make this a smooth transition. Karl was her own personal choice to take over this most lucrative sales area. Sally will not have time to introduce Karl personally to her long-time clients, but she doesn't want him to have to walk in cold with no introduction at all. Because Sally communicates best face to face, she has asked you to write a letter of introduction for Karl to each of her major accounts. Specifically, she wants to announce her promotion, explain how much she'll miss seeing them on a regular basis, and describe a little about her replacement, who she handpicked because of his excellent track record in the vast open spaces of Montana. Draft a letter for Sally to review.

ACTIVITY 10-9: Credit Request, Small Business

Bill Long has been burned a few times. Receivables are the life blood of a small business, and the two times a big order turned sour, his business, Steinway Glass, teetered on the brink of extinction. Steinway Glass is licensed to sell beer steins bearing college logos to college stores around the country. Bill doesn't worry about the on-campus stores, because of their direct tie to school accounting systems. All payables at these stores are computerized, and he rarely has an invoice out past 30 days. Off-campus stores are a different matter. Most are reliable, but a handful are rather risky—and all it takes is one bad account. Bill has just received an order for 100 steins from Off-Campus Express, an independent store located near Blackwell University in Chicago. He knows nothing about the store, but with the order came a list of credit references. Bill decides to write one of them to ask about their experience selling to Off-Campus Express. The order is for $1,200, and Bill can't afford to be careless with such large amounts. Your task is to write a credit request from Bill Long to Blue Mountain Arts, P.O. Box 4549, Boulder, Colorado 80306.

ACTIVITY 10-10: Credit Request, Sales

The Leadership Connection (TLC) is a Seattle-based consulting group that conducts leadership seminars for middle management in all types of businesses. They have been contacted by Fran Singleton, a seminar marketer. TLC partners John Scofield and Patrick Ubricht have been looking for new markets. Because they aren't well known outside the Pacific Northwest, they haven't had much success in other parts of the country. For this reason, Fran seems like just the type of connection they need. She says she's been in the seminar marketing business for 15 years, and has connections all over the country. Fran matches companies and consultants, and coordinates their schedules. She bills the companies directly and then pays 80 percent of the seminar fee to the client. Her commission is the remaining 20 percent before expenses. TLC wants to check with some of Fran's other clients, to make sure she delivers on her word and pays the 80 percent promptly. She has given them the names and addresses of four other consulting groups that she represents. One of them is Management Renaissance, headquartered at 110 North Point, San Francisco, CA 94120. Write Management Renaissance a letter, requesting a full report on their association with Fran Singleton.

ACTIVITY 10-11: Acknowledgment, Management

Meg Wheatley, president of the Berkana Institute, has been invited to participate on a business ethics panel at the first annual business conference of Brigham Young University's Marriott School of Management. For several years Meg was a faculty member at the Marriott School and would be happy to spend some time on campus discussing one of her favorite topics. She has asked you to send an affirmative response to Cheryl McBeth, 710 Tanner Building, Brigham Young University, Provo, UT 84602. The business conference is June 22, 19XX. The ethics panel is scheduled at 9:30 A.M. in the Varsity Theater.

ACTIVITY 10-12: Acknowledgment, Charity

Paul Oscarson, a noted genetic researcher, has been contacted by the A-T Foundation. The group of parents and physicians have organized to find a cure for ataxia-telangiectasia, a deadly and rare genetic disease that afflicts about 600 children in the United States. Carrie Anderson, president of the A-T Foundation, has invited Oscarson to present his most recent research at a conference on August 25, 19XX. There is no honorarium for this presentation: The A-T Foundation has offered to send Paul a round-trip ticket to St. Louis and put him up at the Marriott Pavilion Hotel, where the conference will be held. Paul understands that Carrie's two sons are afflicted with A-T, and knows that she and other parents are on a tight timetable. The disease puts children in wheelchairs by age 10, renders them unable to move their eyes to read by about age 15, and takes their lives by age 20. There is no cure. Although Paul has a prior commitment that will pay him $5,000, there is no question where he can make the biggest contribution. He sits down to compose a letter to Carrie Anderson, accepting her invitation and even offering to pay his own airfare. "They can use the money to fund more research," he says to himself. Your task is to write this letter as if you were Paul Oscarson.

ACTIVITY 10-13: Confirmation, Community Relations

Professor Jonathan Yossarian's operations management class at Fort Wayne State College has scheduled a tour of the Hammond Steel Mill in Plymouth, Indiana, at 2:00 P.M. on October 20, 19XX. The mill has been newly fitted with the latest in pollution-control equipment, and Hammond is eager to show off its new environment-friendly technology. As head of community relations, it is your task to write Professor Yossarian and confirm his class tour. Yossarian's address is 588 Jacobs Building, Fort Wayne State College, Fort Wayne, IN 46802.

ACTIVITY 10-14: Confirmation, Loan Approval Letter

You are the credit manager for BAMCO Financial Services. Recently, Ms. Laura Hutton applied for a $5,000 signature loan through your branch office. Write a letter to Ms. Hutton informing her that her loan request has been approved. Make up the addresses and any other reasonable information.

ACTIVITY 10-15: Appreciation, Small Business

As a small business person in a competitive business, you decide to make more personal contacts with your customers. Your business rents used cars to people. Most of your customers come to your town to enjoy the nearby ski slopes. Accordingly, your most popular rental vehicle is a four-wheel-drive utility vehicle, the Jeep Wagoneer.

Last weekend, Bill and Harriett Meecham rented a jeep from you. They live in Phoenix, Arizona, and come to your town several times each year to ski. (Their full address is 2443 Greenleaf Drive, Phoenix, AZ 97561.)

Your policy is to write personalized goodwill notes to as many customers as time permits, thanking them for their business and wishing them a pleasant holiday season. These notes are handwritten on company letterhead. Write a note to the Meechams from your company, Rent-a-Tank, Inc., 221 South Main, Snowville, UT 94611.

ACTIVITY 10-16: Recognition, Management

Rewrite the following commendation letter using the principles discussed in this chapter.

December 18, 199X

Tim Smothers
Kearns Probation Unit
4299 West 5415 South
Boise, Idaho

Dear Tim:

A review of your services this past year in the
Probation Division and particularly your assignment
as ranch coordinator was made in our morning director's meeting on this date. Pursuant to that discussion, we feel we should extend this letter of
commendation. We understand that much of the planning responsibility was given to you and that the
implementation and coordinating of the program was
your specific responsibility. Because of your efforts, your division chief, Mr. Harris, has indicated the ranch program became a most effective
treatment program. We understand that much was accomplished at the ranch in terms of improvements
under your personal leadership. Your participation
in all three of the eleven-day programs is acknowledged as a service over and above that which is
usually considered the duty of a probation counselor. Your knowledge and expertise in this particular area are considered also to be a factor in the
success of this program.

Please receive this letter of commendation with
sincere thanks and our appreciation for your contributions to a more effective public service.

Sincerely,

William M. Blake
Director of Court Services

Carlon J. Harris
Chief, Probation Division

ACTIVITY 10-17: Recognition Co-Worker

Sandra Treese, a secretary in your office, was just awarded a professional secretary certification by Professional Secretaries International (PSI). This award is given by PSI to people who complete several years of home study and who master a wide range of secretarial skills. This is the highest honor given by PSI.

You've know Sandra for four years. She is a lively, fun-loving woman with a rich sense of humor. When she laughs (and she does so often), her voice becomes fairly high-pitched—a musical laugh. Over the years you've teased her by giving her the nickname "Squeaky." She accepts the nickname with her characteristic good humor.

ACTIVITY 10-18: Condolence, Small Business

Lisa O'Brien, owner of the O'Brien Group, a marketing communication and advertising agency, learned this morning that Marcus Langford, custodian of the building she leases, lost his father to cancer over the weekend. Marcus, a conscientious and courteous worker, has taken care of the building for as long as the O'Brien Group has been at One Plaza Center. Lisa has asked you to draft a letter to Marcus, expressing the sympathy of the entire O'Brien group at this time of loss. Marcus Langford's address is 937 E. Canyon Street, Albuquerque, NM 87103.

ACTIVITY 10-19: Condolence, Management

Last Sunday evening Larry Mikelson's 12-year-old son, Tommy, was killed in an accident. He was struck by a passing car while riding his bicycle. Larry is manager of another branch of your company in a town 25 miles away. You've known Larry and his family for many years. Last summer you went on a fishing trip with Larry and Tommy. Prepare a goodwill note to send to Larry and his wife, Amelia.

ACTIVITY 10-20: News Release, Public Relations

Is it possible to please shareholders and environmentalists at the same time? Most paper-products companies would say no, but Weyerhaeuser is not only making profits, it is also making inroads with green activists. CEO John W. Creighton, Jr., inherited a company in 1991 that was near the bottom of its industry. Within a year, he had set in motion an 18-month re-engineering effort. In 1994, operating income was up 24 percent. Operating profits for 1995 were expected to soar another 72 percent. Its operating margin in 1994 was nearly 30 percent better than its rivals. Stock price went from a low of 18 in 1990 to nearly 49 in 1994. On the environmental front, Creighton has adopted a cooperative stance, reasoning that Weyerhaeuser's long-term interests are better served by not fighting regulation. Among other changes, Weyerhaeuser has installed new technology in its paper mills that eliminate most chlorines and will meet proposed EPA rules two years earlier than required. Weyerhaeuser has also analyzed the impact of logging on 12 Northwest river basins and came up with tree-harvesting plans that reduce threats to salmon runs. Although Weyerhaeuser will probably never please all environmentalists, it is moving in the right direction, and it is improving its competitiveness in the process.

Write a news release for major newspapers and news magazines to spread the word about Weyerhaeuser's progress under John Creighton. You have received permission to use the following quotation by Alan Copsey, chair of the Washington Environmental Council's forest resources committee: "They're never going to do everything environmentalists wish; if they did, they'd go broke. But they're one of the best at taking care of the land."

PERFORMING
on the Job

CASE 10-1 Online News Release

The following news release appeared in America Online. It looks different from the typical release that might be sent to a local newspaper. The intent here is to reach opinion leaders who use the online service (in this case it was America Online) with an *outline* of a story they could follow up. By calling the contact numbers included in the message, interested parties could get further information. Electronic online services tend to be more concise in conveying the bones of the message.

Read this release and answer the following questions.

Case Questions

1. In what ways does this differ from the news release format recommended in the chapter?

2. Why might this release be more effective in reaching its target audience?

3. Does this kind of release make it easier or more difficult for the receiver to use the information? Why?

CASE 10-2 Chevy Dealer's Customer Letter

Go back to the letter written by the Chevrolet dealer shown on pages 241–242.

Case Questions

1. Based on what you've learned in this chapter, how might you improve on this? Start by listing five strengths and weaknesses.

2. Summarize what you'd do differently if you were to write such a letter.

3. Rewrite it, and explain any changes you would make.

LOCAL AD AGENCIES CLOSE THEIR DOORS FOR A DAY TO DO
GOOD DEEDS

What: The Heart of Advertising. A celebration of
the season through community service by Philadelphia ad agencies. Throughout the month of December,
12 local ad agencies chose to close their doors for
a day and give back to the community. Community
service projects vary, but include rehabilitating a
house with Habitat for Humanity, hosting a trip for
abused children, and delivering meals to people
with AIDS.

Who: Participating ad agencies are members of the
Philadelphia Chapter of the American Association of
Advertising Agencies (Four A's). For complete list
of agencies, contact Rachel Ezekiel-Fishbein at
Earle Palmer Brown, 215-555-5555.

When: Photo opportunities—Friday, December 16, during Earle Palmer Brown Heart of Advertising Community Service Day.

Where: The following four community organizations,
all located in Philadelphia, welcome the media during their Heart of Advertising visits.

1. Habitat for Humanity, 1829 N. 19th Street. Go to
   office at 1829 N. 19th Street for directions to
   house. 8:30 A.M.-4:00 P.M. Volunteers will help

PAGE 1

rehabilitate homes for underprivileged families. On-site contact: Rachel Ezekiel-Fishbein.

2. Pegasus Riding Therapy, 1019 Ripley Street. 9:30 A.M.-11:30 A.M. Volunteers will assist handicapped children with horseback riding therapy. On-site contact: Bridget Boland.

3. Greater Philadelphia Food Bank, 302 W. Berks Street. 10:00 A.M.-3:00 P.M. Volunteers will pack boxes of food for delivery. On-site contact: Bill Melnick.

4. Free Library of Philadelphia/Queen Memorial Library, 1201 S. 23rd Street. 10:00 A.M.-4:00 P.M. Volunteers will help ready the library for reopening by cleaning, shelving books, weeding yard, etc. On-site contact: John Moscatelli.

History: This Four A's-sponsored community service program was initiated in 1991 by Lonny Strum, chairman of the Philadelphia Council Board of Governors of the Four A's and president of Earle Palmer Brown/Philadelphia. Contact: Rachel Ezekiel-Fishbein of Earle Palmer Brown, 215-555-5555.

PAGE 2

CHAPTER ELEVEN

Writing Disappointing or Unfavorable Messages:
Clarity with Sensitivity

LEARNING GOALS

After you have studied this chapter, you should be able to:

- Make a rational decision about using the bad-news format to soften the blow of a letter or memo.

- Apply the BILL approach in an appropriate manner to inform a reader of a disappointing message while trying to salvage goodwill.

- Identify and apply the five steps of a BILL bad-news message format.

- Write an effective buffer paragraph and smooth transition into the reasoning.

- Objectively use decision criteria to explain your decision.

- Articulate a refusal (bad news) tactfully yet clearly using de-emphasis techniques.

- Recognize the desirability of a "lesser alternative."

- Write an effective goodwill close.

- Recognize that some messages may be more effective without using the BILL approach.

The Way It Is . . . A Customer Apology

"I used to shop with you guys all the time, but I've had it. You better get some new people in the Meridian store or I'm history," said the caller, Ed Cruikshank.

It was a Tuesday morning, and Kate could do without this kind of telephone call to start the day. It comes with the territory, however. Kate Olson was general manager for a chain of tire and automotive stores in Wisconsin. Wilbur's Tire and Auto stores were well known. Founded in the 1950s by Kate's grandfather, the business had provided a good living for three generations of her family and hundreds of other Wisconsin residents. Located in 23 small- to medium-sized towns throughout the state, Wilbur's had built its reputation around friendly personal service, fair prices, and honest dealing.

"Gee, I'm sorry you had a problem, Mr. Cruikshank. Can you tell me a bit more about what happened? I'd sure appreciate the chance to try to win you back," replied Kate.

"Where do you want me to start? Slow service, price ripoffs, insulting behavior. One of your guys tried to sell me new struts for my car, and I just replaced them six months ago. I had to wait almost an hour for a simple rotation and balance. And the brake job cost $40 more than your advertising said it would. It dang near breaks my heart to see Wilbur's go down the sewer like that. I'd expect that from some big city outfit, but I always trusted you folks. I want the cost of this "service" removed from the bill. I figure you owe me $76 all together."

The conversation continued for several minutes and Kate asked if she could get back to Mr. Cruikshank by the end of the week. He agreed but said he wanted her explanation and apology in writing. She agreed and went about verifying the customer's complaints.

Tom Burden is the manager of the Meridian store. She called immediately. "Tom, I just heard from Ed Cruikshank."

"I'm not surprised, Kate. He was really steamed when he drove out of here. Let me bring you up to date on our friend Ed."

Tom explained that Cruikshank has a reputation for griping about almost everything. "His car is twenty years old, and he tries to keep it limping along with a minimum of service. He buys the cheapest parts and seldom does routine maintenance. The struts he'd had replaced six months ago came from a salvage yard and were pretty likely to be defective when he installed them. The delay in service was because he had an 8:00 A.M. appointment but didn't show up until 8:45 A.M. The delay was made worse by the first snow of the year that had everybody in town asking us to mount their snow tires. When he was late, I agreed to get snow tires on the local police car—we have a contract with them, you know."

"All in all, Ed's a decent fellow but he gets forgetful and tends to blame everybody but himself. Believe me, I've bent over backward to try to meet his needs, but we just couldn't help the delay yesterday."

After getting more details from Tom, Kate felt that a refund was not warranted. She'd like to keep Ed as a customer, though. He has a lot of friends in town. Now she needs to write her letter to him as promised.

Some business letters convey information the reader is not anxious to hear. Occasionally we need to refuse a request or give some other type of bad news. This chapter talks about the strategies used to handle such situations.

A Strategic Decision: Should I Soften the Blow?

Breaking the bad news to someone requires a strategic decision. Usually, the unpleasant message you are sending will be received by someone whose goodwill you would like to retain—often a present or potential customer. From a strategic standpoint, you must decide if maintaining the goodwill of the reader is important enough to spend

(Reprinted with special permission of King Features Syndicate.)

the extra effort normally required to write a reader-sensitive letter. Often, this decision boils down to a cost/benefit analysis. Will the extra cost be returned in equal if not greater benefits?

Sometimes employees don't have the discretion to compose a careful response. They are under pressure to use standard letter formats or to get the mail out as quickly as possible. This decision generally reflects management's decision to be more efficient. It can, however, damage message effectiveness.

If maintaining goodwill with that reader is not important enough that you are willing to expend some extra effort in writing to him, the alternative is to simply blurt out the bad news and let the PR chips fall where they may. A tactful, carefully arranged bad-news letter costs more to produce but is likely to at least soften any negative impressions your reader has toward you or your organization. The payoff is that we reduce the risk of irritating the reader and improve the likelihood of maintaining goodwill.

These are the options: (1) be blunt and organize your bad-news letter in the same direct manner as a routine letter (BIF pattern), or (2) apply a pattern of organization that attempts to psychologically soothe or at least create understanding of your viewpoint in the reader. If you decide on option 2, here is a way of going about it using a BILL approach.

Reader-sensitive bad-news letters require extra effort. You should first decide if the effort is worth it.

BILL: Bad-News Breaker

Suppose you have received ten exciting job offers (this is a hypothetical example, but wouldn't it be nice?). Because there is only one of you and ten offers to choose from, you know you will have to turn down nine of them. You like all ten of the companies and may want to go to work for one of the other companies later. How do you go about telling the nine other companies "no" without burning the bridge behind you?

Use the BILL approach.

Remember, the big idea is what you want your reader to do, feel, or understand. In this case, you want to make sure your reader understands why you turned down the offer. You want the person you are refusing to be able to say, "I am disappointed that he or she didn't accept our offer, but I can understand the reasoning he or she used. If I had had to face a similar choice, I might have turned down our offer, too."

This is the goal of a good BILL letter: to have the readers see your viewpoint and, although disappointed in the message, feel that they might well have done the same thing if they were you.

One surefire way to *fail* to achieve this would be to write a letter like this message.

The big idea is what you want your reader to do, feel, or understand.

I regret to inform you that I must reject your job offer. I got ten different offers and chose the one that was the best.

Thanks anyhow.

Way BILL Works

By saving the big idea (your refusal, in this case) for a little later rather than hitting the reader between the eyes in the first sentence, you can salvage some good feelings. The BILL approach gives you a chance to explain your reasoning and to try to gain reader understanding before revealing the bad news.

The BILL approach uses five simple steps.

1. Use a buffer to cushion the reader for the news.
2. Make a smooth transition to the reasoning.
3. Present the reasons behind your decision.
4. Deliver the bad news.
5. Rebuild the reader's goodwill.

Figure 11–1 illustrates how to position the five steps in drafting your message.

FIGURE 11–1
Guide for laying out a
BILL message.

1. The cushion or   _____
   bad-news buffer   _____
                       _____

2. Transition to   _____
   the reasoning   _____
                       _____

3. Presentation of   _____
   the reasoning   _____
   behind the news   _____

4. The bad news   _____
   itself (the big   _____
   idea later)   _____

5. The goodwill or   _____
   optimistic close   _____
                       _____

Cushioning the Blow

Before you start laying down your reasoning for the reader, you want to put in a little buffer—to create a positive mental preview.

The buffer paragraph paves the way.

The purpose of the **buffer paragraph,** then, is to prepare the way for your reasoning. You want to put your reader in a receptive frame of mind to hear what you have to say. Your goal: to get the reader to read (preferably with an open mind) the rest of your letter.

A good buffer is neutral or mildly positive.

Just how do you pave the way for your reader? Most experienced writers begin their **bad-news messages** with a neutral or mildly positive statement. They say something with which the reader is likely to agree. For example, consider the bad-news letter you might write to those nine companies. Remember, you wanted to turn down the job offer without closing the door to possible future employment. Here's one way to set up the buffer paragraph.

> **Dear Ms. Roper:**
>
> **Thank you for your recent offer to join Magna-Tech as an assistant controller. As I mentioned to the vice-president of finance, I enjoyed visiting with you and your staff last week to talk about the position. Your company is impressive. Your people were very friendly.**

This example combines both neutral statements ("Thank you for . . .") and more positive, complimentary statements ("Your company is impressive . . ."). Either type of comments may be appropriate for use as a buffer. Some other buffer statements might be:

- Comments about how pleasant your association has been ("I have been a satisfied customer for many years . . .").
- Thanks for the reader's interest in you.
- Thanks for the reader's effort in getting requested information to you.
- Expressions of interest in the reader or the company.

These types of statements set a dispassionate or neutral tone. However, you may want to be more upbeat in your buffer. You can do this by using a statement that the reader will agree with. Go back to the offer-refusal example.

> **Dear Ms. Roper:**
>
> **During my office visit with you last week, I was able to tell rather quickly that Magna-Tech is an exciting place to work. I want to thank you for the time you spent with me discussing the career possibilities with your company. I also want to let you know I appreciate the recent offer you extended to become assistant controller.**

Both the statement that the reader can agree with in the second example and the neutral statement in the first example do the job nicely. We have been able to get the reader into the letter, postpone the bad news, and pave the way for our reasoning.

A good buffer is neutral or mildly positive.

One note of caution: Don't be too encouraging. Don't lead your reader to believe he or she is going to get a good-news message. Keep it neutral or *mildly* positive.

Smooth Transition

Once you have cushioned your reader, the next step is to make the **transition** into your reasoning. The transition should have a natural flow. It should be graceful, not abrupt. A quick shift into your reasons may defeat the purpose of your buffer paragraph. Make the transition smooth.

Smooth transitions aren't all that difficult. Just remember the following two points:

1. Avoid the abrupt *but* or *however.*
2. "Seed" your buffer paragraph with a thought that you can refer to in the first sentence of your reasoning paragraph.

Take a look at the following bad-news letter. Watch the transition closely—you'll see a problem.

Dear Paul:

Thanks for your letter of November 10. I was very happy to hear from you and I'm delighted you're finishing your college work.

I've been giving your proposal to gather some research data in the Orlando District a great deal of thought. Your project sounds interesting, and it is the kind of thing I've personally been interested in for several years. However, after having considered your request, I've decided to decline your offer.

I hope you will be able to conduct your research elsewhere without any difficulty, and I wish you the very best.

Yours very truly,

District Manager

The writer begins with a pretty good buffer in the first paragraph. But then, instead of moving smoothly into his reasoning, the author shifts gears with the deadly *however.* The transition is just too abrupt. As soon as the reader sees *however,* he knows that bad news is coming.

Generally avoid *but* or *however* in the transition from the buffer to the reasoning.

Remember to choose your transition words carefully, and avoid the abrupt *but* and *however.* Don't tip off your reader before you get a chance to explain.

Now that this section has discussed what *not* to do in transitioning, the following one spends some time on what you *should* do. Point 2, identified earlier, suggested that you use **seed words**. These are words or thoughts sprinkled in the buffer paragraph that you can use to sprout your reasoning paragraph. Go back to the earlier examples to identify the cushion seeds.

Examples of Seed Words

During my office *visit* with you last week, I was able to tell rather quickly that Magna-Tech is an exciting place to work. I want to thank you for the time you spent with me discussing the career possibilities with your company. I also want to let you know I appreciate the recent *offer* you extended to become assistant controller.

In this example, you could make the transition by referring back to the visit or the offer. It is better, however, to make the transition with the *offer* or *position* because these seed words are closer to the next paragraph. Here's what the transition paragraph looks like.

> **The position sounds challenging and compares favorably with the other offers I have received. This has made my decision much more difficult.**

The paragraph moves smoothly into a discussion of the reasoning behind the refusal. The reader senses that you are finished with the pleasantries and are getting down to business. The following example uses the *visit* for the transition seed.

> **Thank you for your recent offer to join Magna-Tech as an assistant controller. As I mentioned to the vice-president of finance, I enjoyed *visiting* with you and your staff last week to talk about the position. You answered many of my questions concerning Magna-Tech and the position responsibilities.**
>
> **During our visit, I discussed with you my short- and long-term goals, and. . . .**

Here the focus on what was talked about during the writer's visit, particularly those "short- and long-term goals," sets the stage for a reasoning section. The reasoning will now allude to goals different from those discussed at the visit as a reason for refusing the job.

Please, Let Me Explain

If you've been successful up to this point in your bad-news letter, your reader is in a neutral or mildly positive frame of mind and knows you are getting ready for your explanation or reasoning. Before you can continue by citing your reasons, you need to be sure exactly what your reasons are. You need to clarify in your own mind why you are sending out the bad-news message. Jot down your reasons in specific terms. These notes will form the foundation of your reasoning section.

Consider your reasoning from the reader's viewpoint.

Once you have solidified your line of thought, the next step is to put on your reader-viewpoint hat. Ask yourself: How will the reader respond to what I have to say? What is the best way to lay out my logic so the reader will understand it? Is there any possible benefit to the reader from this bad news?

Generally, one of the best approaches to laying out your reasoning is to go from the facts to the conclusion. In this way, your reader shouldn't be able to anticipate your refusal. Begin by simply stating the specific facts. Then show how these facts lead to your bad-news conclusion. Let's take a look at our offer-refusal examples.

> **The position sounds challenging and compares favorably with the other offers I have received. This has made my decision much more difficult. To narrow down the choices, I have compared my goals with those of the companies from which I have received offers. In addition, I have tried to the best of my ability to determine if there was a good personality fit between the company and me. After taking all this into consideration. . . .**

Here is another example.

> **During our visit, I discussed with you my short- and long-term goals. We were both interested in seeing if there was a fit between what each of us were looking for. After careful introspection. . . .**

Explanation of Decision Criteria

In both examples, the reader becomes aware of criteria that were used to decide which offer to take. Notice, however, that the level of detail is not very deep. Your reasoning may be specific and much more detailed. This is where you try to anticipate the reader's reaction. You will have to decide how much of an explanation your reader needs.

Pitfall of Hiding Behind Policy

When "policy" is the reason for a refusal, briefly explain the reasons behind the policy.

One pitfall business writers should avoid is the tendency to hide behind company policy. Often, business writers must refuse a request because the company prefers not to do what's been requested. But don't just say to your reader, "That's against our company policy," without any further explanation. Company policy is, or should be, based on reasons. To simply cite "policy" without getting into the underlying reasons for that policy is like answering "because" when asked "why?"—neither one is a satisfying answer.

Delivery of Refusal

Be tactful but conclusive in the refusal.

The key in delivering the refusal is to be tactful but conclusive. The actual refusal or bad news should be carefully worded and carefully placed to avoid undue emphasis on it. At the same time, the message should be clear so there is no misunderstanding on the part of your reader. If your message is perceived as something less than final, your reader may repeat the request. You might end up with a pen pal. That can be expensive.

One technique to soften the blow while delivering the bad new is to phrase the bad news in the passive voice ("your request must be denied") rather than the active voice ("I am denying your request"). Another technique is to position the actual refusal where it naturally receives less emphasis. The positions of strongest emphasis (which should normally be avoided for bad news) are at the beginning and end of each paragraph, and the total letter. Figure 11–2 shows these positions.

Put your refusal in the middle of the letter.

The top positions are emphasized because they are the first words the reader sees in each paragraph. The end positions are those phrases that tend to linger in the reader's mind and are thus emphasized.

The two strongest **emphasis positions** in the whole letter are the first and last phrases written. Your refusal or bad-news phrase would be best positioned toward the middle of the letter for de-emphasis. However, don't focus attention on the refusal by putting it in a separate paragraph by itself in the middle of the letter. Attach the refusal near the end of the reasoning section.

Take a look at refusals in our continuing examples.

> **. . . In addition, I tried to the best of my ability to determine if there was a good personality fit between the company and me. After taking all this into consideration, it seems that it would be best for both of us if your offer is not accepted at this time.**

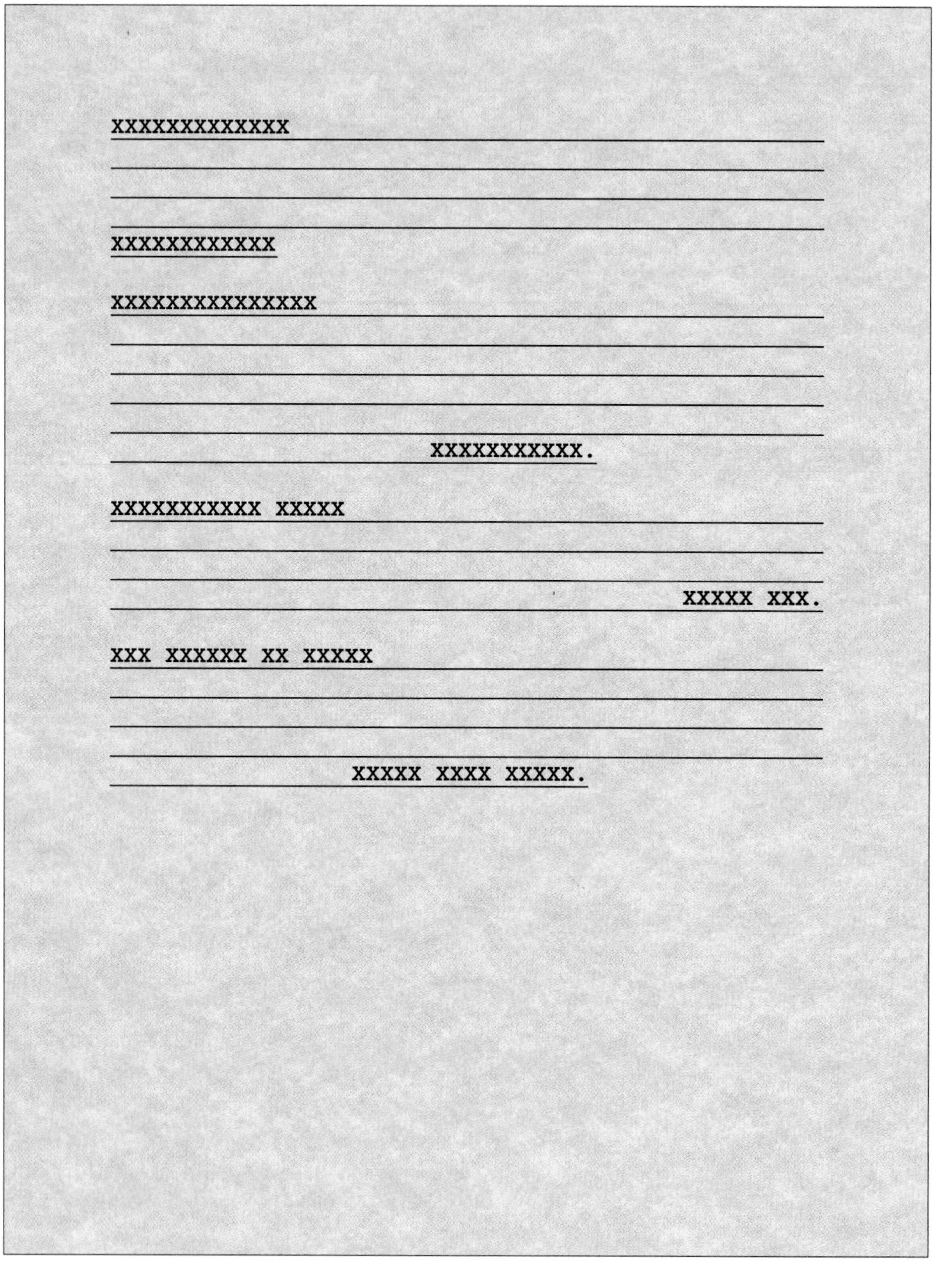

XXXXXXXXXXXX
_____
_____
_____

XXXXXXXXXXX
_____

XXXXXXXXXXXXXXX
_____
_____
_____
_____
        XXXXXXXXXX.

XXXXXXXXXXX XXXXX
_____
_____
_____
              XXXXX XXX.

XXX XXXXXX XX XXXXX
_____
_____
_____
     XXXXX XXXX XXXXX.

FIGURE 11–2

Positions of emphasis in a bad-news message.

Here is another example.

> **. . . We were both interested in seeing if there was a fit between what each of us was looking for. After careful introspection, I have decided to accept an offer with another company.**

The first example uses the passive voice to make the refusal. In addition, it hints at the fact that the decision is in the best interests of the company. The second example also employs an indirect approach, which declines the offer by stating that you have accepted someone else's offer. Both refusals are explicit without being vivid.

Refusal Language

The reasons presented should be logically and clearly presented. Avoid jargon or complexities that the reader may not comprehend. Also avoid the overuse of negative language or words that have undesirable overtones. These can be a real turnoff to your reader. If your decision was based on prudent reasoning, there is no need to sound judgmental in your tone—or to apologize. Be especially careful to avoid words and phrases that may imply a judgment of your reader. The following list illustrates the kinds of hidden meanings that may be conveyed to your reader.

WORDS AND PHRASES HAVING UNDESIRABLE OVERTONES

If You Say	You Imply
I must differ with you about . . .	I must be right; you're wrong.
I question your . . .	You're probably lying.
I repeated to you . . .	How often must I tell you?
Why didn't you . . . ?	You are so stupid, forgetful, and negligent.
You apparently overlooked . . .	You are careless.
You were misinformed . . .	Somebody lied to you, but I didn't.
Your complaint . . .	Gripe, gripe, gripe!
You contend . . .	Arguing again, are you?
You did not include . . .	Carelessness!
You do not realize . . .	Stupid—you couldn't possibly understand.
You failed to . . .	You loser . . .
I cannot understand your . . .	You don't make yourself clear.

Offer of Lesser Alternative

When offering an alternative to a request, make it easy for the reader to accept.

Often, offering the reader an alternative to the original request is a good strategy. The alternative should be explained in a positive tone, conveying the assumption that it will be accepted. Figure 11–3 illustrates such an effective refusal.

When offering an alternative, make it easy for the reader to accept. Many letters simply toss the ball back to the reader. Here is an example of the refusal alternative section of such a letter.

> **After checking my travel schedule for the remainder of the year, I find I will be out of town on the date you wanted me to visit your group.**
>
> **If some other date would be acceptable or if another person from our company could be of help, please contact me again.**

SYNECTIC SYSTEMS, INC
3322 Tryon Blvd
Charlotte, NC 28336

September 20, 1998

Mr. Bob Gambrell, President
Young Businessmen's Federation
119 North Central
Charlotte, NC 28104

Dear Mr. Gambrell:

We appreciate your interest in the kinds of employee motivation programs we are developing here at Synectic Systems. Your request that I speak to your group in November is personally flattering and has been considered carefully.

After checking my travel schedule for the remainder of the year, I find I have a conflict with the November 19 date you mentioned. I will be attending a conference in New York and will not return until November 22. May I suggest an alternative?

Dr. Elliott Anderson has recently joined our organization. He brings excellent academic background and seven years' industrial psychology experience with a major manufacturing organization on the West Coast. He is anxious to know more people in the area and has indicated a willingness to talk with your group on November 19.

Elliott is an excellent speaker, and I'm sure you'll enjoy his presentation. He will be calling you to confirm this early next week.

Again, we appreciate the opportunity to speak to your fine group.

Cordially,

George Bell

George Bell
President

FIGURE 11-3
A refusal letter offering
a lesser alternative.

A letter such as this one fails to achieve closure—the problem remains unresolved. If your letter must refuse a request, do so in explicit terms so there is no misunderstanding. If you offer an alternative, follow through on the new idea. Don't just give the problem back to the reader and start the whole message-response cycle over again.

Offering a **lesser alternative** should not be used as a way to cop out on saying no. It should be used only when you genuinely want to offer an option to the reader.

Always try to reach closure so that additional correspondence is not necessary.

Decision to Leave 'em on a Good Note

Once you have clearly and tactfully delivered the bad news, it's time to begin repairing any damage to the goodwill between you and the reader. This is where the optimistic or **goodwill close** comes in.

Your Decision: Don't Over Apologize

Leave out the apology in a goodwill close.

If, in fact, your decision has been based on sound, adult reasoning, there is no need to apologize. An attempt to apologize may imply that you're really not so sure you did the right thing. It could tear down all the work you did in the reasoning section of your message. The effusive apology may cause your reader to question your reasoning. "The lady doth protest too much" implies underlying guilt.

Consideration of Your Next Meeting with the Reader

As you compose your closing remarks, think about your relation with the reader and visualize the next contact you hope to have with that person. How will that next contact benefit the reader? Will the reader benefit from a continued association with you or your company?

When your refusal is to a customer, you may want to express confidence that a good business relationship will continue. For example, in refusing a customer's claim for an adjustment, you might close as follows:

> We appreciate your patronage at March's Department Stores these past twelve years and look forward to a continued relationship. For your information, our summer presale (for charge customers, such as yourself) begins May 25. Most of our merchandise will be marked down at least 15 percent. We hope you will be able to stop in to take advantage of the great summer values.

Let's take a look at a goodwill close for our offer-refusal example. Notice how the thrust of the close is to keep the "employment door" open.

> Again, I want to thank you for the time you spent with me during the interview process. I was impressed with Magna-Tech and its people. If at some future date another opportunity arises with Magna-Tech, please keep me in mind.

Examples of the BILL Approach

Writing the goodwill close completes the BILL approach. As mentioned, you would set up the five elements of the bad-news messages, step by step. Now, look at a complete bad-news letter that makes good use of the BILL strategy.

PACIFIC AIRLINES
"WE ALMOST ALWAYS GET YOU THERE ALIVE"
Airline Parkway
San Jose, CA 99888

March 13, 1998

Mr. Tim Naranja
339 East 3900 South
Ogden, OH 47101

Dear Mr. Naranja:

Ben Brennon shared your letter with me and asked
that I reply on his behalf. Please accept our
apologies for the delayed arrival of Flight 191 on
January 15 and the further delay in your arrival on
Lanai.

Although we appreciate the extraordinary planning
you made to reach Lanai on January 15, I'm sure you
will understand that unless Pacific Airlines is involved in making those plans, we cannot accept the
responsibility for expenses incurred as a result.
We recognize the inconvenience the delay caused
you, however, and want to share in your unexpected
costs. Our check for $50 is enclosed.

I hope your visit to the Islands was pleasant and
that you'll be traveling with Pacific again soon.

Sincerely,

Patricia A. Bosworth

Patricia A. Bosworth
Passenger Service Manager

FIGURE 11–4
A bad news message
using the BILL
approach.

In Figure 11–4, Ms. Bosworth is responding to a claim letter from Mr. Naranja that he had sent to the company president, Ben Brennon. On a business trip to Hawaii, Mr. Naranja was delayed on a Pacific Airlines flight from Los Angeles to Honolulu. The delay caused Mr. Naranja to miss a connecting flight to Lanai and also left him stranded for three days, unable to complete his business. Mr. Naranja wrote to Pacific requesting that they pick up the tab for at least the first night's lodging, which was $90.

Realization that Not Everyone Likes BILL

As you can see, the reader-sensitive message requires more thought and effort than a routine letter or memo does. The BILL approach, however, has important advantages: (1) by placing the bad news a little later, you have the opportunity to explain yourself first; and (2) by using a buffer and an optimistic close, you can retain the goodwill of the reader.

Even though the BILL approach is widely regarded as an effective way to deal with potentially sticky situations, not everyone agrees that it's worth the effort. One communication consultant advocates "directness in 'no' letters—not rude bluntness but straight-to-the-pointness." Using the job-applicant refusal letter as an example, the consultant said, "I believe we patronize an unsuccessful applicant when, from whatever motivation, we lead him through a circuitous route to the core of our message." His alternative is to write something like the following:

> **Dear Applicant:**
>
> **If it disappoints you to learn that we have selected another candidate to fill the position for which you applied, we want you to know that this reflects no unfavorable assessment of you or your excellent qualifications.**[1]

This consultant is primarily critical of the bad-news letter that sounds overly optimistic in the cushion section only to shift gears with the reasoning paragraph. Although the transition from buffer to refusal is sometimes too abrupt, don't throw out the time-tested BILL approach for a more direct one.

Some people can accept the more direct format without being offended. On the whole, however, many cannot. Play it safe, and stick with the BILL approach if you have any doubts about your reader's reaction.

Apology Letters

Apology letters should be straightforward and sincere, addressing as many of these reader wants as appropriate.

Figure 11–5 is a standard letter used by the U.S. Postal Service to accompany damaged mail. This letter is usually stuffed into a plastic envelope along with the remains of the damaged mail. Figure 11-6 shows a more direct and less defensive apology. Which do you prefer?

Occasionally it becomes necessary to apologize on behalf of yourself or your organization. When people are upset, they typically want some or all of the following from you:

UNITED STATES POSTAL SERVICE

Dear Postal Customer:

The enclosed was found loose in the mail or has
been damaged in handling in the Postal Service
(whichever is applicable to the enclosure).

We realize your mail is important to you, and you
have every right to expect it to be delivered intact and in good condition. The Postal Service
makes every effort to properly handle the main en-
trusted to it, but due to the large volume, occasional damage may occur.

When a Post Office handles in excess of six million
pieces of mail daily, it is imperative that automated methods be used to maintain production and
ensure prompt delivery of the mail. Damage may occur if mail is not sealed properly or bulky contents are enclosed. When this occurs and our
machinery is jammed, the faulty envelope may be
damaged, and other properly prepared mail may be
damaged as well. We are constantly striving to improve our processing methods to reduce the inci-
dence of damage.

If the enclosed was damaged during the handling, we
extend our sincere apologies for any inconvenience
you may have experienced.

Sincerely,

Jane Freeman

Plant Manager
Processing and Distribution

- To be taken seriously
- To understand their problem and the reason they are upset
- To be compensated
- To get their problem handled quickly
- To avoid further inconvenience
- To be treated with respect
- To have someone punished for the problem
- To assure them that the problem will not happen again

FIGURE 11-6

A second postal service apology letter.

UNITED STATES POSTAL SERVICE

Dear Customer:

Please accept our apologies for the damage that occurred to the enclosed letter. We know that your mail is very important, and that you expect it to be delivered in good condition. We regret any inconvenience you have been caused.

Although the Postal Service makes every effort to deliver the mail in good condition, occasional mishaps do occur. We sort mail on high-speed automated equipment in order to handle the huge volume we receive (over 165 billion pieces a year) at the lowest possible cost. Mail can be damaged when bulky contents are not securely sealed. When this happens, machinery can jam and damage not only the improperly prepared envelopes, but others as well.

Again, we apologize.

Sincerely,

Joe Brown

United States Postal Service
Salt Lake City, UT 84199-9702

Customer service expert Ron Zemke wrote a column about this post office message in *The Service Edge*.[2] In it he recommends the following rules of thumb for apologizing:

1. Apologize clearly and without equivocation for the mess, mistake, or error.

2. Accept responsibility when appropriate; remain silent if the error is the customer's.

3. Do not use the report of the error as an opportunity to instruct the customer. Revelation of error is not a teachable moment.

4. Tell the customer what you are going to do to correct the mistake. If possible, ask the customer to participate; frequently you'll find some good ideas of what an acceptable fix should look like.

5. To atone, give the customer a token of repair—a complimentary dessert, a no-charge delivery, or some sort of free add-on—to demonstrate your sincerity.

Understanding the Basics

SUMMARY OF KEY IDEAS

• Many times you will have to write letters or memos that your reader is not going to be happy to get.

• Common bad-news topics include refusals, denials, some announcements, poor performance, and apologies.

• Breaking bad news requires a strategic decision as to whether you want to exert the effort needed to retain the goodwill of the reader.

• The purpose of the BILL approach is to give you a chance to explain yourself by placing the big idea later.

• The buffer paragraph paves the way for your reasoning.

• Neutral or positive statements make good buffers.

• The transition from the cushion to your line of reasoning should be smooth, not abrupt. Your transition should help the reader sense that you are finished with pleasantries and are now getting down to business.

• Before sending out your bad-news message, make sure you know what your reasons for the bad new are—specifically.

• One of the best ways to lay out your reasoning is to go from the facts to the conclusion.

• Hiding behind company policy is *really* bad news.

• In delivering the refusal, be sure to be tactful but conclusive. Put your bad news in the middle of the letter.

• The purpose of the optimistic close is to repair any damage to goodwill between you and your reader.

• Apologies have no place in an optimistic close.

• Some people believe the bad-news message should be straight to the point.

• Apology letters should be clear, accept responsibility, avoid "teaching" the reader, explain how the problem will be fixed, and give the reader a token of repair if possible.

KEY TERMS AND CONCEPTS

bad-news messages	seed words	emphasis positions
goodwill close	lesser alternative	apology letters
buffer paragraph	transition	

1. Why is the BILL approach usually more costly to produce? When is this added cost justified?

2. What is the goal of an effective bad-news letter?

3. Describe the five parts of an effective BILL-format bad-news letter.

4. Explain the use of "seeds words" in the transition from the buffer to the reasoning phase.

5. If the reason for a refusal is "company policy," how should this be handled?

6. Where are the psychological emphasis positions in a letter?

7. Why do we recommend that you *not* apologize in the goodwill closing of the letter?

8. What arguments could you offer for *not* using the BILL-format bad-news letter?

9. What do upset people want from those who caused them problems?

Banks Use Gentler Approach with Credit Card Deadbeats

The era of ominous warning letters and threatening phone calls to credit card deadbeats may be ending. Banks apparently are turning to a kinder and gentler approach to force customers behind on their credit card payments into compliance—and to keep them as customers.

According to an Associated Press report,

> Some big banks have successfully experimented with a more customer-friendly approach— mailing the deadbeats a kindly "we-feel-your-pain" videotape that implores them to confer with a credit officer and set up a reasonable repayment schedule. With cutthroat competition for good customers, bankers believe that it's better to go easy on these people, rather than risk losing them— and their payments—for good.

Chase Manhattan Corp. began sending such a tape to hundreds of its customers in August. It features an actor who plays a bank representative saying, "Together, we can work it out," and the tape repeatedly urges delinquents to call an 800 number on the screen. Customers who call the bank will be treated with dignity and not raked over the coals, claims the seven-minute video, which *AP* says cost the bank $37,000 to produce and $3.50 each to mail.

Chase decided to try the videos nationwide after a test conducted last fall with 10,000 West Coast customers improved collections. Chase sent the video to select cardholders who had not paid their bills in three months and had not responded to repeated phone calls or mailings. The result: The bank heard from 28% more people than before the videos were sent.

Bank One has been sending its own tape to 1,000 customers a month, and an AT&T credit card subsidiary plans a video test as well. Credit counselors said the videotape strategy isn't necessarily a public relations gimmick; people who owe money often are depressed and have lost their pride. The tape might get them to respond because it's a different, unusual approach, they say.

("Banks Use Gentler Approach with Credit Card Deadbeats," *The Service Edge,* September, 1994, p. 4. Reprinted with permission.)

Applying Your Knowledge

1. Describe what you see as advantages and disadvantages of using videos for such bad-news messages.

2. How does this video approach enhance or detract from efficiency? Effectiveness? (Go back to Chapter 6 to review the differences, if necessary.)

Applying Your Skills

ACTIVITY 11-1: Bad News, Real Estate Management

Here's a letter from an apartment-management company to the tenants of the Pineview Apartments.

Can you do better? Rewrite the letter using the BILL approach.

PineView Apartments
Where the Pines Can Be Viewed:
Omaha's Prestige Address

August 2, 1997

Residents of Pineview Apartments
7350 West Springfield Glen
Omaha, NE 34567

Dear Resident:

This letter is to serve as notice of the annual
rental increase that will take effect September 1,
1997. With the September 1997 payment, all rents
will be increased $40. We have tried very hard to
keep our cost down to a minimum while at the same
time trying to maintain the property in a clean and
good condition. We can all relate to the impact the
rate of inflation has had on everyone. If we were to
raise our rent to meet our increased expenses, we
would be announcing an increase of $66 to 68! We,
therefore, think that the $40 increase is reason-
able.

We have been able to keep our increases to an annual basis. We fully intend to continue this policy. It is important to realize, however, that when
we are paying for the heat, there must exist the
possibility of a mid-year adjustment to compensate
for any unusually high rate increases from the
utilities. We have not had to do this in the past,

— PAGE 1 —

and we don't intend to do it in the near future, but it would be necessary if rates increase very much. This year's increase is actually less than last year's. We have really had to commit ourselves to keep our expenses down this year in order to keep the rental increase down to only $40.

We hope that you are happy with your accommodations and that your stay with us is a pleasant one. Please contact your resident manager if you have questions or other requests: Jennifer Castleton, 555-2664 (day), 555-4605 (evening).

Sincerely,

Robin Winnegar
Account Manager

- PAGE 2 -

ACTIVITY 11-2: Bad News, City Management

This letter from a city zoning technician uses the BIF approach to deliver the bad-news message. If you were Dr. or Mrs. Smith, how would you react to getting this letter? Would BILL be appropriate in this situation? If so, why? If not, why not? Should the city be concerned about the goodwill of the city inhabitants? Try rewriting this letter using the principles discussed in the chapter.

THE CITY OF ATLANTA
The Cultural Center of Georgia
Office of Community Development
1450 Peachtree Street
Atlanta, GA 40522

November 30, 1997

Dr. and Mrs. Guy Smith
25019 Maple Lane
Athens, GA 21212

Dear Dr. and Mrs. Smith:

It has been brought to our attention that your house at 25019 Maple Lane is currently being rented to four singles who occupy the basement apartment. This is a violation of Section 24.20.020 of the Atlanta City Zoning Ordinance and must, therefore, be corrected.

We do have a letter on file in our office that was presented to us by yourselves at the time the building permit was issued. This letter states that you are fully aware of the Atlanta city zoning requirements for this area and intend to comply with them. It appears, therefore, that your intentions have been purposely misrepresented to the city. I hope this is not the case.

In view of the above circumstances, we would like you to contact our office within ten days to discuss

---

```
this situation and make arrangements for bringing
this violation into compliance with the law. If I
do not hear from you, it will be necessary to take
appropriate legal action to obtain compliance with
city ordinances. I can be reached at 375-1822, ext.
185.



Sincerely,

Office of Community Development

Roland Houser

Roland Houser
Zoning Technician
```

ACTIVITY 11-3: Bad News, Customer Relations

Write a letter to Mrs. Susan Gruber (134 Elmer Place, Chicago, IL 60601), a safe-deposit-box holder in your bank. Let her know that her box rental has expired, and she must either renew her box or remove the contents. Relate to Mrs. Gruber that box rentals have increased 100 percent over last year, from $12 to $24. Don't forget that your bank manages Mrs. Gruber's income trust of $250,000.

ACTIVITY 11-4: Bad News, Sales

Write a memo to your supervisor (Sharon Aarons, sales manager, Arapaho Plastic Packages Corp.) explaining that you have missed your monthly sales target for food products packages by 50 percent. The original target was $50,000 for your region. Your five sales representatives worked hard but just couldn't quite close the necessary sales. One of your representatives had an emergency appendectomy during the month. The FatMutt dog-food cannery deal fell through when they elected to stay with aluminum cans instead of your plastic pouches. Your chief competitor, Canadian Can & Carton Corp., has taken away several of your existing customers by cutting their container costs by 5 percent.

ACTIVITY 11-5: Bad News, Finance

Write a memo to the president of your company (Home Entertainment Products, Laser Division) detailing the findings of your research project. Essentially, the findings include the following:

• The company has sufficient cash flow to operate only three months at the current level.

• The new record-playback laser disk is not selling well against competition.

• Some of the top management have determined that the company is going under and are beginning to send out their resumes.

You have been with the company only six months since your graduation in business administration from a well-known West Coast university. You were hired into the brand new Internal Consulting Department, which has yet to prove its worth to the company.

ACTIVITY 11-6: Refusal, Human Resources

In the letter on page 302, Ms. Bromford must turn down an applicant for a job for which he is not physically qualified. How well does Ms. Bromford succeed? See how much better you can write this letter. Be sure to use the principles covered in the chapter.

ACTIVITY 11-7: Refusal, Customer Service

Write a letter to Mary Kronig (321 Carlson St., Freeport, ME 04101), letting her know her credit-card request has been denied. Mary is 24 years old, single, and employed part-time at Cougar Motors in downtown Freeport, Maine. Mary is just finishing her bachelor's degree at the local college. About once a month, she drops into your women's shop to buy clothes. Because she is a regular customer, your boss suggested that Mary apply for a charge card. In checking with the local credit bureau, you found that she is heavily in debt and has a long history of late payments and several defaults in earlier loans.

ACTIVITY 11-8: Refusal, Literary Agency

Sam Nelson, a ghostwriter and literary agent, has been hired to write a self-improvement book for

Ba[...]
succ[...]
chapt[...]
Two [...]
a $100,[...]
son for [...]
tute is wi[...]
sell at its s[...]
Sam, Gold[...]
Their offer i[...]
its parent cor[...]
Goldman wou[...]
Sam must now [...] ...nt at St. Peter's Press, [...], even though, personally, he thi[...] ...s would be a better choice from a pure[...] ...ishing standpoint. Your task is to compose this letter, explaining why an admittedly inferior publisher is getting Goldman's book.

ACTIVITY 11-9: Refusal, Customer Service

For the past ten years, Top Management Book Club (TMBC) has been offering a great deal to executives. A new club member can order four books for $1 each (plus shipping and handling) with no obligation to buy any more books—ever. Robin Miller, a customer service representative for TMBC, has been processing new memberships when her computer flags one of them. John Grisbold of 428 Washington Avenue, Cincinnati, OH 45202, the computer says, has joined TMBC four previous times, received the initial order, and then canceled his membership without buying any books at regular club prices. TMBC has enacted a new policy that automatically rejects the repeat membership of anyone who ever belonged to the club but canceled without buying a book. Grisbold falls into this category four times over. Robin must now write a brief letter to Mr. Grisbold, explaining the reason why TMBC is rejecting his membership application. Write this letter as if you were Robin Miller.

ACTIVITY 11-10: Lesser Alternative, Law Office

Lee Galeez, an attorney in the injury claims business, ran a full-page, color advertisement on the back cover of the local telephone book last fall. Since then he has been deluged with new clients. He hired two recent law school graduates to help with the caseload, but he's still swamped. Today he received a letter from Carl Neubold, a retiree who claims he was bitten by his neighbor's pet iguana and suffered

August 4, 199X

Mr. Ralph Tidwell
79 East Zina Avenue
Florissant, MS

Dear Mr. Tidwell:

We must refuse your request for a job in our Loading Department. It is simply impossible for us to
give you the job of materials handler specialist.

We are certain that you understand that our labor
requirements in the Loading Department are for persons who are quite strong and who can do heavy
physical work, lifting and carrying for long periods. If we were to hire people like you with histo-
ries of heart trouble and back strain particularly
men who are 59 years old, then our insurance rates
would skyrocket. That would be bad business.

Please accept our best wishes for the success of
your hernia operation. Once again, we are sorry we
cannot give you the job.

Sincerely,

Rosemary Bromford

Rosemary Bromford
Manager of Personnel Placement

---

nerve damage to his finger. Two years ago, Lee would have jumped at this case, but now it doesn't look as promising as all the automobile-accident claims he has lined up. He has asked you to fire off a quick letter, rejecting Carl's inquiry. Then, as an afterthought, he suggests that you refer Mr. Neubold to Buck Short, a classmate from law school. Carl Neubold's address is 201 Meadow Road, Edison, NJ 08817.

ACTIVITY 11-11: Lesser Alternative, Labor Relations

Wendy Pack, quality assurance manager for Robotix, Inc., has a dilemma. She started an employee suggestion program two months ago, and she desperately wants it to succeed. She realizes that to have the employees support the program, she must use a good percentage of their suggestions, even if some of them are not particularly effective. She has also made it a policy to send a brief memo to each employee who submits a suggestion, either telling them that Robotix is implementing their idea or explaining why the company can't use their suggestion at this time. Today she received two suggestions that would have the same effect, but one is far more expensive than the other. Phyllis Carpenter, a line worker in robot assembly, suggested that two workstations be realigned to eliminate a recurring bottleneck. Harry Simons, a supervisor on the same line, recommended adding an additional worker to solve the bottleneck problem. Wendy has asked you to write a memo to Harry, thanking him for his suggestion but explaining that another suggestion solved the problem at no additional cost to the company.

ACTIVITY 11-12: Lesser Alternative, Labor Relations

Midwest Airlines has taken a hit because of recent fare wars. The company has had record losses in each of the past six quarters. CEO Eddie Richterbaker must cut costs somehow or watch Midwest fly off into the sunset. He has decided that the best solution is to cut several less popular routes. This would result in the termination of 10 percent of Midwest pilots and flight crews. When this decision was brought before the pilots, they came up with an alternative: Convert five L-1011 planes into cargo jets, and pick up a share of the expanding Pacific Rim cargo market. This alternative would save all the pilot jobs and 20 percent of jobs for the flight crews. Eddie liked this suggestion and asked his financial people to analyze this proposal. Eddie was disappointed to learn that, based on projections, Midwest would be able to acquire only enough of the cargo market to justify the converting of three planes. He must now break the mixed news to his pilots and flight crews. Draft a letter from Eddie to the affected Midwest employees. Explain that 4 percent of the pilots and 9 percent of other flight crew members would be laid off. This is better than he originally hoped for but worse than the pilots' suggestion promised.

ACTIVITY 11-13: Lesser Alternative, Customer Service

Your employer, THC, a health insurance provider, has received an application from Warren Harris, a self-employed roofer. As you look through his application, you notice several red flags. Harris has a his-

tory of high blood pressure and a bad back from 20 years of roofing. His wife takes several medications that suggest chronic problems that will only get worse with time. You must write Warren a letter, rejecting his application. Because you don't want to leave him high and dry, you decide to refer him to a competitor, Healthway, Inc., a provider with a greater tolerance for risk and (consequently) much higher rates. Harris's address is 2104 W. Florist Ave., Milwaukee, WI 53209.

ACTIVITY 11-14: Apology, Hospital Administration

The hospital administrator at a university hospital received a disturbing letter one day. In this letter an upset husband and father explained how his wife had given birth by emergency cesarean section to a three-month-premature baby—at your hospital. While the baby had received excellent care, the attention received by his wife had ranged from merely negligent to grossly incompetent.

The letter than attacked the nursing staff in the maternity ward. They were inattentive, failing consistently to answer the nurse button, once making her wait 20 minutes when the intravenous line fell out of her arm and dripped all over the bed. The husband claimed that he had to perform many of the nurse's duties himself. When the nurse wouldn't answer her page, he would go looking for help, and would find a group of five or six other nurses standing at the station, "just shooting the breeze." When he asked for help, their response was "Her nurse must be busy." He called this an "it's not my job" attitude.

The final criticism was leveled at certain charges on their hospital bill, including a $12 charge because he stayed in her room the night the baby was born. "Where else was I to go?" he asked. "My wife was in terrible pain, and my baby was fighting for his life." In his opinion, this was a Mickey Mouse policy.

Assume you are the hospital administrator. You realize that this family went through a trying ordeal. They probably do not have good cause to sue the hospital for malpractice, and the letter didn't threaten legal action. There is another concern here, though. What if all these allegations are true? They certainly are from this man's perspective. He and his wife were undoubtedly angered by the lack of care given in the hospital. This suggests a severe quality problem. You want to get to the bottom of this, but first you must write him a letter, apologizing for the negative experience he and his wife had at your hospital. Outline specific actions in the letter that you are taking to investigate and correct the situation.

ACTIVITY 11-15: Apology, Management

In the late 1980s, Audi, a division of Volkswagen AG of West Germany, made a terrible public relations move. Many Audi 5000 owners had complained of a "sudden acceleration" problem, where the car would suddenly and unintentionally accelerate. In one month this problem resulted in 513 accidents, 271 injuries, and 5 deaths, according to the National Highway Traffic Safety Administration. Audi's initial response? The company claimed that drivers were unintentionally pressing the accelerator instead of the brake. A big mistake. As one marketing professor put it, "When somebody is shelling out more than $20,000 for a car, he doesn't want to be told he doesn't know how to drive it." This stance resulted in a 20 percent drop in sales the next year. Assume you were responsible for Audi's next move. What would you have done? Draft a letter to Audi 5000 owners, explaining what the company is willing to do to correct the problem.

ACTIVITY 11-16: Apology, Customer Service

National Bank of South Dakota has received a letter from a disgruntled Visa card holder. "In January I called with a concern and one of your customer service people told me they would extend my introductory 6.9 percent interest rate another six months. When I got my statement this month I noticed that I am being charged 18.9 percent. What's the deal?" National Bank keeps no records of telephone conversations, so there is no way to verify this. Bank policy, however, states that the customer is always right. Write to Vic Garcia of 300 North Minnesota, Sioux Falls, SD 57117, apologize, and verify in writing that the 6.9 percent rate will be in effect for another full year.

ACTIVITY 11-17: Apology, Information Systems

Emily Ransom, information systems manager at Harris Business School, supervises the maintenance of the alumni database. Students enter data from surveys sent to each alumnus into the database, so that the school has current information on names, addresses, telephone numbers, occupations, contributions, and so forth. This information is published biannually in an alumni directory that interested parties can purchase for $25. The latest directory was mailed a month ago. Last week Emily received a nasty letter from Charles Mason, an alumnus who was upset about his own listing in the directory. "On your survey I listed my occupation as 'mort. sec.,' which, as any idiot would know, means mortgage securities. You listed me as a mortgage secretary. I am humiliated and infuriated at your incompetence. Strike my name from your mailing lists. I never want to hear from you again, and you can bet I'll never contribute any more of my hard-earned money to the Harris School of Incompetence." Emily realizes this is probably a lost cause, but she has asked you to compose a letter over her signature to Mr. Charles Mason, Acme Financial Services, 411 Pearl Street, Jackson, MI 39205.

PERFORMING
on the Job

CASE 11-1 Unfilled Bags[3]

The maker of the popular Hyponex brand pine bark mulch said Friday it is replacing bags sold at the 124 Kmart stores in the Carolinas and one in Georgia, because some bags sold were not full.

Garden products giant Scotts Co., which makes Hyponex Pine Bark Nuggets and Mulch, said it has cut prices and alerted customers of the problem in the meantime. Mulch is used by gardeners to keep soil moist and suppress weeds around bushes and plants.

In a search of seven N.C. cities, state Department of Agriculture investigators found last week that Hyponex mulch bags, which were labeled 2 cubic feet, were understuffed by 6 percent to 10 percent. They ordered Kmart to stop selling the bags, and Kmart in turn asked Scotts to replace the bags. The investigation was prompted by a tip from a competing maker of mulch.

In response to the investigation's findings, Scotts sent signs to local stores alerting customers to the problem. Kmart has been compensated for the mistake, and the bags were replaced. The affected Kmart stores began selling the new bags at a discount Monday, said a spokesman for Marysville, Ohio-based Scotts.

"We moved to fix the problem as soon as we found out about it," a Scotts spokesman said. "All we know is that it was a manufacturing problem. It could have been a mechanical problem or human error."

Neither Kmart nor Scotts was fined by the N.C. Department of Agriculture for the mistake. Under-stuffed Hyponex products were also found at Home Depot stores in Charlotte and Raleigh, according to Ron Murdock, program manager for the measurements section of the standards division of the department.

The Scotts' spokesman said the company is investigating the Chester and Jackson plants to figure out how the problem occurred. Assembly lines at the two plants have been adjusted to fill bags to the full 2 cubic feet.

At the Kmart in Pineville, Hyponex pine bark is selling for $1.20, down 24 cents from its usual price.

"The customer is making out like a bandit on these," said Jason Smith, the manager of the lawn and garden department at the Pineville store. Smith said the Pineville store hasn't received any underfilled bags of Hyponex mulch.

"Scotts has been very good about it," Smith said. "I think they took care of the problem."

Murdock said Scotts is being "most cooperative in this thing and trying to get replacement product and picking up bad product."

Case Question

1. Assume the role as spokesman for Scotts. Prepare an open letter to customers that could be printed in newspapers throughout the state.

CASE 11-2 Canceled Symposium

The following campus memo was sent to faculty members about one week before a scheduled symposium was to take place.

CAMPUS MEMORANDUM
UPPER STATE UNIVERSITY

TO: All Faculty

FROM: Sal Swinyardson, Retail Institute

DATE: July 28, 1998

RE: Faculty Retail Symposium at Sunbird Resort

Thank you for your willingness to participate in our Faculty Retailing Symposium. We have appreciated your cooperation and support of the Retail Institute program.

We had assembled an impressive two-day symposium—one that would educate and enlighten those in attendance. However, we seem to have unforeseen scheduling conflicts that have hindered attendance. We have done everything possible to make the symposium work, but as the symposium dates grow nearer, we have been forced to admit that the conflicts are insurmountable ones.

Therefore, it is with deep regret that we are postponing the program until a better time frame can be found. We will be in touch with you.

Once again, thank you for your willingness to participate in and support our program. We look forward to the rescheduled symposium.

Case Questions

1. What is your overall reaction to this message?

2. Assuming that readers will be disappointed by this message, what could have been done to make the memo more effective?

3. How would you rewrite this to be more effective?

Persuasive *and* Sales Messages:
Getting Results

LEARNING GOALS

After you have studied this chapter, you should be able to:

- Define persuasive communication.

- Identify five types of persuasive messages.

- Describe the difference between persuasion and manipulation.

- Identify the four elements of the ANSA approach.

- List at least five popular attention-getters.

- Describe five key principles in capturing the reader's interest.

- Phrase a persuasive appeal either positively or negatively.

- Identify the elements of successful need development.

- Identify and describe five types of evidence that can be used to convince the reader that your offer fills his or her need.

- Identify the key elements of an action close.

- Describe the distinction between features and benefits.

- Rewrite poorly organized persuasive messages to improve their impact.

The Way It Is . . . Getting Readers to "Just Do It"

Action! That's what you're after in a persuasive message. A good persuasive business letter or memo persuades the reader to *do* something—something the reader would not normally do without some prodding. Persuasive communication goes beyond simply providing information to your reader and convincing him or her that you are right. The persuasive message influences your reader to act on your request.

The effectiveness of the persuasive message can often be judged by the action that results. The effective sales letter sells. The effective collection letter collects. The effective fund-raising letter fills the coffers. The worst thing that can happen to you is to have your reader finish your persuasive message and say, "That's nice." Well, that's *not* nice, because you want results.

To get results, you will generally need to appeal to the emotions of your reader. The persuasive message, then, is similar to the bad-news message discussed in Chapter 11—both messages work on the reader's emotions to some extent.

With a bad-news message, you anticipate your reader's disappointment and put the bad news a little later in your letter. The purpose of using this approach is to soften or downplay the emotional response. With the persuasive message, you want to use reader emotions for a different effect: You want to create enough enthusiasm and positive emotions toward your request to motivate your reader to action. As with the bad-news message, you place your big idea or request for action a little later in your message to build up to it.

The following letter has been used for years to sell subscriptions to the *Wall Street Journal.* The fact that it continues to be used tells us that it is obviously effective. As you can see, it's a bit longer than many business messages, but persuasion often requires more elaboration than BIF approach letters.

Many keys to successful persuasion are employed in this letter. When you have finished reading this chapter, you will be able to identify these techniques and use similar ones to produce effective persuasive letters yourself.

Goal of Persuasive Messages

Although persuasion always seeks some sort of action, persuasive communication is not limited to sales letters. Other types of **persuasive messages** are the following:

- Requests for favors
- Proposals
- Some invitations
- Memos urging cooperation
- Requests for cooperation in policy or performance requirements changes
- Job-application letters (this is a special case, treated separately in Chapter Thirteen.)
- Requests for donations
- Some claim letters

THE WALL STREET JOURNAL

World Financial Center, 200 Liberty Street, New York, NY 10281

Dear Reader:

On a beautiful late spring afternoon, twenty-five years ago, two young men graduated from the same college. They were very much alike, these two young men. Both had been better than average students, both were personable and both—as young college graduates are—were filled with ambitious dreams for the future.

Recently, these men returned to their college for their 25th reunion.

They were still very much alike. Both were happily married. Both had three children. And both, it turned out, had gone to work for the same Midwestern manufacturing company after graduation, and were still there.

But there was a difference. One of the men was manager of a small department of that company. The other was its president.

What Made the Difference

Have you ever wondered, as I have, what makes this kind of difference in people's lives? It isn't a native intelligence or talent or dedication. It isn't that one person wants success and the other doesn't.

The difference lies in what each person knows and how he or she makes use of that knowledge.

And that is why I am writing to you and to people like you about *The Wall Street Journal*. For that is the whole purpose of The Journal: to give its readers knowledge—knowledge that they can use in business.

A Publication Unlike Any Other

You see, *The Wall Street Journal* is a unique publication. It's the country's only national business

FIGURE 12–1

The Wall Street Journal promotional letter.

daily. Each business day, it is put together by the world's largest staff of business-news experts.

Each business day, The Journal's pages include a broad range of information of interest and significance to business-minded people, no matter where it comes from. *Not just stocks and finance,* but anything and everything in the whole, fast-moving world of business. . . *The Wall Street Journal* gives you all the business news you need—when you need it.

Knowledge Is Power

Right now, I am looking at page one of The Journal, the best-read front page in America. It combines all the important news of the day with in-depth feature reporting. Every phase of business news is covered. I see articles on new taxes, inflation, business forecasts, gas prices, politics. I see major stories from Washington, Berlin, Tokyo, the Middle East. I see item after item that can affect you, your job, your future.

And there is page after page inside The Journal, filled with fascinating and significant information that's useful to you. The *Marketplace* section gives you insights into how consumers are thinking and spending, how companies compete for market share. There is daily coverage of law, technology, media and marketing. Plus daily features on the challenges of managing smaller companies.

The Journal is also the single best source for news and statistics about your money. In the *Money & Investing* section there are helpful charts, easy-to-scan market quotations, plus "Abreast of the Market," "Heard on the Street" and "Your Money Matters," three of America's most influential and carefully read investment columns.

If you have never read *The Wall Street Journal,* you cannot imagine how useful it can be to you.

A Money-Saving Subscription

Put our statements to the proof by subscribing for the next 13 weeks for *just* $44. This is among the shortest subscription terms we offer—and a perfect way to get acquainted with The Journal.

FIGURE 12-1 cont'd

Or you may prefer to take advantage of our *better buy*—one year for $149. You save over $40 off the cover price of The Journal.

Simply fill out the enclosed order card and mail it in the postage-paid envelope provided. And here's The Journal guarantee: should The Journal not measure up to your expectations, you may cancel this arrangement at any point and receive a refund for the undelivered portion of your subscription.

If you feel as we do that this is a fair and reasonable proposition, then you will want to find out without delay if *The Wall Street Journal* can do for you what it is doing for millions of readers. So please mail the enclosed order card now, and we will start serving you immediately.

About those two college classmates I mentioned at the beginning of this letter: they graduated from college together and together got started in the business world. So what made their *lives* in business different?

Knowledge. Useful knowledge. And its application.

An Investment in Success

I cannot promise you that success will be instantly yours if you start reading *The Wall Street Journal*. But I can guarantee that you will find The Journal always interesting, always reliable, and always useful.

Sincerely,

Peter R. Kann
Publisher

PRK:id
Encs.

P.S. It's important to note that The Journal's subscription price may be tax deductible. Ask your tax advisor.

FIGURE 12-1 cont'd

Although these other types of persuasive communication are not sales letters in the strict sense, they do attempt to *sell* an idea or request.

All this talk of *action, results, influence,* and *persuasion* may sound a bit manipulative. The fact is, persuasive communication is a daily occurrence. Think back for a minute to the beginning of the day and count how many times people have tried to persuade you today. Everyday we are bombarded by television or radio commercials, junk mail, and requests from other people.

Persuasion, in its best form, is not manipulation. Persuasion is the art of influencing people to act in their own best interest. Manipulation, conversely, is somewhat different. The manipulator tries to persuade others to take action solely to benefit the manipulator.

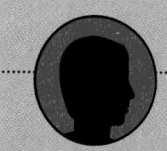

COMMUNICATOR'S PROFILE

Weston Cook, Salomon Brothers, Investment Bank

Weston Cook is a young executive in a high-pressure business: investment banking. His organization is "very meritocratic," meaning that people advance based on what they accomplish. "A person's ability to communicate effectively and convincingly in both written and oral form is critical to achieving a high level of success on the job."

The major communication challenge facing his organization? "Time. In this profession time is a rare asset. Important ideas can be brushed under the carpet if your communication is not relevant to the listener's agenda. People must be aware of the benefits of talking with you and understand through concise communication how the organization's interests will be promoted [by listening to your ideas.]"

Weston spends 40 percent of his work day writing correspondence (e-mail or paper). Another 30 percent is spent on the phone and the last 30 percent in meetings or one-to-one communication. In other words, his whole job in this world-famous financial institution is communication!

Psychology of Persuasion

Persuasion presupposes some resistance.

Persuasive communication presupposes some resistance to what you have to say. That's natural. After all, your message calls for action. Action implies change, and change requires effort—that your reader would probably just as soon avoid. It's your job to motivate your reader to expend the needed effort to change. To do so, you will need to make some guesses about your reader's needs, wants, and motives.

Knowing your reader's need level helps you be more persuasive.

Most people are persuaded for one of two reasons: to gain a benefit or to avoid a loss. The trick is to know which benefits your reader would like to obtain or avoid

Nike's "Just Do It" slogan is an example of influencing people to act in their own best interests. (Courtesy of Jim Cummins/FPG International.)

losing. Careful thought about your message receiver can improve your persuasive results. The more you can put yourself in another's shoes, the more effective you will be in persuading that person.

Persuasive Requests: Use BILL

Resistance to change is a formidable competitor of persuasion.

The persuasive business message is *action* oriented. It seeks to get the reader to *do* something he or she normally would not do without some prodding. The letter's effectiveness can be judged by the action that results. (Messages and letters also refer to any other print materials that may accompany them. Brochures, flyers, product samples, and multimedia sales aids are often used as part of the persuasive effort.) The effective sales letter sells. The effective collection letter collects. By their fruits shall they be evaluated.

Letters that persuade people normally require a slow, deliberate approach. They need to be phrased in terms of *the reader's* interests, not the writer's. They need to employ vivid language that conveys clear images. The underlying theme of the entire letter should be one of explaining the benefits of your proposal to your reader. The letter should follow a systematic arrangement that leads the reader inevitably to the desired action. One such pattern of arrangement is described next.

ANSA Approach to Persuasion

In theory, successful persuasion is simple. All you have to do is help your reader get the answer to his or her problem. The key word is *answer*. With a little mnemonic magic this becomes ANSA (answer spoken with a Boston accent), which stands for the following:

Attention

Need development

Solution to the problem

Action

Memory aids, such as the ANSA mnemonic, really will help you remember not only the four parts to the approach but the key to successful persuasion—providing answers.

ANSA suggests a pattern of arrangement, but it need not be rigidly applied.

The **ANSA approach** works in almost all written and oral persuasive settings. Though the following sections discuss each part as if it were one isolated step in a four-step sequence, the truth is these parts often overlap. Sometimes the parts are even presented in a different order with the solution presentation coming before need development. Other times, when the need is evident, more emphasis is placed on getting attention and convincing the reader your product really is the answer. With this understanding clearly in mind, the following sections examine each part of the ANSA approach separately.

A Is for Attention

You don't have much time to get your reader's attention.

Everyone gets persuasive messages in the mail. Most are called direct mail—mass-mailed persuasive messages, which some people refer to as junk mail. Only about 30 percent of the people who receive such sales letters read the persuasive message, whereas 45 percent open and glance at the mailing. The rest of the people throw direct mail away, unread.

Our point is this: You as a persuader don't have much time to grab the interest of your reader. Granted, many of your persuasive messages will not be of the direct-mail variety. From our experience with persuasive communication, the conclusion is still the same—you don't have much time to get your reader into the message.

How do you turn a "glancer" into a reader? You have to arouse interest and get the glancer to pay attention. That's the first step. If you are successful, your reader will want to finish the rest of your message.

Sounds simple enough, but how do you get your reader's eyes to focus on your message? To answer that one, take a look at some popular attention-getters. While you're looking over these examples, see if you can spot some common concepts for sparking interest. There are at least five that we've been able to isolate.

1. Quote from a famous person	"Know thyself," Socrates admonished. At the North Island Institute, you get a chance to come in contact with the real you.
2. Story	The customers were lining up for blocks behind the sales cash register. "I hope I get there before they run out," an elderly woman intoned. Wouldn't you like lines like this at your store? Let's find out what's going on and see how you can make this happen for you.
3. Astonishing fact	More money is spent on alcohol rehabilitation in this country than on primary education.
4. News announcement	"The 199X tax act is the middle income earner's act," say the experts. Did you know that under this act, you can. . . .

5. Proverb	Time is money. Unless. . . .
6. Bargain	Designer jeans at half price!
7. Solution to a problem	Finally, a plastic that resists the subfreezing cold in your area.
8. Split sentence	Come on in . . . and see the selection of fall merchandise our buyers have just acquired for you.
9. Free gift	Welcome to the area! Please accept this coupon for a free gift as a little neighborly token.
10. Question	How would you like to save $2,000 a month in your department?
11. Free sample	Because you've recently purchased one of our executive shirts, we thought you'd like to complement your wardrobe with one of our new wool blazers. Inside, you'll find swatch samples to give you a feel for the quality material that goes into our coats.
12. Interesting anecdote	The other day I tried to explain to my son what would happen if we got into a car accident. We even discussed the possibility of my dying. My son didn't seem concerned. He said, "Well, we will just have to get a new daddy." "Don't you wish it were that easy?"
13. Outstanding feature	Handwarmers that do the job without the hazard of fire. We finally got them in stock.
14. What-if opening	What if Harry came to you and said, "We need to reduce our staff by 10 percent"? Susan, that day is coming. Seriously, we need to sit down and talk about staff cuts.
15. Analogy	Gold jewelry—the only gift worth its weight.

Before you read on, take a few minutes to jot down the common concepts you see in these examples.

Key Principles in Arousing Interest. The following list is by no means conclusive. If you fail to use these five concepts, however, you may fail to grab your reader's interest.

1. Use a position of emphasis.
2. Write in the second person.
3. Go heavy on the action verbs and concrete nouns.
4. Be original.
5. *Relate your attention-getter to the needs of your reader.*

How did you do in your analysis of the examples? We hope you identified the fifth idea. It is probably the most important key to a successful attention-getter. Let's talk just a bit about each of these concepts.

The first line is a strong emphasis position.

Position of Emphasis. In most letters, the *first line* is one of the strongest positions of emphasis. Don't waste this spot on droll nonessentials. Put your attention-getter right there on the first line.

Chapter 11 showed you how to de-emphasize bad news by *avoiding* emphasis positions. In persuasive messages, use emphasis positions to focus the reader on important information.

Second Person. Baby, it's you, you, you, ... Look at examples 1, 2, 4, 7 and 8 in the list of popular attention-getters. Each of these directly or indirectly uses the second person, "you." This makes the reader think that you have addressed the message to him or her, and you have! The use of the second person personalizes the message.

Action verbs and concrete nouns create vivid mental pictures.

Action Verbs and Concrete Nouns. Would you want to receive a persuasive letter that starts like this?

Dear Customer:

We here at the Porterville Mall have recently expanded our facility to include a number of new stores. That's exciting to us. Now we have a new toy store, book store, nail boutique, and mid-Eastern vegetarian clinic.

Boring! Who cares about the Porterville Mall and its expansion? If you want to succeed in getting your reader's attention, personalize the letter with "you." Show the readers what's in it for *them*.

Action verbs and **concrete nouns** are pretty loud words. To persuade, you need to create vivid mental pictures in your reader's mind. The *Wall Street Journal* letter at the beginning of this chapter is rich with words that create clear mental pictures.

If you want to arouse interest, you need to help the reader see your product or idea and visualize how it is going to help him or her. Use action verbs and concrete nouns liberally.

Be Original: I Coined This Myself. The quickest way to turn your letter glancer into a letter discarder is to be trite—a user of tired, worn-out ideas. Think about the last detergent commercial you saw. If the commercial claimed the product was "new and improved," did you really listen? I mean, how many times can you really improve soap? One place you don't want to follow the leader is in persuasive letters. **"Me-too" messages** almost always end up in the trash.

Be original. Be different.

How Will This Benefit My Reader? A successful attention-getter relates your product or idea to the needs of your reader. Psychologists typically cite four categories of appeals you can use to gain reader attention. We can appeal to the reader's needs for *health, wealth,* and *pleasure,* and to his or her *curiosity.* In organizations, you might add appeals to the need for *success, power* or *status enhancement,* and *self-satisfaction.* Such attention-getting appeals may be phrased positively or negatively. Positive appeals focus on what the reader stands to gain; negative appeals accentuate what the reader might lose if he or she does not pay attention to your message. Examples of such appeals are presented in Table 12–1.

N Is for Need Development

Presenting a need upsets the reader's sense of psychological balance, motivating him to a solution.

Often the attention-getter combines interest-creating information with a description of a problem (like the *Wall Street Journal* letter). Television commercials also typically follow this pattern. They present an unpleasant situation in such a way that you can identify with the victim of (say, "ring around the collar,") or the restaurant hamburger with little meat ("Where's the beef?").

Why does agitation move the reader to action? Psychologists explain this in terms of *balance theory.* People prefer to be in a state of psychological balance or equilibrium; they want perceptions to fit together, make sense, seem rational, and be comfortable. When you expose a problem that your reader can identify with, you create a feeling of tension and imbalance in the reader; it's agitating! To reduce tension, the reader will try to restore psychological balance. That balance comes about by doing what the persuader suggests. At least that's how it's supposed to work.

Our intent should be to articulate a problem that can be solved by the product we want you to buy. Although television spots exaggerate, this persuasion pattern of

TABLE 12-1

ATTENTION-GETTING APPEALS

Success	Power and Status Enhancement	Self-Satisfaction	Curiosity
Positive Appeals			
Acting will lead to the reader's success in accomplishing goals	Acting will improve the reader's power and status.	Acting will lead to a sense of satisfaction for the reader.	Acting will answer questions the reader would like answered.
Example: "You can break into the million-dollar sales club. . . ."	*Example:* "Want to get others to perk up and listen when you have something to say?"	*Example:* "How would you like to be your own boss?"	*Example:* "How would you like to know your competitor's exact pricing tables?"
Negative Appeals			
Not acting will lead to the reader's failure to accomplish goals.	Not acting will cost the reader loss of power or status.	Not acting will lead to dissatisfaction or missed opportunity for the reader.	Not acting will leave important questions unanswered.
Example: "Can you be satisfied with another average sales year?"	*Example:* "Are other young executives passing you by?"	*Example:* "How much longer can you take the drudgery of your 9-to-5 job?"	*Example:* "Is what you don't know about the competition killing you?"

attention, **need development**—followed by solution—is often an effective one. In the following letter excerpt, the persuasive intent is to get the reader to contribute to the university radio station. Here is the opening need-developing phase.

> **With the recent change of WBCY-FM to a rock music format, those of us who enjoy bright, easy listening stereo radio are stuck. There remains only one such station in our community. And because of this no-competition situation, that station has increased its advertising time and reduced the amount of music.**

> **I still like the mellow, contemporary sounds of our one remaining station, WEZC-FM, and I suspect you do too. But it seems absurd that a city this size cannot offer more than one high-quality station. What would we do if WEZC would follow their competitor into the lucrative rock radio market? We'd all suffer the loss. East Dogpatch needs another FM station to play the kind of music contemporary young adults enjoy.**

That's the need-development phase. If your readers agree that there is a potential problem here, you have met the first requirement of a persuasive message. Now you can begin to explain how the problem might be solved with additional information such as the following:

> **Now you and I can play a part in filling that need and guaranteeing the continuation of our kind of music. The state legislature has pledged $70,000 in matching funds to WFAE-FM, the university radio station, if we can raise only $20,000.**

Once the opening appeal has succeeded in gaining the reader's interest, the writer's job is to explain how the need aroused can be satisfied. You can now show the reader the **personal benefit** to be gained.

Importance of "You" Viewpoint. Many persuasive requests run afoul when the writer forgets the "you" attitude. The following letter illustrates this. The letter was used by a political candidate to raise money for his campaign. It was printed on campaign letterhead paper, personally signed, and was a generally attractive document. Consider the content, however.

The tone in this letter is "I" oriented. The use of the dollar figure at the top of the page is fairly effective—it does spark curiosity of the reader. The use of exclamation points and underlining for emphasis seem out of place. Exclamation points give us the image of a circus barker. Avoid them.

Suppose you were working on this candidate's campaign. How would you rewrite this message to create a **"you" viewpoint?**

First, consider what the reader potentially has to gain by doing the desired action (sending in $21.83). We may want to appeal to the reader's need or desire to have good people elected to public office, assuming that they perceive this candidate to be a good person. More specifically, most people are likely to feel a sense of status enhancement in having a friend they supported get elected to office. A positive appeal may imply that their contribution will result in the candidate's election and that his election will give them some special influence in the legislature. Thinking along these lines, you might rework this letter, adding a "you" orientation.

```
                          $15,279.47

The figure above is the amount that I must raise to
win election to the North Carolina House of Repre-
sentatives.

You are one of 700 friends I feel that I can count
on. I'm asking for your financial support in the
amount of $21.83!!!

July 25th is the date we must have all money on
hand!!!

Please make checks payable to Alan Jones for N.C.
House and forward to John S. Fredericks, Treasurer,
2011 Doughton Road, Charlotte, NC 28207.

Thank you for your consideration.


                              Sincerely,

                              Alan Jones

                              Alan Jones
```

5 Is for Solution to the Problem

Once you have the reader's attention and have developed a need, your job is to explain to the reader how to satisfy that need. You want to show the reader what's in it for him or her. You want to give the reader *the* solution, and to convince your reader you really do have the solution, you'll need to present believable evidence. Such evidence can take the form of

- A description of benefits your product or idea has to offer
- Third-party quotes or testimonials
- Enclosed product samples or free trial offers

$15,279.47

The figure above is what is will cost to put *your* representative in the North Carolina House.

You are one of 700 friends I value deeply. Your past friendship and support have led me to believe that we share similar concerns for our state government and that I can effectively represent your interests in Raleigh. To bring this about, I'm asking for your financial help. Your contribution of only $21.83 puts us in a position where we can, and will, win the election on November 7.

To meet our campaign expenses, the money needs to be in the hands of John Fredericks, my campaign treasurer, by July 25. With your help, your voice will be heard in the upcoming legislative session.

Cordially,

Alan Jones

Alan Jones

- A special price or cost justification
- Answers to possible objections about your product or idea

A skilled persuader refers to product features only as they relate to reader benefits.

Feature-Benefit Distinction. Of these types of evidence, the most important one is the description of benefits your product or idea offers—*not product features.* The skillful persuader alludes to the product's features only as they relate to the reader's benefit. The features are attributes of the product or idea you are selling. The benefits are what the features mean to the customer.

One of your authors used to work with sales representatives for a large office-products manufacturer. The copying machines he sold had many impressive features.

They had the ability to copy on both sides of the sheet of paper automatically, to reproduce from light originals, to reduce the original onto a sheet half the size, and so on. These, at the time, were features unique to this company's products.

Time after time, sales representatives tried to sell these features but failed to sell the product. The successful persuader was the one who tied features to benefits.

> **This machine copies on both sides of a sheet [feature]. And what this means to you, Mr. Customer, is that you can cut your paper costs significantly, reduce postage costs, perhaps even reduce the need for additional filing cabinets. This feature can save you a lot of money [benefits].**

Remember, a feature is simply some aspect or characteristic of your product. An automobile may have a V-8 engine, a vacuum cleaner has a hose attachment, and a photocopier can copy on both sides of a sheet of paper. These are features.

A *benefit,* however, is a "what-this-means-to-you, the-customer (or reader) statement." The hose attachment gets into corners and *makes your home cleaner and more attractive.* The photocopier allows you to *save on paper and postage* because it copies on both sides.

One of the best examples of a benefit statement was seen on the box that holds attachments for a vacuum cleaner. There written in large letters were the words: "More Free Time for You." It didn't say "This machine really sucks up dirt," or "Your house will be cleaner." It got to the ultimate benefit: more free time.

Take a further look at this **feature-benefit distinction** by examining some excerpts from persuasive letters.

Feature	Benefit or What This Means to You
The Western Silver Card provides you with a $2,000 line of credit.	You can use this line of credit to get $2,000 cash when you need it most. Your Western Silver Card will even help you with your line of credit when you're traveling in the United States or abroad.
World magazine carries articles on a wide range of interests.	*World*'s articles are thought provoking. Its color photographs and lavish reproductions of great art are a treat for the eyes. Through its pages you may share a 100-foot-high platform with an arboreal naturalist under the mysterious vegetation canopy of a Costa Rican rain forest.

Let's apply this feature-benefit distinction to a persuasive request made to another department. Figure 12–2 is an effort to persuade one manager that another manger's suggestion is good enough to warrant payment.

Helen is translating the features of her idea to the benefits by explaining "What this means to you."

MEMORANDUM

TO: Jackson Gray, Manager
       Installations and Repair

FROM: Helen Baker, Manager
       Commercial Operations

DATE: April 19, 199X

RE: Operational Problems

Would you like to know why almost 15 percent of our
orders are being worked later than the time agreed
on with the customer? And why both your service index and mine are among the lowest in the division?
I'd like to find out before we get a lot more heat
from the area manager.

Jack, we've talked about this ongoing problem for
several months, and neither of us seems to be able
to pinpoint the problem. Here's an idea I'd like to
share with you.

My district manager has just hired a management
trainee named Gail Engles. Gail is a recent Ohio
State graduate with a major in business systems—
exactly where we seem to be having problems. We
could turn her loose with a stopwatch and some
checksheets to see where our operations are fouling
up. She could trace sample orders through the whole
system.

Because Gail hasn't yet been assigned permanent duties, the only cost to us is that she'd have to be
paid out of our temporary help or overtime budget.
And we'd be obligated to use her only as long as
she's needed. I think we should take advantage of
this.

I'd appreciate it if you'd do two things. First,
check to see if you can cover one-half of her
salary costs for two or three weeks. Her base
salary is $2,300/month. I'll pay the other half.
Second, go with me to the district manager's office
to make the request. I think he'll be glad to see
our interdepartmental cooperation on this.

I'll call next Monday, April 23, to confirm all
this. I really think this will improve our customer
service and help us avoid some future grief from
the area people.

FIGURE 12–2

Persuasive
memorandum.

Features	What This Means to You
Gail majored in operations management.	Her training can be usefully applied to our problem.
Gail has been trained in business systems.	She can trace orders through the system to pinpoint problems.
Gail is not yet permanently assigned.	We can pay her out of our temporary budget and use her only as long as needed.

Testimonials and references help build credibility.

Testimonials and References. To help build the credibility of your product or ideas in the reader's eyes, sometimes it helps to use third-party quotes. These can be references to authoritative sources or customer testimonials. You might use such an **authoritative reference** in a proposal or memo, where you think quoting an authority will help your position. **Customer testimonials,** conversely, help convince your prospective customers that they will like your product. For example, Debbie Fields says, "I tried Mama's chocolate chip cookies, and they are the best I've ever eaten."

Be sure that the testimonial is strong. The more specific it is and the more recognizable the testifier, the better.

Samples and offers change readers' attitude by changing their behavior.

Product Samples and Trial Offers. The purpose of using a product sample or trial offer is to get your reader to use the product. Here, the persuader hopes to change readers' behavior (get them to use and buy!) by sampling the product. This, in turn, should cause the reader to have a favorable attitude toward the product and to purchase it. If you think your product will stir up lots of resistance in the mind of the reader, product samples and trial offers may be an effective way to overcome the reader's defensive attitude.

Price Information. If low price or cost is one of your convincing arguments, make sure the fact stands out by putting it in a position of emphasis. Otherwise, you'll probably want to de-emphasize the monetary aspect of your product by burying the information in the middle of a paragraph that justifies the price or cost. Make sure you mention price *after* you've talked about the benefits of the product or idea to your reader. Also, it is a good idea to state price in terms of small units. For example, $5 each sounds a lot better than $500 per hundred. Magazines that cost only 33 cents a day sound better than $120.45 a year.

Anticipating Objections. One of the best ways to overcome reader resistance is to **anticipate and address objections** to your persuasive message.

For example, suppose you wanted to propose that your department upgrade its computer system. The obvious objection that comes to mind is the cost. A lesser objection might be the time needed to train the department personnel on the new machine. Now that you have anticipated these objections (and as many other possible objections as you can guess at), you can address them in your proposal. You might overcome the cost objection by showing how the cost will be offset by increased worker efficiency.

It sometimes makes sense to address anticipated objections early in the message. Let's say, for example, that you are trying to overcome the objection that "all janitorial supply firms carry basically the same products, so why change?" You might include information like the following:

> **You say that all janitorial supply firms are the same. You feel that they all carry look-alike products.**
>
> **Up until now, we would have agreed with you. For the past five years, Buffalo business people have had little choice in buying products to keep their buildings sparkling clean, sanitary, and safe. But Janit-all has changed that.**
>
> **Now you have a wider-than-ever line of top-quality products to choose from—many never before available. . . .**

A Is for Action

If you've been successful up to this point, you have grabbed the attention of your reader, agitated the reader into recognizing an unfilled need, and proposed the solution to meet that need. Now all that's left to do is to get your reader to act. That's the purpose behind the action close. An effective action close makes the difference between a nice, informative message and one that gets results.

The **action close** seeks to do two things: First, it should persuade your reader to do something specific; second, it should remind your reader of the benefit one can expect from taking this action. By reminding the reader of the expected benefits, you actually resell your product or idea.

The action close should remind the reader of the benefits of your proposal.

In addition to clearly stating what should be done and reminding the reader why, the action close should set a deadline or provide some other incentive to act soon. The action close should also make it easy for the reader to comply. Often, a mailback reply card, self-addressed envelope, telephone number, or promise of a follow-up call or visit makes it easier for the reader to respond to your persuasive request.

The tone of the action step should be assumptive. You should be moving from conditional phrasing, such as "If you do it," that you used at the beginning of your message to the more definitive, "Here's how you do it." Assume that your reader has understood and agreed with your reasoning, and now simply needs to be pushed a bit to obtain the benefits you promised. There is no need to be hesitant. Remember, what you're telling your reader to do is for the reader's own benefit.

Figures 12–3 to 12–9 are examples of persuasive letters, the arrangement of which may be worth emulating.

NEIGHBORHOOD CHILDREN'S FUND
2800 Amherst Drive
Snyder, NY 14226

June 26, 199X

Dear Mr. Skabota:

It's not often that I request your help in a worthy cause. But now, I need you.

Since 1966, The Neighborhood Children's Fund (NCF) has provided services to needy children in our community. Now, our challenge is to provide desperately needed assistance in paying overnight expenses at inner-city medical centers specializing in pediatric medicine.

Most of us rely on the community for the success of our business. Many of us grew up here and want to give something back to the community. I've become involved with NCF because I'm impressed with what they do and how hard they work to get a difficult job done. Their results are measurable, and their goals are admirable.

Generally, we request that businesses of your size consider a monetary contribution of $1,000 or 1 percent of monthly payroll. Of course, these are only guidelines. I urge you to consider giving what you can afford this year. I would appreciate your approval of my request because your help is sorely needed.

At NCF, we work hard to make a meaningful contribution to the community. I'm confident you'll agree that our work is important and support us as best you can.

Sincerely,

Monica Moe

Monica Moe

FIGURE 12-3

Request for a favor, gift, or donation.

MOM'S
GOOD EATS, CLEAN PLATES
121 Main Street
Homey, IL 61667

August 25, 199X

Dear Ms. Jamisin:

It can be tough, but we sure try.

At Mom's Restaurants, we strive to give our cus-
tomers the best food, quality, value, and service.
We've built our business around that commitment.
Judging by the relationship we've had with Systo
Food Wholesalers, you've adopted a similar commit-
ment.

From time to time we review certain policies and
procedures that may inhibit our ability to bring
real value to our customers. In the process, we occasionally find that a supplier's business practice
presents a roadblock. Such is the case with Systo;
we are having a problem with food deliveries during
our busiest time: lunch hours. Having our employees
inventory and assist with stocking goods detracts
from our need to serve our customers. Also, your
truck often blocks valuable parking spaces needed
for our customers.

Won't you please arrange for delivery before 11:00
A.M. or after 2:30 P.M.?

I'm confident that once you are aware of the problem, your current delivery schedule causes us,
you'll resolve it to our mutual satisfaction.

Thank You for your prompt attention. And thanks for
your role in providing quality food for our customers.

Sincerely,

Erma Cook

Erma Cook

FIGURE 12–4
A proposal or change
in policy.

SpamCo, Inc.
Organic Health Foods
2 Bucolic Lane
Yazoo City, MS 22200

September 16, 199X

Hello, Mrs. Buchannan:

I know you're busy, so I'll be brief—SpamCo, Inc.
can save you time and money.

We'll save you time because once you've done business with us, you'll spend less time shopping for
the best deal and the best service. You'll save
money for the same reason—value.

Have you ever wondered where world-class athletes
buy their food suppliments? Have you ever wondered
where top health food restauranteurs get their superior, organically grown vegetables and seafoods?
Many of them come to SpamCo. We've been in the community for more than twenty-three years (long before health food was widely popular!) providing
free delivery of the widest possible variety of nu-
tritionally superior foods and diet supplements.

Attention to detail and an absolute commitment to
quality set us apart from our competition. But you
don't have to take our word for it—we'll be happy
to refer you to some of our customers for an objective opinion. See the enclosed testimonials.

Can we talk about establishing a wholesale account
with SpamCo for you? I'd like to show you how we
can provide the absolute highest-quality products
at prices much lower than you'd expect. I'll call
within the next week to arrange an appointment, or
you can call me if you'd like to meet sooner. We
look forward to meeting and serving you.

Sincerely,

Benoit Cochon

Benoit Cochon
Owner

FIGURE 12-5
Request for an
appointment or
opportunity to meet.

MEMORANDUM

TO: Sarah McKissin

FROM: Bob Robust

DATE: June 26, 199X

RE: Giving our Clients Exceptional Seminar Value

You were chosen to be part of the Quest Seminars team partly because of your willingness to strive consistently for excellence in performing your job as a professional trainer.

But, hey, you know that. You're among the best in the field.

So why this memo? A reminder.

Our client can get similar services from several other training companies. Some of them are closer to home and may even offer more attractive pricing. How do we compete? By offering the best, most consistently pleasant, useful, and professional programs available. Seminar quality is what sets us apart and distinguishes us from the competition.

Clients must believe they're getting exceptional training value for their money from us at Quest. As we grow, it becomes increasingly difficult to give all clients the high level of service they've come to expect from us. And yet, it's increasingly critical that customers perceive our service to be superior.

To accomplish this, it will take every employee making the effort every day. It will take our unified dedication to finding ways to improve, even when that means changing old ways. I'm asking you to seek out those things that may inhibit our ability to deliver quality programs and share your ideas with your team leader.

Together we can continuously upgrade our services for the better.

Let's make quality a priority!

FIGURE 12–6

Memo asking employees for a commitment.

GLORIA'S GIFTSHOP
PRETTY, NEAT STUFF
133 State Road
Bemidji, MN 16778

March 15, 199X

Mrs. Petula Clark
455 Paucity Lane
Minneapolis, MN 78871

SUBJECT: Your Gloria's GiftShop Account
         Account # 12-671
         Amount due: $179.54
         Date due: February 15, 199X

Dear Mrs. Clark:

I'm sure you have been busy. Perhaps you haven't
noticed that your payment for your January purchases to Gloria's GiftShop is past due.

If your payment was made since the date of this notice, please disregard this letter. And thank you
for your business.

If your payment has not been made, please do so
now. You can preserve your good credit by visiting
us or mailing your payment promptly.

Thank you.
Sincerely,

Bruno J. Gloria

Bruno J. Gloria
Owner

FIGURE 12-7
Collection letter—first
request.

GLORIA'S GIFTSHOP
PRETTY, NEAT STUFF
133 State Road
Bemidji, MN 16778

April 1, 199X

Mrs. Petula Clark
455 Paucity Lane
Minneapolis, MN 78871

SUBJECT: Your Gloria's GiftShop Account
         Account # 12-671
         Amount due: $179.54
         Date due: February 15, 199X

Dear Mrs. Clark:

We have made several attempts to contact you by
telephone to remind you of your obligation to Gloria's GiftShop. Your account payment is seriously
past due, and you have not returned our telephone
calls.

At this point, you must take immediate action to
bring your account up to date. Until you do, we
must suspend available credit on your account. If
you cannot make your payment today, call Johnathan
Gloriana at 222-5555 immediately to let us know
when you will.

We realize there may be a good reason why you have
not paid your bill. But because you have not returned our calls, we do not know what that reason
is. You have been a valuable customer to Gloria's.
We do not want to see you jeopardize your credit
history and the record of continued business you
have established with us over the years.

Please visit us to make your payment, or call immediately.

Thank you.
Sincerely,

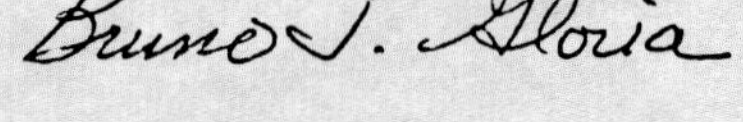

Bruno J. Gloria

Bruno J. Gloria
Owner

FIGURE 12-8
Collection letter—
second request.

GLORIA'S GIFTSHOP
PRETTY, NEAT STUFF
133 State Road
Bemidji, MN 16778

April 15, 199X

Mrs. Petula Clark
455 Paucity Lane
Minneapolis, MN 78871

SUBJECT: Your Gloria's GiftShop Account
        Account # 12-671
        Amount due: $179.54
        Date due: February 15, 199X

Dear Mrs. Clark:

The matter of your past-due account has been referred to our legal counsel for collection. To avoid additional expenses that may be incurred in the collection process, it is critical that you pay the total amount past due within five days of this letter.

If payment is not received by that time, your account will be considered in default, and the company's legal counsel will begin the litigation process to recover the amount due us. After this point, you may be liable for the legal expenses incurred by Gloria's GiftShop.

To avoid the permanent loss of your account with Gloria's GiftShop, and to preserve your credit standing, please make your payment within the next five days.

Thank you.
Sincerely,

Bruno J. Gloria

Bruno J. Gloria
Owner

FIGURE 12-9
Collection letter—third request.

Here are two examples of action closes.

Drop the enclosed card in the mail—today, while you're thinking about it—and I'll send you a free examination copy of the *Executive Planner.* You'll be surprised how much time this modern management tool will save you. It'll be substantial!

Pick up the telephone *now* (24 hours a day), and we'll enroll you. All this—and more—is yours for a mere $21 a year. This is a bargain if there ever was one—*and a tangible expression of your support* for America's National Museum—your active commitment to preserving, using, and expanding the vast body of scientific and cultural knowledge that is America's most valuable resource.

Sincerely,

Roger Keatsworth

P.S. *Send no money now.* But to ensure receipt of the thirteen-star flag poster offered during our current drive, *please be sure* your enrollment form arrives *before* Veteran's Day, November 11, accompanied by your control number. We will also send your membership card and an invoice for your first year's dues.

Persuasive Messages: Complete Samples

Although this chapter has focused on the ANSA model, it is not the only arrangement of ideas that can persuade.

However, it is important to use some psychological principle and not just experiment. If you don't have a better idea, use the proven model of ANSA.

Understanding the Basics

SUMMARY OF KEY IDEAS

• A persuasive message attempts to persuade the reader to do something he or she would not normally do without prodding.

• The persuasive message tries to create positive emotions in the reader.

• Manipulation occurs when the influencer gets others to take action that is not in their own best interests.

• Persuasive communication presupposes some resistance to what you have to say.

• Most people are persuaded because they want to either gain a benefit or avoid a loss.

• Most readers will not give you much time to grab their attention.

• There are at least five key psychological appeals for arousing your reader's attention.

• The first line in a letter is a strong position of emphasis.

• The use of the second person helps personalize the message.

• Action verbs and concrete nouns create the vivid mental pictures needed to persuade your reader.

• Trite attention-getters really don't get much attention from the reader.

• The overall purpose of stirring up your readers is to make them desire your product, service, or idea. You create desire by exposing a need and then offering a solution or answer to fill that need.

• You can convince your reader that you have the answer to his or her need by presenting believable evidence.

• A skillful persuader refers to the product's features only as they relate to the reader's benefits.

• Testimonials and third-party references can build credibility for your product, idea, or proposal.

• Product samples and offers change the readers' attitude by changing their behavior.

• Generally, the mention of price or cost should be placed in a de-emphasized position—unless it is a major selling point.

• One of the best ways to overcome reader resistance to change is to anticipate objections to your product or idea.

• The action close should convince your reader to act and remind them of the expected benefits from taking action.

KEY TERMS AND CONCEPTS

persuasive messages	anticipate and address objections	feature/benefit distinction
manipulation	customer testimonials	avoid a loss
attention	authoritative reference	position of emphasis
action close	ANSA approach	action verbs
second person	need development	concrete nouns
personalize	solution presentation	easy reply
your viewpoint	positive/negative phrasing	"me-too" messages

QUESTIONS FOR FURTHER THOUGHT

1. What is the role of psychology in the creation of persuasive messages? Why does use of a persuasive model increase likelihood of success?

2. What types of evidence do you generally find to be the most persuasive?

3. Describe situations where the use of the ANSA model would be ineffective? What approach would you use instead?

4. Why is an action close especially important in business communication?

They Laughed When I Sat Down to Write

"You cannot bore people into buying." The years I spent writing direct mail copy drilled that classic line into my head. That's why I love junk mail! It provides the best writing course in the world. Every word is designed to produce results. The pros have five seconds to hook you. If you don't call that 800 number, they're fired.

So they know how to use word and phrase cues like no one else in business: "Cent" is masculine; "penny" is feminine. "Take the quiz inside" beats "take the test inside" (people love quizzes, hate tests). "Postage-free" beats "postage-paid." With upscale customers use "complimentary," not "free." "Do you make these mistakes in English?" beats "Are you afraid of making mistakes in English?" And always include a 'P.S.'; 80% of all direct mail recipients read them.

You can use the same kind of psychology to make sure your own memos get read. Here are some corporate writing tips that can be found in your direct mail:

Emphasize control. "The Optima Card puts the right person in charge of your interest rate. You." People want to be in control of their lives. For a memo, "This seminar puts the right person in charge. You."

Tap into fear. A great headline: "I'll never lose my job. I'll never lose my job. . ." It tapped right into my sense of security (and fear of insecurity). In a memo, you could ask, "What is the one mistake that could ruin us?" Or simply begin by saying, "Protect yourself."

Promise to unlock a puzzle. "The Deaf Hear Whispers" compels you to read on. For a letter to your sales force:

"How I doubled my client list in one evening."

Promise exclusivity. "Quite frankly, our credit card is not for everyone. And everyone who applies for membership is not approved." If it works for them, it can work for you. "I'm sending this to only a select few."

Tantalize. "Think how wonderful it would feel to walk without pain." This can be applied to most company problems. For a memo: "Think how wonderful it would be to reduce our inventory costs."

Show what's in it for me. "Save up to 60% on the books you order." For a letter: "Save up to 60% on our long-distance calls."

Use headline grabbers. "Golf pros banned from using new 'hot' ball; flies too far." To announce a training program: "Learn to use a computer in less than an hour."

Paint a picture. "Listen to 500 dolphins shrieking in panic as they gasp for air." For a memo: "Listen to 500 angry customers screaming for refunds unless you. . ."

Stress convenience. "Never waste another evening returning videos. We pick them up." Tell your employees how you can make their lives easier. To promote your travel desk, write: "Never stand in line for another ticket."

Emphasize the negative. "Are you making these seven common mistakes in your golf game?" In your office, ask: "Are you making these seven common mistakes in your entries?"

Play on underdog appeal. Remember the brilliant ad, "They laughed when I sat down at the piano"? People love underdogs who succeed. Use, "They laughed when I ordered 100 new. . ." or "They thought I was nuts when. . ."

Ask provocative questions. "When an employee gets sick, how long does it take your company to recover?" For a memo: "Are our pumps costing more to operate than they should?"

Use the "barker" technique. "Call your friends . . . check your fuse box . . . and get ready to rock . . . because we're bringing the world's loudest, most awesome. . ." Those people are excited! Show passion and excitement in your letters. "This company is about to take off like never before!"

Appeal to curiosity/greed. "If you think you could never get a boat, a car and a trip for $22.50, think again." For a memo: "If you thought we can't earn $100,000 with this new product, think again."

Elicit guilt; stress urgency. "In the 10 seconds it took you to open and begin to read this letter, four children died from the effects of malnutrition or disease." Ow! Right to the heart. Perhaps you could use: "In one week our company will waste $10,000 unless you. . ."

Use bullets. People skip-read. Pros bullet important points. For example, when selling driving glasses they write:

- Beat headlight glare.
- Drive through blinding rain.
- Increase vision and safety.

P.S.: Don't throw away that direct mail! It'll beat any writing course you ever took.

Applying Your Knowledge

1. Direct mail is a special type of business communication that lives or dies by its results. Collect several pieces of "junk" mail and analyze it to see how the writers use the techniques discussed in this article. Make a list of techniques found for each piece of mail.

2. What might be the down side of using these techniques? How could they damage a message's effectiveness?

Applying Your Skills

ACTIVITY 12-1: Request for Action, Human Resources

Critique the following request for a favor, using the ANSA approach for persuasive communication.

Then rewrite the letter, using the principles of persuasion discussed in the chapter.

Ms. Melissa Sanders
28506 Leacrest Drive
Springfield, MO

Dear Ms. Sanders:

We would like to ask your help in making Missouri
Stone & Gravel a better place to work.

While you were employed by our company, you no
doubt formed many opinions about our organization
that would be of value to us in improving our personnel policies and practices. Further, we would
appreciate knowing the actual reason(s) for your
leaving. Frequently, in the process of terminating,
even when an exit interview is conducted, not all
the pertinent information is obtained.

I wonder if you would be kind enough to help us by
completing the enclosed form and providing any additional information or opinions you think we
should know. Your candid and specific answers will
be very helpful to us.

Thank you for whatever assistance you are able to
furnish. Your comments may be influential in improving our work environment and may benefit some of
your former associates. Our best wishes for success
in your new endeavors.

Sincerely,

Alice Cox

Alice Cox
Regional Director of Human Resources

Enclosures

ACTIVITY 12-2: Request for Action, Fund Raising

A common form of persuasive letter is for the purpose of fund raising. Analyze the following fund-raising letter, and determine if it meets the ANSA requirements of persuasive letters. Would you donate to Upper State University (USU) after receiving this letter? Try rewriting the letter in a more positive tone.

OFFICE OF THE PRESIDENT

It's not like you. . .
to forget us. (You've been a steady, loyal contributor to USU in the past.) However, unless our records are wrong, you seem to have missed your much-appreciated contribution to USU in the 199X-9X Annual Giving Campaign. Moreover, in a matter of just a few weeks, we will be closing our books on this year's effort.

All of this means, of course, that time is running out—for you and for us.

Perhaps you will be able to take a moment now to return your contribution in the enclosed reply envelope. Your gift of $10, $25, $50—whatever you can afford to give—will help us move the university steadily toward the excellence we expect. In terms of things that matter most, I think you will agree that this is a rewarding investment.

Thank you for your past support and for all you have done, in a variety of ways, to further the development of this institution and the deserving young people who study here.

With best wishes,

Adelaine T. Simpson

Adelaine T. Simpson

WORKING FOR WHAT YOU BELIEVE IN
The Annual Campaign for Upper State University

ACTIVITY 12-3: Request for Action, Human Resources

Prepare a persuasive memorandum to your boss requesting funds to attend a national conference of middle managers on the impact of artificial intelligence on office automation. The conference is slated for February 26 and 27 in Honolulu, Hawaii. The registration fee for the conference is $495 with an additional $695 for charter airfare, and $650 for hotel and meals. Although the conference could help you achieve potential cost savings in your position as office manager, your boss looks on winter conferences suspiciously. He is concerned that they may be seen as a waste of organization funds.

ACTIVITY 12-4: Request for Action, Advertising

One advertising approach uses a stack of mail-back cards describing offers for a family of similar products or services, such as business opportunities, office products, and so on.

Evaluate the effectiveness of this card on the basis of attention getting, appearance, persuasive appeal(s), action step, and general appeal. Do you think it is likely to meet its objective? Why, or why not?

ACTIVITY 12-5: Request for Action, Marketing

Your business, a garden center, is located on State Street, the main thoroughfare in Orem, Utah. Unfortunately, State Street is undergoing major pavement reconstruction. Although you are happy with the city's decision to resurface the street, it may put a kink in your bottom line. Road construction has caused many drivers to opt for alternate routes. Your big worry is that you will lose regular customers to competitors who are unaffected by the construction. You have a mailing list of your most frequent customers over the past five years. Write a letter to these customers, thanking them for their loyalty, apologizing for the inconvenience, and encouraging them to come to Eden's Garden for their landscaping needs. Explain that your parking lot is connected behind the building to the parking lot of the Mountain Green Medical Clinic. Mountain Green has no objections if your customers drive through its parking lot to reach yours. The Medical Clinic is located on Orem Boulevard between Fourth and Fifth South. You have also decided to offer a free potted flower to each customer who brings this letter to the garden center.

ACTIVITY 12-6: Request for Action, Shipping

Carl Higashi, shipping manager for The Light Side, a mail order catalog for exotic lamps, has just received a call from Susan Nay, a customer who had ordered the popular Pit Bull Desk Lamp. The lamp arrived, says Susan in about a thousand pieces. The Light Side ships everything through National Parcel Service (NPS), and this is no new problem. It has happened at least four times in the past month. Carl asks Susan to tape the box up and send it back cash on delivery. When it arrives a couple of days later, Carl is amazed. The lamp was packed with enough styrofoam peanuts to feed a plastic elephant, but the box looks as though a real elephant sat on it. Carl drops the box on your desk and asks you to write a letter to NPS, requesting reimbursement of $18.68 for freight to and from Akron, Ohio, and politely reminding them to pay more attention to boxes labeled "fragile." NPS local headquarters are at 5400 N.W. Broken Sound Boulevard, Boca Raton, FL 33487.

ACTIVITY 12-7: Request for Action, Publications

Pat Cochran is the publications director for Random Access, Inc. (RAI), a producer of memory chips for personal computers. RAI's small publications department is responsible for product brochures, magazine advertisements, and an internal newsletter. They also publish instruction booklets for RAI's popular do-it-yourself random access memory upgrade kits. In the past, Pat and her two assistants have written the copy in-house, then passed it on to a local graphics company for design and printing. Last week, however, RAI president Mark Wheatley requested that all department heads decrease costs by 10 percent.

Pat has analyzed her department and thinks that the easiest way to save money would be for the publications department to join the desktop publishing revolution. The only problem she sees is that to reduce costs substantially over the long haul, she must invest a few thousand dollars up front. For starters, she needs new computers and software. This means purchasing three Macintoshes at approximately $5,000 each (including monitors, additional memory, and software) and another $4,500 for crash Mac courses to get Pat and her two assistants up to speed on the new computers. This initial investment of $19,500 should yield savings of about $15,000 a year.

Pat has asked you to write an internal memo to Mark Wheatley, explaining the situation and justifying a negative net cash flow of $4,500 first year. (Net profit, you may wish to point out, should be positive because the computers are capital equipment and can be depreciated over five years). Persuade Mark that this is the best way to save money in the long run. Anticipate any objections he may have.

ACTIVITY 12-8: Request for Action, Accounting

Ben Counter, a certified public accountant who balances the books for five small businesses, swallowed hook, line, and sinker a salesman's pitch for Accountax. This software package promised to pay for itself by saving Ben huge amounts of time and effort. Ben likes some features of the program, specifically, the receivables and payables modules, but overall Accountax is costing him more and more as time goes by. He's putting in longer hours on each client's books, and his long-distance bill doubled last month. Ben has made numerous calls to the software company to overcome mysterious glitches and gaps in the programming. Accountax, apparently, was released without sufficient testing. Not one to admit he made a mistake and just scrap the new software, Ben has decided to write Accountax, Inc., and make a suggestion instead: If the software company would install a 1-800 help line until the program has been cleaned up, it would save users hundreds of dollars and lots of frustration. Accountax, Inc., is headquarted at 7650 Benassi Drive, Gilroy, CA 95020. Write this letter as if you were Ben Counter.

ACTIVITY 12-9: Request for Action, Job Candidate

Sandra Brookhaven interviewed for a job yesterday with Blake Modersitzki at Novell Inc. The position she is seeking is in marketing, and she feels good about the interview. Her strong point is her background—two years at IBM followed by five years and four promotions at Adobe—but she is smart enough to know that lots of overqualified applicants don't land the jobs they want. Sandra doesn't want to be pushy, but she thinks a short note thanking Mr. Modersitzki for the interview and expressing her enthusiasm for Novell's products would add a few percentage points to her chances. Write this letter as if you were Sandra Brookhaven, and address it to Blake Modersitzki, Novell Inc., 1555 North Technology Way, Orem, UT 84057.

ACTIVITY 12-10: Claims, Customer Service

Select a product you have purchased that you are not at all pleased with. Write a three to five-paragraph letter to the manufacturer, expressing your dissatisfaction. Specify the action you would like to see the company take to correct the problem.

ACTIVITY 12-11: Adjustment, Accounts Payable

Roger Terry, president of the funcompany, a small business that produces humorous day planners, was looking over his most recent UPS bill and noticed and unusual charge. A 102-pound air shipment from Clark Enterprises in Phoenix to M. I. Data Serve in Browndear, Wisconsin. The total charge was $181.35. "That can't be right," he thought. "Someone must have made an error entering orders into the computer and put my account number on someone else's shipment." Write a letter to United Parcel Service, P.O. Box 630016, Dallas TX 75263, as if you were Roger Terry, explaining the mistake and asking it to be corrected. The invoice number in question is 83E314-255.

ACTIVITY 12-12: Claims, Purchasing

Keri Patterson, who works in the purchasing department at Executive Training Associates in Princeton, New Jersey, received the memo on the following page from Jason Pathweaver in technical support.

Write this claim letter, notifying Global Computer Supply that you have also attached a copy of the invoice and the canceled check. Global Computer Supply is located at 11 Harbor Park Drive, Port Washington, 11050.

ACTIVITY 12-13: Sales, Marketing

Prepare a direct-mail sales letter in which you explain the advantages of your new portable hot tub. Be sure to explain that the cost ($1,599) is lower than that of a stationary hot tub. The tub can be moved from residence to residence and it requires only 110-volt electric hookups with no special plumbing. Invite your prospective customers to a free demonstration this Friday night at the West Park Mall. Feel free to add any additional promotional data you believe would be pertinent to your intended reader. Your company is Portatubby, Inc., 1211 Soothe Drive, Burbank, CA 94101.

ACTIVITY 12-14: Sales, Marketing

Parry Evans, president of the Executive Intelligence Book Club (EIBC), approached you yesterday with a new assignment. EIBC's executive committee has decided it needs to dramatically increase club membership. EIBC will, therefore, introduce a new promotion offering five books for the price of one, with no obligation to buy anything, ever. A letter from Parry Evans will accompany a brochure depicting 50

```
TO:       Keri Patterson

FROM:     Jason Pathweaver

DATE:     October 25, 199X

SUBJECT: Fax Switch model DLE-200


A month ago I requested a fax switch, which you
promptly ordered from Global Computer Supply. I in-
stalled the switch, and from the start it never
worked right. Some fax transmissions would be
routed to the fax machine, others to my answering
machine. Since yesterday, though, all incoming
faxes are being routed to my answering machine,
none to the fax machine. Please write Global Com-
puter Supply, explain the problem, and ask for a
refund. Let's pick up a more reliable brand at Ra-
dio Shack. I have a friend who bought one there and
has never had trouble with it. Thanks for your
help.
```

of EIBC's best-selling books and will be mailed to 50,000 executives across the United States. Parry has asked you to write a "persuasive" letter for him, one that will "make these executives understand why they need to read our books." EIBC sells books on management, leadership, quality control, finance, sales, investing, economics, organizational change, and human resource issues. "This letter had better be good," Parry warned you. "We sell dozens of books on how to be a super salesperson; if we can't set a good example, we have no business selling sales books in the first place."

ACTIVITY 12-15: Sales, Marketing

Your Pen, Inc., an imprinter of quality pens, is about to implement an aggressive direct mail campaign. The goal of this campaign is to get companies around the country to engage in a little high-class self-promotion by giving their customers a quality Your Pen. Your Pen, unlike dozens of its competitors, does not sell cheap, heavy-point pens bearing the company's name and address in ugly white lettering. It sells Faber Castell's top-of-the-line Uni-ball fine-point pen with the purchaser's name, address, and phone number in fancy gold lettering. The idea is that by giving away a useful, quality product your company's name will stay in your customer's pockets and purses and on their desks rather than finding a quick resting place in their round files. "This is Your Pen, not a throwaway" is the motto of the campaign. Write a letter from Your Pen to potential customers, explaining the benefits of giving customers a free pen that they will use every day. Companies can buy Your Pens for the following prices: 50 pens for $125, 100 pens for $200, 500 pens for $800, 1,000 pens for $1,500, or 5,000 pens for $6,000.

ACTIVITY 12-16: Sales, Small Business

It has been your secret dream for years to own a small bookstore, and when the Bookshelf, a local used book store you have frequented for years, became available, you put together the necessary financing and snatched it up. Now you're faced with a dilemma. To pay off the load and turn a profit, you need to double the store's clientele. You determine that a direct mailing to 2,000 individuals who either work or study at the local university would be your best strategy. The Bookshelf trades and sells all kinds of paperbacks and a few hardcover books. Customers can either buy the books at half the cover price or trade books at a $.50-per-book fee. For instance, if a customer brings in five books with a combined cover price of $19.95, she can trade for any number of books, so long as the combined cover price doesn't exceed $19.95. If she wants only one book, and the cover price is $6.00, the she pays $.50 for that book and, a credit of $13.95 is entered on her account.

You suspect that most people don't know how used book stores do business. You also suspect that most people have a few books sitting around gathering dust that they will never read again. You feel you've isolated a segment of the population that likes to read. If you catch their eye with the right opening line, they will read your letter and see the benefits of trading for used books instead of spending money on new ones. Write a persuasive direct mail letter that will bring new business to your used book store.

ACTIVITY 12-17: Sales, Marketing

Stan Linsley, D.M.D, is having a white sale and he's asked you to write the copy for a direct mail promotional piece. Dr. Linsley is offering an introductory bleaching special and will announce it through direct mail to 4,000 homes in your city. For a limited time, individuals can whiten their smiles for only $99 (regular price is $325). This introductory bleaching includes a consultation appointment, upper and lower custom trays, a leading home bleaching system, and a follow-up appointment. The only challenge in this assignment is that everything you write must fit on one side of a postcard. Dr. Stan is convinced that brevity is a virtue and that most people (especially advertisers) say little with far too may words. Linsley's dental practice is located at 945 N. Marshall Street, Winston-Salem, NC 27101; the telephone number is (919) 727-1010.

ACTIVITY 12-18: Collections, Management

Critique the letter on page 345, identifying any reasons why the letter might be effective.

ACTIVITY 12-19: Collections, First Letter, Accounts Receivable

The Book Distributors Corporation (BDC) is a book wholesaler located in New York City. BDC shipped 20 cookbooks to the Book Corner, 3600 Main Street, Shrewsbury, MA 01545 on October 19, 199X. The entire order came to $587.94. It is now January 20, and the Book Corner has not paid its bill. Terms were net 30, and interest accrues at the rate of 1.5 percent per month. Write the Book Corner an initial collection letter, reminding them of their overdue invoice and requesting prompt payment. The invoice number is 992345.

ACTIVITY 12-20: Collections, Second Letter, Accounts Receivable

After receiving your first letter, the Book Corner wrote back saying the cash is short, but they will try to pay by the end of February. It is now March 20, and no check has arrived. Write a second letter to the store, requesting immediate payment and warning that legal action may follow.

ACTIVITY 12-21: Collections, Final Attempt, Accounts Receivable

On March 25, Ms. Lucinda Prentice called you and introduced herself as the owner of the Book Corner. The books were damaged on the way to her store, she says, and she had to sell them at a 50 percent dis-

```
                    April 4, 199X


                    Mr. Ralph Bradshaw
                    2019 Ortega Way
                    Winter Garden, FL


                    Dear Mr. Bradshaw:


                    You know—

                    • How hard it is to ask for money
                    • And say just enough to get it
                    • Without offending

                    Your remittance may be on its way. If not, we know
                    you will send it immediately. In either case, thank
                    you.



                    Sincerely,

                    Robert Hernandez

                    Robert Hernandez
                    Vice-President

                    RH:mz

                    P.S. This statement reflects the balance on your ac-
                    count, 0028919, as of March 15, 199X. If payment
                    has already been made, please disregard this state-
                    ment.
```

count. She offered to pay half the invoiced amount and call it even. You don't believe her, but tell her you'll talk to your supervisor. You do just that and she says to give it one more try, then turn the bill over to an attorney. Write Ms. Prentice a letter, demanding either full payment or proof of damage to the books. You realize that you will lose money on this small account even if the attorney manages to get the full payment. Be as creative as you can in persuading Ms. Prentice to pay. If you can get 75 per-cent of the invoice, it will be better than hiring an attorney. Then you can chalk it up to experience and deal with the Book Corner on a cash-only basis in the future.

ACTIVITY 12-22: Collections, Accounts Receivable

Sally LeGrande brought her two-year-old in to the Cottonwood Medical Clinic on December 15, 199X, and Dr. Carney examined him and prescribed an antibiotic for strep throat. After three months, Sally had not paid the bill, so you called, and she said, "I'm a single mother, I'm working two jobs, and I haven't got enough money to even pay the rent and buy food. There's no way I can pay $36 for an office call. Besides, why should I pay some rich doctor a lot of money to tell me something I already knew? Sorry. Chalk it up to charity." She then hung up. You have tried calling again, but as soon as you introduce yourself, Sally hangs up. Dr. Carney suggested that before you turn the bill over to a collection agency, that you try a different approach. "A different approach," you say, "what kind of different approach?" "I don't know," he answers. You think about it and decide to write Sally a letter, explaining that you understand her difficult situation. If you appeal to her sense of decency and offer her the chance to pay the bill in six monthly installments of $6 each, then maybe she'll feel inclined to try. Sally lives at 720 Roosevelt Road, Chicago, IL 60607.

PERFORMING
on the Job

CASE 12-1 **Dairy Queen Dilemma**

The following letter was triggered by an irate reader who read this news announcement in the paper. Prepare a response to Mrs. Flanagan.

News Release[1]

Owners Updated One of Indiana's Oldest Dairy Queen Stores Last Week—at Least to the Automobile Age

The Dairy Queen stand at 2902 Parnell Ave. opened a drive-through last Monday.

The renovation also established picnic tables in front of the store in a newly landscaped area enclosed by trees, shrubs and planters.

It was the first physical change at the 800-square-foot shop since it opened in 1949.

Serving motorists in their cars is not a radical concept, but owners Gavin and Kim Hart said they were cautious about the renovation.

"We had some concern that people didn't want us to change what was here, so we tried to keep as much of the old-fashioned walk-up [atmosphere] as we could," said Gavin Hart.

A contractor built the drive-through with the same type of materials used in the original structure, he said.

Some of the shop's regular customers have grown up within a few blocks of it. They said they understood the need for improvements but hoped changes would be minimal, Gavin said.

The store doesn't have indoor seating, so the drive-through will allow customers to buy its ice cream, soda and sandwiches without getting wet when it rains, he said.

— PAGE 1 —

The Dairy Queen sells 9,000 to 10,000 gallons of ice cream annually, and the addition of a drive-through could boost sales by 30 percent, Gavin said.

Much of the new business is likely to come in the form of impulse buying by motorists driving from events at the Memorial Coliseum, which is a few blocks away, he said.

The business employs eight workers and probably will add two positions to handle drive-through business, Gavin said.

The Dairy Queen also will remain open four weeks longer each year, as its business becomes less dependent on good weather, he said. The business will operate through the end of October and open every March 1, instead of closing in mid-October and opening in mid-March.

Dear Dairy Queen Manager:

I get so damn sick of "progress" sometimes, don't you?

I was real upset to see that you are going to change the DQ near my home on Parnell. I like it the way it's been for as long as I can remember. Why mess with a good thing? My grandkids love it the way it's been.

Forget the "modernization." I want it the old way.

Mrs. Doris Flanagan

Mrs. Doris Flanagan

CASE 12-2 We Want You Back

The following letter illustrates a manager's attempt to win back some lost customers. It is based on a real case:

October 1, 1998

Barney F. Hansen, President
ReallyBig Tire Stores & Auto Service Centers
123 Main
Bison Breath, ND 85678

An Open Letter to the People of Bison Breath

Some time ago, we discovered that our previous manager and his staff were not taking care of out customers at our Bison Breath store. This is certainly
not in keeping with ReallyBig Tire's guarantee of
customer satisfaction, qualified technicians and
friendly service. We were extremely disappointed to
hear this, and we tried to move quickly to correct
the situation.

The previous manager was discharged, and on June 27
we transferred Craig Cunningham into the Bison
Breath store. Craig is a competent, courteous manager with years of experience in the tire and automotive industry. Craig, his wife, and family are
long-term residents of nearby Eastville. Since
Craig has been your store manager, we have had many
positive comments on his service and dedication to
customer's needs.

To show our good faith, and to welcome folks back
to our store at 123 Main, we will perform a full
lubrication service; change the oil with up to five
quarts of Pennzoil oil, install a new oil filter,
and lube the chassis for only $5.95 on presentation
of this letter at the store.

We are happy to be part of the growing Bison Breath
community and will do our best to offer tires and
automotive services at the lowest prices in Nebraska with the finest service anywhere.

Sincerely,

Barney F. Hansen, President

cc: Honorable Janet Williams, Mayor
    City of Bison Breath

Case Questions

1. How effective do you think this letter would be?

2. To what extent does Hansen's letter follow the model described in this chapter?

3. Rewrite the letter applying the ANSA model. (You may add other details as needed.)

Communicating about Employment:

From Resume to Interview

LEARNING GOALS

After you have studied this chapter, you
should be able to

- Explain the importance of the
  resume, cover letter, and interview
  in the job search.

- Describe the major parts of a
  standard resume and application
  letter.

- Describe and present pro and con
  arguments for the use of optional or
  creative additions to the standard
  resume content.

- Describe some expressions or ways
  of wording information that should be
  avoided in the resume.

- Review sample resume parts and
  express why certain examples would
  work best for your resume.

- Recognize the benefits and limitations
  of preparation for a job interview.

- Describe the five most frequent
  complaints recruiters voice about
  interviewees.

- Identify four major ways that
  candidates can overcome the common
  interviewee pitfalls.

- Describe the kinds of information one
  should gather about an organization
  before interviewing.

The Way It Is . . . Hiring Employees Today

The hiring process at many companies is more sophisticated than ever. With the trend toward keeping a smaller core of key employees while outsourcing more work or hiring temporary workers, companies are increasingly careful about who they hire. After all, hiring means making a long-term commitment. It's not easy to fire ineffective workers. They are often protected by union agreements or legal requirements companies must follow.

A classic example of how big companies are approaching hiring is described by Greg Gardner in the *Detroit Free Press*.[1] Gardner writes about the U.S. automotive industry's process:

"Even as the car companies pare production payrolls to become more efficient, they will need a stunning number of new employees in the next decade because 260,000 of their 400,000 hourly workers will either retire or be eligible to retire by 2003.

"As a result, the automakers are entering a period in which they will be hiring at a rate unseen since the early 1960s." He goes on to say that times have changed. "There was a time when a plant manager who needed help just called the nearest employment office, asked for 100 workers and hoped for the best. Little testing was done. If a person was not cut out for life on the factory floor, everyone found out the hard way."

Those days are gone. Ford, GM, and Chrysler see this as an unprecedented opportunity to redefine how American automotive workers do their jobs, and then fill those jobs with a new generation of highly qualified, highly motivated employees.

Today's automotive company applicant now faces a six-hour battery of tests spread over two days. The survivors come back for an interview the third day. The screening process is competitive.

That doesn't mean you need a graduate degree in physics. Nimble hands and physical endurance are still important. A reliable work ethic certainly helps. You won't qualify for an interview, however, without demonstrating basic reading and math skills. What you absolutely must show is an ability and willingness to work on a team.

Gardner goes on to illustrate: "Just ask Debra Scacella. A Roseville, Michigan, mother of two spent a recent afternoon in a hotel room with five strangers trying to find faster and smarter ways to assemble a simple device of plastic plates held together by nuts and bolts. The exercise tries to measure whether an applicant merely follows orders or suggests changes, whether she keeps to herself or reaches out to help coworkers, and whether she gives equal attention to productivity and quality."

People from the company's testing services are in the room making notes on each applicant's performance. They identify who is quick to propose changes, who is holding back, and who is trying to involve everyone in the group.

"You're under a lot of pressure trying to do your best," Scacella said. "It takes a lot of concentration and you try to stay calm."

As business technology grows more sophisticated, workers who use it will need a broader range of skills and be constantly ready to learn new ones.

The increasing use of careful selection techniques doesn't mean companies have been choosing the wrong type of person in the past and that's the problem. It's just that times have changed and so has the way people work. Employees used to tell a person, " 'Here's what we want you to do and we'll come by later to see if you're doing it.' That won't work anymore. The workers of tomorrow will constantly redefine their jobs according to the questions they're able to ask," says Gardner.

Understanding the Challenge

There is no magic
formula.

If you're looking for a single, foolproof, magic formula for getting a great job, you may be disappointed. There is no such formula. There are some tips you can use to improve your chances for success, however. This chapter explains some of these.

A job search may be
your most important
sales campaign.

There is no "one best way" to apply for a good job. Indeed, there are as many different approaches as there are creative people seeking jobs. Ultimately, a successful job search boils down to the ability to sell yourself. For many, the job search is the most important sales campaign of their life.

So consider these premises:

1. There is no single best, surefire way to conduct a job search.

2. The job search is a sales campaign, and each candidate needs to recognize the importance of salesmanship.

3. Creativity and attention to details often separate the successful candidate from the dismissed one.

Perhaps the best way to start the job-search process is to become familiar with what others have done or are doing to get good jobs. This chapter suggests several ideas and a few "do's and don'ts" for your consideration. Sort out these thoughts and determine which may work best for you.

Your Resume Is Your Sales Literature

In almost every selling situation you need to provide some written materials. In the job search, these materials include a resume and an accompanying cover letter.

A resume is a
condensed, efficient
description of you.

A **resume,** also sometimes referred to as a data sheet or vita, is a condensed, efficient description of your personal characteristics, experiences, accomplishments, and so forth. If the resume is done well, it will also clearly imply how these traits will be useful to an employer.

As you apply for a job, the resume becomes your "sales brochure." As a brochure, it should meet all the qualifications of high-quality business communication described previously. It should be carefully thought out, well arranged, and neatly typed or printed, presenting an attractive and informative document.

Resume readers tend to
read between the lines.

Because the resume is an abbreviated information sheet, its readers will tend to read between the lines. The items that you print on that sheet will suggest broader characteristics to the reader. If you remember this point, you can use it to make your resume better. Here are some short examples.

If your resume includes a statement like, "I reduced costs of manufacturing . . . ," the reader may add to that an interpretation that you are profit conscious, and that perhaps you could help reduce costs for the reader's company, too.

If, conversely, you indicate that while you were a supervisor, you "fired thirty-two unproductive workers," the reader may interpret that behavior (reading between the lines) as indicating that you are impetuous, impatient, or insensitive. You may come across to that reader as being a "hatchet man."

Be sensitive to the unspoken implications of your resume. When you make a statement about things that you have accomplished, be sure that it reflects positively on you and your work characteristics.

Standard Parts of the Resume

Lead off your resume with your strongest selling point.

A resume can and should be a creative document. It should include any and all bits of information that will help present an impressive picture of you as a job candidate. There are, however, certain standard parts that are included in almost every resume. The order in which you arrange these standard parts will depend on which are your better selling points. Typically, resume writers lead off with their strongest selling point. If, for example, you have just graduated from college but you have limited work experience, your education is your stronger selling point. Your education should be presented early in the resume. If, however, you have worked for ten years in a particular field, you would probably want to lead off with such experience. The three parts of almost any resume follow.

Education. This includes information about your higher **education** (normally, if you have attended college, you would not include your high school) and training while you were getting that education. Readers of your resume will probably want to know what your major courses of study have been, and what kinds of grades or honors or scholastic achievement you have made.

In cases in which your major course of study is one not clearly understood by the reader (for example, most business people know what an accounting major does, but they may be less clear as to what a person who majors in "human resource development" does), include brief descriptions of some of the courses that you've taken.

Readers want to know about your results more than your job title.

Work Experience. The reader of the resume wants to know what kind of **work experience** you have. He or she wants to know the positions you held previously but, more important, what your responsibilities were and what results were obtained while you were a worker.

Occasionally, students come to us and say, "I've had no formal work experience." By this they usually mean that they have not been hired for paying work. It's not necessary, however, that your job be a paying, traditional job. We have talked to several students who have not had a need to work part-time but who have spent time in volunteer organizations. Some have worked as helpers in hospitals or in nursing homes, or have handled accounting, bookkeeping, or newsletter preparation for their church, and so forth. The point they need to convey in a resume is that they have had some experience in an organization and that that experience taught them something. What it taught them is potentially useful to their future employer.

Personal Data. The reader of your resume wants to get some picture in his or her mind about what you are like. You are not, however, required by law to divulge some aspects of your personal life, such as marital status, age, ethnic background, plans to have children, and so forth. Nevertheless, some people choose to indicate their age, height, weight, marital status, and some other bits of information. Memberships held in various organization, especially leadership positions, can be useful aspects of your **personal data** that tend to reflect positively.

Optional or Creative Additions to Your Resume

In addition to the three standard parts—education, work experience, and personal data—some people choose to prepare several other items with their resumes. These may be printed on or attached to the resume. They may also be prepared to give to an interviewer in addition to the resume.

Career Objective. There are pros and cons to indicating a **career objective** early in the resume. If you have a clear, specific idea of exactly the type of job you want (and you're really not interested in any other type of job), then a career-objective statement may be useful. In such a case, the career-objective statement should be clear and specific. For example, you may say, "I want to work as a general accountant for a Big Six accounting firm with eventual promotion to a management capacity." That is a specific objective, which would get a positive reaction from a person seeking to hire an accountant.

We have found, however, that those who may be less clear about what job they want accomplish little by including a career-objective statement. The statements that they do write tend to be so vague as to have little meaning to the reader. For example, a person who writes, "I am interested in a career position that will give me the opportunity to advance into management and work with people" tells the reader little.

Personal History. Some people choose to write a **personal history** in a narrative form that gives the employer a clear picture of them. This can be useful, but it tends to make the resume long. We have, however, seen examples of such a personal-history statement that cause the applicant to come alive and be projected as an interesting person in the mind of the reader. Page 358 shows an abbreviated example of a personal-history statement.

The writer of this personal history was successful in his job search and received several favorable comments on his approach.

Remember, however, that the personal history is not a traditional resume component; when using it, you may run the risk of appearing ignorant of resume conventions. Conversely, some readers, especially in more creative organizations, may like it. Use your best judgment; if in doubt, however, you would do well to stay with the traditional approach.

Another nontraditional component you may want to consider in a resume is a statement of your goals.

You may want to let your reader know where you are going with your life.

Your Personal Goals. Business organizations are goal oriented. Business people tend to be attracted to applicants who have these same goal-directed habits. It may be useful to the reader to come to understand some of your specific goals and objectives. On page 359, there is an example of some goals that one person presented in a resume to a major company.

Samples of Work. Sometimes it is useful to include samples of the kinds of work that you have done. This is particularly appropriate if you are looking for a job in photography, art, drafting, architecture, or several other areas where illustrations of what you have done would be useful to the person reading your resume.

Do not load up your resume so that it runs too long, however, by including an excessive number of samples. Instead, bring some of the sample documents or drawings with you when you come to the job interview. Or you may indicate on your resume that samples of your work are available in case the reader would like to study those before you have your job interview.

What to Avoid in Resume Preparation

Although the resume is a document about you, it is important not to toot your own horn too loudly. For example, avoid words of self-evaluation like, "I did a 'fantastic' job in achieving new record sales."

It's fine to show in some objective way that you have been successful in past work. Be careful, however, of the superlative terms that are not clearly substantiated.

Personal History

This brief personal history is to aid you in evaluating what kind of employee I might be. I have written it with honest candor and hope it will be useful to you.

As a young boy, I grew up in Pikeville, Kentucky. I had numerous opportunities to work, and thus at an early age learned the importance of doing my best. By the time I had reached eleven, summers were spent mowing lawns and doing odd jobs in the neighborhood. My performance was highly received, because frequently I'd be requested to maintain as many as twenty to twenty-five lawns per week.

Leisure activities included a variety of outdoor recreation, ranging from football to camping. Even though I thoroughly enjoyed all forms of physical activity, I had always had a desire to play professional baseball. This desire propelled me to practice long hours. The apex of my baseball career arrived when both the Cincinnati Reds and the Philadelphia Phillies requested that I participate in their tryout camps. With continued effort and practice, I feel I could have had a successful professional baseball career, but with deep and serious introspection, I determined that I wanted something else. Further education, a stable career, and a close family became more important than the fulfillment of my childhood dream.

On graduation from high school, I determined that I could further my education by joining the United States Army. Although most people look upon the military as an undesirable experience, I decided to make my two years as rewarding as possible. Working as a financial analyst of the pay records provided a good foundation and excellent training for a future career in finance. As I excelled in this field, further responsibility was given to me, including the training of all new finance personnel in my section. Coupled with the benefits listed earlier, serving in the armed forces allowed me the opportunity to reflect on the freedom of this land and my responsibility in maintaining it.

```
Lifetime Goals
─────────────

1. Professional

   • Maintain high integrity at all times
   • Achieve executive-level position in a retail
     organization
   • Serve actively in community organizations
   • Continue to study and learn a wide range of
     areas

2. Personal

   • Raise a close family
   • Be a good financial provider

Short-range Goals
─────────────────

1. Professional

   • Graduate from college with honors
   • Secure employment in a company with a strong
     management-training program
   • Continue advanced management courses in
     evenings

2. Personal

   • Pay off all education expenses within two
     years
   • Purchase a home
```

Describe your
accomplishments in
objective terms.

Instead of saying that you "greatly increased sales," why not indicate the dollar volume or your ranking among salespeople and show how that improved? In other words, measure your accomplishments and talk about these in objective terms.

This point suggests another. Do talk about end results that you've achieved on your jobs or at school. Don't be shy about this, but simply state them in factual, objective terms.

Use clauses instead of
complete sentences.

Another related point: Try to avoid the use of the word *I*. Resumes can be written that avoid the use of *I* entirely. Information in narrative form is presented in clauses, not complete sentences. In other words, instead of saying "I was promoted to . . .," the resume would simply say, "Promoted to. . . ." The reader knows that the resume is about you.

Avoid apologizing. Many people, especially those who are a little uncomfortable with their lack of experience, apologize in the resume. Do not, for example, say, "My work experience is limited. The only job I ever held was in the mailroom." Instead, talk in positive terms about what it was that you accomplished as a mail clerk. If, in fact, the mail-clerk job was the only work you've ever done, break it down into some specific responsibilities. For example, you may find that these responsibilities could be described as follows:

Opened all mail received at headquarters

Accounted for up to $10,000 in daily cash and check distribution

Accounted for and distributed several thousand dollars in U.S. government postage stamps

Operated the copying machine and made thousands of copies of letters and other documents   *(list continues on page 361)* *(list continues on page 361)*

(DILBERT reprinted by permission of United Feature Syndicate, Inc.)

Carried confidential messages to and from the various branches of the organization

Supervised a crew of three others during especially heavy mailing season

Put your best foot forward; avoid the negative.

By describing in full detail the work that was done, even in what seems like a rather lowly position, some positive characteristics make this candidate look good.

A final point to avoid is negative information about you and your experiences. A resume should put your best foot forward. It is not necessary to include such items as having been terminated from previous jobs, having failed in particular assignments, and the like. Readers know that you're human and that everyone makes some mistakes. It is not necessary to put these things in writing, especially in your job-application resume.

Elements to Include

Probably the most important single thing to include in your resume is some indication that the company will benefit from hiring you. Reader viewpoint, discussed earlier, is important in your resume. As you put forth information about you and your characteristics, try to help the reader relate these to benefits that will be received by hiring you.

Padded Resume May Get You a Hard Time in Court[2]

by Kerri Smith

If you still need a reason to stop padding your resume or fibbing on job applications, here it is: Employers can use that information to laugh you out of court if you ever sue the company no matter how legitimate your complaint.

Courts call this information "after-acquired evidence." Recently the U.S. Court of Appeals for the Sixth Circuit ruled that after-acquired evidence is a "complete bar to any recovery by the former employee where the employer can show it would have fired the employee on the basis of the evidence."

Here's an example of what we're talking about: Say you apply for a job at XYZ Corp. You fudge employment dates and write "resigned to take a better job" instead of admitting being fired for tardiness. After all, you figure, that was the year your baby-sitter situation was out of control. Surely there's no need to share that disastrous episode.

XYZ Corp. hires you and life is good.

Five years later, a new boss at XYZ targets all the 40-plus workers. You lose your job and file an age discrimination lawsuit. The attorney says you can't lose.

But you do lose. That's because XYZ Corp. hired an investigator to verify the resumes and job applications of former employees. Citing information supplied by the investigator, XYZ Corp.'s attorney got your case dismissed by saying the company would not have hired you had it known your true employment history.

Employment attorney Gilbert Roman of Denver says companies increasingly are using after-acquired evidence, more commonly referred to as resume fraud, to wiggle out of tight spots.

"In a perverse twist, companies are now encouraged to rummage through employees' files in search of some flaw," Roman said. "Then they use that flaw as a license to walk free from whatever discriminatory action they may have taken."

Roman said attorneys for the National Association for the Advancement of Colored People, the American Association of Retired Persons and several other civil rights organizations protested the Sixth Circuit decision mentioned above. The U.S. Supreme Court will hear the case this fall.

It's true that most workers will never have to sue their employers. But the ominous rise in use of after-acquired evidence as a legal defense is just one more reason why it's foolish to lie on a resume.

Try, if you possibly can, to indicate such characteristics as initiative, responsibility, dependability, cost-consciousness, and people skills. These are the kinds of characteristics that are frequently looked for in new employees.

Examples of Resume Parts

On the following pages are examples of how others have set up various parts of their resumes.

Education Examples

```
Bachelor of Science degree, University Studies,
Ohio University, April 1997; grade-point
average: 3.6

Pertinent Coursework:

Administration of Health     Health Care Law
Care Organizations           Financial Management

Introduction to Hospital     Managerial Economics
Administration

Financial Management of      Statistics
Hospitals

Personnel                    Public Relations

Labor Relations/             Medical Sociology
Collective Bargaining
```

Florida State University, Tallahassee, Florida

Degree: Bachelor of Arts received June 1986

Major: English

Minor: Broadcast management

Honors: Dean's List for three years. Top 10
            percent of class.
            Earned academic scholarship, two
            years.

Activities: Literary Club, secretary. Published
            two short stories in national maga-
            zine. Intramural softball.

Master of Public Administration, 1997

University of Washington, Seattle

Among the pertinent courses taken: Public Finance,
Public Personnel Administration, Organization and
Management, Accounting and Information Systems,
Statistics, Intergovernmental Relations, Municipal
and County Management.

Certificates: International City Managers Association for Municipal Management, 1995.

```
Undergraduate Education

Bachelor of arts, 1996, University of Wyoming

Major:          Political Science

Minor Fields: Philosophy, English

Scholarships: Academic Leadership Scholarship,
              1995-96
              Farmington Oil Co. Scholarship, 1994

Associate of Arts, 1994, Carper Community College

Major:          Auto technology
```

**Experience
Examples**

Experience   Internship: Texas State Legislative
              Auditor General's Office

              • Audited Texas Mental Health
                Centers' unit cost data

              • Prepared tables, charts, and
                graphs for audit report

              • Initiated and conducted audit
                interviews with agency person-
                nel

              Bookkeeper: E-Z Auto Parts

              • Prepared daily bank deposits and
                kept general journal

              Editor: Bountiful High School Year-
              book

              • Edited and approved all copy,
                layouts, and pictures

Recent Employment History

Summer 1995—Avtel Electronics Inc. of Covina, California. Worked with the material control supervisor and a management information systems consultant. Converted the company's accounting, inventory, and purchasing systems to a form that was compatible to storage in a data bank and one that gave management more relevant information for decision making.

September 1993 to February 1994—Managed a drive-in restaurant in Phoenix. Sales of more than $10,000 per month.

September 1982 to August 1993—Managed an instant printing service store in Chandler, Arizona. Sales of $127,000 per year.

```
Work
Experience  United States Steel Corporation, Geneva
            Works, Orem, Utah. Involved with prod-
            uct testing in Metallurgical Chemical
            Inspection Department (May 1993 to Au-
            gust 1995).

            Department of Economics, Brigham Young
            University, Provo, Utah. Teaching as-
            sistant for the Introductory Economics
            Courses (December 1995 to April 1996).

            Security Pacific National Bank, Glen-
            dale, California. Management trainee
            with exposure to customer relations,
            operations, loan department, and teller
            work (June 1987 to September 1987).

1989-93     Bell South Corp., Orlando and Jack-
            sonville, Florida. Commercial manager
            responsible for work force of 7 super-
            visors and 32 nonmanagement service
            representatives handling 40,000 cus-
            tomer accounts. Duties included train-
            ing and development, employee and
            public relations, and achievement of
            company objectives in sales, customer
            service, and collection.

            On later staff assignment, developed a
            monthly results booklet that was the
            subject of articles in two professional
            newsletters. Also did personnel assess-
            ment workshops, business office audits,
            and implementation of job enrichment
            programs.
```

Career Objectives Examples

```
Employment
Objective        Seeking a responsible administra-
                 tive or management position with
                 a government agency. It is impor-
                 tant that the position provide
                 sufficient challenge and freedom
                 so that I can use my individual
                 initiative and creativity to
                 solve problems and accomplish the
                 agency's mission.

Employment
Objective        My emphasis of study and interest
                 has been local government. There-
                 fore, I would prefer a position
                 that is either directly involved
                 in local government or one that
                 is indirectly involved through
                 intergovernmental relations.

Career Objective A career requiring strong analyt-
                 ical, leadership, and decision-
                 making skills in the area of
                 financial or investment analysis.

Career Objective Responsible management position
                 in an entrepreneurial private
                 business. Emphasis on program
                 planning, monitoring, and evalua-
                 tion.

Career Objective A position offering maximum expo-
                 sure, responsibility, and growth
                 potential in the field of systems
                 management.
```

Miscellaneous Examples

Language Proficiency	Worked for two years (1990–92) as a Red Cross volunteer in Brazil using the Portuguese language exclusively.
Language Skill	Family lived in Ecuador for three years while my father managed an oil refinery. I speak Spanish fluently.
Language	Have traveled extensively and speak three Asian languages.
Other Background	• Junior Class president, Boise State College • Member, Curriculum Innovation Committee, Boise State College • Participant, Honors Program, Boise State College • First runner-up, All-American Family Pageant, Lehigh Acres, Florida, 1983 • National Honor Society, Boise High School • Various Oratorical Awards • Eagle Scout • Speak French fluently
Special Interests	Private pilot (eight years), clarinet since 1978, oil painting, skiing, jogging, golfing, and writing.

Sample Resumes

Finally, take a look at two complete sample resumes (Figures 13–1 and 13–2). Again, these are only suggested arrangements that should be tailored to meet your reader's needs.

```
                    SUSAN ERIKA TIMMONS


Home Address:                      University Address:
132 Redmont Road                      4011 Union Street
Rochester, NY 14624                    Alfred, NY 14872
(716) 248-4336                        (605) 343-3033

Employment
Objective      To secure a position that would apply
               my educational background in market-
               ing. The ideal position would include
               personal contact with the public and
               steadily increasing responsibility.

Education:     Alfred University
               Bachelor of science degree in business
               administration, May 1997
               Major: Marketing
               Monroe Community College
               Associate of Science in business ad-
               ministration, May 1993

Course
Emphasis:      Marketing Management, Consumer Be-
               havior, Sales Management, Promotional
               Strategy, and Marketing Research

Honors:        Alfred University Presidential Schol-
               arship Dean's List (grade-point aver-
               age: 3.73)
               Business Honors program
               College Scholar scholarship winner
               Graduated with high honors

Experience:    Student Aide, September 1996 to May
               1997
               Herrick Memorial Library—Alfred Uni-
               versity
               Clerk, March 1994 to August 1995
               Roses Variety Store, Alfred, New York

Activities:    American Marketing Association (stu-
               dent chapter, vice-president)
               Alfred University Women's Business As-
               sociation

References:    Available on request
```

FIGURE 13-1

Sample resume #1.

```
James (Jamie) Thomas West      771 Capital Drive
                               Williamstown, VA 27331
                               (703) 226-0819

Career
Objective     To pursue a career within a consumer
              goods industry, leading to profes-
              sional opportunities in advertising,
              brand/product management, and market
              research and development.

Education:
1993-96       Florida State University, Tallahassee,
              Florida
              Major: Radio/TV Production, Communica-
              tion Theory
              Minor Interest: Mathematics, Architec-
              ture
              Graduate of a three-year bachelor of
              science program; grade-point average:
              3.3

Work
Experience:   Summer
1993          Motorola, Inc.—Chicago, Illinois
              Research analyst and coproject direc-
              tor.
              The assignment was to design and im-
              plement an exploratory market research
              program that would (1) indicate the
              existence of a mass consumer market
              for radio paging products, and (2) de-
              scribe the market and determine appro-
              priate channels of distribution, price
              elasticities, and product form charac-
              teristics. Also assisted in the design
              of a CB radio product trade-up re-
              search program.
```

FIGURE 13-2
Sample resume #2.

```
1991            Marshall Fields—Evanston, Illinois
                Assistant manager of a textbook ware-
                house dealing primarily with inventory
                levels and order processing.

1989-1991       American Airlines—Chicago, Illinois
                Ticket agent and public service repre-
                sentative at O'Hare Field, Chicago.

Outside
Activities:     Disk jockey on campus radio station
                WFSU, intramural sports, Sailing Club
                cochairman, 1995 Homecoming activi-
                ties, Young Alumni Council, member of
                Psi Upsilon fraternity, and host of
                employment program Careers '95.

Other
Interests:      Photography, golf, hang-gliding, and
                surfing.
```

FIGURE 13–2 cont'd

Cover Letter

When applying for a job by mail, you'll need to enclose a cover letter of application with your resume. The cover letter is a persuasive message. A review of ideas in Chapter Twelve will be useful. In addition, the following information can help you compose an effective job-winning letter to accompany your resume.

Address your cover letter to a specific person.

Always address an application letter to a specific person. Too often, letters addressed simply to the personnel manager or manager of employment fail to get the personal attention you desire. Don't get lost in the paper jungle of the employment department.

Use names from recruiting literature or newspaper ads, or telephone the company to determine the best person to write to. When in doubt about which of several possible contacts to use, write to the person of the highest organizational position (within reason). That person will usually refer it to the one who makes hiring decisions. That referral in itself can add valuable credibility to your application. It can imply that the boss wants the resume carefully reviewed.

What Goes into an Application Letter?

Cover or **application letters** should include the following:

1. Reasons for the letter
2. The specific position or type of work for which you are applying
3. A reference to your enclosed resume with a brief highlight of the key features you have to offer to that particular company
4. A request for an interview

The goal of the cover letter is to get the reader to review your resume.

The effective application letter will not only create a positive image; it will have two other key results: (1) get the reader to look at your resume and thus gain additional insights about how you might fit into the organization, and (2) motivate the reader to set up a selection interview with you.

Letters should be individually typed and not just copies of a mass-produced letter. The appearance of the letter itself must create a positive image for you.

Following are examples of openings, middles, and closings for application letters and with these examples are several complete sample letters.

Sample Application Letters

Examples of Openings

- Mr. James E. Pietre, director of personnel for Union Camp Corporation in Wayne, New Jersey, has informed me of the job opening in your Personnel Department. I am interested and feel confident that I can suit the needs of the job of a personnel interviewer.

- Will you please consider me for the secretarial position advertised in the *Times*? Because of my education and experience as a professional secretary, I feel confident and competent in my ability to work for your firm.

- Last December, while you were auditing Bay Area Shippers, I talked with you concerning my interest in accounting. At that time, you asked me to call on you when my education was nearing completion. Since that time, I have continued my studies in accounting and am now ready to pursue a career in that field.

- Do you have an opening in your fabrication shop for a skilled welder? My qualifications include an associate's degree in welding from Piedmont Tech, more than five years of work experience, and a genuine interest in further developing expertise in steel fabrication.

Examples of Middles

- In addition to major requirements in accounting and finance, my program of studies included courses in business communication and speech.

- Through my involvement with several organizations on campus, I have become more aware of the importance of running effective meetings.

- My most valuable education, though, has been working as a secretary to one of the top executives at the university.

- The practical courses I have taken at L.A. Trade Tech have taught me important skills in upholstering and furniture manufacture.

Examples of Closings (Action Steps)

- The enclosed data sheet gives you additional information about my background. After you have a chance to verify some of the things I have said about myself, please call me about the possibilities of working for your company. Also, please let me know if you wish additional information. I'll be glad to send it to you promptly.

- Will you give me a chance to show you what I have to offer your company? I feel that I can contribute to the pleasant atmosphere I find in your organization.

- May I have an interview to give you an opportunity to learn more about me and to give me an opportunity to learn more about you? Please call me at (201)999-9384, and I can make travel arrangements.

- I will be in the Los Angeles area April 24 to 29, and I am eager to discuss with you the asset of having an accountant with strong communication experience. Will you please let me know by April 10 if I can come in and talk with you at some time during that week?

Examples of Complete Letter Text

- Will you consider me for a business internship in San Francisco? I am currently enrolled in the M.B.A. program at Indiana University and am interested in increasing the depth of my management skills through a practical application of my education.

    I have received an undergraduate degree in chemical engineering and want to work for a company in which this education would be an asset.

    My engineering experience has increased my desire to work in the engineering field. This experience has also acquainted me with Bechtel's outstanding reputation within the industry.

    The enclosed resume outlines additional educational and work experiences.

    I will be in the Bay Area from December 23 to January 2 and would appreciate the opportunity to talk to you or someone in your organization. I look forward to hearing from you.

- As graduation approaches, I would like to apply for a position in your fabrication shop. My training at erie Technical College has given me thorough experience in the uses of virtually every type of welding equipment.

    For the past two summers I have worked for Morrison Steel Products, helping to assemble their specialized truck bodies. My supervisor at Morrison, Mr. Don Carter, has written a letter of commendation for me and stands ready to recommend me to you.

    Enclosed is a resume describing my education and work experience in more detail. I am available for an interview at your earliest convenience. Please call me at (716) 849-3933.

- Is there a place at Save-Mo Industries for a thoroughly trained secretary with excellent computer skills? My recently completed training at Bryant Business

College has helped me develop these skills, and I would like the chance to demonstrate how I can put them to work for you.

The enclosed resume describes my education, software expertise, and work experience. You will note that my grades were nearly straight *As* and that I placed second in the nation in the Secretarial Keyboarding Skills competition last May.

Technical skills aren't all I'd like to bring to Save-Mo, however. Ambition, enthusiasm, and a sincere desire to become an administrative assistant are at the heart of my career plans.

If this brief description meets requirements for work in your office, I'd like to talk further with you. May I call for an interview next week?

- With two years' experience as a bookkeeper at the Dick Warren Ford dealership and a soon-to-be-completed college degree in accounting, I'm eager to apply for the position you advertised in the *Herald*.

  Your advertisement calls for a permanent resident with accounting skills and a desire to work into management. This description matches my abilities.

  As a lifelong resident of Kansas City, I have been looking forward to a career in the financial industry. (In fact, I have long been one of your satisfied customers.)

  The enclosed resume will give you additional information about my interests and background. Please let me know when we can get together to talk further about a career with U.S. Savings and Loan.

  You can reach me at my home (after 4:00 P.M.) at (215)221-4113.

Interviews to Get the Job

All the effort put forth to prepare a good resume and effective job-search letter culminates in the job interview.

Selection interviews are part of a process to see if there is a "fit" between the candidate and the company.

There are several types of job interviews. Some are used to screen possible job candidates, ultimately, more in-depth interviewing is used to make a final selection. Normally, candidates undergo a series of discussions with several different people.

Any selection interview is a joint process in which both participants—the interviewer and the prospective job candidate—have their own purposes in mind. Ideally,

Focus your energy on preparation for job interviews. (Courtesy of Mike Malyszko/FPG International.)

each is attempting to measure the strengths and weaknesses of the other. The interviewer is looking for good employees. The interviewee is shopping for a job position that suits his or her career interests and needs. A great deal of what happens in the job interview hinges on the personal chemistry that comes about as these people talk with each other. That chemistry is subjective. Some people just hit it off better than others. You don't have much control over such things, so don't worry about them too much. Instead, focus your energy on the kinds of things that can be better controlled. In a word, *preparation* is the key.

The Interview Is Two-Way Information Sharing

Your chief jobs in the interview situation are to (1) sell yourself, and (2) find out how well the job and the company suit your needs. Each of these purposes is important. Remember that companies need employees! Don't go into a job situation with your figurative "hat in your hand," begging for a job. Go into it rather viewing it as an opportunity to explore and satisfy your needs as well as the employer's.

The most frequent complaints recruiters have about interviewees provide an excellent starting point to help you prepare and accomplish a successful interview.

Complaints about Interview Preparation

Ill-Prepared for the Interview. Job candidates too often have little information about the company or the job. They have no good questions to ask and often no interview training. As a two-way communication experience, it is as important for you to have prepared questions as it is for the interviewer. Find out as much as you can about the company before the interview. The more you know, the more impressive you will be to the interviewer.

Vague Interests. Candidates often lack career goals—tend to not know what job they want. As part of your preparation, think about career objectives and long-range plans. Have specific answers prepared.

Unrealistic Expectations. Candidates lack flexibility, are too concerned with salary, or seem to have a "What can you do for me?" attitude. Students are seen as immature because they have unrealistic or impractical ideas of what companies can offer. Learn what to expect. Get an idea of what starting salary is realistic and how long it takes to move up in an organization.

Complaints about the Interview

Poor Communication Skills. This is the most frequent complaint expressed by interviewers about job candidates. The candidates come across as evasive, by not answering questions directly and confidently. They seem poorly organized by giving rambling responses. They talk too little or talk too much. They seem ill at ease and are nervous.

Lack of Motivation and Enthusiasm. This is another complaint often heard by interviewers. Candidates are apathetic, lack interest, do not sell themselves, or are too agreeable. These perceptions probably arise from the presentation skills of the interviewee. Vocal variation, effective nonverbal behaviors, and good people skills will overcome this problem.

Awareness of the ideas covered throughout this book can go a long way toward improving your interview skills. The principles for preparing a good presentation can also be used in preparing and conducting an interview.

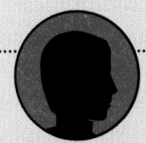

Self-Check Your Attitudes toward the Job-Finding Process[3]

"If you don't expect to find the best job available, you probably won't," says attitude expert Elwood Chapman.

To earn a position equal to your potential, it is vital to maintain a positive attitude over an extended period. To measure your current attitude toward the job-finding process, complete this exercise. Circle the appropriate number between the opposite statements. For example, if you circle a 5, you are saying no improvement is possible.

	High				Low	
I like searching for prospective employers and setting up interviews.	5	4	3	2	1	I hate having to find a prospective employer.
I love the challenge of an employment interview.	5	4	3	2	1	Interviews bother me.
The prospect of a professional job search excites me.	5	4	3	2	1	I am depressed before I get started.
An interview can be a dignified experience.	5	4	3	2	1	Interviewing is a demeaning experience.
Going through a dozen interviews to get the best possible job does not bother me.	5	4	3	2	1	I hope my first interview is my last.
Selling employers on my talents is fun.	5	4	3	2	1	Having to sell myself is embarrassing.
I want to learn everything I can about the job-finding process.	5	4	3	2	1	I would rather have someone just offer me a job, or pay an agency.
Interview mistakes can be a positive learning experience.	5	4	3	2	1	Interview mistakes leave me totally discouraged.
Finding a job is a game; I am going to win!	5	4	3	2	1	Finding a job is like going to the dentist.
I plan to complete three interviews next week.	5	4	3	2	1	I am taking next week off; job searching is tiring.

Total Score _____

If you rated yourself above 40, you have an excellent attitude toward the search ahead. If you rated yourself between 25 and 40, you appear to have some adjustments to make. A rating under 25 indicates you are not mentally prepared for your search.

Complaints about Interview Follow-Up

Many interviewees never follow up, thus wasting an opportunity to make a good impression.

This one is simple: *Too few candidates follow up at all!* They leave the interviewer and never again speak to him or her. Often interviewers see this lack of communication as a lack of interest. Some intentionally wait to see if the candidate has the initiative to follow up.

The simplest form of follow-up is a thank you note expressing appreciation for the interview and restating your desire to work for the company. Many applicants never do this.

How to Avoid Common Complaints about Interviewees

Four ways to best prepare for a job interview include the following:

1. Understand yourself and what you are seeking.
2. Learn something about the organization.
3. Assemble materials to take to the interview.
4. Practice effective communication skills.

Understand-ing Yourself: A Look In-ward

Self-analysis is an excellent place to begin a job search.

Before you go into any job interview, be sure you understand yourself and what you want. Give serious thought to your interests, needs, values, and goals. Know what kind of job you are seeking.

One interesting approach to such self-analysis is to develop a **dream list.** To do this, simply take a tablet or some sheets of blank paper and make a list of your skills, your interests, and your desires. Do not censor your thinking at this point. Simply throw out on the paper as many ideas as you come up with. Focus primarily on what it is you would like to have in your career. List as many details as you can to develop an ideal job description.

As you make this list, include details about your personal life, your financial situation, your family relationships, and any other aspect of the ideal career that you picture for yourself. Visualize your job title, responsibilities, the way you will dress when you go to work, the nature of the work itself, the potential headaches, and the amount of enjoyment. Make as long a list as possible. Quantity is important here. Do not think about each idea too carefully. Simply scratch it down on sheets of paper.

(FRANK & ERNEST reprinted by permission of Newspaper Enterprise Association, Inc.)

A "dream" list can help sort out conflicting desires.

Once you have roughed out a dream list like this, let it cool off for a few days. Then review what you have written, this time more critically. Take a look at each item, and see if it might conflict with others. Typical conflicts arise when you want the ideal job that would give you "lots of opportunity for travel" but at the same time express a high interest in "spending time with the family." When you visualize working in a high-technology computer center but would really enjoy coming up with creative displays for merchandise in a store, another conflict results.

These kinds of potentially conflicting ideas can pose interesting self-evaluative questions. Where do you draw the line? At what point would it not be worth it to you to work long hours at the cost of your family time? What ethical considerations or stress factors would influence the kind of job you would like to have? Ask yourself a lot of tough questions, and try to develop a clear picture of what would, indeed, be an ideal type of job for you. Then write out a careful description of that ideal job.

Do Your Homework: Research the Organization

You must learn about a company *before* an interview.

There is no way an interviewer can give you a complete picture of the organization he or she represents in the time that you will have together in the interview. It is important for you to come into the interview having done your homework. Get information about the company before you interview. If possible, visit the company and ask questions of people who work there. Most people are cooperative in giving such information to you.

If you are applying to work in a large company you can look up articles about the company at the library. You can also contact companies directly for copies of their annual reports. Among the kinds of information you may be able to get before the interview are the following:

- Nature of the organization's products or services
- Typical path for advancement opportunities
- History of growth and potential for future growth of the company
- Possibilities for personal growth within the company
- Approximate salary range you might expect
- Challenges and opportunities the company is facing in the marketplace (e.g., fast growth or stiff competition)

By taking the time to gather such information, you can create accurate expectations in your mind. With this information, prepare some questions to ask the interviewer.

People normally enjoy talking about their work. Some of the best interviews result from letting the interviewer do much of the talking. Remember that a common interviewer complaint is that candidates do not ask intelligent questions.

Take Materials with You

The interview is an opportunity to sell yourself. Take along some of your own sales literature, such as your resume and anything else that might help your presentation. Extra copies of the resume are especially important if you will be meeting several people.

For many types of jobs, samples of your work can show your abilities. If the job will involve writing, take along sample papers you have written. If you did a research project in school that may be of use to your potential employer, have a copy available.

Do not forget the little things, too. Be sure to take a pen and something to write on. Your daily planner or a calendar may be useful as well. Do not forget the list of questions you want to ask the interviewer. Have these written down and handy for reference.

Communicate Skillfully in the Interview

The **personal chemistry**—how well you hit it off—established between you and the interviewer comes from both verbal and nonverbal cues. Be sensitive to both forms of communication.

Be prompt and prepared for the interview. Tardiness shows a lack of respect for the other person's time as well as a lack of self-discipline. Be dressed appropriately, as you would dress after you get the job. (It helps to know the company's dress code, if any.)

When you are introduced, be responsive and shake hands warmly. Respond to the introduction and be prepared to tell the interviewer who you are (even if he or she probably knows your name already).

Follow the interviewer's lead.

Follow the interviewer's lead. Do not try to take over the interview but rather respond to the climate the interviewer sets. Such questions as the formality of address (should you call the interviewer Ms. Jones or Christy?) can be determined by the interviewer's lead. Be sensitive to the way he or she is communicating and respond in like manner. Usually it makes sense to be a bit overly formal rather than too familiar, at first. If people want to be called by their first name, they will tell you so.

Be a good listener, but do not forget to sell.

Be a good, active listener. Remember, listening is not a passive activity that you sit back and do when you are not talking. Instead, it should be an active mental process. When you listen to people actively, you listen for key ideas, arrange those ideas in your mind, and provide intelligent responses to them.

Do not forget to sell yourself in the interview. It is important to focus on your features—your experiences, education, and talents as they relate to benefits for that company—the what-this-means-to-you statements. Draw the link between **features** and **benefits** as clearly as possible. Do not assume that the interviewer will automatically see how your experience fits with the company's needs.

Here are some examples of features-and-benefits statements as they might be used in a job interview.

Never underestimate the importance of your appearance in a job interview. (Courtesy of Steve Weber/Stock Boston and Superstock.)

Feature Statement Alone	Feature Tied to a Benefit
I worked for a temporary help placement office for two years.	I worked in the temporary help placement office where I learned how to select employees like those your company hires.
I sold shoes in the summer.	My summer sales job in a shoe store taught me how to work with even the difficult-to-please customer—the kind of customer with whom your people must deal.
I worked my way through school.	I worked my way through school so I know the importance of watching my expenses carefully, just as your employees do.

Answer questions positively, stressing your positive features and downplaying anything negative in your resume. Volunteer information and be rather pointed in explaining how you are exceptional or unique in some important way. Do not be too bashful.

Use **assertiveness**—pleasant directness—in expressing your feelings honestly and taking charge of your rights responsibly. Avoid negative comments that tear down others. Never speak unkindly or negatively about other people or other organizations you have worked for. Be objective, frank, honest, and consistent in your answers.

One important thought to remember is that not every question requires an immediate response. Indeed, the **use of silence** can be very valuable in a job interview.

For example, a young graduate was excited about being offered a position by a particular company. The recruiter concluded a series of interviews with the statement, "John, we would like to invite you to join our retailing team. We would like you to start the first of next month, and we are prepared to pay you $22,000 a year." In John's mind he was delighted to receive this offer, but on the outside, he skillfully used the technique of silence—in this case a pause of only about 30 seconds—in which he made no response at all. He merely thought it over in his mind. The interviewer, however, did make a response. After this half-minute of silence, the interviewer came back and said, "Okay, John, we can make that $25,000." In less than a half-minute, John increased his salary by $3,000 by using that thoughtful pause.

The use of silence tends to put the burden on the other person. Many people will quickly fill the gap by providing some additional information or, as in this case, by upping the ante by $3,000!

It is not always appropriate to use silence, however. Some questions can be answered quickly and openly, and should be handled that way. Don't hesitate to use the slower, more thoughtful responses, especially when a difficult question is being asked. Do not appear flustered, simply appear to be organizing your thoughts in your mind.

When preparing, ask yourself tough questions.

A Few Words about Salary

Know the going rate for the job for which you are applying. This will help you avoid asking for an unreasonably high amount while also ensuring that you get a fair salary.

Remember, too, that salary isn't everything. Put the dollar amount in perspective. More important questions may be the following:

- Is this the type of work I enjoy doing? Will it be personally rewarding?
- Is this the type of organization with which I want to be associated? Are these the kind of people I'd enjoy being around?
- Are there benefits or advancement opportunities that can compensate for a lower salary?

Questions for which You Should Be Prepared

In preparation, be sure to ask yourself some of the tough questions—interviewers call them *blockbuster* questions. These may be vague, such as, "Tell me about yourself," or convey an implied antagonism, such as, "What good are you?" If you are not prepared for something like this, it can throw you off. The questions are designed to put you under some stress. Be prepared with a thoughtful, concise, and effective answer.

Anybody can handle the easy questions. Be prepared for the tough ones.

When handling any question, be sure to listen to what the interviewer is requesting. Do not hesitate to ask for clarification or to restate in your own words what you think he or she is asking. Be sure you know the question before you go off half-cocked with an answer.

Although interviewers do use various strategies, the questions asked are often similar. On page 384 you'll see a list of questions for which you would be wise to prepare. First, here are a few words about your rights.

Illegal or Inappropriate Questions

There are legal limits on what recruiters may ask.

Laws designed to reduce unfair job discrimination are enforced in the United States by the Equal Employment Opportunity Commission (EEOC). (Other countries have similar agencies.) The EEOC has determined that some questions are not to be asked of job applicants. Some **illegal questions** include the following:

Questions about Race or National Origin

- Where were you born?
- Are you of the _____ race?
- Do you believe that your race will be a problem in your job performance?
- Where were your parents born?
- Of what country are you a citizen?

Questions about Age or Handicaps

- What do you think about working for a person younger than you are?
- Do you have any handicaps?
- As a handicapped person, what help will you need to do your work?
- How severe is your handicap?
- How old are you?

Questions about Your Religion

- What church do you attend?
- What is your religion?
- Are you a _____ ?

- Do you hold any religious beliefs that would prevent you from working certain days of the week?

Questions about Marital/Family Relationships
....

- Do you have plans for having children?
- What does your husband/wife do?
- What happens if your spouse gets transferred to another city?
- Who will take care of your children when you work?
- Are you in a relationship currently?
- How would you react to working for a man/woman?

Identifying such illegal questions is only part of the challenge. Many interviewers may not be aware that they are asking illegal questions. In fact, surveys show that interviewees face a high probability of being asked an illegal question.

Your Options When Asked Illegal Questions

When you are asked an illegal question, how do you respond? Several options are available.[5]

Answer the Question. Many job candidates simply answer the question. Unfortunately, this may encourage the interviewer to ask more illegal questions. Nevertheless, in many cases, the question is asked innocently and will not be used unfairly against the candidate.

Ask How the Question Relates to Job Qualification. Example: "I am not sure how this question pertains to my qualifications for this job. I would be happy to answer if I can understand how it pertains to my qualification."

Direct Refusal. Examples: "I am sorry, this is not a question I am willing to answer"; or "I am sorry, this is not a question I am willing to answer because this information is personal."

Acknowledge Concern and Ask for Information. Example: "I am not sure what you want to know by asking that question. Could you tell me what it is you want to know?"

Answer the Underlying Concern Expressed by the Question. Examples: "I take it that your question about my plans for child care is a concern about the likelihood that I may be absent from work when they are ill. I want to assure you that I see myself as a professional person and will behave in a professionally responsible manner when they are ill." Or, "I am married. If you are concerned about how my marital status might affect my staying with the company, I can assure you that I am a professional and intend to continue working regardless of events in my personal life."

Terminating the Interview. Example: "It is interesting that your company uses such questions as a basis for hiring. I expect to file a complaint with the EEOC because you discriminate on an illegal basis."

Commonly Asked Questions

There is no substitute for practice when preparing for a job interview. What follows is a list of questions frequently used by recruiters.

From the list, select ten questions you might have difficulty with. Have a friend ask you those questions and tape record your responses. Ask others to give you feedback on the answers you give. Remember to relate your answers to the potential needs of the company (features to benefits) as discussed in this chapter.

(Note, questions with an asterisk may be illegal. Select at least two of these for practice and decide how you will handle them.)

   1. In what school activities did you participate? Why? Which did you enjoy the most?

   2. In what type of position are you most interested?

   3. What jobs have you held? How were they obtained, and why did you leave?

   4. What courses did you like best? Least? Why?

   5. What percentage of your school expenses did you earn? How?

   6. How did you spend your vacations while in school?

   7. What do you know about our company?

   8. What qualifications do you have that make you feel you would be successful in your field?

   9. What kind of salary are you looking for?

 *10. How do you feel about your family?

  11. If you were starting school all over again, what courses would you take?

 *12. Do you have a girlfriend/boyfriend? Is it serious?

  13. How much money do you hope to earn at age _____ ?

  14. Why did you decide to go to the school you attended?

  15. What do you think determines a person's progress in a good company?

 *16. Where did your family originally come from? What kind of a name is yours?

  17. Why do you think you would like this particular type of job?

 *18. What is your father's occupation?

 *19. Tell me about your home during the time you were growing up.

  20. Do you prefer working with others or by yourself?

  21. What kind of boss do you prefer?

 *22. Can you take instructions from a woman/man without feeling upset?

 *23. Do you live with your parents? Which of your parents has had the most profound influence on you?

  24. How did previous employers treat you?

  25. What have you learned from some of the jobs you have held?

  26. What interests you about our product or service?

  27. Have you ever changed your major field of interest? Why?

(continued)

(continued)

28. What do you know about opportunities in the field in which you are trained?

*29. How long do you expect to work before having children?

*30. Do you own any life insurance?

*31. Do you have any debts?

*32. How old were you when you became self-supporting?

*33. Do you attend church?

34. Do you like routine, repetitive work?

*35. When did you first contribute to family income?

36. What is your major weakness?

37. Will you fight to get ahead?

38. What do you do to keep in good physical condition?

*39. How do you usually spend Sunday?

*40. Have you had any serious illness, injury, or handicap?

41. What job in our company would you choose if you were entirely free to do so?

*42. Is it an effort for you to be tolerant of persons with backgrounds and interests different from your own?

43. What types of books have you read?

44. Have you plans for further education?

45. Have you ever tutored another student?

46. What jobs have you enjoyed the most? Least? Why?

47. What are your own special abilities?

*48. How would your husband/wife feel about your working here?

*49. Would your children be able to handle your overtime work?

50. Do you think that grades should be considered by employers? Why or why not?

It is hoped that your interviewing experiences will not end because of illegal questions. You do have legal rights, however. The idea is to participate successfully in the job-search process—to get a job. Be somewhat tolerant of the interviewer. You may be an interviewer one day, and the challenge of selecting employees without discriminating unfairly calls for some careful communication skills.

Understanding the Basics

SUMMARY OF KEY IDEAS

• No one, surefire way to conduct a job search exists; individual salesmanship, creativity, and attention to detail are important to success.

• Resumes are abbreviated information sheets. Those who review them tend to read between the lines and draw certain unstated conclusions.

- Standard parts of virtually all resumes include statements about the candidate's
  - Education or training
  - Work experience (paid or volunteer)
  - Personal characteristics and interests
- Optional or creative additions one may want to add to or use to accompany a resume include such things as
  - Career objective
  - Personal history
  - Personal goals
  - Photograph
  - Samples of work
- Avoid resume wording that tends to exaggerate, express ideas in nonmeasurable phrases, is too "I" oriented, apologizes, or unduly presents negative ideas.
- Be sure to let a company know how it will benefit from hiring you (features/benefits).
- Application letters that accompany a resume should include
  - Reason for the letter
  - Position being applied for
  - Reference to enclosed resume
  - Highlight of a key selling point
  - Request for an interview
- A job interview may be one of the most important communication events in a person's life.
- Although personal chemistry between interviewer and interviewee plays an important role, a person can improve his or her chance for success in the interview by careful preparation.
- Job candidates should see their major purpose as selling themselves, and finding out how the job and company suits their personal needs.

- The five most common complaints recruiters have about interviewees are
  - Poor communication skills
  - Being ill prepared for the interview
  - Vague interests
  - Lack of motivation
  - Unrealistic expectations
- Candidates can avoid common pitfalls by better
  - Understanding themselves
  - Understanding the organization
  - Assembling materials for the interview
  - Practicing communication skills
- Looking inward and systematically analyzing personal career expectations can help focus a candidate.
- Researching the organization before interviewing should help the candidate to better understand the company's
  - Products or services
  - Organization structure
  - Growth potential
  - Plans for coping with change
  - Growth possibilities for employees
  - Approximate salary ranges
- Being prepared with good questions helps make the interviewer feel more at ease and illustrates the candidate's preparation.
- Take along pertinent materials to the interview. These may include extra resumes, samples of work, pen and paper, and your prepared questions.
- Be sensitive to both verbal and nonverbal cues that come across during the interview.
- When selling yourself, relate your features to potential benefits you can offer the organization.
- Don't feel compelled to respond instantly to all questions. Silence can be an effective tool.

KEY TERMS AND CONCEPTS

resume	career objective	assertiveness
personal data	personal history	features and benefits
work experience	personal chemistry	computer scanning
dream list	education and training	use of silence
illegal questions	cover or application letters	

1. In this chapter, your authors recommend leading off your resume with your strongest selling point. Many resumes begin with personal data, such as date of birth, and so forth. Because such personal characteristics are seldom a candidate's strongest point, this contradicts the authors' advice. Which approach do you think is better? Why? (Remember that there are no absolute right or wrong approaches to resume writing!)

2. How do you react to the example of the "personal history" presented in this chapter? Do you think it might be helpful in your job search? Could it hurt your chances? Develop a list of arguments for and against the use of such a personal history in your job search.

3. What are the two main purposes of the job interview?

4. Name the five most frequent complaints recruiters have about interviewees.

5. What is a "dream list," and how can it help you prepare for job interviewing?

6. What should you know about any company with which you interview?

7. What materials should you take with you on a job interview?

8. Why is it illegal to ask some questions in an interview?

9. What types of questions are not to be asked?

10. What options do you have if asked an illegal question?

ANOTHER Look

How to Impress a Computer with Your Resume

You loaded your resume with power verbs and printed it on classy-looking gray linen stock. So how is it the big companies haven't come calling?

Probably because you never got past their computers. It's estimated that up to 80 percent of medium- to large-size companies will use computers to process resumes by the end of the century—and computers don't care about your fancy linen paper. (That's why so many companies ask applicants to fax resumes; those faxes go right into the database.) To make your resume stand out to a computer, you need to know what the scanning software is looking for, says Joyce Lain Kennedy, senior author of *Electronic*

Resume Revolution and a syndicated columnist.

A primer on the new rules:
- List companies, titles and jargon. Action verbs such as "managed," "developed" or "instituted" don't score with computers searching for job-specific nouns such as "MBA" and "engineer" or keywords like "will relocate."
- Use white paper and simple, high-contrast printing. Colors, including gray, inhibit letter-background contrast. For the same reason, don't get fancy with typefaces, boxes and graphics.
- Be detailed. More information means more potential keywords.

Don't worry about exceeding one page—computers don't care.
- Use 10- to 14-point type, nothing smaller.
- Don't fold. Cramming your resume into a business envelope creates creases that make scanning difficult.

Resumix, a company that sells resume-scanning systems, offers a free pamphlet on preparing computer-scanned resumes. Send a self-addressed, stamped envelope to Resumix Pamphlet Offer, 2953 Bunker Hill Lane, Santa Clara, CA 95054.

(*Men's Health*, March 1995, p. 28.)

Applying Your Knowledge

1. Review the essential and nonessential elements of a resume that were presented in this chapter. Plan your resume by listing the elements you think you can use as your "selling points." Then, make notes on the information you will include under each element.

2. Using the advice of Joyce Kennedy and the models of this chapter, prepare a draft of your resume. Show your draft to someone or several people whose objective opinion you respect. Use the feedback you receive, and continue to work on your draft until you feel confident about the final product. Remember that a resume is always a work in progress. It needs to change as you and your circumstances change.

Applying Your Skills

ACTIVITY 13-1: Tying Features to Benefits

Describe one or more benefits an employer might receive for each of the following features:

1. I have three years' experience in one of your competitor's stores.

2. I have been active in athletics.

3. I taught myself twelve different computer software programs.

4. I am active in several school clubs.

5. I jog regularly and play basketball.

6. I teach a youth group at my church.

7. I was an Eagle Scout.

8. I left college after my sophomore year but returned to complete my degree after three years in the army.

9. I keep careful personal financial records.

10. I lived in South America as a child.

ACTIVITY 13-2: What Employers Want

We began this chapter with a description of how automotive companies—and many other employers—have made their hiring process more sophisticated.

Review this "The Way It Is" segment, and identify at least five characteristics employers seem to want in new employees. List these below:

1.

2.

3.

4.

5.

How can you project clear "between the lines" messages in your cover letter, resume, and interview to indicate that you possess such characteristics?

Create a planning sheet listing the five key employer wants and specific phrases you could use to hit these "hot buttons."

What This Employer Wants

Key phrases in my cover letter

Key phrases in my resume

Key phrases in my interview

ACTIVITY 13-3: Research Target Companies

Select three companies with which you would be interested in interviewing. Research these companies, and prepare a description of each that could be presented orally to your class. Be sure that you include the six key areas of information described in the chapter under "Research the Organization."

Present your finding orally or in writing, as your instructor requests.

ACTIVITY 13-4: Create Your Application Letter

Develop an application letter to one of the three companies you have researched. Tailor the letter to what you think the company may need. Be prepared to explain your thinking.

ACTIVITY 13-5: Practice Answering Questions

Refer back to the list of most commonly asked questions in this chapter. Randomly select ten questions and prepare a brief, written response. (You may want to use an outline rather than a narrative answer.) Ask an associate to then fire these questions at you (in no particular order), and respond orally. Don't use your notes.

Compare your written answers to those given orally. Ask for feedback from your questioner. How can you improve your answers?

PERFORMING on the Job

CASE 13-1 Bill's Resume Strategy

The college years have been fun for Bill Brantwood. He is a bright 23-year-old who took his time getting through his bachelor's degree program at St. Harry's College. It is now March and graduation is coming up in a few months.

St. Harry's is a well respected small liberal arts school of about 800 students. Several major companies have recruited successfully on campus but this year the economy is in a downturn and campus recruiting is down significantly.

Bill has earned a modest 2.8-grade-point average. He spent a lot of time in extracurricular activities as president of a fraternity, cross country team captain, baseball team member (third base), player in a country-rock band (lead guitar and vocals), and director of all homecoming weekend activities in his senior year.

Because Bill's family is wealthy, it has not been necessary for him to work or pay anything toward his college education. He received a generous allowance from his parents each month. During the summer months, he vacationed, spending a lot of time at the beach.

During an interview with his college advisor he was asked what he planned to do after graduation. "I don't know for sure," he replied. "Maybe I'd like to get a job in an office somewhere," was all he could come up with.

Case Questions

1. What challenges does Bill face in achieving a career position in a business organization?

2. If you were to advise Bill in the preparation of his resume and cover letter, what would you suggest?

3. What are some potentially difficult interview questions Bill may face and how should he handle these?

CASE 13-2 I Need This Job

Sariah Jerris was a bit nervous about the interview. This company seemed exactly right for her, and she wanted to work there. She had spent almost four years with an advertising agency in New York as a graphic artist and all around idea person. The agency was known for its creative, sometimes outrageous, ad campaigns. The people there were casual, funny, and often eccentric. It was a fun place to work and Sariah had no plans to leave.

But all that changed when Sariah and her husband Frederik divorced last fall after a turbulent three-year marriage. Her supportive family in Bakersfield encouraged her to come home. Now she was looking for a similar job in a much smaller city, and she thought she might have found it.

Looking around the lobby she saw framed samples of art work and creative advertisements. The people she'd seen so far seemed interesting. Donnie Donnerson, the head of the creative staff greeted her warmly and invited her into his office. It went down hill from there.

After several minutes of general questions, Donnie drew his chair closer to his desk, folded his hands and looked directly into Sariah's eyes. "Can we cut all the job interview crapola, and just talk?" he asked. "Sure, I guess so," she replied.

"We're a pretty informal shop here and frankly, the most important thing I need to know is how well you'd fit as a colleague and friend. That's what our business is all about. So I'm going to ask you a few questions you maybe haven't been asked before. First, let's start with the divorce—I assume you're divorced, right? What was that all about?"

Case Questions

1. Assume that Donnie is persistent in asking a series of very personal questions. What options are available to Sariah?

2. Put yourself in her shoes. Remember that you'd really like the job and there aren't a lot of other ad agencies with openings. What would you do?

PART FOUR

Report Writing Skills

for Effectiveness

amid Change

Some of the prominent criticisms of government and some large organizations are their maze of complex rules, regulations, and reporting requirements. Businesses and individuals have become deluged with requirements for written information and extensive explanations ranging from the tax forms to environmental impact studies to progress reports and product documentation (instructions).

With that said, there remains value in documenting information not only so that it can be shared but so that the writer is forced to think through the proposal or idea. This point does not advocate nor condone excessive reporting, but rather indicates the value of thinking on paper—of articulating thought in ways that can be done only in written documents.

As with other aspects of communication, the trend is toward briefer, more efficient documents. The formal business report that has traditionally taken a large segment of any business communication class is found infrequently in real companies. In small organizations, the segment of the economy where the most jobs are being created (and the best opportunities often reside), you will seldom see a formal business report other than business plans, proposals, or requests for funding. There are however, exceptions to this statement depending on the nature of the business.

CHAPTER 14

Using Reports and
Proposals: Organizing
and Articulating Thoughts

CHAPTER 15

Writing the Report:
Getting It Down on Paper

Using Reports and Proposals:
Organizing and Articulating Thoughts

LEARNING GOALS

After you have studied this chapter, you
should be able to:

- Describe the purpose and
  characteristics of a successful
  business report.

- Answer four key questions as you plan
  the business report.

- Describe and use four basic ways to
  find information to be used in
  reports.

- Plan and budget resources involved in
  producing a report.

- Identify different types of short
  reports.

- Write short reports and proposals.

- Define the key elements of an
  effective proposal.

The Way It Is . . . A Good Report Gives Readers What They Need to Know

The following story illustrates a typical situation calling for a business report: During its first three years in business, Comatose Waterbed and Stereo, Inc., has enjoyed tremendous success. From a single 1,500-square-foot store on Bailey Avenue in Buffalo, Comatose has blossomed into a five-location business. Sales this year have increased by an astounding 560 percent over last year. The owners, Marge and Tony Bastioni, are delighted. But now they've set their sights even higher.

Last Tuesday morning, Tony Bastioni visited with Chico Roberts, manager of the Tonawanda store. Their conversation went something like the following:

Tony began, "Chico, your store is the best in the company. You've done a heck of a job, and Marge and I appreciate your efforts."

"Thanks, chief, " said Chico. "This company has been good to me, too."

"That's why I wanted to talk to you," Tony continued. "I want to expand beyond Western New York. I'm play-

ing with the idea of offering Comatose franchises nationwide. And I'd like your help."

"What can I do?"

"You've got your degree in business administration, and my guess is you could pull together some information I need. What I'd like you to do, Chico, is take a few days off and put together a report for me. I need to know the advantages and disadvantages of franchising our company. If franchising looks like a good alternative, I'd also like some suggestions about how to market the franchise, what locations would be most promising, where to advertise, and how much to charge."

"Sounds like a big order, Tony. Let me go over to the university library and see what I can dig up. I'll write you a proposal first before putting together a full-blown report."

"Great. Let me know how much time and whatever other help you'll need. And Chico, this is *really* important to our company."

Organizations depend on good information.

Business and organizations today depend on good information to make decisions. The job success of leaders and followers alike often depends on having useful information in digestible forms. Reports of various types, ranging from a simple computer printout to an extensive printed analysis running hundreds of pages, provide such data.

This chapter examines people-generated reports that gather a variety of types of information into a useful format to prompt action. These reports may be **routine,** such as those that provide production figures, membership data, and sales results, or **special reports** (like the one Tony asked Chico for) that deal with specific organizational questions or issues, and generally include more than just raw data.

Three Purposes for Business Reports

When a report project is assigned, the person or group doing the work should be told their specific purpose—the extent and nature of the information-gathering task. There are three general purposes for business reports.

Professionals rely on reports for making business decisions. (Courtesy of Superstock.)

- To supply data (an *informative* or routine report)
- To make some analysis and integration of the data (an *interpretive* report)
- To specify a recommended action (an *analytical decision* report)

Reports can inform, interpret, or recommend decisions.

Regardless of the type and extent of the report, its emphasis should be on functional communication of ideas that will help solve organizational problems and keep the company on track, working toward its objectives. A good definition of a business report is

an orderly and objective communication of factual information which serves some business purpose.

Report writers should make the document's organization obvious to readers.

Two other characteristics in this definition deserve emphasis. First a report is *orderly;* it is carefully prepared so that its contents are arranged in a predetermined fashion. Report writers should use content setup, accessing, and internal summaries (see Chapter Eight) to make the report's organization *obvious* to readers.

A second key term is *objective.* A report should contain findings and analysis, not express undocumented opinions. Special emphasis is placed on facts, hard data, and documentation. The report writer should be especially careful to separate facts from inferences (see Chapter Four), and to provide adequate *support* for all key ideas (see Chapter Eight).

When opinion, guesses, hunches, or predictions are made, they should be clearly labeled as such so the reader will not mistakenly assume they are facts. Objectivity requires such clarification. It also demands that all relevant data or evidence be presented in such a way that they do not stack the deck in favor of or in opposition to a particular viewpoint.

The successful report gives its readers factual, useful information. It attempts to present such information in an unbiased, objective, and orderly manner. By so doing, it can best fulfill its purpose of supplying information, analyzing data, or recommending action.

Four Key Questions for Planning the Business Report

Reports involve research, and research involves *planned inquiry*. One of the most important and time-saving steps in report preparation is to think through the research project along general lines before you dig in. Ten or 15 minutes of concentrated thought may save hours of wheel spinning, wasted effort later. Thinking should include jotting down your thoughts. Start this thinking-through process by answering several questions.

- *Why is this report being prepared?* Usually because management needs specific information to make a decision.
- *How will I know when the purpose has been achieved?* When the report requester's questions are clearly answered, and a course of action is recommended.
- *Who will be reading this?* Often the intended audience will affect the way in which one chooses to present information in a report.
- *Where can I get the best possible information?* That's a tougher question. Your choices are between **secondary sources** (information others have written about the topic) or **primary research** where new information is generated.

For secondary sources, a library or an online data service is a good place to start. For primary research data, you'll need to design your study and data-gathering approach carefully. Techniques, such as interviews, surveys, focus groups or questionnaires, may be needed.

Four General Ways to Find Information to Use in Reports

Let's take a broader look at the four basic ways to find out what we need to know: reading, interviewing, observing, and reasoning.

1. *Reading.* Many managers, on the day after graduation, promptly forget where the university library is. Yet libraries exist for the sole purpose of dispensing information. Become familiar with the library resources available in your area. You'll probably be amazed at what modern libraries have.

   Better yet, learn to use online database services such as CompuServe, America Online, Prodigy, and the Internet. These can bring important reading materials to a computer screen near you. Anything that appears on your screen can be saved in a file and printed.

   The term *reading* is used here in a general sense to include not only graphic or printed matter, but also audiovisual materials such as films, tapes, and pictures. Most of what you'll ever need to know has been recorded somewhere at some time. Your challenge is to find relevant material.

   Fortunately, finding the right manuscripts, books, articles, statistical tables, computer databases, and the like is today easier than ever. If you cannot get what you need via your computer, ask a librarian to help you.

   Thanks to modern library technology, it is possible to search through huge amounts of information quickly. A typical computer search can go through 10 to 15 years of an index in just a few minutes. A computer search can

Today's database services bring enormous amounts of information right to your computer.

also help you find items you would otherwise miss or give you access to materials that your library does not have—you can search several libraries from a single location. If your library does not have the information you need, they can often retrieve it from another library across the nation.

The downside to this may be the embarrassment of riches: You can quickly find yourself inundated with far more information than you, or your reader, could ever digest. Your job as a reporter is to condense and synthesize your message into that which is relevant.

2. *Interviewing.* Interviewing an expert or source person is a valuable way of gathering information. Any person who is intimately familiar with a specific problem or issue—who has firsthand knowledge—may legitimately be considered an ex-

Interview the people closest to a problem.

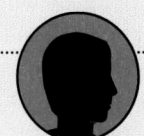

COMMUNICATOR'S INVENTORY

Checking Your Style

Which information-gathering style is most like you? For each of the following situations, circle the number that would most closely approximate how you would feel or respond to each situation. Circle 1 if the statement on the left of the page is always true.

Circle 7 if the statement on the right of the page is always true. Circle 4 if both statements are equally true. If one statement is more often true, but not always, circle a number in between.

1. When I am working on a problem . . .
I try to solve it myself.

      I get help from others.

         1   2   3   4   5   6   7

2. When I need information from others . . .
I always go to the top leaders.

      I ask people closest to the problem regardless of their organizational level.

         1   2   3   4   5   6   7

3. I usually limit my interviewing to . . .
Whomever I can reach conveniently.

      Anyone who may have useful ideas.

         1   2   3   4   5   6   7

4. I believe that . . .
If a person can't express an idea clearly, it's probably a bad idea.

      Some people have good ideas but just can't explain them clearly.

         1   2   3   4   5   6   7

5. I usually find that . . .
Top managers always understand organizational problems best.

      People at all levels understand problems and may have good suggestions.

         1   2   3   4   5   6   7

A total score above 25 usually reflects a more effective information-gathering style.

pert. This means that the assembly-line worker, the data-input operator, or the building maintenance worker may be the person you need to talk with, even though their formal organizational position does not call for decision making. Many organizational problems are solved by going to those who are seldom sought after for managerial advice. When you have the opportunity to go to the people involved, you should use it. This can be the strongest data-gathering approach for many problems. It also empowers employees by making them feel a part of decisions.

3. *Observing.* When you can't find exactly what you need to know by reading or interviewing, you must sometimes observe for yourself. Direct observations should not be casual or haphazard. They should be planned in advance. If you simply go into an organization, look around, and draw conclusions from one or two observations, you run the risk of getting contaminated data—a distorted picture. Decide in advance exactly what is to be observed and precisely when it is to be observed. A reasonable number of different observations should be made, and, when possible, the **reliability** of these observations should be established. Reliability is simply the likelihood that, on subsequent observation, essentially the same things will be observed. Using multiple observations or multiple observers helps improve reliability. In short, don't jump to conclusions based on one or two casual looks.

Always prepare a data-gathering form before using an observation technique.

Usually it is helpful to design a data-gathering form or tally sheet to categorize events witnessed. The more thorough the preparation of such a form, the clearer your categories and the better your information.

4. *Reasoning.* The fourth general way to get information for reports is reasoning from what you have learned. Drawing conclusions based on evidence gathered may be the riskiest step in the research process. Your conclusions can be only as good as your evidence and reasoning. There is no foolproof way to eliminate personal biases from this process, but it is important to be aware that your own viewpoint may prevent you from seeing other possibilities.

Organizational decisions are based on reasoning from the known (the information gathered) to the unknown (the predicted results of a course of action). If the reasoning processes are valid and the decision implemented, it should be an effective decision; this is the final test.

These, then, are four major ways to find out what you want to know for a written report: reading, interviewing experts, observation, and reasoning.

Report Formatting

The following guidelines represent a standard report format but are not the only way to format reports. Because of the wide variety of computer software available, you may want to deviate from these suggested guidelines. Learn the various features available in your own software, and use them to make your reports easier to produce and more creative. Always remember the importance of *accessing* key information.

Margins (Figure 14–1)

In most cases, set your top margin at 1.5 inches on the first page and 1 inch for following pages. Set the right, left, and bottom margins at 1 inch for all pages.

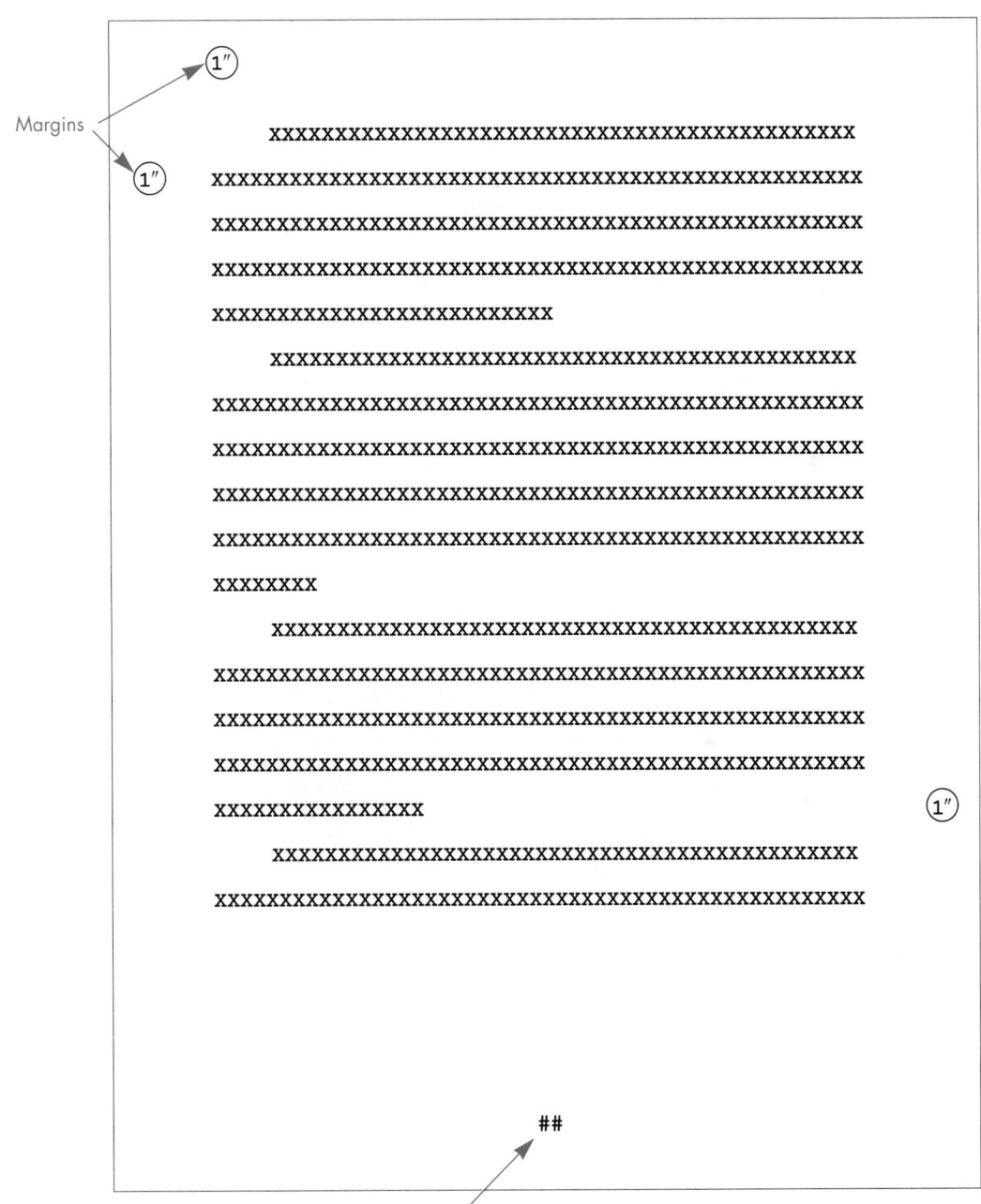

FIGURE 14-1
Margins, pagination, and spacing.

If your report will be bound, add 0.5 inches to the left margin to allow for the binding.

Pagination (Figure 14-1)

The first page is usually not numbered. All following pages should have page numbers either 0.5 inches from the top right or 0.5 inches from the bottom center.

Spacing (Figure 14–1)

Single-spaced reports can often be difficult to read if the paragraphs are long. Either keep paragraphs short or use double-spacing. The first line of each paragraph should be indented 0.5 inches from the left margin. (If you choose to single space, double space between each paragraph.)

Headings (Figure 14–2)

Title heading. Should be typed in all capital letters and centered horizontally. Triple-space after the title if there is no secondary heading. If using a secondary heading, double-space only after the title.

FIGURE 14–2
Headings.

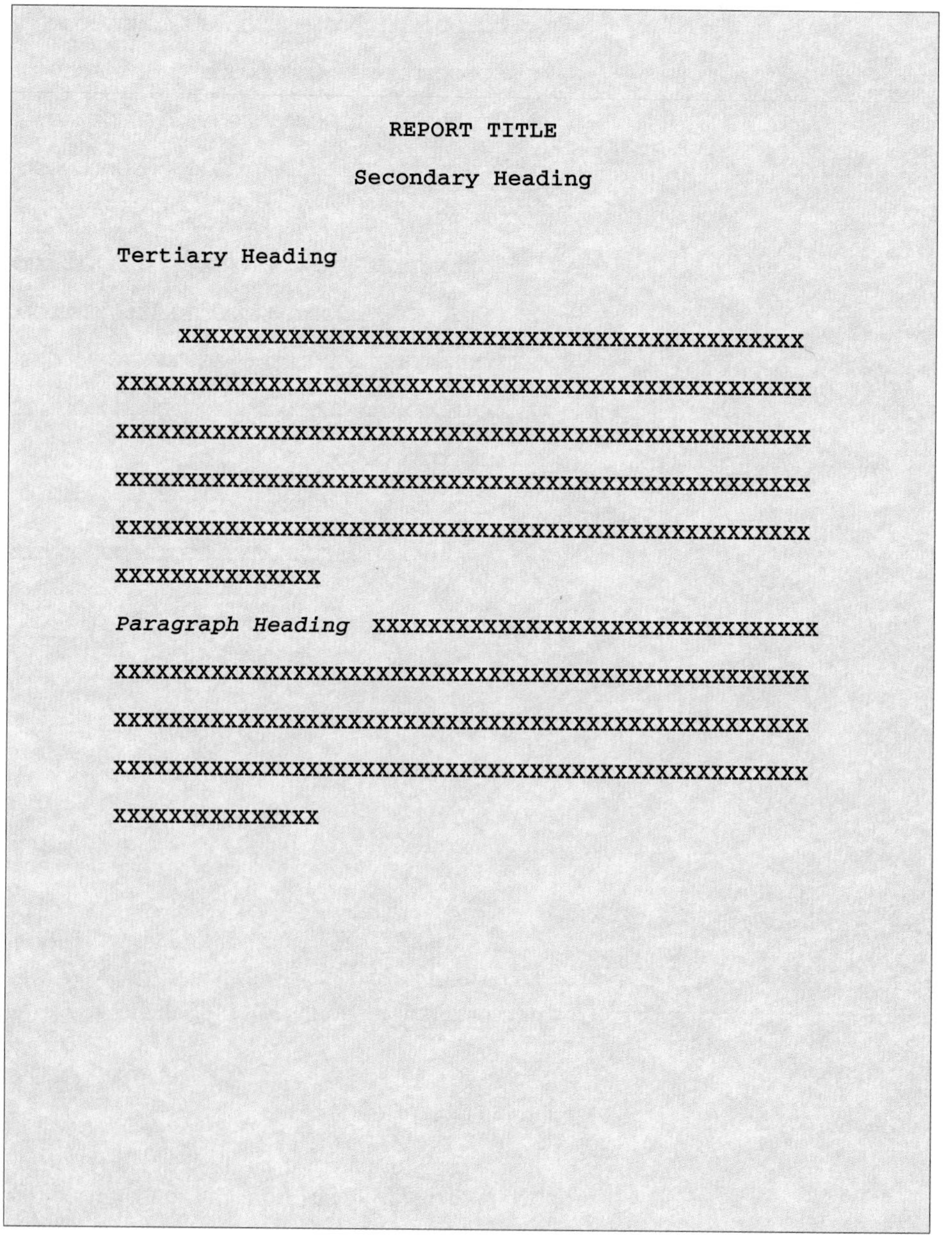

```
                          REPORT TITLE
                       Secondary Heading


     Tertiary Heading

          XXXXXXXXXXXXXXXXXXXXXXXXXXXXXXXXXXXXXXXXXXXX

     XXXXXXXXXXXXXXXXXXXXXXXXXXXXXXXXXXXXXXXXXXXXXXXXXX

     XXXXXXXXXXXXXXXXXXXXXXXXXXXXXXXXXXXXXXXXXXXXXXXXXX

     XXXXXXXXXXXXXXXXXXXXXXXXXXXXXXXXXXXXXXXXXXXXXXXXX

     XXXXXXXXXXXXXXXXXXXXXXXXXXXXXXXXXXXXXXXXXXXXXXXX

     XXXXXXXXXXXXXX

     Paragraph Heading  XXXXXXXXXXXXXXXXXXXXXXXXXXXXXXXXX

     XXXXXXXXXXXXXXXXXXXXXXXXXXXXXXXXXXXXXXXXXXXXXXXX

     XXXXXXXXXXXXXXXXXXXXXXXXXXXXXXXXXXXXXXXXXXXXXXXX

     XXXXXXXXXXXXXXXXXXXXXXXXXXXXXXXXXXXXXXXXXXXXXXXX

     XXXXXXXXXXXXXX
```

Secondary heading. Should have each major word capitalized and should be centered horizontally. Double-space before and triple-space after the secondary heading.

Tertiary heading. Has each major word capitalized, is underlined (or italicized), and is left justified (flush with the left margin). Double-space before and after the tertiary heading.

Paragraph heading. Has only the first word capitalized, is underlined or italicized, ends with a period, and is indented 0.5 inches from the left margin. Double-space after the paragraph heading.

FIGURE 14–3
Quotations.

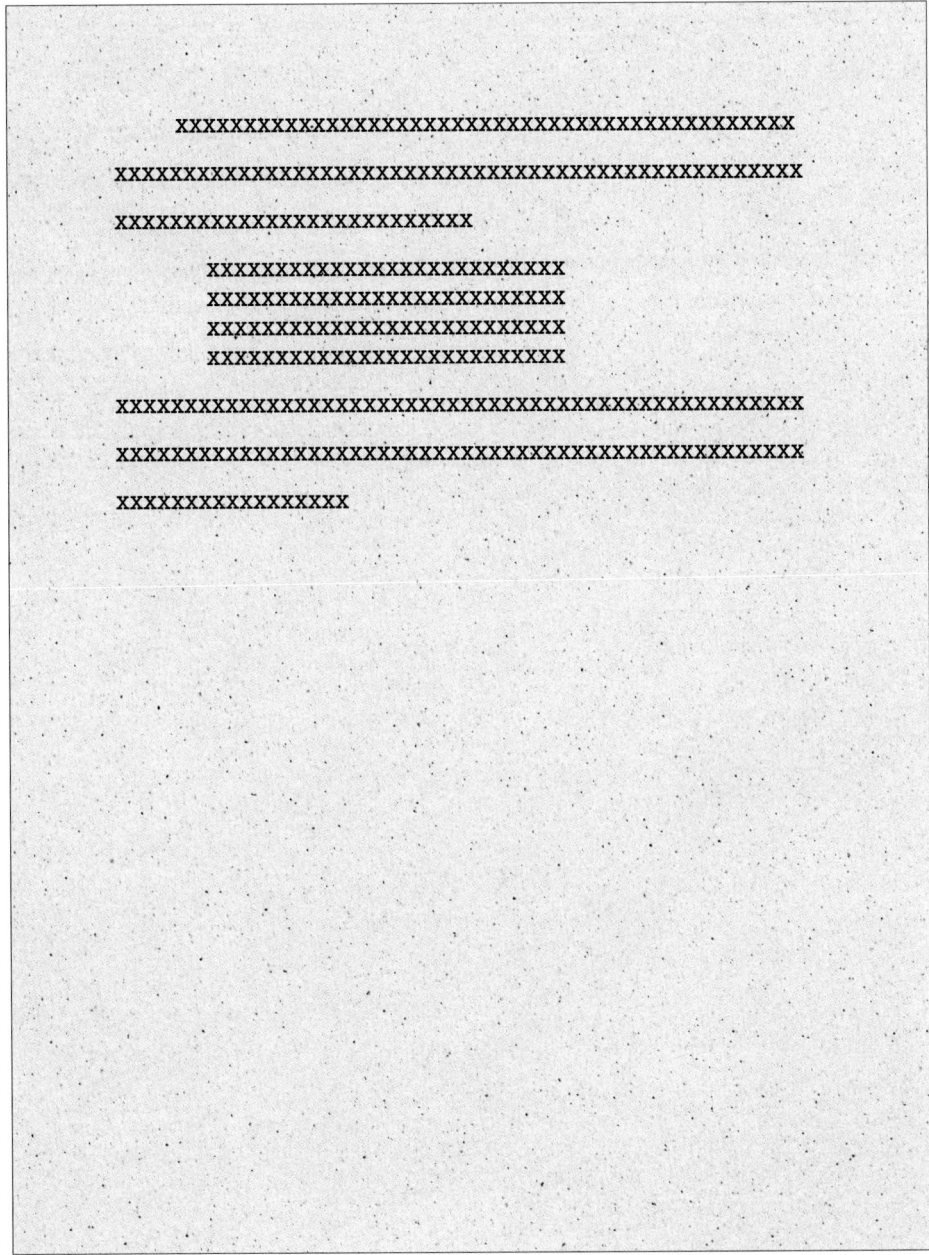

Quotations (Figure 14–3)

If a quotation is longer than two lines, it is indented 0.5 inches from both left and right margins. Quotations are usually single-spaced, preceded and followed by a double-space.

Listings (Figure 14–4)

Listings are indented 0.5 inches from the left margin. Single-space items longer than one line; indent second and following lines under the first word, not the number; and double-space between items.

FIGURE 14–4
Listings.

```
        XXXXXXXXXXXXXXXXXXXXXXXXXXXXXXXXXXXXXXXXXXX

    XXXXXXXXXXXXXXXXXXXXXXXXXXXXXXXXXXXXXXXXXXXXXXXX

    XXXXXXXXXXXXXXXXXXXXXXXXXXXXXXXX

    1.  XXXXXXXXXXXXXXXXXXXXXXXXXXXXXXXXXXXXXXXXXXXXXX
        XXXXXXXXXXXXXXXXXXXXXXXXXXXXXXXXXXXXXXXX.

    2.  XXXXXXXXXXXXXXXXXXXXXXXXXXXXXXXXXXXXXXXXXXXX
        XXXXXXXXXXXXXXXX.

    3.  XXXXXXXXXXXXXXXXXXXXXXXXXXXXXXXXXXXXXXXXXXXX
        XXXXXXXXXXXXXXXXXXXXXXXXXXXXXXXXXXXXXXXXX
```

Documenting Sources Used

Many different styles can be used when citing sources used in preparing your report. Consult your organization's style guide if it has one; otherwise use a reference manual for specific formatting possibilities. Regardless of which style you use, every source reference should include the following:

Author(s)

Date of publication

Source title

Where published

Publisher

Page number(s)

Internal Citations or Footnotes/Endnotes

If you choose to use internal citations, quoted material is cited directly within the report. Each citation is followed directly by the author's surname and year of publication, with page numbers included in the reference list that follows the report. Example: "Use a BIFF approach for bad-news" (Stead, 1996).

If using footnotes, they are numbered within the text with references located at the bottom of the page on which the number appears. Endnotes are like footnotes except the references are all located at the end of the report on a separate page labeled "Notes." It would be advantageous to learn how to use the automatic footnote function in your software package when using footnotes in your reports.

Reference List

The reference list is located at the end of the report on a separate page and includes a title, such as References or Bibliography, followed by three spaces. Items in the list should be single-spaced and in alphabetical order with double-spacing between items. Begin the first line of each item at the left margin with following lines indented 0.5 inches.

Good Reports Are Realistic about Purpose, Time, and Cost

Virtually any topic can be researched to death. At some point, the cost of a new tidbit of additional insight becomes prohibitive.

Common sense limits the need placed on how much is spent on a report. It would be irresponsible to spend $50,000 on research to answer a $100 question. The benefits must exceed the cost.

Be sure that the report's cost is justified.

The magnitude of the problem's effects on the organization provides a good indicator of a project's value. A decision on what hours to open the cafeteria calls for a quick, short report, at most. An analysis of a problem on which the future of the company hangs—say, an unwanted takeover attempt, or a need to combat a competitor's actions—would be a no-holds-barred research effort. Any reasonable expenditure would be justified.

Budgeting Report Costs

How much can a person write in an hour or a day? It depends on the complexity of the material being written, the depth of the analysis, the familiarity the writer has with the material, and the writer's ability, motivation, alertness, and energy level.

Before word processing, analyses of productivity revealed that the professional writer averaged from one to three hours of actual writing a day. Some writers can go for ten hours a day for a week but then they'd run dry for a month.

How much could be written in one to three hours? Again, of course, it varies. The typical professional writer often can complete only a few pages of final copy a day. This may sound like a small output. It makes more sense, however, when you consider all the steps involved: research, rough drafts, planning of illustrations, final drafts, and proofreading.

Creative editing or the arranging of work contributed by several participating writers into a final report can take as long as original writing. So a team-written report of thirty pages would take about a month to prepare.[1]

Word processing makes report writing much more efficient, but it is still an expensive medium.

Word processing has boosted writing productivity enormously, especially when ideas, data, and files can be downloaded into a report without retyping.

Nevertheless, reports are still a costly medium. Sometimes there is no good substitute for a written report to meet the information needs of an organization. As discussed in Chapter Six, there are several significant advantages to the use of this medium including the capability of conveying complex information in an orderly fashion, the presence of hard copy for future reference, and the relative formality a report affords to important matters. A report can be used efficiently—read when most convenient and when the reader is particularly alert or motivated. Perhaps the greatest value of report writing, however, is that it forces sound thinking. By articulating thoughts on paper, any holes in logic quickly become evident.

Report Length and Degree of Formality

Because of the wide range and variety of shapes and sizes, business reports are often difficult to define. We have chosen a wide definition by breaking all reports into two types: long and short. Typically, the longer the report, the more formal it is. The formal report is often bound, printed on quality paper, and implies an official source. It presents important information and often reaches readers outside the organization. The long report may be divided into several parts, which the next section discusses.

The short, and usually less formal, report covers less important information such as progress reports, travel and expense reports, minor requests, and routine status reports. These reports can take the form of a letter or memo and can be handwritten—but are usually printed on preprinted forms or sent electronically by e-mail. A short report is usually two to five pages.

Proposals for Long Reports

Writing a **proposal** is one way to avoid the problem of spending too much on formal reports. The proposal itself is a short report that lays out a working plan for the long, decision-making report.

The well-written proposal crystallizes the writer's thinking and lets the reader know what to expect from the final report. Typically, it includes

- Background information where appropriate
- A clear statement of the problem or issue to be dealt with
- A statement of the goal of the report

- A description of what research steps will be taken to arrive at a conclusion
- An estimate of the cost of preparing the report

These elements are outlined in Figure 14–5.

The proposal is helpful for the researcher because it

1. Permits him or her to think—on paper—about the research steps to be taken
2. Provides an opportunity to discover a possible error or faulty thinking early in the project, where it's less likely to do serious damage
3. Serves as a guide throughout the investigation

In addition, the carefully prepared proposal will include material for writing the introductory section in the final report.

The report proposal should be addressed to the person(s) who will formally authorize the research project. Typically, it is presented in memo format and seldom runs longer than two or three pages. Note: You need not use exactly the same headings. Be descriptive, but don't feel bound to this precise wording.

Background

Before spending time, effort, and money, the decision maker should understand the conditions that gave rise to the problem or issue to be researched. This section puts the project into context and paves the way for a more specific definition of the immediate problem the writer will study. Although the background section may tell readers things they already know, it provides an opportunity for the writer and the person who authorized the report to be sure they are on the same wavelength. It is far better to catch any misunderstandings here than after an extensive study has been completed.

Statement of the Problem

Clearly defining the research problem is crucial to the ultimate success of the project. This section of the proposal needs to include more than a one-sentence definition. Remember that your reader is likely to view the nature of any given problem a little differently from the way you do—our experiences and worldviews make this inevitable. So, in addition to stating your view of the problem, you'll need to explain why you see it that way. You must also convince your reader that yours is an appropriate view and definition of the issue.

Be careful of emotional language that may be overly judgmental or convey biases. An objective, unemotional *statement of the problem* should be your goal. The following examples illustrate this.

Emotional/judgmental. Supervisors are incapable of writing good performance reviews.

More objective. Most first-line supervisors are writing performance reviews that do not meet company standards.

A common error made in preparing this part of a proposal is to state the problem in terms that are too broad. When the problem is too grandiose or unusually wide in scope, the report loses focus. Here are examples.

Too broad. This report will study the effects of foreign competition on our business.

More objective. This report will study the marketing strategy of the three foreign competitors that are having the most impact on our share of the market in cable television: Sony, Panasonic, and Mitsubishi.

RESEARCH PROPOSAL

Title of Project

Give the project a title that describes your study. For example, "A Comparison of Light Pickup Trucks for Customer Delivery Services by Allgood Business Products, Inc."

by Your Name

Introduction and Background

Briefly introduce the study. If you want, you may also summarize earlier research in the area.

Objectives of This Report
or Statement of the Problem

State your overall objective in one sentence. Make sure it is focused. You may then break this objective down into any number of supporting objectives.

Likely Significance of the Findings

Summarize the benefits to the scientific community as well as the benefits to other populations (e.g., specific groups, the nation, mankind as a whole, etc.).

Research Techniques to Be Used

Describe the research plan, indicate the specific steps you plan to follow when doing the research. As you describe the steps, indicate when you expect each step to be completed. (If the study is part of a larger project, you may want to start this section off with an explanation of the larger effort.)

If you plan to conduct a quantitative analysis, describe in your plan the instruments and statistical analyses you plan to use.

At the end of your plan, indicate the outcomes you expect (e.g., presentation to management, publication in the *Journal of Business Communication*, distribution to the board of directors, etc.).

Budget

Itemize your expected expenses, indicating what you need and how much it will cost.

FIGURE 14–5

Elements of a research proposal.

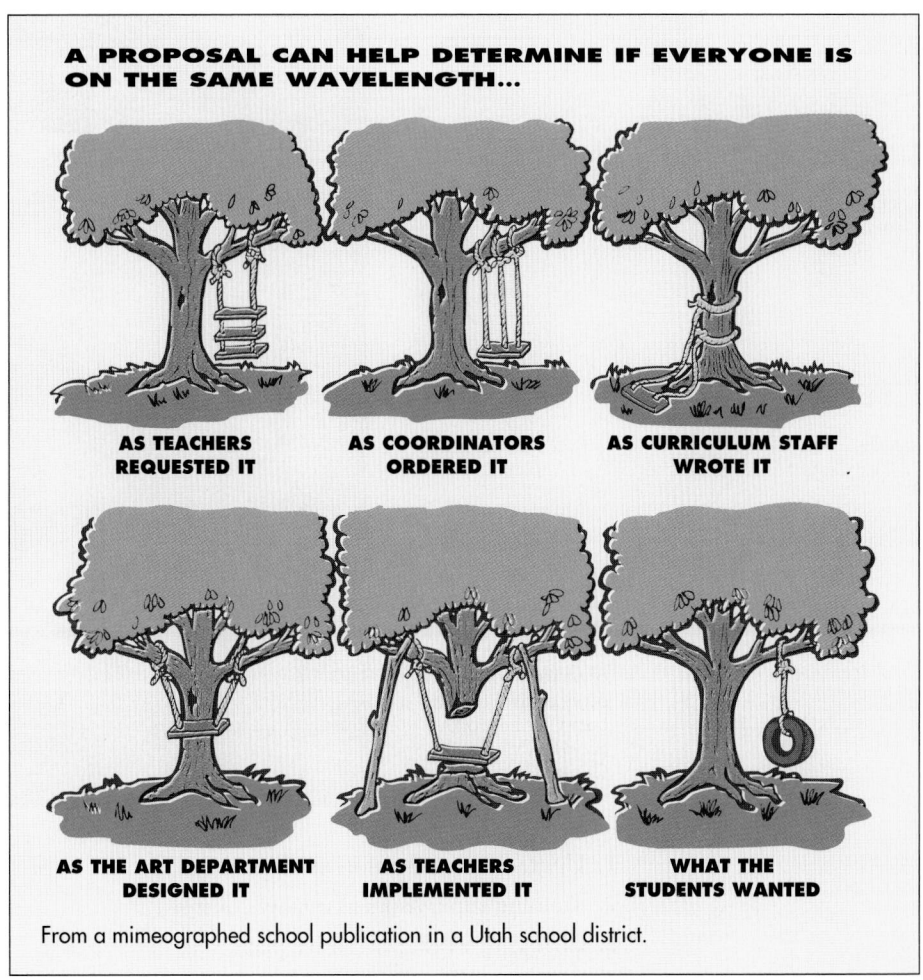

A PROPOSAL CAN HELP DETERMINE IF EVERYONE IS ON THE SAME WAVELENGTH...

AS TEACHERS REQUESTED IT

AS COORDINATORS ORDERED IT

AS CURRICULUM STAFF WROTE IT

AS THE ART DEPARTMENT DESIGNED IT

AS TEACHERS IMPLEMENTED IT

WHAT THE STUDENTS WANTED

From a mimeographed school publication in a Utah school district.

Too vague or ill-defined. This report will examine safety problems in our manufacturing operations.

More specific. This report reviews lost-time accidents reported in the past twelve months in our manufacturing plant and corrective actions taken to prevent recurrence.

Goal of the Project

Be sure the **statement of your goal** or objective fits the statement of the problem. The readers of your proposal should understand from this section exactly what they will be getting. You should state this in concrete, specific language. This section may include a list of goals rather than a single one. If a list is used, cite the most significant goal first followed by supplementary objectives. Avoid unclear generalities.

Too vague. This report will suggest some ideas for changes to cope with rising labor costs.

More specific. This report will recommend a systematic approach to offset rising labor costs in the assembly plant via

Literature searches and data gathering can be simplified with the use of online information services available on computer networks. (Courtesy of Charles Gupton/Uniphoto Picture Agency.)

1. Upgrading production machinery
2. Training supervisors in quality control
3. Changing worker incentive plans

Research Procedures

In this section of the proposal, methods for gathering and processing information should be spelled out. Because no research project is completely new, you may begin by citing previous work done in the area by others. As anyone who has ever written a major term paper will attest, this "literature search" can be tedious, but it does provide a sound foundation for the recommendations offered by the project.

If you need to collect data for the report, details of your methodology, timeframe, and analysis should be stated.

The proposal reader needs to know how you are going to find the information needed to solve the problem posed. Your choice of methods is, of course, limited by the available resources (time and money, for example).

Cost of the Project

The final section of the proposal tells your readers what the project will cost, so that they can decide if it is worth the expenditure. If the writer is on the organization's payroll, it is usually sufficient to list the staff members involved and estimate the number of work hours needed plus other material expenses such as photography, artwork, printing, and postage. If the proposal is prepared by an outside consultant, a charge for professional services will also be included.

Although all this sounds like a great deal of information, the final version of the report proposal is seldom more than a few pages. Figure 14–6 shows an example of such a proposal.

September 12, 199X

TO: Lynn McClurg, Vice-President of Training

FROM: Sharon Seamons, Staff Assistant

RE: PROPOSAL FOR AN ANALYSIS OF AVAILABLE
       TRAINING SOFTWARE

BACKGROUND

Mr. McClurg, as you are aware, our company has recently diversified into two new areas of operation,
fast-food merchandising and dairy products processing. Since this diversification, pressures to provide a wide range of additional training programs
have mounted.

Our experiences in past expansions attest to the
fact that computerized training packages are effective in developing a wide range of technical and
managerial skills. In addition, a wide range of new
software, now available, may meet our needs.

STATEMENT OF THE PROBLEM

The diversity of software poses opportunities as
well as a problem. The problem is that the company
lacks the information necessary to make an intelligent comparison among the many software packages.
Information is needed to compare the content,
costs, and potential usefulness of these packages
in the light of our company's needs.

GOAL OF THE PROJECT

The goal of this project is to narrow the field of
alternatives to three software packages for fast-
food managers and three for the dairy people. Information will be gathered to support the
selections. Each selection will be evaluated and
ranked from most appropriate to least appropriate,
based on findings of the research. Final recommendations will be made.

THE RESEARCH PROCEDURES

The information presented in this report will be
gathered from three main areas.

1. Directories of software located in recent technical publications found in the local univer-

FIGURE 14–6
Proposal report.

Writing Your Way to Success

After being chosen one of a select few college juniors to be a summer intern at a major accounting firm, Craig worked long, demanding hours to prove his worth. At summer's end, he hoped for a letter of recommendation to take with him on job interviews during his senior year. But he didn't get one. He was told that although his math was excellent, his writing was not. His written reports to his supervisors lacked clarity, used words incorrectly, and contained multiple basic errors.

Craig, never having felt particularly talented at writing and shocked to discover how important writing would be to his career success, came to me for advice. Here's what I told him the first time we talked.

1. Remember that writing is an attitude as much as an activity.
Don't worry about talent because good writing doesn't jump magically onto a page. Do worry about fluency. It comes as a result of practice, habit, and the absolute conviction that you can master what you need to know. No matter what your age, it's never too late to develop fluency. Be guided by the old adage: *"Genius is 90% perspiration and 10% inspiration."*

2. Keep moving or you'll stand still.
A hand moving a pen or fingers typing at a computer trains your mind as well as your muscles to get words onto paper. To become a fluent writer, you must budget time every day to practice. Force those sentences out of you, reach for the precise word you want, stretch to express the ideas you are thinking about. Even fifteen concentrated minutes a day can be enough, though longer is better. Unless you discipline yourself into the habit of daily writing, you'll miss out on your potential to move ahead as a writer with confidence.

3. Expect to rewrite.
A damaging myth holds that good writers write perfectly the first time. Nonsense. Writing IS revising: trying one way then another until it comes close to what you want. Will it ever get there? Probably not, because good writers know that there's always another way, and still another way, to express ideas clearly and effectively. When you start writing something, your purpose is to get words onto paper so that you can revise them. In fact, one useful daily self-drill is to write a sentence and then see how many different ways you can rewrite it by changing words, sentence structure, rhythms. If you hesitate to tackle one of your own sentences, pick one from this article (or anything else you're reading) and rewrite it various ways.

4. Have a critical eye but not a critical heart.
As you read and reread your drafts, evaluate them with intense concentra-tion but without emotion. You are looking at ink, nothing more. When you see words, sentences, ideas that can be improved, tinker with them freely until you have something better. But never allow yourself to engage in negative thinking about your intelligence, your ability to learn, or your potential for success. Negative thinking is the biggest trap of all. Do you know a key reason that so many people develop writing blocks? Because, without realizing it, they are rebelling against a standard so rigidly high that they can't ever achieve it; they are angry for expecting so much from themselves. Forget perfection—if such a thing exists for writers—and aim for progress, for fluency.

Craig, as you can imagine, was surprised that my first round of advice had nothing to do with techniques of writing style, ways of organizing material, or grammar, spelling, and punctuation. I explained that those things matter, but they follow only after a person adopts a conscious, upbeat philosophy about writing. If it seems hard to get over negative thinking about yourself as a writer, repeat the four principles I gave Craig. Without them, no one can expect to write their way to success.

Lynn Quitman Troyka, "Writing Your Way to Success," *Keys to Success,* January 1994, p. 11. Reprinted with permission of Prentice Hall/Allyn & Bacon College Divisions.

APPLYING YOUR KNOWLEDGE

1. Create a sign to put on your word processor summarizing the four key points in this article. Put the ideas in your own words, but make it a visible and constant reminder to you.

2. Elaborate on the idea of "hav[ing] a critical eye but not a critical heart." How can this idea help you be a more effective writer and editor?

Applying Your Skills

ACTIVITY 14-1: Report Analysis

Review one report you've received recently. (If you don't have any real reports, take a sample report from this or another business writing textbook.) Copy down just the headings used in that report. Does the arrangement make sense? Are the headings informative or simply topical? If topical headings were used, change them to informative. How could such a change affect the report's readability?

ACTIVITY 14-2: Gathering Information Through Reading

Go to the periodicals in the library and gather information on the comparative advantages and disadvantages of IBM PCs and Macintosh computers for personal and business use. Summarize the data in a short report.

ACTIVITY 14-3: Gathering Information through Interviewing

Find two individuals who work in jobs you think you'd enjoy and interview them, using a set of questions you have designed beforehand. Learn about their responsibilities, the decisions they make, the reports they prepare, the reports they receive from others, the things they like about their positions, the things they don't like, the most challenging aspects of work, the most rewarding aspects, the organizational culture, and so on. Summarize your findings. After these interviews, which if either of these jobs would you prefer?

ACTIVITY 14-4: Gathering Information through Observing

You're thinking of opening a fast-food restaurant near the university and want to adopt the best possible service philosophy for this type of business. First, you have to learn about different types of fast-food operations. Spend 30 minutes at the local McDonald's, 30 minutes at Wendy's, and another 30 minutes at one other fast-food restaurant of your choice. Observe the operations and take notes. Compare the three in a memo to Paul Miller, a friend who is going to help finance this venture. Discuss the strengths and weaknesses of each service philosophy and outline which aspects of each you plan to adopt.

ACTIVITY 14-5: Gathering Information through Reasoning

You are the sole proprietor of a small business that sells T-shirts imprinted with humorous sayings. In your first year you marketed your shirts locally and had a fair degree of success, so you are now looking at new and larger markets. You don't have enough money to conduct much market research, so you are relying on your limited knowledge of various markets and your abundant supply of mental prowess. Reason through the following markets, listing the good and bad points of each market, given your particular product and your limited resources: large discounters, department stores, gift shops, college stores, catalogs, direct mail, grocery stores.

ACTIVITY 14-6: Planning a Report, Alumni Magazine

You are the new editor of *Campus Reflections,* a magazine that goes out quarterly to all alumni of the university. You have been asked by the university's director of alumni relations to prepare a report for him, outlining how you intend to improve the magazine and make it more interesting to the school's alumni. You have decided that the best way to achieve these objectives is to send a survey to a sampling of alumni and incorporate their feedback into a basic plan for improving the magazine. Design a survey for readers to gather the necessary data.

ACTIVITY 14-7: Researching a Report, Supermarket Prices

Assume that three local supermarkets each claim to have the lowest prices in town. Design a method of researching this claim, incorporating such variables as sales prices, store brands, and loss leaders. Then visit the three stores, conduct your research, and prepare a short report to the management of each store, divulging your findings.

ACTIVITY 14-8: Researching a Report, Textbook Costs

Many students at your university are concerned about the amount of money they spend each year on textbooks. Plan a method of gathering information and conduct research on the average cost of textbooks for students in three diverse majors at your university. Write a short report in the form of a giate Connection, detailing the three options and all relevant prices (price to The Collegiate Connection, price to retailers, and suggested retail price).

ACTIVITY 14-14: Proposal, Publications

Sandy McCormack has just been hired as editor of *Management Exchange,* the magazine that Jefferson State College's business school sends out three times a year to its 25,000 alumni. Dean Porter has been concerned about the cost of the magazine and has asked her to look into the situation and recommend some changes that won't decrease the quality of the magazine, since it is the school's "showpiece." Sandy gets the magazine's financial statements from the dean's office and immediately sets to work.

Within two weeks she has learned several interesting things about the magazine. First, the former editor (who left for a corporate job) had hired two student assistants who, as far as Sandy could tell, had done most of the work on the magazine. She figured that she could handle all the editorial work on a 32-page magazine that was published only three times a year. This would save $10,000 on student labor. Second, the last three issues of the *Management Exchange* had been designed at University Graphics for a total of $16,500. Sandy was competent with QuarkXpress and Adobe Illustrator, and could save the school at least half of the graphics expense by pulling much of the design in-house. The only problem was that her office was equipped with a 386-SX PC with only 2 megabytes of random access memory. To be compatible with both University Graphics and most printers, she would need a Macintosh, at least a Power Mac 7100, and some new software. This would cost the school about $4,000, but would save twice that the first year. Finally, after checking with University Graphics about where and how the magazine was printed, she discovered that the Uni-

versity Press was printing each issue on a sheet-fed press. The total printing cost was $65,000 for the past year. Sandy solicited several bids from independent presses in the community and found that she could save $14,000 by printing the magazine on a web press at Excel Lithography. Quality would decrease slightly on the web press, but only a trained eye would notice the difference.

These three changes would save the school about $28,000, but there were other issues to be addressed. The student labor was expensive, but it was a good experience for students to work on the actual production of a magazine. The $10,000 could be seen as an investment in two students' education. The school provided funds for research and teaching assistants. These positions were similar in many regards. If experience were the main issue, perhaps students enrolled in a new desktop publishing course could help on the magazine as part of the course curriculum. The school had a long-term relationship with University Graphics. To disrupt that relationship suddenly might have unexpected ramifications. Still, desktop publishing is the wave of the present, not just the future, and more and more publishing will be done in-house and not in dedicated design shops. Certainly University Graphics was aware of this. Regarding the change from sheet-fed to web press, Sandy compared several samples provided by Excel Lithography and felt the dean would not think the slight difference in quality was worth $14,000 a year.

Write Dean Porter a proposal for reducing costs on *Management Exchange* as if you were Sandy McCormack. Discuss cost savings, as well as the other related issues. Make your proposal convincing. The dean wants to save money and wants to feel good about it.

PERFORMING
on the Job

CASE 14-1 Request for Education Reimbursement

Sue is an employee of Sintac Oil Company. She is attending night school to earn a bachelor's degree in business management. The following is a description of her efforts to be reimbursed for one particular class.

> I had a recent personal experience, applying for reimbursement, that is an example of company communication. There are formal and informal steps that must be adhered to applying for this reimbursement. There is a standard form that must be completed and signed by the immediate supervisor and forwarded to the Human Resource (HR) department. HR reviews the course and, on approval, forwards it to the administrative vice-president (AVP). The AVP reviews HR's decision, and approves or denies the request. The form is returned to HR, which informs the employee informally of the approval or denial.
>
> The last class I enrolled in was Religion of Western Culture. Three weeks before the start of the course, I completed the necessary form and sent it to HR. Within a week, HR requested a course description. Not only did I submit a course description, but I telephoned the professor who informed me of the relationship of this course to business. I prepared a letter relaying the conversation with the professor and sent it with the description to HR.
>
> After several weeks, I questioned HR only to find out that the reimbursement had been denied. What frustrates me is everything I turn in for the education reimbursement benefit is formal and in writing. The response from HR is informal and verbal. I would like to have written information on why they would not pay for the course, just as they require me to petition them in writing.

Case Questions

1. What could Sue do in a formal, written proposal to improve the reimbursement procedure?
2. To whom would such a proposal be sent?
3. Describe the title, introduction, background, and objectives of such a proposal.

CASE 14-2 Proposal Skimming

Southwick Software Solutions (SSS) works as an independent contractor to develop software documentation, procedures manuals, and business proposals. Starting as a one-person operation with five clients five years ago. SSS now has 35 clients, 15 contract writers, and a new full-time marketing director. Beth Southwick, CEO, is attempting to meet the challenge of increasing, steady growth. Her original business plan did not anticipate the current need for office space and equipment. To keep up the high-quality service to her clients, within the next quarter she must purchase additional computer equipment, office furniture, and a copy machine.

Her immediate goal is to identify a few vendors and then choose from that list. Among all the vendors with whom she has met, three sell copy machines. This past week she received proposals from all three. She knows she is not sure which equipment and service will best meet her needs. Feeling some pressure to make a decision, she skims the beginning of the three proposals.

Proposal 1 Our streamline "CopyCat" copier has simple, easy-to-read digital controls that put all the copying functions at your fingertips. It makes 18 copies per minute on a variety of paper including address labels and most letterhead. For special applications, you can reduce or enlarge the copy size in 5 percent increments from 65 to 130 percent.

Proposal 2 Takasaki "Copy Jet" System Cost
Twenty-four month lease/purchase: $200 per month, system includes

> Copy Jet Copier
>
> Cabinet-console
>
> Paper cassette
>
> Enlargement and reduction capabilities
>
> One hundred-sheet stack bypass attachment

Proposal 3 Your copying needs are complex and vary from day to day. The nature of your business requires that copies have a consistently high quality and that the machine be able to

- Produce color copies
- Collate and staple
- Feed originals automatically

After her review, Beth narrowed her choice to one and picked up the telephone to call.

Case Questions

1. What was Beth looking for in the proposals?

2. Which vendor came out on top and why?

3. What focus did the other two proposals use that caused them to miss Beth's needs?

4. Is "proposal skimming" something that occurs often in the world of business? Why? Why not?

Writing
the Report:
Getting it Down on Paper

LEARNING GOALS

After you have studied this chapter, you should be able to

- Understand the greatest value of report writing.

- Describe the five most common reports used in business and the professions.

  Conquer the fear of getting started.

  Apply four steps in preparing an effective report.

- Recognize the layout elements of business reports.

-

The Way It Is . . . Getting Thoughts Down on Paper

One of the toughest steps in writing long or short reports is getting started. Getting your thoughts and the information you've gathered onto that ominous blank sheet of paper or blank computer screen can be a daunting chore. You don't have to worry anymore, however. A simple four-step process will turn your mountain of raw data into a compact, effective draft report. Follow these steps, and you'll end up with well-organized and even sensibly written documents.

Why is getting started such a problem? In many cases, the writer's expectations are at the heart of the problem. Among the common unrealistic expectations—those that cause pressure on the writer and hinder getting started—are the following:

1. *The expectation that you have to write in final, polished form or it's not worth putting on paper at all.* In reality, no one can compose finished-quality reports off the top of the head. Writing anything more than a few lines is almost always a three-step process: thinking it through, developing a rough draft, and polishing the final product.

2. *The expectation that the deadline is unrealistic and cannot be met.* "I can't have it finished by then!" is a common first reaction to a request for a report. Maybe you can't, or perhaps the quality will suffer if the project is rushed too much. Don't let the deadline paralyze you, however. It's certain that *nothing* will get done if you don't get started! In many cases, writing projects are not as time-consuming as you may think—especially if you learn the tricks of the trade.

3. *The expectation that you will experience writer's block.* Sometimes you may experience **writer's block** simply because you *expect* to block—you've had trouble getting started on past projects and assume the same problems will arise this time. Forget the past. The key to overcoming these unrealistic expectations lies in *action*—doing something instead of just sitting there!

4. *The expectation that you'll demonstrate only your ignorance by writing the report.* Relax. You're bound to know more about the topic than your boss. If the boss already knew all the answers, it's unlikely that you'd be assigned the task in the first place. Besides, if you are a conscientious worker, you'll find out all that you need to know. Others won't be willing to spend time and effort to get the information needed for your report.

Clearing of Deck for Takeoff

Putting all the negative expectations aside may be easier said than done. One way to cope with such mental clutter is to first deal with physical clutter around you. Start your writing task by having a good place to write. Take a few moments to clear off your desk or table; set up a good lamp; gather the paper, pencils, and other materials you'll need; and, by all means, turn off the radio or television. You'll be amazed at how a quiet, functional work area can help reduce the expectations that may be holding you back.

Before talking further about getting started, the next section discusses additional types of reports you are likely to face in the business or professional world. Chapter 14 focused on the longer, more formal report—one that requires in-depth analysis and often acceptance of a proposal before the project begins. A more common writing task that affects almost everyone in business is the informal, and often shorter, report.

Informal (Short) Reports

Short reports are used to inform readers about routine activities or to answer specific questions. Many organizations must submit reports to state or federal agencies to keep their accreditation or funding. Virtually all organizations require performance reports on employees. Many companies file routine reports covering a wide range of organizational activities.

The skills necessary to write short reports are among the most important you can develop. You will be required to prepare short reports often on your job; business and industry would not be able to function without them. The following is a list of the **typical short reports** you can write:

• Audit report	• Laboratory report	• Research report
• Compliance report	• Library report	• Research study
• Design report	• Manager's report	• Sales report
• Evaluation report	• Operations report	• Situational report
• Experiment report	• Periodic report	• Status report
• Feasibility report	• Production report	• Task report
• Incident report	• Progress report	• Test report
• Investigative report	• Proposal	• Trip report
• Justification report	• Recommendation report	• Weekly report

Although these kinds of reports are normally brief, you should take the time and effort to plan and write them well.

Although the following sections won't discuss each of these in detail, they examine five of the most common reports you are likely to encounter in business and the professions:

1. Task reports
2. Periodic reports
3. Progress reports
4. Meeting minutes
5. Trip or conference reports

Task Reports

Many professionals deal with a variety of tasks and assignments that require feedback through reports. These reports are often used to make recommendations such as for buying new equipment, changing an existing policy, or creating a new program; or they could be used to report an inspection of a plant site, a program objective, or the effectiveness of personnel. Performance reviews are perhaps the most common form of the task report.

Periodic Reports

Periodic reports are often recorded on prepared forms and are the most familiar of short reports. As the name suggests, periodic reports provide readers with information at regularly scheduled intervals: daily, weekly, monthly, quarterly, and yearly. They summarize regular activities and events performed during the reporting period as well as irregular events that must be brought to the attention of the reader.

Progress Reports

Progress reports are used to inform the reader about the status of an ongoing project or assignment. These reports may be external (informing customers regarding the headway of a project) or internal (advising management of the status of activities). Progress reports are typically organized in either chronological or priority order. In your introduction, specify the nature and purpose of the project, providing enough background to make your reader comfortable. Describe the work completed and the work in progress including personnel, methods, activities, and locations. Anticipate possible problems and offer solutions. Discuss future activities including the projected completion date.

Meeting Minutes

Minutes are a record of meeting discussion and decisions. Meeting minutes often serve as official (sometimes even legal) records, which provide a review of the meeting for both those who attended and those who did not. When you are in charge of preparing minutes, remember the following guidelines:

1. Provide identification: date, time, location, meeting type, members attending, and person presiding.
2. Maintain an objective tone: no editorializing or subtle slanting of statements.
3. Summarize when possible.
4. Express motions and amendments precisely: maker, seconder, and margin by which the motion passed or failed.
5. Record time of adjournment, and time and date of next scheduled meeting. Attach relevant announcements, agenda, or handouts.

Meeting minutes (summary) record what happened and may be required by law.

Trip or Conference Reports

Conference reports describe three to five things learned.

Most business professionals will have the opportunity to attend a convention or conference and may be required to submit a report when they return. The report should include what was learned about new procedures, equipment, laws, and supply information affecting the products, operations, or service of the firm. The key to writing a good trip report is the ability to select the most relevant material and organize this material into a coherent report. Do not give a travel log, but instead concentrate on from three to five important topics that your reader will find interesting.

Main Points to Remember about Short Reports

The following are the key points to remember about short reports:

1. They are generally organized in one of three different formats.
   - *Memo format.* Internal short reports are often just two- to three-page memos.
   - *Prepared form format.* Many short reports are routine and require a special form.
   - *Letter format.* External short reports are usually part of a short letter.
2. Short reports are a few pages at most and get to the point quickly. Avoid tangential or irrelevant information.

3. They should anticipate the types of information the readers will need and how this information will be used. The important information in a progress report is not the same as that in a periodic report.

4. They should organize the introduction, body, and conclusion clearly and logically.

5. They summarize and offer conclusions when possible.

Figure 15–1 is a sample progress report using the memo format.

FIGURE 15–1

Sample progress report in memo form.

DATE: April 12, 199X

TO: Bonnie Erehart

FROM: Wilbur Rite

SUBJECT: Proposed Methods and Procedures for
         Gathering Information on Your Becoming a
         Licensed Private Pilot in the Cloud County
         Area

STATEMENT OF THE PROBLEM

On March 16, 199X, you asked me to find out everything you will need to know to become a licensed
private pilot. Because you will be in this area for
at least two years, you wanted to know where to go
in Cloud County for qualified instruction.

WHAT I NEED TO KNOW

To make an informed recommendation I must find out

• Which airports in Cloud County offer student pilot instruction

• Where they are located and the distance from your
  home

• What is the extent of their facilities and student pilot services

• What is the reputation of the operation and the
  competency of the personnel

• How well the student pilot programs prepare you
  to meet Federal Aviation Administration (FAA) requirements for licensing

• What additional FAA requirements you will need to
  know about

HOW I AM GETTING THE INFORMATION

To gather the information I first called each airport in Cloud County to find out if they offer a
learn-to-fly program. If they did, I scheduled an
interview with an instructor and arranged to be
shown around the airport.

I wrote to the FAA asking them for any information
they could give me on what steps must be taken to
become a private pilot.

Finally, I planned to check with several members of
the local flying club, Wings Way, to see what I
could discover about the individual airport,
specifically the maintenance of equipment and teaching ability of instructors.

WHAT I HAVE FOUND OUT SO FAR

Who Offers Qualified Instruction The following are
the names and addresses of four local airports offering complete learn-to-fly packages:

1. Cloud Air Park, Cloud County Lane, Cloudland (13
   miles from your home)

2. Fly by Night Airport, Route 355, Shillington (17
   miles)

3. Park Air Depot, Junction Hill Road, Junction (8
   miles)

4. Belleton Air Park, R.D. 1, Belleton (22 miles)

In telephone interviews with the managers of all
four airports, I found that total costs for package
deals, including flight training and ground school
instruction, range from a low of $2,150 at Park Air
Depot to $3,220 at Cloud. From what I can determine
so far, prices seem closely related to airport facilities, the type and number of airplanes used for
training, and services offered the student. Thus
far, I have visited Cloud Air Park to interview Mr.
Rickenbacker, the flight instructor, and to tour the
grounds.

What the FAA Requires An aspiring pilot must successfully meet requirements set by the FAA to be
licensed. To become a student pilot, he must pass a
medical examination. To become a licensed private
pilot, he must pass a *written* examination and a
practical (flying) examination.

FIGURE 15–1 cont'd

The medical examination is given by three local FAA-certified physicians (see attached list for names and addresses). Preparations for the thorough written test is available in the ground school training offered by the local airports. I will include in the final report a booklet I received from the FAA explaining the test and giving sample questions. Requirements to take the practical examination are met by completing any one of the local learn-to-fly programs.

WHAT I WILL DO SOON

Airport Visits Within the next week I will visit Fly by Night Airport, Park Air Depot, and Belleton Air Park. At each airport, I am scheduled to talk with an instructor and to be shown around.

Flying Club Interview After the airport visits, I have appointments with three members of Wings Way at separate times to discuss their judgments of the airports and the personnel. In an earlier telephone conversation with the club president I was impressed with his openness and eagerness to help. I hope that my talks with the three pilots will give me an "inside" look at what is involved in learning to fly in general and what these specific airports have to offer.

FAA Material For the final report, I intend to distill much of the thorough information I received from the FAA into a checklist and to explain each examination as it applies to you. For example, I will call one of the local medical examiners to discuss with him what the examination covers and what it costs.

As planned, I will have the full report with a recommendation of which local airport can best serve you by May 16, 199X.

FIGURE 15-1 cont'd

Regardless of report length or formality, writers always face the challenge of getting words onto paper and overcoming the kinds of false expectations that lead to writer's block. The first step is often the most difficult; the next section suggests ways to handle this challenge successfully.

Raw Writing to the Rescue

One of the best ways to get words on paper is through a direct approach called **raw writing.** Such an approach works especially well if you don't have much time, and you have plenty to say. It's great for functional writing tasks like memos, reports, somewhat complex or sensitive letters, or papers for which you don't want to engage in much new thinking. Raw writing is also good if you are inexperienced or nervous about putting thoughts on paper. Applying this idea calls for a simple four-step process.

1. *Know you reader.* Start off by thinking carefully about the person who will be reading what you write. Ask yourself such questions as: What does the reader already know about the topic? What does the reader need to know? What kind of information is likely to persuade the reader? These will help you focus on reader benefits, and better capture his or her attention. Jot down your answers to such questions.

2. *Set your time clock.* Once you've focused your mind on the reader, determine a realistic amount of time you'll need to convey your message. If you are writing a relatively simple letter, a few minutes may be plenty of time. A more complex report may take hours of writing time after the raw data have been collected. At any rate, set a deadline. Then divide the available time *in half.*

3. *Use half your time for fast writing.* The first half of your allotted time should be used to get something—anything!—down on paper. (the following paragraphs describe this process). When the time is up, stop immediately!

4. *Use half your time for polishing.* The second half of your allotted time should be used to revise and polish the draft you made in the first half.

> In raw writing, the important point is to get your ideas down on paper—fast!

Write fast. Don't waste time or energy worrying about how to organize it, what to start with, paragraphing, wording, spelling, grammar, or any other matters of presentation. Just get ideas down helter-skelter. If you can't think of the right word, just leave a blank. If you can't make it the way you want to say it, say it the wrong way. (If it makes you feel better, highlight those wrong bits to remind you to fix them later.)[2]

Okay, time's up. Stop your fast-and-loose scribbling of every idea and feeling. It's time to shift your mental gears. Put on a new hat. You are now a ruthless, tough-minded, skeptical, rigorously logical *editor.*

> **Process of Starting over Again: From Mess to Masterpiece**

Even if you feel frustrated at not having written enough or figured out exactly what you are going to say, stop. You have used up your allotted time for raw writing. Even if you think that what you have done so far is poor, if you steal any more of your revising time for more raw writing, the total product will be even worse. Besides, you'll have ample opportunity during the revising process (described later in the chapter) to figure out what else you might want to say—to add a few of the missing pieces.

Organization and Writing of Individual Report

The following are four steps for preparing an effective report.

Step 1: Overview of Your Project

Start by thinking with a "broad brush." Plan how you will articulate three important steps.

1. Clearly define the problem(s) the report will *focus* on or the question(s) the report will seek to answer. What does your reader need to know?

2. Spell out the *criteria* that are likely to be used to make a final decision or recommendation. Identify the factors that will decide the issue. For example, a business decision may hinge on costs, labor availability, expected customer acceptance, and legal requirements. The best decision, then, would be one that is cost-effective; has the people available to do it; would meet customer approval; and is within the laws of the community, state, and federal government.

3. Identify the *sources of information* or evidence, and the methods of gathering the information selected. Will you be using the local library, online databases, interviews, or statistical data from within the company?

Write your responses to these questions! Then, if you are writing this report for someone else, check with the person to be sure that you are both on the same wavelength. Report writing is too costly to risk trekking down the wrong road.

Step 2: Preliminary Information Gathering

Ambiguity is inevitable at the beginning of a report project.

During the initial-fumbling around stage it is better to err on the side of jotting down too much information than on the side of letting something potentially important slip by.

Even the most carefully planned report project involves a period of sorting through chaos and searching for useful data. Ambiguity is normal in the early development stages. If there were no uncertainty, a report would not be needed.

The initial-fumbling-around stage (IFAS) often takes the form of surfing the Internet, leafing through books and periodicals, or conducting some loosely structured interviews with people who know something about the report topic. A common mistake for many is that they fail to write down this preliminary information because they are not sure where—or if—it will fit in the final report. During the IFAS, it makes sense to err on the side of gathering a little too much information rather than on the side of letting something important slip away.

Don't be too selective during the IFAS. Reconcile yourself to the fact that you won't use every tidbit of information you gather. That's okay, but get all that might be relevant onto note cards or your computer files.

Even with today's word processing, many writers still find it useful to gather preliminary ideas on note cards first. Often, the 3- × 5-inch cards work best because you can carry them around in a pocket or purse, and capture that inspiration as it strikes.

Software equivalents of old-fashioned note cards are available too. One is called *NoteCard*™ and is paired up with *Citation*™, which allows you to store, sort, and retrieve ideas and their sources. Other programs imitate the old way of sorting and arranging the cards. One called *Cork Board*™ is a computerized version of sticking note cards on a bulletin board to see how the ideas can best be fit together. As you become more comfortable with computers, these replace the manual functions of jotting and sorting note cards.

Pulling in Past Reports. You should seldom have to draft a common report completely from scratch. If you or a colleague have written a similar report in the past, you can often borrow parts for the current report you are writing. You must be careful to make sure the material in the past report is current and applicable.

Using Prepared Formats. Many software packages guide you through various types of reports, organizing according to a set pattern. For example, several packages will talk you through the development of a business plan or employee evaluation reports. These can take some of the guesswork out of typical reports but you run the risk of creating a cookie-cutter approach that may not be appropriate for your specific need.

Tracking note sources. As you gather preliminary information, be sure to identify the specific source and whether you are quoting directly or paraphrasing.

Typically, you will be taking three types of notes: *direct quotes, paraphrased quotes,* and *your own ideas.* For each type, the source can be identified in parentheses following the note. If you copy a **direct quote,** use quotation marks and ellipses and brackets as necessary. When you omit words in quoted materials, you should use a series of three spaced periods called ellipses points to indicate the omission. The omission must not detract from or alter the essential meaning of the sentence. Brackets are used to insert a word or phrase of your own to clarify the context of the quote for the reader. Examples:

> **Technical material distributed for promotional use is sometimes charged for, particularly in high-volume distribution to educational institutions, although prices for these publications are not uniformly based on the cost of developing them. (Without omission)**

An example of the use of ellipses follows:

> **Technical material distributed for promotional use is sometimes charged for . . . although prices for these publications are not uniformly based on the cost of developing them. (With omission)**

An example of the use of brackets follows:

> Those who learn to write better reports tend to become more demanding in what they expect of the reports they receive. "When 800 people took my course at Standard of Ohio," says [Albert] Joseph [president of the Industrial Writing Institute], "they began to ridicule the reports that still were written in the old style. The environment has changed."

Without the brackets, you would not know who Mr. Joseph is.

Paraphrased material should convey the same thought as the original text but use different words. When gathering paraphrases, omit the quotation marks, but do cite the source of the idea.

One other type of preliminary note is often overlooked by researchers: *your own thoughts*. As you read and gather data, ideas are going to be triggered in your own mind. Don't let these get away. Jot them down immediately and identify them as your own simply by putting your initials in parentheses at the end of the note.

Here are examples of each type of note.

- Direct quote

  And unfortunately, the beginning report writers tend to overlook the preparation stage, sometimes even ignoring it completely, preferring to get into the more active job of gathering information. (Hatch, 1995, p. 245)

- Paraphrased quote

  Beginning report writers tend to overlook the preparation stage, preferring to get directly into information gathering. (Hatch, p. 245.)

- Own idea

  One problem leading to our poor-quality reports may be that less-experienced writers are not spending enough time in preparation before they gather data. (JAS)

  Jim Stead's initials appear in the "own idea" example.

For every source you cite in your preliminary note taking, be sure to make up a bibliography or citation card. This card records all the pertinent publishing information (for materials in print), or time and place of interview data. On the top of page 434 are examples of several citation cards.

Step 3: Review of Materials and Creation of Preliminary Outline

The next broad step in report production is to develop an outline showing a logical arrangement of the major ideas you want to cover. Having been immersed in data gathering will prepare you for this step. You will undoubtedly note common themes among the materials you gather and should be able to classify some of these.

Your written notes provide the raw materials. Now you'll want to rearrange them freely until each piece fits into some sort of logical sequence.

- Citation for book

  Paul R. Timm and Kristen B. DeTienne, *Managerial Communication,*
  3rd ed. (Englewood Cliffs, NJ: Prentice Hall, 1995), p. 344.

- Citation for periodical

  Jim Stead, "Why Credit Unions Rip You Off," *U.S. News and World*
  Report, **July 17, 1997, pp. 27–28.**

- Citation for interview

  Interview with Harry Thompson, CEO of Comotose Waterbed, Inc.,
  July 12, 1996 in Cleveland, Ohio.

As you organize these ideas, start with a clear description of the report's problem definition and decision criteria. Let's say, for example, your report examines the feasibility of renovating an older shoe store in your city's downtown shopping district. The central question is: Would such a business decision be profitable to the company?

Assume that your information gathering reveals the following facts:

- Fewer shoppers use downtown stores than five years ago, but there has been a slight uptrend in the past two years.
- Tax incentives are available to companies that expand or locate new facilities downtown.
- Renovation of old stores is less expensive than a move to a new location, and re-modeling contractors are eager for the business.
- The Downtown Business Association is supporting a redevelopment program for the downtown area by recognizing the civic pride of companies who stay.
- Shoppers who do use downtown stores spend less than those who use our suburban mall stores.
- The state legislature is considering a bill to provide low-cost loans to businesses that renovate or relocate in urban areas.
- Many downtown shoppers are elderly and cannot travel to suburban stores.

How could this information be arranged? A review of the facts shows that there are essentially three classes of information presented here.

1. Information about shoppers and potential profits follows:

   - There are fewer than in the past, but numbers are improving.
   - Shoppers spend less downtown than in suburbs.
   - Many are elderly.

2. Information about costs follows:

   - It would be less expensive to renovate.
   - Remodeling contractors want business.
   - Tax incentives are available.
   - Low-cost loans are possible in the future.

3. Information about PR benefits follows:

   - Downtown Business Association offers recognition.
   - Renovation demonstrates service to the elderly.
   - Redevelopment shows civic pride.

Once these areas have been identified, each major section should be numbered (1 to 3 in the preceding example). Then each note or bit of data gathered should be examined to see where it fits best. If you are working with hard copy (e.g., cards or other written notes), sort the data into stacks according to the number assigned. If a note doesn't seem to fit, set it aside for now. It may be useful in later drafts of the report, or it may be irrelevant to the topic and can be discarded.

If you are working on a computer, use the software's sorting features to segment the larger report into several smaller, easier-to-deal-with sections. At some point, most people will want to print out a draft, and mark it up for further editing or rearrangement. Some people can do this on the computer, but others still prefer a paper copy and a sharp pencil.

When this draft of major ideas is pasted together (literally or electronically), go back through the draft and add transitions tying the data together. Here you will want to insert appropriate setup paragraphs and internal summaries, and review the document for any holes in the information presented.

Then you should review once again to see if the accessing is appropriate. Use verbal and visual accessing techniques to help the reader get to the meat of the message. Use short paragraphs and enumeration. Also look for opportunities to show information graphically instead of just with words. Illustrations, figures, tables, and photographs all can add an important dimension to your report.

At this point, your report may look pretty messy. You are likely to have cut and pasted, or scribbled lots of notes in the margins. You may have used pens or pencils of several colors. That's fine; this is a working draft. Better to rearrange it here than to determine prematurely that what has been written is the final product.

Remember, no one writes perfect material the first time. All writers edit, rearrange, and re-edit—often many times—before being satisfied with the professionalism of the final product.

Step 4: Editing and Polishing of Report

Once you have created and reworked several drafts of your report, you should be ready to edit and polish the final product. The next task calls for some "heartless" editing. This means setting aside your pride in authorship and asking difficult questions. Does this arrangement make sense? Have I worded this the best possible way? Will my reader know what this means?

Review each heading, thought, sentence, and phrase to be sure it carries its own weight. Delete superfluous words and phrases; eliminate redundancies. Be sure to set aside the draft before editing. A fresh look often reveals editing opportunities not seen immediately after writing the draft.

Some Samples. Figure 15–2 is a sample of a formal report showing typical parts and formats. Please recall, however, that the following are samples and suggested formats. Remember a theme that this book has repeated: Communication is an art. Your creativity may suggest ways to format reports differently, but if you wish to follow a generally accepted model, this is a good one.

FIGURE 15–2

Long formal report.

THE EFFECTS ON THE AMERICAN MUSIC
INDUSTRY OF MANDATORY RECORD LABELING
FOR POTENTIALLY OFFENSIVE MATERIAL

Presented to
Tipper Gore
Parents Resource Music Center

Prepared by
Robert Baker
November 4, 199X

EXECUTIVE SUMMARY

Ever since the 1990 trial of 2 Live Crew
for charges of obscenity, well-publicized
controversies have arisen over mandatory
record-label warnings. This report examines
the Parents Resource Music Center's (PRMC's)
role in encouraging legislation mandating
record-label warnings.

Three main topics are addressed in this
report.

1. Disputes, based on the First Amendment, over the legality of record-
   labeling laws

2. Public opinion regarding record labeling

3. Economic effects of record labeling

The study shows that, on grounds of the
First Amendment, the legality of mandatory
record-labeling laws is questionable.

Despite the questionability of such laws,
most parents, concerned about what their
children are listening to, support record
labeling.

The third major conclusion from the report is that, because of lost revenues that
would result from banning the sale of labeled records to minors, record-labeling
laws will cause detrimental economic effects

to the music industry and to state governments.

Because of conflicting interests between
the First Amendment rights and the wishes of
parents, the best solution is to continue
to support record companies' existing
voluntary-labeling policies instead of
pushing for mandatory-labeling legislation.
Supporting the voluntary-labeling policies
will bring the advantages of record labeling
without the disadvantages of making record
labeling mandatory.

Contents

THE EFFECTS ON THE AMERICAN MUSIC INDUSTRY
OF MANDATORY RECORD LABELING FOR POTENTIALLY
OFFENSIVE MATERIAL

Introduction

During the past few years, mandatory record labeling for potentially offensive material has sparked quite a bit of debate. Many people have expressed their concerns about not being informed of offensive lyrics contained in various records; consequently, these people favor record labeling.

Conversely, many recording artists, record companies, and freedom-of-speech advocates oppose these mandatory labeling practices.

The purpose of this report is to show both the positive and the negative sides of mandatory record labeling. Conclusions will be reached as to whether or not such a labeling system is necessary and beneficial for the American market. From the conclusions, recommendations will be made about whether or not the music-recording industry should be required to put warning labels on potentially offensive material.

Statement of the Problem
This report examines the effect on the American music industry of mandatory record labeling for potentially offensive material.

Purpose of the Study
The following questions will be answered by the conclusions of this study:

1. Should record-labeling laws governing lyrics be enacted and enforced?

2. Is the music industry effectively and voluntarily labeling questionable lyrics?

3. Do parents desire to see record-labeling laws?

4. Would mandatory-labeling laws cause decreased revenues for record companies?

Background of Record Labeling
In 1990, rap group 2 Live Crew and several retailers who sold 2 Live Crew's records were arrested, and later acquitted, on charges of obscenity.[1] This publicity brought the issues of censorship and record

---

[1] Arthur S. Hayes, "First Amendments Lawyers Are Upbeat over Chances to Win Obscenity Cases," *The Wall Street Journal*, February 12, 1991, p. B-8.

labeling to the forefront. As a result, various state legislators made several unsuccessful attempts to enact mandatory record-labeling laws to warn consumers of potentially offensive lyrics.

FIRST AMENDMENT RIGHTS FOR RECORD LABELING

Perhaps the biggest topic in the record-labeling issue is whether or not mandatory record-warning labels would violate the First Amendment. As one might expect, diametrically opposed views exist on this matter.

Arguments for Legality
In 1987, Congress's in-house research service concluded that Congress, with authority from the commerce clause of the Constitution, could legally regulate the music industry. The major conclusion of the congressional report stated that Congress could require warning labels for records with explicit lyrics and could restrict minors' access to those records. However, the report also concluded that any restrictive laws must not be so broad as to infringe on adults' rights to have access to the same material.[2]

[2]Bill Holland, "Congress Can Regulate Lyrics, '87 Study Says," Billboard, June 10, 1989, pp. 1, 84.

Arguments Against Legality
In direct contrast to the congressional report are the opinions of several authorities, including James Fitzpatrick, a Washington, DC, attorney. Fitzpatrick believes the conclusions of the report are not justified; he also asserts any Congress-imposed labeling system would be "extreme" and would represent an "unfounded reading of the cases" referred to in the congressional study.[3]

In addition to Fitzpatrick, many others believe such legislation would be crossing the line of unconstitutionality. Commenting on the obscenity trial of 2 Live Crew, Jeff Ayeroff of Virgin Records said the following:

> Playing with the Bill of Rights is much more offensive to me than 2 Live Crew. I don't like the record any more than anybody else, but this is America. Supporting the Bill of Rights doesn't mean you're in favor of pornography. It means that you live in a country that must, for its own sake of existence, tolerate obnoxious things.[4]

[3]Ibid., p. 84.
[4]Kim Neely, "Rockers Sound Off," Rolling Stone, August 9, 1990, p. 27.

Jason S. Berman, president of the Recording Industry Association of America, also believes any state labeling laws would be in violation of the First Amendment.[5]

Todd Lewis, a programmer for an urban-formatted radio station in Cincinnati, admits that some songs' lyrics may be too descriptive. At the same time, however, Lewis still believes the artists' rights for self-expression must be defended.[6]

Barbara Dority, a board member of the American Civil Liberties Union, strongly opposes record labeling. She asserts the following:

> These heavy-handed attacks on the freedom of expression of young musicians are direct assaults on everyone's First Amendment rights of free speech and political dissent. We *must not tolerate* government censorship. We must stand together against this tyranny![7]

[5]Jason S. Berman, "Censorship Must Be Opposed," Billboard, July 7, 1990, p. 11.
[6]"Record Labeling Could Have Radio Fallout?" Broadcasting, April 30, 1990, p. 58.
[7]Barbara Dority, "Civil Liberties Watch," The Humanist, September/October 1990, p. 36.

Indeed, some states have proposed legislation banning the sale of a record to a minor that "contains references to such acts as murder, suicide, rape, or illegal use of drugs or alcohol."[8] With threatened legislation mandating record-warning labels, most record companies initiated a voluntary-labeling program. Therefore, many states have determined that mandatory-labeling laws are not necessary. Consequently, many legislatures backed off and repealed the proposed labeling bills.[9] If the voluntary program is ineffective, however, many state legislatures will once again sponsor mandatory-labeling bills.[10]

One debate is about whether potentially offensive lyrics even deserve the protection of the First Amendment. The Supreme Court has said that "music, *as a form of expression and communication,* is protected under the First Amendment." However, types of expression such as *obscenity* have been ruled *not to be speech at all* [emphasis added]."[11]

[8]"Music Biz Braces for Louisiana Lyrics Bill," Variety, June 17, 1991, p. 80.
[9]Charles Fleming, "Stickers for Minors a Major Headache," Variety, July 25, 1990, p. 63.
[10]Bill Holland, "Assault on First Amendment Stirred Industry to Action," Billboard, January 5, 1991, p. 81.
[11]Jason S. Berman, "Censorship Must Be Opposed," Billboard, July 7, 1990, p. 11.

The First Amendment is intended to protect free speech that is not "obscene." For something to be obscene as defined by the Supreme Court, three criteria must be met.

The "average person" must find the work appeals to "prurient interests," that it "depicts or describes in a patently offensive way sexual conduct," and that it lacks serious artistic value.[12]

Although many offensive songs may meet the first two criteria, almost all songs in question will still have artistic value.[13]

Indeed, after the quick acquittal of 2 Live Crew on charges of obscenity, many First Amendment experts concluded obscenity laws will not be effective in limiting the free speech of music.[14]

The acquittal of retailers on obscenity charges has further convinced music-industry defense lawyers they can win on First Amend-

[12]Peter Katel, Shawn Lewis, and Peter Plagens, "Mixed Signals on Obscenity," *Newsweek*, October 15, 1990, p. 74.
[13]John T. Mitchell, "Are We Losing Our Freedom to Sing?" *Los Angeles Times*, October 8, 1990, F-3.
[14]Jose de Cordoba and Christi Harlan, "Rap Group's Acquittal Seen as Warning to Prosecutors," *The Wall Street Journal*, October 22, 1990, p. B-3.

ment rights.[15] For example, one lawsuit against a Texas retailer was dropped because the prosecution "couldn't prove the sexually explicit lyrics [of 2 Live Crew album] were obscene."[16] In fact, in one obscenity case, the jury decided "that even offensive art is protected by the First Amendment and that people have a constitutional right" to have access to such questionable material.[17]

People need to remember what may be offensive to one person may not be offensive to another.[18] The First Amendment exists for the very purpose of protecting people from other's opinions.[19]

PUBLIC OPINION OF RECORD LABELING

A second point of analysis in this report is the public opinion regarding record labeling. Once again, diverse interests are involved.

[15]Hayes, "Obscenity Cases," p. B-8.
[16]"Charges Dropped in Texas Obscenity Case," *The Washington Post*, December 11, 1990, p. D-2.
[17]Joseph Kalik, "Not, What Is Art? But, What Is Freedom?" *The Wall Street Journal*, November 12, 1990, p. A-5.
[18]"Should Dirty Lyrics Be against the Law?" *U.S. News & News Report*, June 25, 1990, p. 24.
[19]Mitchell, "Freedom to Sing," p. F-3.

Parental Concerns
The foremost advantage of a mandatory record-labeling system is many parents across the nation are worried about what music their children are purchasing and listening to. The following poll results come from *The Atlanta Journal and Constitution*:

Question: How concerned are you about the influence of rock music lyrics on young children? Are you very concerned, somewhat concerned, not very concerned, or not at all concerned?

Very	38 percent
Somewhat	32 percent
Not very	19 percent
Not at all	10 percent[20]

Under proposed legislation, records containing offensive lyrics—especially those with sexually explicit lyrics—would be labeled for the intent of keeping those records out of the hands of minors, or at least to inform parents of what their children are listening to.[21,22]

[20]Bob Dart, "Record Industry: We'll Label; Don't Legislate, "*The Atlanta Journal and Constitution*, May 10, 1990, p. G-4.
[21]Holland, "Assault on First Amendment," p. 81.
[22]Berman, "Censorship Must Be Opposed," p. 11.

When asked about parents' responsibility for what their children listen to, Bob Martinez, governor of Florida, said the following:

Parents ought to feel that their children can go into any record store and not be able to buy this material. They can't buy liquor and they have to be 18 years old to see nude movies. We do have a responsibility to protect our young.[23] With an opposing view on record labeling, rock artist Ozzy Osbourne said, If I don't want my kids to listen to a certain form of music, or read a certain form of book, or watch a certain form of pornographic video, I make sure they don't. People are blaming the artists when they should take a good look in the bloody mirror.[24]

[23]"Should Dirty Lyrics Be against the Law?" p. 24.
[24]Neely, "Rockers Sound Off," p. 27.

Retailer Concerns

Not only are parents concerned about records containing offensive material, but many retailers also are concerned. Even with only the possibility of legislation, many retailers are being intimidated. Many have pulled potentially offensive records from their shelves and restricted access of other records to adults only.[25]

ECONOMIC EFFECTS OF RECORD LABELING

When looking at the possibility of virtually eliminating a whole segment of a market, one cannot overlook the economic consequences.

Declining Revenues
for the Music Industry

One magazine did a worst-case-scenario analysis to figure the possible lost revenues if laws banning minors' purchases of rap and heavy-metal records—the most likely to get warning labels—passed. If *all* minors stop buying *all* rap and heavy-metal records, the lost revenues for the music industry could exceed $540 million annually.[26]

---

[25]Jon Pareles, "In Rap Music, the Beat and the Lawsuits Go On," The *New York Times*, October 23, 1990, p. C-14.
[26]Fleming, "Stickers for Minors," p. 63.

In addition to lost sales from minors, some record stores might decide not to sell objectionable material at *all*. A proposed lyrics bill in Louisiana would make selling a labeled record to a minor illegal. This bill would undermine the voluntary-labeling program, because to keep retailers from getting in trouble for selling labeled records, record companies would simply *not* label their records.[27]

Declining Revenues for States

In addition to the music industry losing sales, states imposing a record-labeling requirement could face consequences, too. For example, because of its proposed lyric legislation, Louisiana has already been informed that it will not be a candidate to house the Grammy Hall of Fame.[28]

Along with the loss of sales revenues for the music industry discussed earlier, local businesses and government could lose out in income. In Louisiana, where the controversial lyrics bill was introduced earlier this year, the music industry brings $1.4 billion in income to the state annually.[29]

---

[27]"Music Biz Braces," pp. 80–81.
[28]Berman, "Censorship Must Be Opposed," p. 11.
[29]"Music Biz Braces," p. 81.

SUMMARY

Three main issues exist regarding mandatory record labeling. The biggest issue is whether or not record-labeling laws would violate First Amendment rights to free speech.

The second main issue concerns public opinion regarding mandatory record labeling. Parents, concerned about the effects of music lyrics on their children, make up the main group advocating record labeling.

Finally, mandatory record labeling would bring about economic effects. The consequences would affect both the music industry and individual states' economies where labeling laws are passed.

CONCLUSIONS

Based on the analysis of this study, the following conclusions are made:

1. The legality of record-labeling laws remains questionable, although most cases to date have ruled against lyric legislation.
2. The music industry already almost universally uses warning labels voluntarily. To introduce mandatory-labeling laws could cut back on the effective-

ness of the current voluntary-labeling program.
3. Most parents want records to be labeled to be aware of what music their children are listening to.
4. Mandatory-labeling laws could cause falling revenues for both the music industry and state economies.
5. Other consequences similar to Louisiana's not being considered for the Grammy Hall of Fame could result for states that pass mandatory-labeling laws.

RECOMMENDATIONS

Based on the conclusions of this study, the following recommendations are made:

1. PRMC should not push for legislation requiring record labeling. Because of the controversy concerning First Amendment rights for record labeling, the PRMC should let the current music-industry practice of *voluntary* labeling suffice.
2. The PRMC should encourage continued voluntary record labeling.

3. The PRMC should encourage parents to use the labels voluntarily placed on records to help select the materials their children will listen to.

4. The PRMC may also wish to pursue a further study into a more detailed labeling system similar to the rating system used by the Motion Picture Association of America.

BIBLIOGRAPHY

Berman, Jason S. "Censorship Must Be Opposed." *Billboard,* July 7, 1990, p. 11.

Dart, Bob. "Record Industry: We'll Label; Don't Legislate." *The Atlanta Journal and Constitution,* May 10, 1990, p. G-4.

De Cordoba, Jose, and Christi Harlan. "Rap Group's Acquittal Seen as Warning to Prosecutors," The *Wall Street Journal,* October 22, 1990, p. B-3.

Dority, Barbara. "Civil Liberties Watch." *The Humanist,* September/October 1990, pp. 35-36.

Fleming, Charles. "Stickers for Minors a Major Headache." *Variety,* July 25, 1990, 1 ff.

Hayes, Arthur S. "First Amendment Lawyers Are Upbeat over Chances to Win Obscenity Cases." *The Wall Street Journal,* December 11, 1990, p. D-2.

Holland, Bill. "Assault on First Amendment Stirred Industry to Action." *Billboard,* January 5, 1991, 7 ff.

——. "Congress Can Regulate Lyrics, '87 Study Says." *Billboard,* June 10, 1989, 1 ff.

Kalik, Joseph. "Not, What Is Are? But, What Is Freedom?" *The Wall Street Journal,* 12 November 1990, A5.

Katel, Peter, Shawn Lewis, and Peter Plagens. "Mixed Signals on Obscenity." *Newsweek,* October 15, 1990, p. 74.

Mitchell, John T. "Are We Losing Our Freedom to Sing?" *The Los Angeles Times,* October 8, 1990, p. F-3.

"Music Biz Braces for Louisiana Lyrics Bill." *Variety* June 17, 1991, pp. 80-81.

Neely, Kim. "Rockers Sound Off." *Rolling Stone,* August 9, 1990, 27 ff.

Pareles, Jon. "In Rap Music, the Beat and the Lawsuits Go On." The *New York Times,* October 23, 1990, pp. C13-C14.

"Record Labeling Could Have Radio Fallout?" *Broadcasting,* April 30, 1990, p. 58.

"Should Dirty Lyrics Be against the Law?" *U.S. News & World Report,* June 25, 1990, p. 24.

Preparation of Formal Reports

For career-conscious students, learning to write reports is an essential part of education. As Keithley and Schreiner state, "Preparing readable reports is an inevitable part of a career in business, industry, education, or science."[3]

Placement Guides

Although the new writer and the typist share responsibility for the preparation and ultimate success of a report, the writer must usually accept final responsibility. Turabian says,

> The writer is responsible for the correct presentation of his or her paper. The typist should be held responsible only for the mechanical details having to do with spacing [margins, heading placement, page numbering, and footnote placement], neatness, and the general appearance of the final copy.[4]

Spacing

Reports such as school papers, formal reports, and manuscripts to be submitted for publication, are usually double-spaced. Where single-spacing is used, double-space between paragraphs.

Margins

Leave a bottom margin of at least 1 inch. Leave 1-inch top and side margins on all pages, with the following exceptions:

1. On the first page of the report, leave a top margin of 2 inches before typing the title of the report.
2. Leave a left margin of 1-1/2 inches on all pages of a left-bound report.

Indent the first line of a paragraph five to ten spaces. For quoted matter of four or more lines, use single-spacing and indent the quotation five spaces from the left margin. Indenting in this manner sets the quotation off; therefore, quotation marks are not required.

Headings

Main heading (title). The main heading is typed in all capitals or italics and is centered over the line of writing. A secondary heading, when used, is typed a double-space below the main heading in capital and lowercase letters, followed by double- or triple-space. When no secondary heading is used, double- or triple-space after the main heading.

Centered headings. First-level headings such as "Placement Guides" in this report are centered over the line of writing in capital and lowercase letters, and are underlined.

Side headings. Side headings (e.g.,"Spacing," "Margins," etc., in this report) are typed at the left margin, and are underlined or italicized. Begin main words with a capital letter. Spacing is the same as that for centered headings. Side headings of this kind are considered second-level headings and are subordinate to first-level headings used.

(continued)

(continued)

Paragraph headings. Paragraph or third-level headings are used as guides to information subordinate to that under side or second-level headings. A paragraph heading is indented, followed by a period, and underlined or italicized. Generally, only the first word or proper nouns are capitalized.

Page numbers. For unbound or left-bound reports, number all pages after the first page (the first page need not be numbered) at the top right or top center of the paper. Begin typing the narrative leaving a 1-inch top margin. On pages that begin with a major heading (such as the first page of the bibliography), you may place the number at the foot of the page, centered.[5]

Footnote Placement

Footnotes are typed on the same page as their reference and are typed at the foot of the page, regardless of the fact that the page may only be partially filled. The footnotes are preceded by a single line one and a half inches long, which is followed by a double space.[6] Underline or italicize titles of complete publications; use quotation marks with parts of publications. Word processors will automatically place footnotes in the proper position, thus eliminating a time-consuming task typists used to do.

Endnote Placement

Endnotes are typed on a new page placed at the end of the report. The heading "Notes" or "Endnotes" is typed 2 inches from the top edge and is followed by a double-space. Again, word processors will order and place endnotes automatically. Use either endnotes or footnotes to cite references, but don't mix the two.

General Appearance

As a report writer, typist, or both, remember that first impressions are important. Jackson emphasizes the point that people are influenced by the appearance of a page before they become aware of its content.[7] Therefore, an effective writer should make certain that any report leaving his or her desk is technically correct in style, is neat, and is printed on high-quality bond paper.

Understanding the Basics

SUMMARY OF KEY IDEAS

• Getting started can be the most difficult part of writing a report.

• Overcoming unrealistic expectations about writing can help writers break through writer's block.

• Several types of short or routine reports are commonplace in business including task reports, periodic reports, progress reports, meeting minutes, and trip or conference reports.

• Short reports often take the form of elaborated memos.

• Individual report writing can be streamlined starting with a four-step process. The process begins with focusing the topic, gathering information, and arranging this information into preliminary drafts. It ends with polishing the final draft.

• A sample report shows the conventions used by many business report writers regarding format and organization.

KEY TERMS AND CONCEPTS

direct quote

paraphrased material

source bank

report proposal

raw writing

secondary sources

typical short reports

writer's block

QUESTIONS FOR FURTHER THOUGHT

1. Why is it important to understand the difference between draft documents and final reports?

2. What is "raw writing," and how can it help overcome writer's block?

3. Explain the four-step process for report writing described in this chapter.

4. What are some patterns of arrangement that may make sense in the body of a major report? (Hint: Check back to Chapter 8 for ideas.)

5. What are some arguments for following a standard format in report writing? Under what conditions might you want to use a different format?

6. What are some advantages of patterning your writing after reports written by others in your company? What possible disadvantages?

Note Jotting Made Simple

How many times have you found yourself scrambling for something to jot a note down on? And what were you in the middle of doing when you started scrambling? A business luncheon used to be my favorite place for doing this. I tore up more napkins at these functions, only to find a rolled up ball of napkin fragments in my pocket when my suit came back from the cleaners. I've also written on sugar packets, doggie bags, and newspapers—to mention just a few. I've often thought it would be interesting to conduct a survey on the most unusual things people have used as notepads.

I found a solution to my dilemma: three by five cards. They're perfect. You can write down quite a bit of information on one of these cards, and they fit right in your pocket or purse. Not only that, but when you get to the office you can easily file them for future reference.

NOTES IN THE OFFICE

You may find 3 × 5 cards quite handy when you're talking on the telephone. It's pretty simple to slip a card out of your pocket to jot something down. I've also found it helpful as I walk down the hall at work. I don't know about you, but normally I find myself in and out of several conversations between the time I leave my work station and the time I return. Sometimes I get distracted enough that I don't even remember what my original intentions were—the 3 × 5 card can be useful for directing efforts, too.

Before you leave your office to go talk with someone else, jot down what you need on one of your cards. As you get involved in side conversations heading to your destination, make pertinent notes for future reference. It's likely that you'll agree to get back to somebody on something, and if you jot down a reminder on a 3 × 5 card it will save you the embarrassment of later having to admit that you forgot. Then if you get to the point at which you forget what you originally set out to do, just glance at the 3 × 5 card before you start down the hall and you're back in business.

MORE HELPFUL HINTS

Another way you can use a 3 × 5 card is to jot down reminders of things you know you need to do (or maybe you remember something that you forgot to do) on your way home from work. Maybe you need to pick up a birthday card or some groceries. It may seem simplistic, but writing these things down on a 3 × 5 card can make a difference in your own life.

You can use a 3 × 5 card as a bookmark and make notes on it about specific pages in the book you may want to refer to at a later date. I've also had success in using them to remind me of things I need to do in the heat of a busy day. Just jot down your reminder note on the bottom half of the card and fold it in half—it works just like a place card.

This little practice has served me well at times when I was interrupted by a phone call while I was in the middle of something important. I'd agree to do something for the caller, hang up the phone, and get right back into what I was doing before the phone rang. Invariably, I'd forget what it was I'd agreed to on the phone. But when I jot down this information on my 3 × 5 card and fold it, I have an instant reminder right on my desk. You can create a mini "to do" list this way as well.

If you happen to be partial to colors, 3 × 5 cards come in a variety of shades. I prefer white unlined cards because there's nothing to restrict creativity. And one final point: You may also find that at the end of a particularly hectic day or at the end of a particularly unpleasant task, chances are you'll get immense pleasure from ripping up those 3 × 5 cards. It beats $100 a pop talking to a therapist!

(Jim Woodford, "Note-Jotting Made Simple," originally appeared in *Supervisory Management*, May 1992. Mr Woodford is a management consultant in Xenia, Ohio. Reprinted with permission of Jim Woodford.)

Applying Your Knowledge

1. As this article suggests, note cards can be handy for capturing and organizing ideas, bits of data, and quotes. What are some other approaches?

2. How has technology affected "note jotting?" Review some computer publications to determine what software programs can fulfill this task. Report your results in memo format.

Applying Your Skills

ACTIVITY 15-1: The Four-Step Process, Short Report

Use the four-step method described in this chapter to draft a report. For this exercise, use a fairly simple problem for which data are readily available. Critique the method. What were its strengths and weaknesses? How can you improve on it to make it work better for you?

Here are some possible report questions.

• Should your school require license tags for all bicycles used on campus? Assume you are a university administrator.

• How effective is the customer support at local computer stores? Assume that you are responsible for customer service for a chain of such stores.

• Should your company invest in motivational seminars? Assume that you are the training director for a medium-sized manufacturing company.

• Examine the advantages and disadvantages of purchasing versus leasing a new automobile. Assume that you could qualify for such a lease.

ACTIVITY 15-2: Expectations and Writer's Block

Out of the four "negative expectations" writers have, describe at least two that you have experienced in your writing efforts.

• The expectation to write in final, polished form: When? What happened?

• The expectation that a deadline can't be met: What happened?

• The expectation to experience writer's block: What happened? How did you break the block?

• The expectation to demonstrate your ignorance in your writing: What happened?

ACTIVITY 15-3: Check Your Writing Environment

Describe the physical location where you do your writing.

• Type of desk or workstation:

• Equipment:

• Lighting:

• Privacy:

• Comfort:

• Other:

Based on the preceding information, are there ways in which your physical surroundings could be improved? Consider and list the improvements you can put into place.

ACTIVITY 15-4: Who Uses Reports?

Find out the most used report by interviewing friends, coworkers, business acquaintances, and faculty. Ask which of the following they use most often, for what purpose, and in what kind of format they exist.

• Task report:

• Periodic report:

• Progress report:

• Meeting minutes:

• Trip or conference report:

ACTIVITY 15-5: Raw Writing

Do some "raw writing." Apply the four-step process of (1) knowing your reader, (2) setting your time clock, (3) using half your time for fast writing, and (4) using half your time for polishing to the following:

You have 30 minutes to formulate the basis for a report to be presented to your supervisor on how flextime can benefit your department's productivity. Alternatively, you may pick another topic that may be more relevant to you at this time. Once you have decided on the topic, go through the raw-writing steps in the allotted time. After the 30 minutes, analyze the process as to its value.

ACTIVITY 15-6: Human Resources Report

As human resource research supervisor of First Bank, a large urban bank with many branches, you were asked five months ago to investigate why there is high turnover among bank tellers. You set up an exit-interviewing process and discovered that of fifty tellers who resigned during that time, 27 gave the stress of handling money transactions as the main reason; 5 said they were going to other financial institutions; 5 said they wanted to work part-time; and 8 others gave personal reasons.

You have the following recommendations for slowing turnover:

Use flex-time schedules

Use more part-time employees

Review the current teller wage scale

Investigate training programs for handling stress on the job

Implement a personality questionnaire of job applicants to test "job fit"

You believe that anything to reduce turnover will be worthwhile because the cost of training new tellers is high. Prepare a report for Ronald E. Liason, vice-president of human resources, that presents your findings and recommendations. Mr. Liason is open to change, but needs facts and numbers to help in the decision-making process.

ACTIVITY 15-7: Recommending Topics

You are a member of a trade association. You have been asked by those in authority to suggest possible topics for a three-hour workshop at the upcoming national convention. You are not responsible for facilitating the workshop, only suggesting possible topics. Prepare a report suggesting three topics, any one of which will be appropriate. Present the rationale for your choices and how they will compliment the convention. Prioritize your choices according to your rationale, and indicate how each topic will assist participants attending the workshop.

ACTIVITY 15-8: Short Report

You are marketing director for CalendarSavers, a company that sells screen saver calendars for computers. Your product is just like a wall calendar, except that it appears on people's computer screens instead of on their walls. You sell several models: Back to Nature, Norman Rockwell, French Impressionists, Scenes from National Parks, Sunsets, Seasons, Animals of the Wild, Seascapes, and Famous Buildings. The relevant monthly calendar and photograph take turns on the screen, fading in and out every 20 seconds. You've sold these for two years at office supply and computer stores, but decided this year to try a new market—traditional bookstores, where wall calendars are a big item.

In accordance with this new strategy, you paid for a small booth at the American Booksellers Association (ABA) Trade Show in Chicago this spring. Nancy Lucia, president of CalendarSavers, has asked you to write a short report about your success in this new market. The show, you decided was worth the investment, more because of connections you made than actual sales. You signed on five good sales reps for New England, the deep South, and California,

and you had a calendar distributor express interest in carrying your screen savers in his catalog. Write Nancy Lucia a short report, indicating that the ABA Trade Show was a good first step in a new market, well worth a follow-up appearance next year.

ACTIVITY 15-9: A Short Report

You are involved in a three-month summer management trainee internship at Webber Manufacturing (five hundred employees). Your supervisor, Paul Brown, has asked you to prepare a report on employee participation in decision making. He wants to know what is currently being done in business and industry. He also is curious about what other manufacturing companies like Webber are implementing, and how they are measuring and rewarding increased productivity. Paul would like your report in one week and is giving you the time you need to research and prepare. He appreciates brevity and will not accept a report longer than five pages.

ACTIVITY 15-10: Long Report

Max Esplin at Nu Skin has asked you to evaluate the proposal from Custom Planners (see Case 14–12) and write a detailed report for him. Address each issue from a biased perspective: You are the liaison between Nu Skin and Franklin Quest and enjoy working with the larger company. Besides the fact that changing horses midstream would cause you a great deal more work, you don't see cost savings as a big issue, because the kits are paid for in full by the distributors, and none of them seems to complain about the cost.

ACTIVITY 15-11: Long Report Requiring Additional Research

You work for the Center for Corporate Values, a think tank that keeps an eye on business ethics. Robert Cotter, president of the Center, has asked you to analyze trends in executive compensation. Most of the relevant statistics can be found each year in an April issue of *Business Week*. Cotter wants you to compare this year's compensation for top corporate executives with last year's figures, evaluate CEO pay in relation to corporate profitability, and determine which industries have the greatest discrepancy between executive compensation and corporate profit. He also wants you to choose at random ten Fortune 500 companies, obtain a copy of their most recent annual report, and compare top executive pay with average employee wages. Write a detailed report that considers the following questions using specific examples:

1. Which industry pays its chief executives most? Does this same industry show greater profits than other industries?

2. How much has average pay changed for chief executives over the past year?

3. A significant portion of executive pay comes in the form of stock options. Is this portion increasing or decreasing? What effect will this have on executive pay in the future?

4. How does average change in pay for executives compare with change in pay for the average worker in the ten companies you evaluated?

5. What corporate or individual values could possibly account for the trends and comparisons outlined in your report?

6. Is this something the average citizen or corporate employee should be concerned about?

7. Discuss some possible ramifications of the trends and statistics cited in your report.

PERFORMING
on the Job

CASE 15-1 Performance Reviews as a Type of Task Report

A performance review is an opportunity for communication between supervisor and employee. This opportunity should come periodically and should be aimed at setting goals and discussing standards between the person who assigns the work and the person who performs the tasks.

The objective of a performance appraisal is to establish goals and clarify standards so that no misunderstanding can occur. The performance review is intended to benefit only the employee but should also bring out important information that the appraiser can use.

Some benefits that people can gain from regular, effective performance appraisals are the following:

- Insights into the work being done
- Extended opportunities for the employee
- Reduced employee anxiety
- Feedback on individual performance

Each of these benefits can increase the productivity and usefulness of the employee and work group.

The performance review is an excellent tool, *if* it is used effectively. That's a big *if,* however. Too often, poorly prepared or improperly conducted performance reviews undo in an hour all the good supervisor-employee relationships that have developed over months or even years. There is always this downside risk. On the positive side, though, an *effective* review session can go a long way toward clarifying expectations and objectives for both supervisor and worker, and can provide a base for supportive, mutually helpful work relationships.

Most workers react well to individual one-on-one attention from their boss, so long as the conversation is constructive and nonthreatening.

The written report is a crucial part of the performance review process for these reasons.

1. It forces the supervisor to think through the evaluation objectively.
2. It requires the supervisor to be orderly in presenting the evaluation and to support key points.
3. It provides a permanent record of what was covered in the interview. Often companies have employees sign the evaluation report indicating that they have received the message. (This signature doesn't signify that they necessarily agree with the assessment, only that it has been presented to them.)

By definition, a performance review or appraisal is a formal, carefully planned interview session with an accompanying written report. Those three elements—planning, interviewing, and reporting—are crucial.

1. Prepare a brief task report critiquing the performance of an imaginary employee, Rose Bailey. Rose works for you in a retail store selling clothing. She meets company goals for sales (in fact, she is at 110 percent of her sales target), and is almost always friendly and considerate. Her appearance at work is good, and she goes the extra mile in giving good customer service. Her weaknesses seem to be excessive absenses (she missed twelve days of work in the past six months, six of which were due to a case of the flu; however, the others were not for illness). She came to work more than fifteen minutes late seven times. On three occasions, she made errors in handling customer transactions that resulted in the customer being shortchanged. This seems to indicate some carelessness in handling cash.

Make up additional details, and write a brief performance report in memo format to be used in connection with a performance interview. Be sure to include a place for her to sign the review.

CASE 15-2 Much-Desired Position

A retail organization that employs approximately 150 people recently had an interesting situation occur while trying to fill a position in their marketing department. Positions in the marketing department are few and far between. This new position was designed to assist the marketing director with various tasks and responsibilities. This opening generated a great deal of interest among the employees. Some of the reasons for the interest included the following:

1. Higher pay range
2. Tasks and responsibilities with a great deal of variety
3. Opportunity to work with other companies, vendors, and members of the media
4. Chance to work in a small, two-person department
5. Opportunity to be creative

Employees are given three days in which to respond to "inside" job postings. They are required to put their "notice of interest" in writing and submit it to the human resource department. There were 14 notices of interest turned in, which was the largest number ever showing interest in any position in the ten-year history of the company.

The marketing director and the human resource director discussed the large number of applicants and attempted to narrow the field by having the applicants write their responses to six statements. The statements included (1) List any college level classes you have satisfactorily completed in Marketing, Journalism, Public Relations, and English. When? Where? (2) Describe your experience with photography, layout editing and market research. (3) Describe your experience and knowledge of desktop publishing software. (4) Describe your experience and knowledge of the retail market and customer service. (5) Describe your experience with speaking in front of groups. (6) Describe your definition of marketing.

All statements had to do with the qualifications of the position. A copy of the job description was made available at the time the job was posted so that all could review the qualifications. Five of the 14 applicants responded to the memo. After preliminary and secondary interviews, the position was filled by an applicant from outside the organization.

Case Questions

1. The marketing director and the human resource director wanted to narrow the field. Was their method or requesting feedback in writing reasonable? Why? Why not?

2. Why do you think so few responded in writing to the memo?

3. What would you have written if you were one of the 14 applicants who met only a few of the qualifications but had a strong desire to be involved in marketing?

4. Why do you think the position was filled from outside the organization?

PART FIVE

Speaking *and* Listening Skills *for* Effectiveness *amid* Change

Most people's daily communication involves speaking and listening. The ability to listen, digest, and articulate ideas in ways that create understanding and hold listener interest cannot be overvalued.

In business and the professions, career success depends on the ability to express ideas, instruction, and information. For many people, such communication—especially when standing before groups as a "presentational speaker"—can be daunting. As humorist George Jessel said, "The human brain is a wonderful organ. It starts working as soon as you are born and doesn't stop until you get up to deliver a speech."

This part contains important information applicable to preparing and delivering a speech (or business presentation), but it also focuses on key skills that enhance listening, using visuals, and participating in groups and teams.

Active Listening:
The Master Key

LEARNING GOALS

After you have studied this chapter, you
should be able to:

- Describe the differences between
  hearing and listening.

- Distinguish among internal,
  environmental, and interactional
  factors that complicate the listening
  process.

- Explain how information overload and
  underuse of listening capacity can
  cause communication problems.

- Describe the problems of self-
  centeredness and self-protection as
  they apply to listening.

- Identify two behaviors to employ for
  better listening.

The Way It Is . . . The Nature and Challenge of Listening

Listening means the difference between passing or failing a test, making or losing a sale, getting or losing a job, motivating or discouraging a team, mending or destroying a relationship. Listening, however, has gotten a bad reputation as a passive state. To the contrary, listening is simply the precursor of successful activity.[1]

Most people are not good listeners. Typically, people listen at about 25 percent of their potential, which means that they ignore, distort, or misunderstand 75 percent of what they hear. This problem is significant for businesses and professions. When communication breaks down, costly mistakes are made.

The major reason people listen poorly is because they have no intention of listening well. They are too preoccupied with themselves. They are too focused on getting what they want done or heard; they have no time to be interrupted by someone talking to them. They are like the communicator who is so wrapped up in his own message that he can't assimilate the other person's view. Common understanding—the goal of communicating—never emerges from such one-way communication.

Listening may be the most important of all communication skills.

How many times have you heard people complain, "You just haven't heard a word I said to you. Nobody listens to me around here. I might as well be talking to the wall." If you haven't, you must be living on another planet. The lack of effective listening may be the most common communication problem in most organizations (including families). Managers need to have their "ears on" regularly. They need to be particularly aware of the importance of effective listening to their organizations and to employees.

Ironically, of the four basic communication skills—reading, writing, speaking, and listening—only one is not formally *taught*. Elementary schools focus heavily on the first three and assume that students are picking up listening. After all, some people reason, listening is really just a matter of sitting back and letting the talker have his or her say. Of all the communication skills, however, listening may actually be the most important. It deserves more attention than it typically gets.

This chapter considers the nature of listening; defines some common barriers to good listening; and offers some pointers on how to become a more skillful, active listener.

Difference between Hearing and Listening

Three elements complicate the listening process: internal, environmental, and interactional factors.

Many of us confuse hearing with listening. In reality, they are two different processes. *Hearing* is purely physical activity by which acoustic energy in the form of sound waves is changed to mechanical and electrochemical energy that the brain can understand. All of this has little to do with listening. *Listening* refers to the psychological processes that allow you to attach meaning to the patterns of energy "heard." All the potential problems, which typically arise from differences in perception, come into play in the listening process.

The "cocktail party effect" provides a good example of the difference between hearing and listening. At a cocktail party there are usually several conversations going on simultaneously in the same room. Everyone present at the party is aware of these

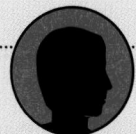

How Good Are Your Listening Habits?

Circle the number that best indicates how strongly you agree with each of the following statements. According to this scale, 1 means you strongly disagree, and 5 means you strongly agree; 2 to 4 show relative strength of agreement.

1. I always focus on people when they talk to me so that I can best understand what they are saying.

           1 2   3   4   5

2. I never let my mind wander during conversations.

           1 2   3   4   5

3. Listening is one of my best communication skills.

           1 2   3   4   5

4. Listening is the single most important communication skill needed for business or professional success.

           1 2   3   4   5

5. People, in general, are not very good listeners.

           1 2   3   4   5

6. Listening is seldom taught in school despite its importance to career success.

           1 2   3   4   5

7. I understand the uses of different types of listening for different situations.

           1 2   3   4   5

8. Self-centeredness is a key cause of poor listening.

           1 2   3   4   5

9. People can listen a lot faster than they can talk.

           1 2   3   4   5

10. I recognize in myself a need to be a more effective listener.

           1 2   3   4   5

The maximum possible score on this self-evaluation is 50. The higher your score, the more in tune you are with the need for and challenges of effective listening. If you scored more than 35, you are on track with your assumptions about listening. The rest of this chapter gives you some powerful insights into the process of listening and some key tips for personal improvement.

conversations in that they can be heard. Conversely, you usually have to make a conscious effort to listen to any one of these conversations. You are physically capable of changing all or most of the acoustic energy in the room into electrochemical energy. You are much less capable of attaching meanings to all the electrochemical impulses.

What Contributes to Listening?

Before you can begin to improve your listening skills, you need to understand the demands placed on your listening capacities. These demands fall into three categories or elements of the listening process: internal, environmental, and interactional elements.

Internal Elements Affecting Listening

As just noted, listening involves attaching meanings to words or sounds you hear. Two preconditions must be met concerning **internal elements.**

1. The words or other sounds used by the message source must be received by the hearer.

2. The listener must possess a set of meanings or referents for these sounds.

Overhearing someone speaking an unfamiliar foreign language is an obvious example of a breakdown in this second step. If the sounds have no referent, you cannot understand. Listening is the way you put sounds and their meanings together to create understanding.

Environmental Elements Affecting Listening

The **environmental elements** involved in the listening process include the factors of the communication environment, which determine what you are able to listen to and what you cannot. These factors include the following:

- Individual listening capacity
- Presence of noise
- Use or misuse of gatekeepers

Listening capacity can be damaged by too much or too little information.

Individual Listening Capacity. Listening capacity can be diminished in two ways: It can be overloaded with too much information, or it can be underused. In both cases, listening tends to break down.

Examples of listening breakdowns caused by an exceeded listening capacity can be found in your everyday experiences. Only so many messages can be heard and responded to in any given day; only so many telephone calls can be answered at one time. Once your capacity to accomplish these tasks has been reached, you develop defensive mechanisms for coping. You develop psychological strategies for selecting what you will attend to and what you will tune out.

These selection mechanisms, although often unconscious, are normally based on your individual needs, which change from time to time. When your capacity for paying attention to incoming information is exceeded, the impact on your listening is difficult to predict. Only one point is certain: You are likely to miss some messages.

People are capable of listening faster than others can talk.

The opposite problem, in which environmental demands cause us to underuse our listening capacity, is also widespread. Most people speak at the rate of about 120 words per minute (except for auctioneers or disk jockeys), yet our normal capacity for listening—assigning meanings to words—is about 500 words per minute. The problem is that you listen faster than anyone can talk to you, providing ample time for your mind to wander far afield. Listening to others becomes a tedious task, forcing us to slow down your thinking to stay synchronized with those speaking to you.

Noise may be either external—a factor of the environment—or internal—within yourself.

Noise. The presence of **noise** is another environmental element affecting listening. Noise refers to any stimuli irrelevant to the conversation. Such noise may be either environmental (e.g., the sound of machinery, other conversations, buzzers, or bells) or internal (e.g., a headache, your dislike of the person to whom you are listening, or preoccupation with a meeting with the boss later in the day). Whatever the source, noise distracts us from the business of listening.

Gatekeepers preview incoming information before passing it on to others.

Taking an important telephone call in the kitchen can present several challenges. You are likely to be distracted by the sound of a dishwasher in midcycle, the television in the adjoining room, and even the conversation that was interrupted in midsentence that your partner is trying to finish with sign language. All this is noise that will likely damage your ability to honestly listen.

Gatekeepers. One way people deal with the problems of exceeded listening capacity and excessive noise is through **gatekeepers,** who preview incoming information to determine if it is appropriate to the needs of the organization or an individual. If the gatekeeper sees a message as irrelevant, it will be withheld from the system. In this sense, a gatekeeper is a person whose job it is to do some of your listening for you. The person may be a secretary, administrative assistant, or any other person you turn to for organizational information. In many instances, these individuals determine what needs your attention and what doesn't.

Although gatekeeping has its benefits, it also poses problems. When you finally do get the information, it has been through at least two sets of interpretations: your gatekeeper's and your own. There is no guarantee that you are listening to the message as originally intended. Your gatekeeper may accidentally filter out messages that you need to hear.

Interactional Elements Affecting Listening

In contrast to the environmental elements of the listening process, the interactional elements concern internal psychological processes that are not as easily identified. Two such psychological elements deserve careful consideration: self-centeredness and self-protection.

Effects of Self-Centeredness on Listening. Self-centeredness refers to the degree of "vested interest" you may have in your own viewpoint. When a difference of opinion arises among people, your vested interest in your ideas can create a listening barrier.

It isn't difficult to understand why this occurs. When you have taken the time to formulate an idea, you usually verbalize that idea in the presence of others. In essence, you have made a public commitment to that position, and it becomes embarrassing for you to change. At the same time, the people you are interacting with have also publicly committed themselves to their opinions.

Being publicly committed to a viewpoint can make it difficult for you to listen to other views.

Because listening is a psychological process, based in your individual needs, you think and listen from a self-centered orientation. As a result, you don't listen to *what* the other person is saying; you listen instead to how their views affect your position. In other words, you are "listening" through a predetermined set of biases, looking for flaws in your "opponent's" views rather than seeking common understanding. You develop a mind like a steel trap—closed.

Here's an example of the effects of self-centeredness on listening. In a recent training session and workshop for personnel managers, a group was split into several male-female pairs. Each pair was given a different conflict situation to discuss and solve.

In one discussion problem, the pair was asked to role play the following situation as husband and wife: "The husband has a good job in his chosen profession in the city where the couple resides. The wife has just completed her master's degree and received only one job offer in her chosen profession, but it would require the couple to move to a distant city. Although the husband has tried, he has been unable to find a job in that new city."

An analysis of the resulting interaction revealed the self-centeredness concept in action. Both participants made a valiant effort to appear to understand the other's position; however, the communication revealed that neither was as interested in listening to the other for the sake of gathering conflict-reducing information as much as to find a means of convincing the other person of their own viewpoint. Few of the participants developed a genuine understanding or a satisfactory solution.

The listening behaviors here are not unique. In your daily interactions you can find yourselves listening to other people solely for the purpose of finding the weaknesses in their positions so that you can formulate a convincing response.

Another example of the self-centeredness problem arises when you listen to the other person only long enough to key an answer in your own minds. At that point, you may stop listening and begin to plan what you'll say in response. The other person is still talking, and you still hear them but are no longer listening.

Self-centered listening has a direct impact on the amount of information you receive. Because research indicates that the more information you have, the better decisions you are able to make, such blocking out of relevant information cannot help but lower the quality of your decisions.

Effects of Self-Protection on Listening

A second interactional element affecting the listening process is **self-protection.** You "protect" yourself by playing out an anticipated communication interaction in your own mind before the real interaction ever occurs, to make sure you don't get caught saying something stupid. In essence, then, you are practicing by listening to yourself listen to others.

A serious listening problem arises when you engage in conjecture by listening to yourself listen to others, by anticipating what might be said and reacting to that instead of the actual situation. Both of these interactional elements—self-centeredness and self-protectiveness—affect the listening process in that they tend to orient your listening behavior toward biased interpretations of messages.

These three elements of the listening process—internal, environmental, and interactional—pose potential problems requiring *active* effort. Listening must be recognized as more than something you sit back and do to kill time when you're not talking. As communication scholar Harold Janis has said, "Listening . . . is not merely hearing; it is a state of receptivity that permits understanding of what is heard and grants the listener full partnership in the communication process."[2]

We sometimes listen only to formulate our own argument. (Courtesy of Brad Markel/ Gamma-Liaison, Inc.)

What can you do to improve your listening skills? A good starting point would be to recognize the two major types of listening and some good listening habits to adopt.

Two Major Forms of Listening: Support and Retention Listening

Support Listening

Support listening consists of hearing and remembering what others say with a minimum of emotion or observable reaction. The idea is to focus on listening to another so as to learn what that person thinks and feels. Avoid speaking except to encourage or cause the other person to speak.

Support listening consists of three responses.

- Open question
- "Uh-huh" technique
- Content reflection

Support listening puts the responsibility for continuing the conversation on the other person.

An open question cannot be answered with a simple yes or no statement. The **"uh-huh"** technique is the simplest kind of oral response and consists of saying "uh-huh" or "hmmm" as the other person talks. Content reflection involves repeating, mirroring, or echoing the content of a statement made by another person in the form of a question. Each reaction is designed to cause the speaker to keep speaking and the listener to keep listening.

Support listening places the responsibility for continuing a conversation, dialogue, or interview on the other person. If you ask the question, "What do you think about our firm?" and then look intently and inquiringly at the person to whom you addressed the question, the responsibility for continuing the dialogue is placed firmly on the other person. The commitment is equally strong when you simply say "uh-huh" or "hmmm" when the other person makes a comment. The effect is essentially the same when you echo the idea just stated. Support listening establishes that you want the other person to either begin or continue talking. When you respond this way, you create an expectation that can be fulfilled only when the other person talks and when you listen.

Each skill of support listening encourages the other to talk. The following dialogue illustrates support listening:

Rita: Doris, how do you feel about the department? (Open question)

Doris: Working in this department is extremely difficult.

Rita: Uh-huh. ("Uh-huh")

Doris: What I mean is that I have problems getting along with Dan.

Rita: Hmmm. ("Uh-huh")

Doris: He just can't accept the fact that I'm his boss.

Rita: Dan can't accept you as his boss? (Content reflection)

Doris: That right! He's always making snide comments about women bosses.

Rita: What kinds of things does he say? (Open question)

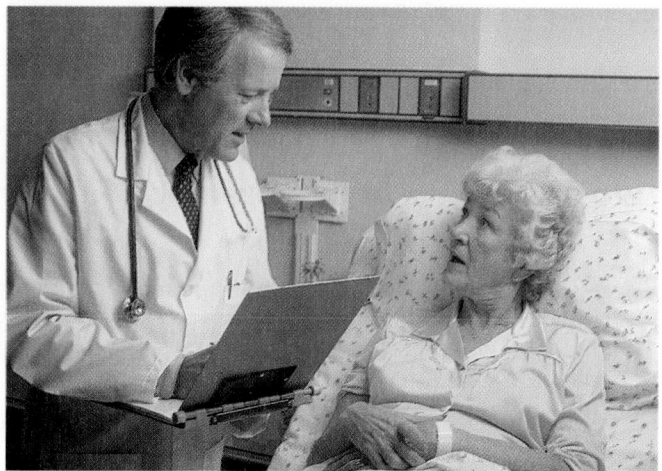

Support listening is grounded in positive reinforcement. (Courtesy of Hemley & Savage/ Uniphoto Picture Agency.)

Support listening is grounded in the theory of positive reinforcement. People like to talk to others who support them, or at least do not deny or reject them. Psychological theory suggests that if you react or respond in a supportive manner to something the other person said, he or she will feel that the comments have been accepted and will continue to talk. If you begin talking and get positive reactions in return, you will tend to continue talking. Each support listening skill provides positive reinforcement by indicating that you have an interest in what is being said and care enough to listen.

Although each type of response can be used individually and independently, the techniques of support listening are most effective when they are used together. The open question is often used to start the conversation, after which a content reflection or an "uh-huh" response is given. Thereafter, as the conversation runs through a sequence of interactions involving reflections and "uh-huh" responses, another open question can be asked.

Begin the conversation or interview with an open question.

Arlene: **How have you been getting along with George?**

Then look at the other person and lean slightly toward him or her. Indicate that you are listening by nodding your head occasionally as the other talks. Vocalize your support by giving an "uh-huh" response:

Sally: **I really appreciate all that he does for me.**

Arlene: **Uh-huh.**

Sally: **He really seems to care about me.**

Arlene: **Uh-huh.**

The "uh-huh" response provides support and indicates that you are following the conversation.

Or you might want to secure information about a topic. In that case, content reflection and additional open questions are appropriate.

Skills and techniques of effective interpersonal communication work only if you care about the other person.

Sally: I simply can't stand this place any longer.

Arlene: You can't stand being here any longer?

Sally: You said it! If I have to work with George any longer, I'm going to go out of my mind.

Arlene: Well, how do you feel about George as a manager?

Support listening is a basic technique that shows support and encourages the other person to continue talking. Support listening is essentially nonevaluative—it avoids expressing approval or disapproval—and requires careful hearing of the other. How well support listening works depends on the sincere interest of the user. If the listener is not sincerely interested in what the speaker has to say, then the technique is merely a gimmick. In those instances, the speaker usually recognizes what is happening, refuses to cooperate, and focuses on the technique rather than on communicating. Remember that the combination of facial expressions, tone of voice, and body language plays a vital role in support listening.

Good listeners invite people to talk by commenting on their body language. Shy people may need encouragement to talk to you, particularly when they are unsure if you'd be interested in what they have to say. You can convey to them that you are ready and available to listen by commenting on their nonverbal cues. "You look puzzled"; "You look happy, what's up?"; or "You look down a lot. Are you discouraged about something?" The person may not take your cue, but he or she has had an open invitation to respond with meaningful conversation.[3]

Retention Listening

In an interview with *U.S. News & World Report,* Lyman K. Steil makes the following points about **retention listening:**[4]

1. Because of the listening mistakes of workers (and most make several mistakes each week), letters have to be retyped, appointments rescheduled, and shipments rerouted. Productivity and profits decline.

2. A simple $10 mistake by each of the 100 million workers in America would add up to a cost of $1 billion.

3. "Good" or effective listening is more than merely "hearing." Effective listening involves
   a. Hearing.
   b. Interpreting (which leads to understanding or misunderstanding).
   c. Evaluating (weighing the information and deciding how to use it).
   d. Responding (based on what we heard, understood, and evaluated).

4. When all four stages (hearing, interpreting, evaluating, and responding) are considered, people on average listen at an effective rate of 25 percent.

5. The ability to listen is not an inherent trait; it is learned behavior that has to be taught. Unlike reading, writing, speaking, and many other subjects, however, it is not systematically taught in our schools.

6. People have not been taught to listen well. They spend 80 percent of their waking hours communicating and 45 percent of their communication time listening (with speaking, reading, and writing taking up the other 55 percent).

7. Listening is more complex than reading. If we misread something or are distracted, we can go back and read it again. But listening is transient: "The message is written on the wind. If we don't get it the first time, there usually is no going back."

8. According to a recent study, managers rate listening as the most important competency among the abilities they considered critical for their managerial success. "The higher one advances in management, the more critical listening ability and skill become." Most problems in business arise because management fails to listen.

9. Most people recognize the lack of listening skills in others but consider themselves good listeners. Listening exercises usually demonstrate that people are not as good at listening as they thought they were before the exercise.

Steil makes eight points that he thinks are important for anyone to operate effectively as a retentive listener.[5]

Active listening requires effort.

1. *Resist distractions.* This point emphasizes the importance of concentration. Force yourself to keep your mind on what is being said.

2. *Be an opportunist.* Do your best to find areas of interest between you and the speaker. Ask yourself, "What's in it for me? What can I get out of what is being said?"

3. *Stay alert.* It is easy to daydream if the speaker is a bit boring. Force yourself to stay alert, even if the speaker is slow and boring. If your thoughts run ahead of the speaker, use the extra time to evaluate, anticipate, and review.

4. *Identify the speaker's purpose and adapt to it.* What is the speaker trying to do? Is the speaker informing, persuading, or entertaining? Whatever the speaker's purpose, identify and adjust to it.

5. *Listen for central themes rather than for isolated facts.* Too often people get hopelessly lost as listeners because they focus in on unimportant facts and details, and miss the speaker's main point.

6. *Plan to report the content of a message to someone within eight hours.* This forces the listener to concentrate and remember. It is a good practice technique.

7. *Develop note-taking skills.* There are many approaches to note taking. Whichever approach you use, the simple process of writing things down as you hear them helps you retain what you hear, even if you do not read the notes later.

8. *As a listener, take primary responsibility for the success of two-way communication.* Don't blame the other person for your listening inadequacies. Listening is your responsibility, not the speaker's.

The effective communicator can listen both supportively and retentively. Be aware of both types of listening, and practice the skills presented in this chapter.

Some Poor Listening Habits to Avoid

Most people didn't become poor listeners overnight; they learned how to be a poor listener over a period. Here are four habits that most people resort to, even though they do no good.

Faking Attention

Faking attention is an attempt to be polite to someone during a conversation and results in what someone called the "wide asleep listener." This is usually accomplished by looking directly at the speaker when you are really thinking about something else, automatically nodding responses, or even saying "yes" and "uh-huh" to conversations you have mentally tuned out. When you have agreed to listen to someone, commit yourself to expending the needed effort to listen and give that conversation your active attention.

Changing Channels

A second habit to avoid is changing channels in the middle of a presentation or conversation. When something appears to be too dull, difficult to comprehend, or time-consuming, the poor listener will tune out. Because you know there is plenty of thinking time between the speaker's thoughts, you think switching back and forth between several conversations without losing any information is possible. This assumption is often incorrect, however.

Listening for Only the Facts

Another habit to avoid is listening for only the facts. Much of what people communicate is feelings, impressions, and emotions; factual messages are often wrapped up in these. For example, a student came to her instructor's office, and in the course of the conversation she appeared upset about something. When she explained to the professor that her husband had just been terminated from his job, the instructor expressed what he thought was appropriate concern and soon changed the subject. Shortly after, the student abruptly left the office, apparently angry with the instructor. He had listened to the facts of what she'd said but completely missed her meaning.

From the instructor's perspective, these were the facts.

1. Her husband was a capable young man who was unhappy with his present employer and had been looking around for another company.
2. This couple was young, and had no children and few financial burdens.
3. Her husband had recently been offered another comparable position, which he turned down because it paid about the same as he was now making.
4. Her husband had just lost his job.

Sometimes you need to listen to what people are *not* saying.

In his listening process, the instructor associated the new fact (point 4) with facts he already knew (points 1 to 3) and concluded that there was no real serious problem. The husband would find a new and probably better job soon.

So why did the student storm out of the office? The instructor had listened for only the facts while the student wanted to talk about feelings and concerns she had. She wanted him to listen to what she was *not* saying. What she needed was someone to share these thoughts with, and perhaps get some comfort from. Many messages convey emotion as well as information. Listening for only the facts is often not enough.

Interrupting

Don't let requests for clarification sound like interrogation. Let the speaker finish before asking questions.

One more bad habit is interrupting a speaker before he or she has finished expressing an idea. Interrupting in the middle of the message can disrupt both speaker and listener. It sounds like an interrogation. Hold back on frequent use of questions like "What do you mean?" and "Why do you say that?" until you are sure the speaker is finished. Then if you need clarification, ask for it.

Some Positive Steps to Better Listening

Avoiding poor listening habits is only part of the process of becoming a good listener. You also need to take some positive steps to improve your listening effectiveness. Among these are the following.

Solicit Clarification

When a message is unclear, it is important that you let the sender know it. People who hesitate to ask for clarification usually do so because

- They are afraid to appear ignorant.
- They think they can figure the message out on their own—eventually.
- They don't want to take the time or expend the effort to make sure they understand.

Asking for clarification shows interest and willingness to risk appearing uninformed for the sake of understanding.

By failing to ask for clarification from the sender, you force yourself to rely too heavily on your own guesses for help in interpreting messages. When you ask questions about the meanings of a message, any implication that you lack knowledge will be more than made up for by your sincere desire to understand. This is flattering to others. It conveys a regard for people who speak to you. When you solicit clarification, ask open-ended questions.

Minimize the Number of Gatekeepers

As noted earlier, gatekeepers result in our listening to someone else's version of the message. Whenever possible, avoid sending an intermediary to get the story from the source and then reporting back to you. Avoid requesting that someone tell their story to your secretary or administrative assistant and then let that person synthesize the information for you. Avoid channeling through someone else something that will eventually end up in your office.

You can force yourself to listen from another's viewpoint.

You'll notice that the preface of this recommendation is "whenever possible." No professional can listen to everything everyone wants to say. To reduce the probability of information overload, you need to develop a clear policy on what information needs your direct personal attention and what can be satisfactorily handled by others in the organization.

Try Counterattitudinal Advocacy

Counterattitudinal advocacy (CAA) is a big term for a simple process. It means to take the other person's position—to advocate or express a viewpoint that runs counter to your own attitude. The objective of CAA is to reduce the degree to which a listener listens through his or her own biases. CAA forces the listener to listen objectively and understand rather than to listen only until a response is cued.

Here is how CAA works: You, as a listener, simply make a commitment to *restate* and *defend* the position that is "counter to your attitude," that is, opposite to your position. You can implement this by honestly trying to restate to others exactly what you hear them expressing. This includes both the facts and the emotions you think are being conveyed. Use your own words to express the idea you hear the other person saying. Then ask if your interpretation is accurate. If not, restate it again until agreement is reached. What happens is that by committing yourself to restate and defend someone else's position, you must listen more effectively to that position to understand what you are defending.

There are additional implications that can be especially useful in conflict management. By defending a position counter to your own, you force yourself to consider information that you avoided when advancing your own position. You have forced

10 Keys to Effective Listening[6]

10 Keys to Effective Listening	The Bad Listener	The Good Listener
1. Find area of interest	Tunes out dry subjects	Opportunizes, asks "what's in it for me?"
2. Judge content, not delivery	Tunes out if delivery is poor	Judges content, skips over delivery errors
3. Hold your fire	Tends to enter into argument	Doesn't judge until comprehension is complete
4. Listen for ideas	Listen for facts	Listens for central themes
5. Be flexible	Takes intensive notes using only one system	Takes fewer notes. Uses 4–5 different systems, depending on speaker
6. Work at listening	Shows no energy output. Attention is faked	Works hard, exhibits active body state
7. Resist distractions	Distracted easily	Fights or avoids distractions. Tolerates bad habits, knows how to concentrate
8. Exercise your mind	Resists difficult expository material; seeks light, recreational material	Uses heavier material as exercise for the mind
9. Keep your mind open	Reacts to emotional words	Interprets color words; does not get hung up on them
10. Capitalize on fact that *thought* is *faster* than speech	Tends to daydream with slow speakers	Challenges, anticipates, mentally summarizes, weighs the evidence, listens between the lines to tone of voice

yourself to listen to ideas through someone else's biases. The end result is a better understanding of the entire situation rather than just *your* position.

This process does not obligate you to cave in to the views of others when you honestly disagree. It simply provides one way of better understanding where those you disagree with "are coming from." In some cases, disagreements evaporate when you clarify each other's position. You recognize that you don't really disagree in principle; you are simply expressing similar ideas in different or confusing ways.

Other Tips for Effective Listening

You can do many different things to improve your listening skills. Here are some additional tips.

- Remember that your listeners may not process information in the same way you do. Different people have different learning styles.
- Take notes. Writing down major ideas and important facts may help you to listen and remember more effectively. However, it's important for you to be selective. Don't try to write down everything.
- Show your interest. It is discourteous to fidget or look bored. If you have committed to listen to the speaker, then give your full attention and show that you're listening.

Motivation to Listen Better

Most thoughtful business people recognize the need for careful listening. They spend more time in listening than any other communication activity. Listening is crucial to customer satisfaction, which, in turn, is critical to professional success. John Wade, a media consultant, says: "At first contact with an individual, I spend a good deal of time just listening, gathering information, picking up clues about self-perception and self-esteem before I ever give advice."

How do you motivate others to listen? A cartoon suggested one way. It showed the boss talking to employees at a meeting saying: "Now pay careful attention. I'll let you know at the end of the meeting who will write up the minutes." When everyone in the organization begins to listen as though they were going to have to write up the minutes, understanding will advance by a quantum leap. Listening improvement starts at home with yourself.

A common theme throughout this book is the need to create understanding via a circular process of communicating and receiving feedback so that the next message can be better than the first. Listening is the way we do this in everyday life.

Understanding the Basics

SUMMARY OF KEY IDEAS

- Hearing differs from listening in that hearing is a purely physiological activity, whereas listening also involves the psychological processing of sounds.

- The following three types of factors complicate the listening process and pose potential barriers.

  Internal elements within the listener's mind.

  Environmental elements surrounding the communication.

  Interactional elements that arise especially from listener self-centeredness and self-protection.

- Communication problems can arise from information overload or from underuse of our listening capacity.

- Interactional elements of the listening process encompass the problems of self-centeredness and self-protection.

- A good listener adopts two types of listening: support and retention.

- To be a better listener, avoid poor listening behaviors like the following:

Faking attention.

Changing channels.

Listening for only the facts.

Responding in a way that turns people off.

Showing impatience.

Overusing gatekeepers.

• To improve listening effectiveness, use the following behaviors (in addition to avoiding those listed as potential barriers):

Solicit clarification.

Use CAA.

Minimize the number of gatekeepers.

KEY TERMS AND CONCEPTS

support listening

"uh-huh" technique

environmental elements

self-protection

retention listening

hearing versus listening

internal elements

listening capacity

noise

gatekeepers

self-centeredness

counterattitudinal advocacy

QUESTIONS FOR FURTHER THOUGHT

1. How do hearing and listening differ?

2. What is meant by the "cocktail party effect"?

3. What are the three major elements that complicate listening? Give examples of each.

4. What happens when people experience communication overload?

5. What do environmental and internal "noise" mean?

6. How do "gatekeepers" complicate the listening process?

7. What are self-centeredness and self-protection as they relate to listening?

8. What is CAA, and how can it be used to clarify understanding?

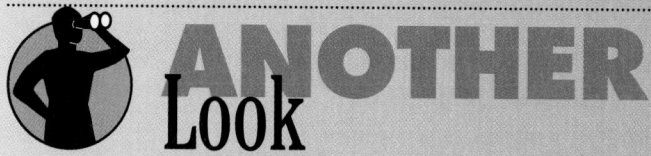

The Costs of Lazy Listening

1. A sales manager for a large company asked his accounting department how he could charge off a hundred-thousand-dollar error caused by a dispatcher who routed a fleet of drivers to deliver building material to the wrong state. The dispatcher heard the city (Portland) but not the state (Maine). The result was eight trucks three-thousand miles off course in Portland, Oregon. . . .

2. Three computer sales representatives from different companies presented their products to a historian who had special application needs. The historian was a dealer in rare manu-scripts and explained to each sales representative what computer functions were required. Two of the sales representatives did not listen and presented products that were inappropriate. The third understood what the historian wanted, and she got the order. The manuscript dealer was impressed with only one thing, and it wasn't the hardware, because he didn't know much about computers. He did know that two people didn't listen and the third did. He bought his computer from the person who listened. . . .

3. Linda recently cut short a business trip to attend an important invest-ment dinner meeting with her husband. She hurried from the airport, dressed for dinner, and met her husband at the restaurant. An hour and a half later, their financial advisor had not arrived. A phone call deducted they were at the right restaurant but on the wrong night. The dinner was rescheduled, but Linda sacrificed profitable business she would have closed had she kept her original trip schedule.

(True stories excerpted from Diane Bone, *The Business of Listening* [Menlo Park, CA: Crisp Publications, 1988], p. 5.)

Applying Your Knowledge

1. How could the sales manager, sales representatives, and Linda have avoided the communication failures?
2. What could the customer in the second example do to improve the likelihood of being listened to?
3. How could the problems have been avoided in each case?

Applying Your Skills

ACTIVITY 16-1: Listening Intentions

This chapter discusses various aspects of the listening process. An excellent place for self-evaluation is the listening habits Communicator's Inventory on page 457; please complete it if you have not already done so. Another aspect of listening are your "listening in-tentions." Can you be focused on the speaker to come to a common understanding? Is listening some-thing you can intend to do? Intention is defined as a determination to act in a certain way. List some benefits of intending to listen to others in the follow-ing situations:

- Conversation with a friend:
- Task discussion with a coworker:
- Attending a meeting of some sort:
- Making a car purchase (or other major purchase):

Remember, your intentions create how you behave. You can intend to be good listeners as a starting point for better listening skill.

ACTIVITY 16-2: Listening Examples

From your responses to the Communicator's Inven-tory you completed on page 457, give an actual example of your behavior for each of the ten statements listed in that exercise. This will give you some ideas as to how your intended behavior matches actual behavior.

ACTIVITY 16-3: Listening History

Think back over your life time. Ponder the lessons of listening you have had. Where did you learn to listen? From whom? Where were you? To whom did you listen and why? Here are some guides to help you ponder you listening history.

- Parent/guardian:
- Grandparents/uncles/aunts:
- Friends/playmates:
- Other adults:
- Teachers:
- Public speakers:
- Celebrities:
- Other role models:
- Formal education/classes:

Consider the good and the bad habits you have experienced. You can learn from both and realize where some of your thoughts and habits of listening originated. Attempt to incorporate the positive experiences in your listening behavior.

ACTIVITY 16-4: Listening Elements

For each of the three elements, which many times complicate the listening process, give an example in your experience.

- Internal elements (attaching meaning to words or sounds):
- Environmental elements (capacity, noise, and gatekeeping):
- Interactional elements (self-centeredness and self-protection):

ACTIVITY 16-5: Whole Body Listening

Good listeners give both nonverbal and verbal signs that they are listening. Check the whole-body listening characteristics you include in your listening behavior.

	Yes	No
• Conveying a positive encouraging attitude	☐	☐
• Using attentive posture	☐	☐
• Being alert but comfortable	☐	☐
• Nodding to acknowledge the speaker	☐	☐
• Maintaining good eye contact	☐	☐
• Listening for feelings	☐	☐
• Using the appearance of a listener	☐	☐
• Ignoring distractions	☐	☐

If you checked "No" to some items, consider why you don't feel comfortable using these behaviors. Could you acquire them with practice? Remember, how you look and act as listeners determines your listening style.

ACTIVITY 16-6: Noise Factors

Noise refers to any element that is irrelevant to the conversation or presentation. List the types of noise you experience most often in situations in which you need to practice active listening. Categorize these types of noise as external or internal.

List how you can cope with these distractions or what you can do to avoid them.

ACTIVITY 16-7: Listening Similarities

Define the following terms as they relate to listening behavior:

- Self-centeredness:
- Self-protection:
- Gatekeeping:

Discuss any similarities between these three aspects of listening.

ACTIVITY 16-8: Open-Ended Questions

Practice formulating open-ended questions by changing the following yes/no questions to open-ended questions.

- Do you feel okay?
- Do you like the new supervisor?
- Have you been here before?
- Have you taken a class from Professor Hansen?
- Did you understand what I just said?

PERFORMING
on the Job

CASE 16-1 No One Listened to Bill

Bill started working for First State Bank (FSB) six months ago. He had several years experience in the financial services industry before joining FSB. Because of FSB's stable work force, Bill started in an entry-level teller position with intentions of moving into a loan position as soon as he could. That opportunity came within three months when Bill transferred to another branch of FSB as a loan processor. He was the only man in a five-person department supervised by Connie Larkin. Bill seemed enthusiastic about his new position and was eager to make recommendations to his supervisor and bank management based on his previous experience with various forms of credit.

After making several recommendations, Bill became upset that no changes seemed to be occurring. He expressed his frustration to coworkers and customers that his suggestions and recommendations were not being listened to. In an effort to be heard, he sent an emotion-filled letter to each of the board of directors of FSB. The letter questioned management's ability to lead, decisions that had been made, and the organization's possibility for continued success because it was so "mickey mouse." At the next board of director's meeting, Bill's letter was high on the list to be discussed. Two directors thought Bill should be terminated, but most of the directors believed more information would be helpful to know why Bill felt so strongly. The board requested the CEO to meet personally with Bill and listen face to face to clarify the validity of his statements. That meeting occurred with the CEO, Bill, and a representative from Human Resources. Information was shared, and questions were addressed. Both sides realized better organizational communications would be necessary in the future. Bill resigned two weeks later.

Case Questions

1. Did Bill's letter do him any good?
2. Did Bill's letter encourage others to listen to him?
3. As CEO, how would you feel going into the meeting with Bill? What would be your listening strategy?
4. Why do you think Bill felt he was not being heard?
5. Should Bill have been terminated without a meeting with the CEO? Why?

CASE 16-2 The Roof Is Leaking

The following conversation occurred between the owner of MicroWorld and the manager of the building where MicroWorld was leasing office and storage space.

> Something is terribly wrong with the roof. Water is leaking in our storage area right above our new stock. We were able to cover our storage racks with tarps yesterday and last night. We're expecting a large delivery of computer parts tomorrow. I have no other storage facility and I can't

have these parts getting wet because we need them to finish a pending project that is critical to our long term success. This problem with the roof must be taken care of *immediately!*

The manager said the following to the owner: "I'll send a maintenance technician to your office to assess the problem, and then we'll contact the roofer who issued the warranty on the roof *right away."* After hanging up the telephone, the manager began thinking, "Stan is working on another call right now, and he has two more lined up. I can't pull him off those jobs, and we're really shorthanded this afternoon. The only other maintenance technician on duty is Grant, and he's working on an air-conditioning unit. I'll write a service request. Maybe Grant can take a look at the roof later this afternoon. In any case, I'll make sure that either Stan or Grant handles the problem first thing in the morning."

Case Questions

1. Do you think the owner feels the manager listened to him and understood his concern?

2. Did the manager really understand the owner's concern that the roof be fixed immediately?

3. What do you think the owner understood when the manager told him he would contact the roofer right away?

4. Should the manager call the owner back and explain his situation? Why? Why not?

CHAPTER SEVENTEEN

Preparation
of the Presentation

Briefings and Oral Presentations

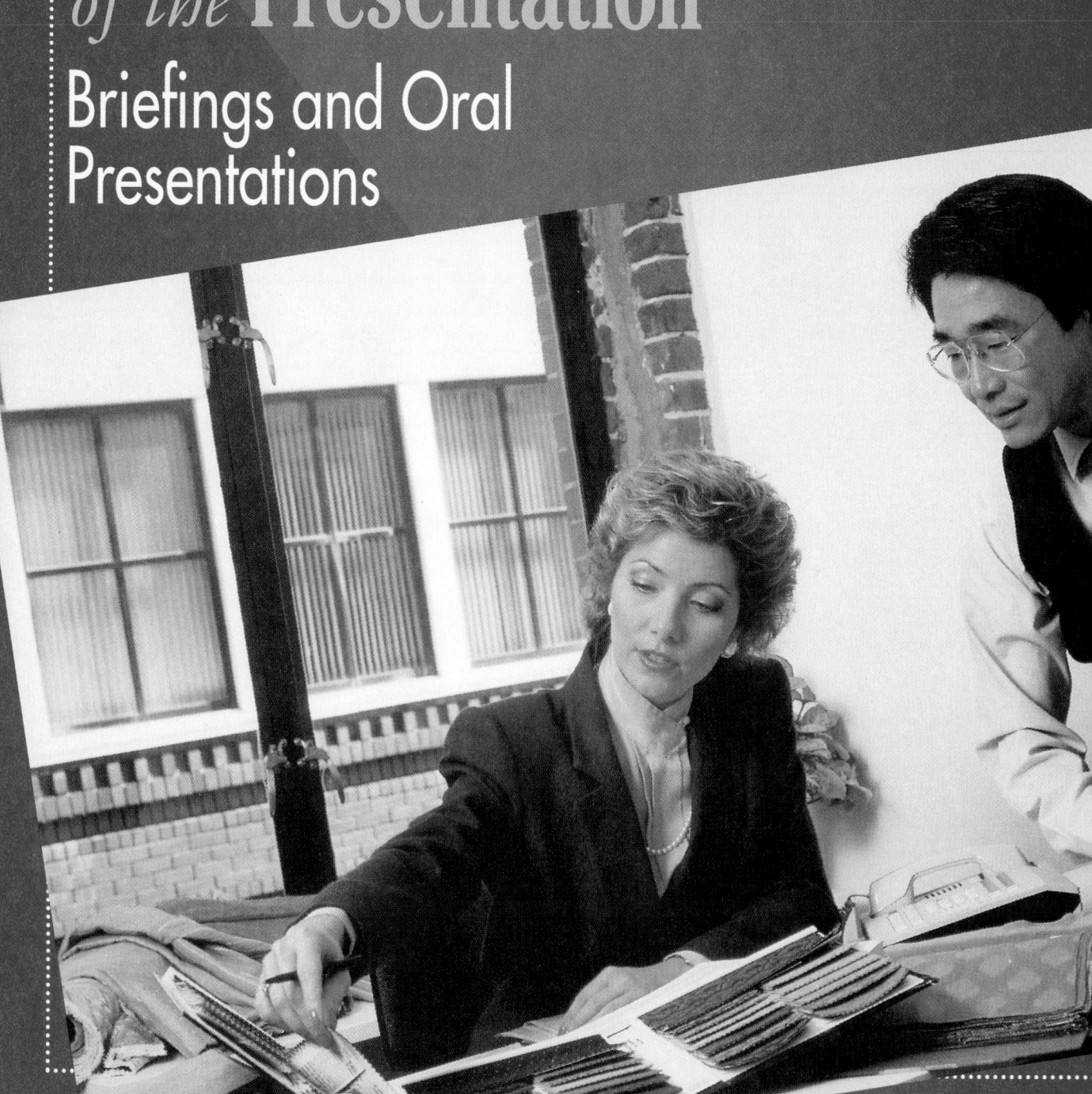

LEARNING GOALS

After you have studied this chapter, you should be able to:

- Identify and distinguish among four types of briefings commonly used in organizations.

- Anticipate the kinds of questions your listeners are likely to ask and conduct a systematic listener analysis.

- Recognize and use listener expectations to improve the clarity of your presentation.

- Plan the contents of a briefing by identifying and supporting main ideas, developing an effective introduction, organizing key points for maximum impact, conveying credibility, and presenting an effective conclusion.

The Way It Is . . . Here are Some Great Ideas

"I have a whole bunch of great ideas for our new business," said Terry enthusiastically. "My mind is swimming with the possibilities. Let's see, where should I begin?"

"I really appreciate your excitement, Terry. That is why we wanted to bring you on board. Marcus and I are not as creative as you are. We are good at administering the company but really need your fresh thoughts," responded Marilyn. "Let's schedule a time on Monday morning when you can give us your game plan."

"That will be great," said Terry. "I will spend the weekend organizing some thoughts. There are so many possible directions we can go. Let me sort them out and recommend a course of action."

"Sounds great. We will schedule the conference room for an hour on Monday at 9:00 A.M."

That weekend, Terry did "swim" in thoughts. She quickly realized that she had more ideas than Marcus and Marilyn could possibly digest in one presentation. The challenge she faced was how to extract the best ideas and present them clearly.

In another office, the telephone rings. It's Sean's boss asking him to "take a few minutes at Friday's staff meeting to bring everyone up to date on the program to convert the office's telecommunication system." Just as he ponders how he'll do this, one of the newer clerks comes to his office door. "I'm having a difficult time figuring out this filing system, Sean. Where do we keep the completed orders? How can I tell if an order is completed or pending? Everybody seems to be doing things a different way. I'm confused, boss." Then there's the six-page document that arrived in this morning's mail from the corporate benefits office. "Please be sure that all affected employees understand these benefit changes," it says.

Another typical day for two business communicators.

Business professionals are often asked to present proposals, explain new products, and give progress reports. Often, the best medium for conveying such information is the oral presentation. The thought of giving a talk in front of others has a way of unraveling even the most self-confident individual. Surveys have indicated that of all things people fear, giving a public speech is at the top of the list. Comedian George Jessel once said, "The human brain is a wonderful organ. It starts to work as soon as you are born and doesn't stop until you get up to deliver a speech."

Although briefings are somewhat different from public speeches, they can sometimes be anxiety producing. This chapter discusses tips for preparing an effective oral presentation. Chapter Eighteen focuses on the delivery of that presentation.

Many people hold a deep fear of speaking before a group.

The Purpose of Typical Business Presentations

Effective presentations and briefings provide people with digestible *information*. Information is the oxygen of a working organization; it reduces uncertainty and clarifies scope, purposes, and direction for workers. In other words, *business presentations answer questions.* The following four types of presentations are commonly used in organizations:

1. Persuasive
2. Explanatory
3. Instructional
4. Progressive

An element of *persuasion*—getting agreement or action from the audience—is present in any briefing, but the first type focuses on this extensively. An attempt to sell your colleagues or boss on an idea for accomplishing a goal, a different method of handling a process, or the need for a different work schedule are types of persuasive briefings. The key feature of a persuasive briefing is that it attempts to get others to "buy" an idea, plan, or recommendation. "Buying" generally involves more than simply agreeing with what you say. It means getting some desired *action* from your listeners. The success of your briefing will be readily observable by how much of the desired action actually occurs.

In *explanatory* or *instructional* briefings, you are not trying to sell anything but are providing opportunities for the listener to gain knowledge, understanding, or skills. *Explanatory* briefings generally present a "big picture" overview, such as orienting new employees to the company, acquainting staff members with what is involved in opening a new branch or division in the company, or showing how each function of the organization fits in with the others. *Instructional* briefings get more specific. They teach others how to do or use something, such as a new machine, pro-

Persuasive presentations seek specific action from listeners. What do you want them to *do*?

Instructional presentations should include testing for listener learning.

Business presentations answer questions. (Courtesy of Tim Brown/Tony Stone Images.)

cedure, or paperwork system. This usually involves more audience involvement, such as testing for knowledge gained.

The *progress report* brings audience members up to date on some project with which they are already familiar. Examples of this may be reports on a research project, development of a new product, or the process of checking your success against objectives or goals.

Regardless of the type of presentation, an important starting point in preparing the talk is to consider your audience carefully. Make educated guesses about how listeners are likely to react to your message before you even begin the briefing. Here are some ideas on listener analysis.[1]

Listener Analysis: A Starting Point

Listener analysis is the process of putting yourself in the listeners' shoes. Before preparing an oral presentation, list all possible questions your talk might provoke in the minds of your listeners. Don't just ask the obvious ones; dig a little to anticipate what else might be on the minds of your listeners. A talk that fails to address relevant listener concerns falls flat. Having all the answers, but to the wrong questions, doesn't help.

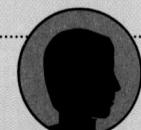

COMMUNICATOR'S PROFILE

Errol A. Griffin, Executive Vice President, Orange County Federal Credit Union

When asked what communication processes have been especially successful in his organization, Errol Griffin didn't hesitate to say "I strongly believe in the old adage, 'If it is worth saying once, it's worth saying again!' " While the concept of repetition may seem inefficient or unnecessary to some people, it is effective. Errol believes in "repeating organizational philosophy; spreading good, bad, and insignificant news; and encouraging others to repeat and summarize. This allows for a demonstration of a clear understanding on behalf of the speaker and the listeners and is very effective for successful communications. LET ME REPEAT!"

Errol goes on to say that really successful communicators "know the predispositions, needs, joys, and fears of their audience. Communicating is like dating," he says. "A blind date may be successful, but it's much more of a challenge. Doing your homework and knowing your subject matter is a must. Applying the same due diligence to knowing who you are addressing is just as important.

"It is difficult to arrive at a common ground for a multileveled audience, but it is possible to make sure that your communication *to* a large group is also *with* the individuals that comprise the group." Audience analysis helps you do this.

Discover Your Listeners Before Communicating with Them

Listener analysis is crucial to communication effectiveness.

The more you know about your listeners, the better your chances are of being effective. The most serious mistake any communicator can make is to fail to understand his or her audience. By making some careful judgments or guesses about the people you talk to, you can adjust your message to hit them where they live.

Listener analysis means making guesses based on as much information as you can reasonably gather. From these guesses you can determine how best to formulate your message for maximum impact. The process is not mysterious; you make guesses about others' behaviors every day. When you walk down a busy street, you guess that others will go to one side of the sidewalk or the other. You also may anticipate the possibility that the person walking in front of you may suddenly stop to look in a shop window.

More to the point, when you convey a message to someone, you picture mentally how that person is likely to react. When you inform your spouse that mother is coming to visit for a month or that the kitchen sink is clogged up again, you can predict fairly well the kind of reaction you will get. Professionally, you also learn to predict responses. The orthodontist learns to anticipate the response to the announcement that Sandra needs $4,000 worth of braces. Sales representatives anticipate buyer objections ("It'll only get 16 miles to the gallon") and deliver carefully prepared responses ("But with its larger gas tank, the Speedfire V-8 can go more than 500 miles between fill-ups!"). Listener analysis and the prediction of responses are normal and natural activities for people in all walks of life.

After Anticipating the Listeners' Questions, Ask Yourself a Few

The ancient philosopher Seneca said, "Our plans miscarry because they have no aim. When a man does not know what harbor he is making for, no wind is the right wind." If you don't know where you are going with an oral presentation, you'll never know whether or not you've succeeded.

Once you've anticipated your listeners' likely questions, ask yourself these questions as you plan your oral presentation.

- What exactly do you hope to accomplish?
- How will your listeners respond after you finish?
- What specific actions would you like to see from your listeners?

How to Predict Listener Responses More Accurately

Listener analysis helps you to better predict audience responses.

You can learn to predict listener responses by carefully considering the following:

1. Your own experiences with situations or topics similar to the one you will be speaking about
2. Your understanding of the actions, thoughts, values, and emotions of your listeners, or other people who are similar to your listeners

Because each communication situation and each person is unique, you cannot predict with 100 percent accuracy. You can improve the prediction of likely responses with careful listener analysis.

Weston Cook of Salomom Brothers Investment Bank says: "By "priming the pump" (having one-on-one conversations) before a more formal presentation, a person can make allies to an idea or proposal or at least help bring to light any significant time bombs that may need to be addressed."

Listener analysis is a *questioning* process. The answers aren't always clear, but the process is essential to effective communication. Chapter Five describes four approaches to audience analysis—whether that audience is receiving written or spoken messages. To review this material, see pages 116–122.

Planning of the Content of Your Talk: Identifying Main Ideas

Once your purpose is clear and your listeners have been analyzed, you need to sort out the main ideas of your presentation. Main ideas are the concepts that your listeners must understand for your talk to succeed. These ideas should be stated in the form of conclusions you want your listeners to reach. For example, your main ideas that support the thesis, "We need to hire a plant safety inspector," may be the following:

1. It is essential that the company get the expertise needed to cope with its increasing accident rate and more frequent government inspections.
2. The costs of hiring a safety expert would be offset by reduced lost-time injuries and avoidance of government penalties.
3. This company cares about its employees' well-being and is committed to creating a safe and pleasant place to work.
4. A search committee must be appointed to find a qualified safety inspector.

For some presentations, there is only one main idea that will be approached from several directions. A progress report may simply stress that "We are on target" or "We will meet our objectives despite certain temporary setbacks."

When developing these **key ideas (main points)** or concepts—those the audience *must* understand if you are to be successful—be sure to

1. State the key ideas as conclusions, preferably in complete sentences.
2. Be sure each idea leads to a specific objective, such as securing agreement, convincing, or gaining a desired action. (In the preceding example, the first three ideas aim at getting agreement or inducing belief. The fourth seeks action.)
3. Express ideas in thought-provoking ways.
4. Use only a few main ideas. Three is an ideal number; listeners can't remember more than five.

Because you are still in a planning stage at this point, don't be overly concerned with the supporting details of the talk. Do be sure that you have focused on main ideas. The main ideas of the "safety inspector" briefing just mentioned might be identified like the following:

1. Company records showing increased accident rate and increased number of government inspections
2. Estimate of cost of employing a safety inspector
3. Amount of fines levied by government inspectors in similar industries
4. Description of company policy and programs that indicate high concern for employees' well-being

Using a preliminary plan as a guide will help focus your energy toward the goal of your presentation. It also helps reduce wasted time and results in a more cohesive briefing.

Once your preplanning is complete, it is time to assemble the contents of your briefing. The three major parts of the presentation are the introduction, body, and conclusion. Transitions tie each of these together.

Presentations have three major parts: introduction, body, and conclusion.

If your introduction fails to gain sufficient attention and interest, your message will not be received. Typically, audiences are alert as a speaker begins to talk. Their attention span curves downward as the presentation goes on and then perks up as the speaker gives his or her concluding remarks. If your conclusion is not effective, audience retention of what has been said suffers. For these reasons, special emphasis should be placed on preparing strong introductions and conclusions.

Introductions: Gaining Attention and Interest

The introduction that just gets attention does only part of the job. You can get attention by pounding on the desk, tapping a water glass with a spoon, shouting obscenities, or telling a joke. Yet none of these devices does what an introduction should do. An effective introduction creates appropriate expectations in the minds of your listeners. It prepares them to receive your message.

Sometimes a simple statement of the topic is sufficient. Sometimes the presenter would be wise to use techniques of the public speaker to grab the audience members' attention and get their minds on what will be covered. Among the techniques effectively used by speakers are the **startling statement** or statistic, the **rhetorical question,** a quotation, a definition, a short narrative, or **audience participation.**

Startling Statement or Statistic

"The river behind our assembly plant has been declared a fire hazard." "By the year 2000—fewer than five years from now—we will run out of the primary materials we use to manufacture our products." These kinds of straightforward statements can get your listeners' attention if they are interestingly worded and not too complicated. The natural reaction is to perk up and mentally ask for more information.

Likewise, statistics can often be worded in ways that grab our attention. "Today more than 64 percent of our female employees use day care facilities for their children at a cost of more than $90,000 per year." "Today, on May 10, you begin working for yourself and your family. Since the first of the year, you've been working to pay your taxes." Statistics can be expressed in many ways to make them sound smaller ("only 93 cents per day") or larger ("over its contract life the service will cost $75,000"). Your wording depends on your intent.

Rhetorical Question

This is the use of thought-provoking questions for which you don't expect an answer. "Just how much more government interference can our company take?" "How would you feel if you were turned down for a promotion because you had a physical handicap?" Sometimes a whole series of these is effective.

- What will you do when there is no gasoline to drive your car?

    When there is no fuel to heat your home?

    When our electrical generators go silent?

    When the oil supply is shut off?
- What will you do?

Be careful not to overwork this approach. Remember that there is always the danger that someone will *answer* your question and completely deflate your introduction. "How many more people do we have to lose to the competition before we wake up?" If someone in the audience deadpans, "11," your introduction may fizzle.

Quotation, Definition, or Short Narrative

Often a short story, quote, or light remark can effectively lead into the body of your talk. A briefing advocating expenditures for additional training might build on a quote from Benjamin Franklin: "If a man empties his purse into his head, no man can take it away from him." If a person invests in learning, he or she has made the greatest investment.

Everybody loves to hear a story. So it's no surprise that the narrative or short anecdote, especially if a personal example, often works beautifully. Simply relate your interesting experiences as though you were telling a friend. Strive for a conversational tone. Don't drag out the story; use it only as a lead-in to the meat of your talk.

> A man went into a clothing store to buy a suit. The salesman asked him his name, age, religion, occupation, college, high school, hobbies, political party, and his wife's maiden name.
>
> "Why all the questions?" the customer asked. "All I want is a suit."
>
> "Sir, this is not just an ordinary tailor shop," the salesman said. "We don't merely sell you a suit. We find a suit that is exactly right for you.
>
> "We make a study of your personality and your background and your surroundings. We send to the part of Australia that has the kind of sheep your character and mood require.
>
> "We ship that particular blend of wool to London to be combed and sponged according to a special formula. Then the wool is woven in a section of Scotland where the climate is most favorable to your temperament. Then we fit and measure you carefully.
>
> "Finally, after much careful thought and study, the suit is made. There are more fittings and more changes. And then. . . ."
>
> "Wait a minute," the customer said. "I need this suit tomorrow night for my nephew's wedding."
>
> "Don't worry," the salesman said. "You'll have it."[2]

"Now *that's* customer service!" the speaker concluded. The audience enjoyed it, and the speaker had their attention.

A word of caution: Always *practice* a joke or story *out loud* several times to be sure it *sounds* as good as it reads. Pay special attention to the exact wording of the punch line.

Audience Participation

Asking a few key questions of specific listeners or having the group take a "quiz" or participate in a simple activity may be a good way to get them in tune with your talk.

"I'd like to ask for your candid remarks about the new building proposals. Martha, what concerns do you have?" Be sure you don't put people on the spot. Be sensitive to your tone of voice in asking the questions. Don't do anything that's likely to embarrass your listeners or make them uncomfortable. In short, use this approach with discretion. Don't drag it out too long, and be sure to show your listeners how this relates to your theme and purpose.

Statement of Topic or Reference to Occasion

A simple statement of the theme is seldom an effective introduction. Be more creative than that.

If your audience is already interested in what you'll be saying, a simple statement of your topic may be sufficient. "I am going to outline the new sales representative compensation program." Reference to the occasion may sound like this: "As you know, Tom has asked me to take a few minutes at each staff meeting to update you on new software available."

Other introductory approaches and combinations will also work. The key word in developing effective introductions is *creativity*. Avoid the path of least resistance—the simple statement of your purpose—if there are any more interesting ways open to you; usually there are.

Some Surefire Ways to Flop

An inadequate introduction can seriously damage your talk by failing to gain attention, setting an inappropriate theme, and destroying your credibility. Here are some surefire ways to fall on your face.

The Apologetic Beginning

The **apologetic beginning,** or the "unaccustomed-as-I-am-to-public-speaking" type of remark, has no place in a presentation. Neither do opening statements like, "I'm here to bore you with a few more statistics" or "I'm pretty nervous, so I hope you'll bear with me." If you haven't prepared well enough to be effective, it will become obvious to your audience soon enough. You accomplish nothing by announcing it.

The Potentially Offensive Beginning

An off-color joke, a ridiculing statement, or use of the same, standard opening remark regardless of the audience or occasion will eventually get you in trouble.

The story is told of a rather timid governor who spoke to the inmates of a men's penitentiary. He began conventionally with "Ladies and . . . ," but there was laughter before he could get out the word "gentleman." After he recovered, he began a second time with "Fellow inmates," and again there was a burst of laughter. A moment later he blundered on with "Glad to see so many of you here." Undoubtedly, more planning should have gone into the governor's opening remarks to make them appropriate to his audience.[3]

Other openings may be inappropriate because they are trite or excessively flattering, or just plain phony: "I am filled with a deep sense of personal inadequacy when I presume to speak authoritatively in the presence of so many knowledgeable people."

John Wade advises: "Highly successful business communicators never resort to off-color or vulgar stories to make a point. They possess a degree of elevated dignity in demeanor that makes it easy to respect and trust them."

The Gimmicky Beginning

Apologetic, offensive, overused, and gimmicky openers often fail.

Resist the temptation to use a **gimmicky beginning:** blow a whistle, sing a song, role play a violent scene from a play, or write the word "sex" on the blackboard saying, "Now that I have your attention. . . ." These just don't work. They tend to put your audience members on the spot—they don't know how they should respond. It's embarrassing and distracting.

Your introduction should be brief and direct. It should get the audience members' attention and prepare them for what is to follow. Just ask yourself, would this introduction get my attention? If not, rework it. The introduction is probably the single most important segment of your talk, so plan it carefully.

The Body: Now that I Have Your Attention

If the introduction has been effective, it sets the stage for the body of your presentation. The body then presents main points, elaborates on them, clarifies, and summarizes so the audience will remember what you've said. The number of main points should be limited to as few as will cover the material adequately. With too many main points, your listener's retention will suffer. Research shows that most people's short-term memory is limited to about five items. To be safe, try to keep main points to three or four if possible. If you must cover more than that number, provide listeners with a written list or outline.

Organization of Main Points

The arrangement of **main points** will vary depending on your purpose. The following describes some available options.

Direct Plan. This arrangement begins with the main idea or the general conclusion of the briefing followed by supporting information. This is the BIF approach we described in Chapter Eight. Here is an example.

A direct order arrangement puts the big idea first followed by support.

> **The coming year should be our most profitable year since 1991 [main point and big idea]. In the last 6 months, orders for our minisatellite dish have increased by 86 percent; costs of materials have remained stable and are projected to increase by not more than 2 percent in the coming year; and our recent contract with the union freezes wages and benefits at present levels for the next 18 months [supporting details].**

Organize details under their main point. The main points should be prioritized so that the most important, or dramatic, point comes first. The selection of these priorities may be a judgment call for the presenter, but it should be based on audience needs and interests.

The direct organization is appropriate for most business presentations. It is efficient and hits the high point immediately while the audience's attention level is still high.

Indirect Plan. The indirect or *inductive* order starts with details or supporting information and builds up to the main point. Main points are arranged in ascending order of importance so that the *big idea* or major conclusion comes last. This is the BILL approach discussed in Chapter Eight. Here is how the preceding example would look if arranged inductively.

> **Our recent contract with the union freezes wages and benefits at present levels for the next 18 months. Costs of raw materials for our products have remained stable and are projected to increase by not more than 2 percent in the coming year. In the last 6 months, orders for our minisatellite dishes have increased by 86 percent [all supporting detail].** *The coming year will be our most profitable year since 1991* **[main point].**

An indirect pattern saves the main idea until after the support has been presented.

The indirect arrangement works best when the speaker sees the need to be persuasive, when the briefing's purpose is to get the listeners to believe or to do something they are not likely to otherwise believe or do. If the conclusion were presented first as in the direct plan, the listener may be defensive or even argumentative, tuning out the evidence that supports that conclusion. The indirect plan avoids this by putting the evidence first, using convincing detail to lead to the general conclusion. Much resistance can be overcome with skillful use of indirect arrangement of ideas. Many speakers also choose the indirect plan when they are delivering bad news.

Problem-Solution Plan. Another arrangement useful in persuasion is the problem-solution approach. Here, the speaker clarifies and amplifies some need. This is done to get the listener to be concerned about the problem in personal terms. Once this point is reached, introduction of your solution is welcomed, and acceptance is likely.

Television advertisements often use an abbreviated form of this plan. They introduce a problem (an upset stomach, unreliable telephone equipment, or "that embarrassing dandruff") and then solve the dilemma by introducing their product.

Here's an example of how a business presentation uses a problem-solution pattern of arrangement.

> In the past six months our use of long-distance telephone service has increased by 71 percent with no noticeable decrease in the use of letters or teletype. As a result of this increase, our monthly telephone bills now exceed $1,850 per month. Even if the usage could be held at this level, that's $22,200 per year for long distance—as much as we'd spend on an extra, desperately needed clerical employee. Although the increase is alarming, the prospect of not being able to put a lid on it is what really bothers me. Without better control, our profit picture and individual earnings are going to be hurt [need development and personalization of problem].

> There is a way we can deal with this that I think you'll like. A telecommunication company representative has been talking to me about installing a new long-distance calling system. Here are some cost figures [solution].

Cause-Effect Plan. By clarifying how one event or action causes another, the speaker can recommend changes in one to bring about corresponding changes in the other. This arrangement can be useful in either explanatory or informational presentations or, when followed by a call for action, in persuasion.

Chronological Order. This organization plan simply arranges points as they occur in time. A presentation to new employees on the company's history would probably use this plan.

Topical or Spatial Order. Space order typically moves from examples that are near to those far away or vice versa. For example, a progress report on computerization may begin with the local branch and move to outlying branches or other cities.

Increase of Magnitude of Difficulty Pattern. A briefing on the effects of the economy on a business may develop from relatively local, temporary factors over which the organization maintains some control to the more complex national or worldwide condition that is beyond its control. For example, a slowdown in sales in a downtown shoe store may be attributed to the following:

- Fewer sales made per employee
- Increased competition from newer stores in outlying shopping malls
- Higher crime rate in the vicinity of the store
- Higher unemployment rate because of a layoff at a major local employer
- Delays in getting high-demand shoes from distributors
- Worldwide shortage of quality leather

Each of these points represents increasing difficulty for the local business person.

Order of importance plan. This arrangement presents the most significant or noteworthy point first, with other developments following in descending order of importance.

Table 17–1 summarizes the ways of arranging the body of your oral presentation.

TABLE 17–1
ARRANGING THE BODY OF A PRESENTATION

Type of Briefing	General Objective	Organization of Body
Persuasive	Get audience to accept ideas and do something ("sell" them something)	*Inductive pattern:* Show several specific cases or lines of reasoning that lead up to general conclusion/action step. (Use when audience resistance to your key idea is expected to be strong.)
Explanatory or instructional	Inform audience members (teach them something)	*Deductive pattern:* Present the conclusion and explain how it was arrived at. (May also be used in persuasive talks when the key idea is not likely to turn off your listeners.) *Chronological pattern:* Show how events developed over time. *Topical or spatial pattern:* Give examples from different places or categories that relate to the topic. *Increasing difficulty pattern:* Starting from something already known, add to it to explain more complex or unusual concepts. *Chain-of-events pattern:* Show how different steps or procedures lead to a certain conclusion.
Progress report	Inform or update knowledge	*Chronological or chain-of-events pattern:* As above. *Order of importance:* Present the most significant developments first.

Development and Support of Main Points

Most main points take the form of simple declarative statements. Few of these can stand alone. Support, elaboration, clarification, and proof can shore up these themes, and result in audience acceptance and agreement. Several types of support are discussed subsequently.

Specific details or explanation of the main point are probably the most common, though not always the most effective, way to build support. Here you simply explain in other words what you have asserted. This support may be prefaced by remarks, such as "Let me explain why I've said that" or "Another way to say this might be. . . ." Some speakers rely too heavily on this type of support when other, more interesting approaches could be used, some of which are discussed subsequently.

Comparisons or analogies often result in strong support. Frequently these take the form of a narrative. Here is a recent example overheard at a convention. A young professor asked an older, well-established author how long it took him to complete his recent book. The author responded with a narrative about a wartime experience in Europe in 1945. The author, who was then a soldier in recently liberated Paris, approached a sidewalk artist whom he had observed painting. He asked if the painting was for sale and the artist responded, "Yes." When informed of the price, the soldier replied, "But it only took you an hour to paint that!" The artist responded indignantly. "But I have prepared all my life." The young professor got the point of the analogy and felt a bit embarrassed for even asking the question.

Such parables provide long-lasting and thought-provoking support to a speaker's points.

Examples, especially those of a personal nature, add support to main points and also lend credibility to the speaker. Some speakers are unduly hesitant about using personal experiences. These provide support of a firsthand nature and can be convincing.

Be certain that your example is typical of and pertinent to the point being supported. An isolated incident or fluke occurrence will be obvious to your audience, and should not be presented as illustrative of a general condition. For example, let's say that your main point is, "Morale in the plant is low." Yet you do not support it with a single example of one employee's complaints about working conditions. If you string together a series of isolated examples, you develop support for your theme.

- *Main point.* Employee morale is low.
- *Supporting examples.* The following are the supporting examples:

  Six different workers have complained about the excessive heat in the plant.

  Absenteeism is up 20 percent over last month.

  Three workers quit, citing unbearable shop conditions.

  Four grievances have been filed with the union.

Statistics provide support when they are used ethically. There are many well-known ways to distort information using statistics, but there are also many ways to lie. The problem is that some speakers don't really understand how statistics are derived or what they have when they get them.

There are two general types of statistics: descriptive and inferential. *Descriptive* statistics can take a large quantity of numbers and make another, much smaller set of numbers out of it with the essential information remaining intact. In other words, they condense or describe the original mass of data to make it more intelligible. *Inferential* statistics predict conclusions based on evidence provided by samples and mathematically calculate probabilities that a given conclusion is so.

Sometimes statistics confuse more than they clarify or support. In briefings, speakers should determine what level of statistical expertise their audience has before relying heavily on the more sophisticated statistics. Most people can readily grasp de-

Statistics can be of two types: descriptive and inferential.

scriptive statistics but are rather confused by inferential statistics. A speaker recently misused actuarial data compiled by an insurance company to project life span based on health habits. He told his audience such things as, "If you smoke more than two packs of cigarettes a day, subtract eight years from your life; if you live in the country, add two years to your life." By the time he finished, half of the audience members thought they would live forever, and the other half wondered why they were not already dead. The point is that actuarial data on life expectancies are complex statistics. If you do not thoroughly understand the implications of complex statistics, do not use them.

Four points will help you develop an idea using statistics.

1. Round out large numbers so your listeners can digest them.
2. Interpret the numbers in some meaningful way. Percentages seem to be the easiest for most to grasp.
3. Be sure to compare "apples to apples." One speaker expressed relief that the unemployment rate was only 6 or 7 percent, whereas in Israel, "1 person in 18 is unemployed!" That is virtually the same percentage.
4. Use charts and graphs to help your audience understand the statistics.

Use statistics sparingly. They should not be considered the only type of support but should be part of an assortment of developmental approaches.

Formal quotations or *testimonial statements* can be effective if you choose to quote an authority who is

1. A recognized expert
2. In a position to know about the specific point you are trying to support
3. In general agreement with other authorities on the subject
4. Free from prejudice that would distort his or her view

Testimonial quotes can be powerful if the source is seen as credible.

The person quoted need not be a world-renowned expert; he or she may well be someone within the organization with considerable experience or training in the area being discussed. In deciding whether an authority is free of prejudice, consider what the person quoted may stand to gain or lose. You would probably not quote a television advertising salesperson's views on the relative merits of newspaper versus broadcast promotions.

Audiovisual aids may be used in conjunction with several other types of support. There is an increasing awareness of the importance of supplementing the spoken word with another medium. As was mentioned in Chapter Six, communication effectiveness is enhanced by use of more than one medium. Visuals can range from a simple chalkboard or flip chart to the highly sophisticated multimedia productions involving slides, movies, special lighting effects, and elaborate sound systems. In most business presentations, you can often use a wide variety of devices, such as charts, graphs, overhead projectors, slides, movies or videotape, tape recordings, and models (more on such visuals in Chapter Eighteen).

Transitions, Summaries, and Conclusions

Transitions are statements or questions that help provide coherence in the talk by showing connection between separate thoughts or parts of the presentation. Some examples follow:

- "Now that we have seen the sales results, let's consider the effect on profits."
- "Having said that, I'd like to suggest another viewpoint."
- "How does this impact our business? Let's look at two key ways."
- "If you'll keep these three points in mind, I'll show you how we can. . . ."

Few listeners can follow a message without clear transitions.

Transitional words and phrases help your listeners shift gears, readjust expectations, and mentally recap what has been covered. Without adequate transitions it is almost impossible for listeners to follow even a moderately complex line of thought. As the speaker, you also get important advantages from the liberal use of transitions. They give you extra moments to check your notes, change physical position, reestablish eye contact with your audience, check for listener feedback, or adjust a visual aid.

Likewise, summaries and **conclusions** serve to help your listener remember important information. Four goals should be accomplished as you end most presentations. (The exception may be the simple progress report.) You should

1. Summarize key points.
2. Restate your central theme.
3. Point to the listeners' need to know what you've just told them and remind them of the urgency (or at least importance) of that information.
4. Provide them with a clear action step, a prescribed behavior, or mental activity they should initiate.

Summaries are especially useful to recap the *key ideas* (but not too many details) of your talk. Repetition helps your listeners remember; so use this important tool as you lead into your close. Avoid introducing any new material at this point. It may confuse your listeners.

Everything you have done to develop this presentation comes to a climax at the conclusion. So a most important question goes back to your conceptual planning—what was your specific intent? Picture yourself as a listener and ask the tough question: "What does this all mean to me?" Your talk should provide a clear answer.

Use of an Action Step

Action steps are appropriate for all kinds of briefings. The action step tells your listeners what you want them to *do* or *think* (preferably, *do*). (This is how Chapter Eight defined a "big idea." It is the reason for the communication.)

Your audience has a right to expect and receive guidance from all your research and preparation. If you don't provide such guidance in the form of a clear, action-oriented conclusion, you have probably let your listeners down. The actions you advocate should be ones you can realistically request from your listeners. Your conclusions need not be elaborate or drawn out. If the rest of the talk is well done, the conclusion will be self-evident, and you need only restate and bring a sense of finality.

Understanding the Basics

• The general purpose of any business presentation is to answer questions—to provide usable information.

• Analyzing your listeners (audience) before developing the presentation increases your chance of communication success. This analysis calls for making educated guesses about your listeners.

• Listener analysis should be an ongoing process that is done before, during, and after the presentation.

• The presentation model will increase message retention in your listeners by presenting the information in an organized fashion.

• Special attention should be given to the introduction, arrangement of key ideas, support for each key idea, transitions, conclusion, and action step.

KEY TERMS AND CONCEPTS

listener analysis	transitions	gimmicky beginning
rhetorical question	action steps	types of support
apologetic beginning	startling statement	conclusions
key ideas (main points)	audience participation	types of presentations

QUESTIONS FOR FURTHER THOUGHT

1. What is listener analysis? How can it improve a talk?

2. How do listeners' expectations of the speaker affect the messages they receive?

3. How can a speaker accomplish ongoing listener analysis?

4. What are the three key elements of any talk, and how can you make the most of these?

5. Discuss the importance of an effective introduction. How can you make the most of this part of a presentation?

6. What demographic characteristics will affect the way a listener responds to your talk?

Speechwriters of the World, Get Lost!

By Phil Theibert

I have been a corporate speechwriter for over 10 years. I don't mean to offend anyone, but most of the speeches top executives give stink. And because executives are surrounded by people wanting favors, or contracts, or simply by people who've grown accustomed to getting a regular paycheck, they never hear the truth about their speeches.

If you're giving a speech, let me offer some advice. First, write it yourself. Don't have a speechwriter do it for you. Speechwriters justify their jobs by putting in witty quotes, amusing anecdotes and reams of statistics. This may impress the speaker, but it also creates a Tower of Babel that no listener cares to scale.

Why? Well, here's a dirty little secret few speechwriters will tell you: Audiences rarely care how witty or amusing you are. They have two goals in mind. They want to hear your points as directly and simply as possible, and they want to get the hell out of there.

The best way to approach a speech? Forget about eloquence. We don't live in an age of eloquence. Over half the people in your audience have grown up with MTV. Their attention span is limited to sound bites on the evening news. There are only two elements that make a speech great: sincerity and brevity.

I've often talked to chief executives and they want to know what they should say. That's easy. Tell the audience what you really believe in your heart. And if you don't give a damn about the topic, don't give the damn speech. If you don't care, your audience surely won't.

If you're giving a speech, dig down deep, find out what your beliefs really are, and hit your audience between the eyes with them. And don't forget that any speech is only 20% text and 80% speaker. If you're not sincere, if your soul doesn't come through in that speech, you will hear snoring from the front row all the way back to the exit door.

Another thing. There was once a president from Missouri. He believed in plain speaking. "Plain speaking" really comprises just three simple rules. Communication gurus can't justify their existence if you remember these points:

1. Tell them what you're going to say.
2. Say it.
3. Tell them what you said.

Let me give you two quick examples I've pulled from speeches that have crossed my desk. Some slight editing has been done to spare the executives in question any anguish.

A bad example: "My associates know I have an abiding interest in the personality and the writings of Winston Churchill. If you examine his speeches, his 'History of the English-Speaking Peoples,' and his history of the Second World War. . . ."

Okay, enough. First, nobody really cares about old Winston anymore. Most of the people he inspired are dead. I'll make you a bet that half your audience will have trouble even identifying who he was. And that holds true with any audience. Second, the speech is not about Winston, it's not about your admiration for Winston . . . in fact, I'm not quite sure what the speech was about. I never got down that far.

Contrarily, here is a good example taken from a fund-raising speech: "Plain and simple, we need money to run the foundation, just like you need money to develop new products. We need money to make this work. We need money from you. Pick up that pledge card. Fill it out. Turn it in at the door as you leave. Make a statement about your commitment . . . make it a big statement."

I like that closing. Boom, boom, boom. Here are the facts, now act on them.

Remember: Keep it simple, keep it plain, tell them the truth and get the hell out of there. Be brief, be sincere.

Finally, when it comes to bad or uncomfortable news, people want the truth right between the eyes. If someone listens to your speech and says, "I don't agree with what he says, but he gave it to me straight," you have done your job.

(Phil Theibert, "Speechwriters of the World, Get Lost!" *The Wall Street Journal*, August 2, 1993, p. A-16. Reprinted with permission of The Wall Street Journal, © 1993 Dow Jones & Company, Inc. All rights reserved.)

Applying Your Knowledge

1. On what points does Theibert's article agree with the ideas in this chapter? Disagree?

2. Defend or argue against his statement, "When it comes to bad news, people want the truth right between the eyes."

3. What two things do audiences want from a speech?

4. What does the author suggest to organization leaders who ask what they should say in a speech?

5. To what extent do you agree that "any speech is only 20 percent text and 80 percent speaker"?

Applying Your Skills

ACTIVITY 17-1: Articulating Themes and Key Ideas

What follows are some central themes for presentations. Based on your own experience (no research is needed), see if you can come up with several key ideas for each. The first one has been done as an example.

Central Theme

1. People should rent formal attire rather than purchase it.
2. Recycling alum inum is good for everyone.
3. Your school should offer more evening (or day or weekend) classes.
4. Your company should organize athletic teams for employees.
5. You need a laptop computer to be fully efficient.

Possible Key Ideas

a. Formal attire is worn on only rare occasions.
b. Formal attire is expensive to purchase, and it is seldom worn more than a few times.
c. Storage of formal attire is inconvenient.
d. Renting formal attire costs about 85 percent less than owning.

ACTIVITY 17-2: Pinpoint Potential Questions

Some key ideas follow. For each key idea, write one or more potential questions a listener is likely to ask. (Later sections suggest ways to *answer* the questions. For now, see what questions spring to mind for each of these key ideas.) The first one has been done as an example.

Key Idea

1. A mandatory safety course would reduce motorcycle accident injuries.
2. A student credit card is a better idea than using cash for bookstore purchases.
3. Sales profits rose 80 percent this month.
4. We anticipate stronger demand for our products in July.
5. My leadership experiences in school will help me be more effective on the job [in a job interview presentation].
6. The construction of phase one should be completed by September 15 [in a progress report].
7. The teachings of Aristotle are still important for today's communicator.
8. Customers are different today from five years ago.

Potential Questions

a. Would such training reduce accidents?

ACTIVITY 17-3: Getting It Down on Paper

Go back to your responses to Activity 17–2. Having identified your main points and developed support for each, you are now ready to organize the presentation. Select three potential questions from Activity 17–2. Determine how your audience is likely to respond, and then develop answers and support. Write your ideas using two columns as shown.

Potential Listener Questions	Answers and Types of Support

Key Idea 1:
Audience Attitude
  Accepting
  Skeptical
  Opposed

Key Idea 2
Audience Attitude
  Accepting
  Skeptical
  Opposed

Key Idea 3
Audience Attitude
  Accepting
  Skeptical
  Opposed

ACTIVITY 17-4: Teaching a Simple Skill

Think of a fairly simple task you could teach someone else. Using Pitone's ideas, outline a four-step training presentation. If you can't think of a topic, try one of these.

- How to mow the lawn
- How to change oil in a car
- How to create a word chart on the computer
- How to access the Internet
- How to shine shoes
- How to wash and wax a car properly

ACTIVITY 17-5: Create a "Game Plan"

Respond to the two scenarios at the beginning of the chapter. How can Terry best organize a presentation for Marcus and Marilyn? How should Sean respond to the demands for communication he receives?

What kinds of presentations are called for? How might these be structured?

ACTIVITY 17-6: Identifying the Fear

Speaking before a group (large or small) can produce fear in the presenter. Make a list of the three main fears you have when assigned to give a briefing or make a presentation. Explain why you experience these fears, and comment as to how you might overcome them. Use the following headings:

Fear	Why I Have This Fear	Possibilities for Overcoming Fear

ACTIVITY 17-7: Listener Analysis

This chapter has discussed the importance of finding out as much as possible about your audience before making a presentation. For each of the following, list some suggestions for gathering information about your audience.

1. A briefing to the six-member senior management team on this month's financial success of the company.

2. A presentation to a group of first-line supervisors on the sales objectives of the organization.

3. Instructing coworkers on a new procedure.

4. Making a presentation on "Listening Skills" to a group of employees from several different organizations in your local area.

ACTIVITY 17-8: A Pleasing Introduction
Go back to Activity 17–7, and formulate an introduction for each of the four presentations listed.

PERFORMING
on the Job

CASE 17-1 Giving It Their Best Shot

Just over a year ago Jerry started a small business with his son, Jim. Jerry is in his late 40s and has been in various management positions since graduating from college more than 25 years ago. Jim is beginning his second year of law school and, like his father, enjoys entrepreneurial projects. This new venture excited Jerry and Jim because it dealt with a golf-related product (both are avid golfers). Much thought and planning went into the business plan, concept, and necessary legal maneuvers to ensure intellectual property protection with trademarks. Design and artwork of the company logo involved a professional graphics artist to provide a suitable image.

Jerry decided to attempt a joint venture with a large, well-known, and successful golf products company to find the necessary capital to put the product into production. He obtained information about this large company by calling and requesting information from its Marketing and Investor Relations departments. Contacts in both departments were more than willing to share information about their company. Jim gathered as much information as possible from a variety of sources at the university library. Jerry and Jim thoroughly reviewed all the information in depth and prepared what they believed to be an excellent presentation on the possibilities for a joint venture. After a great deal of effort, Jerry and Jim were able to meet with three company representatives to give a one-hour presentation on their product and their intentions for a joint venture. The reaction to the presentation was positive. The company representatives appreciated the research Jerry and Jim had done, and the ideas they had come up with. Two follow-up meetings were held in which details of a joint venture were finalized and licensing agreements signed. A joint venture was formed. Both Jerry and Jim thought their presentation was the key to their success. They had truly given it their best shot, and it paid off.

Case Questions

1. What were the reasons for the presentation being a success?
2. How do you visualize Jerry and Jim making the actual presentation?

CASE 17-2 All Is Not Well

Kristine is a graduate student at a local university about to finish her master's degree in the field of health and nutrition. Before taking a full-time position as a director of wellness for a local company, she was working as a wellness counselor for a company called Corporate Well Being (CWB). CWB had several corporate clients it was providing wellness services to on an ongoing basis. These services included health testing and training of the client's employees in health-related subjects.

Kristine had been assigned to give monthly training classes at a local company where approximately 30 employees were taking part in the program. In addition to the monthly classes, Kristine met with each of the participants in a once-a-month "private counseling session" to check progress and set goals. After two months, three participants notified CWB that they would no longer be participating in the program. Monthly class attendance fell from an average of 25 to an average of 10. By the fourth month, the owner of CWB contacted participants as to why they were not taking part as they had done previously. Some of the responses were the following:

- "I don't feel comfortable."
- "The classes just aren't that interesting."
- "Kristine seems to have a difficult time relating to us."
- "It seems as though we are just a training ground for graduate students doing internships."

Case Questions

1. What kinds of problems exist for CWB in this case?
2. Can the relationship between the company and CWB be improved? How?
3. What "presentation-type" issues are demonstrated in this case?
4. Do an audience analysis for CWB to assist in resolving this problem. Recommend a plan of action.

CHAPTER EIGHTEEN

Delivery
of Oral Presentations

Conveying Your Message
with Impact

LEARNING GOALS

After you have studied this chapter, you should be able to:

- Name and give example of six kinds of nonverbal variables that can affect the speaker's total image.

- Identify six common mistakes that can nonverbally detract from the speaker's message.

- Describe five aspects of voice and paralanguage that affect delivery.

- Explain the advantages and disadvantages of notes versus a manuscript.

- Describe eight techniques for making the most of a question-and-answer session.

PERFORMANCE CHALLENGE

The Way It Is . . . Overcoming Nervousness When Speaking before Groups

Barry had done an excellent job of preparing his presentation. He was sure that the committee was going to like his ideas. He had planned a creative introduction and a solid conclusion. Each main idea was clearly supported with a story, example, or statistic. He had developed some nice visuals. In short, this was a good presentation.

All that remained was for Barry to get his message across to his listeners. He was a little nervous but felt generally confident. Delivery time is when all the preparation pays off—or flops.

Inevitably, the first concern most people have about delivering a presentation is nervousness. Anxiety studies have shown that speaking before groups is often rated as more fearful than death! It certainly doesn't have to be that way. In fact, people can quickly learn to control speaker anxiety and use it to improve their speaking rather than detract from it. All that is needed are understanding and application of some simple yet powerful ideas that this chapter covers.

If people have any self-regard, they'll be concerned about how others see and respond to them. This concern naturally leads to some nervousness. The skillful speaker seeks to *control* this nervous energy, not eliminate it. As the Toastmaster's handbook says, effectiveness training in speech "won't completely eliminate those butterflies in the stomach, but it will keep them flying in formation."[1]

Communication professors Harold Zelko and Frank Dance talk about developing your "coping quotient" by reducing the number of factors you must give conscious attention to. As different aspects of presentational speaking become natural and spontaneous, you can channel your concentration toward the specific purpose of your briefing. It's like typing or playing a musical instrument. So long as you must consciously think about how each finger should be positioned to print a letter or produce a note, you will never be effective in putting together the entire composition.

Ways to Control Speaking Anxiety

Here are several ways to reduce **speaker anxiety** or the number of specific factors that call for your attention to bring the presentation comfortably within your coping quotient.[2]

Prepare

Prepare your talk almost to the point of overpreparation.

There is absolutely no substitute for adequate preparation. If you are well prepared, your capacity to cope with problems rises significantly. Nothing reduces anxiety like being well prepared to the point of being overprepared—that is, totally confident of your grasp of the subject matter. Preparation should go beyond the content and delivery of the presentation to include practice in handling anticipated questions.

Be Idea Conscious, Not Self-Conscious

Having your specific purpose in mind helps reduce overconcern for irrelevant details. You are most effective when you don't think of each step or procedure needed to complete a task, but instead focus on the desired result and let your subconscious mind help you get there. The baseball outfielder going after a high fly ball doesn't consciously think, "I'll take six steps to my left, two steps forward, raise my glove with my left hand and shield my eyes from the sun with my right hand." Instead, he fixes his eye on the ball and visualizes the desired result of catching it. His unconscious success mechanisms go through the mechanics of bringing that to pass and free him from concerns about tripping over his shoelace, taking the wrong-sized steps, or raising his glove too late.

The same principle applies in presentational speaking. Overconcern with mechanics can only be distracting and anxiety producing. Zelko and Dance give this example.

Focusing on yourself rather than your message is the equivalent of saying "cheese" for a photograph instead of really smiling.

Self-consciousness tends to be self-destructive. If you are overly worried about the way you look, you often over-compensate and this draws to yourself attention which would not ordinarily be centered on you. It's when you are trying to walk nonchalantly that you walk stiffly or affectedly. It is when you are trying to smile naturally ("Say 'cheese' ") that your smile tends to look artificial. If you are caught up in a conversation or in telling a story and the conversation or the story causes you to smile, you are usually unaware of the smile itself, and it is at that point that the smile is, and appears, most natural. Similarly with speaking in public. When you are caught up in the message of your speech, when you are interested in communicating the ideas of the speech to the listeners, you are not usually uncomfortable or noticeably concerned with how you look or how you sound—it's the idea that is at center state, not the self. Simple remedies: Be audience-centered; be message-centered; not self-centered.[3]

Relax

If you still feel that flush of nervousness just as you're being introduced, don't worry about it. It's perfectly natural and seldom visible to your audience. When you get up to speak, take a moment to arrange your notes; look at your audience and smile; and take a few slow, deep breaths.

The more successful experiences you have, the easier speaking becomes.

Once you've had a few successful speaking experiences, your **coping quotient** quickly increases. You get to the point where you welcome the opportunity to stand up before a group with your well-prepared talk.

Use Your Background and Experience

Every speaker brings unique experiences, attitudes, and ideas to any presentation, yet for some reason, speakers tend to depreciate the value of such experience and ideas and instead turn to other, more "authoritative" sources. There are, of course, situations where it's important to cite recognized authorities on a topic, but don't hesitate to add your own ideas too. People can better explain and answer questions about *personal* experiences. Preparation for this presentation makes you a bona fide authority in your own right.

Recognize that Your Listeners Want You to Succeed

When people have taken the time to assemble for the purpose of hearing what you have to say, they don't want to feel the time has been wasted. Even the hostile listener wants you to explain yourself clearly, if for no other reason than that he or she can then attempt to shoot down your ideas. Let's face it—a poor presentation can be just as embarrassing and uncomfortable for the listeners as it is for the speaker. Your audience wants you to succeed.

Conveying of Your Credibility

Effectiveness in articulating a message can convey the single most important factor in determining overall success: your **credibility.**

Credibility arises from personality characteristics that permeate all our interactions with others. In organizations where you are likely to have repeated communication opportunities with the same people, what you said or did yesterday or last month may well have bearing on your credibility today.

Aristotle's treatise, *The Rhetoric*, was probably the first book on communication theory. In it, he explains three types of arguments one may use to convince an audience: logical appeals *(logos)*, emotion appeals *(pathos)*, and ethical appeals *(ethos)*. Of these three, *ethos* is the strongest. Over time the concept of ethos has come to refer to the credibility of the message source. People who are held in high esteem because of perceived intelligence or ethical standards are far more likely to be effective communicators.

Research into what creates credibility has concluded that four factors determine your perceived credibility in a given situation.

1. *Expertise.* How well informed you are about a given topic affects credibility. The highly credible source is likely to be one who has experience and training relevant to the topic, and who effectively conveys this competence to the audience. Demonstration of understanding of the issues discussed, and use of firsthand experience or personal examples is one way to build this expertise factor.

2. *Trustworthiness.* When a speaker is seen as being sincere and unbiased, credibility will be enhanced. One way to convey such an impression is by using facts and reasoning carefully and usually avoiding overuse of emotionalism in language. Also, recognizing and presenting opposing viewpoints can demonstrate the propensity to weigh alternatives carefully and examine issues judiciously. The absence of secret motives, such as personal gain or special advantages for the individual's work group, will also strengthen trust in the speaker.

3. *Composure.* Whether a person is seen as poised, relaxed, and confident as opposed to nervous, tense, or uncomfortable affects credibility. These perceptions arise from our audience's awareness of cues, most of which are nonverbal. Appearance, posture, mannerisms, and purposefulness of movements combine to create an impression of personal composure. There is such a thing as being *too* composed. The meticulously groomed, carefully rehearsed, and precisely choreographed presentation might be a bit suspect. Being too perfect may cause others to question your trustworthiness. This image created by looking sharp and acting confidently—with an added dash of humility—seems to be the kind most of us prefer.

4. *Dynamism.* A fourth factor believed to affect source credibility is a sense of personal dynamism: the tendency to be active, outgoing, talkative, or bold. The very introverted, shy, or apprehensive individual is usually seen as less credible. As with composure, this can be carried too far. The stereotyped hotshot used car salesman or the loud-mouthed joker may be dynamic but not credible. In many situations, the soft-spoken voice of quiet reasoning is welcomed. Research showing a relationship between dynamism and high credibility has been less convincing than that relating high credibility to expertise, trust, and composure.

Ted Koppel, anchorperson for ABC News Nightline, is the epitome of the poised, relaxed, and confident image every speaker would like to convey. (Courtesy of Scott Peterson/Gamma-Liaison, Inc.)

Credibility permeates all the activities of a communicator. In many cases, it arrives before you do in the form of others' past impressions. The speaker whose credibility is not yet established must make a conscious effort to demonstrate these characteristics to the audience. The speaker who is already high in credibility must reinforce that view. The speaker with low credibility must expend considerable effort to create more favorable images. These changes in attitudes toward the low-credibility speaker take time and usually require repeated demonstrations of change.

The organization of a presentation can do much to build credibility as well as improve audience comprehension and retention. Studies have shown that the speaker who is well organized in his or her presentation is regarded as a more credible source than a speaker who is disorganized. This was determined by measuring audience attitudes toward the speaker after presenting essentially the same speech in either organized or disorganized fashion.[4]

Specific Delivery Techniques

No matter how well you've planned and prepared the presentation, your success will still depend in large part on the delivery. Delivery is a combination of many factors that collectively produce a total impression upon your audience. Overcoming excessive anxiety and developing credibility are important. In addition, here are some techniques to apply.

Eye Contact

It is a cultural expectation for most people to look into the eyes of the receiver when communicating. When addressing a large group this can become a problem. The best bet seems to be to look at one individual for a few seconds and then move on to another. Don't just scan over the crowd—really look *at* individuals. Be sure you get to almost everyone in the room at some point. Be aware of tendencies to look too much at one particularly attractive or attentive person while ignoring the bored person in the back of the room.

Gestures and Movement

Your sense of personal dynamism or self-confidence comes across via such body language as gestures, posture, and mannerisms. Gestures can be useful to punctuate what is being said. They should be spontaneous and natural, yet used purposefully. Everyone has different tendencies to use or avoid gestures. For some, it feels uncomfortable to point or raise hands in exclamation. For others, it may be said that if you tied their hands they'd be speechless.

There are several common mistakes people make with gestures.

1. They fail to use them where they can be useful for emphasis.
2. They use the same gesture repeatedly to the point where it becomes monotonous, distracting, or even annoying.
3. They use gestures that cannot be seen clearly; a hand motion hidden from audience view by a podium is of no value.

Gestures and body movement—if purposeful—provide nonverbal punctuation for your message.

Body movement is another important way to bring life to a talk. Pausing between points in the briefing and physically moving to another place in the room helps your listeners know that you have completed one point and are now ready to address another. This pause helps your listeners follow your logical development. If you cannot freely move around, you may still use the pause and a shift in position, or a change in the direction you're looking, to indicate the same things. Whenever possible, avoid the speaker-behind-the-podium format. If a mike is needed, a cordless, clip-on microphone is best for freedom of movement.

Pronunciation

Be careful not to mispronounce. As with other distractions, such goofs may not seriously change meaning but will reflect on your credibility. One audience at a university was unsettled to hear a professor pronounce the word library as "liberry." People sometimes mispronounce "satistics" and supervisors explain "pacific" examples. Folklore at an air force training school relates how pilots were surprised to hear that "humid air" is responsible for many plane crashes. This culprit was really "human error."

Voice

Work for variation in voice pitch, rate, and loudness to hold your audience.

A clear, strong voice increases the probability of audience understanding. Clear articulation of the language is important, but other voice characteristics, such as variation in pitch, loudness, and rate of speech, have as much or more impact. The range of pitch one uses may be wide, allowing for effective vocal emphasis, or narrow, resulting in what is commonly called a monotone voice. Over time, a committed monotone can put virtually anybody to sleep.

The key word to keeping listener attention is *variation*. Two common voice variation problems come up often. First, male speakers seldom have enough variation in pitch. Men seem to think that it sounds macho to talk in only a deep tone, and they do so continuously. Tremendous emphasis can be made by raising and lowering the pitch, yet many speakers don't want to "risk" it.

Second, some female speakers have a different problem: They tend to lose the conversational tone in their voice when addressing a group. Their voice sounds theatrical, artificial, and forced. Occasionally this comes out sing-songy. This latter problem results from habitual pitch change patterns that become monotonous and distracting. It also arises from overdoing voice *intensity,* perhaps in an effort to sound assertive.

Some people are overly loud, whereas others are so soft-spoken that they need to "speak up." Most business presentations can be made at a conversational level, although additional emphasis can be achieved by variation. Don't assume always that a louder voice commands more attention. Often the quiet, firm voice—the one the listener has to lean toward and work to hear—is the most powerful.

One other distracting vocal use is what is called "up-talk." Here the speaker raises intonation at the end of a statement to make it sound like a question. Try saying the following sentences using up-talk—raising your intonation on the italicized word:

- She's very good at everything she *does.*
- The management is concerned about the *costs.*
- I'm interested in getting some information about your *vacation plans.*

Notice how up-talk creates a note of uncertainty in what is spoken. Unfortunately, some people habitually use up-talk without noticing how it can undermine their assertiveness and make them consistently sound tentative.

"Uptalk" can be annoying and makes assertions sound like questions.

Verbalized Pauses

Few things can drive your audience up the wall like the liberal use of verbalized fillers, such as "ah," "um," "uh," and (the popular favorite) "ya know." Some intelligent and apparently rational men and women salt their every utterance with these expressions until their listeners want to scream at them, ya know?

The human talker abhors a vacuum. When the detested monster, silence, raises its ugly head, some beat it to death with ah, uh, um, or ya knows. Do yourself a favor; ask others you speak with to point out when you are drifting into this habit. Commit yourself to listening for and eliminating your own filler words. Rid yourself of the fear of silence.

Why do some people fill the air with nonwords and sounds? For some it is a sign of nervousness; they fear silence and experience **speaker anxiety.** Recent research at Columbia University suggests another reason. The Columbia psychologists speculated that speakers fill pauses when searching for the next word. To investigate this idea, they counted the use of filler words used by lecturers in biology, chemistry, and mathematics, where the subject matter uses scientific definitions that limit the variety of word choices available to the speaker. They then compared the number of filler words used by teachers in English, art history, and philosophy, where the subject matter is less well defined and more open to word choices.

Twenty science lecturers used an average of 1.39 uhs a minute, compared with 4.85 uhs a minute by thirteen humanities teachers. Their conclusion: Subject matter and breadth of vocabulary may determine use of filler words more than habit or anxiety.[5]

Whatever the reason, the cure for filler words is preparation. We reduce nervousness and preselect the right ways to say ideas through preparation and practice.

Emphasis

Putting more stress on certain words can have interesting effects on meaning. Think of the different inflections you could give the question "What do you mean by that?"

- *What* do you mean by that?
- What *do* you mean by that?
- What do *you* mean by that?
- What do you *mean* by that?
- What do you mean by *that?*

Professional communicators are sensitive to these kinds of differences. Listen carefully to the words emphasized by the radio announcer. "*Big Jim wants* to sell you a car" is likely to come across differently from, "Big Jim wants to sell *you* a car," or, better yet, "Big Jim wants to sell you a *car*." The last of these three examples focuses your attention on the product, whereas the first one focuses on what Big Jim wants. Who cares what Big Jim wants?

After the Presentation: Handling Questions

Prepare to handle questions; don't leave the question-and-answer sessions to chance.

For most business presentations there is a considerable amount of audience give and take, often in the form of a question-and-answer session following the talk. Sometimes a great deal of meaningful information is exchanged in such sessions. When the audience is large, or your topic is unusually controversial and you don't want to risk undermining your presentation, you may want to avoid the question-and-answer session altogether. If you do accept questions from the audience, remember that the fundamentals of handling questions are simply (1) repeat or restate the question, (2) anticipate and be prepared to handle them, and (3) keep control of yourself and the audience.

Listen to the questioner's question. If you are unclear what is being asked, seek clarification, or restate the question to be sure you are dealing with the same issue. Don't switch topics and use the question to go off on a tangent and restate some earlier point. (Some politicians are famous for doing this.)

Preparing for questions should not be a problem if the presentation is well planned. In each step of content development, you should put yourself in the shoes of your listeners and anticipate likely questions or reactions. Brainstorm all such possible objections with the help of others, and work out the best possible answers. Then have an associate fire the tough questions at you and practice your response.

Keeping control of the situation requires some effort when you face hostile or surprising questions. Don't get paranoid about the questions asked. What may at first sound like a real zinger may simply be a listener's way of testing you under fire or even confirming his or her *agreement* with your view. If you don't know the answer, say so. Don't try to fake it. Remember how important trustworthiness is to your credibility.

When hostile or loaded questions arise, take them in stride, and don't heckle back—maintain your dignity and good appearance.

Promotion of Listener Participation

Often it is desirable to get your listeners vocally involved through **listener participation.** In smaller groups, you may find it useful to encourage your listeners to ask questions *as you present your talk*. For some topics and audiences, you may prefer that listeners hold their questions until *after* you've presented your talk. In some cases you may want to *ask* questions to check for understanding and gain commitment as you go.

How can you encourage questions from listeners so you'll know they got the message? The tone you set in handling the first few questions will have an impact on future question-and-answer interaction. Here are a few tips on how to maximize this give and take.

- Avoid embarrassing listeners by putting them on the spot with one of your questions.

- Avoid expressing negative evaluations of questions received—verbally or non-verbally. All questions asked should be regarded as requests for more information. Such requests show listeners are interested in gaining an understanding of what you have to say. That's the same goal you have! Accept the old dictum that "The only stupid question is the one you don't ask."

- Restate the question for the rest of your audience before answering it, especially when all listeners may not have heard it originally.

- When a listener makes a statement, react to it (even if it doesn't require an answer). Don't just let a remark hang there in dead air. Say something to indicate agreement, disagreement, or at least appreciation for sharing the thought. A simple "thanks for sharing that idea with us, Sue," or "good point, Chris," can go a long way toward encouraging additional participation.

- Don't let a single questioner dominate. Encourage everyone who has questions or comments to speak up. If you have one person who is persistent in overparticipating, you may suggest that you'll get together with him or her after the presentation to clarify things.

- In some cases, you may want to plant one or two questions to ensure that the question session will get off the ground. Prearrange to have a few important questions asked, preferably questions that will stimulate further comments from others.

- Don't let the questions get too far afield of your topic. If they do, you may wind up spending too much time on irrelevant issues.

- Answer questions directly and candidly. If you don't know an answer, say so. Don't try to bluff. If it's an important enough question, offer to find out and get back to the questioner.

- Be patient. Some of your listeners won't grasp the message as quickly as you may think they should. Keep trying to help them understand.

One final thought. When you feel you have presented your talk as effectively as possible and you've handled a reasonable number of questions—quit. Don't drag it out. As an anonymous wag once said, "No speech can be entirely bad if it is short."

Creation of Your Personal Delivery Style

Anything you do or say (or don't do or say!) can be interpreted by others as having some meaning. Much of your image or style is projected nonverbally, that is, without words. Although you can't account for all possible interpretations of your nonverbal behaviors, you can become aware of some that most often convey meaning. Three kinds of nonverbal variables can be important in oral presentations. Be aware of the potential impact of these.

1. Appearance
2. Facial expression and eye contact
3. Voice cues and paralanguage

Appearance   You never get a second chance to make a first impression, says the old adage. Much of that first impression comes from the way you look. Your dress and grooming lend themselves to the total impression you convey to others.

Clothing should be appropriate to the occasion and it should not be so extreme in style that it draws attention away from your message. In other words, your tie or jewelry shouldn't talk louder than you do!

Perceived attractiveness increases the credibility of a speaker, and gives him or her a persuasive advantage over a less attractive person. Much of this attractiveness comes from your dress and grooming.

Facial Expression and Eye Contact

Smile! People relate well to a pleasant face, one that appears comfortable. A smile is often the best way to do this, although there are situations in which a smile would be inappropriate.

A videotape of one aspiring speaker showed him maintaining a serious facial expression—almost a scowl—throughout the presentation. When he viewed the tape, he was shocked at how this demeanor conveyed just the opposite of what he was hoping to project. He is a nice guy selling a pleasant message, but his face conveyed an intensity that scared people off.

Vocal Cues and Paralanguage

Paralanguage refers to that which accompanies what is said, not the message itself. It is *the way* something is said and not *what* is said. Examples of potentially distracting paralanguage might be a

- Breathy, whining, or strident voice
- Bombastic or rapid-fire delivery
- Dull, expressionless recitation

Vocal cues include emphasis and tone of voice that can change the meaning of a message. A man who is obviously enraged (as indicated by his nonverbal cues) who shouts, "I am not angry!" is contradicting the meaning of his words. Another example is a disappointed person who tells the boss, "Yeah, that'll be fine."

Other vocal cues come from *articulation,* the process of shaping sounds using the tongue, lips, jaw, and so forth. The sounds of the English language cannot be articulated clearly through half-closed mouths. Get the jaw moving—it's hinged for that purpose—to avoid mumbling or slurring words. Some common problems follow:

- Omitting final consonants ("goin'" instead of going; "havin'" instead of "having"; "ya" instead of "you")
- Omitting other sounds ("liberry" instead of "library"; "tempature" instead of "temperature"; "binness" instead of "business")
- Inserting additional sounds ("athalete" instead of "athlete"; "off-ten" instead of "often" (the *t* is silent)
- Distorted sounds or mispronunciations ("crick" instead of "creek"; "flustrated" instead of "frustrated")

When in doubt about how to pronounce a word, check the dictionary or ask someone else who would know. This applies to people's names too. You don't make many friends by mangling their names.

The delivery critique form in Figure 18–1 can be useful in getting feedback on your delivery style. (Your instructor will have extra copies of this in the supplemental materials that accompany this text.) Ask people you trust to give you the feedback you need.

Delivery Critique Form

Speaker: _____ Date: _____ Occasion: _____

1. Identify anything distracting in the opening moments of the talk. Check appearance, posture, body positioning, and use of space.

_____

_____

2. How was the eye contact? Did it create a sense of communication? Did the speaker look too much at some people and not enough at others?

_____

_____

_____

3. How effective were the speaker's gestures, facial expressions, and movement? Identify anything distracting.

_____

_____

_____

_____

4. Identify any mispronounced or unclearly expressed terms.

_____

_____

5. How was the voice? Was the volume appropriate? Was there sufficient variation in pitch and rate to hold listener interest? Was emphasis appropriate and helpful to understanding?

_____

_____

_____

_____

6. Identify any filler words and their frequency.

_____

_____

FIGURE 18–1

Delivery critique form.

Memory Devices: Notes versus Manuscript

A formal manuscript—a word-for-word copy of the talk—is seldom used in oral presentations. The only advantage of a manuscript is that it allows for precise expression and a written record of what exactly was said. This can be important in diplomacy and some formal negotiations. The drawback is that speakers sound as if they are reading (which they are) instead of communicating conversationally with listeners.

Extemporaneous speaking (from a few notes) is most common in business presentations.

For most presentations, it makes more sense to extemporize—use notes. The amount of detail in one's notes will vary, but extemporaneous speaking always permits more flexibility. You can more easily adjust to your audience. The late Senator Everett Dirksen enjoyed this speaking flexibility: "I always extemporize. I love the diversions, the detours. Without [detailed] notes you may digress . . . you may dart . . . and after you have taken on an interrupter, you don't have to flounder around with a piece of paper to find out where the hell you were."

How much should you put in your notes? When in doubt, leave it out. More speakers err on the side of too many notes than too few. Detailed notes become a security blanket. The more you have written, the more you are likely to look at them. The danger in having such notes is that you lose eye contact with your listeners.

Many speakers prefer to use note cards rather than sheets of paper. They're less distracting. Others have found that good visual aids (which Chapter Nineteen discusses) can take the place of notes.

Nothing can substitute for practicing out loud.

Regardless of whether you use notes, visual aids, or a manuscript, it is crucial that you practice the presentation *out loud* before actually delivering it. There is *no* substitute for this rehearsal.

If you are embarrassed to practice before family or friends, find a quiet spot with a mirror to practice. Better yet, videotape your talk in advance. Modern, low-cost videotaping is one of the great breakthroughs in communication training. Use it.

When you review your video or watch yourself in the mirror, be critical. It's better to catch potential weak spots in the presentation here than to have the "real thing" fizzle.

The Language of Feelings

Affective language conveys feelings, not just facts or data.

Much of what you say in presentation uses simple **reporting language.** It describes without conveying much emotion. Yet it is emotion that holds peoples' interest.

Contrasting with report language is **affective language**—words that go beyond purely factual information. Just as literary writing sounds and feels different from a newspaper story, so too does affective language differ from reporting.

Expressions of feeling convey urgency or enthusiasm, which is likely to be contagious. Your audience will "catch the vision" of what you say when they better understand your feelings.

Direct Address or "This Means You" Statements

One affective device is simply direct address to the listener. The speaker makes "this means you!" statements. Each day, you may recognize examples of this approach in television and radio commercials. The announcer "personally" addresses each of the several million people who may be listening and attempts to make them feel that he or she is speaking to them as individuals. The direct address technique is now also

Direct address
statements create the
impression of one-to-one
communication.

common in the written media. As the beginning of this book indicated, computers have been taught to program letters to include the name of the addressee several places within the body of the message. These "personal letters" have been shown to be effective in helping to raise funds for political candidates and getting people to enter *Reader's Digest* sweepstakes. They create the impression of one-to-one communication.

Direct address shows your listeners how your message applies to them and how it can meet their individual needs in some ways. This technique relates closely to the notion of tying features to benefits that we talked about in Chapter 12. Remember, a feature is a characteristic of the product being sold (e.g., this copy machine can duplicate on both sides of a sheet of paper). The benefit is a "what this means to you, the customer" statements (you can cut your postage and paper costs by up to 50 percent). Personalizing your messages by telling the listener that this applies to his or her specific interests and needs is an important and simple technique for holding interest.

Figurative Language

Another effective element is the use of figurative language devices, such as metaphor, simile, and hyperbole. Figurative expressions are frequently useful because they conjure up a humorous or thought-provoking image in the mind of the listener. Although they may be nonsensical if interpreted literally, they nevertheless can create interest when you hear them spoken figuratively. **Hyperbole** is the use of an intentional exaggeration not expected to be taken literally. Expressions, such as "the purchasing agent has *a basket full of money* to spend on office equipment," or "Harry wouldn't recognize a bargain if *it carried a neon sign*," or "by the time he finished speaking the audience was *comatose*," make a point in an imprecise but rather interesting way. Be careful to avoid clichés that deaden the effect. Look for fresh, imaginative expressions.

Metaphor is used figuratively to suggest a resemblance between things that are not literally associated. Educator John Dewey used the following metaphor that effectively conveyed his feelings about the process of intelligence quotient testing:

Metaphor and simile
will stick in your
listener's mind.

This intelligence-testing business reminds me of the way they used to weigh hogs in Texas. They would get a long plank, put it over a crossbar, and somehow tie the hog on one end of the plank. They'd search all around till they found a stone that would balance the weight of the hog and they'd put that on the other end of the plank. Then, they'd guess the weight of the stone.

A metaphor like that one will stick with the listeners long after your talk is over.

Simile is a figurative comparison usually using the terms "like" or "as." In simile, you would avoid saying "he is a moose" (hyperbole) and instead say, "He is *like* a moose."

Many figurative expressions are used so frequently that they become trite or overworked to the extent of being nearly meaningless. Expressions, such as "awesome," "blowout sale"; "mind-boggling"; "killer!"; "bottom line"; and many other terms fall in this category. Metaphor, hyperbole, and simile can add life to your style, but they do so at the cost of technical accuracy and objectivity. A clever and original metaphor can be fun to use and helpful to your audience. An overworked one will have no benefit and may even irritate your listeners.

Humorist Percy H. Whiting wrote a book based on his many years of experience called *How to Speak and Write with Humor.* His advice includes the following comments:

> **The surest way never to achieve brightness or wit in writing, conversation, or public speaking is to depend for your laughs on clichés and slang—or the worn-out humor of somebody else.**
>
> **People use clichés, slang, and profanity because they're too lazy to think up equivalent expressions of their own. So they use phrases that others invented and thus lose the chance to get practice in making humorous remarks. This "lazy man's language" can be produced by anyone with a reasonably good memory, substantially without mental effort.[6]**

Don't Tell Jokes—Use Wit

The most interesting and entertaining people you know never tell jokes, at least not in the "Did ya hear the one about. . . ." sense of that term. They do spice up their conversation, though, with humorous devices.

Almost any presentation—or any kind of communications for that matter—can be improved by a little wit. Being funny does not always come naturally. Yet anyone can learn to say funny things by applying certain humorous devices in original and creative ways. The following sections identify some of these devices.

The next time you hear a humorous remark or story, or you read cartoons that make you chuckle, analyze them and try to figure out what makes them funny. More often than not, you'll find one of the following techniques at work:

1. *Incongruous list.* This is an easy technique to use. The **incongruous list** involves simply including a totally out-of-place item in a list of serious items. If the item

Standard humor devices can add life to any presentation.

If you are not good at telling jokes, leave it to the professionals like Jay Leno of the Tonight Show. (Courtesy of John Barr/Gamma-Liaison, Inc.)

is sufficiently ridiculous, you'll get a good laugh. A cartoon showed a dignified gentleman addressing what appeared to be a corporate board of directors saying,

> **Gentlemen, my talk today is entitled "Corporate Responsibility, Sound Fiscal Policy, Profitability, and Madonna's latest movie."**

This technique is easy to use. Simply look through your talk, and see where you've used a list of articles or events—then slip in one ridiculous, out-of-place item. Here is another example from a cartoon.

> **Man listening to a taped message on the telephone: "The time is 3:10 P.M. The Temperature is 72. The air quality is acceptable. The barometer is 29.94. The fish are jumpin' and the cotton is high."**

2. *Exaggeration.* **Exaggeration** can also add vitality to your speech *provided the audience knows your kidding.* You have to make the exaggerated part so absurd that no one would mistakenly think you're serious. This technique has long been a mainstay of American humor from the "tall tales" of Paul Bunyon and Big John Henry to the writings of modern-day humorists like Dave Barry. As with the incongruous list item, exaggeration can be thrown into a talk almost anywhere without having to "set up" your listeners that a joke is coming. The element of surprise makes it fun to use.

> **A radio announcer caught me off guard when he informed listeners, the day after a particularly violent thunder shower, that "there's a 40 percent chance of afternoon and evening thunder showers and winds gushing from 15 to 3,000 miles per hour!"**

Practice exaggerations. Don't just mildly exaggerate—make it preposterous. Any speech that will be improved by a bit of humor is a good place to use exaggeration . . . [but] don't overdo it. Too much exaggeration is tiresome.

3. *Juxtaposition.* Adding an inappropriate, out-of-place, or inconsistent item or comment can provoke humor if it throws one off the train of thought and creates

COMMUNICATOR'S JOURNAL

Exaggeration

Complete these statements in your journal using exaggeration.

1. Tom typically shows up for class about _____ late.
2. Sarah's car is her pride and joy. She's spent at least $ _____ fixing it up.
3. Mom is no crazier than any other mother with _____ kids would be.
4. With all the good service we are giving, I'm sure we can expect the first month's sales to be about _____ units.

surprise. This technique works essentially the same as the incongruous list. Notice humorist Woody Allen's juxtaposition of a religious theme with the worldly.

> If only God would give me some clear sign! Like making a large deposit in my name at a Swiss bank.

> I don't want to achieve immortality through my work. I want to achieve it through not dying.

Here are some other variations of juxtaposition.

> "How're you getting along?" the veteran salesperson asked the new rep.
>
> "Rotten. I got nothing but insults every place I called."
>
> "That's funny," the older man mused. "I've been on the road 40 years. I've had doors slammed in my face, my samples dumped in the street. I've been tossed down stairs, been manhandled by janitors—but insulted? Never!"[7]

> I was going to buy a copy of *The Power of Positive Thinking*, and then I thought, What the hell good would that do?
>
> —Ronnie Shakes.

4. *Humorous quote or definition.* Any library will have several books of quotations, many of them witty, which can spice up a presentation. Often these use the techniques of juxtaposition, exaggeration, or incongruous lists. Here are a few of our favorites.

> I have a scheme for stopping war. It's this . . . no nation is allowed to enter a war till they paid for the last one.
>
> —Will Rogers

> If you're not the lead dog, the scenery never changes.
>
> —Anon.

> I am kind of a paranoid in reverse. I suspect people of plotting to make me happy.
>
> — J.D. Salinger

> Do something every day for no other reason than you would rather not do it at all.
>
> — William James

> What you think about expands into reality. I never think about what I don't want to expand.
>
> — Wayne Dyer

> The secret of being a good manager: "Keep the five guys who hate your guts away from the four who are undecided.
>
> — Casey Stengle

You will find interesting, quotable quotes in a wide range of sources from *Sports Illustrated* to the *Bible*. Almost every book will have a few. It's a good idea to keep a pack of 3- × 5-inch cards handy to jot these down when you come across them. Then toss the cards into a file box, and use them as the occasion arises or create a database in your computer. Software programs (e.g., *The Humor Processor*) come with thousands of jokes and quotes that can be modified in several ways. It is less important how you gather funny or thought-provoking material than that you do so.

5. *Insult*. This is one of the oldest forms of humor and one that is still popular. Some comedians make their living insulting others. Use insults carefully lest you cross the line of a good-natured barb that deflates the ego a bit. For example, one speaker was talking about his boss, who sat at the head table.

> "Folks, I want you to know that my boss, Pete Zaleski, is a fine leader, a sensitive and effective supervisor, a friend, a counselor, a skillful executive, an honest man, a man of great intelligence. . ."[pause]. The speaker, holding his speech notes, then turned to his boss and said, "Pete, what else does this say? I can't read your writing."

The popular honorary dinners have taken the insult to hew heights (or depths). I heard of a roast of a professor by some students that concluded (after citing all the educator's eccentricities) by excusing him his many shortcomings because it was widely known that Professor Hanson "is insane." That barb may have crossed the line between a good natured insult and slander. (Then again, it may have hit too close to home!) Be careful if you use the insult as a humorous technique. The insult, or satirical humor, can be "a two-edged sword that my cut deeper than intended, miss the marks, or decapitate the source on the return swing."[8]

6. *Anticlimax*. The techniques of **anticlimax** uses sudden collapse from a serious crescendo; falloff in dignity is so extreme as to be ludicrous. Here are some examples.

> A demure young bride, a trifle pale, her lips set in a tremulous smile, slowly stepped down the long church aisle on the arm of her dignified but aging father.
>
> As she reached the low platform before the alter, her tiny slippered foot brushed a potted fern, upsetting it. She looked down at the spilled dirt seriously, and her childlike eyes rose to the sedate face of the minister. "That," she said "is a hell of a place to put a plant!"[9]

> The trouble with heart disease is that the first symptom is often hard to deal with: sudden death.

> — Michael Phelps, MD

7. *Understatement.* Closely related to the anticlimax is understatement. Again, there is a "sudden collapse form a crescendo" when you lead up to a potentially powerful point and then present that point in restrained terms. Your conclusion is represented less strongly than the facts would bear out. George Santayana's quote about philosophy is a classic.

> It is a great advantage for a system of philosophy to be substantially true.

Another example follows:

> On a television program seen some years ago, songwriter Don Schiltz (who wrote the Kenny Rogers's hit *The Gambler*) used this technique beautifully. Schiltz had just won the Country Music Association's award for best song of the year. As he came forth to accept the prestigious award he said, "You know, this is the first song I've ever had recorded." [Pause, then in a matter-of-fact tone:] "I find this encouraging."

When the facts and reasoning presented are exceptionally strong, an understated conclusion can be powerful as well as interesting.

8. *Play on words.* One final humor and interest technique is the play on words. Occasionally these work, but they often miss the mark in oral communication. The pun (one form of play on words) can be dangerous. Either they bypass the listener entirely or, when recognized, elicit a groan. Nevertheless, here are examples of word plays.

> During one of his many presidential election campaigns, comedian Pat Paulson proclaimed, "I'm not a right nor a left winger. I'm sort of middle of the bird."

> Horse sense is stable thinking.

> She thinks the white male rat is a redundancy.

Many humorous devices overlap the categories described and incorporate several gimmicks. The best advice for putting lively humor into a presentation is to plan, prepare, and practice it. Avoid the use of clichés or worn-out phrases. Then experiment with ways of humorizing your talks to give them sparkle and interest.

Humor and clever wording are not the only ways to create feeling and interest. Although these techniques for arousing listener involvement are useful in their place, often the most powerful emotional reactions can come from objectively presented facts themselves. When factual data are presented explicitly and clearly, they can lead the listener to the conclusion you are trying to make without additional techniques.

The creative use of a variety of interest-building devices is a key to effective speaking. Some of the best speakers shift smoothly from wit to the effectiveness of facts. Holding your listeners' interest is an art, not a science. This chapter has suggested some devices that, when skillfully used, can "add a little life to your style." Try them, and see how your listeners react.

Understanding the Basics

• Some anxiety is perfectly natural when you are speaking before groups. You should expect it and strive to make it work for, not against, you.

• You can bring the level of speaker anxiety within a manageable range (improving your coping quotient) by being well prepared and idea conscious, learning to relax, and not being self-conscious.

• Your listeners want you to succeed.

• Gestures and body movements convey dynamism. They also serve to emphasize and provide nonverbal transitions, indicating the flow of your message for the listener.

• Facial expression and eye contact may be the most important nonverbal communicators. People expect eye contact when communicating with others.

• Your personal characteristics project a total image as you speak to others. Much of this image comes across through your voices. Avoid annoying vocal mannerisms, such as lack of variation, verbalized pauses, and up-talk.

• Audience participation, with question-and-answer sessions being the most common form, leads to the creation of better understanding. The speaker often sets the tone and climate for such give and take.

• Affective language conveys more than factual data; it expresses feelings.

• Direct address or the use of "this means you" statements personalize messages for listeners.

• Metaphor, hyperbole, and simile conjure up thought-provoking images that hold listener interest.

• Some figurative expressions are overused and become trite. Avoid use of clichés and other overused phrases. Achieve brightness or wit in expression by being original.

• Wit can be developed through creative use of light humorous devices.

> Incongruous list
> Exaggeration
> Juxtaposition
> Humorous quote or definition
> Insult
> Anticlimax
> Understatement
> Play on words

• Powerful emotional reactions can arise from explicitly presented and unembellished facts.

• Creative use of a variety of interest-building devices is a key to speaking effectiveness.

KEY TERMS AND CONCEPTS

speaker anxiety	simile	reporting language
credibility	metaphor	affective language
idea conscious	coping quotient	hyperbole
exaggeration	listener participation	anticlimax
verbalized pauses	incongruous list	

QUESTIONS FOR FURTHER THOUGHT

1. What is a coping quotient? How can you expand it so that you'll be more relaxed as speakers?

2. What is meant by the statement, "Self-consciousness tends to be self-destructive"?

3. How do nonverbal aspects of delivery affect your listeners? Give examples.

4. How can you encourage questions from your listeners?

5. How can you add life to your style? Describe five ways and give an original example of each.

Education of a Wandering Man

The well-known author Louis L'Amour published a biography called *Education of a Wandering Man* in which he talks of his experiences in developing his excellent communication skills. In the following excerpt, L'Amour speaks of the challenge of becoming an effective speaker, even for the well read and successful.[10]

Shortly before World War II, I was invited to attend a lecture at the University of Oklahoma. Two quite gifted speakers were each to talk for a few minutes, and the feature of the evening was to be an address by George Milburn.

An Oklahoman who had made a name for himself in the short story field, Milburn . . . was a gifted writer. But George was a writer, not a speaker, and this was his first time as the latter. Obviously, he had written a good speech, but he just could not put it together. He fumbled and floundered and we all suffered with him. Finally, he seemed to get started, and then a train whistle blew somewhere outside and it might as well have cut his throat.

All present were in sympathy with him, but sitting there I suffered as much as he did, I believe, for I could see myself in the same position. At the time I did not have the courage to stand up and say my name in public. What I had seen happen to George Milburn could happen to me, and because I was confident that I was going to "make it," I knew it would happen.

What to do? I knew I would never attend a class, as I would avoid even trying to speak, so I decided the thing to do was to take the bull by the horns and just start speaking. I let the word get around that I was open for speaking engagements, knowing that sooner or later I would be challenged and have to make good. . . . It came about just that way.

The night before the speech I did not sleep. The day of the lecture I decided I could not go through with it. A lady was driving some distance to pick me up and I called her to beg off. It was too late. She was already on her way.

All I wanted now was to get out of it, any way I could. I was sure I would make an unholy fool of myself trying to speak to any sort of crowd, yet I could think of no way out. With a dreadful sinking feeling, as of a man going to his execution, I got in the car and we turned to leave. I thought of jumping out. I thought of everything. . . .

There was no way out. I had gotten myself into this fix and must see it through. On stage I reached into my pockets for my notes and they were not there. . . . So I began to talk without them, and somehow the evening passed and everyone seemed pleased. Especially me, as I was off the hook.

That was the beginning, and many years ago, but I firmly believe that if I could become a speaker, anybody can do anything if he or she wants to enough. Since that time I have ap-peared on the platform with a former President of the United States, a Supreme Court Justice, and many others. Education takes many forms and this was an important part of my education. Of course, if one is to speak, one must have something worth saying, and say it intelligently. The important lesson to be learned is that one's principal enemy in such cases is oneself.

A thing to remember is that the audience wants you to be good. No matter whether they know you or not, they do not want to be bored, so whether you realize it or not, they are pulling for you.

This is an age of communication. At one time or another, nearly everyone will have to stand up and sell his bill of goods, whatever it may be.

All young men and women owe it to themselves to be able to write a letter on not more than one page, to set forth an idea or possible plan. That same young person should, in a few brief spoken words, be able to deliver that idea orally.

No need for details, for if the idea is expressed well, there will be questions, and the details can come later.

That day back in Oklahoma when I decided to become a public speaker was one of the most important in my life.

(Excerpt from EDUCATION OF A WANDERING MAN by Louis L'Amour. Copyright ©1989 by Louis D. L'Amour and Katherine E. L'Amour 1983 Trust. Used by permission of Bantam Books, a division of Bantam Doubleday Dell Publishing Group, Inc.)

Applying Your Knowledge

1. What points about speaker anxiety discussed in this chapter are reinforced by this Louis L'Amour excerpt?

2. Louis L'Amour describes his experience from years ago. To what extent do would-be speakers face the same hurdles today, or have things changed?

Applying Your Skills

ACTIVITY 18-1: Changing Meanings

See how the meaning of the sentence below is changed by putting the emphasis on a different word. Strongly emphasize the underlined word. Then write down the implied message. I'll do the first one:

1. <u>I</u> think Homer can do that. (Implied meaning: Other people probably don't think so, but I do.)

2. I <u>think</u> Homer can do that.

3. I think <u>Homer</u> can do that.

4. I think Homer can do <u>that</u>.

ACTIVITY 18-2: Discover Your Filler Words

Tape-record your next presentation or conversation. Then count the number of filler words you use. Identify your most used verbalized pauses and commit to reducing their use.

List your results (fillers used and number of times each).

ACTIVITY 18-3: Clear Articulation

Many radio and television announcers develop outstanding articulation by practicing tongue twisters. Try the following ones. Start by saying them slowly and firmly, so that each sound is clearly formed. Gradually increase to your normal rate of speed.

1. Sid said to tell him that Benny hid the penny many years ago.

2. Fetch me the finest French-fried freshest fish that Finney fries.

3. Three gray geese in the green grass grazing; gray were the geese, and green was the grazing.

4. Shy Sarah saw six Swiss wrist watches.

ACTIVITY 18-4: Visualize Success

One of the best ways to "prepare" for a presentation is to give that presentation in your mind. Schedules do not always allow for enough time to rehearse physically; thus, it becomes necessary to incorporate alternatives. Try visualizing yourself giving the presentation. Do this completely in your mind. Picture the following:

1. What the room looks like

2. What the seating arrangement is

3. What the audience looks like

4. What the temperature in the room is

5. How well you are prepared

6. How organized your presentation is

7. How well your introduction stirs attention

8. Go through your main points and support material

9. Use your visuals to enhance your verbal expression

10. Answer questions confidently

11. Summarize and conclude

12. Listen to the applause

Try to include picturing with as many of your senses (hearing, sight, touch, taste, and smell) as possible. Your brain is a powerful tool that will influence your physical characteristics in a positive way. Remember to picture yourself actually giving the presentation successfully. This is a way of mentally rehearsing.

ACTIVITY 18-5: Just Relax

As mentioned in the chapter, relaxing is one of the three ways to control speaking anxiety. Here is a breathing exercise for you to try. Breathe in through your nose to a slow count to four: 1 . . . 2 . . . 3 . . . 4. Now exhale through your mouth to another slow count to four: 1 . . . 2 . . 3 . . . 4. Do this four or five times. Don't worry about hyperventilation; you hyperventilate when you don't exhale. As long as you exhale after each inhale, you will be fine. This has helped many speakers relax before starting. Try it!

ACTIVITY 18-6: A Story from Your Past

Think of and briefly list some of the main ideas from a past experience in which you learned something about yourself. This chapter discusses the importance of personal background and experience. Many times experiences have had great impact on your life.

Now, list three ways in which this story might be used to illustrate a point in an oral presentation.

1.

2.

3.

ACTIVITY 18-7: Speakers Exhibiting Four Credibility Factors

Give an example of speakers you have experienced exhibiting any of the following four credibility factors

Explain what you experienced.

	Speaker	Experienced
1. Expertise		
2. Trustworthiness		
3. Composure		
4. Dynamism		

PERFORMING
on the Job

CASE 18-1 **It's Not Easy in Front of a Group**

For the past few years, Central Savings Bank (CSB) has been implementing more aggressive techniques of generating additional business. Incentives have been put in place for front-line employees who sell additional financial products and services to existing customers. They also receive incentives for cross-selling new customers additional products when they are opening their accounts at CSB. In addition to individual incentives, an annual bonus has been put in place for all employees. This annual bonus is based on service quality to customers and net profit for CSB.

Many employees participate and earn extra income by selling customers additional services and products. Each month in staff meetings, the highest-achieving employees receive special recognition for their accomplishments. The incentives and bonus have proved to be positive factors in CSB's effort to implement its plan.

In the last staff meeting it was decided by management that the top three "incentive earners" would take a few minutes each to tell an experience of their success. Each of the three employees were notified one week prior to the meeting and told to take 3 to 5 minutes in sharing their story with the rest of the staff. All seemed agreeable and willing to participate.

During the staff meeting when it came time for the three employees to share their stories, an interesting thing occurred. They all made poor presentations. All seemed nervous. They spoke to the floor and could hardly be heard (a microphone was offered, but all declined). They lacked any kind of enthusiasm in telling their stories, and each took fewer than two minutes. Management was visibly disappointed.

Case Questions

1. Why did these employees have such a difficult time telling their stories to the staff?

2. Was management's idea to have staff members present stories a good one? Why? Why not?

3. Do you think the employees just failed to do any kind of preparation?

4. Management at CSB wants this practice to continue in monthly staff meetings. What recommendations do you suggest to improve it?

CASE 18-2 **Your Question Please**

A well-known professor (Dr. Stuart) from an Arizona University was asked to give a presentation at the Phoenix Convention Center to a group of 300 to 400 executives from around the United States. Dr. Stuart is highly sought after as a speaker. He has written numerous books, articles, and papers in the area of marketing along with ongoing research in the area. The convention organizers felt fortunate to get him as a speaker. Dr. Stuart agreed to give a two-hour presentation on the second day of the convention (Tuesday). His topic would be "relationship marketing."

On the second day of the convention, approximately 350 executives settled into an auditorium to hear the presentation on relationship marketing. All went well. Dr. Stuart was well prepared and spoke eloquently on the topic he loved. He seemed to adjust well to the fact that his presentation took place immediately following lunch at 1:30 P.M. His presentation was done with the lights dimmed because he made use of numerous transparencies projected on a large screen in the front of the auditorium.

At the conclusion of his presentation, he spent some time answering questions from members of the audience. Most were general questions about his research findings, clarification of terms, or future projects. However, a gentleman stepped to one of the microphones for audience questions and wanted to know something specific.

"In your presentation today you stressed the importance of training our employees to be relationship oriented. This is just fine provided you have the time to train. In my business we deal with the public from the time we open early in the morning until the time we close late at night. How do you suggest I get my employees trained to build relationships with customers?" asked the audience member.

Dr. Stuart seemed somewhat surprised by the question. "Well, each situation is different. I would have to look at your situation in more detail to be able to give you advice or a recommendation," he said.

After this answer, the gentleman who asked it turned and, rather than returning to his seat, walked directly to the nearest exit and left the room. It appeared his question had not been answered to his satisfaction.

Case Questions

1. Describe Dr. Stuart's credibility.
2. Do you think most of the audience enjoyed the presentation? Why?
3. Describe the challenges for Dr. Stuart giving a presentation after lunch in a room with the lights down low.
4. Why did the gentleman walk out of the room after Dr. Stuart answered his question?

CHAPTER NINETEEN

The *Visual* *Presentation* *of* Information

Getting the Picture

LEARNING GOALS

When you have studied this chapter, you should be able to:

- Describe four ways visual information improves both oral and written communication.

- Identify six types of direct visuals, and give examples of their use.

- Name nine key rules for the effective use of direct visuals.

- Name the three most common types of projected visuals, and describe their advantages over direct visuals.

- Name six suggestions for the effective use of projected visuals.

- Know how to position listeners and visuals to boost communication effectiveness.

The Way It Is . . . The Medium Is the Message

Doris Steenburg, a financial manager and a reluctant speaker, is asked to give a 15-minute presentation at a quarterly management meeting. She comes to the front of the room with an ominously large stack of overhead transparencies. After fumbling for the on-off switch, she turns on the projector. All eyes in the room shift to the glaring blank screen, but she hasn't put up a transparency yet. She just felt she would be more comfortable with the projector switched on. She begins her presentation, moving rapidly through 20 transparencies.

Her transparencies were produced on the office copier from pages of her latest report. Because her copier hasn't been well maintained, the print quality is fuzzy. In spots, the clear plastic transparencies are smudgy. They average 18 to 25 lines of information per page. Some included charts and graphs, but many were just text and numbers. The type is so small the managers in the front have to squint to read it. She hasn't put frames on her transparencies, so some of them stick together, and others float in static electricity and refuse to sit on the projector straight.

Doris is aware that these black-on-white transparencies aren't exactly state-of-the-art visuals, so she tells her audience, "You probably can't read this, but . . ." several times during the presentation.

If Doris is lucky, her visual aids and the way she uses them are standard-operating procedure in her organization. If so, the worst she's done is to look average in front of management, missing a great opportunity for sharing her professionalism. If her audience is accustomed to well-prepared visuals, used skillfully, her professional image just took a dive.[1]

Remember the conversation in Chapter One about people's preferences for visual, auditory, and kinesthetic stimuli? Although people process information through each of these senses (assuming that none is impaired), they typically allow one of them to be dominant. For about 70 percent of people, that dominant stimulus is visual. This majority of all people prefers to receive information visually.

People you communicate with today were raised with much visual stimulation: television, movies, video games, and color printing. They are not accustomed to processing spoken words alone. They want to see something.

Visuals Aid Message Comprehension

Studies of listener comprehension repeatedly come to the same conclusion: Visual aids help listeners get the message. Typical of these studies was one by Robert S. Craig of the U.S. Public Health Service who reported that . . . "when knowledge was imparted to a person by *telling alone,* the recall three hours later was 70 percent, and three days later only 10 percent." When *showing alone* was used "the knowledge recall three hours later was 72 percent, and three days later about 35 percent." However, when *both telling and showing* were the teaching tools, the recall three hours

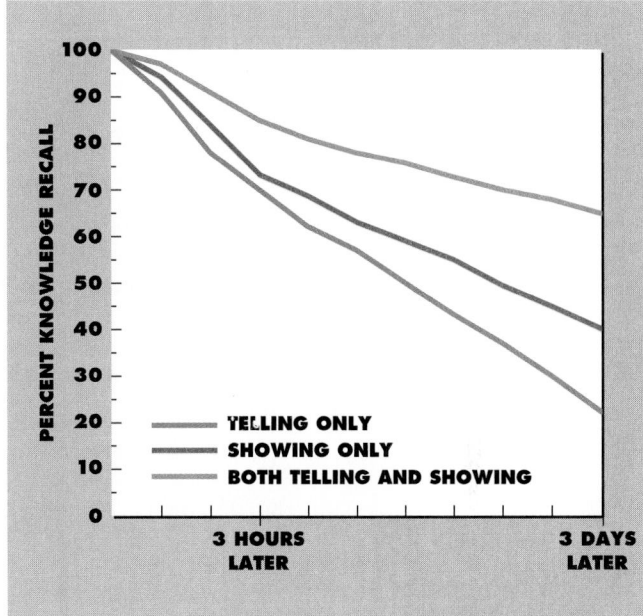

FIGURE 19–1

Listener comprehension increases with the use of visual media.

later was 85 percent, and three days later 65 percent.[2] This study was done when visual media were far less commonplace, and expected, than today (see Figure 19–1).

Robert L. Montgomery, a veteran teacher of public speaking, strongly encourages heavy use of visual aids. He relates that "the American Management Association, which has been training people in management throughout the world since 1923, says that they found through testing that there is only a 10 percent return on an average lecture, but this percentage jumps to as high as 50 percent when there are visual aids and audience participation as well."[3]

The heavy use of audiovisual materials started during World War II when the military services were faced with a tremendous task of quickly and efficiently training millions of people. Men and women of different educational backgrounds had to be trained in many different skills needed for the war effort. This training had to be done quickly and thoroughly. Social scientists then found that about 85 percent of learning is achieved through the visual stimuli—what you see. When visual aids are added to spoken instruction, 35 percent more information can be absorbed in the same amount of time, and retention is about 55 percent better.[4]

Now that you are dizzy with statistics, here is another one that's easy to remember: Kodak Corporation estimates that "Your audience remembers 20 percent of what they hear and 80 percent of what they see."

Although this chapter talks more about oral presentations than written documents, many of the principles for effective visuals apply to both. Any document can be made better with graphic displays of information, just as any presentation similarly benefits.

Although this chapter seems to emphasize oral presentations, many of the same principles of visual communication apply to written documents.

Visuals Help the Audience and the Communicator

The visual display of information is vital to the communicator because it serves at least four important functions:

1. It helps crystallize abstract ideas in the minds of message receivers.

2. It helps listeners and readers retain information—illustrated ideas linger in the mind.

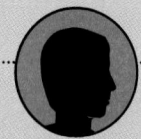
3. It helps fight listener or reader boredom, daydreaming, confusion, and apathy. It perks up interest.

4. In oral presentations, it serves as a guide to keep a speaker on track by doubling as notes.

Consider how visuals help you as a communicator. You should recognize visuals as an internal part of your presentation or document, not an afterthought tacked on.

As you develop the content of your message, visuals can help in organizing ideas strengthening the impact of the message, creating continuity of thought, providing variety, and clarifying important concepts or associations.

> Think about opportunities for visuals as you plan a document or presentation.

Proper Use of Visual Aids

Studies repeatedly indicate that visual materials reinforce virtually any message. Here are a few thoughts to remember when using such visuals.

1. Each visual should be planned to drive home a *single* point. The quickest way to lose the effectiveness of an audiovisual aid is to overcomplicate it or try to convey too much information. This is especially true with charts or illustrations. Keep them simple and concise. Never display a chart or graph that your audience cannot comprehend in 30 seconds. You can accomplish this by sticking to one key point and removing any superfluous materials.

2. You should know exactly *when* to present your illustration (or where to place it in a document) so it coincides with your message. Reveal the chart or illustration only when you are ready to present it. Otherwise, it will distract or confuse your reader or listener.

3. In written documents, you should always refer to the visual in the text. For example, say "As you can see in chart 3 . . .," or "The table below summa-

rizes. . . ." Numbering any visuals is preferred so that you can precisely refer to the one you want to highlight.

4. If you use slides or overhead transparencies that require dimming the lights, you should remember that you are losing some important speaker-to-audience variables. Some communication experts discourage the general use of slides for this reason. Physical presence has a great deal to do with psychological motivation. When the lights go out, you lose eye contact with your audience. You become an impersonal voice in the dark—at best, a mere narrator. Nevertheless, there are many strong arguments that favor the use of such visuals, especially if you can maintain eye contact.

5. Be sure you know how to work all equipment you may use. Slide projectors, tape recorders, videotape playback units, and the like all have their own idiosyncracies. For example, more than a few users of videotape playback are unaware that each time they hit the "stop" button, the tape would rewind several feet. When the tape started again there was a distinct sense of *déjà vu,* the illusion of having previously had a given experience. It is better to use the "pause" control instead. Machines differ, so be sure to check out its features in advance.

Another common equipment problem is bulb burnout on an overhead or slide projector. Most machines have a backup bulb, but speakers are wise to check both bulbs before the presentation.

By and large, flip charts, posters, and overhead transparencies are the simplest types of visual aids for oral presentations. They give good value for the money. An added benefit is that any of them can be easily transformed into a printed handout and given to your audience after the presentation.

Computers can easily produce graphics that can be converted into simple visuals. Software presentation programs are widely available. Some examples of such software are WordPerfect Presentations, Aldus Persuasion, and Microsoft's Powerpoint. These can prepare computer-generated visuals that can be projected onto a large screen.

If computer projectors are not available, these programs can print out color images on paper (which can be made into transparencies via a color photocopier) or on a disk that can be taken to a copy service that will transfer the images directly onto slides or overheads. Today, anyone can create professional quality visuals quickly and fairly easily with such software.

A few cautions: Don't let the visuals drive the whole presentation or document, and don't get too clever so that they overwhelm the message.

This chapter focuses on visuals you can prepare without professional help.

The following sections elaborate on three classes of visuals and offer suggestions for effective use of each. The three types are direct visual, projected visuals, and dynamic visuals. The emphasis will be on the kind of visuals you can prepare and use without calling for professional preparation.

Direct Visuals

Direct visuals are drawings, graphics, illustrations or photos that can be viewed without special equipment. These are the only kind of visuals you can use in written documents. In oral presentations, these can range from the simple flip chart or white board to three-dimensional model or mock-up.

Probably the single most important thing to remember about the direct visual is to keep it simple and concise. This is especially true of graphs, charts, or other illustrations. Simple design lingers in the mind of the receiver.

Here are some types of direct visuals and suggestions as to how to make them.

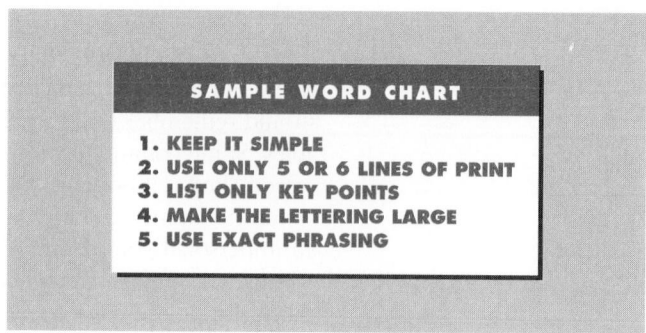

FIGURE 19-2
Word chart rules.

Word Charts. A **word chart** states key ideas concisely and directly. It is probably your simplest visual. In preparing word charts, economy of language is crucial. Be sure that the lettering is large so that everyone in your presentation audience can read it. The sample chart illustrated in Figure 19–2 shows you some rules for making word charts.

When using word charts in presentations, you are not limited to poster board mounted on a tripod. One alternative is to make boxes of three-sided charts that stand alone. On each side of the visual is a different word chart. Other sets of word charts or simple graphs can be stacked inside each other and removed as needed. This approach has the added advantage of avoiding the common problem of charts that slip off the tripods or fall off the wall. These three-dimensional charts can be placed on a table or on the floor (if your listeners can see them there) as you speak. The added advantage is that they are different from visuals most people have come to expect, so they hold attention better (Figure 19–3).

Flip Charts. Flip charts use large tablets of paper on an easel. They are inexpensive and can be adapted to a variety of situations. You can prepare them in advance and add to them during the presentation, or use them for recording ideas shared by oth-

FIGURE 19-3
A three-sided word chart.

FIGURE 19–4
Flip Chart.

ers. Flip charts are usually informal and work best with small- to medium-sized groups (Figure 19–4).

Flip charts require good handwriting but allow creativity in drawings as well as words. Use broad-tip marking pens in a variety of colors, and practice different lettering styles.

Figure 19–5 shows some examples of drawings you can make using just four basic shapes. The drawings in Figure 19–6 combine these basic shapes with a few simple cartoon features and can result in a variety of symbols.

Pie Charts. A pie chart is a simple, circular illustration that is divided into segments to show part-to-whole comparison. It can effectively show only a few broad divisions. If you hand draw pie charts, remember these points:

1. Cut segments of the pie accurately, usually beginning at the top and moving clockwise for each new segment.

2. Label each "slice," showing what it represents and the percentage it represents.

3. Use large, clear lettering for the chart. A simple, hand-drawn pie chart is shown in Figure 19–7, page 535.

If you use a graphics software package on your computer, it will automatically slice the pie correctly for you. It can also make it look three-dimensional and do other things with colors, as shown in Figure 19–8, page 535.

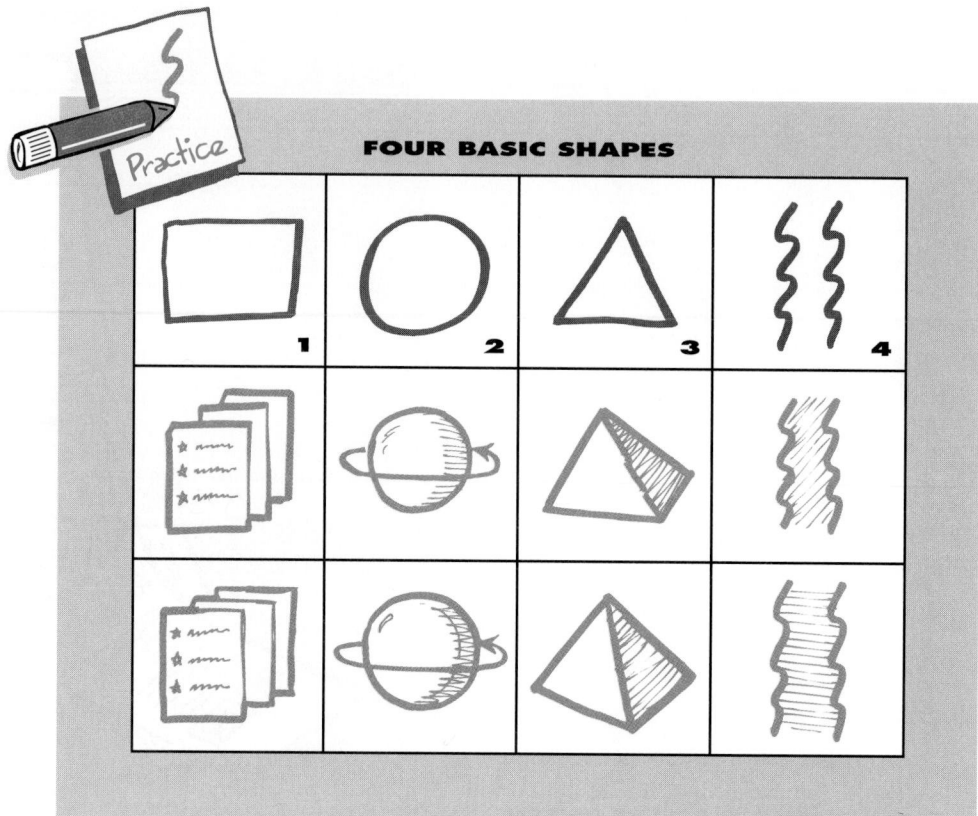

FIGURE 19–5

Many drawings evolve from just four basic shapes.

Line, Bar, and Column Graphs. A line graph is a "trendy" way to show a continuous picture of trends or changes over time as shown in Figure 19–9, page 535. It can also show simple comparisons of trends as in Figure 19–10, page 536. Avoid having too many lines on the chart. Color coding can be helpful to clarify the message. These were generated on a computer. Hand drawing these is rarely done anymore. Software does it better and faster.

Comparing graphs with different scales can mislead.

If you'll look again at Figure 19–10, notice a potential problem that could be misleading to the viewer. The drop in the value of the dollar appears to be as great as the increase in the sale profit. A more careful look at percentage changes, however, tells a different story. Sales profits go from around $200 per unit to $360 (a 180 percent increase), whereas the dollar value went from around $.50 to $.45 (a 10 percent decrease). The different scales on the vertical axis of the graphs suggest a more dramatic change than actually occurred. If the two graphs were displayed together, implying a comparison, a misleading conclusion may be reached by the viewer. The data are distorted.

The bar chart or column graph can quickly compare quantities. The **bar chart** uses a horizontal design; **column graphs** are vertical. Figure 19–11 on page 536 shows a bar chart and a column graph.

Dry-Mounted Photographs. Photographs or drawings can provide excellent visual support in documents. Photographs or pictures large enough for a presentation may be flimsy and difficult to handle if on lightweight paper.

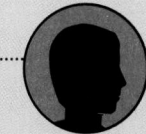
Learn a Few Lettering and Drawing Tips

Even if your handwriting isn't legible, and you can't draw a straight line (actually nobody can), you can learn lettering and drawing styles with a little practice. Use a felt-tip pen to practice the following styles.

Write your name and the alphabet in each letter style. Then practice the basic drawing shapes as shown.

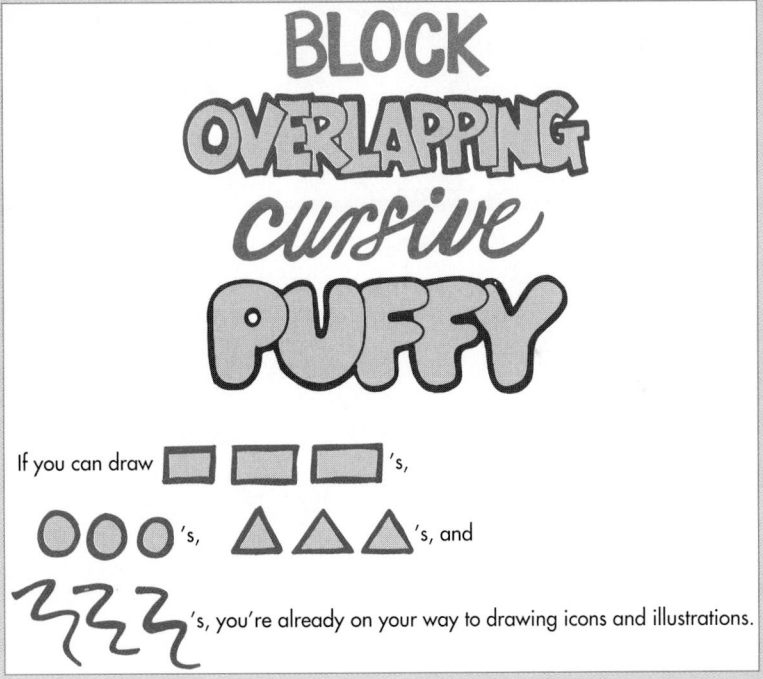

One simple and relatively inexpensive technique for overcoming this disadvantage is dry-mounted photographs. Dry mounting sticks material to backings, such as poster board. Dry-mounting tissue—a thin sheet of rice paper coated on both sides with heat-sensitive adhesive—is placed between the visual and the backing material. When heat is applied, the adhesive softens and adheres the visual to the backing.

Dry mounting adds professionalism as well as durability to visuals and beats fumbling with flimsy photographs or paper illustrations.

Props or Models. When your audience is relatively small, you may want to use props or models. A nuclear reactor engineer used a prop to gain audience surprise and got the attention of his audience with this statement: "This small piece of atomic fuel weighs a little over 2 pounds, yet is capable of generating the heat equivalent of over 2,000 tons of coal."

FIGURE 19-6
Polishing the four basic shapes created cartoon icons.

When giving a talk to explain the workings of a new machine or to sell a product, it makes sense to have the machine or product there as a prop.

In a written document, an enclosed sample of the product can serve as a prop.

Effective Direct Visuals. Direct visuals are inexpensive and appropriate in most documents or oral presentations. When designing and using them, remember these key rules.

1. Keep them simple.
2. Keep them clear. (Use different colors and so forth to highlight key information.)
3. Refer specifically to the visual in document text.
4. Place the visual where it can be seen by everyone. (Don't stand in front of it as you explain the material.)
5. Don't talk to the visual aid; maintain eye contact with your listeners.

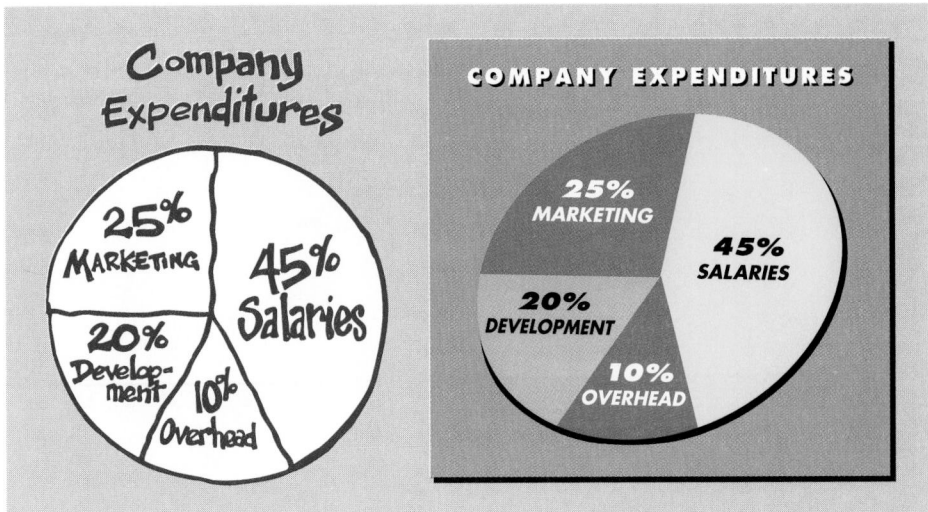

6. Display the visual only when it is in use. (Showing it too early or, in some cases, leaving it up too long, can be distracting.)

7. Be sure it's large enough to be seen by everyone.

8. Use visuals to support important ideas in your message. (The time and effort of creating visuals conveys to your readers or listeners that your message is important. Make sure it really is.)

9. Strive for professionalism in the design of your visuals. Get artistic or computer help when necessary.

Projected Visuals

The three most prominent **projected visuals** are overhead transparencies, slides, and computer projections. Software packages coupled with a color printer capable of printing on transparencies can produce easy overheads. Slides generally have to be prepared using equipment not readily available in most offices. Quick-print office service stores and photograph shops can usually make these. Computer projections use a

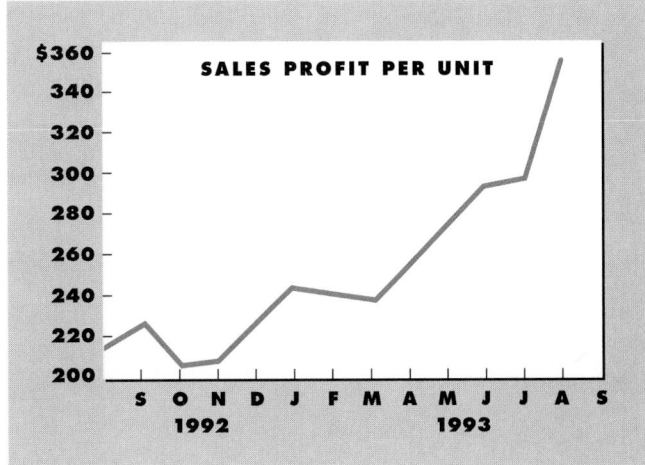

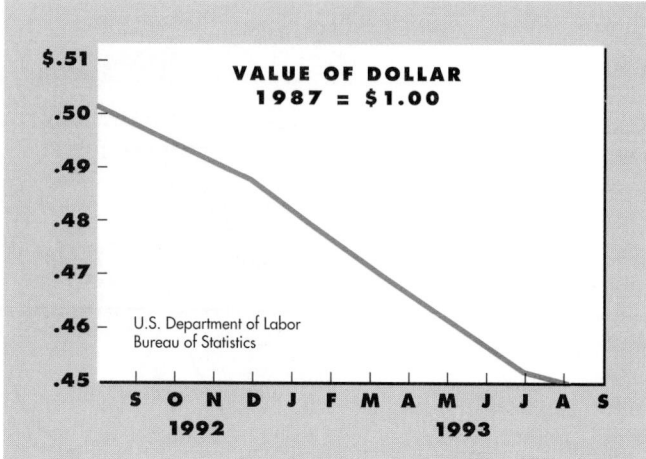

FIGURE 19-10

A line graph showing comparisons and trends.

device such as a liquid crystal display (LCD) plate to throw an image onto a screen. The technology in this area is changing rapidly, and the process of creating professional visual presentations is getting easier for those willing to learn the technology.

Projected visuals have two major advantages over direct visuals when used in oral presentations.

FIGURE 19-11

A bar chart and column chart.

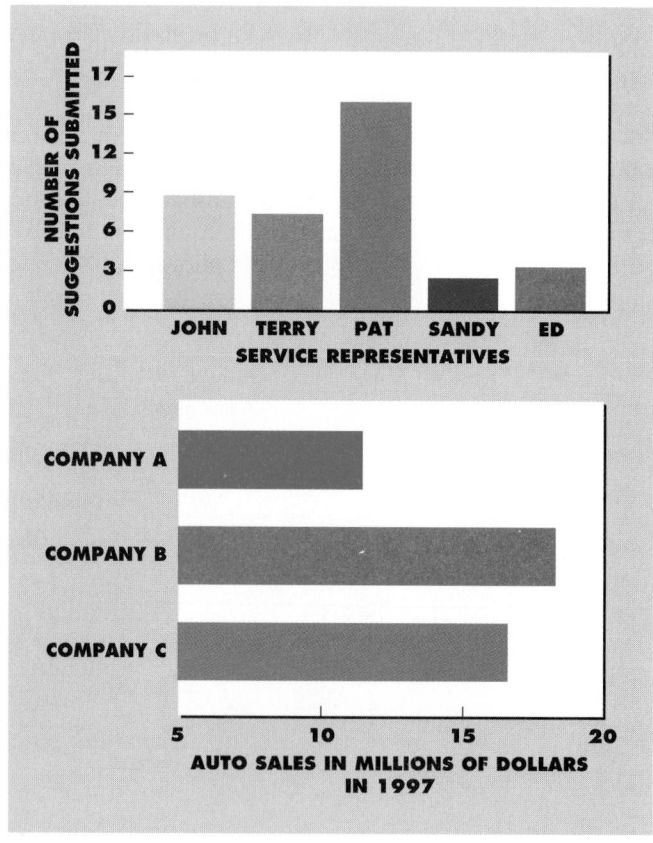

Telling and showing works best to get your audience to understand and remember information. (Photo by John Coletti, courtesy of Stock Boston.)

1. They are less cumbersome to use.

2. They can be used with large audiences who may not be able to see direct visuals.

Overhead Transparencies. Today's transparency projectors are often portable, quiet, and capable of reproducing a sharp image. The transparencies themselves can be made simply, often using a xerographic copy as a master. This enables the presen-

Computer image projectors work well with large audiences. (Charles Arrico/ Courtesy of Superstock.)

ter to get cartoons, newspaper clippings, line drawings, and illustrations of many different types and quickly convert them into **overhead transparencies.** In addition, felt-tip pens that write on transparencies are readily available. These let the speaker put a transparency on display, and then add to it in his or her own handwriting. In situations in which a chalkboard or flip chart is not available, a presenter can simply write on a blank transparency sheet as he or she speaks. This would be projected on a wall or screen for easy viewing by the audience. This has the added benefit of allowing the speaker to maintain eye contact while continuing to face the audience as he or she writes on the transparency.

Another use for the overhead transparency projector is the display of cartoons. Cartoons can frequently convey in few words an important concept or idea. Cartoonists often use stock symbols to communicate messages rapidly without too much detail. It is a simple process to make overhead transparencies of cartoons you have clipped from newspapers or magazines. These can add a great deal to your presentation if they fit into the flow of thought. (Note: If cartoons are used as a standard sales presentation or on company literature, you must get **cartoon permission** from the artist. The artist can be reached through the syndicate that distributes the cartoon to newspapers and magazines. You will usually have to pay a fee, depending on your intended usage.)

The most common error in using transparencies: too much information on each visual.

The most common mistake in using transparencies is putting too much information on each page. The rules for making word charts discussed earlier also apply to transparencies. Keep them simple.

Many presenters mount transparencies on cardboard frames or plastic sleeve "flip frames." This makes you look more professional and keeps the transparencies from sticking together or sliding because of static electricity buildup. Another advantage is that the frames provide a good place to write your notes and key ideas.

Slides. **Photographic slides** can be produced inexpensively and can provide a professional image to your presentation. There are at least three sources of good slides. First, the speaker (or his or her staff) can take photographs of precisely the slides needed for the planned presentation. Second, photographic slides can be purchased or shot to order by a professional photographer. A third option is to turn to computer technology.

Computer graphics can be created in-house or by professional organizations (see Figure 19–12). Some companies will take your data (which may be transmitted by a modem directly to the producer's computer) and create colorful, attractive slides. This service is becoming more widely available. Check local quick-print shops to see what capability they have.

A computerized slide production facility works this way: Working at a keyboard, the artist keys your data into the system's computer. He or she designs formats or retrieves them from the computer's memory bank, plots data points, changes copy sizes, composes, and illustrates as needed. A wide range of colors can be rendered, giving the slide the communications impact required. As these elements are integrated, they are instantly displayed on a monitor for the artist's approval. During this creative process, the artist can experiment with different colors and layouts.

The result can be highly professional slides. Such professionalism costs much more than homemade slides. Companies pay up to several hundred dollars for some complex slides. A more typical cost is $10 to $50 each.

Effective Projected Visuals. Here are some suggestions for boosting your effectiveness with projected visuals.

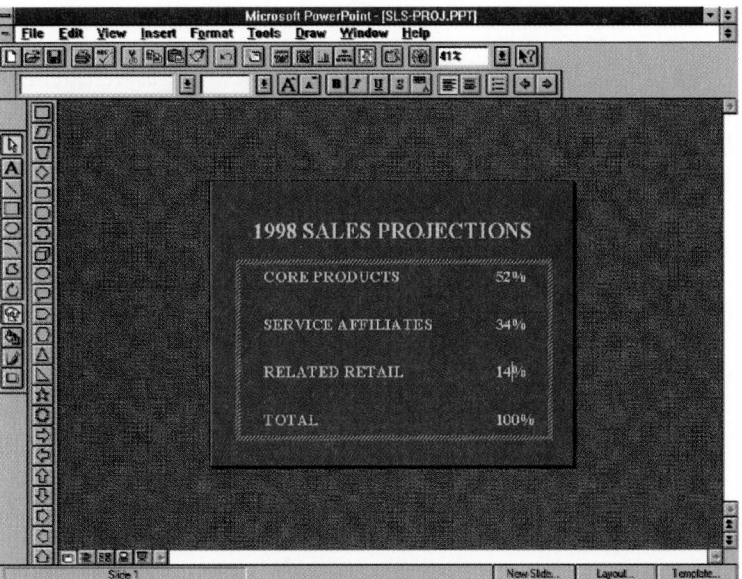

FIGURE 19–12

Professional quality graphics can be generated easily using computer software.

1. Use slides or transparencies. These are especially useful in showing entire structures of complicated pieces of equipment, or for the comparison of data such as graphs and charts. Don't let your talk become just a commentary on your slides or transparencies.

2. Leave the lights on while you show the slides. This is probably the easiest remedy for the worst drawback to the use of slides. Most slides, if properly prepared, can be seen with normal projection equipment if the lights in the room are slightly dimmed. By keeping the room lighted, you avoid the problem of losing listeners who tend to doze off in the darkness. You maintain eye contact with them more effectively, and you'll be able to see and talk with them.

3. Use a remote-control device that allows you to change the slide without physically touching the projector. When showing transparencies, to be as unobtrusive as possible, don't stop in the middle of a thought or abruptly change the visual. When preparing for your presentation, think about when the transparencies must be changed, then strive to do so smoothly and with minimal distraction to your audience.

4. Don't turn away from your audience and talk to the image on the screen. This is a particular problem when speaking to a larger group and using a fixed microphone. Each time a new image appeared on the screen, some speakers turn toward that image and away from the microphone, causing their voices to fade.

5. Turn the transparency or slide projector off when not in use. If you leave the light on on a blank screen, it can be blinding.

6. Finally, keep your slides to a reasonable number. Don't overkill your audience, and don't expect the slide show to be a substitute for a good presentation.

If you do use a lot of slides, try this: Eliminate the abrupt shift from one slide to the next by using two projectors hooked up so that instead of changing slides on one machine, the first slide fades out (as the lamp is turned off) while the second slide fades in (as its lamp is turned on). While the lamp is off, the first machine advances to the next slide, ready to turn back on when the second machine shuts off. (Your photograph supply dealer can explain how to make this hookup.) The effect is professional and smooth. This may be worth setting up for a presentation that will be given repeatedly, such as a new employee orientation or public relation displays.

Dynamic Visuals

Dynamic visuals show motion and sound. The most common types are movies and videotapes, but computer presentation packages can now produce dynamic visuals on disk too. Traditionally, the cost of producing dynamic visuals has been high, but that is changing rapidly.

Videotapes can be produced almost as easily as audiotapes using a camcorder. Be careful of random movement that can make your viewers dizzy. Use a tripod to steady the camera whenever possible. Videocassettes are easy to store and play back. The cost of equipment is also reasonable.

Dynamic visuals can be especially useful in training situations. Participants in role plays, for example, can benefit from an objective view of themselves in action. It can be a real eye-opener.

With the explosion of commercial videotapes, you may find prerecorded tapes that fit in nicely with your presentation. If so, don't reinvent the wheel—use them. You may use only segments of the commercial program or the whole tape. The quality of such tapes usually exceeds home videos because of the professional lighting, sound recording, and content preparation.[5]

Positioning Your Listeners and Your Visuals

To get ideas across and encourage participation, you should be aware of options in seating. Don't feel locked in "theater-style" rows of seats or even a conference table. Move the furniture around!

When possible, have listeners' backs to doors or windows that may distract them (Figure 19–13). Also move chairs to be sure they can see your direct visuals (Figure 19–14). The presenter is the round dot in each figure.

A Final Thought about Audiovisual Aids: Check Them Out in Advance!

Everyone has seen presentations where the gremlins inside the microphone, projector, or computer caused something to go dead, burn out, or malfunction. It is crucial for you as a speaker to be as well prepared as possible for such problems. Be sure to arrive early enough to test equipment. Bring spare projector bulbs. Check out the videotape player, slide projector, and computer hookup. Make sure your tape or slide tray is cued up to the right place before you begin. Don't rewind or advance a tape while your audience waits. Know your equipment, and use it smoothly.

FIGURE 19–13

Positioning of listeners.

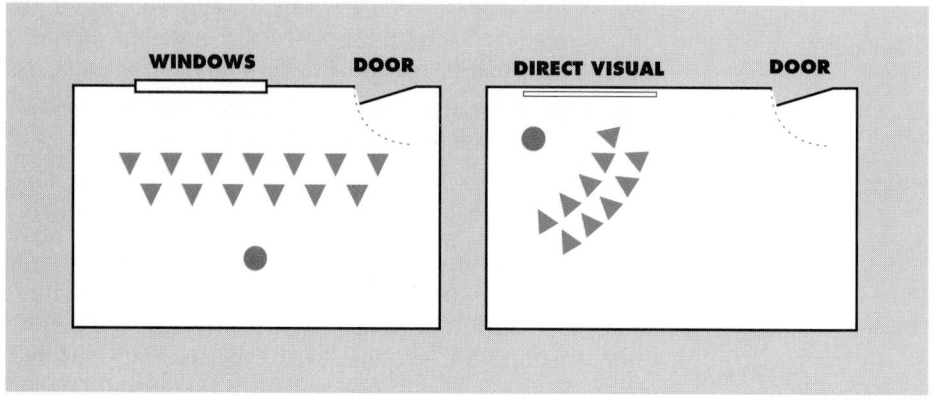

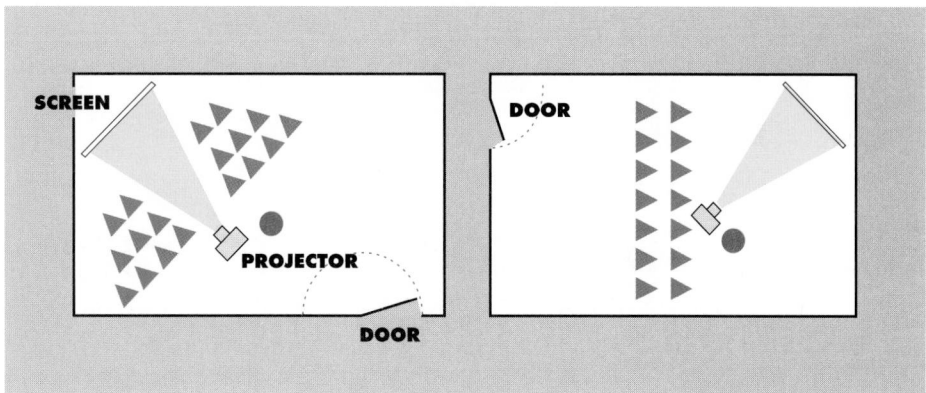

FIGURE 19–14

Positioning projected visuals.

Understanding the Basics

SUMMARY OF KEY IDEAS

• Visuals used in both written documents and oral presentations will simplify, clarify, and improve receiver comprehension.

• Plan for the use of visual displays of information as you develop your document or talk.

• Direct visuals are used in written documents and oral presentations. Projected and dynamic visuals are for oral presentations only.

• Direct visuals include word charts, graphs, pie charts, bar charts, drawings, and models or photographs.

• Projected visuals include slides, transparencies, and computer projections.

• Dynamic visuals show motion and sound. These are becoming more widely used in oral presentations and are now relatively easy to prepare.

• Always check any projection or sound equipment before using it in an oral presentation.

KEY TERMS AND CONCEPTS

pie chart	dynamic visuals	photographic slides
bar chart	direct visuals	word chart
column graph	dry-mounted photographs	cartoon permission
line graph	overhead transparencies	projected visuals

QUESTIONS FOR FURTHER THOUGHT

1. Why are visuals useful in almost any written document or oral presentation?

2. What mistakes did the plant manager make in the opening story for this chapter? List four specific things you'd do differently.

3. When would you use a flip chart rather than word chart posters?

4. What are the two main advantages of project visuals versus direct visuals?

5. What is the most common mistake made with both word charts and transparencies?

6. What are dynamic visuals? What advantages and disadvantages do they offer?

7. Where should a screen used with projected visuals be placed in a room? Why?

Using Color to Create High Impact Business Presentations

When you combine colors creatively, you can portray themes, convey ideas, and stimulate your viewers to take action. The information below offers some tips for creating the moods you may need to project. Use these suggestions to help form your own ideas and themes.

A common mistake, especially of people new to designing with color, is to include so many colors that they achieve only discord. Remember: less is more. Be careful not to use combinations of too many vivid colors: think about limiting vivids to accent areas.

Select object colors after choosing a background. Pick the color for the largest area first, then think about the smaller areas. If the subject matter dictates your selection of accent color, choose a background that is compatible and that creates harmony. For example, if you are designing an ad for Florida oranges, you might want to use sunshine yellow and orange as accents, with a darker color as background.

Warmth: Create a warm color scheme by using warm colors. Use reds, oranges, and yellows if you want to project HOT! Stick to oranges, yellows, and warm browns to turn down the heat a little. If you need to include cooler colors like blue, green, or gray, warm them up by adding yellow (to blue or green) or red (to gray).

Coldness: Create a cold color scheme by using cool colors: tints of blue, green, gray, and purple. Be careful when including any warm colors because they will take away from the chill of the piece.

Distance or Depth: Create an impression of depth or distance by gradually moving from light colors (near) to dark colors (far). You can use different colors or shades of the same color. You can also create depth by placing warm-colored images on cool-colored backgrounds. The warm-colored images will appear closer to the viewer.

Excitement: To generate excitement, combine red with bright, unusual secondary colors like magenta, orange, and chartreuse. Some of these combinations clash, which enhances the excitement. Black can be added to help ease vibrating effects and increase contrast, an important element in exciting designs.

Tranquility: Reverse the principles of creating exciting designs and you will have guidelines for tranquil pieces. Use pale, cool colors, grays, and secondary shades (which tend to be more tranquil than primary colors). Keep contrast to a minimum to limit excitement.

High-Tech: The look of the high-tech age is achromatic and highly contrasting. Use a basic palette of white, black, and shades of gray, and include sparks of vivid color to add interest.

Elegance: Two-color combinations of gold, silver, black, white, red, brown, and navy blue create the feel of elegance. The combination of black, gold, and white appears particularly expensive.

Luxury: Create a feeling of affluence by using the traditional colors signifying wealth and luxury: rich reds, golds, purples, and black.

Cleanliness: Use combinations of white and blue or white and green to create crisp, clean, or pure images. Packaging of most bathroom cleansers, bleaches, first-aid products, and toothpastes uses these colors to project a squeaky-clean and sanitary image.

Violence: Combinations of red and black are often used to create a violent feeling, since black symbolizes death and red symbolizes anger and action. Think about the packaging of items like insecticides, suspense novels, and horror-movie posters.

(Excerpted from *Graphic Design and Color in Today's Office* by Suzanne M. Topping, © Eastman Kodak Company, 1990.)

Applying Your Knowledge

1. Assume that you are to give an oral presentation to a group of Denver business people. Your intent is to sell them on using the new taxi service described in Case 19-2 on page 546. Sketch out at least four visuals you would use to convey your message. Identify each type of chart, illustration, photograph, and so forth. Explain colors you would use.

2. If you knew that you would be making this same presentation to many groups, how would you go about constructing reusable presentation visuals?

Applying Your Skills

ACTIVITY 19-1: Summarize What You Know about Visuals

Create a checksheet. In your notebook, describe the advantages and disadvantages of each visual when used in oral presentations.

	Advantages	Disadvantages
Transparencies		
Slides		
Flip charts		
Posters		
Dry-mounted photographs		
Samples and models		

ACTIVITY 19-2: Presenting to the Board

As an employee of fast-growing Nanotech Electronics, the board of directors has asked you to give a briefing on the company's research and development activity. You asked your administrative assistant, Cornell Hubbel, to gather some information for you to use in the report. This morning as you arrived at your executive office, Cornell was waiting for you with a copy of the brief report as shown below.

Hubbel thought it would be a good idea just to hand out this written summary to the board. You don't think so.

Describe the conversation you would have with Cornell to help him improve the presentation of the report. Be sure to explain what you suggest he do. Also, explain why you think the improvements are necessary. Be specific.

Cite several opportunities for using visuals (graphics) in any written materials you'd give the board as well as in your oral presentation.

ACTIVITY 19-3: Prepare a Vertical Bar Graph

Prepare a vertical bar graph from the following data: Sugar producers have been able to boost prices significantly in the past few years because of tight supplies. Prices went up 17 percent in 1997, 13 percent in 1996, and 8 percent in 1995.

ACTIVITY 19-4: Prepare a Horizontal Bar Chart

Using the information on rapidly growing occupations (page 544), prepare a horizontal bar chart showing the top ten occupations in ascending order by percentage of growth.

ACTIVITY 19-5: Rewrite a Memo-Report

Using the concepts discussed in this chapter on business graphics, rewrite the following memo-report by Jennifer Wong on page 545. Add some graphics to the text.

Nanotech Electronics' Research and Development Activity

Nanotech Electronics has always considered a heavy commitment to research and development (R&D) expenditures an essential part of its overall corporate strategy. In 1987, R&D outlays totaled $90 million. Since that time, expenditures for corporate R&D have grown as follows: $95 million in 1988; $105 million in 1989; $140 million in 1990; $210 million in 1991; $200 million in 1992; $190 million in 1993; $203 million in 1994; $230 million in 1995; $275 million in 1996; and $305 million in 1997. Estimated expenditures for 1998 are projected at $360 million.

Although R&D growth has not been linear, the general trend has been upward.

TEN MOST RAPIDLY GROWING OCCUPATIONS*	
Occupation	Growth in Employment 1978–1990 (%)
Employment interviewers	66.6
Computer programmers	73.6
Paralegal personnel	132.4
Tax preparers	64.5
Office machine and cash register servicers	80.8
Computer systems analysts	107.8
Food preparation and service workers, fast-food restaurants	68.8
Data-processing machine mechanics	147.6
Computer operators	87.9
Aero-astronautic engineers	70.4

*U.S. Department of Labor (March 1992)

ACTIVITY 19-6: What You Like and Why

Put the following visual aids in order with the one you enjoy most as the first and the one you enjoy least as the fifth, based on your experience as an audience member. Indicate why you have set the priority as you have.

1. Video
2. Flip chart
3. White board
4. Overhead transparencies
5. Slides

ACTIVITY 19-7: Show Them about Yourself

You have been assigned to give a five-minute presentation to introduce yourself to the class. Make a list of at least eight models or props you could use as visuals in this presentation. Be creative.

TO: Ramsey Nelson, Chief Operating Office

FROM: Jennifer Wong, Personnel Manager

DATE: September 30, 19XX

RE: A Look at Current Employee Breakdown and
         Recommendations for Changes in Employee
         Distribution

At your request, I have examined our company's employee breakdown and tried to find some of the weak links that are causing delays in our operations.

The company is broken into five divisions: Marketing, Sales, Production, R&D, and Administration. There are 750 employees below the executive level: 70 in Marketing, 400 in Sales, 200 in Production, 40 in R&D, and another 40 in Administration.

In Marketing we have 12 group managers, 48 product managers, and 10 secretaries and staff. In Sales we have 15 district managers, 85 sales managers, 280 salesmen, and 20 secretaries and staff. In Production there are 18 foremen, 53 supervisors, 126 factory workers, and 3 secretaries. In Administration we have 8 department heads, 26 salaried employees, and 6 secretaries and filing clerks.

After surveying managers and employees and observing the divisions in action, we have drawn two conclusions as to the reasons for the delays in our operations. First, we have too many managers. The managers tend to bicker and quarrel over even the smallest detail. Second, we are extremely shorthanded on secretarial and clerical staff. The secretaries in Production and R&D in particular are inundated with reports and paper work.

For the depth in which this survey was taken, we do not feel properly informed for specific recommendations. However, as the rule of thumb, it appears that we should cut our management staff by at least 10 percent, and increase our secretarial and clerical staff by at least 15 percent.

PERFORMING
on the Job

CASE 19-1 Consulting with Doris

Go back to the opening story at the beginning of this chapter. Assume that you have been hired as a consultant and assigned to work with Doris Steenburg. Describe, in detail, what you would recommend she do to improve her use of visuals. List at least ten ideas.

CASE 19-2 Selling New Taxi Service[6]

Use the following information to complete the application activity on pages 542–43.

Betting that corporate customers who visit Denver will support an upscale taxi service, Centennial Sedans, which opened Monday, has launched itself with a fleet of 11 new Cadillac Fleetwoods.

"We are not a limo company," said Karrie Howard, Centennial's sales director. "We have upscale taxis, charge flat rates and offer impeccable service without the ostentation of the limo."

Howard said Zone Cab studied the market in Denver and identified a niche to serve customers—both local and from out of town—who wanted a luxury-car service that was dependable and available by reservation up to six months in advance.

Howard says the company estimates that a major share of its business will be with customers who will fly into Denver International Airport [DIA] and then go to major corporate offices in the metro area.

Each sedan will be driven by chauffeurs in black suits, and the vehicles will be equipped with such conveniences as cellular phones and special reading lights.

Howard stresses that she believes the convenience of a simple phone call to make a reservation for a sedan will appeal to many customers.

And she adds that the flat-rate cost, which will be quoted when the reservation is made and can be paid for by credit card, is an added feature. The flat rate is for the service of the sedan; up to four persons may ride at no additional cost.

"We only charge for pickup and delivery. If we get slowed down by traffic or a snowstorm, that is our loss," Howard says.

Comparable costs: Centennial's charge from DIA to downtown is $55; Yellow Cab fare averages $36 to $37, but the Yellow Cab fare can be lowered when customers share a cab.

Optimistic about the future of Centennial's service, Howard said the company planned to add about four Fleetwoods—Cadillac's largest sedan—each month to its fleet. No vehicle will remain in the fleet longer than three years and each will be inspected weekly. Howard also said each vehicle will carry $1 million in liability insurance.

Participation
in Meetings *and* Teams

You Can't Go On Meeting Like This

LEARNING GOALS

When you have studied this chapter, you should be able to:

- Participate in or lead problem-solving meetings more effectively.

- Recognize the common business pitfall of overused or ineffective meetings.

- Rate yourself as a meeting participant.

- Describe the three phases of a participative, problem-solving meeting.

- Distinguish between the two general reasons for meetings.

- Explain the advantages and disadvantages of meetings.

- Be alert to four ways the group process can backfire, resulting in poor decisions.

- Name eight ways to effectively participate in meetings.

PERFORMANCE CHALLENGE

The Way It Is . . . You *Will* Participate

Meetings are a fact of life in every organization. Unfortunately, many of the meetings held are far less productive than they might be. As Chapter Six discussed, meetings can be an expensive medium of communication. Good business communicators learn when and how to make the most of meetings, committees, and small teams. This chapter shows you how.

The following story illustrates some ways that meetings can go wrong. After you have read this chapter, you will be able to identify, and avoid, many of the problems.

The president of Moose Lips Corporation meant well, but somehow things just didn't work quite the way he thought they would. Matt Bayless had built Moose Lips from a one-man operation working out of his garage to the largest manufacturer of camping and recreational gear in the Pacific Northwest. Despite rapid financial growth, Matt had the uneasy feeling that things wouldn't continue to be so good. He was disturbed by a marked rise in production costs and an increase in competitor activity. Nothing specific, but he was just uncomfortable.

Then he hit on an idea.

After dusting off a management textbook he'd read in college, Matt decided to use **participative decision making** (PDM) to cope with the company's problems. "Sure, that's it," he decided. "We'll have a big meeting and get some new ideas."

His memo to all employees went out the next morning. Everyone was "invited" to participate in an all-day retreat at the Homestead Resort and Conference Center about 20 miles out of town. The agenda was set: The employees would all get together to "share their ideas" on how to retain market share and "any other topics relevant to the success of their business." The entire company would be shut down all day Friday while its 126 employees met.

A few days before the big meeting, word filtered back to Matt that several Moose Lips employees had been mouthing off about having to spend a whole day at the Homestead.

They already were feeling a lot of pressure to keep up with their work, and, in fact, they were coming up on the busiest time of the year for several departments. Besides, no one seemed to understand what was supposed to be accomplished at the proposed meeting.

Matt was upset by the grumbling. After all, participative decision making was supposed to make the workers feel good. Everything he read said PDM is the way to go. So he sent another memo to answer their objections. He explained in a tone that didn't succeed in concealing his irritation that although no specific proposals were expected to be voted on at this meeting, he felt the opportunity to "share input" was important, and he expected everyone to be there.

The big day came, and 118 people showed up for the all-day retreat. In the opening session, the president said that he was concerned about the company's market share and production costs. He then indicated that, to be systematic, the morning would be spent in 12-member "buzz groups" dealing with the market share. Each group would report back to the whole assembly just before lunch. The afternoon would follow a similar schedule but would deal with production costs.

The buzz groups were assigned randomly, and everyone—including Matt and the other company officers—participated. By 5:00 P.M. when the meeting broke up, it was clear that most participants were frustrated by the whole process. Employee grumbling had become a dull roar. No one, including Matt, could clearly describe what had been accomplished. The net cost to the company went far beyond the rental cost of the facilities, and the catered coffee breaks and lunch. The cost included well over a thousand person-hours. You know what was accomplished? You guessed it: Nothing!

The challenge of meetings is to produce good results and avoid the pitfalls. (Courtesy of David Hanover/Tony Stone Images.)

This chapter talks about how to maximize your work in meetings, whether you are leader or a participant.

If you've worked in an organization for a while, you'll probably agree that the preceding story isn't too far-fetched. Indeed, meetings are widely misused.

Nevertheless, an effective meeting can accomplish a great deal. The challenge is to produce good meetings while avoiding the pitfalls. This chapter discusses that challenge from two viewpoints: first, how you as a participant can make the most of meetings; and, second, how you, when a leader, can maximize meetings results. (Obviously, you have more influence in a leader role than as a participant.) Randy Myer, Director, Investor Service Centers, Charles Schwab & Co. has this opinion: "The effective communicator conducts efficient, focused, and planned meetings. The value of time is acknowledged. An effort is made prior to the meeting to ensure that all participants are prepared. If not, the meeting is rescheduled."

Types of Meetings

Organizations use meetings for two general reasons.

- To inform (advise, update, and sell)
- To make decisions (solve problems and set goals)

Informative meetings are mostly presentations with question-and-answer sessions.

Informative meetings use much more one-way communication from leader to participants than do decision-making meetings. As such, the informative meeting is

Rate Yourself as a Meeting Participant

Answer yes or no to each of the following questions based on how you participate in meetings. Be honest.

1. Do you enjoy most meetings?

2. Do you understand the specific purpose of the meetings you attend?

3. Do you understand your roles in meetings attended?

4. Do you hold back on judging the ideas of other people until they've been fully explained?

5. Do you complete your "homework," such as looking up information or studying proposals before the meetings?

6. Do you arrive at meetings a few minutes before they are scheduled to begin?

7. Do you engage in side conversations while the meeting is in progress?

8. Do you look for excuses to leave meetings for reasons such as nonemergency telephone calls?

9. Do you ask clarifying questions when you are not sure about something?

10. Do you use both support and retention listening techniques?

11. Do you actively participate in discussions when you have something worthwhile to contribute?

12. Do you suggest ways to stay on the subject or move the group process along toward a conclusion?

13. Following meetings do you follow-up with agreed-on action?

14. Do you contribute to improving meetings by giving feedback to the people who conduct them either by a note, telephone call, or visit?

Except for questions 4, 7, and 8, a yes response is preferred. If you answered no to the others and yes to questions 4, 7, and 8, your contribution to meetings is less than it can be. Read on to find ways to improve your meeting effectiveness.

easier to lead. It is really a presentation to a group with perhaps some question-and-answer interaction. The key to success in such a meeting is planning and preparation of the information to be presented.

Decision-making meetings involve much more give and take. They succeed or fail in large part based on the climate of openness and free expression created. Climate arises from the participants' feelings about how freely they can participate.

Productive Participation

A good meeting participant contributes to three phases of a meeting

- Preparation
- Active participation
- Postmeeting follow-up

Preparation

The following points highlight ways to prepare for a meeting:

- Clarify the purpose for the meeting and, more specifically, your involvement in it. Ask the person who calls the meeting what he or she wants from you: "How can I best help the meeting succeed?"

- Research the meeting topic. Make notes of ideas you want to offer. Having these ideas already thought through and supported with details will help you present them more clearly. Don't come to the meeting with an idea to sell without first listening to the give and take of others.

- Arrive at the meeting a few minutes early. Be fresh and organized. Greet others cheerfully, and contribute to a friendly, positive climate.

Come prepared to share your ideas but also be ready to hear others.

Active Participation

Many of the communication techniques discussed throughout this book apply in meetings. Your participation affords opportunities for minipresentations and the skills used for other presentations apply.

Think before you speak, yet don't hold back too long. Make your points in clear, organized ways with support for your key ideas. Use the delivery techniques discussed in Chapter 18 to convey enthusiasm and sincerity.

Contribute your ideas freely. That's why you were invited to the meeting. Likewise, listen to other participants. Consider their ideas carefully. Add your thinking by hitchhiking on the ideas of others. That is how groups can make better decisions than individuals.

Play by the rules of the game. If the leader seeks your creativity in brainstorming, stick to the guidelines (see box below). If the group wants to define certain decision criteria, don't jump ahead to advance a solution.

The term **brainstorming** is often used loosely to mean generating creative ideas. Actually, the term was coined by advertising executive Alex Osborn many years ago. It refers to a specific process, requiring adherence to clear rules.

Hitchhiking on ideas of others can lead to better group decisions.

The rules for effective brainstorming are the following:

1. Don't criticize *any* ideas.
2. No idea should be considered too wild.
3. The *quantity* of ideas generated is most important.
4. Seize opportunities to improve or add to ideas suggested by others.

The process of setting decision criteria is used after some potential solutions have been generated. Groups step aside from the possible solutions for a moment and ask the following question: What would the *ideal* solution to the problem be like?

The criteria spell out this notion of an optimum or ideal solution in detail. For example, a problem of deciding what kind of car to purchase might establish criteria like these.

- Must get 30 miles per gallon or better
- Must seat five people comfortably
- Must be American made
- Must sell for less than $16,000

Postmeeting followup brings closure to the activity. (Courtesy of Ken Levinson/ Monkmeyer Press.)

Decision criteria help answer the question, "What would the ideal solution be like?"

Once the criteria are clearly stated, the group can compare each recommended car against the criteria to narrow the field and result in a decision. Taking time to specify criteria of an ideal solution is an important step in the group process.

Postmeeting Follow-Up

After a meeting, give feedback as part of **postmeeting follow-up** to meeting leaders or participants who have made good contributions. Let them know that you respect their communication skills and enjoy working with them. This can help build future rapport, making the next time your group meets more comfortable.

If you disagree with group members, reassure them that you still value them as friends but have a different viewpoint. Respect differences.

Be sure you know what follow-up is expected of you. Make notes of what you've agreed to do. Then do it promptly and report completion to your leader.

Good meetings usually keep **minutes,** a written record of major ideas, solutions, and actions agreed on. Typically, one person is asked to take the minutes from the beginning of the meeting. This summary is typed and copied for group members to review later.

Follow-up actions after a meeting can help improve future meetings.

Another idea for postmeeting follow-up that is often overlooked, but can be useful: Send a note or call the group leader to provide feedback. Tell him or her what you liked about the process or suggest ideas on how the group might be more effective. Be tactful and remember that the leader's job may be a difficult one.

Finally, evaluate the meeting on a checksheet like the one on page 555.

Effective Leadership

The first question a leader should ask: "Is this meeting likely to be useful?"

The first step to being a good leader is to understand the advantages and disadvantages of meetings. When the disadvantages outweigh the advantages, don't have a meeting.

Advantages of Meetings

An obvious advantage of group decision making is that a variety of viewpoints can be brought to bear on the problem. This can be useful *if* the group has developed

Meetings Evaluation Check Sheet

Consider the typical meeting you attend whether in business, at church, in a club, a school project, etc., Compare your meeting to the characteristics of an effective meeting discussed in this chapter. Check those statements that apply to meetings you attend:

____ 1. An agenda is prepared prior to the meeting.

____ 2. Participants at the meeting have an opportunity to contribute to the agenda.

____ 3. Advance notice of meeting time and place is provided to those invited.

____ 4. Meetings facilities are comfortable and adequate for the number of participants.

____ 5. The meeting begins on time.

____ 6. The meeting has a scheduled ending time.

____ 7. The use of time is monitored throughout the meeting.

____ 8. Everyone has an opportunity to present his or her point of view.

____ 9. Participants listen attentively to each other.

____ 10. There are periodic summaries as the meeting progresses.

____ 11. No one tends to dominate the discussion.

____ 12. Everyone has a voice in decisions made at the meeting.

____ 13. The meeting typically ends with a summary of accomplishments.

____ 14. The meeting is periodically evaluated by participants.

____ 15. People can be depended upon to carry out any action agreed to during the meeting.

____ 16. A memorandum of discussion or minutes of the meeting is provided to each participant following the meeting.

____ 17. The meeting leader follows up with participants on action agreed to during the meeting.

____ 18. The appropriate and necessary people can be counted on to attend each meeting.

____ 19. The decision process used is appropriate for the size of the group.

____ 20. When used, audiovisual equipment is in good working condition and does not detract from the meeting.

Number of Statements Checked ____ × 5 = ____ Meeting Score

A score of 80 or more indicates you attend a high percentage of quality meetings.

A score below 60 suggests work is required to improve the quality of meetings you attend.

ways of *processing* the ideas that come up. To be successful, the group must develop ways of:

- Sharing ideas so that members can build on, or compare and contrast one another's insights
- Resolving differences among group members, which, if left unattended, would lead to excessive conflict and prevent eventual agreement
- Drawing out useful information from all participants while toning down those who tend to dominate

When such conditions are present, synergy can result. Synergy is what happens when the group's decision is better than any decisions that could have been made by individuals working on the problem alone. With synergy, the outcome is better than anything that could happen if you followed individual solutions.

So, the primary advantage of decision-making meetings is that groups can reach synergy—if the conditions are right.

In addition to the way the group airs information and builds consensus, the nature of the problem will also determine the likelihood that synergy will result. Studies show that groups are better at solving problems that require the making of relative rather than absolute judgments. That is, groups can better solve problems for which there are many potential solutions. Problems having only one correct answer are more "structured" and can often be better solved by a motivated individual—or by a computer.

The group process can be more successful than people working alone when the problem is complex, having many parts and requiring several steps to follow. Groups also seem better at dealing with controversial or emotionally charged problems. A problem is emotionally charged when people have taken strong moral or ethical viewpoints, and cannot feel good about a compromise or another viewpoint. Their strong feelings make them less flexible.

A second advantage to group decision making is that participants are likely to feel a stronger commitment—or, at least, less resistance—to a group solution they've helped make. Similarly, when those participating are commissioned to execute the decision, they will do so more faithfully because they understand how the decision was reached. This level of commitment is difficult to achieve when someone else makes the decision without consulting others.

Disadvantages of Meetings

When leaders opt for group problem solving, they give up some control over the decision process. They give the group some power that was theirs to exercise. Although giving up control can result in more useful decisions, there remains some risk that the decision won't be what the leader would like to see happen.

Conversely, some managers use meetings as a way to pass responsibility to others instead of having to make a difficult or painful decision. They use meetings as a substitute for action. Consciously or unconsciously, they hope that by "talking it out" they can avoid the unpleasant necessity of acting.

The meeting as a substitute for action can become a bad habit. A "when in doubt, call a meeting" attitude can eat up enormous amounts of time and energy. In the end, the tangible result is nothing, except possibly some social satisfaction from sitting around gabbing.

Another disadvantage of group decision making is that meetings cost too much time and money. A group decision takes more time than a leader's decision, and the costs of such time can really add up. If it takes a 12-member committee three hours

With synergy, the outcome is greater than the sum of all individual contributions.

Some problems are more suitable to group discussion than others.

A "when in doubt, call a meeting" mind-set wastes a lot of time and money in organizations.

to make a decision, and the average committee member's salary is $35,000 a year, the decision costs more than $600. This estimate includes only direct labor costs.

Consider the ripples of psychological costs to the individual and the organization, which can be staggering. For example, work done by subordinates is often tied up while the boss is in conference. Talented employees do monotonous busywork while waiting for direction from the absent leader. Customers are annoyed that they cannot talk with someone tied up in a meeting. The meeting goer's work piles up, so that he or she is faced with a stack of telephone messages to respond to, a pile of papers in the in-basket, and half a dozen people who just have to talk about some pressing matter when the meeting ends.

Ways Meetings Can Go Bad

Effective leaders recognize that the group process can backfire, resulting in poor decisions, when

- Group members lack hard data about the topic of discussion. The outcome of such a group will be no more than pooled ignorance. If the issues require specialized expertise, go to an expert. Don't muddy the water by using a committee.

- Excessive conflict prevails within the group. In meetings, some conflict is potentially useful—it can help refine and improve ideas. But when participants in a group get into no-holds-barred, bitter arguments, the effect on both relationships and quality of decisions can be disastrous.

- The group takes excessive risks. Some groups make more daring or more risky decisions than its members would ever make if working alone. Social pressures from within the group can result in the group members recommending extreme solutions that they wouldn't dream of taking responsibility for as individuals.

Groupthink or individual dominance can destroy the group process.

- The free flow of information in the group is impeded by groupthink or individual dominance. The term *groupthink* describes a condition that can arise in groups that are particularly cohesive, or like-minded. In such groups, the desire for agreement and harmony becomes stronger than their desire for a good decision. Critical thinking and objective analysis of ideas are seen as less important than a smooth-running group.

A second type of pressure that censors the free flow of information is individual dominance. In many groups, certain people come to dominate the discussion. They can do this when others see them as

- Personable and having a pleasant personality

- Unusually articulate

- Persistent in pushing their own views

- Holding an organizational leadership position

President Matt Bayless (in our opening story) ran a serious risk of censoring the Moose Lips group discussion by assigning himself and his vice-presidents to discussion buzz groups. Many employees would feel uncomfortable disagreeing with the boss.

Individual dominance wears down the group and results in less give and take.

Although individual dominance can speed up the decision process, it does so at the risk of reducing decision quality. The dominant member's ideas may not be the best ones, but they often find "acceptance" among the group that has grown weary of resisting.

Effective leaders recognize advantages and limitations to the use of meetings. When a meeting is called for, they work to create a climate that is conducive to a free flow of information, comfortable with some disagreement, and supportive of each other.

Speaking Up—Whether Leader or Participant

Your effectiveness in meetings will call on the entire range of communication skills discussed in this book. To make the very best of meetings, remember these tips also.

1. Know why the meeting is being held and why you are being invited to attend. Understand your roles.

2. Be on time, and be ready to participate through advance preparation.

3. Stay focused on the topic. (It often helps to put the theme—the central question—on a board or flip chart, and refer to it regularly.)

4. Don't cause problems for the leader. Help him or her to help the group succeed. Avoid getting into side conversations, dominating the discussion, interrupting the meeting, or getting overly emotional.

5. Be open and supportive of the ideas of others. Listen actively. Ask clarifying questions. Express approval when appropriate.

6. Try to help the leader control the meeting. If arguments break out, try to clarify both viewpoints objectively. If the group members wander off the topic, suggest that they refocus on the key question.

7. Pay attention. Make notes. Be an active participant. Try to make the process as effective as possible (even if you'd prefer to not be in the meeting at all)!

8. Remember that much of your value to organization comes from your ideas and contributions to the group. Give the benefit of your experience and viewpoint.

Understanding the Basics

SUMMARY OF KEY IDEAS

• Group problem solving can be a powerful tool when both leaders and participants understand its strategies and weaknesses.

• An effective meeting participant contributes in meeting preparation, active participation, and post-meeting follow-up.

• Brainstorming is a specific idea-generating technique with four clear rules.

• Setting decision criteria involves identifying factors that would be present in an ideal solution to the problem.

• Informative meetings differ from decision-making meetings.

• Effective leaders understand the advantages and disadvantages of the group process.

• Meetings can fail when participants lack basic information, allow excessive conflict to occur, take excessive risk, or allow groupthink or individual dominance to emerge.

participative decision making	brainstorming	informative versus decision meetings
postmeeting follow-up	groupthink	synergy
minutes	decision criteria	pooled ignorance
hidden agenda	agenda	individual dominance

QUESTIONS FOR FURTHER THOUGHT

1. How can you best prepare in advance for a meeting?

2. What kinds of things can you do after a meeting to affect the quality of future meetings?

3. How do the two general types of meetings differ? What is the key to success for each type?

4. What is "groupthink," and why is it dangerous?

5. How can you help the group stay focused on the topic?

Meetings

Keeping Briefings Brief

Nothing saps the spirit like watching, powerless, as a meeting wanders into oblivion. But Flight Time International makes meetings work. A tight agenda holds meetings to less than half an hour; shared responsibility keeps attendees alert and teaches them new skills. And having written minutes reinforces follow-up action.

The 14 employees at the Brookline, Mass., travel agency take turns hosting weekly updates. Beforehand, the host asks the others how long they'll talk and on what topic, and then sets the time and the agenda. Everyone agrees to keep things short. The one-page agenda lists items such as "Paul—newsletter update (three minutes)." The meeting may start with sales quickly listing new customers and deals closed; then accounting might talk about setting up escrow accounts for certain clients. The format extinguishes rumors, says marketing vice-president Paul Thurman. "Everyone hears things simultaneously, firsthand."

Playing host gives employees experience in organizing and running meetings. For his part, Thurman is working on correcting his sloppy note-taking skills: "I've gotten better now that people are depending on me for a permanent record," he says.

The host enforces the agenda. For instance, Thurman says, "Jane, one of the founders, may get too detailed and start talking about pricing a particular trip instead of general pricing policies. I'll say, 'Maybe we can talk about this at lunch. Let's get back on track.' " When a less forceful host allows lengthy digressions, other attendees take it upon themselves to interrupt.

The host also takes meeting minutes, types them up, and circulates them. The minutes are to be read and initialed by everyone; they can also be referred to later if follow-up tasks have been left undone.

Phaedra Hise, "Keeping Meetings Brief," *Inc.* Magazine, September 1994, p. 122. Reprinted with permission.

Applying Your Knowledge

1. Summarize the importance of using an agenda during and after a meeting.
2. If you were asked to be the host of a meeting, what specific steps would you take to prepare for the meeting?

Applying Your Skills

ACTIVITY 20-1: The Moose Lips Mistakes

Go back to the story at the beginning of this chapter. Put yourself in the shoes of Matt Bayless, the company president and describe how you would better meet the need to get useful input to solve organizational problems. Be specific.

What Went Wrong? See if you can identify some of the specific causes of the "Moose Lips" Conference failure.

Identify steps that could have been taken to make the Moose Lips Conference more successful.

ACTIVITY 20-2: The Advantages of Meetings

Summarize in your own words the two major advantages of meetings:

ACTIVITY 20-3: The Disadvantages of Meetings

Summarize in your own words the two major disadvantages of meetings.

ACTIVITY 20-4: How Meetings Go Bad

Summarize in your own words the four ways meetings can lead to poor decisions.

PERFORMING
on the Job

CASE 20-1 The Seville Manor for the Elderly

The Seville Manor is a facility providing apartments for elderly individuals or couples. Various support services, caring supervision, and skilled personnel are all available on site.

The Seville Manor is managed by Mary Ruth, Shelley, and David. Mary Ruth and Shelley are registered nurses; David is a recreational therapist. The three of them have worked diligently with the aged population in a variety of settings. The skills and backgrounds of all three provide the expertise required to assess, plan, implement, and analyze accurately strategies designed to meet the needs of the residents. They also know how to deal with the type of stress that comes from caring for older adults.

Mary Ruth, Shelley, and David have maintained a workable and satisfying working relationship during the five years their business has been operating. They consider themselves partners, but Mary Ruth is considered the group leader and has the title of administrator of Seville Manor.

The working relationship of the three partners is one of open communication. They meet informally whenever necessary to discuss problems, situations, or issues that come up. There is also a formal meeting once a month to review major issues and how the function of Seville Manor is helping the elderly residents on a continuing basis.

Several months ago, a new service was added to the existing services available to residents. Ted, a massage therapist and physiotherapist, had convinced Mary Ruth, Shelley, and David to add a program of massage and exercise to help residents feel better and maintain the physical strength needed to do daily activities. The program has had success.

As time went by, Ted spent more time meeting with David. The fact that David had two women for partners and that one of them was the administrator seemed to surprise Ted. Three months ago Ted asked David if he could participate in the monthly meetings. David discussed Ted's request with Mary Ruth and Shelley, and as a group they made the decision to include Ted.

Ted has attended two monthly meetings. At the first meeting he contributed little to the discussion. When he did speak, it was to boast about the success of his program. At the second meeting, he spoke in an authoritarian manner when addressing Mary Ruth and was openly critical of how the status of the residents was being analyzed.

Case Questions

1. Do you think Ted's attitude in the meetings will change in the future?

2. Describe the purpose of Ted's meeting with David.

3. If you were Mary Ruth, how would you handle Ted's meeting participation?

CASE 20-2 Jake Calls a Meeting

Western Finance has a management team consisting of four people. The CEO is Blaine, who has been with the organization for eight years. Marketing and personnel functions are the responsibility of Betty, who has been with Western for five years. Accounting and finance is overseen by Norris, who joined the team four years ago. Jake is the newest member of the group. As general manager, he is responsible for the daily operations of Western. Jake began with Western 18 months ago. Western is a fast-growing company and has many challenges. The management group works fairly well together. However, an interesting meeting occurred about two months ago.

Jake requested the meeting. He was about to depart for a two-week vacation but wanted to resolve an issue before leaving. He told Blaine the reason for wanting a meeting was to "clear the air" between himself, Betty, and Norris. Blaine felt good about getting the group together and scheduled the meeting. Once the meeting started, the interaction went as follows:

Jake: I requested this meeting because I feel caught in the middle between Betty and Norris. If I am speaking with Betty, Norris thinks we are discussing him or the way he is running his department. If I am speaking to Norris, then I feel Betty is nervous that we are discussing her. I base my perceptions on comments that I hear from both Betty and Norris. Employees are starting to notice the animosity, and we are not being as effective as leaders. Would it be possible for you two to share your concerns openly with the group so that we might try to come to a solution?

Betty: I'll be glad to start. Norris and I have known each other since high school. We never were good friends. Our interests seem to be in different directions. I must admit, we do see things differently here at Western. He seems to disagree with anything I say or want to do. He makes sarcastic comments and says "he's only joking." I, for one, don't think his comments are funny. Jake, I'm sorry if you feel caught in the middle. I try not to let what Norris does or says affect me one way or the other. [Betty spoke for nearly 20 minutes in detail about her concerns. She made several recommendations as to what she could do to improve the situation. After she was done, the group turned to Norris for his comments and reactions.]

Norris: I really don't see any problem. I think everything is going OK. [He then remained silent until Jake began again.]

Jake: Well, I don't know what we have accomplished, but I have one final thing to say. Norris and Betty, I like you both, and I enjoy working with each of you. Norris, in the future when I'm talking to Betty, it will be about business—nothing personal about anyone. Betty, in the future when I'm talking to Norris, it will be about business—nothing personal about anyone. I am simply letting you know what my communicative behavior with this group will be—strictly business, nothing personal.

Case Questions

1. Was this a productive meeting? Why or why not?
2. Why do you think Blaine did not get involved in the discussion?
3. Was Jake's conclusion reasonable for the productivity of the group?
4. Do you think Jake will be able to carry out his intentions?
5. Would another meeting help? Should Blaine talk to each group member individually?

PART SIX

Reference Tools
for Communication Effectiveness *amid* Change

A Review
of Grammar, Punctuation, *and* Usage[1]

For many people, grammar ain't no fun. But it is a tool of the business communicator's trade. Effective grammar improves your chances of getting your messages across.

You do not write to achieve good grammar; rather, you use grammar to achieve clear-to-the-reader writing. If the writing is clear, the grammar will be good.

Grammar, then, is secondary to your primary goal of communicating. No matter how much you use words, however, there comes a time when you aren't sure whether you've structured your message just right.

This appendix presents a concise review of some rules of basic language usage. Specifically, these topics are covered:

- Agreement (subject-verb and pronoun-antecedent), beginning on this page.
- Modifiers (adjectives and adverbs), beginning on page 578.
- Prepositions and other connectives, beginning on page 584.
- Punctuation, beginning on page 588.
- Number usage, beginning on page 595.

Agreement: Subjects and Verbs

What Is Agreement?

Agreement is simply a matter of deciding whether we're talking

1. About one person (singular) or about more than one person (plural)
2. About ourselves (called "first person"—"I," "we," etc.) or about the reader or listener (called "second person"—"you," "your," etc.) or about someone else (called "third person"—"he," "she," "they," "it," etc.)
3. About a woman, about a man, or about people or things in general regardless of gender

Agreement Means that All Parts of the Sentence Agree with One Another. Once you've decided exactly whom or what you're talking about in relation to these three characteristics *(number, person,* and *gender),* you have to make sure all parts of each sentence "agree" with (are consistent with) all other parts of the sentence. In particular, you have to make sure that each verb agrees with its subject and that each pronoun agrees with its "antecedent" (the word the pronoun refers to—the word the pronoun replaces in the sentence).

Subjects Has to Agree with Their Verbs

"Subjects *has* to agree with their verbs"? An obvious error in subject-verb agreement, isn't it? Many subject-verb agreement problems are no more difficult than that— making sure that a plural subject like "subjects" has a plural verb like "have." Rarely will you make such a mistake—your ear will tell you if you've chosen the wrong verb to go with the subject you are using. For example, notice how the verb "write" changes in these sentences, depending on the subject of each sentence:

I *write* a department management report every week.

She *writes* a department management report every week.

They *write* a department management report every week.

In your everyday speech and writing, you probably have few problems with agreement between subjects and verbs. You would never write "they goes" or say "he were." And you know without thinking that "they is here" and "he write" are wrong.

Even though subject-verb agreement (or lack of agreement) is usually very easy to hear, it is sometimes difficult to work with the following kinds of subjects:

1. Two or more subjects joined with "and"
2. Two or more subjects joined with "or"
3. A subject that comes before a prepositional phrase like "of the records," for example
4. A subject that comes before a parenthetical phrase like "in addition to" or "as well as," for example
5. Singular subjects like "each," "everyone," "either," and "neither"
6. Subjects like "all," "some," and "most" that sometimes are singular and sometimes are plural
7. Collective subjects like "jury" and "committee" that sometimes are singular and sometimes are plural

Subjects Joined with "and"

The word "and" means about the same thing as a "+" in math—it means "both." So whenever we join two subjects with the word "and," we're obviously talking about more than one—about *both*—and we have to use a plural verb, as in these sentences:

Understanding English grammar *and* knowing how to use grammar effectively *are* important to a good writer.

The investment broker *and* her assistant *were* at the meeting yesterday.

Notice that in these sentences, two distinct, separate subjects are joined by the word "and." In fact, the two subjects in each sentence could be split and used in two separate sentences (this time with singular verbs, of course) without modifying the wording of the subjects themselves, as shown here:

Understanding English grammar *and* knowing how to use grammar effectively *are* important to a good writer.

becomes

Understanding English grammar *is* important to a good writer.

and

Knowing how to use grammar effectively *is* important to a good writer.

Knowing whether subjects can be split apart and used in separate sentences is important. By being able to split the subjects, you know that you are in fact dealing with *two* subjects joined with "and" instead of with just *one* subject that has the word "and" included in it. For example, which of the following subjects are plural (two *separate* subjects joined with "and")? Which of them are singular (a *single* subject that happens to have the word "and" in it somewhere)?

1. My friend and associate
2. My friend and my associate
3. Ham and eggs
4. The ability to type accurately and to proofread thoroughly
5. The ability to type accurately and the patience to proofread thoroughly

Subjects 1, 3, and 4 are *singular* subjects (subjects that identify just one person or thing) that have the word "and" in them. But Subjects 2 and 5 are *separate* subjects joined with "and."

Thus, we could construct the following sentences using these subjects:

1. My friend and associate *is* attending the meeting.
   (You could not separate "my friend" and "associate" into separate sentences without adding another "my" before "associate.")

2. My friend and my associate *are* attending the meeting.
   (You could separate "my friend" and "my associate" into separate sentences: "My friend *is* attending," and "My associate *is* attending.")

3. Ham and eggs *is* my favorite breakfast.
   ("Ham and eggs" is one breakfast dish—one menu item. Thus, we would not communicate the same idea if we said "Ham is my favorite breakfast" and "eggs are my favorite breakfast.")

4. The ability to type accurately and to proofread thoroughly *is* important to a typist.
   (The *real* subject in this sentence is "ability"—you could not separate "the ability to type accurately" and "to proofread thoroughly" into two sentences.)

5. The ability to type accurately and the patience to proofread thoroughly *are* important to a typist.
   (The real subjects in this sentence are "the ability" and "the patience"—subjects that you could separate into two sentences: "The ability to type accurately is important" and "The patience to proofread carefully is important.")

In summary, separate subjects joined with "and" need a plural verb. But if the two subjects are not really separate subjects—if, instead, they are closely related ideas that cannot be separated into two sentences—you use a singular verb.

Subjects Joined with "or" or "nor"

When we join two singular subjects with "or" or "nor," we have to use a singular verb, as in these examples:

John *or* Mike *is* coming to the meeting.

The letter *or* the report *was* sent late. Neither the police officer *nor* the fire fighter *was* injured in the accident.

Because "John" and "Mike" are joined by "or," we know that John and Mike are not *both* coming to the meeting—only *one* of them will come. And because "the letter" and "the report" are joined by "or," we know that *both* the letter and the report were not sent late—only *one* of them was.

However, what happens if we join two *plural* subjects with "or" (or "nor"), as in "the books *or* the tapes"? And what happens if we join a *singular* subject and a *plural* subject with "or"?

Because "or" indicates a choice between two or more things, couldn't the verb be either plural or singular?

The Subject Closest to the Verb Determines the Verb. One simple principle will solve this problem: When two or more subjects are joined with "or," the subject closest to the verb determines whether the verb should be singular or plural. For example:

The *book* (singular) *or* the *tapes* (plural) *were* (plural) sent.

The *books* (plural) *or* the *tapes* (plural) *were* (plural) sent.

The *books* (plural) *or* the *tape* (singular) *was* (singular) sent.

The *book* (singular) *or* the *tape* (singular) *was* (singular) sent.

Generally, when you join a singular subject and a plural subject with "or," try to put the plural subject last so that the sentence will have a plural verb. Doing so will usually make the sentence sound more natural, as shown here:

The Smiths *or* John *is* coming. (Sounds a little awkward.)

John *or* the Smiths *are* coming. (Sounds more natural.)

Subjects with Prepositional Phrases

Often, a singular subject will be followed by a prepositional phrase that contains a plural word as the object of the preposition. For example, notice the plural words that are objects of the prepositions "of," "in," and "at" in the following sentence parts:

An examination *of* the *records* . . .

The spectator *in* the *bleachers* . . .

The worker *at* the *controls* . . .

When a verb follows such plural words, many understandably (but mistakenly) make the verb plural (as in "the worker at the controls *are* . . ."). But the plural word ("controls") that follows the preposition is not the subject of the verb that follows—the singular subject that precedes the prepositional phrase is the subject (*"the worker* at the controls *is* . . .").

In other words, prepositional phrases do not affect agreement between the subject of the sentence and the verb. As a matter of fact, you could mentally block out the entire prepositional phrase from the sentence while you decide whether to use a singular or a plural verb.

In "an examination of the records," for example, you can block out the prepositional phrase "of the records"—"an examination" remains as the subject (and it is singular, not plural). In "the spectator in the bleachers," you can block out "in the bleachers"—"the spectator" is the singular subject. And in "the worker at the controls," you can block out "at the controls"—"the worker" is the singular subject. Thus, all these subjects would be used with singular verbs, as shown here:

An *examination* (of the records) *is* recommended.

The *spectator* (in the bleachers) *was* late for the game last week.

The *worker* (at the controls) *performs* the job very well.

When a plural subject is followed by a prepositional phrase, the verb must be plural. You seldom make mistakes in subject-verb agreement in that kind of sentence construction. The following sentences probably sound correct to you without your having to think about them:

Very thorough *examinations* (of the records) *are* recommended.

The *spectators* (in the bleachers) *were* late for the game last week.

The *workers* (at the controls) *perform* the job very well.

Even if a singular word acts as the object of the preposition that follows a plural subject, you seldom make the mistake of using a singular verb—the plural verb sounds right to us (and, luckily, is correct!).

Singular Subjects Like "Each" and "Either"

Often, subjects like "each," "either," "neither," and "everyone" are followed by prepositional phrases containing plural words: "each of the men," "either of the children," and so on.

You've just learned that to determine whether a singular verb or a plural verb is needed, you can block out the prepositional phrase in such constructions. In a phrase like "every one (of the workers)," the subject ("every one") is singular. Whether words, such as "each" and "neither," are singular or plural is less obvious to most of us.

Some Words Are Always Singular. Because "each" can be thought of as really meaning "each *one*" and "either" can be thought of as really meaning "either *one*," and so on, the following words are always singular:

anybody	everything
anyone	neither
any one	nobody
anything	no one
each	nothing
either	one
every	somebody
everybody	someone
everyone	some one
every one	something

Thus, we use singular verbs with them:

Each of the men *is* applying for the promotion.

Either of the children *sings* well.

Neither of the applicants *was* qualified for the position.

Every one of the secretaries *was* fired.

Something is wrong here.

Subjects Like "All" and "Some"

Unlike the "always-singular" pronouns you just read about, words like "all" and "some" can be either singular or plural. Whether to use a singular or a plural verb with such words depends on how the word is used.

Notice that in the following sentences the words "some," "all," and "most" are used both with singular verbs and with plural verbs, depending on whether the words refer to something that can be counted or to something that is only a single part of a larger unit:

Some of the old equipment *has* been painted to match the new equipment.

Some of the new machines *were* ordered two weeks ago.

All of the work *was* completed before the deadline we agreed to.

All of the custom wheels *were* stolen from us last night.

Most of the planning *is* being done by the personnel department.

Most of the office workers *are* planning to attend the company luncheon.

None of the work *has* been finished.

None of the workers *were* injured.

Collective Subjects

Subjects that describe collections of people or things are called "collective subjects." The following are just a few of the many collective subjects you may use in your speech or in business or other writing:

committee	crowd
jury	team
family	staff
class	tribe

Like the singular or plural words you just studied, collective subjects can be used with either singular verbs or plural verbs. To know whether a collective noun is singular or plural, answer these questions:

1. Do I want to show the reader that this action is being performed by several individuals or that this action is being performed by several people or things that are acting as a single unit?

2. Does this action or situation require more than one performer or can it be performed by a single group or unit?

Notice how collective subjects have been used correctly with either singular or plural verbs in the following sentences, depending on the writer's purpose or on the nature of the verb:

The *crowd* is running onto the football field.

The *crowd are* losing their hats in the wind.

The *team is* winning its games this year.

The *team are* doing well in their off-season jobs in various parts of the country.

My *class wants* me to discuss subject-verb agreement today.

My *class are* preparing their reports that are due at the beginning of class tomorrow.

Agreement: Pronouns and Antecedents

Pronouns are the generic words used to replace nouns. They include the following words which appear in almost every sentence we write or say:

I	me	my	you	your
we	us	our	he	him
his	she	her	hers	his
they	them	their	theirs	who
who/whom	whose	it	its	that
which	there	this	these	those

As with subjects and verbs, pronouns and their antecedents must agree. The antecedent is the noun that comes before the pronoun—not so far before that it has been forgotten or obscured.

Two rules apply to the link between pronouns and their antecedents:

1. Every pronoun must refer clearly to one and only one specific noun in the same sentence or in a preceding sentence.

2. Every pronoun must agree with its antecedent in terms of number, person, and gender.

Those two rules identify two essential parts of agreement between a pronoun and its antecedent: *reference* and *agreement* or *consistency*. Reference and agreement both deal with the link or relationship between a pronoun and its antecedent, and although the two terms are closely related in meaning, they have separate definitions.

1. Reference identifies how clearly the pronoun refers to or is linked with its antecedent.

2. Agreement identifies consistency between the pronoun and its antecedent in terms of number, person, and gender. Even if a pronoun has clear reference to a particular antecedent, agreement is faulty if the pronoun and the antecedent are not consistent in number, person, and gender.

Pronoun-Antecedent Reference

Writers are sometimes so familiar with what they are trying to say that they assume everyone else automatically knows what word each pronoun refers to. As a result, we sometimes see a sentence like this:

When the guests arrive, take their coats and hang them in the closet.

Hang the guests in the closet? Or their coats? The writer meant "hang their coats in the closet," but couldn't someone assume that "them" refers to guests just as easily as it refers to coats? An easy way to check for clear antecedent reference is the following:

1. Draw a circle around the pronoun.

When the guests arrive, take their coats and hang them in the closet.

2. Draw arrows from the circle to every word in the sentence (or perhaps in a preceding sentence) that the pronoun might likely be replacing or referring to in the following:

When the guests arrive, take their coats and hang them in the closet.

If you can draw only one arrow, you know that pronoun-antecedent reference is clear. If you can draw more than one arrow or if the arrow can't be pointed at any particular word, you know that pronoun-antecedent reference is not clear.

Pronoun-Antecedent Agreement or Consistency

Now Let's Check for Agreement. After you check to see that a pronoun has clear reference to its antecedent, your next task is to see that the pronoun *agrees* with its antecedent. As you've already read, *agreement* refers to consistency between the pronoun and its antecedent in these areas:

Number—singular or plural

Person—first, second, or third person

Gender—male, female, or neutral

In addition, relative pronouns must agree with their antecedents in one other way: "human" or "person" pronouns must be used to refer to people, and "nonperson" or "thing" pronouns must be used to refer to things other than people.

Agreement in Number

Certain words are always singular and therefore take singular verbs and other words are always plural and therefore take plural verbs.

Likewise, those same words must always be referred to by singular or plural pronouns, as in the following examples:

Everybody is invited to choose *his or her* own research topic. (singular)

Some of the managers are being asked to bring *their* departmental reports to the meeting. (plural)

Much of the work has been done, but *it* has not been done well. (singular)

The *company* is selling *its* old equipment to interested employees. (singular)

When *one* first sees the Grand Canyon, *he* (or *he or she* or *one*) will be surprised by its size and its beauty. (singular)

As the *workers* punched in this morning, *they* were told about the strike plans.

Grammatically, "they" is still considered plural by most writers and should be used to refer to plural—not singular—antecedents. Whether you adopt "they" as a singular pronoun in your own writing should depend to a great deal on your intended readers—would they rather see "he" or "she" used to refer to a singular antecedent or would they rather see "they" used to refer to a singular antecedent?

Agreement in Person

Readers are easily confused by illogical shifts within a sentence from one viewpoint (person) to another. For example, the following sentence begins in second person (referring directly to the reader) and then shifts to third person (referring to someone other than either the writer or the reader):

When *you* choose a long-distance telephone company, *one* should consider the company's billing practices.

Such shifting from one person or point of view to another makes the sentence sound awkward and poorly planned. Thus, to avoid illogical shifts in person within a sentence, follow these basic rules:

1. Use first-person pronouns to refer to first-person antecedents (first person includes words like "I," "my," "we," and "our").

2. Use second-person pronouns to refer to second-person antecedents (second person includes words like "you" and "your").

3. Use third-person pronouns to refer to third-person antecedents (third person includes words like "he," "she," "it," "one," and "they").

Agreement in Gender

The most obvious gender-agreement error would be to refer to a man as a "she" or to a woman as a "he." But few writers make such obvious errors—when such errors are made, they are usually the result of typographical error.

The more subtle gender-agreement errors have to do with using all masculine pronouns ("he," "him," "his") or all feminine pronouns ("she," "her") to refer to antecedents such as "managers," "secretaries," "workers," "one," and so on—antecedents that are neutral in terms of gender.

For years, pronouns like "he" and "him" were used to refer to neutral antecedents, and such masculine pronouns were accepted as being neutral and as being acceptable references to both men and women. But in recent years writers have attempted to avoid using masculine pronouns—or feminine pronouns—to refer to neutral antecedents. Many people view the use of masculine or feminine pronouns with neutral antecedents to be a stereotyped or sexist use of language.

For example, someone who writes "an effective secretary will take messages for *her* supervisor when *he* is away from *his* desk" sends a message to the reader that all secretaries must be women and that all supervisors must be men. Thus, the sentence would be improved if it were written this way:

An effective secretary will take messages for his or her supervisor when the supervisor is away from his or her desk.

To avoid the wordy constructions of "he or she" and "his or her," the sentence could be written this way:

Effective secretaries will take messages for their supervisors when the supervisors are away from their desks.

As mentioned in the preceding paragraphs, some writers have chosen to use pronouns like "they" and "their" to refer to singular antecedents in order to avoid the "he or she" constructions. However, most people think of "they" as being plural, and whether you choose to use "they" as a singular pronoun must depend on your audience and on your personal feelings about language.

Until more of our society accepts "they" as a singular pronoun, perhaps the safest way to write is to use "they" only with plural antecedents and to use either "he or she" or "he" with singular, neutral antecedents. Remember, though, that the use of "he" with neutral antecedents will be looked on by some readers as being unacceptable sexist usage.

Agreement in the Use of Relative Pronouns

The last way in which pronouns and antecedents should agree is in the proper use of the relative pronouns to refer either to persons or to things. Also, the proper choice of relative pronouns to introduce either essential or nonessential clauses (although not strictly an agreement problem) is important to effective writing.

The basic rules governing the use of relative pronouns with either human or nonhuman antecedents and to introduce either essential or nonessential clauses are summarized as follows:

1. "Who," "whom," and "whose" refer to humans (although "whose" is also used to refer to things other than humans) and can introduce either essential or nonessential clauses.

2. "That" refers to things other than humans and is used to introduce essential clauses.

3. "Which" refers to things other than humans and is used to introduce nonessential clauses.

For example, instead of saying "the police officer *that* made the arrest," say "the police officer *who* made the arrest." Instead of saying "the company *who* bought the materials," say "the company *that* bought the materials." (Some writers use "that" with a human antecedent; but using "who," "whom," and "whose" has a more personal, human-sounding effect and will always be correct.)

The difference between "that" and "which" is often confusing. The key to choosing between these two pronouns is knowing whether the clause to be introduced is essential or nonessential. *Essential clauses* limit—or more narrowly define—the meaning of the antecedent. An essential clause differentiates its antecedent from other persons or things that otherwise would be named by the same expression. For example,

The car *that I bought yesterday* is missing.

The essential clause "that I bought yesterday" differentiates or identifies *which* car is missing—"the car that I bought yesterday" as opposed to another car that I may have purchased a year ago.

Nonessential clauses give additional or supplementary information about the antecedent. The nonessential clause could be removed from the sentence without changing the meaning of the sentence or the identification of the antecedent. For example,

My new car, *which I bought yesterday,* is missing.

The nonessential clause "which I bought yesterday" could be eliminated from the sentence without changing the meaning of the sentence: "My new car is missing." The nonessential "which I bought yesterday" is not needed to identify or clarify *which* car is missing—I have only one *new car.*

Notice, too, that essential clauses do not have commas before or after them. Nonessential clauses, on the other hand, are always set off with a comma before and a comma after. When referring to a human antecedent and therefore using "who," "whom," or "whose," a writer must remember that the only signal the reader will have as to whether the relative clause is essential or nonessential is whether the clause has commas around it.

Now compare the differences between the following examples of essential clauses and of nonessential clauses (note especially the use of "which" or of "that" for nonhuman antecedents and the use of commas or no commas to indicate either essential or nonessential relative clauses):

Essential Clauses

The lake *that* we visited last year is now severely polluted. (identifies *which* lake is polluted)

The teacher *who* wrote the text book is Mr. Allen. (identifies *which* teacher)

The computer *that* I bought was defective; the computer *that* my friend bought has always worked well. (identifies *which* computer didn't work and *which* computer did work)

Nonessential Clauses

Snowflake Lake, *which* we visited last year, is now severely polluted. (additional information only—is not needed to identify *which* Snowflake Lake)

Our teacher, *who* wrote the text book, is Mr. Allen. (additional information—"our teacher" is not identified or differentiated by "who wrote the text book")

My computer, *which* I bought a month ago, was defective; Fred's computer, *which* he bought at the same time, has always worked well. (additional information—not needed to identify or clarify which computer worked and which did not)

Modifiers: Adjectives and Adverbs

Effective Use of Modifiers Is Essential to Good Writing. You can see that learning to use modifiers effectively is essential to good writing. Part of learning to use modifiers effectively is knowing the difference between the two major types of modifiers: adjectives and adverbs. Once you've learned how to distinguish an adjective from an adverb and how to use each, you'll be ready to study the rules for using adjectives and adverbs effectively.

Adjectives and adverbs—the two kinds of modifiers or describing words—can be distinguished from each other by the kinds of things they describe. Adjectives describe things, and adverbs describe action or other describing words.

Adjectives

Adjectives are words that describe nouns or pronouns (things). Adjectives answer these questions: "What kind of [thing]?" "Which [thing]?"

For example, in the following sentence what word answers the question "What kind of car?" or "Which car?"

The man who was driving the truck didn't see the red car.

"Red" describes what kind of car or which car, so we know that "red" is an adjective.

Thus, if a describing word makes sense when it is placed with a noun and if it answers the question "what kind of [thing]?" or "which [thing]?" it is an adjective. For example, the italicized words in the phrases that follow are adjectives:

the *quick* car

the *national* economy

the *friendly* neighbor

the *rolling* stone

the *tired* worker

the *up-to-date* report

the *updated* schedule

the *increasing* demand

the *tentative* agreement

the *responsive* control panel

Not all adjectives are just one word. Notice the multiple-word adjectives in the following sentences:

The *half-done* report is on the desk.

He gave us a "get-lost-before-I-get-mad" look.

The man *who wanted the report* was referred to us.

In the first sentence, the words "half" and "done" are joined to describe which report or what kind of report. Likewise, the words "get lost before I get mad" are joined to describe what kind of look someone gave us. In the last sentence, the words "who wanted the report" are used to describe which man.

Although "half-done" and "get-lost-before-I-get-mad" come in front of the nouns in the first two sentences, "who wanted the report" comes after the noun. Adjectives that come after the noun are usually relative clauses or participles. Notice the relative clauses and participles used in the following sentences:

The report *giving these details* was submitted. (participle)

The report *that gives these details* was submitted. (relative clause)

The worker *selected for the award* is a painter in the finishing department. (participle)

The worker *who was selected for the award* is a painter in the finishing department (relative clause)

Remember that not all -ed and -ing verbs are participles—they are participles only if they act as describing words.

In summary, adjectives are words that describe things. Most adjectives can be placed in front of a noun, but many adjectives come after the noun. No matter where the adjective is placed, it answers the questions "What kind of [thing]?" and "Which [thing]?" Adjectives can be single words, groups of words, relative clauses, and participles.

Adverbs

Adverbs are words that describe verbs (action), adjectives, or other adverbs. Adverbs answer these questions:

Where?

When?

How?

How much?

So, a word is an adverb if it can be placed before or after a verb or another describing word and if it tells the reader where, when, how, or how much. Notice the adverbs in these phrases:

Do the job *quickly* (do the job *how?*)

It is good *enough* (*how* good?)

It was *very* expensive (*how* expensive?)

Read the letter *immediately* (*when?*)

Don't leave it *there* (*where?*)

Notice that many adjectives can be made into adverbs by the addition of -ly, as in these examples:

Adjective	+	Ending	=	Adverb
real	+	-ly	=	really
quick	+	-ly	=	quickly
sure	+	-ly	=	surely
national	+	-ly	=	nationally
immediate	+	-ly	=	immediately

Modifiers: The Rules

Now that you're familiar with the two kinds of modifiers and how to distinguish one from the other, you're ready to learn the rules or guidelines that help us use modifiers effectively.

1. Do not omit the -ly ending from adverbs.

You know that we use adjectives to describe things and adverbs to describe actions or other modifiers. That sounds easier than it actually is sometimes.

In conversation, we often use adjectives improperly in place of adverbs, by dropping the -ly ending from the adverbs. For example, we incorrectly say things like "I was sure lucky" and "the work went real good" instead of "I was surely lucky" and "the work went really well."

Especially in writing, the adverb form should be used to describe verbs and other describing words:

He *surely* is lucky to get the prize money.

I am *really* pleased to hear of your promotion.

I think you did *well* yesterday.

2. Use adjectives after linking verbs.

Remember that a linking verb is a very like "feel" or "is"—a verb that links the subject to a description or identification of itself. For example, the linking verbs in the following sentences link the subject to an adjective that describes the subject:

The perfume smells *good*.

He is *lucky*.

The weather seems *stormy*.

The new car looks *good*.

Because the words that follow the linking verbs in the preceding sentences describe the subject—a thing—they are adjectives. They do not describe how the action of the linking verb takes place, so they are not adverbs. Thus, the key to knowing whether to use an adjective or an adverb after what you think might be a linking verb is to ask yourself, "Does this word describe the subject (a thing), or does it describe how the action takes place?"

What about this sentence?

I feel badly about the mistake.

Right or wrong? Is "feel" a linking verb in this sentence? Does "badly" describe "I" or does it describe the action named by the verb "feel"? With a little thought, you'll realize that it describes "I"—and it should say

I feel *bad* about the mistake.

If you're not convinced that you should say "I feel *bad* about the mistake," look at these two sentences and see which you think is right:

I feel *well* about the achievement. (adverb)

I feel *good* about the achievement. (adjective)

You probably chose "I feel *good*"—because "good" is an adjective that actually describes "I" and not "feel." Likewise, "bad" is an adjective that actually describes "I" and not "feel" in "I feel *bad* about the mistake."

On the other hand, the adverb "badly" in the following sentence describes the action named by the verb "played"—not the subject "I"—and is correct:

I played *badly* in yesterday's game.

3. Keep related words together.

The idea of keeping related words together as closely as possible is probably the whole idea behind studying modifiers. Adjectives should be placed right next to the things they describe, and adverbs should be placed right next to the action or the other modifiers they describe.

The most common problem with keeping related words together is the simple misplacement of an adjective—especially an adjective like "only," "just," "about," or "almost." Notice that in the following sentences the adjectives are not as close as they should be to the words they are actually meant to describe. Circles and arrows indicate better placement:

> I almost have enough money to start a new company.
> Please bring the speaker a cold glass of water.
> He only has $5 to spend at the store.
> Checks are only accepted with valid identification.

Relative clauses are often mistakenly placed too far from the words they are intended to describe, but remembering to keep related words together will help you to avoid mistakes such as these:

> The man is here *who quit.*
> The report is very good *that he wrote at home yesterday afternoon.*

These sentences would have greater effect if they were rewritten like this:

> The man *who quit* is here.
> The report *that he wrote at home yesterday afternoon* is very good.

Just as an artist must place the colors in a painting in the right places to get the picture across, we as writers must place the colors (describing words) in just the right places to get our picture across to the reader.

4. Avoid dangling modifiers.

A dangling modifier is an adjective that does not refer clearly to a specific word or group of words in a sentence. Thus, because the modifier is not "tied" to something in the sentence, it "dangles."

Notice that in the following sentences the adjective phrases dangle because they do not refer clearly to a particular word or group of words in the sentences or are not as close to the words they describe as they could be:

> *Having rotted in the cellar all winter,* my brother was unable to sell the apples.
> *To be sure the report would be delivered on time,* "URGENT" was written across the front of the envelope.

Does "having rotted in the cellar all winter" refer clearly to whatever it is supposed to describe? And does "to be sure the report would be delivered on time" refer clearly to whatever it is supposed to describe? No.

In the first sentence, the participle phrase "having rotted . . ." is supposed to describe "the apples," but it is placed right in front of "my brother" instead. And in the second sentence, the infinitive phrase "to be sure . . ." is supposed to describe "we" or "I" or someone else not named in the sentence, but it is placed in front of "URGENT" instead.

To correct these dangling modifiers, we could rewrite the sentences as shown here:

> Having rotted in the cellar all winter, *the apples* could not be sold by my brother.
>
> To be sure the report would be delivered on time, *we* wrote "URGENT" across the front of the envelope.

The reason we have such problems with dangling modifiers is this: The subject of the modifier is not named in the phrase. That is, in phrases like "to convince the mayor of his plan," "hoping to finish before 5:00," and "selected as Mother of the Year," the person or thing being talked about is not identified. Therefore, we always assume that the phrase is talking about the subject of the main clause that follows the phrase. Sometimes that doesn't seem to make sense—and we know then that the modifier dangles.

5. Avoid overusing modifiers.

Modifiers are used to make meaning more clear or more vivid—to show contrast or to give emphasis. But "all emphasis is no emphasis," that is, use of too many modifiers detract from the effect they are meant to have, just as typing a letter in all capital letters destroys the emphasis the typist had hoped to achieve.

6. Use comparative modifiers to compare two things and superlative modifiers to compare more than two things.

Adjectives and adverbs are often used to compare two or more things. When only two things are compared, the adjectives and adverbs should be comparative modifiers used with words like "more" and "less" and adjectives with "-er" added to them (like "greater" and "smarter"). For example,

> This half is *better* than that half.
>
> Of the two, John is the *smarter* student.
>
> Betty is a *faster* typist than all the rest of our typists.
>
> He is *more* capable than she is.
>
> He is *less* capable than she is.

Conversely, when more than two things are compared, the adjectives and adverbs should be superlative modifiers—used with words like "most" and "least" and adjectives with "-est" added to them (like "greatest" and "smartest"). For example,

> She is the *tallest* member of the team.
>
> He is the *smallest* quarterback to play in the NFL.
>
> She is the *most* qualified of all the applicants.
>
> He is the *least* nervous of all the contestants.

8. Hyphenate compound adjectives.

Often, a noun is described by a group of words that act together to provide a single description of the noun. For example, the words "up," "to," and "date" work together to provide just one description—not three—of the noun "report" in "the up-to-date report." This group of words is called a compound adjective.

What Is a Compound Adjective? A compound adjective is a group of words that provides a single description of a noun that follows. Hyphens are used between the words to make the words appear as a single unit. That is, the hyphens "glue" the words together and let the reader know that the words are to be read as a single adjective.

Thus, proper hyphenation of compound adjectives increases understanding and speeds the reader along. Notice the proper use of hyphens to form compound adjectives in the following sentences:

> The Small Business Administration approved a small-business loan for $2 million.
>
> He said that the large-appliance industry has been weakened by the recent economic depression.
>
> The well-known reporter walked to the front of the room to announce his discovery.
>
> Just-in-time inventory has been adopted by more than one American company with success.
>
> His "better-late-than-never" attitude kept him from hearing the opening remarks of many meetings.

Each compound adjective in these sentences provides a single description of the noun that follows it, regardless of whether the adjective has two, three, or more words in it.

The decision to place a hyphen between two words or to leave the hyphen out, will often have a significant effect on the meaning of a sentence. In the following pairs of sentences, the only thing different between the sentences in each pair is the hyphen, but notice how the meaning of the sentence changes:

> We need more qualified workers. (We need what? Greater numbers of qualified workers.)
>
> We need more-qualified workers. (We need what? Workers who are more qualified than the workers we have now.)
>
> The large appliance industry is suffering. (Which industry? The appliance industry, which is large.)
>
> The large-appliance industry is suffering. (Which industry? The industry that produces large appliances.)
>
> The small business computer costs $4,000. (Which computer? The business computer, which is small.)
>
> The small-business computer costs $4,000. (Which computer? The computer that is designed for small businesses.)

Remember that hyphenated compound adjectives are used only before nouns. When they come after nouns, they are not hyphenated:

> The up-to-date report was submitted on time. (comes before the noun)
>
> The report was up to date. (comes after the noun)
>
> It was a well-written report. (comes before the noun)
>
> The report was well written. (comes after the noun)

Prepositions and Connectives

Putting Ideas Together

Words, phrases, and clauses in a sentence—ideas—can be joined in various ways. They can be joined to show that one idea continues or adds to the thought expressed in another part of the sentence:

> I learned the material, *and* I did well on the test.

To show that one idea presents a new or separate thought from what is presented in another part of the sentence:

> I learned the material *by* attending class and *by* taking notes in class.

Or to show that one idea is really a "subpart" of another part of the sentence:

> I learned the material *by* attending class and taking notes.

Connectives Connect Ideas and Show Relationships. Letting your reader know when your sentences change thoughts, continue thoughts, or add thoughts is an important part of good writing. Prepositions and other connectives are the signals you use to show those changes to the reader. Connectives not only connect or join ideas but also show the relationship between ideas.

Connectives include prepositions (words like "in," "by," "to," "among," and "between"); conjunctions (joining words) like "and," "but," "so," and "because"; relative pronouns, including "that," "whether," "whichever," "whatever," "whoever," "who," "whom," and "which"; and relative adverbs like "where," "when," and "while."

Effective use of connectives often centers on making sure that connected ideas or sentence parts are parallel. This discussion of connectives starts with an explanation of parallelism; then you will be ready to study the rules governing the use of prepositions and other connectives.

Parallelism and Connectives

Parallelism is often defined simply as "consistency." More exactly, though, parallelism is defined this way: Equal grammatical structure for items that are of equal rank or importance.

If you fail to use connectives properly to show parallelism or equal importance of two ideas, your reader will assume that the ideas are not equal in importance. As a result, your reader may not receive the message you meant to send.

For example, assume that you write the following sentence in a letter:

> Please send $10 *to* Alex and me.

Assuming that your reader is willing to comply with your request, how much money will he or she send? Just $10, and you and Alex will have to be happy with taking home just $5 each. But now let's assume that you write this sentence in a letter:

> Please send $10 *to* Alex and *to* me.

Again assuming that your reader will comply with your request, how much money will he or she send? Twenty dollars—$10 to you and $10 to Alex. Why?

In "send $10 *to* Alex and *to* me," "Alex" and "me" are treated as separate, equally important parts of the sentence. That is, they are expressed as parallel items in the sentence, because they have the same grammatical structure—"*to* Alex and *to* me."

Prepositions as Connectives

Just as all connectives join sentence elements and show the relationships that exist between the elements, prepositions connect a word, phrase, or clause with something else in the sentence and show the relationship between the two elements. Prepositions can be classified as being either simple prepositions, compound prepositions, or prepositional phrases. Here are a few examples of each kind of preposition.

Simple Prepositions

in	at	by	to
on	of	off	over
like	out	through	with

Compound Prepositions

about	above	after	against
among	around	behind	between
beside	outside	toward	except

Prepositional Phrases

according to	inasmuch as
because of	contrary to

Despite the great number of prepositions in the English language (remember, the prepositions just listed are only a few of those you use), most have no problem deciding which preposition to use in most writing or speaking situations. The choice of one preposition over another often just seems right, and you use prepositions without thinking much about them.

For example, most would say "I was interested *in* the project," not "I was interested *for* the project." "In" naturally sounds right, whereas "for" is awkward and unnatural.

The choice of some prepositions is not always as easy as the choice between "interested in" and "interested for." For example, many of us misuse "between" and "among" because we haven't developed a sense of which preposition is right in a particular situation. In such cases, we can rely on rules of usage to guide our choice.

In the case of "between" and "among," the rule of usage tells us to use "between" when referring to just two things and to use "among" when referring to more than two things. For example, "the subject was discussed *between* the two employees" but "the subject was discussed *among* the three employees."

1. Use simple prepositions instead of wordy prepositional phrases.

For many years, business writers have been criticized for making their letters and reports hard to understand and pompous sounding. Part of this problem comes from the use of prepositional phrases in place of simple prepositions that express the same ideas. For example, the wordy prepositional phrases in the left-hand column of the following listing can usually be replaced by the simple prepositions shown in the right-hand column:

Wordy Prepositional Phrase	Simple Preposition
inasmuch as	because, since
for the purpose of	to
in the event that	if
in order to	to
prior to	before
subsequent to	after
in regard to	about

In the following sentences, notice the improvement in sentence readability that is brought about by the use of a simple preposition in place of a wordy prepositional phrase:

Inasmuch as we were late for the meeting, we missed the new product announcement.

becomes

Because we were late for the meeting . . .

In the event that he attends the meeting, ask him for a copy of the report.

becomes

If he attends the meeting . . .

Subsequent to receiving your request for information *with regard to* the new store, we called the New Haven office.

becomes

After receiving your request for information *about* the new store . . .

2. Use a preposition at the end of a sentence if the preposition sounds natural and is needed.

More than one English teacher may have taught you that ending a sentence with a preposition is a situation "up with which we cannot put." The fact is that you do end sentences with prepositions in much of your writing. When you force yourselves to avoid ending a sentence with a preposition, you are often left with an awkward and unnatural-sounding sentence (like the phrase "up with which we cannot put" in the first sentence of this paragraph).

Conversely, some prepositions are not needed at the end of a sentence and can be omitted. In fact, we should omit some prepositions from the end of a sentence to avoid sounding uneducated. For example, language-usage books indicate that many educated people view a sentence like "where are you *at*" (or "at" used even in the middle of a sentence with "where") as an indication of a writer's or a speaker's lack of education.

In deciding whether to end a sentence with a preposition, you should consider two important questions:

1. Does ending the sentence with a preposition sound natural—would rewriting the sentence to avoid ending it with a preposition make the sentence sound awkward or artificial?
2. Is the preposition necessary—or can the preposition be omitted without any loss of meaning?

When the word "where" is used in the sentence, a preposition—especially "at"—is rarely, if ever, needed. Be careful to avoid ending "where" sentences with prepositions unless you're sure the preposition is necessary, as in "where did he come *from?*"

3. Omit unneeded prepositions.

Especially in talking—but in writing as well—you often use prepositions that are not needed. Sometimes you even needlessly use two prepositions together, as in "He is sitting *in at* the desk." More common uses of unneeded prepositions are found in sentences like these:

Let's try *out* the new procedure.

I will type *up* the report.

Where did you sit *at* when you saw the concert?

Add *up* the sales figures.

Let's start *in on* the report in the morning.

By avoiding unnecessary prepositions (the italicized words in these examples) in our writing, you will be able to communicate much more clearly and concisely.

4. Include all needed prepositions.

Two kinds of sentence structures require prepositions that we often leave out: sentences with connected parallel elements (elements of equal importance) and sentences that include split constructions.

Connecting Parallel Elements. Because elements of equal rank or importance should be treated with equal grammatical structure, be sure to repeat the preposition before the second of two connected elements. For example:

We told the job applicants *to* submit a completed application form and *to* call next week for an interview time. (two elements of equal importance—"to submit" and "to call" are separate actions)

The students prepared for the test *by* studying the textbook and *by* taking careful notes in class. (two elements of equal importance—"studying the textbook" and "taking notes" are separate actions)

Many writers repeat the preposition before each of three or more parallel elements, as in "we sent letters *to* Bob, *to* Carol, *to* Ted, *to* Alice, and *to* Algernon." Other writers prefer not to repeat the preposition before each element in a list of more than two parallel elements, believing that the sentence sounds more natural and is less wordy when the preposition is not repeated, as in "we sent letters to Bob, Carol, Ted, Alice, and Algernon."

Completing Split Constructions. As mentioned earlier, your sense of what sounds right usually tells you which preposition to use to "complete" or "go with" particular words. You say "interest *in*" but "obligation *to*." You say "looking *for*" or "looking *at*" but "aware *of*."

When in one sentence you use two words that are completed by different prepositions, be sure to include both prepositions:

She was interested *in* and prepared *for* the new job in the accounting department.

The mayor was involved *with* and committed *to* the conservation program.

The students were active *in* and impressed *by* the social club's activities.

I was aware *of* but not excited *about* the proposal to build a new school.

Punctuation: Does a Comma Go Here?

"Does a comma go here?" is probably one of the most-asked writing questions. The comma is probably the most-used (and the most-*misused*) punctuation mark.

Learning to use commas correctly is really a matter of two simple steps:

1. Don't stick a comma in a sentence just because the sentence "sounds" like it "needs" a comma, and don't leave out all your commas just because you're afraid of using them incorrectly.

2. Learn the "names" or functions of the commas; then use the "right" commas to get your point across.

Step 1 is sometimes hard to take. So stop right now, take a deep breath, look yourself squarely in the eye, and promise that you'll quit punctuating by ear and that you'll quit leaving commas out because you're afraid of them.

Now you're ready to take step 2—learn the various functions that commas perform so that you can use them correctly.

Introducing Commas with Names!

Each time you use a comma to perform a certain function, we can "name" the comma after that particular function. For example, a comma that follows an introductory phrase like "for example" at the beginning of this sentence can be called an "introductory comma." And a comma that is used before a conjunction like "and" to join two main clauses can be called a "conjunction comma."

There are two comma families, and the family names identify the two major functions performed by commas: separating sentence elements and enclosing sentence elements.

The "Separate" Family

Conjunction comma

Series comma

Introductory comma

Explanation comma

"And"-omitted comma

The "Enclose" Family

Parenthetical comma

Nonessential comma

Renaming comma

Dates and addresses comma

"Hey, you!" comma

Commas that Separate. Generally speaking, commas in the "separate" family are used just one at a time (commas from the "enclose" family are used in pairs). The following paragraphs introduce each "separate" comma and give simple examples of each.

Conjunction Comma. The conjunction comma is used—with a conjunction like "and," "but," or "so"—to separate two main clauses. The choice of either "and" or "but" or another conjunction depends on the relationship you want to show between the two main clauses; but be sure to include a conjunction—a conjunction comma without a conjunction cannot do its job properly. Notice the use of the conjunction comma and a conjunction to separate the main clauses in the following sentences:

> The attorney filed the appeal today, *but* the judge will not make a decision on it until next week.

> The material used in our suit coats is the very best available, *and* we guarantee you will be satisfied with every coat you purchase from us.

> I scored 97 percent on my final exam, *so* I think I will probably earn an A in the class.

Series Comma. A series comma is used to separate items in a list of three or more items. (Two items do not make a list.) Items in a list can be single words, phrases, or clauses. For example,

> We purchased books, papers, pencils, and erasers. (words in a list)

> He studies for an hour in the morning, at noon, and in the evening. (prepositional phrases in a list)

> John typed the letter, Mary copied it, and I mailed it. (main clauses in a list)

Notice that in each of the preceding sentences, a series comma is included before the last item in the list. Although this comma before the "and" or the "or" in a list is really optional, it is a clear signal to your reader that the next item is the final one in the list. In many sentences, omitting the last comma results in a somewhat confused sentence that will probably have to be read at least twice for clear understanding. For example:

> We invited Ted and Mary, Max and Jackie, Ed and Sandy and Paul and Helen.

The grouping of names in this sentence would be much clearer to the reader if the last series comma were included, as has been done here:

> We invited Ted and Mary, Max and Jackie, Ed and Sandy, and Paul and Helen.

Introductory Comma. The introductory comma separates introductory words, phrases, and dependent clauses at the beginning of a sentence from a main clause. Often, the introductory word or phrase is a conjunctive adverb. For example:

> Therefore, we signed the papers as he requested. (introductory word)

> In addition, we agreed to rewrite the contract next week. (introductory phrase)

> When the check arrived, we were disappointed to learn that only $50 was being refunded to us. (introductory dependent clause)

Explanation Comma. The explanation comma separates a clause or phrase of explanation or clarification at the end of a sentence from the main clause. The explanation comma is very much like the introductory comma, except that it precedes something that has been added to the end of a sentence and the introductory comma follows something added to the front of a sentence, as shown in following examples:

Hoping to be on time for the meeting, I ran up the stairs. (introductory phrase followed by an *introductory* comma)

I ran up the stairs, hoping to be on time for the meeting. (explanatory phrase preceded by an *explanation* comma)

Here are a few more examples of the explanation comma used to separate a main clause from an explanatory phrase or clause at the end of the sentence:

I hurried through the examination, knowing that I could not provide the correct answers.

We were late for the conference, as we had thought it started at 4:00 P.M. instead of 2:00 P.M.

Please don't turn in your application form after 5:00 P.M., because we will not be able to accept it.

"And"-Omitted Comma. The "and"-omitted comma separates consecutive or independent adjectives that would otherwise be separated with the word "and." Thus, as you learned in Topic 15, if you can insert the word "and" between two adjectives, you can use an "and"-omitted comma instead:

The report had a long, wordy conclusion. (long *and* wordy)

The sharp-looking, expensive car was totally demolished in the accident. (sharp-looking *and* expensive)

WordPerfect is a well-planned, professional, easy-to-use word-processing software package. (well-planned *and* professional *and* easy-to-use)

Commas that Enclose. Unlike "separate" commas, which are used just one at a time, "enclose" commas are usually used in pairs. Just as a left parenthesis is the beginning marker and a right parenthesis is the ending marker of something being enclosed, one "enclose" comma acts as a beginning marker and another "enclose" comma acts as an ending marker of something being enclosed. Thus, "enclose" commas can often be used in place of parentheses, as in these examples:

The new accountant (whom you hired) is not doing a very good job.

The new accountant, whom you hired, is not doing a very good job.

The "enclose" family includes parenthetical commas, renaming commas, date and address commas, and "hey, you!" commas. The following paragraphs provide a brief introduction to each kind of comma and give some simple examples.

Parenthetical Comma. The parenthetical comma, as its name implies, is used to enclose thoughts that could be enclosed in parentheses. Such thoughts are usually interjections or interruptions to a sentence, as in these sentences:

The man was, as you know, fired from his last four jobs.

The equipment, in the meantime, sat idle and became rusty.

We did not, however, forget that you were interested in taking over the project.

Chris, when the box arrived, was in the middle of calling to find out when the box was going to be sent.

Notice that parenthetical commas can be used to enclose interjections or interruptions that are single words (such as "however"), phrases (such as "in the meantime"), or dependent clauses (such as "when the box arrived").

Renaming Comma. The renaming comma is used to enclose a word or group of words that renames a person or thing already named in the sentence. For example,

Bill Jones, the president of Interwest Health Services, will speak at the luncheon. ("the president of Interwest Health Services" renames "Bill Jones")

Pam Adams, a business education teacher in the Murray School District, has received the district's "Teacher of the Year" award again this year. ("a business education teacher in the Murray School District" renames "Pam Adams")

Paul Thompson, dean of the college, will speak to us tonight. ("dean of the college" renames "Paul Thompson")

We sent the checks to the president, Marlow Marchant, and to the vice-president, Alan Kimball. ("Marlow Marchant" renames "the president," and "Alan Kimball" renames "the vice-president")

Date and Address Commas. Date and address commas are, as the name implies, used to enclose information in dates and in addresses. In dates, use commas to enclose each element that renames or clarifies the first element named:

On Friday, December 22, we will hold the department Christmas party. ("December 22" clarifies "Friday")

On December 22, 1987, we will hold the department Christmas party. ("1987" clarifies "December 22")

On Friday, December 22, 1987, we will hold the department Christmas party. (both "December 22" and "1987" clarify "Friday")

In addresses written in sentences, use commas to enclose each major element except the first:

Send your payment to Accounts Payable Department, Kimball & Company, 1234 South Logan Avenue, Suite 211, Salt Creek, ID 85032. (notice the commas enclosing "Suite 211," which is a major element of the address)

In addresses written in "envelope format," also enclose major elements with commas (if the major element ends a line of the address, use only the first comma of the pair):

Accounts Payable Department

Kimball & Company

1234 South Logan Avenue, Suite 211

Salt Creek, ID 85032

"Hey, You!" Comma. The "hey, you!" comma is more formally called the "direct address" comma. It is used in pairs to enclose interjections used to get the reader's attention—usually the person's name:

> Thank you, Bill, for your time and effort on this project.
>
> Sue, can I take half a day off today?
>
> I can understand your wanting the job, Kim.

As with other "enclose" commas, the "hey, you!" comma is used only once if the portion of the sentence being enclosed either begins or ends the sentence.

Punctuation: If Not a Comma, What?

If not a comma, what? How about semicolons, colons, dashes, and hyphens? All these marks can be used to good effect by a skillful writer. These marks can provide important and meaningful clues to help the reader grasp the real message behind your words.

The semicolon, the colon, the dash, and the hyphen are briefly introduced and explained in the following paragraphs.

The Semicolon or "Super Comma"

The difference between the semicolon and the conjunction comma, then, is that the semicolon needs no help from a conjunction or from any other kind of word to join two main clauses. It is stronger or more powerful than a conjunction comma and can therefore be called a super comma.

> We locked the office and went home; we would not return until the following Tuesday.
>
> The test has never been validated as an employment device; therefore, we must find another method of screening applicants.
>
> Forty applicants qualified for the secretarial job; only one person can be hired.

At times, the semicolon will be used with a conjunction to separate two main clauses. Whenever either of two main clauses contains some kind of comma, use a super comma in place of a conjunction comma to separate the clauses. This beefing up of the conjunction comma into a super comma gives the reader a stronger signal that one main clause has ended and that the second main clause is going to begin. If you still want to include a conjunction like "and" or "but" to show the relationship between the two clauses, that's fine:

> We were, as you can guess, surprised by his answer; *but* we did not let his lack of support stop us from completing the project on time.
>
> The machine failed to perform as promised; *and*, as a result, we will expect a refund immediately.

The super comma really performs just two functions. The first function is the one we just discussed—that of joining (or separating) two main clauses:

The second function of the semicolon is that of clarifying items presented in a list (a series) when at least one of the items in the list has a comma in it. In that situation, the super comma replaces the series commas so that they are not confused with other commas used in the series. For example, notice the confusion resulting in the following sentence from the lack of something stronger than a comma:

We presented the secretarial seminar in Houston, Texas, Salt Lake City, Utah, Denver, Colorado, Reno, Nevada, and Los Angeles, California.

At first, the list appears to contain nine or ten places. On closer examination, though, you can see that only five places are named. Notice how much clearer the sentence becomes when the super comma is used in place of the series commas:

We presented the secretarial seminar in Houston, Texas; Salt Lake City, Utah; Denver, Colorado; Reno, Nevada; and Los Angeles, California.

Thus, the semicolon or super comma could at times also be called the "series semicolon."

Separating main clauses and replacing series commas are the only two functions of the semicolon. Do not use the semicolon to separate dependent clauses, to follow introductory phrases, to enclose parenthetical information, or to introduce lists.

The Colon or "Super Period"

Like the semicolon, the colon can be used to separate two main clauses in certain situations. When the second of two main clauses is the expected or natural explanation or result of the first clause, a colon can be used to introduce the second clause, as in this sentence:

His prediction came true: we never did finish the manuscript.

Because the colon acts much like a period in ending the first main clause but also shows the relationship between that clause and the following one, the name "super period" is appropriate—it does more than a simple period can do. And calling a colon a super period helps us remember this basic rule: Use a colon only where you could use a period—after a complete thought (main clause); do not use a colon after only part of a sentence.

Remembering that basic rule is especially important when you use the super period in its one other role—that of introducing a word, a phrase, or a list. If the word, phrase, or list is preceded by a complete sentence, a colon can be used as an introduction. For example,

Please purchase the following items: a pen, a pencil, and an eraser.

His talents are many: he paints, he writes, he acts, and he sings.

His answer was simple: no.

These are the people who have been invited to participate in the program: (1) John Able, (2) Mary Baker, (3) Jeff Cardwell, and (4) George Durrant.

One exception to the rule that a colon must come after a complete thought is this: When part of a sentence is used to introduce items that will be typed in a displayed list beginning on a separate line from the introductory sentence fragment, a colon may be used to end the partial sentence. In other words, the following use of the colon is correct and acceptable:

He mentioned several important supervision principles in the writing seminar. They are to:

1. Orient employees
2. Explain specific duties
3. Observe outcomes
4. Provide feedback

The Dash— Two Hyphens

Before we start talking about how to use the dash, let's get our terms straight: In typewritten material, the dash is formed by typing two hyphens together (--). In printed material (like this textbook or a magazine), the dash is usually shown as one long hyphen (—). But many students who proofread aloud insist on reading a dash as "dash-dash"—but it is simply a "dash" or, if you wish to be overly careful in your proofreading, a "hyphen-hyphen"!

There. Now that we've cleared the air about what a dash really is, let's get to the important stuff.

The dash—like the colon—can be used to separate two main clauses when the second clause is the natural or expected result or explanation of the first clause. The dash acts somewhat as an arrow would—it alerts the reader to important or emphasized points of information. For example:

He was right about one thing—we never did finish the manuscript.

His answer was very clear—no.

In addition, the dash is used in place of parenthetical, or renaming, commas as a way of emphasizing the enclosed part of the sentence. The dash is particularly useful when the enclosed part of the sentence is an interruption of the normal flow of the sentence, as in these examples:

His attempts to cover his error—attempts that were weak and poorly planned at best—were seen by us as being sufficient reason for his dismissal.

We were—fortunately—able to finish the project before Christmas.

The dash is also helpful when one parenthetical word or phrase (or other enclosed sentence part) is enclosed within another enclosed sentence part. Without the dash, we end up writing something like this:

The information manager, recruited, we believe, from OSU, is doing a great job.

With the dash, the sentence is much easier to read. Notice that dashes can be used to enclose either of the two parenthetical sentence parts, depending on where we want to place emphasis in the sentence:

The information manager—recruited, we believe, from OSU—is doing a great job.

or

The information manager, recruited—we believe—from OSU, is doing a great job.

As you might have guessed, parentheses could also be used to enclose items in a sentence, so the sentence you just read could take one of these forms as well.

The information manager—recruited (we believe) from OSU—is doing a great job.

The information manager (recruited—we believe—from OSU) is doing a great job.

The information manager (recruited, we believe, from OSU) is doing a great job.

The information manager, recruited (we believe) from OSU, is doing a great job.

The difference among all these sentences is simply that of emphasis—dashes tend to emphasize enclosed items, commas merely identify the enclosed items as being parenthetical or nonessential, and parentheses tend to deemphasize the importance of enclosed items.

The Hyphen— Half a Dash

You've already learned that the hyphen (-) is used to join two or more words that act together as a compound adjective to provide a single description of a noun that follows, as in these sentences:

His below-par game was the cause of his depression Monday.

The small-computer industry is one of the largest in America today.

In addition to being used to form compound adjectives, hyphens are also used in some nouns and adverbs like the ones listed here:

Hyphenated Nouns

mother-in-law

father-in-law

commander-in-chief

governor-elect

vice-president (also vice president)

co-worker

Hyphenated Adverbs

full-time

part-time

Also, "self-" words are always hyphenated (except *selfsame, selfish, selfless*, etc.):

self-service

self-examination

self-evaluation

Number Usage

Following are widely recognized number-expression rules for communications in the business world. They also cover the most frequently occurring number-expression situations.

Rule 1 is, in reality, two rules. It is often referred to as the "rule of ten." The two rules reflected in Rule 1 are the two fundamental rules for expression of numbers in business writing. All other rules could be viewed as exceptions to these two fundamental rules.

1. Use figures to express definite numbers over ten. Write out numbers from one to ten inclusive.

NOT: He requested eleven copies of the production report.

BUT: He requested 11 copies of the production report.

NOT: The Engineering Department has 9 more days to do the research.

BUT: The Engineering Department has nine more days to do the research.

2. Spell out numbers that begin sentences.

NOT: 53 executives participated in the study.

BUT: Fifty-three executives participated in the study.

OR: The study involved 53 executives.

3. Express numbers in a connected group in the same manner. If the largest number is more than ten, express all numbers in the group in figures.

NOT: The purchase order covered two typewriters, one photocopy machine, and 12 transcribers.

BUT: The purchase order covered 2 typewriters, 1 photocopy machine, and 12 transcribers.

4. Write percentages in figures followed by the word *percent* (except in statistical material).

NOT: The interest rate will be six percent.

NOT: The interest rate will be 6%.

BUT: The interest rate will be 6 percent.

5. Except in legal documents, write amounts of money in figures. Express even sums of money without the decimal and ciphers. Use figures without the decimal and spell out *cents* when stating cents. Express round amounts of money in millions or higher in combined word and figure form.

NOT: The cost of the book is five dollars.

BUT: The cost of the book is $5.

NOT: Please put this $.10 in petty cash.

NOT: Please put this ten cents in petty cash.

BUT: Please put this 10 cents in petty cash.

NOT: The cost of the building is projected to be about $10,500,000.

BUT: The cost of the building is projected to be about $10.5 million.

6. When even dollars are typed in the same sentence with expressions of mixed dollars and cents, use ciphers to make the figures consistent. Repeat the dollar sign before numbers written in succession.

NOT: Bids on the item were $55, $62, and $65.70.

BUT: Bids on the item were $55.00, $62.00, and $65.70.

NOT: Sales figures for the event were $615, 725, and 1,001.

BUT: Sales figures for the event were $615, $725, and $1,001.

7. Use figures to express whole numbers with fractions. Spell out fractions that stand alone.

NOT: We estimate the two and one-fourth more days will be required.

BUT: We estimate that 2¼ more days will be required.

NOT: We will complete the job in ½ the time we anticipated.

BUT: We will complete the job in one-half the time we anticipated.

8. Use figures to express time when A.M. and P.M. are used. Use a colon to separate the figure for the hour from the figure for the minutes. Do not use the colon and ciphers with even hours unless the even hour is in the same sentence with an uneven hour. Spell the hour in full when *o'clock* is used.

NOT: The meeting adjourned at four-thirty P.M.

BUT: The meeting adjourned at 4:30 P.M.

NOT: Appointments are scheduled for 9:00 A.M. and 11:00 A.M.

BUT: Appointments are scheduled for 9 A.M. and 11 A.M.

NOT: The meeting will begin at 9 A.M., and a refreshment break will occur at 10:30 A.M.

BUT: The meeting will begin at 9:00 A.M., and a refreshment break will occur at 10:30 A.M.

NOT: I will meet you at 7 o'clock sharp.

BUT: I will meet you at seven o'clock sharp.

9. When the word *number* precedes a number, express *number* as a capitalized abbreviation (singular—No.; plural—Nos.) and use a figure to express the number itself.

NOT: Your report is number seven on the agenda.

BUT: Your report is No. 7 on the agenda.

10. Use figures to express distances (except fractions of a mile or of a kilometer), measures, dimensions, weights, and temperatures.

NOT: three meters; ¼ kilometer; two grams; three meters by five meters; seventy degrees; ten tons

BUT: 3 meters; one-fourth kilometer; 2 grams; 3 meters by 5 meters; 70 degrees, 10 tons

11. Express decimals in figures. If a decimal is not preceded by a whole number, use a cipher before it (unless the decimal itself begins with a cipher).

NOT: The correct figure is .55 gram.

BUT: The correct figure is 0.55 gram.

NOT: Third quarter sales showed an increase of only .82 percent.

BUT: Third-quarter sales showed an increase of only 0.82 percent.

12. Use cardinal numbers (1, 25, etc.) when the day follows the name of the month. Use ordinals (first, 1st, etc.) when the day precedes the name of the month.

NOT: The report is due on February 7th.

BUT: The report is due on February 7.

NOT: Mr. Smith will arrive on the 21 of April.

BUT: Mr. Smith will arrive on the 21st of April.

How to Organize and Format Documents

Outlining Mechanics[1]

Before you write a document, you should create an outline to guide your writing. The following text explains how to prepare an outline and how to evaluate the outline, thus making sure it is complete and structurally sound.

Prepare an Outline

Title the Document. The first step in creating an outline is to create a title, which defines the subject matter of the document. The title must accurately describe what the text is all about. For the planning phase, use a *functional* title rather than a creative, attention-getting one. For example, use "Why XYZ Corporation Should Build a New Shipping Facility in Atlanta" rather than "Atlanta: City of Growth." A functional title is helpful in reminding you of the document's objective.

Determine the Categories. The material you write in your text should be divided into relatively small segments for easier reading. Therefore, you need to determine the *categories* into which the text can later be *classified*. For example, a written proposal to change the location where employees of a company may park their cars might include the following categories: (1) Current Policy, (2) Proposed Policy, (3) Advantages of the Proposed Policy, and (4) Implementation Procedures. The names of these categories can be used later as headings (i.e., titles) of the various parts of the report.

Depending on the length of the text you are planning to write, the main categories could be subdivided into even smaller subcategories. Longer documents need more categories because readers comprehend better if they can read smaller sections of material rather than one huge mass of information. A short document might have only three main categories, such as Introduction, Analysis, and Conclusion; a longer document might have six main categories with one or more levels of subcategories under each of the six main categories.

For example, an outline for a document describing 500 major tourist sites in the western United States would be somewhat overwhelming if the sites were simply listed from 1 to 500. An improvement would be to group the sites by state (e.g., Arizona, California, Oregon, etc.). Further, within each state the sites could be grouped according to type (Historic Buildings, Parks, Resorts, etc.). The resulting outline would thus have three levels of categories under the title, as follows:

Title: The 500 Most Popular Tourist Sites in the Western United States

Level 1 Categories: Arizona, California, Nevada, etc.

Level 2 Categories: Historic Buildings, National Parks, Resorts, etc.

Level 3 Categories: Names of the specific tourist sites

Thus, Zion Canyon would be a subcategory of National Parks, which would be a subcategory of Utah, which would be a subcategory of the title (The 500 Most Popular Tourist Sites in the Western United States). Even within the Zion Canyon category, you could have additional subdivisions, such as Accommodations, Maps, Fares, and Weather.

Organize the Categories. The following sections indicate ways to organize the categories:

- *Hierarchy.* Different levels of categories must be organized into a hierarchy, with the title at the top of the hierarchy. In the hierarchy, the various levels of categories and subcategories should be indented and identified according to the following pattern:

Title
  I. First first-level category
    A. First second-level subcategory
      1. First third-level subcategory
        a. First fourth-level subcategory
          i. First fifth-level subcategory
            (a) First sixth-level subcategory
            (b) Second sixth-level subcategory
          ii. Second fifth-level subcategory
        b. Second fourth-level subcategory
      2. Second third-level subcategory
    B. Second second-level subcategory
  II. Second first-level category

Using this approach, an outline with two levels (I, II, etc., and A, B, etc.) would appear as follows:

Title: Results of Management Audit of Administrative Services Division
  I. Introduction
  II. Information Services
    A. Computer Systems
    B. Records Management
  III. Human Resources Department
    A. Employment
    B. Benefits
    C. Training and Development
  IV. Accounting
  V. Accounts Payable
  VI. Accounts Receivable
  VII. Marketing
    A. Advertising
    B. Sales
  VIII. Conclusions and Recommendations

- *Sequence.* In addition to the hierarchical organization, each section must be sequenced appropriately. Categories can be considered as one of two types: *nouns* (person, place, thing, or idea) or *verbs* (actions or events). Noun categories tell about something at a specific point; they include such descriptions as who, what, why, and where. Verb categories describe something that moves or changes over a period; they involve time-sequence information, such as when each of several events occurred or how to perform the steps in a procedure.

Noun categories are sequenced according to *quantity* (e.g., more before less), *quality* (e.g., better before worse), *space* (e.g., high before low), *alphabet* (e.g., *A* before *B*), or some other comparative or otherwise logical measure. *Verb* categories are usually arranged chronologically according to *order of occurrence:* sooner before later (e.g., procedure 1 before procedure 2, cause before effect, stimulus before response, problem before solution, and question before answer).

A noun category example (sequenced from highest to lowest quality) follows:

Comparison of the Top Three Job Finalists

- Chris Gudeman
- Pat Robinson
- Kim Martin

A verb category example (sequenced according to the order in which the steps must be performed) follows:

How to Perform the Inventory Tagging *Process*

- Receive purchase notification
- Assign inventory identification (ID) number
- Create ID tag
- Place ID tag on inventory item

Evaluate the Outline

After the outline is completed, evaluate it to make sure it is structurally sound. To perform the evaluation, use the Structured-Text Evaluation Procedure (STEP). STEP consists of evaluating each *module,* or group, of categories, starting at the first-level categories and then progressing module by module to the most detailed level of the hierarchy. (A module is one group of parallel categories, such as I, II, and III, or A, B, C, and D. Each occurrence of a I, A, 1, a, i, or (a) in an outline signifies the first item in a module.)

Using STEP, you conduct five tests on each module as follows:

1. *Inclusion (or presence) test.* Given the title or heading of a module, are all appropriate items included? If not, restrict the scope of the title or heading to fit the items that are present, or add the missing items. Make sure that every module contains at least two items (e.g., A *and* B; 1 *and* 2).

2. *Exclusion (or absence) test.* Given the title or heading of a module, are all inappropriate items excluded? If not, delete the inappropriate items, or expand the title or heading to fit all the items in the module.

3. *Hierarchy (or horizontal) test.* Are the items in the module hierarchically parallel? If not, shift the problem items to the appropriate level (e.g., from the A, B, and C level to the 1, 2, and 3 level) and make other adjustments necessary to ensure hierarchical parallelism. In most cases, there is no specific right or wrong hierarchy, because most subject matter can be organized in a variety of ways. The writer must decide which organization seems most logical in each circumstance.

4. *Sequence (or vertical) test.* Are the items in the appropriate sequence? Determine whether the module is of the noun or verb type, and then decide which se-

quence seems to be most appropriate for each module. Be sure to make this determination from the standpoint of helping the reader.

5. *Language (or wording) test.* Are the items in the module grammatically parallel? If not, change the wording to achieve parallelism. (This test is important only if the items are used as headings or subheadings in the final text. If they are not, skip this test.)

These tests can be easily remembered by thinking of the words *presence, absence, horizontal, vertical,* and *wording.*

The following examples show how the STEP tests are performed on the first module (first-level categories) of the "Results of Management Audit of Administration Services Division" outline.

STEP Test 1. The following is an example of the inclusion test:

Results of Management Audit of Administrative Services Division

    I. Introduction
   II. Information Services
  III. Human Resources Department
   IV. Accounting
    V. Accounts Payable
   VI. Accounts Receivable
  VII. Marketing
 VIII. Conclusions and Recommendations

Are all units in the Administrative Services Division present? No; the Purchasing Department, a small department with no subunits within it, is missing and needs to be included.

STEP Test 2. The following is an example of the exclusion test:

Results of Management Audit of Administrative Service Division

    I. Introduction
   II. Information Services
  III. Human Resources Department
   IV. Accounting
    V. Accounts Payable
   VI. Accounts Receivable
  VII. Marketing
 VIII. Purchasing
   IX. Conclusions and Recommendations

Are any units included that are not part of the Administrative Services Division? Yes; Marketing is not part of the Administrative Services Division and should be excluded.

STEP Test 3. The following is an example of the hierarchy test:

Results of Management Audit of Administrative Services Division

   I. Introduction
  II. Information Services
 III. Human Resources Department
  IV. Accounting
   V. Accounts Payable
  VI. Accounts Receivable
 VII. Purchasing
VIII. Conclusions and Recommendations

Are all the items in the module hierarchically parallel (on the right level)? No; Accounts Payable and Accounts Receivable are divisions of Accounting. Therefore, they should be shifted to the second level as subdivisions A and B under Accounting, and be tested as a separate module.

STEP Test 4. The following is an example of the sequence test:

Results of Management Audit of Administrative Services Division

   I. Introduction
  II. Information Services
 III. Human Resources Department
  IV. Accounting
       A. Accounts Payable
       B. Accounts Receivable
   V. Purchasing
  VI. Conclusions and Recommendations

Are the items in the most appropriate sequence? This module is a *noun*-type module; therefore, it will not be arranged in a time sequence. Items I and VI are arranged in the order in which the writer wants the reader to encounter them in the report. Items II to V could be arranged by order of size (e.g., largest to smallest) or by order of management problems identified in the audit (e.g., most to least). However, an alphabetical arrangement seems to be more appropriate.

STEP Test 5. The following is an example of the language test:

Results of Management Audit of Administrative Services Division

   I. Introduction
  II. Accounting
       A. Accounts Payable
       B. Accounts Receivable
 III. Human Resources Department
  IV. Information Services

V. Purchasing

VI. Conclusions and Recommendations

Are the items parallel in language? No; items II, III, IV, and V are departments, but only item III includes the word "Department." Therefore, "Department" should be added to items II, IV, and V.

The Revised Outline. With all the necessary changes made, module I to IV now passes all five tests.

Results of Management Audit of Administrative Services Division

I. Introduction

II. Accounting Department

  A. Accounts Payable

  B. Accounts Receivable

III. Human Resources Department

  A. Employment

  B. Benefits

  C. Training and Development

IV. Information Services Department

  A. Computer Systems

  B. Records Management

V. Purchasing Department

VI. Conclusions and Recommendations

After the tests are completed on the first module, they are repeated on all remaining modules. For this example, you would next complete the STEP tests on the three remaining modules in the following order: (1) II, A and B; (2) III, A to C; and (3) IV, A and B. (Note: This structure might change during the evaluation process, resulting in either more or fewer modules to be tested.)

If there were additional levels of submodules, they would be identified and tested in the same manner. For example, if Employment had two subdivisions, it would be identified as module III, A, 1 and 2, and would be tested after module III, A to C.

Figure 1 illustrates the STEP Report Form used to record the test results of each module. This form is particularly useful when you evaluate the structure of another person's writing. Usually, the other person will give you just the text without a table of contents or outline. When this occurs, briefly scan the text (headings, topic sentences, etc.) and create an outline as you go. Then complete the STEP tests on all the modules in the outline you have created; record your evaluations on the STEP Report Form; and give appropriate feedback to the writer.

Conclusion

The STEP procedure is a comprehensive, yet relatively simple, writing tool. The five STEP tests encompass every type of change you can make in an outline: (1) addition, (2) deletion, (3) horizontal movement, (4) vertical movement, and (5) change of wording. Tests 1 and 2 help ensure that the proper *content* is included in each mod-

FIGURE 1

The STEP Report Form, Showing Changes Previously Made in the First Module and Changes that Should Be Made in the Other Three Modules.

```
Title: Results of Management Audit of Administra-
tive Services Division

Module: Title, I to VIII
1. Presence. Add "Purchasing."

2. Absence. Eliminate "Marketing."

3. Hierarchy. Put "Accounts Payable" and "Accounts
   Receivable" as subdivisions of Accounting.

4. Sequence. Arrange in alphabetical order.

5. Language. Add the word "Department" to items II,
   IV, and V.

Module: II, A and B
1. Presence. Add "Payroll" and "Budget."

2. Absence. Okay.

3. Hierarchy. Okay.

4. Sequence. Arrange in alphabetical order.

5. Language. Okay.

Module: III, A to C
1. Presence. Okay.

2. Absence. Okay.

3. Hierarchy. Okay.

4. Sequence. Arrange in alphabetical order.

5. Language. Okay.

Module: IV, A and B
1. Presence. Add "Reproduction Services."

2. Absence. Okay.

3. Hierarchy. Okay.

4. Sequence. Okay.

5. Language. Okay.
```

ule; tests 3 and 4 make sure the items are properly *placed* (horizontally and vertically), and test 5 guarantees proper *language* parallelism.

Four important benefits come from faithfully using the STEP tests. First, the tests help ensure the structural soundness of text. Second, they also help produce clearer thinking. These tests methodically challenge your thought processes, helping assure that no content or organizational considerations are overlooked. Third, the STEP process helps you compose text more efficiently; writing becomes a straightforward process of expanding the outline rather than a perplexing process of not knowing what to write next. Fourth, your text will be easier to read and understand, which is something readers greatly appreciate.

Business Letter Formats

Key Parts of a Business Letter

Refer to Figure 2 captioned "Business Letter Parts." You'll see the major parts that constitute most business correspondence. As a general rule, your business letters should include these elements.

The Letterhead. To project a favorable image, most organizations use letterhead stationery. This letterhead is often designed by advertising agencies, communication consultants, or local printers.

Where letterhead stationery is not used, you should type the name of the person sending the letter, and his or her address at the top of the page above the date line.

The Date Line. The date line refers to the date the letter was written. Eliminate the date if you anticipate there will be a long delay between the time the letter is prepared and the time it is mailed.

The date should be written in either of the following formats:

August 5, 199X

5 August 199X

Do not type the date in straight numbers, such as 8/5/9X as this can be confusing. In the United States, this would be read as August 5, 199X; in much of Europe and Latin America, this would be read as May 8, 199X. The date line should be at the left margin.

A proper inside address ensures delivery.

The Inside Address. The inside address is the name and address of the person to whom you are writing. This is the same address you'll duplicate on the front of the envelope you'll use for mailing.

The information included in the inside address should be accurate and complete to ensure delivery. Usually this includes the name of the person who is going to receive the letter, preceded by the person's title (e.g., Mr., Mrs., Ms., or Dr.); the person's area of responsibility; the name of the organization the person works for; and, finally, the complete address of the organization. When the degree designation or initials are the same as the person's title, only one should be used.

Incorrect: Dr. Gerry Lockyer, M.D.

Correct: Gerry Lockyer, M.D.
or
Dr. Gerry Lockyer

For correspondence you are answering, the inside address information can be drawn from the letter to which you're responding. If you do draw your information from the organization's letterhead, be sure to reproduce the address exactly as indicated on the original letter. Figure 3 illustrates several examples of inside addresses.

When writing addresses, use the U.S. Postal Service state abbreviations for an American audience. These two-letter abbreviations are written in capitals with no punctuation. They allow post office scanners to sort mail more quickly and provide a cross-check against the zip code to be sure the mail is going to the right place.

The Salutation. The salutation line allows you to personalize your message by addressing the reader by name. Your personalized greeting will usually begin with

	HUFFMAN, JONES, & COMPANY
1. Letterhead	Certified Public Accountants
	5308 Derry Avenue, Suite C
	Agoura Hills, CA 91301
	818-706-8328
2. Date line	January 27, 199X
3. Inside address	Mrs. E. F. Bronk
	Vice-President of Manufacturing
	Tramwell Mill Supply
	7926 Chase Lane
	Corvallis, OR 93072
4. Salutation	Dear Ms. Bronk:
5. Body of letter	_____
	_____
	_____
	_____
	_____.
	_____
	_____
	_____
	_____
	_____.
6. Complimentary close	Sincerely,
7. Signature block	
	Randall Johnson
	Sales Manager
8. Initials	RJ/jd
9. Enclosure notation	Enc.

FIGURE 2

Business Letter Parts.

```
Ms. Dorothy Hesse, Manager
Computer Information Systems Department
Pacific Coast Memories, Inc.
One Wilshire Boulevard
Los Angeles, CA 90017
```

```
Robert Z. Lang, M.C.
Topsfield Medical Center
637 Main Street
Topsfield, MA 01983
```

```
Reverend Paul Jacobson
First Church of the Foursquare
23987 West Thistle Street
Cincinnati, OH 45216
```

FIGURE 3
Sample Inside
Addresses.

"Dear," followed by the title of the reader. Typical titles are Mr., Mrs., Ms., Dr., Dean, and Professor. After the title, write the reader's surname, followed by a colon.

Sometimes you will not know the name or title of the person to whom you are writing. This is often the case when you don't personally know the reader, such as when you're writing a letter of complaint, or sending a cover letter and resume to an unnamed corporate recruiting director. In the past, you could handle this situation with the salutation, "Gentlemen":. That won't work today, because such a greeting is often considered sexist. Unfortunately, no alternative has been coined to fill the void. Perhaps the best way to handle the unknown reader is to leave out the salutation entirely. Most readers will never miss it.

Another solution to this dilemma is offered by the Administrative Management Society (AMS) format. The AMS format drops the salutation and the complimentary

RECOMMENDED ABBREVIATIONS FOR STATE NAMES

Alabama	AL	Idaho	ID	Montana	MT	Rhode Island	RI
Alaska	AK	Illinois	IL	Nebraska	NB	South Carolina	SC
Arizona	AZ	Indiana	IN	Nevada	NV	South Dakota	SD
Arkansas	AR	Iowa	IA	New Hampshire	NH	Tennessee	TN
California	CA	Kansas	KS	New Jersey	NJ	Texas	TX
Colorado	CO	Kentucky	KY	New Mexico	NM	Utah	UT
Connecticut	CT	Louisiana	LA	New York	NY	Vermont	VT
Delaware	DE	Maine	ME	North Carolina	NC	Virginia	VA
District of		Maryland	MD	North Dakota	ND	Virgin Islands	VI
Columbia	DC	Massachusetts	MA	Ohio	OH	Washington	WA
Florida	FL	Michigan	MI	Oklahoma	OK	West Virginia	WV
Georgia	GA	Minnesota	MN	Oregon	OR	Wisconsin	WI
Guam	GU	Mississippi	MS	Pennsylvania	PA	Wyoming	WY
Hawaii	HI	Missouri	MO	Puerto Rico	PR		

Source: U.S. Postal Service.

close, both of which are seen as carryovers from a time when business correspondence was much more formal. Instead of a salutation, the letter begins with a subject line. An example of AMS format appears on page 617.

Another salutation dilemma occurs with letters addressed to women. Do you use Ms., Mrs., or Miss? Even if the female reader is married, the use of the title Mrs. can be construed as sexist. It is best to use "Ms." unless your reader signs her name with the title "Mrs." An alternative approach is to include the full name of the reader in the salutation and eliminate the title. For example, if you are writing to Lydia Sproutz, you could use "Dear Lydia Sproutz:" as a salutation.

One final salutation situation bears comment—the unknown reader with the unisex name. Is it Mr. Kim Hall or Ms. Kim Hall? Mr. Chris Thompson or Ms. Chris Thompson? In these cases, omit the salutation line completely. As an alternative, you could include the full name in the salutation and eliminate the title, as mentioned earlier in the Lydia Sproutz example.

The Body. The body of the letter should be carefully centered, both vertically and horizontally, with relatively short paragraphs surrounded by adequate white space.

The Complimentary Close. The complimentary close is a formal way of saying good-bye. It usually consists of words like "Sincerely," "Cordially," or "Respectfully," followed by a comma. When using two-word closes, such as "With regards" or "Yours truly," only the first word is capitalized.

The type of close should match the tone and formality of the letter. For example, "Respectfully yours" would be appropriate for a letter to a person of high respect yet out of place in a personal note to a good friend. In most business correspondence, "Sincerely" works just fine.

```
Three-part signature

Sincerely,




Sandy Blaylock
Vice-President of Finance
```

```
Four-part signature

Sincerely,
Aero Manufacturing & Design Company




Sandy Blaylock
Vice-President of Finance
```

In an attempt to make the complimentary close more meaningful, some companies close their letters with sales-oriented phrases, such as "Comtech is yours truly," "Robertson's is here to help you," or "See your Chrysler Dealer." Chosen with care and discretion, these closes can be effective, especially in sales letters.

The Signature Block. Immediately following the complimentary close, the letter should include either a three- or four-part signature block. The three-part signature includes the signature of the writer, his or her typed name, followed by the writer's title. In the four-part signature block, the name of the company precedes the writer's typed name.

Sometimes the writer isn't available to sign the letter and delegates the signing to a secretary. When this is the case, the secretary usually indicates he or she signed by adding his or her initials just below the signature.

Initials. Initials identify the person who dictated the letter and the one who typed it. The initials are usually typed two lines below the close, with the writer's initials listed first separated by either a slash mark or colon. Often the author's initials are capitalized; the typist's initials are noted in lowercase (e.g., JB/jk or RFK:hc).

Enclosure Notation. If you are going to include an item in the envelope with your letter, you will want to advise you reader by typing the word "Enclosure" or the abbreviation "Enc." just below the identifying initials. If you are enclosing more than one item, indicate this by typing "Enclosures" followed by the number of items: for example, Enclosures 4. Some organizations, including the U.S. government, identify each enclosure as follows:

Enclosures 2

1. HUD Handbook 3001.1
2. Application for FHA Correspondent

Copies. Sometimes you will need to send a copy of your letter to someone else besides the one to whom you are writing. To advise the addressee, type "c:" at the left margin below the enclosure notation or on the line below the identifying initials. If you are going to send copies to many people, list the names according to rank.

Once in a while, you'll need to send a copy to another person without the addressee being informed. In this case, the initials "bc:" (which stand for blind copy) are used. These initials are typed *only on the copy* and *not* on the original letter.

Miscellaneous Parts of the Business Letter

The Attention Line. Sometimes you'll want to address your letter to the organization, but want a particular individual or department to read the letter. This is where the attention line proves useful.

Sample Attention Line.

```
Centa Systems, Inc.
1927 Sand Hill Road
Palo Alto, CA 94001


Attention: Mr. Randy Griffin, Controller
```

The Subject Line. The subject line improves the efficiency of handling correspondence by indicating the topic of the letter. This line makes filing and retrieval simpler and initial understanding of the letter contents easier. If carefully worded, the subject line often replaces much of the first paragraph of the letter.

```
        Ms. Jane Lucas
        Rising Star Productions
        79 East Wind Way
        Boulder, CO 80303

        SUBJECT: Your Order Number 1075


        Dear Ms. Lucas:
```

Generally Accepted Letter Formats

There are four basic business letter formats in common use today (Figures 4 to 7).

- Full block
- Modified block
- Semiblock
- AMS simplified

Memorandum Mechanics

Differences Between Letters and Memos. Memo is an abbreviation for memorandum, which is essentially an *inside letter*. It serves to convey written messages within the organization. For this reason, memos are sometimes referred to as *interoffice correspondence*. A memo serves a slightly different function from a letter and differs from outside correspondence as follows:

It is often less formal.

It may place a little less emphasis on creating a favorable image. The person who receives your memo probably already knows you; you can spend less time on building credibility.

It normally conveys only one theme.

It is usually organized in a direct format.

It frequently employs shortcuts that streamline the message, such as subject lines, frequent enumeration, and so forth.

Memo Construction. A memo has two main parts: a heading and a body. The heading contains five pieces of information and is designed to give the reader the important facts on *who, what,* and *when*. At the top of most memos, you will find the following five items:

1. The words "memorandum," "memo" or "interoffice correspondence," centered at the top of the page. Some organizations use preprinted memo forms.
2. The name(s) of the intended receiver(s). This is called the "to line."
3. The name(s) of title(s) or the writer(s). This is called the "from line."
4. The date the memo was written.
5. The subject of the message. This is called the "subject line."

Figure 8 illustrates a sample memo format.

Three or more lines from top of page	Letterhead
	Date line
Three or more lines from heading	Inside address
Three or four lines below date line	_____
	_____
Double-space	_____
	_____
Double-space	Salutation:
	_____
	_____
Double-space	_____ Body of letter _____
	_____
	_____
	_____.
Double-space	_____
	_____
	_____
	_____.
Double-space	Complimentary close,
Four lines of space for signature	Name Title
Double-space	Initials Enc. c:

FIGURE 4

Full Block Format, with All Elements at the Left Margin.

Three or more lines from top of page	Heading
Three or more lines from heading	Date line
Three or four lines below date line	Inside address
	_____
	_____
Double-space Double-space Paragraph indented	Salutation:
	_____
	_____
	_____ Body of letter _____
	_____
	_____
Double-space Paragraph indented Double-space	_____.
	_____
	_____
	_____
	_____.
Double-space	Complimentary close,
Four lines of space for signature Double-space	Name Title
	Initials Enc. cc:

FIGURE 5

Modified Block Format, with Paragraphs Indented, and Date and Close Centered.

```
| Three or more lines from top of page | Letterhead |
| Three or more lines from heading | Date line |
| | Inside Address |
| Three or four lines below date line | _____ |
| | _____ |
| Double-space | Salutation: |
| Double-space | _____ |
| | _____ Body of |
| | letter _____ |
| Double-space | _____ |
| | _____. |
| Double-space | _____ |
| | _____ |
| | _____ |
| | _____. |
| Double-space | Complimentary close, |
| Four lines of space for signature | Name |
| | Title |
| Double-space | Initials |
| | Enc. |
| | cc: |
```

FIGURE 6

Semiblock Format, with No Indentation, and Date and Close Centered.

Three or more lines from top of page	Heading
Three or more lines from heading	Date line
Three or four lines below date line	Inside address
Triple-space	
Subject line	SUBJECT (All capital letters) (no salutation)
Triple-space	Body of letter
Double-space	
Four lines of space for signature	(No complimentary close)
	NAME (All capital letters)
	TITLE (All capital letters)
Double-space	Initials
	Enc.
	cc:

FIGURE 7

AMS Simplified Format, with No Salutation, Subject Line, and No Complimentary Close.

MEMORANDUM

Six or more
lines from
top of page

Four lines
below heading

TO: _____

FROM: _____

DATE: _____

SUBJECT: _____

_____

Triple-space

_____

_____ Body of

memo _____

_____

_____.

Double-space

_____

_____

_____

_____.

Double-space

_____

_____

_____

_____.

No complimen-
tary close

No signature
block

FIGURE 8

Sample Memo Format.

Memos Use Enumeration. One of the ways to streamline a memo's message is to itemize its main points. Compare the following two memos—one with itemization and one without. Which communicates more efficiently?

Example 1: No Itemization.

MEMORANDUM

```
TO:       Pat Zaleski, Assistant Supervisor

FROM:     Ray West, Manager

DATE:     January 25, 199X

SUBJECT:  Manager's Conference
```

Please contact the people at the Hilton in Greenville to arrange for our upcoming conference. We will need rooms for 30 managers (singles) for the nights of July 13 to 15. Also arrange for a buffet dinner on July 13, a "happy hour" the evening of July 15, and the conference room with tables and seating for 30 people from 9:00 A.M. to 5:00 P.M. all three days. "Breakout rooms" for groups of six to seven near the conference room will be needed for the afternoon of July 14. Be sure they have a 35-mm movie projector, overhead projector, and flip charts. We should also have them bring in coffee, juice, and doughnuts in the morning (about 10:00 A.M.) each day and soft drinks (about 3:00 P.M.) each afternoon.

Thanks for taking care of this.

Example 2: With
Itemization.

MEMORANDUM

TO: Pat Zaleski, Assistant Manager

FROM: Ray West, Manager

DATE: January 25, 199X

SUBJECT: Rooms, Services, and Equipment Needed for
          the Manager's Meeting, July 13 to 15.

Please arrange the following with the people at the
Hilton in Greenville.

Rooms
....

Thirty single rooms for the nights of July 13
to 15

Conference room with tables and seating for 30
from 9:00 A.M. to 5:00 P.M. on all three days

Five "breakout" rooms for the afternoon of
July 14 (six people per room)

Food Service
....

Buffet dinner the evening of July 13

"Happy hour" bar and snacks the evening of
July 15

Coffee, juice, and doughnuts each morning at
10:00 A.M.

Soft drinks each afternoon at 3:00 P.M.

Equipment
....

Thirty-five-mm movie projector (all three days)

Overhead projector for transparencies

Screen

Flip chart-tripod with paper

Thank you for taking care of these arrangements.

Sample Report Proposal (Memo Format)

TO: Ralph C. Wilson, Vice-President of Person-
          nel

FROM: Kathy L. Sanders, Employee Training Super-
          visor

DATE: September 22, 199X

SUBJECT: PROPOSAL FOR AN ANALYSIS OF MULTITASKING
          SOFTWARE FOR USE BY MIDLEVEL MANAGEMENT

Ralph, as we discussed, I am proposing the
following analysis and report on multitasking
software to boost managerial productivity.

BACKGROUND OF THE PROBLEM

As a widely diversified company, we face special
challenges in training our people. Each of our administrative staff deals with a somewhat different
set of managerial problems. Nevertheless, the need
for ongoing training and upgrading productivity of
middle-management professionals is well documented.

Of specific concern is the low level of computer expertise and software use among managers in several
divisions (especially textile processing and machinery support services). Despite the company's
major investment in networked personal computers
(PCs) for each manager, considerable resistance to
this technology is evident. In short, our managers
are not using their PCs to anywhere near their full
potential.

Other potential problem areas are employee productivity and morale. We have seen a marked increase
in absenteeism and product defects, and productivity levels are dropping in most divisions.

These factors played a part in top management's decision to invest more heavily in middle-management
software training. This opportunity provides managerial training in a way that forces managers to
use their computers and, it is hoped, become more
comfortable with the PCs.

STATEMENT OF THE PROBLEM TO BE REVIEWED

Our immediate problem is that we lack expertise in selecting the optimum multitasking software.

GOAL OF THE PROJECT

The project I am proposing will evaluate such software now available.

The selected options will be ranked to aid in the decision process further.

RESEARCH PROCEDURES TO BE USED

The information presented in this report will be gathered from three main sources.

1. A review of relevant publications found in State University's business library. The head reference librarian is well qualified to guide our search and has expressed a willingness to do so. This reference search will use several of the largest computer databases available.

2. Interviews with professionals now using multitasking software for managers. We will talk with at least four local companies who have successfully adopted such software (these companies are not competitors).

3. Manufacturers of software that appears promising (based on steps 1 and 2) will be initiated to demonstrate their products to our analysis team.

COST OF THE PROJECT

Because this research will be done as part of my normal job responsibilities, no special costs are anticipated. I estimate that the study will take approximately 62 work hours to complete. A rough breakdown of time follows:

Planning of library research phase	2 hours
Review of published information	8 hours
Interviews with managers	10 hours
Analysis of data received	6 hours
Attendance at product demonstrations	20 hours

```
        Preparation of final report        14 hours

        Presentation of findings to         2 hours
        board

   Costs of secretarial services, paper, materials,
   photocopying, telephone, and so forth will be ab-
   sorbed by the personnel department.
```

Source Documentation for Business Reports

This section shows how to cite sources of information used in business documents. There are two acceptable forms for citing sources of information used in business reports:

1. A **footnote,** which is a complete source documentation, is printed on the same page as its citation. Word processors automatically place these at the bottom of the page, allocating appropriate space for the note(s).

2. An **endnote** contains the same information as a footnote. Endnotes are listed in order of citation in the text and placed at the end of the document. When you use endnotes, label your list "Notes".

3. A **source list** or **bibliography** may be used to cite general sources used as background information for a document. These may also be referred to as "Works Cited" or "References."

Following are examples of standard formats for footnote and bibliography entries. "F" refers to footnote (or endnote) and "B" designates a bibliography entry. Words shown in italics can also be typed as underlined.

Books

One Author:

F: [1]Paul R. Timm, *Managerial Communication,* 3rd. ed. (Upper Saddle River, NJ: Prentice Hall, 1995), pp. 123–24.

B: Timm, Paul R. *Managerial Communication,* 3rd ed. (Upper Saddle River, NJ: Prentice Hall, 1995).

Two or More Authors:

F: [2]William Jones, Terri Hassom, and Aaron J. Bruce, *The Neuropsychology of Loafing* (New York: Capable Press, 1997), p. 23.

B: Jones, William, Terri Hassom, and Aaron J. Bruce, *The Neuropsychology of Loafing* (New York: Capable Press, 1997).

Editor as "Author":

F: [3]Edward J. Simmons, ed., *Readings in Necrophobia* (Cambridge: The MIT Press, 1999), p. 44.

B: Simmons, Edward J., ed. *Readings in Necrophobia* (Cambridge: The MIT Press, 1999).

Institution, Association, or the Like as "Author":

F: [4]Special Libraries Association, *Directory of Business and Financial Services* (New York: Special Libraries Association, 1998), p. 334.

B: Special Libraries Association, *Directory of Business and Financial Services* (New York: Special Libraries Association, 1998).

Articles in Journals or Magazines

Journals

F: [5]Roberta Q. Jeremiah, "Why Do Managers Constantly Screw UP?" *Management Journal* IV, Issue 6 (January 1998) 34.

B: Jeremiah, Roberta Q. "Why Do Managers Constantly Screw UP?" *Management Journal* IV, Issue 6 (January 1998) 34.

Magazines or Newspapers

F: [6]Paul Craig Roberts, "A Minimum-Wage Study with Minimum Credibility," *Business Week,* April 24, 1995, p. 22.

B: Roberts, Paul Craig. "A Minimum-Wage Study with Minimum Credibility," *Business Week,* April 24, 1995, p. 22.

F: [7]Scott McCartney, "The Multitasking Man: Type A Meets Technology," *Wall Street Journal,* April 19, 1995, p. B1.

B: McCartney, Scott. "The Multitasking Man: Type A Meets Technology," *Wall Street Journal*, April 19, 1995, p. B1.

Interviews

F: [8]James A. Stead, President, National Humongous Corporation, Inc., May 30, 1997, Chicago, IL.

B: Stead, James A. President, National Humongous Corporation, Inc., May 30, 1997, Chicago, IL.

Electronically Transmitted Articles (e.g., Internet or database services). Standards for such documents have not been widely adopted. *The Chicago Manual of Style* recommends that writers should strive for consistency but allow discretion in the specific format used. That's good advice for any citation system. Business readers seldom demand rigid adherence to style-guide perfection. They do, however, need complete citation information so that sources can be looked up if needed. Therefore, be complete and consistent.

Quick Review Checklists

Planning and Managing Business and Professional Writing (Chapter Eight)

1. What is the "big idea" of your message?

   ✓ What do you want your receiver to *do* or *think* after receiving your message?

2. Is this document necessary?

   ✓ Would another medium convey the message more efficiently, effectively, or creatively?

3. Should you use a BIF or BILL pattern of arrangement?

   ✓ Use BIF for routine or direct messages that are not likely to affect the emotions of the receiver.

   ✓ Use BILL if the receiver's emotions are likely to be engaged by the message—that is, if the message will be disappointing or upsetting (bad news), or require the receiver to shift attitudes (persuasive messages).

4. What degree of formality should be used? Will your receiver respond to a casual, conversational tone or would such informality be construed as disrespect?

   ✓ Use a conversational tone—writing the way you talk is a good goal.

   ✓ When in doubt, it is better to err on the side of higher formality.

5. How can you convey clear content to the reader?

   ✓ Preview the intent of your message up front (especially with BIF-approach messages).

6. How can you make the message clear?

   ✓ Review word choices and replace complex terms with simpler words. Clarify or define unfamiliar words or concepts; spell out acronyms the first time they are used.

7. How can you emphasize the most important parts of the message?

   ✓ Use verbal- and visual-accessing techniques.

Projecting Professionalism (Chapter Nine)

1. Have you considered your receiver's feelings?

   ✓ Check the tone of a message and word choices.

   ✓ Anticipate the self-interest of your receivers.

2. Have you phrased ideas in terms of reader interest?

   ✓ Use "reader-important" phrasing.

   ✓ Avoid blanket tone; speak to receivers as individuals.

3. Have you focused on positive wording?

   ✓ Negative wording conveys less information.

4. Could your message be interpreted as abrasive or arrogant?

   ✓ Avoid overuse of the first-person pronouns ("I," "me," or "my").

5. Could your language use convey an offensive tone?
  √ Avoid a preaching, patronizing tone.
  √ Avoid false sincerity.
  √ Avoid sexist or other potentially offensive terms.

Writing Routine, Informative, and Goodwill Messages (Chapter Ten)

1. Is your message direct, complete, and friendly?

2. Does your goodwill message take advantage of the opportunity to strengthen human relations by communicating feelings even though no message is required?

3. Does your message enhance your professionalism?
  √ Check wording for sensitivity.
  √ Check grammar, spelling, mechanics, and polish.

4. What other opportunities for goodwill or FYI messages do you have now?

Disappointing or Unfavorable News (Chapter Eleven)

1. Is it worth the extra effort to attempt to soften the blow of this message?
  √ If you are not concerned about possible hurt feelings or offense, use a straightforward approach.

2. Do your opening remarks create a buffer?
  √ Begin with neutral or mildly positive statements.
  √ Include "seed words" that can later be incorporated into your reasoning.

3. Does your transition to reasoning avoid an abrupt shift?
  √ Avoid abrupt use of "but" or "however."

4. Are your reasons clearly thought out and articulated?
  √ Be specific in explaining your reasons.
  √ Go from facts to conclusions.

5. Is the refusal (or bad news) expressed tactfully yet conclusively?
  √ Use passive voice for de-emphasis.
  √ Check positioning within the letter for de-emphasis. Place bad news in mid-paragraph if possible.

6. Have you added an optimistic close?
  √ Comment on desire to maintain a positive relationship with the receiver.

7. Does your message strive to help your receiver understand and appreciate your reasoning, even though the message is disappointing?

Persuasive and Sales Messages (Chapter Twelve)

1. Does this message clearly seek to get receivers to do something they normally would not do without prodding? Are you clear about what that specific thing is?

2. What benefit can be gained or lost if the receiver acts on your message?
   - √ Consider "what's in it for them."
   - √ Write in terms of receiver benefit.

3. Did you gain attention in an appropriate way?
   - √ Start the message with attention-getting information in the first sentence.
   - √ The opening line is a strong emphasis position. Use this fact.

4. Have you created a mental picture of a problem or dilemma in the mind of your receiver?

5. Have you used the second person ("you" or "your") to personalize the message?

6. Have you used active verbs and concrete nouns to create vivid mental pictures in your message receivers?
   - √ Avoid abstract nouns and verbs.

7. Have you presented clear, credible evidence that can solve the problem or dilemma you described?

8. Have features of your solution or product been clearly related to benefits? Remember the following:

   Features. Characteristics of your product, service, or idea.

   Benefits. A "What this means to you" statement linking the feature to the reader/listener.

9. Have you used testimonials, third-party references, product samples, visuals, or demonstrations as appropriate?

10. Have you included a specific action step?
    - √ Make the action easy and convenient for receivers.
    - √ Motivate *immediate* action.
    - √ Remind receivers of benefits at the end of the message.

Communicating About Employment (Chapter Thirteen)

1. Recognizing that there is no "one best way" for job-getting communication, have you used your best skills of creativity, salesmanship, and attention to detail?
   - √ Avoid "cookie-cutter" resumes and letter formats.
   - √ List your best-selling points before writing a resume.

2. Have you included the traditional parts in your resume, as appropriate?
   - √ Include education and training, work experience, and appropriate personal characteristics and interests.

3. Have you avoided overuse of "I" (and other first person pronouns) in the resume and application letter?
4. Have you carefully considered the "between-the-lines" messages that may be conveyed by your resume and cover letter?
5. Have you clearly linked your "features" with potential benefits you offer the company?
6. Does your application letter include the key elements of the following:
   √ Reason for the letter
   √ Position being applied for
   √ Reference to an enclosed resume
   √ Key selling points
   √ Request for an interview
7. Have you prepared thoroughly for the interview? This can best be done by the following:
   √ Understanding yourself
   √ Understanding the organization
   √ Assembling materials for the interview
   √ Practicing communication skills
   √ Being prepared with good questions to ask the interviewer

Using Reports and Proposals (Chapter Fourteen)

1. Is this report planned with the reader in mind?
   √ Understand *why* the report is produced.
   √ Determine how the success of the report can be measured.
2. Have you applied the four basic ways of gathering information as appropriate?
   √ Read relevant material.
   √ Interview knowledgeable sources.
   √ Observe relevant conditions.
   √ Reason from data gathered.
3. Is the outcome of this report worth the cost of producing it? Could another medium accomplish the task more effectively?
4. Is a short report appropriate?
   √ Use a memo report format.
5. Is a long, more formal report needed?
   √ Begin with a proposal.

Writing the Report (Chapter Fifteen)

1. Have you considered ways to overcome writers' block and begin the major report?

√ Start by scribbling notes.

√ Gather preliminary data.

√ Try "raw writing."

2. Can you clearly state the purpose of the report?

√ Summarize the report's intent in one clear sentence.

3. Have you listed the possible sources of information needed for the report?

4. Have you decided on the format, length, and formality of the report?

Research Techniques for Business and Professional Communication

Getting the Answers You Need

Never have people needed a good crystal ball more than today. The success of today's organizations, more than ever before, hinges on information—a constant flow of new ideas and strategies for providing today's goods and services. Information, carefully cultivated and acted on, is the lifeblood of every successful organization.

To get such information, organization leaders need primary research skills. Research isn't just for professors and graduate students. It is the key to good decisions and organizational effectiveness.

Reference Tool Four provides the keys to effective organizational research.

The Purpose of Research

The purpose of research is to learn something you do not know and to provide useful information to help solve problems. Children learn basic skills by trial and error—trying and failing until they get it right. There is no other way to learn how to walk or catch a ball.

A higher level of learning uses logic that leads to conclusions based on previous generalizations and experiences. Logical thinking puts two different concepts together to form a new conclusion or concept. Research is simply a systematic way of linking information and forming conclusions. It incorporates data-gathering methods to advance your understanding and help you to make better decisions.

Here is a simple example you may have experienced: If you decide to buy a new car, you probably would not just walk into the nearest dealer and grab the first car in sight. Instead, you would do some research. You might

- Read stories in automobile magazines to compare features
- Talk to friends who have recently bought new cars
- Test-drive cars
- Count the number and type of new cars you see on the streets, assuming that if a lot of people are buying a certain model, it must be pretty good

See, you have been doing research all along.

It's not mysterious or exceptionally complex. It can become a day-to-day activity that produces huge dividends in the form of good answers and decisions.

For our purposes, the following definition will apply:

Research is the process of getting dependable answers to important questions using a systematic method of gathering, analyzing, and interpreting evidence. Its end product is knowledge.

Exploratory, Secondary, or Primary Research

When you search through publications—such as books, magazines, newspapers, pamphlets, atlases, or encyclopedias—looking for background information, you are doing *exploratory research*. Exploratory research gives you a frame of reference, or understanding of the issues, and history of the industry you are researching.

Secondary research is the study of the primary research conducted by others that can be extrapolated to apply to your research topic. When you reviewed a copy of *Consumer Reports* before buying a car, you were using secondary research. The use of secondary research techniques allows you to save much time and money by avoiding unnecessary duplication; you must be careful using secondary research, though, because the data may not perfectly fit your needs. The attitude here should be, "Why reinvent the wheel when it's so much easier to read about what others have already done?" Excellent sources of secondary research include trade magazines and government research reports.

Assume that the secondary research effort has not yielded a solid answer to your question. You've read the car magazines but still aren't ready to make a buying decision based on this information. You want to be certain that you are buying the best car for your needs. You will find it necessary to do *primary research*—to collect primary data that must be obtained firsthand from nonpublished information sources. Such information comes from the following four sources:

Observations

Surveys

Interviews

Experiments

In the car-buying example, you may well use all four. You will observe how well the car seems to be built, how it sounds, and how it handles on the road. You may take an informal survey by interviewing some friends who have bought similar cars. You may even try an experiment where you'll try driving several cars over the same roads at the same speeds to see which handles better.

A Research Model

A model is a conceptual representation of the project—the plan. Just as a manufacturer wouldn't design a new product without first building several mock-ups (models), so should the researcher build a model first.

A model presents a framework from which to work. The structure is useful because it assures that researchers, in their excitement to implement a project, do not overlook important steps that, if not considered, might render the research worthless. If you write out a framework before conducting your research, you will be more focused and efficient than if you do not build your model first. The following paragraphs explain the basic parts of a research model.

Introduction. Give a brief history of the research topic. Once the symptoms of an organizational problem appear, do some initial fact gathering that will help to determine the characteristics of the true problem. This fact gathering might include talking to others about the problem and conducting a library literature search on the topic. This fact-gathering process is aimed at refining the researcher's educated guess to a more accurate problem statement.

Objectives. The next step in doing any research is to define correctly the true nature of the research problem. What exactly do you want to know? Getting the right answers to the wrong questions happens more often than you might think. Unless you are working directly on an explicitly identified problem, you really are not doing research; you are simply gathering data.

Specific Problem Statement. The problem statement is exactly what you are researching. It is possible for researchers to get so wrapped up in acquiring new data that they forget to keep a specific research problem in the forefront of their minds. They go off on tangents and diversions from the primary purpose of the study, delaying the research findings and the business decision. During the initial investigation, the researcher must define the scope of the problem and try to determine the cause-and-effect relationships between the variables.

To state a problem that can be researched, it is necessary to write it in a form that includes the following factors:

1. A *relationship* between two variables, or possibly among several variables, is *questioned*.

2. Each variable is *operationally defined*, either within the problem statement or in supplemental statements to it.

3. A *population* for the research is *implied* or identified.

Here is an illustration of these factors as applied to a poorly worded research question: The question, "I wonder why our company's sales seem to be leveling off" is essentially not researchable because it is inadequately defined. What relationships are described? What does "leveling off" mean, and with what is it being compared?

This research question suffers because the terms are not specifically defined. Do the sales refer to product X or products Y and Z? (Maybe X and Y are selling in record numbers, but Z is pulling down the overall results.) Does leveling off mean that the growth of sales is slower than in the past or that there is no growth at all? Finally, what population is implied? Are you talking about all sales to all customers or only particular types of sales to a certain population of customers?

A better research question would be, "Has the cutback in print advertising for product X [one variable] resulted in a decline in sales growth [another variable] for product X over the last six months [time frame]?"

The new question offers the hypothesis that the independent variable—cutback in print advertising—has made a change in the dependent variable—sales over the past six months.

The question could be further improved by spelling out the relationship between the two variables and stating how the variables' advertising and sales were to be measured. An improved research question might become, "Has the 50% reduction in product X's print advertising from January to December 1993 resulted in the low one percent sales growth of product X for the six months of July through December 1993?" This question is now correct and researchable because all variables are *related*, *measured*, and *specific*.

Creating operational definitions is particularly important. These are definitions that reduce ambiguity by describing how something can clearly "fit" the definition. The following are some sample operational definitions.

Term	Operational Definition
Customer	One who visits the store and purchases items. (Note the operations needed to qualify as a customer: "visit store" and "purchase"; a browser wouldn't count.)
Supervisor	An employee who has one or more employees reporting directly to him or her.
Preferred Customer	A customer who purchases more than $X per year, month, or week.
Successful product	A product that produces a 10 percent net profit for at least one year.

| Low maintenance | A machine that requires one or fewer routine service calls per month. |
| Accurate worker | A worker who makes fewer than ten errors per one thousand procedures. |

Purpose Statement. The statement should explain what you expect to gain by doing the research, or, in other words, why you are conducting the research. The trick to writing good purpose statements is not to be so general that nothing really gets answered and not so specific that some of the critical elements are overlooked.

Methodology. Once the research problem has been clearly stated, you can complete the third step of the model or plan. Remember to conduct secondary research first. Primary research can be time consuming and expensive, so finding answers to previously asked questions is always preferable—so long as it applies directly to your business question. In some cases, you will find such information through a thorough library search.

Observation Techniques

Perhaps you never thought of "just watching" as a research technique. It can be one approach but only if done with the purpose of satisfying stated research objectives. All people observe their environment to some degree. That is one reason observation is so frequently used to gather data. Although observation is so commonly used, it is also the most difficult technique to use correctly. Research observation involves much more than casual viewing and a haphazard absorbing of information. Things to be observed must be clearly decided before the observation is attempted. If the variables are not clearly defined, the observer might note one set of items during one observation and another set during another observation.

Advantages and Disadvantages of Observation. Observations are real-world data, not data from a laboratory study designed to duplicate real life. Observations mirror situations as they really exist. Done correctly, the process reduces most bias and distortions.

Further, using observation techniques in connection with mechanical devices (such as rulers, time clocks, or gauges) can produce the most accurate possible data. Any system that produces hard data and consistent measurement will go a long way toward eliminating bias and interpretation errors from the study.

The last advantage of observation is that the results of the study can be verified readily. Managers can go down and check the results through similar observation techniques, and repeated observations can serve to validate the findings.

A disadvantage of observation is that, if observers have not been carefully trained, the data may reflect observer biases. In addition, observers may spend a great deal of time and effort noting the routine, insignificant event. The unusual and potentially useful data are often hidden under a mountain of trivial observations.

Guidelines for Effective Observation. The person making the observations must have a clear understanding of the operational definitions being used for the study. In addition the researcher should do the following:

1. Prepare the forms used to record the data in advance. Pretest these with a pilot study to be sure the observers know exactly how to record observations.

2. Use objective observers, not people who may have a bias. If, for example, you are observing work behaviors in a particular department, it would be best to use observers who do not work there (or better yet do not even know the people being observed).

3. Prepare a schedule of all observations in advance. Indicate who will observe, where to observe, and when to observe.

4. Make your observations methodical by carefully using the same methods of recording data. Although researchers often think of simply tallying observations on a clipboard, some situations may call for measuring devices, such as counters, stop watches, computer monitoring, cameras, video recorders, and other mechanical devices.

5. Minimize the observer's presence in the process. If the observer is blatantly obvious in observing and recording data, the people being observed may act differently from normal, thus masking what really goes on in the company. Also, studies have shown that the very presence of the observer can lead to improved performance in the short run. This is called a Hawthorne effect, named after a factory where it was first noted.

The following sections describe specific observation techniques:

Time-and-Motion Studies. This approach has long been used to attempt to analyze specific actions needed to complete a task. Suppose that you have a few workers who produce substantially more output than the typical person in that job. You may want to use this observation technique to evaluate what the high producers do—specifically—and to compare their movements with those of the less productive workers. When you think you have figured out why the good workers are so good, you can teach other workers the same skills.

In addition to using a time-and-motion approach to increase productivity, it is also used to determine manufacturing costs of a new product and to develop work schedules.

Behavioral Frequency Counts. This observational approach focuses on how often particular behaviors occur in the people being studied during normal day-to-day actions. An example of this is a study that observed the behaviors used by top salespeople compared with behaviors of the rest of the salespeople. The observers found, using behavioral frequency counts, that the best salespeople listened longer, asked more probing questions, and requested the order more often than the average salesperson.

Reports and Written (or Electronic) Documents. Observation techniques can also be used to review written documents. A great deal of data can emerge from a systematic study of records, reports, memos, letters, and electronic documents.

Telephone companies use this in connection with listening in on customer conversations. The conversations are recorded, and any commitments or promises made by the service representative are noted. The service observer then goes through the company's records to see if those commitments were met.

Companies routinely maintain records that provide information on downtime, budget variances, absenteeism, tardiness, output, terminations, work stoppages, overtime, and many other factors. Systematic checking of such data using observational techniques can answer many business questions.

Tallying Observation of Behaviors. Use simple check sheets to record observations. A check sheet is an easy-to-understand form used to answer the question, "How often are certain events happening?"

Once you've determined what is to be observed and recorded, you'll need to decide how often and for how long observations will occur. Design the check sheet to be clear and easy to understand. A sample sales behavior check sheet is shown in Table 1.

TABLE 1
OBSERVED BEHAVIORS

Salesperson	Greets Customer Promptly	Makes Small Talk	Asks Key Questions	Gives Information/ Assistance	Explains/ Clarifies Features	Asks for Order	Writes the Order
1							
2							
3							

Surveys. Generally, the use of survey questionnaires should be limited to research projects where information from other methods is not available. It could also be used to verify results generated from other methods.

Questionnaires are often mailed or otherwise distributed directly to the people who are asked to respond. They work best when respondents know their answers will be kept confidential. Mailed surveys are useful when collecting data from people who may be geographically dispersed, such as customers across the country. This spread-out sample often rules out the use of interviews (except by telephone), observations, and experiments.

Advantages of the Survey Technique

1. *They are inexpensive.* First, surveys are usually less expensive than interviews and experimentation. This is because the survey is not as labor intensive. Once designed, a questionnaire can gather a large quantity of data without requiring a great deal of employee time; therefore, it costs less.

2. *They are easy to administer.* Because, by definition, the questionnaire is an instrument that requires a written response, the administrator does not have to be skilled in interviewing or observing techniques. Generally, a simple group explanation of the questionnaire's purpose or an explanatory letter will suffice.

3. *Responses will have less bias.* The data in such cases may be more accurate because most respondents will be frank and honest when their answers are anonymous.[2]

4. *Management tends to be receptive to the questionnaire approach.* Data so gathered is usually seen as credible. (If handled correctly, it will be credible, but much depends on how well the survey is designed and administered. Garbage in, garbage out, applies here.)

Disadvantages of the Survey Technique

1. *Survey questionnaires are impersonal and structured.* Questionnaire instruments are one-way communications that generally do not allow respondents to clarify answers. This forced-choice format makes for easy data processing, but if the re-

searcher is asking the wrong questions or not allowing for a full range of all possible responses, the data will be contaminated. Survey questionnaires normally do not give people the opportunity to provide unstructured feedback or to elaborate on why they chose a particular rating.

2. *The questionnaire may be subject to overinterpretation.* Some people try to psychoanalyze every question. They read meaning into the question that was not intended and sometimes try to guess at how the researcher would like them to answer. For some people, the survey creates a "test" environment. They feel that they are being evaluated.

3. *The whole process can be time-consuming, especially if the questionnaire is sent through the mail.* Allow ample time for people to respond. Put a due date on the survey, but don't be surprised if responses dribble in well beyond that date.

4. *Low response rates are common with mail surveys.* Although many people can be reached at a relatively low cost with mail surveys, a major disadvantage is a low response rate. Many recipients simply ignore a mail survey.

Overcoming the Disadvantages. The impersonalization problems can be reduced by giving respondents clear oral instructions (if administering the survey personally) or using a conversational, friendly tone in written instructions. Overinterpretation can be reduced by instructing people to give their first impressions and not to attempt to analyze the questions. Time consumption can be reduced by administering the survey to larger groups of people (if possible) and by budgeting enough time to allow for mail delays if using mail surveys. Finally, response rates can be improved by rewarding the respondent with a token of appreciation. Some surveyors attach a dollar bill to a mail survey; others offer to make a donation to charity if the person will complete the survey. Be creative and you can overcome many, if not all, of these disadvantages.

How to Get a Random Sample. Randomness means that any member of the population has an equal chance of being selected for the survey. If your population is defined as people who bought Ford trucks during May of this year, all such buyers have an equal chance of getting your survey. To ensure randomness, use one of these methods.

1. Assign a number to each member of your population. If you have 173 truck buyers, number them from 1 to 173. Then, put slips of paper into a "hat" numbered 1 through 173. As your sample is drawn (suppose you decide to mail surveys to 50 people), check off each name and make your mailing list.

2. A better approach is to use a table of random numbers (Table 2). This table is computer generated to ensure randomness. To use this table, determine that you will select every fifth number until you have a full sample. Close your eyes and point to the starting number in the table. Then go down five numbers at a time, selecting your sample. (Drop off digits as necessary. The example uses only three digits because the population is 173 truck buyers.)

Once you select a sample, stick with it. Substituting hurts randomness, and a nonrandom sample is less reliable than a random one. If carefully selected, a random sample has the best probability of speaking for the whole population.

TABLE 2

RANDOM NUMBERS

36137	42353	54264	01762	61844	70478
06511	50555	87031	32226	42361	48347
37411	30100	36383	78007	66760	02174
30546	17725	62862	63685	76105	46505
06835	07275	12563	43065	88713	15740
88566	78315	62044	77273	16241	42366
65011	14340	00533	77803	55314	37830
82448	66127	10637	62102	34488	50540
87276	62510	57557	61311	73472	71307
42334	88658	86130	87774	87348	76370
60030	05273	17186	18085	53333	81380
32731	43430	18565	15152	07581	23345
60056	28174	73801	16715	03554	50361
14280	52838	70656	28544	11240	47287
87108	68520	58574	13431	07222	70347
37816	84081	70116	86746	40372	78482
33137	37472	52371	28624	07705	50431
30067	87815	42464	43565	70036	74212
88452	32535	25765	28328	67145	05581
05657	73664	15566	25247	18880	35164
50001	86550	23353	38668	37308	05322
16084	13312	67676	13183	04768	76075
15010	07607	66471	20070	28838	66076
25056	85756	58287	27221	37367	31558
10851	53574	23084	00730	65464	28740

Questionnaire Design and Survey Administration

Many of the drawbacks of questionnaire surveys can be overcome by using the ideas presented in this section.

Designing the Questionnaire. The following steps should be used in designing a questionnaire:

1. Determine the information wanted and types of questions needed.
2. Draft and develop the questions.
3. Test the questions.
4. Develop the complete questionnaire.

Step 1: Determine the information and types of questions required. Be sure you have a clear and specific picture of what information you want to get from the survey. Avoid the temptation to toss in a few extra questions that may be interesting but are not germane to your study. Keep it focused. The longer the survey is, the lower your response rate is likely to be.

Next, determine what types of questions would provide the most accurate data. Be sure to consider how the data will be tabulated and analyzed.

Seven types of questions are most frequently used in survey questionnaires. A questionnaire might have any or all of these types of questions.

1. *Close-ended questions.* This is a forced-choice question using an either/or or yes/no response.

   Example. I have good communication with my supervisor.   ☐ Yes   ☐ No

2. *Open-ended questions.* This type of question allows the respondent to give an unlimited answer. It should be followed by sufficient space for the response.

   Example. What problems are you having communicating with your supervisor? [followed by space to respond]

   Warning: Open-ended responses are difficult to quantify. They can be used in surveys to get ideas, examples, and general feelings, but typically an interview is a better medium for this because it allows the researcher to probe and clarify responses.

3. *Checklist.* This type of question presents a list of items where the participant is asked to check those that apply to his or her particular situation.

   Example. Please check the following types of communications that you have with your supervisor.

☐ Informal meetings	☐ After-hours discussions
☐ Formal meetings	☐ Telephone
☐ Written report	☐ Social gathering
☐ Letters	☐ Committee meetings

4. *Multiple choice question.* This type of question offers a number of answer choices from which the respondent is asked to select the most correct one.

   Example. About how often do you communicate with your supervisor?

   - One or fewer times a day
   - Two to three times a day
   - Three to five times a day
   - Six or more times a day

   For a question of this type to be effective, be sure that the choices presented cover *all possible options.* Responses for multiple choice questions should be *mutually exclusive.* Each choice is clearly different from the others. Respondents get irritated when their selection isn't one of the options. (You can add "none of the above" easily enough, but it won't tell you much.)

5. *Ranking scales.* This type of a question requires the participant to rank order a list of items.

   Example. Of the following list of five types of communications that you might have with your supervisor, please place a 1 by the item that is most important to you, a 2 by the item that is second in importance, and so on. All five items should be ranked.

____ Formal meetings	____ Letters or memos
____ Informal conversations	____ Telephone discussions
____ Written reports	

6. *Likert scale.*[3] This type of survey item is generally used to measure attitude toward a concept or idea. It allows the respondent the opportunity to indicate the degree to which he or she agrees or disagrees (usually on a 5- or 7-point scale) with a statement or idea.

   Example. Please indicate the degree to which you agree or disagree with this statement: "I am satisfied with the amount of communication I have with my supervisor."

Strongly Agree	Agree	Neither Agree nor Disagree	Disagree	Strongly Disagree
5	4	3	2	1

7. *Semantic differential.* This is used to measure attitudes by displaying pairs of opposite terms and asking respondents to check which term better describes their feelings toward the concept or topic. Each pair consists of a positive and negative adjective reflecting the extremes such as honest-dishonest, efficient-inefficient, powerful-weak, and so forth. The adjectives are placed at opposite ends of the line, which is divided into an equal number of segments. Respondents can select the degree to which the adjective describes the topic.

Example. The pairs of adjectives are to be considered as they apply to the *XYZ* Corporation District Office. Place an *X* in the space between the two terms that best describe how you see the words reflecting the situation in the district office. Mark only one space between each pair of words.

XYZ Corporation District Office Supervisor Performance Review My supervisor is:

Esteem building :__:__:__:__:__:__: Back biting
Efficient :__:__:__:__:__:__: Inefficent
Not helpful :__:__:__:__:__:__: Helpful

Note: It is important to reverse some of the items so that people don't develop a response set, that is, the habit of marking the same column consistently. In the foregoing example, you see some positive terms on the left and some on the right column as well.

The advantage of using either the Likert or the Semantic Differential scales is that it is possible to begin to calculate a number that reflects attitudes and opinions. The values for each scale can then be added together to get a measure of a person's attitudes toward the subject (in our example, the subject is the district office). The researcher can calculate the mean attitude score for one group and compare it with another group, or remeasure the same people at a later time to see if shifts in attitudes have occurred.

Step 2: Draft and develop the questions. The two most important considerations in developing questions are validity and reliability. *Validity* is the degree to which the item measures what the researcher wants to measure. *Reliability* is the degree to which the item is likely to get the same results consistently.

One method of improving validity is to ensure that the question will not produce a biased response. Emotionally packed words and questions that lead the respondent toward an obviously preferred answer should be avoided. Also, validity can be improved by including several differently phrased questions—each of which is aimed to solicit data about the same topic.

Questions that obtain reasonably consistent results when administered to similar samples (or the same sample at different times) are said to be reliable.

Step 3: Test the questions. Pretest any questionnaire by administering the survey to a small group of people—people similar to those who will be asked to respond to the final version. Responses to the pretest will tell you how well people understand the questions. This feedback will help you refine the questions to eliminate misunderstandings and confusion in the final version.

Step 4: Develop the complete questionnaire. Once the questions have been tested, they should be integrated into a clean, straightforward questionnaire that provides clear instructions on how it should be completed.

Numbering each question and all possible responses will help facilitate the coding process, especially if a computer is used for analysis. Spreadsheet programs are often sufficient for determining the results, although more sophisticated survey-processing software is readily available.[4]

The final version of the questionnaire should be psychologically attractive, leaving ample white space. Don't crowd the information; it'll look imposing to the reader and may reduce the number of responses.

The questionnaire should have as many questions as necessary but as few as possible. Don't overburden the respondent with trivial items. Leave adequate space for fill-in answers. Nothing is more frustrating than trying to put a five-line response into a space where only several words will fit. (This is especially important when using open-ended questions). Consider the following complaint form:

Complaint Form

Write your complaint in the box below. Please write legibly.

☐

Administering the Survey Questionnaire. The method of administering questionnaires depends on the purpose of the research, the method of sampling, the availability of the sample, and resources available to the researcher. The subsequent sections discuss some common administering options.

Group Administering. From the researcher's viewpoint, this is the most efficient. The instructions and introductory information are given at one time, and the completed questionnaires are usually ready for coding within a matter of minutes. This works well when all the questionnaire participants are physically present in a local geographic area.

Survey. When the representative sample is geographically dispersed, mail questionnaires will have to be used. In such a circumstance, a good sales letter needs to be developed to motivate the targeted sample to spend the time necessary to complete the questionnaire. In addition, a self-addressed, stamped envelope should be included.

Using the mail almost always results in a low percentage of responses. People feel less obligation to respond to mailed surveys. Many procrastinate and ultimately fail to respond at all. You can improve mail survey response rates by

1. Including a persuasive letter explaining the benefit to the reader if he or she completes the survey.
2. Attach a tangible reward, such as a dollar bill, a valuable coupon, an offer to donate to a popular charity, or a free booklet. This causes people to feel some obligation to complete the survey.

3. Make the mailout look personal. Use hand written or individually typed names and addresses (rather than labels), a first-class postage stamp (not metered mail), and a simple return address on the envelope that causes the reader to be curious about what's in the envelope.

Checklists. Perhaps the simplest device for collecting survey data is the checklist. The checklist is simply a list of items that the respondent checks off or indicates the appropriate frequency. This can be used as a questionnaire technique or in connection with structured observations. Such an instrument is easy to develop and simple for the respondent to complete.

Example. Ask customers to check off new flavors of ice cream (or new menu items or services) they would like you to sell. Give them a reasonably short list to choose from (five or so).

Interview Techniques

Better to ask twice than to lose your way once.

—Danish proverb

The interview research technique combines observation and questionnaires to obtain a level of data that is deeper and richer than either of the two techniques can produce separately. Researchers who use interviews will not only be able to get verbal responses from the subject but, more important, will also be in a position to observe the subject's nonverbal behavior. Many times the observed behavior of the interviewee will be more meaningful than the words alone.

Interview Design. Because interviews are so commonplace, some people underestimate the need for structuring and planning an interview in advance. Too many choose to fly without a preflight inspection, and the results can be disastrous.

A good interview process calls for the five *C*s.

1. Construct the interview.
2. Commence the interview.
3. Conduct the interview.
4. Conclude the interview.
5. Compile the data and analyze the results.

Each of these five steps applies whether you are interviewing one person at a time or a group.

Constructing the Interview. The first activity before all others is to *state in writing your purpose of the interview.* Be sure to understand what, specifically, you are trying to get from the interview. You will then be ready to construct a list of questions to be asked.

There are two types of interviews—structured and unstructured. A structured interview forces the interview process to follow a predetermined line of questioning; an unstructured interview allows participants to express freely thoughts important to them.

A structured interview is rather like an interrogation, whereas an unstructured interview is more like a conversation. Structured interviews are clearly lead by the interviewer, whereas in unstructured situations the interviewer takes the lead from the interviewee.

Concluding the Interview. Stop the interview when both people have run out of things to say. When this occurs, the interviewer should summarize what was learned, express what he or she intends to do with the information, and what actions may be precipitated from the findings. After this, the interviewer should sincerely thank the interviewee for his or her time and contributions.

Compiling the Data and Analyzing the Results. The data from closed questions can be easily summarized and analyzed using a form much like a questionnaire. Open-ended question data are another matter. With open-ended question information, frequency counts and *content analysis* should be undertaken.

A frequency count simply notes the number of times the same or closely related comments have occurred. Content analysis identifies common themes. Be sensitive to subtle nuances and common threads that run through the respondents' answers. If several respondents verbally or nonverbally refer to a product or person with apparent disdain, you may conclude there is a less than positive feeling toward that product or person.

Three Interview Formats

Three interview formats are used for business research: face-to-face individual interviews, telephone interviews, and group interviews. Advantages and disadvantages of each are described in the following sections.

Face to Face. The face-to-face or personal interview technique is used most often when complete and comprehensive replies are needed. Because interpersonal communication is made up of words, mannerisms, and voice modulation, face-to-face contact provides feedback to the interviewer from all three sources.

Advantages

1. The technique may be the only way to obtain accurate data on complicated or sensitive questions.
2. You get fewer refusals and premature interview termination because the respondent is one on one with the interviewer.
3. The questioning process is generally more thorough.
4. You can build stronger rapport and better respondent cooperation in this more personalized format.
5. The interviewer can get fuller explanations and clarifications through probing (follow-up questions) and observations of nonverbal behaviors. Because of the aforementioned advantages, personal interviews by skilled individuals is normally credited as being the most accurate data-gathering research method.

Disadvantages

1. One-on-one interviewing is definitely the most expensive and time-consuming way to gather information.
2. The interview process requires skilled interviewers to eliminate interview bias.
3. Personal or sensitive information may be withheld because of the recording device or a poor chemistry between interviewer and interviewee.
4. If the researcher is perceived to be the interviewee's boss, people may not level with him or her.

Telephone Interviewing Technique. Everyone has been subjected to telephone interviews, especially by polling organizations or market research groups. The telephone allows data gathering without the cost of actually getting together face to face.

Advantages

1. Difficult-to-contact people who are unwilling to give you the time in person may be open to a telephone call, especially a long-distance call.
2. It is much easier to take notes, tape the interview, and use a script without the interviewee being distracted.
3. The telephone commands attention and privacy, which minimizes interruptions that can occur in a face-to-face interview.
4. The telephone allows for the interviewer to come quickly to the point and establish a businesslike climate without the interviewee feeling rushed.
5. In many instances, people tend to be more candid over the telephone than in a face-to-face interview.

Disadvantages

1. Telephone interviews tend to be shorter than face-to-face interviews, usually not lasting more than 10 to 15 minutes. Because of this, research projects that require gathering a large amount of data per contact are not suitable for telephone interviewing.
2. The interviewer cannot use props, samples, or illustrations as part of the questioning process. This rules out complicated questions that require a demonstration or some type of visual device.
3. The telephone interview is limited to those having telephones. For research within a company, for example, this would probably eliminate assembly-line workers or those who work outside.
4. The telephone does not allow for personal observations of mannerisms, which are some of the best sources of information during interpersonal communications.

Group Interviews. Two types of group interviews are used successfully to collect good research information: panels and focus groups. The following sections discuss the pros and cons of each of group interview format.

Panels are groups of 7 to 12 people who share some organizational *expertise*—for example, a manufacturing company might assemble a quality control panel composed of employees who play roles in the quality process. The panel group is brought together for a few hours and asked questions. The group atmosphere relieves a lot of pressure from each member, allowing a natural flow of opinions based on each member's expertise. This form of research is particularly helpful when you are learning a new topic. You expect to gather a lot of new information from panels of experts.

Panels

Advantages

1. The major advantage to a panel is that the accuracy of information gathered is high. If the panel has been structured, established, and instructed properly, information generated by the panel will be usually better than any information that can be obtained from a single panel member. The combined expertise is better than the ideas of any one member. You achieve synergy.

2. A second advantage is that panels can be reassembled and asked similar questions to test if opinions have changed over time because of test variables.

Disadvantages

1. Panels can be expensive to establish and administer. Taking a group of high-paid experts away from their other work, for example, can be disruptive and costly.

2. It is often difficult to organize a representative panel that reflects the concerns and input of all relevant groups.

3. An ongoing panel may develop groupthink—their own biases that can damage the integrity of the inquiry process. This can happen in panels where group cohesiveness and internal harmony become more important than making tough decisions.

Focus Groups. This is a consumer research technique that has been used since the 19505 to enable market researchers to draw out consumer feelings and opinions of products and services. A focus group is normally a randomly selected group of customers (they typically do not have expertise in the organization) who are invited to share their observations and ideas with organizational leaders.

This group interview process is an unstructured group discussion between the interviewer and a group of 8 to 12 people. Because the interviewer does not ask questions or record answers in a traditional sense, he or she is free to act as a discussion leader or group moderator whose purpose is to direct and focus the group discussion toward the issues being researched. A focus group is like a group of friends who talk about a subject, with one friend who keeps the group on the topic.

Advantages

1. The focus group typically brings in outside ideas from the end user of an organization's goods or services.

2. As the focus group discussion begins to evolve, it is hoped that a spontaneous interchange of ideas will result in a wide variety of insightful and useful data.

Disadvantages

1. Cost and time consumption. Typically participants are paid to participate or, minimally, are given a free dinner.

2. Assembling a random sample of participants may be difficult. Some customers don't have the time or inclination to participate.

3. Qualitative data received may be difficult to interpret, especially when opposite recommendations are offered by people within the group.

Experiments and Tests

All life is an experiment. The more experiments you make the better.

—Ralph Waldo Emerson

The foremost rule of effective marketing applies for many other business functions. Simply stated, it says, "The three most important marketing activities are testing, testing, and testing." Never assume that what has always worked will continue to work. Business success is a constant process of evaluation and improvement. Testing is the research technique that can best help you keep a finger on the pulse of all aspects of organizational success.

Ways to Create a Successful Focus Group Experience

1. Hold the group on neutral ground—a conference room or an off-site hotel.

2. Notify participants where, when, and why the meeting will occur.

3. Provide a relaxed atmosphere with refreshments and allow participants to interact to break the ice before starting.

4. Seat everyone around the table and explain the purpose, why and how the participants were chosen, and how the results of the session will be used.

5. Have all members introduce themselves to loosen up the group and give you feedback on how well each person meets the selected profile.

6. Direct the discussion in a consistently deductive manner, moving from general ideas or impressions to more specific ones.

7. Avoid discouraging novel or unusual ideas. Sometimes these can be useful.

8. Provide equal opportunity for all members to contribute; passive members should be encouraged to interact.

Experiments can be the most reliable and accurate of all the research procedures. They are not used to solicit opinions or ideas from people; rather, they are used to determine *results* of organizational decisions. They don't measure what is said, believed, or felt, but what *happens* when a change is introduced into the equation.

Effective experiments yield hard facts, produce actual results, and deal in reality. Because of the type of information generated by experiments and tests, they are the most powerful business research method to project future results.

The Game Is to Control the Variables

The secret in putting together a successful experiment is to keep all the variables—or anything that could possibly be a variable—constant, except the one being investigated. For example, let's say you are interested in determining the cost-effectiveness of a new direct mail advertising piece. This new mailout includes a different call-to-action incentive for the customer. Let's say that it offers customers who respond within ten days a buy-one, get-one-free deal.

The important thing that needs to be done here is to control all extraneous variables and to make sure that the only difference being measured is the buy-one, get-one-free incentive. This sounds easy but can be a difficult thing to do. To test this offer effectively, you would need to keep the following variables constant:

1. The sales message

2. The document layout

3. Printing and paper quality

4. The mailing schedule (pieces would have to be mailed on the same days of the week or month)

5. The postage amount

6. The mailing lists used (each approach would be equal, and any one prospect in the target market would have an equal chance of receiving either offer)

In Search of Validity and Reliability

You'll want your experiment to have both validity and reliability. An experiment is valid when the results actually measure what is supposed to be measured. In the preceding example, you would be interested in the different effects of the incentive offer. By carefully controlling variables, you can be reasonably sure that a result from a test is due to the test variable. Such a result would be valid.

Reliability is the probability that you would get the same results if the experiment were repeated in the same way. The previous experiment would have reliability if the results could be duplicated consistently, that is, every time you use the buy-one, get-one-free offer, the results will be greater or lesser than from other mailouts.

It's All in the Design. Taking the example of testing a new incentive offer, let's look at several design approaches you can use to build reliability and validity into the experiment on the new mailer.

Let's Give It a Try. The first and most common test method used is what might be called the "Let's Give It a Try" (LGIT) approach. Rearranging a display in a store or putting impulse-buy items near a cash register are examples of LGIT tests.

When the risk of poor results is potentially costly (e.g., the mailing example costs tens of thousands of dollars and will be repeated regularly), a more carefully designed experiment is appropriate.

The problem with the LGIT design is that the experimental variable was introduced without a control (comparison) group or without any specific prior knowledge about the individuals who received the mailer. This does not allow us to evaluate the effectiveness and make a valid comparison between two offers.

Before and After. The before and after experiment design would be an improvement. This experiment design would have you send two mailings—one with the incentive and one without—to the same individuals at different times. The results could then be compared. This is an improvement over LGIT but not that much! The timing really gums things up. All kinds of errors can creep into the experiment. Change occurs over time and introduces factors that will contaminate the results. One obvious possibility is the customer who accepts the nonincentive offer and then gets a better offer for the same product a few months later. How is he or she likely to feel?

Advantages

1. Experiments and tests are the most reliable and accurate of all research methods.
2. The use of control groups (explained in a moment) greatly reduces errors from outside, unforeseen factors.
3. A variety of factors or variables may be tested at the same time.

Disadvantages

1. Cost
2. Need for expertise in research design to isolate variables and create comparable situations

Naturally, this reference tool cannot cover all the techniques and hints of effective researching. The intent is to give a few guidelines so that future research that you conduct will be well organized, with a specific purpose and clear direction. If you implement the ideas this chapter offers, you will improve your efficiency and the relevance of your data to the problem you are researching.

Also, the word "research" strikes fear in many people's hearts. This is usually because they are inexperienced with research, or they are ineffective researchers. This chapter offers a framework for those who fear research, because research is both rewarding and fun.

NOTES

Chapter 1

1. Mark H. McCormack, *What They Don't Teach You at Harvard Business School* (New York: Bantam Books, 1984), p. 25–26.

2. See Don Pepper and Martha Rogers, *The One to One Future* (New York: Currency-Doubleday, 1993), p. 14.

3. Adapted from a discussion by Don Pepper and Martha Rogers in *The One to One Future* (New York: Currency-Doubleday, 1993), pp. 3–6.

4. Quoted in G. Pascal Zachary, "Advertisers Anticipate Interactive Media as Ingenious Means to Court Customers," *The Wall Street Journal,* August 17, 1994, B-1.

5. Donald Adolphson, Matthew DeVries, and Heikki Rinne, "Rethinking Business," *Exchange* (a publication of the Marriott School of Management, Brigham Young University, Provo, Utah), Fall 1994, pp. 6–9.

6. Ricardo Semler, *Maverick: The Success Story Behind the World's Most Unusual Workplace* (New York: Warner Books, 1993).

7. Max DePree, *Leadership Jazz: The Art of Conducting Business through Leadership, Followership, Teamwork, Touch, and Voice* (New York: Dell Publishing, 1992).

8. Adolphson et al., "Rethinking Business," p. 7.

9. Ibid.

10. Excerpted from Robert Barner, "The New Career Strategist," *The Futurist,* September-October 1994, pp. 8–10.

11. Robert Barner, "The New Career Strategist," *The Futurist,* September-October 1994, p. 14.

12. An excellent book on NLP in business communication is Michael Brooks, *The Power of Business Rapport* (New York: HarperCollins, 1991).

Chapter 2

1. Adopted from Robert Levering and Milton Moskowitz, *The 100 Best Companies to Work for in America,* rev. ed. (New York: Plume, 1994), pp. xiv–xv.

2. Quoted from personal correspondence from Walter Neppl to Paul Timm.

3. From a speech by Edwin A. Locke, Jr., "What Price Verbal Incompetence?" Reprinted by permission of Edwin A. Locke, Jr.

4. Some of these ideas were adapted from Bert Decker, *The Art of Communicating* (Menlo Park, CA: Crisp Publications, 1989), p. 37.

5. Jerry B. Harvey and C. Russell Boettger, "Improving Communication within a Managerial Workgroup," *The Journal of Applied Behavioral Science,* 7, No. 2 (1971), 164–79.

6. Adapted from Paul R. Timm, *Basics of Oral Communication* (Cincinnati: South-Western Publishing, 1993), pp. 13–14.

7. Richard C. Whiteley, *The Customer Driven Company: Moving from Talk to Action* (Reading, MA: Addison Wesley Publishing, 1991), p. 27.

8. Excerpted from Bill Maynard in *TeleProfessional,* 209 W. 5th St., Waterloo, IA 50701.

9. Fictional musician "Nighthawk" Cummings in Robert James Waller, *The Bridges of Madison County* (New York: Warner Books, 1992), p. 168.

Chapter 3

1. Adapted from Steve Massey, *Pittsburgh Post-Gazette* (Knight-Ridder/Tribune Business News), transmitted on America Online, April 10, 1995.

2. Much of this information is adapted from Paul R. Timm and Brent D. Peterson, *People at Work,* 4th ed. (St. Paul, MN: West Publishing, 1993), pp. 48–60.

3. David C. McClelland et al., *The Achieving Society* (Princeton, N.J.: Van Nostrand, 1961).

4. John Naisbitt and Patricia Aburdeen, *Re-inventing the Corporation* (New York: Warner Books, 1985), p. 79.

5. Linda and Richard Eyre, *Life Balance* (New York: Ballantine Books, 1987), p. 16.

6. Ron Zemke, "Dusting off the 60s in the 90s," *Training* (June 1991), p. 8.

7. Frederick F. Reichheld, "Making Sure Customers Come Back for More," *Wall Street Journal,* March 12, 1990, p. A-10. Reichheld is vice-president of Bain & Co., an international consulting firm.

8. Reports of a survey in Dan Rode, "Customer Service Relies on Strong Communication Skills," *Healthcare Financial Management,* January 1990, p. 15.

9. Ibid.

10. Timm and Peterson, *People at Work,* p. 43.

11. Vance H. Trimble, *Sam Walton: The Inside Story of America's Richest Man* (New York: Signet Books, 1991), p. 326.

12. Ibid., p. 325.

Chapter 4

1. W. Charles Redding, *Communication with the Organization* (New York: The Industrial Communication Council, 1972), p. 29.

2. Adapted from Paul R. Timm, and Kristen DeTienne, Managerial Communication, 3rd ed. (Englewood Cliffs, NJ: Prentice Hall, 1995) pp. 37–42.

3. Roger Ricklefs, "All the Wrong Moves," *Wall Street Journal,* May 22, 1995, p. R4.

4. William Pemberton, "A Semantic Approach to Counseling," *ETC: A Review of General Semantics,* 13, No. 2 (Winter 1955–56), 83–92.

5. This and other ideas on customer communication can be found in Paul R. Timm, *50 Powerful Ideas You Can Use to Keep Your Customers* (Hawthorne, NJ: Career Press, 1992), see especially p. 24.

6. G. Michael Barton, "Communication: Managing Words Effectively," *Personnel Journal,* January 1990, p. 36.

7. Many of the ideas on writing style are excerpted from John S. Fielden, "What Do You Mean You Don't Like My Style?" in *Harvard Business Review,* May–June 1982, pp. 128–38.

8. Fielden, p. 128.

9. Kevin Goldman, "From Witches to Anorexics, Critical Eyes Scrutinize Ads for Political Correctness," *Wall Street Journal,* March 19, 1994, p. B-1.

Chapter 5

1. "Dubious Award for Ten Advertisers," Reuters news service transmitted via America Online, December 16, 1994.

2. Kenneth Blanchard and Norman Vincent Peale, *The Power of Ethical Management* (New York: Ballantine Books, 1989), p. x.

3. Blanchard and Peale, p. 51.

4. Excerpted from Robert C. Solomon and Kristine Hanson, "Use These 8 Rules of Ethical Thinking," in *The Prior Report,* 10, No. 5a (1994), 9.

5. William Brooks, *Speech Communication,* 2nd ed. (Dubuque, IA: Wm. C. Brown, 1974), p. 259. Brooks's discussion is based on a system of audience analysis originally explained by H. L. Hollingsworth in *The Psychology of the Audience* (New York: American Book, 1935), p. 25.

6. Ibid., p. 265.

7. Deborah Tannen, *You Just Don't Understand: Women and Men in Conversation* (New York: Ballantine Books, 1990) and *Talking from Nine to Five* (New York: William Morrow and Company, 1994).

8. Peggy Taylor, "Can We Talk?" and interview with Deborah Tannen in *New Age Journal* (November–December 1990), p. 32.

9. Transmitted on America Online, from *Inc.* Magazine, March 1992, EST.

10. Paul R. Timm and Brent D. Peterson, *People at Work,* 4th ed. (St. Paul, MN: West Educational Publishing, 1993), pp. 28–29. Used with permission of the authors.

11. Michael Liedtke, *Contra Costa Times,* Walnut Creek, California, Knight-Ridder/Tribune Business News, May 29, 1995.

Chapter 6

1. Some of this material was adapted from Richard Hatch, *Communication in Business* (Chicago: Science Research Associates, 1977), p. 96.

2. From WHAT THEY STILL DON'T TEACH YOU AT HARVARD . . . by Mark H. McCormack, Copyright © 1989 by Mark H. McCormack Enterprises, Inc. Used by

permission of Bantam Books, a division of Bantam Double-day Dell Publishing Group, Inc.

3. Adapted from a discussion by Saul W. Gellerman, *The Management of Human Resources* (Hinsdale, IL: Dryden Press, 1976), p. 61.

4. Ibid., p. 62.

5. *Personnel Journal*, 245 Fischer Ave., B-2, Costa Mesa, CA 92620.

6. Interview with Westin Cook, investment banker with Salo-man Bros., New York, November 22, 1994.

7. Pat O'Donnell, "The Biggest Loser at Solitaire—The Company," *The Wall Street Journal*, December 19, 1994, p. A14.

8. "School Causes Real Stink with Body Odor Letter" (Associated Press) appeared in the Salt Lake City *Deseret News*, September 29, 1994, p. A-12. (Reprinted with permission of Associated Press.)

Chapter 7

1. Peter M. Senge, Charlotte Roberts, Richard B. Ross, Bryan J. Smith, and Art Kleiner, *The Fifth Discipline Fieldbook* (New York: Currency/Doubleday, 1994), pp. 3–4.

2. Deborah Tannen, *You Just Don't Understand: Women and Men in Conversation* (New York: William Morrow-Ballantine, 1990).

3. Deborah Tannen, *Talking from 9 to 5* (New York: William Marrow and Company, 1994).

4. Tannen, *Talking from 9 to 5*, p. 12.

5. Adapted from Lorraine O'Connell, "For Success at Work, Bone Up on Styles of Gender Chat," *The Orlando Sentinel*, November 13, 1994.

6. Patrica H. Westheimer, *Power Writing for Executive Women* (Glenview, IL: Scott, Foresman and Company, 1989), p. 5.

7. Ibid.

8. Some of the material in this section is adapted from a handout for foreign students written by Gary Althen, author of The Handbook of Foreign Student Advising (Intercultural Press, Inc., 1983).

9. Many of the ideas in this section were adapted from Gary Bonvillian and William A. Nowlin, "Cultural Awareness: An Essential Element in Doing Business Abroad," *Business Horizons*, 37, No. 6 (November 1994), 44–50.

10. Excerpted from Ann McGee-Cooper, "Fun at Work," in *At Work: Stories of Tomorrow's Workplace*, (Barrett-Koehler Publishing, 1994), pp. 5, 7. Reprinted with permission.

11. Excerpted from Lorraine O'Connell, "For Success at Work, Bone Up on Styles of Gender Chat," *Orlando Sentinel*, March 19, 1995, p. B-10.

Chapter 8

1. Adapted from Lourdes Lee Valeriano, "Loved the Present! Hated the Manual!," in *Wall Street Journal*, December 15, 1994, p. B-1. Reprinted with permission of the *Wall Street Journal*.

2. John S. Fielden, "What Do You Mean You Don't Like My Style?" *Harvard Business Review* (May–June 1982), pp. 128–38.

3. P. D. Henphill, *Business Communications* (Englewood Cliffs, NJ: Prentice Hall, 1976), p. 27. Reprinted with permission.

4. Bill Repp, "Want Faster, Easier Business Writing? Talk on Paper!" (September 1992), p. 7; and Greville Janner, "Towards a Readable Report," *Accountancy* (January 1993), p. 40.

5. John Leach, "Seven Steps to Better Writing," *Planning* (June 1993), pp. 26–27.

6. Repp, "Want Faster, Easier Business Writing?" p. 7.

7. *Fortune*, February 20, 1995, p. 22. Reprinted with permission.

8. *USA Today*, October 14, 1994, p. B-2.

Chapter 9

1. Gary Blake, "It Is Recommended that You Write Clearly," *Wall Street Journal*, April 3, 1995, p. A-14. (Reprinted with permission of The Wall Street Journal, © 1995, Dow Jones & Company, Inc. All rights reserved.)

2. Daniel Starch, *How to Develop Your Executive Ability* (New York: Harper & Row, 1943), p. 154.

3. Adapted from Lillian O. Feinburg, *Applied Business Communication* (Sherman Oaks, CA: Alfred Publishing, 1982), pp. 118–19.

Chapter 10

1. Robert Levering and Milton Moskowitz, *100 Best Companies to Work For in America*, pp. 269–70.

2. Herta A. Murphey and Charles E. Peck, *Effective Business Communication*, 2nd ed. (New York: McGraw-Hill, 1976), p. 80.

3. James Scott Calvert, "Teaching Business Students to Write the Psychologically Sound Letter of Condolence," an unpublished paper prepared at Utah State University, 1984.

4. Paul R. Timm, *51 Ways to Save Your Job* (Hawthorne, NJ: Career Press, 1992), pp. 23–24.

5. Some of the material in this section is adapted from an America Online description of *The New American Business System* developed by Meridian Learning Systems, 1992.

6. America Online, December 15, 1994.

Chapter 11

1. Frederick W. Harbaugh, in a letter to the editor of *The ABCA Bulletin*, September 1977, p. 28.

2. Ron Zemke, "Don't Muddle Apologies with Accusations and Teaching Points, Just Say I'm Sorry," *Service Edge*, November 1994, p. 8.

3. Excerpted from Tawn Nhan, *The Charlotte Observer*, North Carolina. Knight-Ridder/Tribune Business News, March 26, 1995.

Chapter 12

1. Doug LeDuc, *The News Sentinel*, Fort Wayne, Indiana, Knight-Ridder/Tribune Business News, March 28, 1995.

Chapter 13

1. Greg Gardner in an untitled article transmitted via America Online, April 10, 1995. Knight-Ridder/Tribune Business News.

2. *Deseret News*, July 24, 1994, p. M-7. Reprinted with permission.

3. Adapted from Elwood N. Chapman, *Be True to Your Future* (Los Altos, CA: Crisp Publications, 1990), p. 83. Reprinted with permission.

4. Some of these sample illegal questions and possible responses to them were adapted from Gerald L. Wilson, "Preparing Students for Responding to Illegal Selection Interview Questions," *The Bulletin of the Association for Business Communication*," September 1991, pp. 47–48.

5. Ibid., p. 48.

Chapter 14

1. These productivity figures were adapted from Frederick C. Dyer, *Executive's Guide to Effective Speaking and Writing* (Englewood Cliffs, NJ: Prentice-Hall, Inc. 1962), p. 112.

Chapter 15

1. Patricia C. Weaver, and Robert G. Weaver, *Persuasive Writing* (New York: Macmillan, 1977), pp. 63–64.

2. Raymond V. Lesikar and John D. Pettit, *Report Writing for Business,* 8th ed. (Homewood, IL: Richard D. Irwin, 1991), p. 3.

3. Erwin M. Keithley and Philip J. Schreiner, *A Manual of Style for the Preparation of Papers and Reports,* 2nd ed. (Cincinnati: SouthWestern, 1971), p. 1.

4. Kate L. Turabian, *A Manual for Writers of Term Paper, Theses, and Dissertations* (Chicago: University of Chicago Press, 1973), p. 188.

5. Ibid., p. 200.

6. Keithley and Schreiner, *Manual of Style,* p. 38.

7. Bob Jackson, *What Impresses People* (New York: Blackston Press, 1996), p. 47.

Chapter 16

1. Dianna Booher, *Communicate with Confidence!* (New York: McGraw-Hill, 1994), p. 148.

2. J. Harold Janis, *Writing and Organizational Communication,* 3rd ed. (New York: Macmillan, 1978), p. 492.

3. Booher, *Communicating with Confidence!* p. 153.

4. Lyman K. Steil, interview with *U.S. News & World Report,* May 26, 1980.

5. Ibid.

6. Adapted from Sperry Corporation Listening Program materials by Dr. Lyman K. Steil, Communication Development, Inc., for Sperry Corporation, copyright © 1979.

Chapter 17

1. Information in this section is adapted from Paul R. Timm and Kristen B. DeTienne, *Managerial Communication,* 3rd ed. (Englewood Cliffs, NJ: Prentice Hall, 1995), Chapter 11, pp. 248–68.

2. Myron Cohen, *More Laughing Out Loud* (Secaucus, NJ: Citadel Press, 1960), pp. 169–70.

3. Edward S. Strother and Alan W. Huckleberry, *The Effective Speaker* (Boston: Houghton Mifflin, 1968), p. 167.

Chapter 18

1. Toastmasters International is an excellent organization aimed at improving members' communication and leadership skills. For more information about their programs, consult your local telephone directory.

2. This discussion is adapted from Paul R. Timm, *Basics of Oral Communication* (Cincinnati: South-Western Publishing, 1993), chap. 2. The "coping quotient" idea is found originally in Harold P. Zelko and Frank E. X. Dance, *Business and Professional Speech Communication,* 2nd ed. (New York: Holt, Rinehart & Winston, 1978), pp. 77–79.

3. Zelko and Dance, Business and Professional Speech Communication, p. 78.

4. Larry L. Barker, *Communication* (Englewood Cliffs, NJ: Prentice-Hall, Inc., 1978), p. 241.

5. Michael Waldhold, "Here's One Reason, Uh, Smart People Say 'Uh'," *Wall Street Journal,* March 19, 1991, p. B-1.

6. Percy H. Whiting, *How to Speak and Write with Humor* (New York: McGraw-Hill, 1959), p. 117.

7. *The Reader's Digest Treasury of American Humor* (Pleasantville, NY: Reader's Digest Association, 1972), p. 131.

8. Raymond Ross, *Persuasion: Communication and Interpersonal Relations* (Englewood Cliffs, NJ: Prentice-Hall, Inc., 1974), p. 163.

9. Whiting, *Speak and Write with Humor,* p. 70.

Chapter 19

1. This story is adapted from a similar one in a book by communication trainer, Claire Raines, *Visual Aids in Business* (Menlo Park, CA: Crisp Publication, 1989), p. i.

2. Conwell Carlson, "Best Memories by Eye and the Ear," *The Kansas City Times*, April 19, 1967, p. 36.

3. Robert L. Montgomery, *A Master Guide to Public Speaking* (New York: Harper and Row, 1979), p. 36.

4. Stephen S. Pride, *Business Ideas: How to Create and Present Them* (New York: Harper and Row, 1967), p. 172.

5. One of your authors, Paul Timm, appears in several such professional video programs including *Successful Self-Management, The Power of Customer Service, How to Make Winning Presentations, Winning Telephone Tips,* and *How to Hold Successful Meetings.* These are produced by JWA Video, 411 S. Sangamon, Suite 2-B, Chicago, IL 60607; (312) 829–5100. Programs range from 30 to 50 minutes each and sell for about $100.

6. Adapted from John Eaton, *The Denver Post,* Knight-Ridder/Tribune Business News, America Online, April 5, 1995.

Reference Tool One

1. The authors want to thank Ray L. Young, who developed much of the material in this guide. Ray is a former instructor at the Marriott School of Management at Brigham Young University. He currently is president of OmniTrack, a computer training firm in Alpine, Utah.

Reference Tool Two

1. This section is from a course handout by William H. Baker, "How to Write Structurally Sound Text." Copyright © 1995, William H. Baker, Brigham Young University. Reprinted with permission of the author.

Reference Tool Four

1. This chapter is adapted from Rick C. Farr and Paul R. Timm, *Business Research: An Informal Guide* (Menlo Park, CA: Crisp Publications, 1994). Reprinted with permission.

2. Technically, questionnaire responses are anonymous only if there are no identifying marks on the survey that could be associated with the respondent. If the surveys are numbered or request respondent's name or other identification, the person should be told that his or her answers will be confidential. This means that what they say will not be associated with their name, except possibly by the researcher. The most sensitive issues are better handled via anonymous surveys.

3. Named after its creator Rensis Likert.

4. The following names are titles of sophisticated statistical software programs: SPSS, SAS, SYSTAT, and STATISTICS.

INDEX

G

Gatekeepers, 459
  minimizing number of, 466
Gellerman, Saul, 146
Gender:
  audience, 120–21
  gender-agreement errors, 575–76
Gender differences, in communication, 165–68
Gestures:
  cultural differences in, 172
  in oral presentations, 504
Gilruth, Herb, 1161
Globalization, and communication, 10
Goodwill close, 289
Goodwill messages, 254–64
  appreciation messages, 254–57
  congratulations or recognition messages, 258
  general pattern of, 259–62
  news releases, 262–64
  publicity, 262
  sympathy or condolences, 258–59
Graphics, use of, 128
Green, Steve, 167
Greeting, cultural differences in, 176
Ground rules:
  media, 141–43
    examples of, 142
Group interviews, 649–50
  focus groups, 650, 651
  panels, 649–50
Groupthink, 557

H

Handicap questions, interviews, 382
Handouts, rating as communication form, 144
Handshakes, cultural differences in, 176
Handwritten letters/notes:
  informality of, 149
  rating as communication form, 144
Hard-copy availability, 147
Hatch, Richard, 141
Headings, 402–3
  centered headings, 442
  formal reports, 442
  paragraph heading, 403, 443
  secondary heading, 403
  side headings, 442
  tertiary heading, 403
  title heading, 402
He or *she* construction, 575–76
"Hey, you!" comma, 592
Hiding behind policy, pitfall of, 285
Hierarchy of needs, 57
Hiring challenge, 354
Human needs:
  Maslow's hierarchy of needs, 57–59
    belonging needs, 59
    esteem needs, 59

security needs, 58–59
    self-fulfillment needs, 59
    survival needs, 58
  need for achievement, 59–60
  need for affiliation, 60–61
  need for power, 61–62
Humor, 512–16
  anticlimax, 515–16
  exaggeration, 513
  humorous quote/definition, 514–15
  incongruous lists, 512–13
  insults, 515
  juxtaposition, 513–14
  play on words, 516
  understatement, 516
Hyphens, 595
  and compound adjectives, 582–83

I

I-centered viewpoint, 223
Immediate feedback capacity, 147
Indirect plan, main points, 484–85
Inductive logic, 192–93
Inferences vs. fact, 84–85
Inferential statistics, 487
Informal (short) reports, 425–30
  conference reports, 426
  key points about, 426–30
  meeting minutes, 426
  periodic reports, 426
  progress reports, 426
  sample of, 427–29
  task reports, 425
  trip reports, 426
Information overload, 151–52
Informative reports, 397
Informative subject lines, 194
Initial-fumbling-around stage (IFAS), 431
Initials, business letters, 611–12
Inquiry about product/service, 245
Inside address, 607, 608–609
Instruction manual, 186
Insults, as form of humor, 515
Interactional elements, listening, 459–60
Interactivity:
  between business and customer, 9
  and communication, 9
Intercultural socialization, 174
Interesters, 104
Internal citations, 405
Internal customers, 65
Internal elements, listening, 458
Interpretive reports, 397
Interrupting, 465
Interviews, 375–85
  assertiveness on, 381
  commonly asked questions, 384–85
  drawing link between features and benefits, 380
  dream list, 378

Malespeak, 165–67
Management:
    functions of, 36–37
        commanding and coordinating, 36
        common threads in, 37
        controlling, 37
        organizing, 36
        planning, 36
    and questions, 44
Margins, 400–401, 442
Marital relationship questions, interviews, 383
Mary Kay Cosmetics, 240
Maslow's hierarchy of needs, 57
Mass marketing, 7–8
Mass-produced letters, rating as communication
        form, 144
Meaning:
    concealed, 89–90
    transfer of, 83–84
Mecham, Steven K., 37
Media:
    and changes in business communication, 152–54
    choosing, 139–41
        characteristics/costs, 146–49
        efficiency vs. effectiveness, 145–46
        media expectations, 151
        media mixing, 151
        relative costs, 149–50
    combining for effectiveness, 151
    definition of, 139
    formality of, 149
    ground rules, 141–43
    hard-copy availability, 147
    immediate feedback capacity, 147
    message intensity and complexity, 147–49
    mixing, 151
    people costs, 149
    rating, 144–45
    speed of, 146–47
    technical costs, 149–50
Meeting minutes, 426
Meetings:
    advantages of, 554–56
    backfiring of, 557–58
    disadvantages of, 556–57
    groupthink, 557
    participation in, 550, 552–54
        active, 553–54
        postmeeting follow-up, 556
        preparation, 553
    speaking up at, 558
    types of, 551–52
Memory devices, 510
Memos, 613–20
    construction of, 613
    format:
        report proposal, 621–23
        short reports, 426
    with itemization, 619–20
    request for employee commitment, 330
Message intensity and complexity, 147–49

Metatalk, 103–5
    continuers, 103
    convincers, 104
    downers, 104
    foreboders, 103
    interesters, 104
    pleaders, 105
    softeners, 103
    strokers, 105
Methodology, research model, 635
"Me-too" messages, 318
Miller, Irving A., 9
Misunderstandings, expecting, 16
Mobility, and communication, 9
Models, 533–34
Modifiers:
    adjectives, 578–79
    adverbs, 579
    comparative, 582
    dangling, 581–82
    overuse of, 582
    rules for, 579–83
    superlative, 582
    See also Adjectives; Adverbs
Morale, 47–48
Morand, David, 175
Moskowitz, Milton, 26
Most, 572
Motions, cultural differences in, 172
Movement, in oral presentations, 504

N

Naisbitt, John, 62
National origin questions, interviews, 382
Need development, 319–21
    balance theory, 319
    definition of, 320
    personal benefits to reader, 320
        "you" viewpoint, importance of, 320
Neither, 572
Neppl, Walter J., 32
NeuroLinguistic Programming (NLP), 14
New media, 7–10
    characteristics of, 9
News items, rating as communication form, 144
News releases, 262–64
New technology, characteristics of, 4
Noise:
    barriers arising from, 124
    and listening, 458–59
Nonessential clauses, 577
Nonverbal communication, 90–96
    definition of, 90
    environment and space, 91–92
    eye contact, 96
    facial expressions, 96
    functions of, 96–97
    office arrangements, 94
    and organizational culture, 92